WHO'S WHO IN NELSON'S NAVY

WHO'S WHO IN NELSON'S NAVY

200 Naval Heroes

NICHOLAS TRACY

CHATHAM PUBLISHING
LONDON

MBI PUBLISHING, MINNESOTA

First published in Great Britain in 2006 by
Chatham Publishing
Lionel Leventhal Ltd
Park House
1 Russell Gardens
London
NW11 9NN

Distributed in the United States of America by
MBI Publishing Company
Galtier Plaza, Suite 200, 380 Jackson Street
St Paul, MN 55101-3885, USA

British Library Cataloguing in Publication Data

Tracy, Nicholas, 1944–
Who's who in Nelson's navy ; two hundred heroes
1. Great Britain. Royal Navy – Officers – Biography
2. Great Britain. Royal Navy – History – 18th century
3. Great Britain. Royal Navy – History – 19th century
4. Great Britain. History, Naval – 18th century
5. Great Britain. History, Naval – 19th century
I. Title
359'.0092241

ISBN-13: 978-1-86176-244-3
ISBN-10: 1-86176-244-5

Printed and bound in Great Britain by Cromwell Press Ltd

CONTENTS

Naval Ranks

The following abbreviations are used in lists of ranks:

Adm   Admiral
Capt   Captain
Cmdr   Commander
Lt   Lieutenant
M-C   Master and Commander
R-Adm Rear-Admiral
V-Adm Vice-Admiral

The number in parentheses after a date indicates the relative seniority where more than one officer was commissioned on the same day. Dates recorded for local commissions could sometimes differ by a day from the national calendar because shipboard days began at noon.

ALTHOUGH WRITTEN IN THE 'Year of Victories', 1759, David Garrick's words for 'Hearts of Oak' very much set the tone for Britons' triumphal feelings about their navy during the wars against the French Republic and Empire:

> We ne'er see our foes but we wish them to stay,
> They never see our sails but they wish us away.
> If they run, why we'll follow, and we'll run them ashore.
> And if they won't fight, why, we can do no more.
>
> > Heart of oak are our ships,
> > Jolly tars are our men,
> > We always are ready,
> > Steady, boys, steady,
> > We'll fight and we'll conquer again and again.
>
> They swear they'll invade us, these terrible foes,
> They frighten our women, our children and beaus,
> But should their flat bottoms get o'er in the night,
> Still Britons they'll find on the shore when they alight.
>
> > Heart of oak are our ships, ...

In working through the biographies of the heroes who brought the Royal Navy to life during the wars of the French Republic and Empire, one thing which becomes strongly apparent is the web of personal and service relationships which made up the career of a naval officer. As often as not, it was a world in which boys grew rapidly to manhood under the guidance of their fathers, or their fathers' friends and relations. It mattered greatly which senior officer introduced a young man into the navy by accepting him as volunteer or captain's servant on the quarterdeck of his ship, or rated him as midshipman, and it mattered greatly which very senior officers recognised a young man's potential. Connection made a vast difference between languishing as a lieutenant or being remembered when there were ships needing commanders. Some who were no more than adequately competent were rushed to higher ranks because of the place they held in aristocratic society. And some who might have shone in higher command were doomed to languish because their patrons died suddenly, or failed in their obligations.

The largest group of naval officers were themselves sons of naval officers, with a few sons of non-commissioned naval and dockyard men. Some of the naval families had connections with the aristocracy. A surprising number came from ecclesiastical families.

Apart from connections, and ability, officers were dependent upon the accidents of the service for their promotion. Two of the well-known naval toasts were to 'a bloody war or a sickly season' and to 'a willing foe and sea room'. Hair-raising though they may be, and now banned at least from the Canadian navy, these toasts represented the best hope of promotion, or of dying in the attempt. Those officers who received honours for their services tended to receive many of them, and died loaded with knighthoods, baronies and honorific ranks.

But naval service was not just a 'winner take all' wooden world. It is evident that the Royal Navy was not entirely bound by the demands of family ties. Senior officers could and did recognise the potential of young men of very humble origin, and bring them forward. It was very much in their interest that the officers of the navy should be men of talent and commitment, who would keep their ships afloat and pursue the enemy with determination and courage. The sea is a demanding environment which can be pitiless. In battle, life and reputation depended upon the commitment, training and courage of fellow officers.

The system was not necessarily a fair one: the navy was not a democracy. But it was a system which worked well to ensure the safety of the nation on the seas. Young officers recognised an obligation to their patrons, their 'friends' in the term used at the time. It was a mentoring system which brought out their best. The obligation felt by the junior to his senior, with whom he might be associated for most of his service life, was recognised by admirals in forming the line of battle, when they would ensure that the ships next ahead and astern of their flag were commanded by people whom they knew and on whom they could rely for close support.

As individuals, naval commanders exhibited all the range of human character, from the extreme self-sacrifice of Collingwood, the almost suicidal thirst for glory and public acclaim of Nelson, to the cultivation of Mitchell or Tobin and the arrogance of

St Vincent. The most obvious commonality amongst the leading men of the fleet, inevitably, was their acceptance of the hierarchic discipline which gave them almost unlimited power over their crews. All but the worst commanders were careful of their men, but none are known to have doubted their right to use their men's lives as they thought best, in the interest of their country, but also in the pursuit of their own glory. If they had, they would not have pushed their ways to the forefront of a profession which existed to make war, and which was compensated by a right to seize the property of merchants who were nationals of enemy states.

The circumstances of a war for national survival and social order put an end to the political divisions which had characterised the officer class of the Royal Navy in the preceding two centuries. The period of the wars against the French Republic and Empire contrasts with the unhappy period of the war which began as a rebellion and civil war in the American colonies, during which the British nation and the Royal Navy were bitterly divided and suffered defeats and drawn battles at the hands of the French and Spaniards in the Channel and on the coast of America. Following the peace of Amiens, in 1802, the editor of the *Naval Chronicle* felt impelled to write about the singular success enjoyed by the Royal Navy in the recently concluded war.

> It is a subject of peculiar felicity and congratulation, that during the whole course of the war, an uninterrupted harmony reigned among the Commanders of our fleets. Diversity of opinion in politics, which in former wars had occasioned so much detriment to the service, if it existed, and it is contrary to reason and experience to suppose that it did not exist, caused no animosity between Commanders. All were animated with an equal zeal for the good of the service; and the only rivalship which existed among them, was a glorious rivalship in deeds of arms and feats of valour. NC 8.180

The aristocratic world of eighteenth-century Britain was confronting its greatest test, the popular revolution in France. The echoes of unrest in Britain extended into the fleet, and led to the great mutinies of 1797 that can now be seen as one of the most important events in British labour history. The constant threat of mutiny and even revolution made the Royal Navy of the 1790s altogether a harder place than it had been a generation before, and some officers were hard to the point of brutality. But it is remarkable that they were also so committed. As a group, they were at least as hard on themselves as they were on their ship's companies. Sir Richard Keats, for instance, spent only one night ashore between 19 March 1801 and 22 August 1805. Nor did he find an opportunity to marry until he retired at the age of forty-three. In wartime, marriages were a matter of prolonged absences, which for some such as Samuel Hood were a matter of great sadness. It was an age, however, when people were more inclined to recognise the obligation of duty.

This same recognition of moral obligation, and of a job to be done, was shared by the women who married naval officers. They usually were much younger than were their husbands, usually had to deal with loneliness, pregnancy and child rearing on their own, and often had their husbands return only when broken in body or mind. They were frequently daughters of naval families. Marrying a senior officer's daughter could be an important career move. For a younger man it could mean promotion through forging new patronage ties. No less important, however, was the probability that such unions would ensure her husband a degree of understanding unlikely from a woman who was not brought up to the life she was to lead.

Who's Who in Nelson's Navy: 200 Naval Heroes celebrates the 200th anniversary of the battle of Trafalgar on 21 October 1805, which was the crowning achievement of a generation of naval officers and men. Two hundred is an arbitrary number for this pantheon of heroes, and in fact that limit has been stretched a little. Nor would all the characters be universally regarded as heroes, and it is unquestionably true that many heroes of the lower deck are lost to history. But the stories of the finest achievements of these 200 or more men give a sense of the services of others, now voiceless. In writing their stories, an attempt has been made to bring out what is universal, as well as what was unique. In this way, we read not only about the hours of wrath and exultation, but also about careers in the Georgian navy, and about the texture of its life.

NICHOLAS TRACY
Port Maitland
2006

WHO'S
WHO IN
NELSON'S
NAVY

AUSTEN

ADMIRAL OF THE FLEET SIR FRANCIS WILLIAM AUSTEN, GCB, is best known for being one of the sailor brothers of Jane Austen, the novelist, but his reputation in the navy was based on his daring in-shore work.

The fourth son of the Revd George Austen, rector of Deane and later of Steventon near Basingstoke, Hampshire, and of his wife Cassandra, the youngest daughter of the Revd Thomas Leigh, rector of Harpsden near Henley-on-Thames, Oxfordshire, he was born on 23 April 1774. He began his naval career as a cadet at the Royal (Naval) Academy, Portsmouth, which he entered on 12 April, or possibly 15 September, 1786. Two and a half years later he entered the navy on 23 December 1788 as a volunteer per Admiralty order in *Perseverance*, in which he served in the East Indies under Captain Isaac Smith. On 5 November 1791 he transferred into *Crown* (64) flying Commodore the Honourable William Cornwallis's broad pendant; he followed him into *Minerva* (38), and was commissioned lieutenant on 28 December 1792. He was then appointed to *Dispatch,* armed brig, under Captain John Whitby, and on 23 June 1793 transferred to *Lark*, commanded by Captain Josias Rowley in the Downs and North Sea. Rowley was later succeeded by Captain Ogilvy. On 23 May 1795 Austen transferred into *Andromeda* (32) commanded by Captain Thomas Southeby, who was later succeeded by Captain M Taylor, and served in Baltic convoys. On 13 September he was appointed to *Prince George* (90) flying the flag of Rear-Admiral Hugh Cloberry Christian in command of the expedition to the West Indies, and when she was storm-damaged they moved into *Glory* (90). On 5 May 1796 he was transferred into *Shannon* (38) under the command of Captain Alexander Fraser, for service in the North Sea, but he came ashore on 26 June. On 16 September he was appointed to *Triton* commanded by Captain John Gore in the Channel fleet; on 5 October 1797 he was transferred into *Seahorse* (38) commanded by Captain Edward James Foote; and on 13

February 1798 he was transferred into *London* under the command of Captain John Child Purvis, with whom he served off Cadiz.

He was promoted commander on 3 February 1799, and appointed to *Peterel,* sloop of war, at Gibraltar. In a remarkable action on 21 March 1800 near Marseilles he attacked three French ships, *Le Cerf* armed with fourteen 6-pounders, *Le Joilliet* of six guns, and *La Ligurienne* also with fourteen 6-pounders and two 36-pounder howitzers. *Peterel* was never more than a cable from the shore and was once aground, but succeeded in driving the first two enemy ships onto the rocks, while the third surrendered. In recognition of this accomplishment Austen was made post captain on 13 May 1800, but news of the promotion did not reach him until after he had performed other remarkable services in command of *Peterel* under Sir William Sidney Smith on the coast of Egypt, for which the captain, Pacha, awarded him a rich sabre and pelisse. From 22 October to the end of the war he served as flag captain to Vice-Admiral James Gambier in *Neptune* in the Channel fleet.

Following the renewal of the war in 1803, Austen served for a while as commandant of a division of sea fencibles at Ramsgate as part of the defences of Kent against invasion. This force was recruited from coastal seamen who stood ready to man their boats and hurry to any threatened point on the coast, or attack the rear of an enemy's advanced force. When on 4 May 1804 he returned to sea as flag captain of *Leopard* (50) under Rear-Admiral Louis off Boulogne, he was still serving in the local anti-invasion forces. On 29 March 1805, however, he moved with Louis into *Canopus* (80), which was under orders to join Lord Nelson in the Mediterranean, watching the Toulon fleet.

With Louis he missed the battle of Trafalgar when Nelson ordered the squadron to Gibraltar to resupply. Louis then served in Sir John Duckworth's fleet, and Austen commanded *Canopus* at the battle of San Domingo, after which he was awarded a gold medal and the thanks of both houses of parliament.

He left *Canopus* on 22 June 1806, and on 24 July he married Mary, eldest daughter of John Gibson of Ramsgate, in St Lawrence, Isle of Thanet, Kent. Together they were to have three daughters and five sons.

His was very much a naval family. His brother Charles John Austen had the distinction of being in 1812–14 the captain of *Namur* (90), on board which ship the naval artist Clarkson Stanfield did service as a pressed man. Charles John attained the rank of rear-admiral, and his son, also Charles John, born on 28 May 1821, reached the rank of commander in the post-war navy. Francis Austen's daughter, Mary Jane, married on 10 June 1828 in Titchfield, Hampshire, Captain George Thomas Maitland Purvis, RN. His eldest son was born on 12 July 1809 and christened Francis William after his father. He reached the rank of captain, and was to marry on 13 July 1843 his first cousin, Frances Palmer, third and youngest daughter of his uncle Charles. Francis's third son was the Revd George Austen, who became a naval chaplain, and his fourth son, born in November 1815, was Herbert Grey Austen, who also joined the Royal Navy and reached the rank of commander. His youngest son, Thomas, was the only one to stay out of the navy, taking orders and becoming rector of Barfreston, Kent, but he could not escape it altogether. On 17 July 1855 he was to marry Jane Newnham Collingwood, third daughter of Captain John Clavell, RN.

When Mary Austen died is not known. Shortly after the marriage of his daughter Mary Jane, in July 1828, Francis was married for a second time, to Martha, eldest daughter of the Revd Noyes Lloyd, rector of Enborne, Berkshire. She lived a further fifteen years, until January 1843, but there were to be no further Austen children to grace the quarterdecks of the navy.

Francis's career had kept pace with his family. On 23 March 1807 he had been appointed to command *St Albans* (64), in which he escorted the trade to the Cape of Good Hope and St Helena, and he then escorted transports to Portugal with 2,000 men who fought at the battle of Vimiera, after which he superintended the embarkation of the wounded. Later he was put in charge of the disembarkation at Portsmouth of the soldiers who had survived Sir John Moore's retreat to Corunna. Between 19 December 1810 and 13 May 1811 he flew his flag in *Caledonia* (120) in the Channel fleet, and between 9 July 1811 and 7 May 1814 he flew it in *Elephant* (74) in the North Sea and Baltic.

At the end of the war, on 4 June 1815, he was made one of the first companions of the Bath (CB) when the order was divided into three ranks. He was also accorded the honour and additional salary of colonel of the Royal Marines on 27 May 1825, and five years later, on 22 July 1830, he hoisted his flag as rear-admiral of the blue. The Georgian navy retained the seventeenth-century concept of a three-fleet navy, with blue, white and red squadrons, and promotion within rank from one squadron to the next. Austen's promotions continued to succeed each other in rapid succession. He was promoted on the same day to the white and red squadrons on 10 January 1837, to knight companion of the Bath (KCB) on 28 February 1837, to vice-admiral of the blue on 28 June 1838, to the white squadron on 23 November 1841, and to the red squadron on 9 November 1846. He was promoted admiral of the blue on 1 August 1848, and subsequently to the white on 1 July 1851 and to the red on 3 July 1855. These promotions took place long after he retired from active service, and amounted to honours which increased half pay. In 1854 he was offered appointment as commander-in-chief Portsmouth, but refused on the basis of his age. He was created knight grand cross of the Bath (GCB) on 18 May 1860, rear-admiral of the United Kingdom on 5 June 1862, vice-admiral on 11 December 1862 and less than a year later, on 27 April 1863, admiral of the fleet. He was living at Portsdown Lodge, Hampshire, when he died on 10 August 1865, aged ninety-one.

Lt: 28 December 1792
Cmdr: 3 February 1799
Capt: 13 May 1800
R-Adm: 22 July 1830
V-Adm: 28 June 1838
Adm: 1 August 1848
Adm. of the Fleet: 27 April 1863

D'AUVERGNE

VICE-ADMIRAL PHILIP D'AUVERGNE, PRINCE DE BOUILLON, was a dedicated British naval officer of Jersey origin who had the misfortune to inherit the Norman estates of the duc de Bouillon.

He was born on 22 November 1754 in Elizabeth Castle, Jersey, the fourth son of Charles Dauvergne, who was an officer in the army, and his first wife Elizabeth, daughter of Philip Le Geyt, chief civil magistrate of the royal court and president of the states of Jersey. In 1770 his name was entered on the books of one of the royal yachts by Vice-Admiral Campbell. In 1772 with the patronage of Admiral Lord Howe he joined the *Flora* (32) as a midshipman for several foreign voyages, on one of which he met a party of French scientists in *La Flou* and determined on joining such a voyage. After *Flora* paid off he returned to his studies, but in June 1773 Lord Howe introduced him to Captain the Honourable Constantine John Phipps, later Baron Mulgrave, who agreed to take him on a voyage to Spitzbergen in *Racehorse*, bomb. The young Horatio Nelson was similarly accommodated in the consort *Carcass*.

The following year d'Auvergne joined the *Asia* (64) and sailed with Admiral Vandeput to Boston, where he was nearly arrested by the Americans when he had strolled as far as Concord with the army on the day of the fight at Lexington, 19 April 1775. He was appointed acting lieutenant in *Kingsfisher*, sloop, then joined *Preston* (50), served in the boats during the battle of Bunker Hill, was at the destruction of Falmouth in Casco Bay on 18 October 1775, and then joined *Chatham* (50). On the evacuation of the army to Halifax, d'Auvergne was again made acting lieutenant. He served at the battle of Brooklyn, with the army around New York, and with Rear-Admiral Sir Peter Parker in the *Chatham* against Rhode Island. His service was so satisfactory that on 2 June 1777 Lord Howe commissioned him lieutenant and gave him command of *Alarm*, an armed vessel fitted for river service. His services on the Seaconnet river were cut short by the arrival of a detachment of comte d'Estaing's fleet, and he and the other captains of small craft on the river were obliged to burn their vessels and make the best of their way to New York, whence he returned to England.

He was there appointed first lieutenant of *Arethusa* (32) on the Channel station, but in February 1779 she was wrecked after an action with a French frigate near Ushant, and d'Auvergne was taken prisoner. While in captivity he was recog-

Philip d'Auvergne, Duke of Bouillon, Commodore in His Majesty's Service, engraved by William Ridley from an original miniature, published by Joyce Gold, 103 Shoe Lane, 30 March 1805.

nised by the duc de Bouillon as a scion of his family, but resisted invitations to serve the French.

In the summer of 1780 he was appointed to command the *Lark*, a large armed cutter in which he participated in Commodore George Johnstone's expedition to the Cape of Good Hope and Ceylon. He was made master and commander on 18 August 1781 and sent in *Rattlesnake* (14) to assess the value of Trinidad off the coast of Brazil for a permanent settlement, and there he succeeded in wrecking his ship. He and a few men were ordered to remain there as a mark of possession, and only after three months subsisting on seabirds were they rescued by a convoy of outward-bound East

Indiamen. The court martial dealt leniently with him, and in consideration for his sufferings he was made post captain on 22 January 1784 on his return to England.

He was also tracked down by the duc de Bouillon, who had established to his satisfaction the family connection. D'Auvergne spent the following winter at the duke's seat in Normandy, and was formally adopted as his heir. The adoption was registered by royal licence on 1 January 1787. This proved his undoing following the French declaration of war in February 1793. In June 1794 he was appointed to command the *Nonsuch* (64) and a flotilla of gunboats guarding Jersey and Guernsey, ranked as commodore, and given the job of liaison with the French royalists and émigrés. During the peace of Amiens he travelled to Paris hoping to recover the ducal lands which had been sequestered, but all he got for his effort was humiliation from the French police and the good luck to be expelled from the country. He was employed again as soon as the countries returned to war, and sent back to Jersey, and by the end of the war was a vice-admiral. In 1815 he travelled to Paris again to claim his inheritance at the Congress of Vienna but was rejected. His savings spent in the litigation, he apparently committed suicide on 18 September 1816, aged sixty-one, at Holmes' Hotel, 17 Parliament Street, Westminster. He was buried in St Margaret's, Westminster.

> Lt: 2 June 1777
> M-C: 18 August 1781
> Capt: 22 January 1784
> R-Adm: 9 November 1805
> V-Adm: 31 July 1810

AYLMER

ADMIRAL SIR FREDERICK WHITWORTH WILLIAM AYLMER, BARON AYLMER, KCB, acquired a reputation for boat work and for co-operation with land forces. Perhaps his most valuable part in the war occurred at its end, when in July 1815 he commanded the force which penetrated the Gironde to Bordeaux.

His was a naval family of long descent. He was great-great-grandson of Admiral Matthew Aylmer (first Lord Aylmer), grandson of Captain Henry Aylmer, RN (third Baron Aylmer), and cousin of Admiral John Aylmer. He was born on 12 October 1777, in Twyford near Southampton, the third son of Henry, fourth baron Aylmer of Balrath, county Meath, and of his wife Catherine, second daughter of Sir Charles Whitworth of Leybourne, Kent. He entered the navy on 24 November, or December, 1790 as a captain's servant in *Syren* (32) under the command of Captain John Manley, with whom he served in the Channel. He was rated midshipman on 17 September 1791, and in 1794 followed Manley into *Apollo* (36), on the Irish station. Commissioned lieutenant on 17 December 1796, for rank only, he was appointed to *Swiftsure* (74) under the command of Captain Benjamin Hallowell on 9 January 1797. With him he proceeded to the Mediterranean station, and served as second lieutenant of *Swiftsure* at the battle of the Nile on 1 August 1798. He then appears to have spent some years ashore, but he was promoted commander on 7 January 1802 and appointed to command *Delight*, sloop (18), in which he served in the Mediterranean under Lord Keith. In 1803 he was transferred to *Wasp*, sloop (18), in which he served in the Channel and off Cadiz under Sir John Orde.

Over a year after the return to war following the peace of Amiens, he was promoted post-captain, on 18 May 1805. But not until 1809 was he appointed to command *Narcissus* (32) under Lord Gambier in the Channel. In July he took an active part in the Spanish defence of Santona. His mission at Bordeaux six years later was a delicate one because the population was largely royalist in sympathy, or at any rate preferred peace, but the garrison was imperial. The people of the town of Royan sent a message that

> they would not fire at us, provided we did not assail them. We passed on, with the royal colours of France at our mast-head: the tri-colour flag flew along the batteries, which were all in preparation; but no act of hostility occurred until we reached the heavy battery at Verdun, which opened its fire upon us, and continued it until the ships

reached the anchorage. No injury, however, was sustained, and the squadron did not return a gun, for I was unwilling to disturb the feeling which appeared so generally and so happily to prevail. ^{Marshall 2.951}

Following his occupation of the Gironde, and the end of the war, he was appointed in early 1816 to command of the *Severn* (50) and played an active part at the bombardment of Algiers by the international force under Lord Exmouth on 27 August 1816.

For this service he was nominated CB, and the kingdom of the Two Sicilies made him a knight of the royal order of St Ferdinand and of Merit (KFM) in recognition of his service in carrying to Naples the freed Italian slaves and a sum of money taken by the Algerians. Spain also made him a knight of the royal and military order of St Fernando (KSF). He served as naval aide-de-camp to William IV from 1830 until 1837, and was awarded a good-service pension on 1 July 1851, was advanced in chivalry to KCB on 5 July 1855, and died aged eighty with the rank of vice-admiral on 5 March 1858, at 20 Dawson Place, Westbourne Grove, Sussex.

> Lt: 17 December 1796
> Cmdr: 7 January 1802
> Capt: 18 May 1805
> R-Adm: 10 January 1837
> V-Adm: 8 January 1848 Reserve half pay
> V-Adm: 1 July 1851
> Adm: 11 September 1854

BAKER

VICE-ADMIRAL SIR THOMAS BAKER, KCB, obtained a degree of notoriety in 1800 when he encountered a Danish convoy in the North Sea, and took action which led directly to the battle of Copenhagen less than a year later. He also played an influential part in bringing about the battle of Trafalgar in 1805.

Baker was probably born in 1771 in Kent, a second son. He entered the navy as a midshipman on 23 August 1781 on the storeship *Dromedary* under the command of Captain Stone, with whom he served in the Downs until 26 June 1782. On 27 October he joined *Kite* under the command of

Captain Peyton, and he continued in the Downs until 21 January 1783, when he followed Peyton into *Carnatic* (74) for Channel service. On 15 March he returned to Captain Stone, in *Hermione* (32), and proceeded to go out to Halifax, leaving her on 5 October 1785. It was peacetime, and he obtained employment for the next two and a half years in the East India Company, but on 22 March 1788 he returned to the navy, and joined *Dido* (28), in which he returned to Halifax. He transferred to *Brisk*, ship-sloop (24), on 22 July 1790 for passage home, and after spending the winter ashore, joined *Royal Sovereign* (100) under Captain Parker at Plymouth on 18 May 1791. He transferred to *Dictator* (64) under Captain William Bligh on 24 September, and then returned to Parker in the 12-pounder frigate *Winchelsea* (32) in October, serving in the Channel until he came ashore in February 1792. In August he joined *Minerva* (38) under Commodore the Honourable William Cornwallis, for service in the East Indies, and there he was commissioned lieutenant on 13 October 1792. Four days later he was appointed to *Swan* (10) under the command of Captain LW Halstead.

On 21 December 1793 he left her in England, and was made acting commander of the cutter *Lion*, in which he was employed in the Channel under Rear-Admiral John MacBride, before moving on 20 May 1794 into *Valiant*, lugger, and on 11 November as acting captain into *Fairy* under Vice-Admiral Joseph Peyton. He was formally promoted commander on 24 November 1795 in recognition for satisfactory service in carrying dispatches to the West Indies. In 1796–7 he commanded *Fairy* in the North Sea, and on 13 June 1797 (he remembered it as 18 June when completing his record of service, ADM 9/2 f 51) he was promoted to post captain and appointed flag captain of *Princess Royal* (98) flying Sir John Orde's flag. His probation lasted until 12 July when he was appointed to command *Nemesis* (28), in which he returned to the Downs under Vice-Admiral Peyton.

After three years' service in *Nemesis* he had his first hours of destiny. In order to enforce the blockade of naval stores to French and Dutch dockyards, Baker hailed the Danish frigate *Freya* on 25 July

1800 and said he was sending a boat to examine the merchantmen. The Dane replied that he would fire into the boat if any such attempt were made, and carried out his threat, but missed the boat and hit *Nemesis*, killing a man. There followed a hot action of twenty-five minutes, at the end of which the *Freya* hauled down her colours.

The dispute at law was fundamental to the ability of the Royal Navy to enforce the blockade. The Danes insisted that the escort provided by a king's ship flying a neutral flag should be held as a guarantee of the cargo of the merchant ships except in the approaches to a blockaded port. This same argument continued to be used by the United States as recently as the First World War. Britain, however, had no reason to trust the Danes, and no reason to moderate their policy out of fear of them. Accordingly, Lord Whitworth was sent to Copenhagen, backed by a fleet commanded by Vice-Admiral Archibald Dickson, who obtained a temporary resolution of the problem. However, the Danes then joined with the Swedes and Russians to renew the Armed Neutrality of the American war in the mid-eighteenth century, and it was in order to defeat this conjunction of power that a fleet had to be sent under Sir Hyde Parker to Copenhagen early in 1801, at which time Lord Nelson destroyed the Danish fleet.

The Admiralty approved of Baker's conduct with respect to the Danish convoy, and on 26 May 1801 he was appointed to *Phoebe* (36), which he commanded on the Irish station until 27 May 1802.

Following the peace of Amiens he was appointed to command *Phoenix* (36) on 28 April 1803, serving in the Channel under Admiral Cornwallis. He met *La Didon* (44) on 10 August 1805, and, after an engagement of three hours at pistol-shot range, he captured her. This had an impact on the outcome at Trafalgar on 21 October because *La Didon* was carrying dispatches to Rear-Admiral Allemand, who was at sea with five ships of the line, directing him to concentrate on Vice-Admiral Villeneuve's combined Franco-Spanish fleet. Baker was to influence events leading up to Trafalgar in another way, because he, with his prize, joined *Dragon* (74) on 14 August, and they were sighted

the next day by Villeneuve, who believed they must be the scouts from the Channel fleet. As a result, he turned south to Cadiz to avoid an action.

Baker then took his prize into Plymouth, but he was again to have an impact on grand strategy on 4 November. *Phoenix* formed part of the squadron under Sir Richard Strachan which captured four French ships of the line which had escaped from the combined fleet at Trafalgar. Baker's skill in keeping in touch with the enemy until British ships of the line could come into action was important in bringing a successful outcome.

Baker was honoured on 17 November by being put in command of his prize, *Didon*. In May 1806 he was transferred to *Tribune* (36), in which he was employed for two more years in the Bay of Biscay. He was then appointed, on 21 May 1808, flag captain of *Vanguard* (74) flying the flag of Rear-Admiral Thomas Bertie in the Baltic. Before returning to England in 1811 he took some leave in Sweden, and came home with a bride, the daughter of Count Routh. The couple were to have several children. Baker was employed from 22 November 1811 to 2 August 1815 commanding *Cumberland* (74) under Admiral Young.

He was appointed a CB on 4 June 1815, nominated a colonel of the Royal Marines on 12 August 1819, and promoted to KCB on 8 June 1831. The Dutch court nominated him a knight of the military order of Wilhelm (KWN) in 1816. He returned to active service in 1839, when he was appointed commander-in-chief in the South American station, where he remained until 1833. He had the rank of vice-admiral when he died on 26 January 1845, aged seventy-four, in Walmer, Kent.

Lt: 13 October 1792
Cmdr: 24 November 1795
Capt: 13 June 1797
R-Adm: 19 July 1821
V-Adm: 10 January 1837

BALL

REAR-ADMIRAL SIR ALEXANDER JOHN BALL, BARONET, is best known for his heroic action in towing Nelson's flagship, the *Vanguard*, clear of rocks following its dismasting in the early stages of the 1798 campaign that ended at the battle of the Nile. He also played a distinguished part in the battle itself, and subsequently commanded the Maltese and British forces in the reduction of the garrison Buonaparte had put into Valletta.

Ball had been born at Stonehouse Court, Stroud, Gloucestershire, the fourth son of Robert Ball, lord of the manor of Stonehouse and high sheriff for Gloucestershire in 1748. His mother, Mary, was daughter of Marsh Dickerson, member of parliament for Brackley, Northamptonshire, and lord mayor of London in 1756. He was educated at the Market schoolhouse, Stroud, entered the navy in 1768, and was commissioned lieutenant on 7 August 1778. In his early career he was closely associated with Admiral Rodney. Two days after Rodney's victorious battle of the Saintes, on 14 April 1782, Ball was promoted master and commander, and on 20 March 1783 he was made post captain. With the end of hostilities following the American war, Ball spent some time in France to learn the language and to economise, and it was then that he first met Nelson, who was in France for the same reason. Initially he made a poor impression. Nelson then thought him a 'great coxcomb' because he wore epaulettes, a custom of French origin, only introduced in the Royal Navy in 1795. Probably Ball adopted the practice in order to obtain respect from French officials, and certainly Nelson came to appreciate his qualities.

Ball returned to Gloucestershire in 1784 and remained on half pay until July 1790. He was married on 7 July 1785 to Mary Smith, daughter of John Wilson of Westminster. The couple had a son, William Keith, second baronet of Blofield, Norfolk.

At the time of the Nootka Sound crisis in 1790, he was appointed to command *Nemesis* (28). He continued in command of her until 1793, when he was transferred to *Cleopatra* (32) and served at Newfoundland under Vice-Admiral Sir Richard King. He was appointed to *Alexander* (74) in 1796, and served off Brest and Cadiz until May 1798, when he was sent as part of reinforcements needed if Nelson were to be able to deal with the French armament in Toulon and the coast of Italy. Nelson's opinion of Ball was changed completely by his resolute seamanship, which saved *Vanguard* (74) from disaster. To misquote Samuel Johnson, saving a man's life by towing his ship clear in a heavy swell can concentrate his mind wonderfully.

Ball became one of Nelson's confidants in planning for the battle with the French fleet, which eventually took place amongst the shoals off the mouth of the Nile on 1 August 1798. He placed *Alexander* opposite the French flagship, *L'Orient*. Ball's account, later reported by Samuel Taylor Coleridge, was that the fire which destroyed that ship was caused by an incendiary device which he had made and which one of *Alexander*'s lieutenants threw into *L'Orient*. Apparently Ball had prepared his ship thoroughly for the use of incendiaries:

> All the shrouds and sails of the ship, not absolutely necessary for its immediate management, were thoroughly wetted and so rolled up, that they were as hard and as little inflammable as so many solid cylinders of wood; every sailor had his appropriate place and function, and a certain number were appointed as the firemen, whose sole duty it was to be on the watch if any part of the vessel should take fire. ^{Coleridge 1.549}

Upon the fleet's return to Sicily, Ball was one of the captains who commanded the forces landed from the British squadron to assist at the reduction of Fort St Elmo. Before Naples was taken, however, he was ordered in October 1789 to command the blockade of Malta, which had been captured by General Buonaparte on his way to Egypt. He proved to be the man for the occasion. In a letter to Nelson written off Malta on 25 March 1800, he wrote:

> The inhabitants in the country revolted against the French in the preceding month, whom they were besieging in La Valletta, and what will appear astonishing, 4000 peasants, with only 2000 muskets, kept in awe 6000 regular troops. I had to co-operate with these men, who had chosen for their chiefs a priest and an attorney; but as they did not receive any pay, and only a

scanty allowance of provisions, they soon began to lose that energy which had roused them to vengeance; they were splitting into parties, and the two chiefs opposing each other in every business, which lost them the confidence of the people, who threatened their lives. Anarchy soon ensued: innocent men were put to death, and money extorted from individuals in a very unjust manner. The inhabitants, in the hour of terror and dismay, implored me to assume an authority, and use my efforts to avert the miseries which awaited them. As early as January, 1799, I directed the civil and military affairs of the island; and the inhabitants were so sensible of its good effects, that they sent deputies to His Sicilian Majesty, and to your Lordship, praying that I might be appointed their chief, which has been graciously complied with. NC 25.480 plate 339

It was found to be impossible for him to keep the situation under control ashore when naval duties called him away, so he obtained permission from Nelson to hand over command of his ship to his first lieutenant, Lieutenant William Harrington, who distinguished himself at the capture of the French ship *Le Généreux*. Ball was excluded from the final capitulation of the French garrison at Valletta, and left the island bitterly in April 1801, when he is known to have visited Nelson at Merton. But he returned in June 1802 as the minister-plenipotentiary to the order of St John, who had been masters prior to the French invasion and were to be restored by the terms of the peace of Amiens. The unpopularity of the order to the Maltese was not considered to be important, but there was concern that Tsar Alexander thought he should be elected the order's grand master. Britain had a long-established objection to Russia acquiring a permanent naval base in the Mediterranean, and Alexander was overly receptive to French advances. Accordingly, Ball was instructed to delay any commitment. The renewal of war in 1803 ended any chance the order had, and from then until his death he was the civil commissioner and *de facto* gover-

nor of Malta. For a short time in 1804 Coleridge, the philosopher and poet, was his secretary. Ball endeared himself to the Maltese by refusing to consider Malta a conquered dependency.

In 1801 he was made a baronet, and despite his preoccupation ashore, the navy promoted him rear-admiral on 9 November 1805. He died on 25 October 1809, at San Antonio Palace, and was buried in Fort St Elmo at Valletta, near the grave of General Ralph Abercromby.

Lt: 7 August 1778
M-C: 14 April 1782
Capt: 20 March 1783
R-Adm: 9 November 1805

BARHAM

Admiral Sir Charles Middleton, Baron Barham, was a colossus in the history of the Royal Navy, and one of the architects of the strategy that led to the battle of Trafalgar.

He was born on 14 October 1726, in Leith, Edinburghshire, the second son of Robert Middleton, collector of the customs in Bo'ness, Linlithgowshire. His mother was Helen, daughter of Captain Charles Dundas of Arniston, Edinburghshire, who was a merchant mariner and uncle of Henry Dundas, Viscount Melville. Middleton was credited with three years in the merchant service between 1738 and April 1741 when he entered the navy as a captain's servant. This prior service at sea enabled him to be examined for lieutenant on 4 November 1745, and to be commissioned the next day: he was promoted master and commander on 27 February 1757 and post captain on 22 May 1758. In 1761 he was given command of the 9-pounder frigate *Emerald* (32) with orders to cruise in the West Indies in defence of trade.

Having reached a degree of comfort in his circumstances he asked for the hand of Margaret, daughter of James Gambier, barrister at law and warden of the Fleet prison. This was a naval family. Her uncle was Captain Samuel Mead, RN, and her brother had entered the navy in 1744 and was to first hoist his flag as vice-admiral in 1780. Nevertheless, Margaret's father forbade the marriage. When she left home for refuge with her school friend Elizabeth Bouverie, and from her friend's home married on 12 December 1761, she was disinherited. Charles, Margaret and Elizabeth then lived together. Margaret was a friend of Samuel Johnson and Hannah More, and was one of the first actively to oppose the slave trade. She and Charles had one daughter, Diana, who eventually succeeded to the peerage.

Middleton held the office of comptroller of the navy during the difficult period from 7 August 1778 to 30 March 1790 when the navy for the first time had to deal with revolution in the colonies, the threat of invasion at home and the internal divisions between the 'Montagus' and the 'Keppeletes': those who supported the administration of the first lord, John Montagu, earl of Sandwich, and those who like Admiral Keppel used the revolution as a cause to rally the opposition. From 1784 to 1790 Middleton was also member of parliament for Rochester, Kent, and from 1781 to 1813 he was an elder brother of the Trinity House. He was the driving force behind the introduction into the navy of carronades, short weapons which could fire a heavier shot than an equally heavy long gun, but could only use a smaller propellant charge, and so were limited to close action. A controversial innovation, they were found to be very effective when properly employed. In 1785 he set about reforming the financial administration of the navy. His success as comptroller can be measured by the readiness of the fleet for service at the time of the Nootka Sound incident in 1790, and three years later when the French Republic declared war.

While comptroller he was promoted to rear-admiral on 24 September 1787 in defiance of the customs of the service, a fact that occasioned an outcry from the captains passed over. He was promoted vice-admiral on 1 February 1793 and served as an Admiralty commissioner from 12 May 1794 to 20 November 1795, being promoted to admiral on 1 June 1795.

Ten years later William Pitt brought him out of retirement in the crisis following the impeachment of Viscount Melville to become first lord of the Admiralty from 30 April 1805 to 10 February 1806. He had been made a baronet on 23 October 1781, and on his appointment as first lord, on 1 May 1805, he was elevated to Baron Barham of Barham Court and Teston, Kent. It was as Lord Barham that he issued the operational orders which led to the battle of Trafalgar. His grasp of naval logistics at fleet and shipboard levels was profound, and his belief in his own abilities was supported by an evangelical Anglican faith.

Margaret died on 10 October 1792, and Charles on 17 June 1813, aged eighty-six, in Barham Court, Teston, Kent.

Lt: 5 November 1745
M-C: 27 February 1757
Capt: 22 May 1758
R-Adm: 24 September 1787
V-Adm: 1 February 1793
Adm: 1 June 1795

BARLOW

REAR-ADMIRAL SIR ROBERT BARLOW, GCB, was in command of the brig *Childers* (10) when on 2 January 1793 he came under fire from the batteries of Brest. He hoisted his colours thinking there had been some mistake, but the battery commanders simply hoisted the French Republican flag and opened a determined crossfire which Barlow escaped only because of a breeze which sprang up allowing him to take *Childers* out to sea. These were the opening shots of the war the French Republic was to declare at the beginning of February.

He was born on 25 December 1757 in London, the first son of William Barlow of Bath, Somerset, and his wife, Hilare, daughter of Robert Butcher of Walthamstow, Essex. The Navy Office credited him with serving as an able seaman in *Swift*, sloop, for nearly three years, after which he was rated as admiral's retinue in *Romney* (50) for nearly a year, and then spent nearly two and a half years as masters mate in *Tartar* (28). [ADM 107.7.64] His lieutenant's commission was dated 6 November 1778, and he took part in the 1782 relief of Gibraltar as first lieutenant of *Courageux* (74). He married on 8 September 1785 Elizabeth Anne, daughter of William Garrett of Worthington, Hampshire. From 1786 to 1789 he very successfully commanded the *Barracouta*, cutter, on customs prevention work, and, apparently without any patron urging his advancement, was promoted master and commander on 22 November 1790 and appointed to *Childers*. France having declared war on 1 February, Barlow made the first capture of an armed ship, the privateer *Patriote*, on 15 February off Gravelines.

He was promoted post captain on 24 May 1793 and given command of *Pegasus* (28), which served as one of the repeating frigates at Lord Howe's victory at the Glorious First of June in 1794. It was from the decks and rigging of *Pegasus* that the artist Nicholas Pocock witnessed and recorded the battle. In recognition of his excellent service, Lord Howe persuaded King George to get the Admiralty to transfer him to the larger frigate *Aquilon* (32). He was transferred again in December 1795 to *Phoebe* (44), in which he was to win two single-ship actions. On 21 December 1797, when 180 miles west of Ushant, he captured the *Néréide* (36), and on 19 February 1801 near the Strait of Gibraltar he engaged *Africaine* (44), which was freighted with military stores and 400 soldiers being taken to join the army in Egypt. During the two-hour action at very close range, 200 French were killed and 143 wounded, *Phoebe* losing only one killed and twelve wounded. A butcher's bill like that suggests something of Barlow's capacity as a ship handler and as a leader, but also gives a sickening idea of the desperate courage of the French. In recognition of his service, he was conferred a knighthood on 16 June 1801. He was then appointed to command *Triumph* (74) and served in the Mediterranean until the end of 1804. When she was put out of commission, he was given command of *London* (90), and then *Barfleur* (90), and soon afterwards named flag captain to Lord Keith commanding in the Downs.

He was appointed in the summer of 1806 deputy comptroller of the navy, which office he retained until September 1808, when he was appointed commissioner of Chatham dockyard. He was made a KCB on 20 May 1820, and was superannuated, but was promoted rear-admiral on 24 January 1823, and, returning to active service, was again resident commissioner at Chatham dockyard from 1823 until 1829. He was advanced in chivalry to GCB on 23 February 1842.

Barlow and his wife, who died on 17 September 1817, had two sons and five daughters. His third daughter, Hilare Caroline, when widowed, remarried, and became the wife of the Revd William Nelson, first Earl Nelson, on 26 March 1829. William was Admiral Nelson's brother, and effectively monopolised the honours and awards granted in recognition of the victory at Trafalgar. Barlow's brother was Sir George Hilaro Barlow, baronet, governor-general of India. Admiral Barlow died on 11 May 1843, aged eighty-five, at the Archbishop's Palace, Canterbury.

Lt: 6 November 1778
M-C: 22 November 1790
Capt: 24 May 1793
Superannuated Capt: 31 July 1810
R-Adm: 24 January 1823

BARRIE

REAR-ADMIRAL SIR ROBERT BARRIE, KCB, played a significant part in the war against the United States of America, in the Chesapeake and at Castine. He is remembered in Canada as the superintendent of the naval establishment at Kingston, in present-day Ontario.

He was born probably in 1779, a son to Robert Barrie and his wife, Dorothea. She came from a military and naval family, being daughter of Lieutenant-Colonel William Gardner and sister of Admiral Sir Alan Gardner, Lord Gardner. Robert first went to sea with his uncle in *Europa* (50) about 1787, and served at Jamaica. He was rated a midshipman in *Goliath* (74) by Captain Sir Andrew Snape Douglas, whom he followed into *Alcide* (74), where he served in the Channel fleet. He was one of the young gentlemen who accompanied Commander George Vancouver on the merchant-built *Discovery* (8) in his voyage to the north-west coast of America in 1791 to 1795, during which time he was rated a master's mate. On 5 November 1795 he was commissioned lieutenant in *Queen* (90) flying his uncle's flag in the Channel fleet. He was first lieutenant of *Le Bourdelois*, commanded by Captain Thomas Manby, at the time of the action with a small French squadron near Barbados on 28 January 1801. He subsequently was appointed to *Quebec* under the command of Captain

Charles Grant, with whom he served in the West Indies. On 23 October 1801 he was promoted commander of *Calypso,* ship-sloop, remaining in the West Indies; he was promoted post captain on 29 April 1802, but was not appointed to command *Elephant* (74) in the Irish Sea until 29 February 1804; and on 10 May 1806 he was appointed to command *Pomone* (38). He had a successful career cruising against French trade until 14 October 1811, when he lost his ship running on a rock south-west of the Needles through the error of his pilot in not taking accurate bearings on the light on Hurst Point to the west of the Solent. He was cleared at the court martial, but was not employed again until he took command of *Grampus* (50) on 17 August 1812, for service in the Mediterranean, off Cadiz and in the West Indies. He transferred into *Dragon* (74) on 10 October, for service in North America.

He was commander of the blockade of the Chesapeake during the bitterly cold winter of 1813, and supplied Major-General Ross with the intelligence needed to make possible the capture and burning of Washington. In May 1814 *Dragon* was ordered to refit at Halifax, after which Barrie commanded a squadron which led to the Americans abandoning and blowing up the fort at Castine, Maine. He was sent back to take command of the blockade of the Chesapeake following the failure of the operations against Baltimore, and then was sent to co-operate with the 2nd West Indian Regiment's landing in Georgia just before the conclusion of peace.

He was made a CB on the creation of that order on 4 June 1815, and on 24 October 1816 he married Julia Wharton, daughter of Sir John Ingilby, baronet of Ripley, Yorkshire. She accompanied him to Quebec, where Barrie was commissioner, and then up the St Lawrence river to Kingston in 1819. The two were dominant figures in the community until the Kingston yard was closed in 1834. Barrie had had a son in 1805 named William, whose mother is not now known, and there were unremembered children from his marriage to Julia. After leaving Canada the couple lived in Swerthdale near Lancaster. Barrie had been created a knight

commander of the Guelphic order of Hanover (KCH) in 1824, and was advanced in chivalry to KCB on 4 July 1840, less than a year before he died on 7 June 1841, aged sixty-two.

Lt: 5 November 1795 (1)
Cmdr: 23 October 1801
Capt: 29 April 1802 (109)
R-Adm: 10 January 1837

BAYNTUN

ADMIRAL SIR HENRY WILLIAM BAYNTUN, GCB, was one of Nelson's captains at the battle of Trafalgar.

He was born in 1765 in Algiers, the second son of Edward Bayntun, who was an army officer, consul in Tripoli and later consul-general in Algiers. His mother was Susanna, daughter and coheiress of Sir John Werden, baronet of Leyland, Lancashire, and of Cholmeaton, Cheshire, and half-sister of the duchess of St Albans. Captain George Murray entered his name as captain's servant in the books of *Levant* (28) in the Mediterranean on 20 May 1775, and rated him midshipman on 19 August. On 15 October 1779 Bayntun followed Murray into *Cleopatra* (36), and was serving in her when she acted as Sir Hyde Parker's repeater frigate at the battle of the Dogger Bank. On 29 December 1782 he transferred to *Irresistible* (74) fitting in the Medway, and on 1 March 1783 he was rated as an able seaman on joining *Syren* (32) under the command of Captain William Carlyon for passage to the Leeward Islands. On 9 April he transferred to *Formidable* (90) flying the flag of Admiral Hugh Pigot as commander-in-chief, but five days later he came ashore on his being commissioned lieutenant. For some reason he was not able to join a ship until 23 December, when he was appointed to *Zebra* under the command of Commander Edward Pakenham. He served with him until 23 December 1784, when he joined *Hannibal* (74), which was fitting in the Hamoaze for Rear-Admiral Sir John Jervis's flag.

Between 12 December 1787 and 4 December 1788 he was ashore, but he was then appointed to *Penelope* (32) and served under Captain John Linzee at Halifax. On 20 August 1790, at the time of the Nootka Sound crisis, he transferred to *Prince* (90), on which Rear-Admiral John Jervis was flying his flag. On 5 December he transferred into *Assistance* (50), which was flying the broad pendant of his first friend, Commodore Sir George Murray, who was commanding a squadron being sent to Flushing in connection with the opening of the Scheldt.

After six weeks' leave he followed Murray into *Duke* (90) on 5 February 1793, four days after the French declaration of war, with Captain George Duff commanding the ship. They proceeded to Guadeloupe under the command of Rear-Admiral Alan Gardiner, and on 3 November transferred to *Ulysses* (44) under Commander Sir James Nicoll Morris to take part in Jervis's expedition to capture the French Leeward Islands. On 29 January 1794 he was appointed a second time to serve in Jervis's flagship, which was now *Boyne* (98), but from her he was sent to serve with the army ashore on Martinique. He, was promoted commander of a prize, *Avenger* (16?), during the siege of Fort Bourbon, but he continued serving ashore nonetheless, and was present at the storming of Fort Royal, Martinique. *Avenger* was unsuitable for the planned operation against St Lucia, and on 25 March Bayntun transferred into *Nautilus*. He participated in the capture, then convoyed the French prisoners of war to join their fleet at Rhode Island. He rejoined the army in Guadeloupe.

That mission having been successfully completed, he was posted captain on 14 July 1794 with appointment as flag captain to Rear-Admiral Charles Thompson in *Veteran* (64). He served in her only four days, off Point à Pitre, Guadeloupe, assisting the army. Jervis was then superseded, and Bayntun requested to be transferred into the 12-pounder frigate *Solebay* (32), in which ship he continued in operations supporting the army at Point à Pitre. With *Beaulieu* (40) and *Quebec* (32) he engaged a ship sheltering under a battery and destroyed it.

After finally returning to England, on 26 November 1795 he was appointed to command *Reunion* (36) in the North Sea, where on 25 September of the following year she was wrecked in the Swin while in passage to bring to England

the duke of Württemberg. This led to his return to the West Indies, to Jamaica, in command of *Quebec* and later *Nereide* (38). On 2 April 1801 he was appointed by the Admiralty to *Thunderer* (74), but he exchanged into *Cumberland* (74); he was ordered to fly a broad pendant in charge of a squadron watching Havana. He captured several enemy vessels, including *Creole* (44) from Cape François. On the same day a schooner was captured from Cuba transporting 100 bloodhounds intended for use against the Haitian blacks.

On 15 July he transferred into *Leviathan* (74) and brought home a convoy of 120 sail. For this service he received the thanks of parliament. He then joined Nelson at Toulon and was with him during the pursuit to the West Indies, and at Trafalgar, where he provided close support in the capture of *Bucentaure* and *Santisima Trinidad* and also engaged *St Augustine* (74). He bore the guidon in the water procession before Nelson's funeral.

On 5 November 1806 Bayntun was appointed to *Africa* (64) and employed in the expedition commanded by Rear-Admiral Murray and Brigadier-General Craufurd that was sent to capture Chile, but was afterwards redirected to Buenos Aires, arriving in the Rio de la Plata on 14 June 1807. He came ashore on 20 January 1808. His last operational command was *Milford,* in which he served off Brest and Rochefort from 29 May 1809 to 3 August 1810, and he was then given command of *Royal Sovereign,* yacht, at Deptford, from 1 August 1811 to 30 August 1812.

On 12 August 1809, at Stoke Church, Plymouth, he married Sophia Mayhew of Bath. The couple made their home at Rettenden Hall, Essex, and had one son and one daughter. He was promoted rear-admiral on 12 August 1812, and nominated KCB on 2 January 1815, advancing to GCB on 25 October 1839. Sophia died on 16 September 1830, and Bayntun died with the rank of admiral on 17 December 1840, aged seventy-five, in Bath. He was buried in Weston church, Bath.

Lt: 15 April 1783
Cmdr: 10 March 1794
Capt: 4 May 1794
R-Adm: 12 August 1812
V-Adm: 19 July 1821
Adm: January 1837

Bazeley

ADMIRAL JOHN BAZELEY made his reputation as a fighting captain in the American war, and continued to give vigorous service in the first years of the war against the French Republic.

He was born in March 1741 in Dover, Kent, and entered the navy in April 1755 with the patronage of Captain, later Admiral, Sir Joshua Rowley. For some reason his examination for lieutenant took place in 1760, at the Navy Office, St Mary-le-Strand, Westminster, two years short of the seven years required, and he was commissioned on 7 April 1760.

John Bazeley, Esq.,
Vice-Admiral of the Red Squadron,
engraved by William Ridley from a miniature
painting by Langdon, published by Joyce Gold,
103 Shoe Lane, 1 October 1805.

On 27 April 1765, during the American Revolutionary War, he married Amelia Baker without waiting until he had reached post rank. Her brothers were to become senior naval officers, Vice-Admiral Thomas Baker and Captain John Baker, RN, and she was to be the sister-in-law of Admiral Sir Richard Lee, KCB. But all were Bazeley's jun-

iors, and could not influence his career.

Fortune favoured the brave. In September 1777 Bazeley distinguished himself when in command of *Alert,* cutter, by engaging and capturing the American brig privateer *Lexington*, in recognition of which the Admiralty registered *Alert* as a sloop of war, and promoted Bazeley master and commander on 1 October 1777.

On 15 April 1778 he was advanced to post captain in the *Formidable* (90), Sir Hugh Palliser's flagship, and in her he fought in the unsatisfactory battle of Ushant on 27 July 1778. Following the courts martial on Admirals Keppel and Palliser, Bazeley was so fortunate as to be put in command of the *Pegasus* (28), and even more fortunate in that she was part of Admiral Rodney's fleet, which on 8 January 1780 captured the whole of a Spanish convoy from St Sebastian laden with naval stores and provisions. Eight days later he took part in the chase and capture of Don Juan de Langara's fleet; he then participated in the relief of Gibraltar and proceeded to the West Indies, where he took part in the defeat of the Count de Guichen's squadron, after which he returned to England, bearing Admiral Rodney's dispatches. On 10 September 1781 whilst in command of *Amphion* (32) he supported General Arnold in his destruction of the town and port of New London.

During the peace he commanded the guardship *Alfred* (74) and in her participated in Lord Howe's victory on the Glorious First of June in 1794. In *Blenheim* (98) he participated in Admiral Hotham's action in the Mediterranean in July 1795.

On 1 June 1795 he was promoted rear-admiral, but apart from temporary port commands he was not again employed, although he continued to be promoted, becoming a full admiral on 9 November 1805. Two of his sons followed him into the navy: Vice-Admiral John Bazeley and Captain Henry Bazeley, RN. He died on 6 April 1809, aged sixty-eight, in Dover.

Lt:	7 April 1760
M-C:	1 October 1777
Capt:	15 April 1778
R-Adm:	1 June 1795
V-Adm:	14 February 1799
Adm:	9 November 1805

BEAUCLERK

ADMIRAL LORD AMELIUS BEAUCLERK, GCB, served conspicuously in the Walcheren operation of 1809 as second in command to Sir Richard Strachan, commanding the landing of a division of the army. Later, during Strachan's absence with the army in Flushing, Beauclerk assumed the government of Campvere and command of the fleet and storeships in the Roompot.

He was born on 23 May 1771 in London, the third son of Aubrey, fifth duke of St Albans, and his wife Catharine, daughter of William Ponsonby, second earl of Bessborough. He entered the navy in June 1783 on board *Jackall,* cutter, commanded by Lieutenant Bailley, and served in Newfoundland and the West Indies with Vice-Admiral John Campbell and Commodore Alan Gardner, returning home in 1789 as acting lieutenant of *Europa* (50). He was confirmed in rank on 21 September 1790 at the time of the Nootka Sound crisis. In 1792 he was put in command of *Druid* (32) under orders for the Mediterranean, and following the French declaration of war in February 1793 he served in the Mediterranean fleet under Lord Hood, and was promoted post captain on 16 September 1793 with command of *Nemesis* (28). The following March he was transferred to *Juno* (32) in Admiral Hotham's squadron watching Toulon, and in her he took part in the action of 14 March 1795. *Juno* was one of the escort to the homeward trade in the autumn. After his return to home waters he was transferred to *Dryad* (44), in which he served on the Irish station. On 13 June 1796 he engaged *La Proserpine* (42), which had on board 348 men, as opposed to *Dryad*'s 251, and after an action of forty-five minutes during which the French suffered thirty killed and forty-five wounded, they were obliged to surrender. In late 1800 he commissioned *Fortune* (40) and served in the Channel and in attendance on the king at Weymouth.

On the renewal of hostilities in 1803 he was appointed to command *Majestic* (74) in the Channel fleet; he transferred to *Saturn* (74) in the summer of 1805, and to *Royal Oak* (74) in May 1809. Following the Scheldt operation, Beauclerk was nominated a colonel of marines on 31 July 1810, promoted rear-admiral on 1 August 1811, and given command in the North Sea fleet. At the end of the war he was in command of British forces in Basque Roads, and negotiated a suspension of hostilities with Baron de la Raffiniere, commander-in-chief at Rochelle. He was created KCB on 2 January 1815.

After his eventual promotion to admiral on 22 July 1830 he was advanced in chivalry to GCB on 4 August 1835 and to GCH on 29 March 1831. He was appointed first and principal naval aide-de-camp to William IV, and died on 10 December 1846, aged seventy-five, at the manor of Winkfield, Hampshire.

Lt: 21 September 1790
Capt: 16 September 1793
R-Adm: 1 August 1811
V-Adm: 12 August 1819
Adm: 22 July 1830

BEAUFORT

REAR-ADMIRAL SIR FRANCIS BEAUFORT, KCB, the son of a famous Irish cartographer and priest, is best known for his invention in 1806 of the Beaufort scale of wind measurement, based on the apparent effect of the wind on different classes of ships. In his own day he was known as the author of *Karamania*, a book describing the coast of Asia Minor, on which he commanded the *Frederikstein*, frigate, in 1811 and 1812. His capacity as a hydrographer was unparalleled, and when eventually he was appointed naval hydrographer he vastly increased the production of charts, publishing over 1,000 in the twenty years he was in office.

He was born on 27 May 1774 in Collon, county Louth, the second and younger son of the Venerable Dr Daniel Augustus Beaufort, rector of Navan, county Meath, vicar of Collon and author of a map of Ireland. His mother was Mary, daughter and coheiress of William Waller of Allenstown. He first went to sea in the East India Company, and entered the navy on 21 June 1787 as a volunteer 'on the books' of *Colossus* (74) under Captain Hugh Cloberry Christian. He was rated a midshipman when he joined *Latona* (38) under Captain Albemarle Bertie on 12 June 1790 during the Nootka Sound mobilisation. He came ashore on 27 November, and returned to sea on 10 June 1791, when he was rated midshipman or master's mate in *Aquilon* (32), Captain the Honourable Robert Stopford. He was still serving on board at the battle of the Glorious First of June in 1794, when *Aquilon* served as a repeater for Lord Howe. On 24 July he transferred with Captain Stopford to *Phaeton* (38), which played an important part in Vice-Admiral Cornwallis's defence against superior force on 17 June 1795 by signalling to an imaginary fleet over the horizon.

He remained in his ship when commissioned lieutenant on 10 May 1796, and had risen to first lieutenant by 28 October 1800, when he led a boat attack on a Spanish privateer under the guns of Frangerola and brought away his prize. On boarding her he was wounded nineteen times, suffering injuries including a head wound and several shots in the left arm. This guaranteed his promotion to commander on 13 November 1800, but he needed to come ashore to recover from his wounds in hospital, and was offered in November 1801 a small pension of £45 12s. 5d.

He spent the next two years assisting in the construction of a line of telegraph stations from Dublin to Galway, and on 5 June 1805 he was appointed to command the *Woolwich* (44) armed *en flute* and fitting to transport stores to overseas garrisons. In her he made a voyage to Bombay, and in 1807 he participated in the evacuation of the defeated British troops from Buenos Aires, during which time he undertook a survey of the Rio de la Plata which was praised by Dalrymple, the first naval hydrographer. On 23 May 1809 he accepted command of *Blossom*, ship-sloop, in which he was employed in convoy duty on the coast of Spain. He finally received his commission as post captain on 30 May 1810 in the former Danish *Frederikstein* (36).

In the Aegean he did his best to reduce the number of pirates plundering trade without respect to flag, and he persuaded the Admiralty to commission a survey of the coast. This he was only partly to complete, as he was most severely wounded by a shot from one of the Turkish inhabitants. He survived, however, and on his return to England

devoted himself to preparing charts for publication. These set a very high standard and his account of antiquities on the Turkish coast was very well received by the public. He was awarded a more substantial pension of £250 per annum for his wounds on 2 December 1815.

Having retired from the sea he was able to marry, and on 3 December 1812, at St Mary, St Marylebone, London, he was united to Alicia Magdalena, eldest daughter of Captain Lestock Wilson of Harley Street, London, arbitrator for the East India Company and founder of the shipping company Palmer, Wilson and Co. The couple had four sons and three daughters. The marriage was a very happy one, and it was a terrible blow when Alicia died of cancer on 28 August 1834. For a number of years his sister Harriet kept house for him, and the relationship became virtually a second marriage, but could not be acknowledged. He remarried on 8 November 1838, uniting with Honora, daughter of his brother-in-law, Richard Lovell Edgeworth of Edgeworthstown, county Longford, Ireland. Alas, she became invalided and demented.

Captain Hurd, the second hydrographer of the navy, died in May 1823 but Beaufort was rejected as his successor. The current first secretary of the Admiralty, J W Croker, held the hydrographic service to be a waste of public money. He probably recognised that Beaufort would not be content with a passive sinecure. He was finally appointed hydrographer of the navy in May 1829. For eight years he presided over the Arctic Council, directing the various searches for Sir John Franklin. He was elected a fellow of the Royal Society on 30 June 1814, and was founder and member of the council of the Royal Astronomical Society (1820) and the Royal Geographical Society (1830). He was nominated a civil KCB on 29 April 1848.

He died with the rank of rear-admiral on 17 December 1857, aged eighty-three, in Hove near Brighton, and was buried in Hackney church graveyard, London. Honora died in February 1858.

Lt: 10 May 1796
Cmdr: 13 November 1800
Capt: 30 May 1810
Rear-Adm: 1 October 1846

BEAVER

CAPTAIN PHILIP BEAVER became a protégé of Lord Keith, who noticed his ability. He served in the East and West Indies and the Mediterranean, but he was not lucky either with prize money or with promotion, and died young.

He was born on 28 February 1766, a son of the Revd James Beaver, curate of Lewknor, Oxfordshire. His father's death led his mother, who was not well provided for, to accept an offer of patronage made by Captain Joshua Rowley, and Beaver entered the navy in October 1777 on board *Monarch* (74). On 27 July 1778 he was at the battle of Ushant, and he continued to serve with Rowley during 1779 and 1780, finally being commissioned lieutenant by Rowley on 16 October 1783. During the peace years, apart from the brief mobilisations in 1790 and 1791, Beaver lived with his mother at Boulogne, following which he was employed in a disastrous attempt to colonise Bulama off the coast of Sierra Leone. He arrived back at Plymouth on 17 May 1794, and published an account of his Bulama experiences, *African Memoranda*, in 1805.

He sailed in March 1795 as one of the lieutenants of *Stately* (64) under orders for the Far East, but at the Cape of Good Hope she was attached by Captain Elphinstone, later Lord Keith, to take part in the capture of the Dutch colony. Later, Elphinstone transferred Beaver into his flagship, and they remained together when in 1798 Keith was posted to the Mediterranean, Beaver serving under him as first lieutenant of the *Foudroyant* (80) and afterwards of the *Barfleur* (90). On 28 June 1799 Beaver was promoted commander, and a few months later he was appointed by Keith to the flagship as acting assistant captain of the fleet, in which position he was employed during April and May 1800 in the repeated bombardments of Genoa. On the surrender of that place he was sent home with the dispatches, but he did not receive the customary promotion because by the time he reached London, Napoleon's victory at Marengo had already led to the restoration of Genoa to France.

In compensation, during his return voyage to the Mediterranean he had an opportunity while in Gibraltar to marry his young fiancée, Miss Elliott, who was to present him with six children. And Keith did not let him suffer for Buonaparte's victory, promoting him post captain on 10 February 1801, as his flag captain. He served in the operations on the coast of Egypt, and in June he exchanged into *Déterminée,* frigate, in which he proceeded to Constantinople with dispatches, for which service the sultan presented him with a diamond box. For his services in Egypt he was nominated to the Turkish order of the Crescent. Beaver had been offered a large sum of money, but refused it.

Déterminée was paid off at Portsmouth on 19 May 1802, and Beaver was given command of the sea fencibles of Essex in July 1803. Three years later he was appointed to *Acasta* (40) and served in her in the West Indies until after the capture of Martinique in February 1809. He was then sent home in charge of a convoy and with many French prisoners. He returned to the East Indies in *Nisus* (38) on 22 June 1810 and was employed under Vice-Admiral Albemarle Bertie in the capture of Mauritius in November 1810, and, under Rear-Admiral the Honourable Robert Stopford, in the conquest of Java during August and September 1811. On his return voyage late in 1812 he put into Table Bay, and there he died on 10 April 1813 of a violent inflammation of the bowels. His early death and the bankruptcy of his agent left his widow badly provided for, and she became matron of Greenwich hospital school.

Lt: 16 October 1783
Cmdr: 28 June 1800
Capt: 10 February 1801

BERESFORD

ADMIRAL SIR JOHN POO BERESFORD, BARONET, KCB, was an officer who worked his way to the top of his profession by sheer ability.

He was born in 1767, in Waterford, a natural son of George de la Poer, first marquis of Waterford, and was educated in Catterick Bridge. He entered the navy with the patronage of Lord Longford, and the Navy Office gave him credit for nearly a year and half as captain's servant in *Alexander* (74), in the books of which his name was entered on 20 July 1781, and for nearly two years in *Winchelsea* (32) in which he was rated midshipman on 13 May 1784. He subsequently served as able seaman and midshipman in *Ganges* (74) and *Maidstone* (28) before he passed his examination on 7 October 1787, and was commissioned lieutenant on 4 November 1790. ADM 107.11.289 While serving in *Lapwing* in the Mediterranean he was employed ashore in Genoa and Turin evacuating British residents threatened by the revolutionary excitement. He was at times at considerable risk himself, and eventually escaped disguised as a peasant. In November 1794 he succeeded Captain Penrose in command of *Lynx,* sloop of war, on the American station. When in December the *Thetis* (38), Captain the Honourable Alexander Cochrane, ran aground, Beresford took a prominent part in refloating her after ten days of difficult and dangerous labour. Rear-Admiral George Murray appointed him acting captain of *Hussar* (28) with the rank of commander in February 1795.

During an action with French frigates on 17 May in which Beresford took an active part under Cochrane's orders, two of the enemy were captured, one of which, *Prevoyante*, he was subsequently given to command. His promotion to post captain was dated 25 June 1795. The ship was originally intended for a third rate, but was mounting only twenty-four guns. At his own expense Beresford refitted her at Halifax as a 40-gun frigate, and cruised against enemy trade to recover the expense. It was thus remarkable when he was superseded in command by orders from the Admiralty, on the grounds that she was too large for a first command. He was expected to fit up the second prize, *Raison* (24), again at his own expense. He nearly lost her when surprised by a heavy French frigate, *Vengeance* (52), while his prize crew were on board an American merchantman, but he recovered them and made a strenuous and successful defence, and they parted company in a fog. The French ship had been so badly damaged that it was believed she sank. Beresford had been freighting £200,000 in specie at the time.

In a night action in March 1797 against a brig and a Spanish ship of fifty guns, but mounting only twenty-six and carrying a valuable cargo, Beresford disguised *Raison* as a ship of the line by displaying a double row of lanterns along her hull, and succeeded in capturing both. This was effected so near to the rocks of Little Isaac that Beresford found it necessary to hook his starboard anchor to the prize's fore-chains in order to bring her about onto a safe tack.

In 1798 in command of *Unité* and a 9-pounder frigate *Amphitrite* (28), the old *Pomona* which had been renamed in 1795, he succeeded in taking the fort on Devil's Island near Cayenne by a *coup de main*. He exhibited no less energy in attempting to cut out a French corvette moored close to the fort at Basseterre, but finding the ship chained to the fort, and under a heavy fire, he was forced to abandon the prize. Apart from that setback, he continued to be remarkably successful in taking prizes, and he was transferred into *Diana* (36). In 1801 he was senior officer of frigates under Sir John Duckworth during the operations against the Danish islands. He then returned to home in charge of convoy of 200 sail.

He took the years of peace ashore, but with the renewal of the war in 1803 he was appointed to *Virginia*, frigate, which he wore out in service on the French coast. In August 1804 he was ordered to sail to the American station as a passenger, in order to take command of *Cambrian*, a 44-gun, 24-pounder frigate, and on the death of Sir Andrew Mitchell he succeeded to the command-in-chief, stationing himself at Halifax and being eventually superseded by Admiral Berkeley. Having returned to England he was put in command of *Theseus* (74) and served in the blockade of L'Orient, dealing effectively on 21 February 1809 with the arrival of a battle squadron from Brest which eventually took shelter in Basque Roads. Beresford wrote to Admiral Moorsom, private secretary to Lord Mulgrave, the first lord, suggesting the fireship attack on the ships in the roads which was eventually to be entrusted to Lord Cochrane.

When *Theseus* was paid off, Beresford was appointed to *Poictiers* (74) in the Channel fleet, where for four months he was senior officer before Brest. Later he was sent to Lisbon under Admiral Berkeley, and when the French army retreated from Santarem he was ordered to take the directions of Sir Thomas Williams, whom he accompanied with 600 boats which were used to transport 16,000 men under General Wellington across the Tagus in twenty-four hours. In 1811 Beresford served in the North Sea, where he took part in the blockade of the Texel, and in 1812 he was ordered back to the American station in consequence of the American declaration of war. On 28 October he captured the American sloop *Wasp*. In January 1813 he was ordered to blockade the Delaware with a small squadron; he remained there for four months, and then was sent on a cruise against enemy shipping. In November he returned to England in charge of a convoy.

The end of his active service at sea was marked by the honour of transporting, on 23 April 1814, the Board of Admiralty, the prince regent and King Louis XVIII from Dover to Calais in the *Royal Sovereign,* yacht. He had been created a knight bachelor on 22 May 1812, and he was honoured by investiture as a baronet on 21 May 1814, with promotion to rear-admiral following on 4 June. He was then ordered to stand by to transport the Portuguese prince regent to Lisbon, but the plan was subsequently changed. Nonetheless he was honoured with the Portuguese decoration of the order of the Tower and the Sword (CTS). He was nominated KCB on 12 August 1819, promoted vice-admiral on 27 May 1825, and advanced to GCH in May 1836. In 1820 he was appointed commander-in-chief at Leith, and was there when King George IV made the first official visit by a Hanoverian monarch to Scotland. He also had a second career, in politics, successively holding the parliamentary seats for Coleraine (26 June 1809–12 and 10 June 1814–January 1823), Berwick-upon-Tweed (17 February 1823–6), Northallerton (1826–32), Coleraine again (1832–May 1833) and finally Chatham (1835–7), and serving as a commissioner of the Admiralty from 23 December 1834 to 25 April 1835.

Beresford was married three times, first marrying on 22 June 1809 Mary Ann, only daughter of Captain Anthony James Pye Molloy, RN. The couple had a son, but Mary Ann died in Bermuda on 1 July 1813, and Beresford was married again on 17 August 1815, to Harriet Elizabeth, third daughter of Henry Peirse of Bedale, Yorkshire, and a member of parliament. She was to give birth to two sons and four daughters before she died on 28 February 1825. His third marriage on 26 May 1836 was to Amelia, second daughter of James Baillie and widow of Samuel Peach. There were no children from that union, and his third wife outlived him to 17 December 1862, when she died in Paris. He died with the rank of admiral on 2 October 1844, aged seventy-seven, in Bedale, Yorkshire.

Lt: 4 November 1790
Cmdr: February 1795
Capt: 25 June 1795
R-Adm: 4 June 1814
V-Adm: 27 May 1825
Adm: 28 June 1838

BERKELEY

ADMIRAL THE HONOURABLE SIR GEORGE CRANFIELD BERKELEY, GCB, was one of the breed of eighteenth-century political admirals. Perhaps that provides some explanation for the intemperance of his actions while commander in North America. His orders, dated 1 June 1807, recounted that during the time when the British squadron was at anchor in the Chesapeake, many of their men deserted and 'entered on board the US frigate called the *Chesapeake*, and openly paraded the streets of Norfolk, in sight of their officers, under the American flag, protected by the magistrates of the town'.[NC18.117] Berkeley ordered his captains to stop the *Chesapeake* (44) at sea, and if her commander, Commodore Barron, refused to surrender the deserters, they were to be taken by force. A similar liberty was to be accorded the American to reclaim any US deserters. When *Leopard* (50) commanded by Captain Humphreys encountered *Chesapeake* at sea off Cape Henry on 22 June, the American denied that there were deserters on board, and rejected the offer. In the end a few shots were fired into the US ship before she surrendered to the search, which discovered four deserters, one of whom was later tried and hanged for his insolence to an officer while in Norfolk.

President Jefferson issued a proclamation on 2 July 1807 banning the entry of any British ship of war into American waters, and this led to a British proclamation of 16 October 1807 which amongst other things forbade the forcible searching of foreign warships. The editor of the *Naval Chronicle* was mystified that the government so weakly surrendered what it considered a basic right, but the government's actions did serve to put off until 1812 the evil day when the United States declared war. By then Emperor Napoleon had so embroiled himself in Spain and Russia that the American belligerency was of lesser consequence than it would have been in 1807.

Berkeley was born on 10 August 1753 in Berkeley, Gloucestershire, the third and youngest son of Augustus, fourth earl of Berkeley, and of his wife Elizabeth, daughter of Henry Drax of Charlborough, Dorset. In 1761 he was sent to Eton College, Berkshire, and he entered the navy in 1766. The sea service was a logical career for him, as he was a grandson of Vice-Admiral James Berkeley, third earl, first lord of the Admiralty, who had died in August 1736. His cousin, Augustus Viscount Keppel, was then a post captain commanding the *Mary,* yacht. Berkeley first went to sea under his command in the *Mary*, and served as page to Princess Caroline Matilda, who was being taken to Denmark to be married. In 1767 he joined the *Guernsey* (50), flagship of Commodore Sir Hugh Palliser, on the Newfoundland station, where he assisted in surveys of Newfoundland and the Gulf of St Lawrence being undertaken by John Cartwright and Master Joseph Gilbert, who had served under James Cook in *Resolution* (12). In 1769 Berkeley was appointed to the 12-pounder frigate *Alarm* (32) under the command of Captain John Jervis.

He was given his lieutenant's commission on 5 January 1774, but his career was interrupted when he contested the parliamentary seat for the county of Gloucester. He was back at sea in time to serve as one of Keppel's lieutenants at the battle of Ushant on 27 July 1778, but the political crisis this battle occasioned did Berkeley no good. He was promoted master and commander on 3 September 1778, but when his services to Admiral Lord Shuldham as port admiral at Plymouth during the threatened Franco-Spanish invasion in 1779 led to his being strongly recommended for an appointment to a ship, his political connections prevented the Admiralty employing him in home waters. Instead he was sent to Newfoundland, where on 3 September 1780 he and his cousin Captain George Keppel captured an American packet, *Mercury* (8). On her was travelling Henry Laurens, who was *en route* to the Netherlands to negotiate a loan. This precipitated the British declaration of war against the Netherlands, at a time when any pretext would serve so long as war was declared before the Dutch joined the Russian-led League of Armed Neutrality. Rear-Admiral Richard Edwards, commander-in-chief Newfoundland, ordered the cousins to exchange ships on 12 September, Berkeley taking command of *Vestal* (28), and formally being promoted post captain on 15 September 1780. In 1781 he distinguished himself in the defence of Gibraltar, destroying two gunboats under the walls of the fortress of Ceuta. He was appointed to *Recovery* (32) in January 1782 and served in Vice-Admiral Samuel Barrington's squadron. Following the successful capture of most of a convoy off Ushant between 20 and 22 April, Berkeley was appointed in August to one of the prizes, *Pegase* (74).

Following the American war he returned to active political life, being returned to parliament for Gloucester on 23 April 1783, which seat he held until April 1810. He married Emilia Charlotte, daughter of Lord George Henry Lennox of West Stoke, Sussex, on 23 August 1784. The couple had two sons and three daughters, of whom the elder daughter, Anne Louisa Emily, married in 1807 Captain, later Vice-Admiral, Sir Thomas Masterman Hardy, Lord Nelson's flag captain at Trafalgar. Their third daughter, Georgiana Mary, married in 1811 the man who would rise to be Admiral of the Fleet Sir George Francis Seymour.

Berkeley's political leverage now proved to his advantage. He was appointed to command *Magnificent* (74) in 1786, and from April 1789 to

June 1795 he held the post of surveyor-general of the Ordnance. That appointment did not prevent him returning to sea before the outbreak of war in 1793, and he commanded the *Marlborough* (74) at the battle of the Glorious First of June, during which two French ships struck to him. *Marlborough* was one of six that broke the French line, and was totally dismasted, losing 132 killed and wounded. Berkeley himself suffered dangerous wounds to his head and leg. In recognition, he was promoted colonel of the marines on 1 June 1795, and awarded one of the few medals of merit distributed to captains after that action. His injuries kept Berkeley ashore until 1795, when he was put in command of *Formidable* (90), in which he served off Brest, Cadiz, Ireland and the Texel until 1797.

In the spring of 1798 when the regiment of sea fencibles was being raised in response to the French preparations for invasion, he was appointed to command the division on the coast of Sussex. The following year he hoisted his flag on 14 February 1799 as rear-admiral in the *Mars* (74) and commanded a squadron in the Channel fleet under Admirals Lord Bridport and earl of St Vincent. But his health was affected by gout, and he requested leave of absence before the peace of Amiens in 1802.

Following the renewal of the war, Henry Dundas, Lord Melville, appointed him in December 1804 inspector of sea fencibles, and he undertook a fourteen-month tour of coastal defences. This was critically important work at a time of great anxiety about French preparations for invasion. Following Pitt's death, and Grenville's and Fox's succession to power, Berkeley's political connections again worked for him. He was offered the

The Honourable George Cranfield Berkeley,
Rear-Admiral of the Red Squadron,
engraved by William Ridley from
an original miniature by Miss Page,
published by Joyce Gold,
103 Shoe Lane, 31 August 1804.

command of the North American station. His orders to intercept the USS *Chesapeake*, which cost Captain Humphreys his career, were only a minor setback to Berkeley's career. He was superseded by Admiral Beresford, and returned to Britain in April 1808. Eight months later, in December, he was appointed commander-in-chief on the coast of Portugal, where he was effective in providing close support for the Anglo-Portuguese army under Sir John Cradock, and from April 1809 under Wellington. The ability of Cradock and Sir Arthur Wellesley, future duke of Wellington, to move men and equipment by sea was critical to their successes, and Berkeley's squadron was effective in working with Spanish and Portuguese irregulars in Galicia and northern Portugal, haemorrhaging the corps of Marshals Nicolas Soult and Michel Ney prior to Wellington's defeat of Soult at Porto in May. At Ferrol, Berkeley secured, refitted and took beyond the reach of the French a powerful Spanish squadron.

Evidently the government had been right to forgive him for his intemperance while in command at Halifax. Wellington wrote of Berkeley that 'His activity is unbounded, the whole range of the business of the Country in which he is stationed, civil, military, political, commercial, even ecclesiastical I believe as well as naval are objects of his attention.'[Wellington 30] On 31 July 1810 he was promoted admiral, and the Portuguese prince regent appointed him lord high admiral of Portugal. At the crisis in October, Berkeley provided direct support to the army in the lines of Torres Vedras, with sailors manning batteries and signal posts, and gunboats on the Tagus. When on 5 March 1811 Marshal André Masséna broke camp and retreated, Berkeley was no less supportive in

Wellington's offensive, leading to the capture in 1812 of Ciudad Rodrigo and Badajoz, and the victory at Salamanca, which obliged Soult to raise the siege of Cadiz. In his dispatches, Wellington wrote that he had 'found the Admiral not only disposed to give us every assistance in his power, but to anticipate and exceed our wishes in this way' and 'It is impossible for 2 officers to be on better terms than we are.' Wellington (2) 5.388

In July 1812 Berkeley retired from the sea, and from public life. He did not receive a peerage, perhaps because it was inopportune at the time of the unwanted war with the United States. He was nominated a knight bachelor on 1 February 1813, being raised to GCB on 2 January 1815. He died on 25 February 1818, aged sixty-four, in South Audley Street, Grosvenor Square, Westminster, Middlesex.

Lt: 5 January 1774
M-C: 3 September 1778
Capt: 15 September 1780
R-Adm: 14 February 1799
V-Adm: 9 November 1805
Adm: 1 July 1810

BERRY

REAR-ADMIRAL SIR EDWARD BERRY, BARONET, had already established a reputation for intrepidity and capacity prior to the battle of Cape St Vincent on 14 February 1797, in which he served as a volunteer on board *Captain* (74) flying Nelson's broad pendant. When the fire from the guns of the Spanish *San Nicolas* (80) proved too hot, it was to him that the order to lead the boarders fell. He was reportedly the first into the mizzen chains, and by the time Nelson reached the deck of the *San Nicolas*, Berry had secured her quarterdeck. He then went with Nelson to board the *San Joseph* (112), and made such a favourable impression that Admiral Jervis posted him captain on 6 March 1797. Later in the year, after Nelson had lost an arm in the abortive attack on Tenerife, Berry accompanied him to court: King George expressed his sympathy, but Nelson replied by presenting Berry and saying that 'he still had his right arm left'.

Berry had been born on 17 April 1768 in Norwich, the first son of Edward Berry, merchant in London, and his wife Elizabeth, daughter of the

Revd Thomas Forster of Barbados, rector of Holton, Suffolk. He was sent to be educated at the Norwich grammar school where his uncle the Revd Dr Forster was headmaster. When his father died young, Edward, with the patronage of Lord Mulgrave, entered the navy on 5 February 1779 as an ordinary seaman on board the *Burford* under the command of Captain Peter Rainier. He served in the East Indies, and on 1 February or March 1780 he was rated midshipman. He returned to England at the end of the war in 1783, and joined *Magnificent* (74) under the command of Captain the Honourable George Berkeley in 1786 for six years' service in the Channel, the last two under Captain Richard Onslow, who rated him master's mate. He was rated midshipman when he joined *Duke* (90), apparently before the end of August 1792, for he noted in his précis of service that his captain on joining was Robert Calder. When *Duke* sailed for the West Indies flying the broad pendant of Commodore George Murray, however, command of the ship was in the hands of Captain George Duff. Once on station, he was transferred to *Boyne* (98) flying the flag of Vice-Admiral Sir John Jervis. He had been examined for lieutenant on 3 June 1789, at Somerset House, Westminster, but was not commissioned until 20 January 1794 when he was appointed to *Nautilus*. On 5 November 1795 Jervis appointed him to serve in *Agamemnon* (64) commanded by Commodore Nelson, which was employed in the Mediterranean. Berry soon made a favourable impression, and followed Nelson into *Captain* (74) on 11 June 1796. He was promoted master and commander 'for rank' on 12 November, appointed to command *Bonne Citoyenne* (20) on 18 February 1797, and with breathtaking speed, promoted post captain on 6 March.

In 12 December 1797 he married his cousin Louisa, Dr Forster's daughter. Their decision had been hastened by Nelson's warning four days earlier that he intended to sail soon to rejoin Jervis at Cadiz, from which Berry was to be ordered into the Mediterranean.

On 20 January 1798 Berry assumed command of *Vanguard* flying Nelson's flag as rear-admiral,

Sir Edward Berry, Captain R.N.,
engraved by Daniel Orme, engraver to
His Majesty and the Prince of Wales, from the
original painting in the possession of the late
Admiral Lord Viscount Nelson,
published by Joyce Gold, 103 Shoe Lane,
31 March 1806.

October and arrived on 6 June at Palermo, where two days later Nelson hoisted his flag on board. Nelson was preoccupied with the affairs of the Neapolitan court, and, striking his flag, employed *Foudroyant* as part of Captain Dixon's squadron blockading Malta. On 18 February 1800 she participated in the capture of *Généreux* and on 30 March took part in a hot action which ended in the capture of *Le Guillaume Tell* (80). In the following June the *Foudroyant* carried the queen of Naples from Palermo to Leghorn. As the customary gift, Berry received a gold box, set with diamonds, and a diamond ring. A few months later he left the ship and returned to England. A year to the day following Berry's capture in *Leander* and exchange as prisoner of war he was made a KB.

On 1 November 1800 he was appointed to command *Princess Charlotte*, yacht, and then on 5 April 1801 he was put in command of *Ruby* (64) for employment in the Baltic and North Sea, but he was in her command for little more than a month, and remained ashore throughout the peace of Amiens and for the first two years of the new war.

On 4 September 1805 he was appointed to command the *Agamemnon* (64), in which he took part in the battle of Trafalgar on 21 October 1805, and in Sir John Duckworth's victory at San Domingo on 6 February 1806, although he did not have an opportunity to display his notable courage in either action. On 10 August 1806 he left *Agamemnon,* and he apparently was not employed again until 1812. On 12 December 1806 he was made a baronet.

He took command of a unit of sea fencibles on 10 May 1810, but that force was broken up in 1811. He was appointed to command *Barfleur* (90) on 7 September 1812, serving in the Mediterranean until 27 February 1814. That was his last operational warship. He was honoured with the command of several royal yachts, and in the summer of 1814 he took part in the review at Spithead for the allied monarchs. On 2 January 1815 he was nominated a KCB. On 10 August 1819 he was gazetted colonel of the Royal Marines, and he was promoted rear-admiral on 19 July 1821.

The Berrys had no children, and when Edward

and in May he suffered the loss of his spars in a squall off Sardinia, possibly because of his inexperience. Nelson came to regard him as a fighting blockhead. But Berry made up for the failure by the energy he put into repairing the ship, and he was Nelson's flag captain at the battle of the Nile on 1 August 1798. Later he was to publish the best-known account of the Nile campaign and battle, *An Authentic Narrative of the Proceedings of His Majesty's Squadron under the Command of Rear-Admiral Sir Horatio Nelson, from its Sailing from Gibraltar to the Conclusion of the Glorious Battle of the Nile, Drawn up from the Minutes of an Officer of Rank in the Squadron.*

He was entrusted with Nelson's dispatches to Jervis, now earl of St Vincent, and left *Vanguard* four days after the battle. The ship in which he was taking passage, *Leander* (50), was captured by one of the French survivors of the Nile, *Généreux* (74), after a stiff resistance, and Berry had the misfortune to be taken prisoner. Upon his exchange, he was put in command of *Foudroyant* (80) on 13

Berry died on 13 February 1831, aged sixty-two, in Bath, Somerset, the baronetcy became extinct. He was buried in Walcot church, Bath.

Lt: 20 January 1794
M-C: 12 Nov 1796
Capt: 6 March 1797
R-Adm: 19 July 1821

BERTIE

ADMIRAL SIR THOMAS HOAR BERTIE was best known for being one of Nelson's captains at the battle of Copenhagen, after which he served as rear-admiral in the Baltic from 1808 to 1810. He is also credited with introducing lifebuoys into the navy, after experiments at Spithead in 1778, and later with making an important improvement in the design of the carriages used for carronades, by lowering their centre of gravity. The effect was that a smaller crew was needed and the gun itself was more effective.

He was born on 3 July 1758 in Stockton-on-Tees, county Durham, the sixth child and fourth son of George Hoar of Middleton St George, keeper of the Regalia of England in the Tower of London, and his wife Frances, daughter of William Sleigh of Stockton-on-Tees. To give him a head start in the navy his name was put on the books of the *William and Mary,* yacht, in March 1771, and he was sent first to a navigation school at Stockton, then to Mr Eaton's academy in London, and finally to Christ's Hospital. His true entry into the navy was in October 1773 when he went to sea, serving in the East Indies in *Seahorse* (24), on board which Nelson and Thomas Troubridge were his messmates. He next served with Sir Edward Hughes in *Salisbury* (50), and then under Captain Joshua Rowley in *Monarch* (74), in which he was commissioned lieutenant on 21 May 1778 and served in the battle of Ushant on 27 July. In December he transferred with Rowley into *Suffolk* (74), and served in the West Indies, taking part in Admiral Byron's action with the Comte d'Estaing off Grenada on 6 July 1779. He distinguished himself in two boat actions close inshore at Martinique, and in March 1780 he again followed Rowley, being appointed first lieutenant of *Conqueror* (74).

He fought in Admiral Rodney's three actions with de Guichen on 17 April, 15 May and 19 May 1780, and was promoted commander on 10 August 1782, with appointment to command *Duc d'Estisac* (16) at Port Royal. He remained in her until she was paid off in England in August 1783.

His promotion to post rank was delayed by the end of the war, and he was not to be promoted

Thomas (Hoar) Bertie, Esq.,
Rear-Admiral of the White Squadron,
engraved by R? Page after Lea, published by
Joyce Gold, 103 Shoe Lane,
Fleet Street, 31 July 1811.

until 22 November 1790 at the time of the Nootka Sound crisis. Nevertheless he married on 20 May 1788, in St Marylebone, London, Katherine Dorothy, daughter of the Honourable Peregrine Bertie of Low Layton, Essex, and granddaughter of Willoughby, third earl of Abingdon, assuming the surname of Bertie on his marriage.

After the outbreak of war in 1793 Bertie was not employed until September 1795, when he was appointed to command the *Hindostan* (54) under orders for the West Indies. A severe attack of yellow fever brought him home in October 1796. He was in command of *Braakel* (54) at the time of the trial of Captain John Williamson for misconduct at the battle of Camperdown, and formed part of the court. In October 1797 he was appointed to command *Ardent* (64) in the North Sea fleet. Her small size recommended her for employment in the Baltic force prepared in the winter of 1801 under the command of Sir Hyde Parker, and at the battle of Copenhagen she formed part of Nelson's division. Bertie took the surrender of four Danish ships and floating batteries, and *Ardent* lost 130 men killed and wounded. Following the action he was transferred into *Bellona* (74), whose captain, Thomas Boulden Thompson, had lost a leg. He continued to serve in her under Nelson in the Baltic, and then at Cadiz and finally in the West Indies, returning home to pay off following the peace of Amiens.

On the return to war in 1803 Bertie was appointed to command *Courageux* (74), but resigned his command within a few months because of a family crisis. In December 1805 he was appointed to command *St George* (90), and he remained in her, mostly serving in the Channel, until he was promoted rear-admiral on 28 April 1808, when at the request of Admiral Sir James Saumarez he returned to the Baltic. Poor health obliged him to strike his flag on 19 February 1810, although he was promoted in July, and on 24 June 1813 was made a KB. At the same time the king of Sweden made him a knight of the Sword (KS).

He died on 13 June 1825, aged sixty-six.

> Lt: 21 May 1778
> M-C: 10 August 1782
> Capt: 22 November 1790
> R-Adm: 28 April 1808
> V-Adm: 4 December 1813
> Adm: 27 May 1825

BICKERTON

ADMIRAL SIR RICHARD HUSSEY BICKERTON, BARONET, KCB, was a fighting captain, with active service in three wars, who is best known for his taking second in command under Lord Keith at the blockade of Cadiz in May 1800. The intention was to land an army to capture the town, but at the last minute, with soldiers actually in their boats, the governor warned that a serious pestilence was causing a great mortality in the city.

Discretion appeared the better part of valour, and the British forces were withdrawn.

He was born on 11 October 1759 in Southampton, the eldest and only surviving son of Rear-Admiral Sir Richard Bickerton, first baronet of Upwood, Huntingdonshire, and a member of parliament. His mother was Mary Anne, elder daughter of Thomas Hussey of Wrexham, Denbighshire. His name was entered on the muster of his father's ship, *Marlborough* (74), on 14 December 1771, and subsequently in that of *Princess Augusta,* yacht, on the river Thames in October 1773, but his real entry into the navy as a captain's servant, and later midshipman, took place in June 1774 when he joined *Medway* flying the flag of Vice-Admiral Man and commanded by Captain William Affleck, with whom he served in the Mediterranean. In September 1777 he joined *Invincible* under Captain Hyde Parker for the passage home.[ADM 107-7-19] He was commissioned lieutenant on 16 December 1777, with an appointment to *Prince George* under the command of Captain Middleton, later Lord Barham. He followed

Sir Richard Bickerton, Bart., K.C.,
Rear Admiral of the Red Squadron,
engraved by William Ridley from a drawing by
Maynard, copied from the original painting by an
Italian artist at Malta, published by Joyce Gold,
103 Shoe Lane, 1 June 1805.

Middleton into *Royal Oak* (74) in March 1778, and then to *Jupiter* (50) in May under the command of Captain Francis Reynolds, and was employed in cruises in the Bay of Biscay until 20 March 1779.

On 20 October 1778, while serving as first lieutenant in *Jupiter*, he was in an engagement with *Triton*, a French ship of the line which was eventually forced to retire. The odds were considered such as to constitute a victory, and on Middleton's recommendation, Bickerton was promoted master on 20 March 1779, and the next day given command of *Swallow*, sloop. When the combined French and Spanish fleets entered the Channel that summer, Bickerton was obliged to order the dispersal of the convoy he was escorting, which effected their escape. On 2 January 1780 he took part in the capture of a Dutch convoy carrying naval stores to France, and subsequently was ordered to join Admiral Rodney in the West Indies, where he participated in the capture and looting of St Eustatius.

On 8 February 1781 Rodney made Bickerton post in *Gibraltar* (80), but 'for rank' only, and then immediately moved him as acting captain to *Invincible* (74), in which he took part in the action off Martinique under Admiral Sir Samuel Hood on 29 April 1781. In May he was given his own ship, *Russell* (74), but he only stayed in her until July, when he was appointed to command *Amazon* (28) under orders for the Leeward Islands, North America and home to Portsmouth, where he left her on 7 February 1782. On 4 September he was appointed to *Boyne* (70) for service in home waters, and he came ashore in April 1783 with the conclusion of peace. On 10 January 1787 he was appointed to *Sibyl* (28), in which he served in the West Indies, until October 1790.

On 25 September 1788, in Antigua, he married Anne, daughter of James Athill, MD, of Antigua. They had no children. After the death of his father in 1792 he succeeded to the baronetcy.

With the outbreak of war in 1793 he returned to active service, with orders dated 5 May 1793 to commission the *Ruby* (64) for Channel service. He was transferred to the *Ramillies* (74) in September 1794, with orders to carry General Sir John Vaughan

to the West Indies. From there he proceeded to Newfoundland and at the end of 1795 returned to form part of the North Sea fleet under Admiral Adam Duncan. In 1797 he was transferred to the Channel fleet under Lord Bridport, and in July put in command of *Terrible* (74).

He was promoted to colonel of marines in 1798, and to rear-admiral on 14 February 1799, when he served as second in command at Portsmouth until 7 May 1800. He then sailed in *Seahorse* (38) to join Admiral Lord Keith. At Cadiz on 10 June he hoisted his flag in *Swiftsure* (74), with Benjamin Hallowell as his flag captain. Following the abandonment of the plan to seize Cadiz, the blockade was continued for five months, and then Bickerton sailed with Keith to blockade Alexandria, which capitulated on 27 August to soldiers commanded by Major-General Coote. For his services the sultan appointed him to the order of the Crescent (KC).

Keith returned to England on the conclusion of the peace of Amiens, leaving Bickerton in command and with responsibility for embarking the French army. He remained in the Mediterranean during the peace, with his flag in *Kent,* to which he had shifted in April 1802, and as second in command under Lord Nelson upon the resumption of hostilities, shifting his flag again into *Royal Sovereign* (100) on 26 March 1804, and to *Queen* (90) on 17 June 1805. But he returned to England in *La Decade* in September 1805 with a liver ailment.

He was promoted vice-admiral on 9 November 1805, major-general of the Royal Marines on 20 April 1810, admiral on 31 July 1810, lieutenant-general of the Royal Marines on 5 January 1818 and general of the Royal Marines on 28 June 1830. He was appointed king's counsel on 8 October 1801, and KCB on 2 January 1815.

Following his return from the Mediterranean, he remained ashore. He was a commissioner of the Admiralty from 6 April 1807 until 25 March 1812, and became a director of Greenwich hospital in 1810. He held the parliamentary seat for Poole, Dorset, from 24 February 1808 to 1812, and was a fellow of the Royal Society and vice-president of the Naval Charitable Society. His final naval service was as commander-in-chief Portsmouth between 29 April 1812 and 9 May 1815. He assumed his mother's surname of Hussey before Bickerton on inheriting the estate and manor of Wood Walton, Huntingdonshire, on 16 May 1823, and died on 9 February 1832, aged seventy-two, at The Circus, Bath, his wife living on to 2 March 1850. His estates were inherited by her nephew Vice-Admiral Sir Richard Hussey Moubray, KCB.

Lt: 16 December 1777
M-C: 20 March 1779
Capt: 8 February 1781
R-Adm: 14 February 1799
V-Adm: 9 November 1805
Adm: 31 July 1810

BLACKWOOD

VICE-ADMIRAL THE HONOURABLE SIR HENRY BLACKWOOD, BARONET, KCB, is best known for his brilliant work as commander of the frigate force watching the combined Franco-Spanish fleet in Cadiz, and for delivering it to Nelson's fleet prior to the battle of Trafalgar. His account of Nelson during the final hours before the ships started firing is important both as biographical anecdote, and as commentary on Nelson's tactics.

His birth date is unknown, but he was baptised on 28 December 1770, the sixth and youngest son of Sir John Blackwood, second baronet of Ballyleidy, county Down, and of his wife, Dorcas, eldest daughter of James Stevenson of Killyleagh. His father was member of parliament for county Down and a firm opponent of the union with England and Scotland. After his death, Dorcas was to be created Baroness Dufferin and Clandeboye in July 1800. Henry entered the navy on 1 March 1782 as a volunteer on board the *Artois* (38) under the command of Captain John MacBride. He was rated midshipman on 19 January, or February, 1783 when he joined *Boreas* (28) under the command of Captain Montgomery, whom he followed in October to *Concorde* (32). He reverted to captain's servant when he joined *Druid* (32), again under Captain MacBride, but was rated midshipman on joining *Rose* under Captain Hawkin in April 1784. In July 1785 he transferred to *Trusty* (50) flying the flag of Vice-Admiral Cosby in the

Mediterranean, and remained with him until October 1789, when he joined *Queen Charlotte* (100) flying Earl Howe's flag. After serving as signal midshipman, he was commissioned lieutenant on 3 November 1790 and appointed to *Proserpine* (42). Late in 1791 he obtained leave to study French. When in Paris he was denounced as a spy and had to flee for his life.

Following the French declaration of war on 1 February 1793, he was appointed in March to the 12-pounder frigate *Active* (32) under the command of Captain Nagle, transferring in July to *Invincible* (74) under the command of the Honourable Captain William Pakenham. He served as her first lieutenant at the battle of the Glorious First of June in 1794, and was sent by Captain Pakenham with a message to Admiral Howe, who subsequently ordered Blackwood to take possession of *Le Juste* (84). On the fleet returning to Spithead he was promoted commander in the *Megaera*, fire vessel, the commission being dated on 6 July 1794. He was first made post captain on 2 June 1795 in a somewhat inglorious command, *Nonsuch*, a 64-gun ship reduced to a floating battery at Hull, but in April 1796 he was given a small frigate to command. She was the *Brilliant* (28), and Blackwood established his reputation by making a brilliant defence against two 44-gun frigates, which he managed to elude. This led to his being given in March 1799 a new frigate, *Penelope* (44), serving in the Mediterranean under Rear-Admiral Nelson in the blockade of Malta.

When during the dark night of 30 March 1800 *Guillaume Tell* (86) attempted to escape from Valletta harbour, Blackwood was in place to sight her. He gave chase and engaged her with repeated broadsides into her stern, while avoiding return fire except from the French stern chasers. By dawn *Guillaume Tell* was reduced to head sails and spanker, and was unable to pull away from *Lion* and *Foudroyant*, which engaged her for several hours and brought down her masts. That affected her stability and gave her such a lively motion that she could not keep her lower-deck ports open. It was *Penelope* which took possession of the capture, and Blackwood's reputation was firmly established. On 7 January 1801 he received royal permission to accept and wear the insignia of a commander of the Sicilian order of St Ferdinand and of Merit (KCFM).

After serving under Lord Keith in the Egyptian campaign, for which he was awarded a Turkish gold medal for distinguished services, he returned to Spithead on 19 March 1802, and with the renewal of the war the following year he was given command in June 1803 of *Euryalus* (36). In her he served successively under Lord Gardner on the coast of Ireland, at Boulogne under Lord Keith and off Cadiz under Nelson. It was he who reported to the Admiralty in person that the Franco-Spanish fleet had gone south to Cadiz; he stopped at Merton on his way to London to inform Nelson, who accompanied him to the Admiralty and received his final instructions. Nelson appointed him to command the inshore frigate, and offered him a ship of the line. Blackwood refused as he thought the chance of immediate action would be greater in a frigate, but came to regret it.

At 6:00 A.M. on 21 October 1805, having followed the combined Franco-Spanish fleet all night using shaded light signals to communicate with the inshore squadron of Nelson's fleet, Blackwood was summoned to go onboard the *Victory*. He remained onboard until the shot was falling around the ship. He wrote that Nelson's 'mind seemed entirely directed to the strength and formation of the enemy's line, as well as to the effects which his novel mode of attack was [sic] likely to produce.' When Blackwood was asked by Nelson to estimate the number of captures that might be taken, he replied that 'considering the handsome way in which battle was offered by the enemy, their apparent determination for a fair trial of strength, and the proximity of the land, I thought if fourteen ships were captured, it would be a glorious result.' Nelson insisted that he would be satisfied with nothing less than twenty, but he was clearly nervous. 'He frequently remarked to me' that the combined fleet 'put a good face upon it; but always quickly added, "I'll give them such a dressing as they never had before."' By his leadership from the front, aided by the theatrics of his famous signal to the fleet

that 'England Expects that Every Man will do his Duty,' he insured that that was what transpired. Blackwood tried to persuade Nelson to move his flag into *Euryalus* but Nelson refused, giving 'as his reason the force of example.' And, added Blackwood, 'probably he was right.' In his opinion, Nelson and Collingwood, by their leadership, 'were literally in themselves a host.' However, victory came at a terrific cost. When Nelson bade Blackwood return to *Euryalus* he grasped his hand and said 'I shall never speak to you again.' ^{Marshall 1.462}

Blackwood had hoped that Nelson's signal to come aboard *Victory* would give him a second chance at a ship of the line, but was disappointed. Nelson, however, did entrust him with the unheard-of power to use his name as he thought best to ensure that the ships in the rear of the columns got effectively into action. Late in the battle when *Royal Sovereign* (100) was dismasted, *Euryalus* was ordered to remain within hailing distance to relay Collingwood's signals. Subsequently he shifted his flag into her. After the battle Blackwood was sent with a flag of truce to the governor of Cadiz, offering to land all the wounded Spanish prisoners so they could be cared for in their own hospitals, on condition that they not serve again until exchanged. He was subsequently sent home with Collingwood's dispatches, and with the captive Vice-Admiral Villeneuve. He served as train bearer to the chief mourner, Admiral Sir Peter Parker, at Nelson's funeral.

At the beginning of 1806 Blackwood was given the command of *Ajax* (80), and in her sailed as part of the force under Sir John Duckworth intended to run the Turkish defences of the Dardanelles with the objective of detaching the sultan from his new alliance with France. On 14 February 1807, however, *Ajax* caught fire and was lost. Blackwood was one who escaped the flames by swimming, although he nearly died of exposure, and he took part in the campaign as a volunteer in Duckworth's flagship.

On 22 March 1808 he was appointed to command *Warspite* (80), and he remained in her until the end of the war, commanding the inshore squadron at Toulon in 1810 and returning to the

Mediterranean in 1813. He left her in November, and in April 1814 he was appointed captain of the fleet which was assembled at Spithead when HRH the duke of Clarence hoisted his flag in *Impregnable* (100) to conduct a fleet review for the assembled allied monarchs. Honours continued to be showered on him. He was promoted rear-admiral on 4 June 1814, invested a baronet on 1 August 1814, nominated a KCB on 12 August 1819, a GCH in 1832, and served as groom of the king's bedchamber. In August 1819 he was appointed commander-in-chief in the East Indies, hoisting his flag in *Leander* (50) and striking it on 13 December 1822. He was promoted to vice-admiral on 27 May 1825, and served as commander-in-chief at the Nore from 1 August 1827 to 1830, with his flag in *Prince Regent* (120).

Blackwood was married three times. His first wife, whom he married on 12 January 1795, was Jane Mary, second daughter of Lancelot Crosbie of Tubrid, county Kerry. She died on 19 January 1798, and a little over a year later, on 3 June 1799, he married Eliza, fourth daughter of Captain Martin Waghorn, RN. She had one son, and died on 30 October 1802. He was married for the third time the following 9 May in East Horsley, Surrey, to a daughter of Francis Gore, governor of Grenada. She was to give birth to two sons and a daughter. Blackwood himself died of the typhus or the scarlet fever on 14 December 1832 at the seat of his elder brother, Lord Dufferin, in Ballyleidy, county Down, and was buried in Killyleagh church.

Lt: 3 November 1790
Cmdr: 6 July 1794
Capt: 2 June 1795
R-Adm: 4 June 1814
V-Adm: 27 May 1825

BLIGH

REAR-ADMIRAL JOHN BLIGH, CB, played a remarkable role in the expulsion of the French from Haiti. He was less successful at Curaçao, but ended the war wealthy from prize money.

Bligh was born in August 1770 in Guildford, son of Commander John Bligh, RN, and of his wife, Elizabeth, née Titcher. He was educated at the Royal Grammar School in Guildford, and entered the navy on 22 January 1780 as a captain's servant on board *Nemesis* (28). He was rated midshipman in *Warspite* (74) on 28 August 1782, and served in *Trimmer*, sloop, *Pegase* (74), *Bull Dog* (ship sloop) in which he was rated an able seaman, *Europa* (64), and *Camilla* (20) in which he rated master's mate on 13 September 1786.[ADM 107.11.54] He passed his examination on 6 February 1788, and received his lieutenant's commission on 25 June 1791. At the French declaration of war in February 1793 he was received on board *Courageux* (74) commanded by Captain William Waldegrave, with whom he served in the Mediterranean. After serving under Commodore Robert Linzee in the attack upon St Fiorenzo, and then in the batteries at Toulon, he was transferred into *Barfleur* (90) flying the flag of Lord Waldegrave as a rear-admiral, and served as her first lieutenant in the battle of Cape St Vincent on 14 February 1797. This led to his promotion to commander, on 8 March, and appointment to *Kingsfisher,* sloop, stationed on the Portuguese coast. His commission as post captain followed on 25 April. During the mutinies at Spithead, and whilst in command of the *Latona* (38), he was on 12 May 1797 sent ashore by his crew.

He married on 31 May 1798, in Alverstoke, Hampshire, Sarah, daughter of Henry Sebastian Leeke of Yaxley Hall, Suffolk.

Following the renewal of the war he was placed in command of *Theseus* (74), and on 8 September 1803 he entered Port Dauphin harbour, quickly reduced Fort Labouque by gunfire, and with a few shot brought *La Sagesse* (28) to surrender. The commandant of the garrison immediately sought British protection from the former black slaves who were in the process of claiming control of the country. The guns of the fort were spiked, the ammunition destroyed, and the garrison transported to Cape François. There it was learnt that General Dumont and his suit had been captured by the Haitian general Dessalines, and Bligh was begged to intercede for their lives. This was accorded, and on 18 November Cape François was surrendered to the Haitians. Commodore Barré pleaded with Bligh to take possession of the French squadron there so that they would not be destroyed, and he did so, making it clear he was prepared to respond to any action taken by the Haitians. Marshall comments that 'General Rochambeau who commanded the French garrison, appears on this occasion to have pursued a very extraordinary line of conduct, having proposed to surrender the place to the British at the moment when he had concluded a capitulation with his black opponent, Dessalines.' Marshall 1.816

Following this success, Bligh was put in command of a squadron with orders to attack the Dutch colony of Curaçao, but was unable to make any headway, although he landed 700 men for the purpose and remained on the island for twenty-eight days. He returned home from the West Indies on 30 September 1806 and in March 1807 was appointed to command the *Alfred* (74), in which he took part in the second battle of Copenhagen. Subsequently he served under Sir Charles Cotton on the coast of Portugal. In the summer of 1808 he was employed in response to the request of the people of Figueiras in securing that place, and succeeded in doing so, holding it until Sir Arthur Wellesley was able to bring ashore an army at Mondego Bay. He subsequently assisted at the landing of forces commanded by Brigadier-Generals Anstruther and Acland, and was at the battle of Vimeiro on 21 August which led to the French evacuation of Portugal.

On 14 January 1809 he transferred into *Revenge* (74) as captain *protempore*, and was in danger of capture by a French battle squadron, but he was able to join the squadron commanded by Sir John Poo Beresford, whose tactics led the French to break off contact. On 28 February he transferred into *Valiant* (74) serving under Rear-Admiral Stopford in the blockade of Basque Roads, and he participated in the attack by ships and boats of the fleet following that made by the fireships and explosion ships commanded by Lord Cochrane.

He married for a second time on 17 August 1809, in St Marylebone, London, uniting with Cecilia, daughter of Governor Moultrie.

Bligh's career was capped by his good fortune in capturing on 3 February 1810 a French frigate,

Canonnier, formerly in the British service as *La Minerve*. She had been freighted by the merchants of Isle de France to carry home the loot taken from prizes in the East Indies over a period of three years. Suddenly wealthy, Bligh was also made a CB on 4 June 1815, and promoted rear-admiral on 19 July 1821. He made his home in Fareham in 1823, and died on 19 January 1831, aged sixty-nine, in Gosport.

Lt: 25 June 1791
Cmdr: 8 March 1797
Capt: 25 April 1797
R-Adm: 19 July 1821

BLIGH

ADMIRAL SIR RICHARD RODNEY BLIGH, GCB, is best known for an unequal action on 6 November 1794 when in command of *Alexander* (74) and in company with *Canada* (74). Unable to outrun a French squadron of five seventy-fours, three large frigates and a brig, he fought with them until in a sinking state, and eventually was forced to surrender his ship. *Alexander*'s prolonged resistance enabled *Canada* to escape. Bligh's promotion to rear-admiral had already been announced, on 23 October, but he was not to know about it until his exchange.

Richard was a younger son of Lieutenant Richard Bligh, RN, and his wife Ann, née Page. The date of his birth is unknown, but he was baptised on 8 November 1737 at Holy Trinity church Gosport, Hampshire, with Captain George Brydges Rodney, later Lord Rodney, standing as his godfather. This made inevitable his entry in the navy, in 1750, in *Rainbow* (44) commanded by Rodney. He fought in the battle of Minorca in 1756 as a midshipman in *Ramillies* (90) flying the flag of Admiral John Byng, and was commissioned lieutenant in *Nightingale* (24) in 1757. He continued to follow Rodney during his campaign in the West Indies and was promoted commander of *Virgin*, sloop, by Rodney in 1762, and made post captain in *Camel* on 6 December 1777. His elder brother John, father of Rear-Admiral John Bligh, was commissioned lieutenant two years after him, and did not become master and commander until 1781.

Richard Rodney commanded *Asia* (64) under Lord Howe in the relief of Gibraltar in 1782.

Following his exchange after the loss of *Alexander,* he served, from 1796 to 1799, as second in command at Jamaica under Sir Hyde Parker, who ordered him to return home, against Admiralty regulations, because of a quarrel over Bligh's decision to pardon two of the *Hermione* mutineers, one only twelve years old, and to recommend mercy for a third. He was promoted vice-admiral on 14 February 1799 and admiral on 23 April 1804, upon which he retired.

Richard Rodney Bligh, Esq.,
Admiral of the Blue Squadron,
engraved by William Ridley from a painting
by John Opie, published by Joyce Gold,
103 Shoe Lane, 1 July 1805.

He first married in 1765, Ann, third daughter of Sir Edward Worsley, knight, of Gatcombe Park, Isle of Wight. The couple had one son, Captain George Miller Bligh, and four daughters, two of whom married senior naval officers and three of whom became the mothers of naval officers. His wife died on 7 July 1797, aged fifty-two, and three years later, on 28 June 1800, he married Mary Golightly of Ham Common, Surrey. He was made GCB on 16 May 1820, and

died on 30 April 1821 at his home, Belle Vue, near Southampton, Hampshire. Mary survived him to 4 June 1834.

Lt: 30 September 1757
M-C: 22 October 1762
Capt: 6 December 1777
R-Adm: 23 October 1794
V-Adm: 14 February 1799
Adm: 23 April 1804

BLIGH

VICE-ADMIRAL WILLIAM BLIGH is notorious as the captain of the *Bounty,* on which the crew mutinied and set him adrift in the Pacific Ocean in 1789. His capacity as a seaman was unparalleled, and was amply demonstrated when he navigated *Bounty*'s 23-foot cutter 3,500 miles across the Pacific with the loss of only one man from the overloaded boat. He should also be known as a great warrior, who was one of Nelson's captains at the battle of Copenhagen.

He was born on 9 September 1754 in Plymouth, the only son of Francis Bligh, inspector of the Customs in Plymouth, Devon, and of his first wife Jane, née Balsam or Bond, widow of a Mr Pearce. He entered the navy in 1762 as a captain's servant in *Monmouth* (70), and was rated able seaman in *Hunter* on 27 July 1770, and midshipman or master's mate on 4 February 1771. In September 1771 he transferred to *Crescent* (36), and in September 1775 to *Ranger,* sloop. He passed his examination for lieutenant on 1 May 1776. Unusually, he was rated as a master before he obtained his commission as lieutenant, being chosen by Captain James Cook in March 1776 to command *Resolution* in his third voyage of exploration to the Pacific Ocean.

His abilities as a seaman must already have been evident, but later events were also to show that he suffered from some mental disorder, leading him to employ wild and degrading language which humiliated his officers and men, and also undermined their respect. The Royal Navy saying that there 'is no bastard like a lower-deck bastard' certainly had validity in his instance.

After the three-year voyage Bligh married on 4 February 1781, uniting with Elizabeth, daughter of Richard Betham, at Douglas on the Isle of Man. For Bligh it was a good match. Elizabeth's father counted amongst his friends David Hume and Adam Smith. She was a niece of Duncan Campbell, who was a wealthy shipowner, a contractor for the Royal Navy and overseer of the convict hulks in the Thames. The couple had six daughters.

He was promoted lieutenant on 5 October 1781, and served in a number of ships of the line in the North Sea and the Mediterranean before going on half pay on 13 January 1783. Subsequently he undertook a series of trading voyages to the West Indies in Campbell's vessels, taking with him on two of them Fletcher Christian, whose friendship was to turn to mutiny on the *Bounty* voyage. In December 1787 he sailed in command of *Bounty* on a mission devised by Sir Joseph Banks, president of the Royal Society, to gather breadfruit plants from Tahiti for cultivation in the West Indies. He cleared Tahiti on the return voyage in April 1789, and was removed from command by the mutineers on 28 April when off Togua (Tonga).

After reaching Batavia in *Bounty*'s cutter, and returning to England, Bligh was sent back to the Pacific in 1791–3 in command of *Providence* (10) and *Assistant*, to complete the purpose of bringing breadfruit plants to the West Indies. He had been promoted master and commander and post captain at the end of 1790. The court martial on those of the mutineers who remained on Tahiti and were returned to England by Captain Edward Edwards brought out evidence which stained Bligh's character, but, war having been declared by France in February 1793, he was appointed in April 1795 to command of the *Calcutta* (26), transferring to *Director* (64) in January 1796. He again suffered a mutiny, at the Nore in 1797, after which he apparently ensured that none of his men would be hanged. He participated in the battle of Camperdown on 11 October 1797 in *Director*, and commanded the experimentally armed converted merchant ship *Glatton* (54) in the battle of Copenhagen 2 April 1801. In both battles he exhibited courage and effective ship handling. In May he was also to be elected a fellow of the Royal Society.

He was to suffer another serious insubordina-

tion, by Lieutenant John Frazier on the *Warrior* in 1804, and in February 1805 a court martial brought by Frazier 'reprimanded' Bligh and 'admonished' him to be 'in future more correct in his language'. Sir Joseph Banks obtained for Bligh the position of governor of New South Wales in 1806, but in that role he also failed, and was deposed in 1810.

He was promoted rear-admiral by seniority on 31 July 1810, and died on 7 December 1817, aged sixty-three, in Bond Street, London, with the rank of vice-admiral. He was buried in St Mary-at-Lambeth, Lambeth Palace Road. His wife had predeceased him on 15 April 1812.

> Lt: 5 October 1781
> M-C: November 1790
> Capt: 15 December 1790
> V-Adm: 4 June 1814

BOWEN

REAR-ADMIRAL JAMES BOWEN was the master who piloted *Queen Charlotte* into the battle of the Glorious First of June in 1794. The story goes that on Lord Howe's giving the order 'Starboard!' to cut the French line of battle, Bowen protested, 'My lord, you'll be foul of the French ship if you don't take care.' 'What is that to you, sir?' Howe snapped: 'Starboard!' 'Starboard!' cried Bowen, muttering by no means inaudibly, 'Damned if I care, if you don't. I'll take you near enough to singe your black whiskers.' He passed so close under the stern of the French flagship *Montagne* that the French ensign brushed the main and mizzen shrouds of the *Queen Charlotte* as she fired her broadside into the French ship's starboard quarter.

Bowen was likely born in 1751, in Ilfracombe, Devon, the eldest son of Captain Bowen of the merchant service. He first went to sea as a merchant mariner, and in 1776 he commanded a ship in the African and West India trade. He entered the navy as a master, and he served with Captain John MacBride in the *Artois* (38) and other ships in 1781–9, fighting in the battle of the Dogger Bank on 5 August 1781. He was then appointed inspecting agent of transports in the Thames.

His life was to be changed dramatically when,

following the outbreak of the French Revolutionary War, Lord Howe asked for Bowen as master of his flagship. Following the action on the Glorious First of June, on 23 June 1794, he was commissioned lieutenant, and he was first lieutenant of the *Queen Charlotte* (100) during the action off L'Orient on 23 June 1795, after which he was made commander. On 2 September he was promoted again, to post captain. He commanded the *Thunderer* (74) in the West Indies, transferring in 1798 to *Argo* (44) in the Mediterranean, and took part in the capture of Minorca by Commodore John Duckworth. In 1803 he was appointed to command the *Dreadnought* (98), but shortly afterwards, at the suggestion of the first lord, the earl of St Vincent, he was nominated a commissioner of the Transport Board. He was sent to Ireland in 1803, on the renewal of war, to improve the local naval defences, and in 1805 he was employed laying down moorings for the fleet in Falmouth harbour. In the following year he served as the earl of St Vincent's captain of the fleet off Brest, and in January 1809 he superintended the re-embarkation of the army at Corunna with Captain John Hayes. He was appointed to the Navy Board on 25 February 1816, and continued in that office until 25 August 1825, when he was retired with the rank of rear-admiral.

It is not known when he married a sister of Captain George Nicholas Hardinge, RN, or what even was her name, but the couple had three sons. He died on 27 April 1835, aged eighty-three, in Ilfracombe.

Lt: 23 June 1794
Cmdr: 29 June 1795
Capt: 2 September 1795
Superannuated Capt: 4 June 1814
R-Adm: 18 July 1825

BOWEN

CAPTAIN RICHARD BOWEN was a seaman of immense talent who attracted the attention of such great officers as Jervis and Nelson.

He was born in Ilfracombe, Devon, probably in 1761, the third son of Captain Bowen, who was in the merchant service. Richard first went to sea with his father, and did not enter the navy until he was rated able seaman, and a month later midshipman, in the merchant-built ship sloop *Lighting* (14) on 2 August 1779, too late in the American war for promotion to come rapidly. In the next five years he served in *Buffalo* (50), *Foudroyant* (80), *Dunkirk* which was then a hulk, *Blenheim* (98), *Adamant* (50) and *Latona* (38), as able seaman, midshipman, acting lieutenant, master's mate, and

The late Captain Richard Bowen, R.N.,
engraved by H R Cook, published by Joyce Gold,
103 Shoe Lane, Fleet Street, 31 May 1810.

---

again as acting lieutenant, before passing his examination on 7 November 1787. [ADM 107.10.236] He was then unemployed until 21 September 1790 when he was commissioned lieutenant at the time of the mobilisation on account of Spanish action at Nootka Sound. Three of his brothers also entered the navy: Rear-Admiral James Bowen, Captain George Bowen, RN, and Thomas Bowen, who died as a midshipman in 1790 in the West Indies.

The Nootka Sound crisis being quickly passed, Bowen applied to the Navy Board, which gave him command of a division of three transports bound for Port Jackson in New South Wales. When he arrived there, Lieutenant-Governor King did not think enough rice had been supplied for the colony, and Bowen made a voyage to Bengal via Indonesia before returning to England around the world. War having been declared by France by the time Bowen reached Spithead, he accepted Jervis's offer to serve as fourth lieutenant of his flagship *Boyne* (98). Jervis gave him command of the guard and gunboats at the siege of Martinique, which led to his distinguishing himself by boarding a frigate chained to the walls of Fort Royal. Bowen also distinguished himself in the assault on the fort. He was promoted master and commander on 20 March 1794, and post captain on 23 April.

Being dangerously wounded at Guadeloupe, he was sent home with dispatches, but when Jervis was appointed to take command of the Mediterranean fleet, he appointed Bowen to command the small craft based on Gibraltar. To General O'Hara, Jervis wrote, 'you will find in him the most inexhaustible spirit of enterprise and skilful seamanship, that can be comprised in any human character.' [NC 23.366] In October 1796 while commanding *Terpsichore* (32) he fought and defeated a Spanish frigate, and two months later he also fought and defeated a French frigate, *La Vestale* (36), although he was unable to get her away before the prisoners overcame the prize crew. After the battle of Cape St Vincent he even engaged the Spanish four-decker *Santisima Trinidad*. On 18 June 1797 he cut out a ship from Manila sheltering at Tenerife, but on 25 July, while leading Nelson's landing force at Santa Cruz, he was killed by the same discharge of grape shot which destroyed Nelson's right arm.

Lt: 21 September 1790
M-C: 20 March 1794
Capt: 23 April 1794

BOYLE

VICE-ADMIRAL THE HONOURABLE SIR COURTENAY BOYLE was closely associated with Lord Nelson during the early years of his service life, and well connected to the most influential political leaders through his parents and later through his wife.

He was born on 3 September 1770 in Midgham,

Berkshire, the third son of Edmund Boyle, seventh earl of Cork and Orrery, and his first wife Anne, daughter and coheiress of Kelland Courtenay of Painsford, Devon, and niece of John Montagu, fourth earl of Sandwich, who was first lord of the Admiralty from 1771 to 1782. His father encouraged him when he was ten to take a month-long cruise with the Channel fleet in *Gibraltar* (80) under the command of Captain John Casper Allen, and then to enrol in a naval academy at Greenwich. He tried another short cruise with Sir Hyde Parker in the North Sea in the 18-pounder frigate *Latona* (38), which he joined on 19 February 1781. He had his baptism of fire in the battle of the Dogger Bank on 5 August, and followed Parker into *Goliath* (74) at the end of October for Channel service. He had to come ashore, apparently on 8 April 1782, following a fall from the booms to the orlop, but when recovered was sent as a cadet to the Royal (Naval) Academy in Portsmouth, where he arrived on 18 February 1783.

On 24 March 1784 he was rated midshipman when he joined the *Boreas* under Nelson's command, and thus began a life-long friendship. Nelson's verdict, in a letter to Courtenay's father, was that 'In his professional line he is inferior to none; – His virtues are superior to most.' 'His charming disposition will ever make him friends.' [NC 30.8] He was rated able seaman and midshipman when he joined *Barfleur* (90) on 1 December 1787 under the command of Captain John Knight; on 25 November 1788 he joined *Leander* (50) under Captain John Peyton as an able seaman; and when on 6 June 1789 he joined *Aquilon* (32) under Robert Montagu he was rated an able seaman, but with orders from Rear-Admiral Joseph Peyton to act as lieutenant. On 2 November 1790 he transferred into *Vanguard* (74) commanded by Sir Andrew Hamond, but paradoxically after all that time serving with an acting rank, when he received confirmation of his lieutenant's commission on 22 November 1790 he was put ashore.

He served on board *Roebuck* (44) in the Channel under Captain John May for the month of August in 1791, and then was unemployed again until 1 January 1793, a month before the French declaration of war, when he was appointed to the *Egmont* (74) under Captain Archibald Dickson and joined the Mediterranean fleet. During the months while Spain was still an ally of Britain, *Egmont* recaptured the Spanish registry ship *St Jago* from a French privateer. A lieutenant's share of the prize salvage was £1,400. On 25 June 1793 he was put in command of *Fox*, cutter, for the passage from Gibraltar to England, and on 31 October he was appointed to *Excellent* (74) under the command of William Clement Finch, later succeeded by

The Honourable Courtenay Boyle, R.N., engraved by T Blood from a miniature painting, published by Joyce Gold, Naval Chronicle Offices, 103 Shoe Lane, London, 31 July 1813.

Richard Rodney Bligh, for service at Portsmouth and Spithead. He transferred to *Saturn* (74) under William Lechmore on 14 June 1794, for Channel service, and on 8 December joined the *Mary,* yacht, but was lent to *Jupiter* (50), to which Lechmore had been transferred, and served in the Elbe.

He was promoted commander on 6 April 1795, and on 15 October was appointed to the new fir-built brig-sloop *Kangaroo* (18) on the west coast of Ireland. At the end of December of that year he ran into the French invasion force heading into Bantry Bay. Avoiding any action likely to call at-

tention to his vessel, Boyle worked his ship through the French fleet and then made all sail to Plymouth, riding directly to the Admiralty with the news.

He was promoted post captain on 30 June 1797, and on 16 April 1799 he married Caroline Amelia, daughter of William Pointz of Midgham House, Berkshire, and first cousin of Earl Spencer, first lord of the Admiralty from 1794 to 1801. The couple had three sons and three daughters, of whom the eldest son was Rear-Admiral Courtenay Edmund William Boyle, and his second daughter, Mary Louisa Boyle, was a popular author.

On 15 March 1798 he was appointed to command *Hyaena*, and he was employed in the Channel until 2 March 1799. On 27 June he was given command of *Cormorant* (24), which he had the misfortune to wreck on uncharted rocks near the Damietta mouth of the Nile, following which he was imprisoned in cruel circumstances by the French. After a period of recuperation following his exchange, he was given command of the 18-pounder frigate *Seahorse* (38) on 6 May 1803 with orders to serve under Nelson in the Mediterranean. It was *Seahorse* and another 18-pounder frigate, *Active* (38), which found Nelson at the Magdalena anchorage north of Sardinia in January 1805 with news that the Toulon fleet was at sea. Nelson, although it was dark and the weather tumultuous, immediately directed Boyle to carry two lights at the peak and guide the Mediterranean fleet through the passage of Biche, which is so narrow that only one ship could proceed at a time, guided only by the lights of the ship ahead. Failing to find the French, Nelson ordered Boyle to reconnoitre the Bay of Naples: 'You must recollect that the whole fleet will be waiting for you, before I can proceed further in search of the enemy: therefore, do not anchor or delay. I rely with confidence on your zeal and judgment.' The *Seahorse* found the French back at Toulon on 13 February. On their next sortie, which took them to Cadiz, Martinique and back to Europe with Nelson in pursuit, Boyle was left behind. Using his initiative, by *ruse de guerre* he stopped the Spanish fleet at Cartagena intercepting a British convoy.

His last command was the *Royal William* (100),

to which he was appointed on 1 June 1806, and which he resigned on 22 April 1809. He then embarked on a new career in public service. He had held the parliamentary seat for Bandon Bridge, county Cork, in the short parliament of 1806–7; and he was now appointed to a dazzling succession of desk jobs. He was a commissioner of the Transport Board from 10 June 1809 to March 1817; resident commissioner at Sheerness dockyard from August 1814 to February 1822; deputy chairman of the Victualling Board from February 1822 to July 1823; commissioner of the navy from 3 July 1823 to 4 May 1829; and superintendent of the Transport Service from May 1829 to March 1831. He had been put on the list of superannuated captains on 26 July 1821, but when promoted rear-admiral on 26 February 1831 he was restored to the active list. He was a fellow of the Royal Society, and was nominated a KB on 3 December 1832, and a KCH. He died on 21 May 1844, aged seventy-three, in London.

Lt: 22 November 1790
Cmdr: 6 April 1795
Capt: 30 June 1797
R-Adm: 6 February 1831

BRACE

VICE-ADMIRAL SIR EDWARD BRACE, KCB, played distinguished roles as a captain on the Irish and Mediterranean stations, notably in the defence of Tarifa.

He was a son of Francis Brace of Stagbatch, Herefordshire; the date of his birth is unknown. He was baptised on 2 June 1770, in Kimbolton, Herefordshire. He entered the navy on 15 April 1781 as a volunteer first class, or captain's servant, on board the *Artois* (38) under the command of Captain John MacBride. He was rated an able seaman when he joined *Janus* (32) under Captain John Pakenham on 4 July 1783, for service in the West Indies, where on 1 May 1785 he was rated midshipman. On 27 October 1787 he joined *Victory* (100) under the command of Captain Edward Levison Gower at Portsmouth, and he subsequently transferred to *Gorgon* (44) commanded by Lieutenant Charles Graves at Spithead. On 3 June 1788 he joined *Edgar* (74) under the command of Captain Charles Thompson, for Channel service.

On 12 October 1788 he was rated an able seaman when he joined *Crown* (64) under Commodore the Honourable William Cornwallis in the East Indies, where he was again rated midshipman on 1 October 1790. On 8 November 1791 he followed Cornwallis into *Minerva* (38), where he was again rated an able seaman. He was commissioned lieutenant on 15 March 1792, being appointed 15 May to *Ariel,* sloop, under the command of Captain Edward James Foote, in which he returned to England in 1792; he came ashore on 12 September.

On 1 January 1793, a month before the French declaration of war, he was appointed to *Iris* (24) under the command of Captain George Lumsdaine, with whom he served in the North Sea and Mediterranean, and whom he followed into *Polyphemus* (64) on 10 April 1794 for service in the Irish Sea. On 20 December 1795 he was made acting commander of *Hazard*, cutter, but he returned to *Polyphemus* on 7 March 1796. He was serving as her first lieutenant at the time of her capture of *La Tortue* (44) on 5 January 1797. He was promoted commander on 30 June 1797 and appointed on 10 August to *Kangaroo* (18) on the Irish station, after which he distinguished himself by beating out of Cork harbour in a heavy gale in order to warn British ships of the approach of a French squadron commanded by Rear-Admiral Bompart. When Sir John Borlase Warren brought the French to action on 12 October 1798, *Kangaroo* played an energetic but necessarily limited part.

He was promoted post captain on 22 April 1800, and on 3 September 1800, in Brockhampton near Ross, Herefordshire, he married Elizabeth Fisher.

He was appointed on 27 March 1801 flag captain to Vice-Admiral Gambier in *Neptune* (98). He came ashore on 11 September, and on 1 December took command of *Camilla* (20), and then transferred on 22 June 1802 to *Isis* (50), in which Gambier was flying his flag as commander-in-chief on the Newfoundland station. On 3 April 1803 he was appointed flag captain in *Dreadnought* (98) in the Channel fleet to his old commander, William

Cornwallis, who was now a full admiral. Between 7 September 1803 and 23 March 1805 he commanded *Castor* (26) at Liverpool and in the Downs, and then served again in *Isis* until 27 April 1805, when he was appointed to command *La Virginie* (38). He remained with her for four and a half years in the North Sea and on the Irish station, during which time, at a date not recorded, he engaged and captured a Dutch frigate, *Guederland* (36), in a night action.

On 3 May 1810 *La Virginie* was paid off, and on 23 September Brace was appointed to command *St Albans* (64) off Cadiz under Sir Richard Keats, who entrusted him with command of a squadron convoying Lieutenant-General Graham and his soldiery to Tarifa to co-operate with the Spaniards in the defence of that town. Because of the heavy surf on the beaches, the soldiers were landed at Algeciras and marched along the coast. The guns and munitions were landed through the surf closer to Tarifa, and Graham was enabled to play a major part in the battle of Barrossa in which two divisions of Marshal Victor's army were defeated with the loss of 3,600 killed, wounded and prisoners.

On 1 December 1811 Brace transferred into *Berwick* (74), but he continued his activity harassing the enemy along the French and Spanish coasts, and played prominent roles in the reduction of Genoa in April 1814 and later in the operations against Murat at Gaeta. At the bombardment of Algiers on 26 August 1816 which led to the abolition of slavery there, Brace commanded *Impregnable* (100) flying the flag of Rear-Admiral David Milne as second in command to Lord Exmouth. This time, however, he made a significant blunder, by failing to anchor his ship close under the guns of the batteries, as he had been ordered, where they could not be depressed to register. In consequence he suffered the loss of 210 men killed and wounded.

He had been made a CB on 4 June 1815, and could not be advanced in chivalry following the victory at Algiers because it had been decided that only flag officers should be made GCB. Nevertheless, in recognition of his 'service to humanity', by liberating slaves rather than for his in-

appropriate heroics that killed so many seamen, he was awarded the Netherlands knighthood of the military order of Wilhelm (KWN) and appointed to the Sardinian order of St Maurice and St Lazarus (KML). In recognition of his services at Cadiz in 1811 he was appointed to the Spanish order of Charles III (KCC). He was promoted colonel of the Royal Marines on 27 May 1825, and rear-admiral on 22 July 1830, when he qualified for an appointment as KCB, which was made on 17 October 1834. He was promoted again, to vice-admiral, on 28 June 1838, and died on 26 December 1843 (or 24 January 1844, according to another source), while commander-in-chief at the Nore.

Lt: 15 March 1792
Cmdr: 30 June 1797
Capt: 22 April 1800
R-Adm: 22 July 1830
V-Adm: 28 June 1838

BRENTON

CAPTAIN EDWARD PELHAM BRENTON is best known as the author of a *Naval History of Great Britain from the Year 1783 to 1822* (5 vols, 1823) and *Life and Correspondence of John, Earl of St. Vincent* (2 vols, 1838). He also published *Observations on the Training and Education of Children in Great Britain: A letter to Sir James Graham on impressment: And a translation from the French of M. Ducpetiaux's Work on Mendicity. With an Appendix* (1834). Apart from his work as a defence intellectual and historian, his career nowhere rivalled that of his elder brother, Jahleel. And there are also questions about his scholarship. The opinion of the distinguished nineteenth-century navy historian Sir John Laughton was that 'As an officer of rank, who had been actively employed during the period of his history, his opportunities of gaining information were almost unequalled; but he seems to have been incapable of sifting his evidence, and to have been guided more by prejudice than judgement.' *DNB*

He was born on 19 July 1774 in Newport, Rhode Island, the second son of Rear-Admiral Jahleel Brenton and his wife, Henrietta, daughter and coheiress of Joseph Cowley of Wolverhampton, Staffordshire. He entered the navy on 12 November 1788 as an able seaman in *Crown* flying the broad pendant of the Honourable William Cornwallis, and served in the East Indies, where he was rated midshipman. Having returned to England after the French declaration of war, he joined *Bellona* (74) in August 1793, and served under the command of Captain George Wilson in the Channel fleet. A year later he transferred into *Queen Charlotte* (100) flying the flag of Admiral Lord Hood, with whom he served until 29 May 1795, two days after his being commissioned lieutenant. He was appointed to *Venus* (36) under Captain L W Halstead, with whom he served in the North Sea, following him on 2 February into *Phoenix* (36). He was transferred to *Agamemnon* (64) under Captain Robert Devereux Fancourt in October 1796, and again into *Raven* (16) under Commander John William Taylor Dixon. His ship was wrecked in February 1798, and he was transferred into *Agincourt* (64), which was flying the flag of Vice-Admiral the Honourable William Waldegrave, commanding at Newfoundland. Later she was employed in the Channel and then in the West Indies, and he was transferred into *Theseus* (74) under Captain John Bligh. Having been promoted commander on 29 April 1802, in June he was transferred into *Lark* (16), in which he returned to England. After a year ashore he was appointed to *Merlin* (20) in August 1803 for service in the North Sea and in the Channel, where he distinguished himself on 16 December by destroying the frigate *Shannon* (38), which had been stranded near Cape Barfleur and taken possession of by the French.

He was then moved into the brig-sloop *Amaranthe* (18) and in 1808 he was sent to the West Indies, where, for his distinguished bravery in the attack on a small French squadron under the batteries of St Pierre on Martinique, he was advanced to post rank on 13 December. Sir Alexander Cochrane appointed him acting captain of the *Pompée* (80) bearing the broad pendant of Commodore Cockburn, under whose command he served with a force of seamen landed for the capture of Martinique. Having briefly com-

manded *Belleisle* (74), *Donegal* (76), in which he was acting for Captain Malcolm off Cadiz, and *Cyané* (18) in the western ocean, on 25 September 1810 he was appointed to command the 18-pounder frigate *Spartan* (38) in succession to his brother Jahleel. In 1811 he was sent to North America, where he remained until 15 November 1813, when he returned to England and went on half pay. He did not serve again, with the exception of a few months in the summer of 1815, when he acted as flag captain to Rear-Admiral Sir Benjamin Hallowell in *Royal Sovereign* (100) between 16 April and 5 June, and in *Tonnant* (80) until November.

He had married on 29 March 1803, at St Mary, St Marylebone, London, Margaret Diana, daughter of General Thomas Cox. The couple had a large family. He died on 6 April 1839, aged sixty-four, in London.

> Lt: 27 May 1795
> Cmdr: 29 April 1802
> Capt: 13 December 1808

BRENTON

VICE-ADMIRAL SIR JAHLEEL BRENTON, BARONET, KCB, distinguished himself while in command of *Caesar*, flagship of Rear-Admiral Sir James de Saumarez, when on 6 July 1801 Saumarez attacked a French squadron of three ships of the line sheltering at Algeciras, and was beaten off with considerable loss. The sequel proved Brenton's quality as a captain. Brenton was also hero of several frigate actions, an artist and a defence scholar. He was taken prisoner and severely wounded, but lived a long life.

He was born on 22 August 1770 in Newport, Rhode Island, the first son of Rear-Admiral Jahleel Brenton and his wife Henrietta, daughter and co-heiress of Joseph Cowley of Wolverhampton, Staffordshire. His name was entered into the books of his father's ship, *Tortoise,* as a volunteer, in 1777, when she was in the North American station, and transferred in 1779 to *Strombolo* (14). His family migrated to England as refugees in 1780, and the following year he was sent to school at Enfield, but his name was also transferred into the books of his father's command, the armed ship *Queen*, in which he was employed in the North Sea, and moved in 1781 when he was transferred into *Termagant* (22). In 1783 he was sent as a scholar to the maritime school in Chelsea. In 1785 his name was placed on the books of *Belleisle* (74), which was a guardship in the Medway under Captain Haynes, but it is not known whether he actually served on board. Apparently he travelled with his family in France until 1787 before making the commitment to full-time service in the navy, joining the 9-pounder frigate *Dido* (28) under Captain Charles Sandys as an able seaman and serving in Nova Scotia until October 1789. He joined *Weazle* under Captain Herbert Browel as master's mate for the passage home to England, where he joined *Bellona* (74), which was serving as a guardship at Portsmouth. While on board her he passed his examination on nautical knowledge in March 1790, shortly before the Nootka Sound crisis.

He made the decision to accept a Swedish commission, and on 9 July he took part in the battle of Svenskund between the Russian and Swedish navies, but on 20 March 1791 he was commissioned in the British navy and appointed second lieutenant of *Assurance*, a troop ship under orders for Halifax. He did not sail in her, however, because he was arrested by the mayor of Rochester while he was pressing deserters. After he was released he was appointed on 28 April first lieutenant of *Speedy* (14) and was employed in customs prevention work until his ship was paid off in September. In June 1792 he was put in command of a fore-and-aft-designed sloop *Trepassey* on the Newfoundland station. He was still in her on the French declaration of war in February 1793, when she was employed on the coast of Flanders in the evacuation of the army following the disastrous campaign of the duke of York. He took sick-leave in October. On 6 February 1794 he joined *Sybil* (44) in the North Sea, remaining until November 1795, when he was appointed to *Alliance*, a storeship under orders for the Mediterranean. He protested to the Admiralty, and at Gibraltar to Admiral Jervis, at this demeaning appointment.

Out of consideration for his father, Jervis appointed him first lieutenant of the *Gibraltar* (80) commanded by John Pakenham. She was an unhappy ship. On Brenton's appointment, Pakenham had to ask his officers to make an effort to get along with him, and each other. Jervis believed he had a good effect on the atmosphere in the wardroom. At the end of 1802 *Gibraltar*'s people were to mutiny, although they were easily suppressed, and three of them hanged.

When *Gibraltar* was battered by a gale and ordered home for repairs, Brenton was transferred on 14 January 1797 to a temporary appointment on *Barfleur* (90) flying the flag of Vice-Admiral Waldegrave, Lord Radstock. A month later he served in her at the battle of Cape St Vincent, following which he was promoted to be her first lieutenant. In August he was transferred to *Ville de Paris* (110), and on 22 October 1798 he was put in acting command of his old sloop *Speedy* operating out of Oporto.

His commission was confirmed on 3 July 1799, and several successful actions against gunboats in the Strait of Gibraltar, and the recommendation of Governor O'Hara, led to his promotion to post rank on 25 April 1800. He had been temporarily appointed on 20 February 1800 to command *Généreux,* which had been captured by the blockading forces off Malta. She was undermanned and damaged by a gale, but he got her to sea in May to join the squadron blockading Genoa. From her, he was appointed to *Caesar* (80) on 1 January 1801. Following the action at Algeciras, his efforts and those of *Caesar*'s people to repair her for the renewal of action were to prove of decisive importance. In less than six days they shifted her mainmast, fished and secured her fore-mast, which had been shot through in several places, knotted and spliced the rigging, plugged the shot-holes between wind and water, and completed with stores of all kinds and provisions for four months. The crew worked from dawn to dark and watch and watch all night, and on 12 July warped out of Gibraltar mole while still swaying up *Caesar*'s top-gallant-masts and bending sails. The three French ships had been joined by six Spaniards and passed into the Mediterranean, but Saumarez chased with five British, and in a night action destroyed two and captured a third.

Following his triumphant role in the straits action, and the conclusion of peace, Brenton obtained leave to return home, and on 19 April 1802 he married Isabella, daughter of Anthony Stewart of Maryland. They had been engaged for four years, but her father had made him promise not to marry her until he had reached post rank. She gave him two sons and one daughter.

On 30 October 1802 he was appointed to command *La Minerve* (42) and was almost immediately concussed by a falling block. He was able to resume command in June 1803, but on 2–3 July he had the misfortune to go aground in a fog under the Cherbourg batteries. After ten hours of pounding, and unable to refloat his ship, he was obliged to surrender. Napoleon himself announced the success in the Brussels theatre, and Brenton and all his men were marched 600 miles to the newly established prisoner-of-war facility at Verdun. As the new policy of the French government towards prisoners suggested that his confinement could be protracted, he obtained passports from M. Decrès, minister of marine, for his wife, sister and eldest son to join him. He became a notable figure at Verdun, establishing a chapel and a school for midshipmen. He even obtained permission to spend the winter of 1805 in Tours, and there his second child, Frances Isabella, was born on 15 January 1806. He was not released until December 1806, when Captain Infernet, a nephew of Marshal Masséna who had been captured at Trafalgar, was exchanged for him.

After acquittal at his court martial, Brenton was put in command of *Spartan* (46), joining ship in Italy on 10 February 1807. Admiral Collingwood found him to be rash in his judgements, causing unnecessary losses to ships and men. He was acquitted by a court of enquiry after an ill-judged attack on a polacre off Nice, but Collingwood placed him where he could do little harm, in the blockade of Toulon. In September 1808 he joined Captain Cochrane, commanding *Imperieuse* in the Bay of Rosas and was employed in cruising and in support of the Spanish army. Between October and early 1809 *Spartan* cruised in the eastern Mediterranean; in April he was ordered to convey the British and Spanish ambassadors to Austria from Malta to Trieste; and he then took three frigates, *Amphion*, *Thames* and *Mercury*, under his command.

It was while in charge of this squadron that he proved himself to be an effective commander. He began by driving the French out of Pesaro on 23 April, on 12 May the French garrison on the Croatian island of Lussin surrendered to him and to Austrian soldiers, and in early October he obtained the surrender of the French garrisons on the Ionian islands of Zante, Cephalonia and Cerigo.

Collingwood's opinion of Brenton was changed by these successes, but he was soon to be in trouble again. On 2 May 1810 with *Success* (32) under his command he chased a French squadron of two frigates and a brig into Naples. In order to tempt the French to action, he detached *Success*, with the result that he was heavily outgunned when the French came out on the following day, with drafts of soldiers to give them extra fire-power. After a very bloody engagement, during which Brenton was injured by grape-shot which forced him to hand over command to his lieutenant, he was lucky to disengage with the brig as a prize. Nevertheless, he was offered command of the squadron in the Adriatic, but was compelled by his wounds to return to England.

In recognition of his heroism, Lloyd's Patriotic Fund presented him with a sword valued at 100 guineas, and he was presented with the Sicilian honour of the grand cross of the order of St Ferdinand and of Merit. His convalescence was made harder by the failure of his agent, and the loss of a prize appeal, which left him £3,000 in debt. His friends paid it, and he was awarded a pension of £300 for his wounds, but he had to sell his house in Bath and take lodgings at Paddington. He was invested with the dignity of baronet on 24 December 1812.

When he was able to return to service he was appointed on 29 February 1812 to command *Stirling Castle* (74), and when he found his health would not support active service at sea, on 1

January 1814 he was appointed for a short time resident commissioner at Port Mahon. He then may have spent several months in command of *Dorset* yacht, before appointment on 26 August as resident commissioner at the Cape of Good Hope. On his return, he was appointed to *Royal Charlotte* yacht on 31 July 1821. He was appointed one of the KCBS on 2 January 1815.

His wife had died on 29 July 1817, and on 9 October 1822 Brenton married his cousin Harriet, youngest daughter of James Brenton, judge of the supreme court of Nova Scotia. The couple had one daughter, Harriet Mary, who was to distinguish herself as a poetess and was in 1860 to publish *Evenings with Grandpapa, or, The Admiral on Shore, from the Fireside Stories of Sir Jahleel Brenton.*

Brenton was a reasonably talented artist who had had a picture of the action off Cape St Vincent engraved by James Fittler. Later he commissioned marine artists to make pictures of his actions for the benefit of the wounded and widows. He also published several professional monographs: *The Hope of the Navy; or, The True Source of Discipline . . . as Set Forth in the Articles of War* (London, 1839); *Memoir of Captain Edward Pelham Brenton* (London, 1842); and *Remarks on the Importance of Our Coast Fisheries* (London, 1843). His brother Edward included an account of Sir Jahleel's time as prisoner of war in his *Naval History of Great Britain.*

He was promoted colonel of the Royal Marines on 27 May 1825, was made superannuated rear-admiral on 22 July 1830, and when later restored on the active list, was promoted vice-admiral on 1 July 1840. He was appointed lieutenant-governor of Greenwich hospital on 8 August 1831, and died on 3 April 1844, aged seventy-three, in Casterton, Westmorland.

Lt: 20 November 1790
Cmdr: 3 July 1799
Capt: 25 April 1800
Superannuated R-Adm: 22 July 1830
Restored on the Active List
V-Adm: 1 July 1840

BRIDPORT

ADMIRAL SIR ALEXANDER ARTHUR HOOD, VISCOUNT BRIDPORT, KB, gave service during the war with Revolutionary France which reflected both the capacity he had demonstrated in the Seven Years War, and the difficulty the navy had in dealing with well-connected admirals. His honest dealing with the seamen's delegates during the Spithead mutiny, however, reveals something more unexpected. And his continued service in command of the Channel fleet despite his poor health and the irritation produced by the Admiralty's centralising reforms indicate a high degree of professionalism and patriotism.

He was born on 2 December 1726 into what became one of the most important naval dynasties. The younger brother of Admiral Sir Samuel, Viscount Hood, Alexander was the son of the Revd Samuel Hood, vicar of Butleigh, Somerset, and later of Thorncombe, Devon, and prebendary of Wells. His mother was Mary, daughter of Richard Hoskins of Beaminster, Dorset. Two of his cousins were Captain Alexander Hood, RN, and Vice-Admiral Sir Samuel Hood, baronet, KB.

He entered the navy on 19 January 1741 as a captain's servant in *Romney* (50) commanded by Captain Thomas Smith. He next served for a few months with Captain Thomas Grenville, but then returned to Smith, who rated him midshipman or master's mate on 9 May 1743 in *Princess Mary*. On 2 December 1746 he was commissioned lieutenant on the *Bridgewater*, and he remained in her until she was paid off in October 1748. He was then on half pay until January 1755 when conflict between the French and British establishments in North America led to war. He was appointed to *Prince* (90) under the command of Captain Charles Saunders, was promoted on 23 March 1756 master and commander of *Merlin*, sloop, and was made post captain on 10 June 1756, six weeks before his brother, which meant that he outranked him for the rest of their lives. For the next two years he served as flag captain to Rear-Admiral Charles Saunders in the Mediterranean.

His service during the Seven Years War established a reputation for valour and effective command. On 5 January 1759 he was appointed to *Minerva* (32) in the Channel fleet under Admiral Lord Hawke, and in her he fought at the battle of Quiberon Bay in 20 November. On 23 January 1761 in the Bay of Biscay he engaged for six hours the former British *Warwick*, a razee 60-gun ship, and captured her. In recognition of his ability, in August *Minerva* was attached to the squadron commanded by Lord Anson, first lord of the Admiralty, formed to transport Princess Charlotte, the future queen, from Mecklenburg to Harwich. In September 1761 Hood transferred to *Africa* (64), which had just been launched, and he served in the Mediterranean until the conclusion of the peace of Paris in 1763. It was an indication of the favour he enjoyed that he was provided during the years of peace with an income, by appointment to command the *Katherine,* yacht, and in 1766 he was also appointed treasurer of Greenwich hospital.

He married on 21 August 1761 Mary, only daughter of the Venerable Dr Richard West, DD, archdeacon of Berkshire and prebendary of Durham and of Winchester. She was a niece of Viscount Cobham and sister of Vice-Admiral Temple West, a lord of the Admiralty. On her marriage she entered into a considerable fortune, and Hood insisted that all of it should be settled on her alone. She was twenty years older than he, and it was a love match.

With the mobilisation of ships in December 1777 to deal with the French intervention in the American revolution, Hood was put in command of *Robust* (74) in the Channel fleet under the command of Admiral Keppel. He fought at the controversial battle of Ushant on 27 July 1778, as second to Vice-Admiral Sir Hugh Palliser. 'It would be difficult to select three officers in his Majesty's service, whose character, if impartially considered, must stand higher in general estimation, or whose services have greater claim on their Country, than those of Admiral Keppel, Sir Hugh Palliser, and Captain Alexander Hood,' wrote the editor of the *Naval Chronicle*, 'and yet, when the ill judged advice, or perhaps rather the intended malignity, of false friends, had led these respectable officers to

"cry havoc and let loose the dogs of war;" what tales did calumny, from her murky cell, daily induce the public to consider, and often to believe.' [NC 1.274] Hood felt Palliser had been maligned, but made the mistake of ordering *Robust*'s log to be 'corrected' and of producing the altered version at the court martial. His explanation was accepted by the court, but the public were not convinced.

Hood asked for a promotion or a colonelcy of marines to make it clear that he continued to be approved of by the administration, but the first lord, the earl of Sandwich, dared not go so far, and offered to send him to North America. Hood refused, and resigned command of *Robust*; he returned to the *Katherine* and remained until he was promoted rear-admiral on 26 September 1780. Not until two years later, following the death of Richard Kempenfelt when *Royal George* sank at Spithead, did he hoist his flag on *Glory* (90) in Lord Howe's fleet employed in the relief of Gibraltar. The exact date of his nomination as colonel of marines is not known.

These events during the American war showed the extent to which family and connection were important in Bridport's career. With the conclusion of peace he made the logical step of entering politics. He was elected to the parliamentary seat for Bridgwater, Somerset, in 1784, and held that seat until 1790, after which from 29 December 1790 to 1796 he was member of parliament for Buckingham. His wife Mary died on 12 September 1786, at Cricket Lodge, Somerset, and he remarried on 4 May 1788, uniting with Maria Sophia, daughter and heiress of Thomas Bray of Edmonton, Middlesex. He was promoted vice-admiral in *Prince George* (90) on 24 September 1787, and invested as a knight of the Bath (KB) on 7 May 1788. At the time of the Nootka Sound crisis in 1790 he hoisted his flag in *London* (90) and was also in April 1790 appointed rear-admiral of Great Britain.

With the French declaration of war in February 1793 he hoisted his flag in *Royal George* (100) as second in command of the Channel fleet under Lord Howe, being promoted admiral on 12 April 1794. For his services at the battles of the Glorious First of June he was presented, as were the other squadron leaders, with a gold medal and chain, and on 12 August 1794 he was created Baron Bridport of Cricket St Thomas on the Irish establishment. But he was to be a controversial figure in the naval history of the subsequent six years.

Howe's failing health led to Lord Bridport taking on increasing responsibility within the Channel fleet, although without absolute authority. On 16 June 1795, after escorting the squadron commanded by Captain John Borlase Warren to Quiberon Bay, a squadron detached from the Channel fleet under Bridport's command ran into the Brest fleet under Admiral Villaret-Joyeuse which was at sea to interfere with the landing of the troops carried by Warren's squadron. The next morning Vice-Admiral Cornwallis beat off an attack by the French, but the latter were greatly inferior to the ships of the Channel fleet, both in numbers and in training. The main advantage they enjoyed was good pilots on the confined and dangerous Brittany coast. The main body of the Channel fleet under Bridport's direct tactical command, including eight three-decked ships, overhauled the enemy on the 23rd and captured three of them. The remainder, however, got safely into L'Orient. Bridport did not attempt to blockade them, because of shortage of supplies. Villaret-Joyeuse sent most of the crews to Brest by land. When the coast was clear, the ships were sailed back to Brest three at a time, with the ferry crew returning by road for the second lot.

Limited as was the victory, it had established a moral ascendency over the Brest fleet, and the Channel fleet was broken into small cruising squadrons. In order to deal with the difficulty of Howe's continued nominal authority, and Bridport's resentment, he was commissioned in July as commanding a squadron 'on a particular service', but this did not satisfy him, and in October he hauled down his flag. Nevertheless, he was promoted vice-admiral of Great Britain on 15 March 1796, and on 13 June his barony was placed on the English establishment. He finally agreed to rehoist his flag on 18 December 1796 when the threat from Brest appeared to be growing. Villaret-Joyeuse had warned the French ministry of the marine that his men still lacked adequate training, and the fleet

supplies, but he was replaced by Admiral Morard de Galles, who was given orders to escort an invasion force to Bantry Bay. On 20 December, warning was received of the Brest fleet sailing, and Bridport ordered the Channel fleet to sail from Spithead, but five ships were damaged in trying to get to sea. By the time the Channel fleet was working its way west against the prevailing south-westerlies, the French had defeated themselves and were returning to port.

Worse was to follow. On 15 April 1797, when Bridport ordered the fleet to put to sea from Spithead to deal with new disturbances in Ireland and the threat of another sortie from Brest, the men mutinied for better pay and conditions. This was one of the most important events in English labour history, which for the first time showed that ordinary seamen could organise themselves. It also showed Bridport in a light appreciated more in the present than it was by his contemporaries. The crew of *Royal George* made clear that they had no personal animosity to Bridport, and it was Bridport who forced the Admiralty Board to come down to Portsmouth and take responsibility for meeting the men's demands. Howe, who had finally retired a few days before, was brought back to Portsmouth. The seamen's delegates were not satisfied with equivocal answers, and did not return to obedience until an act of parliament was passed and proclaimed and they were granted a royal pardon. The delegates then permitted Bridport to rehoist his flag on 23 April, and, when he had ensured that the agreement would be honoured, sent him a letter thanking him for his 'open and generous manner' and 'humanity'. He would not permit officers who had been proscribed by the delegates to resume their duties.

For the next three years Bridport commanded the Channel fleet, during a period when the system of blockade of Brest and the Biscay ports was transformed. Supply ships were used to maintain the Channel fleet in more or less permanent stations off Ushant, with a bad-weather rendezvous in Torbay, and the western frigate squadrons based on Falmouth were put under the Channel fleet commander. He was increasingly constrained by detailed orders for ship movements sent from the Admiralty by the first lord, Earl Spencer.

Nevertheless, the blockade failed to prevent another French attempt against Ireland in the summer of 1798, which was defeated only by the squadron on the Irish station. During the following winter the fleet was broken up into squadrons, which Bridport commanded from his house in London. He returned to sea in the spring, and sailed from Spithead on 13 April 1799. But again the French proved able to evade the blockade. The fleet was off Ushant when, under the cover of fog, Vice-Admiral Eustache Bruix slipped out of Brest with eighteen ships of the line, was reinforced from L'Orient, and sailed for the Mediterranean. He was pursued to Toulon by a detachment of the Channel fleet under Rear-Admiral Cotton, and by the Mediterranean fleet commanded by the earl of St Vincent and Lord Keith, but returned safely to Brest in company with the Spanish fleet from Cadiz commanded by Admiral Don Gravina.

To contain this massive force, Bridport was ordered to keep a minimum of twenty-eight ships of the line with him off Ushant, and supply arrangements were increasingly based on Plymouth. The strain was immense, and in April 1800, when the fleet was sheltering in Torbay, Bridport, who had been suffering from poor health for years, hauled down his flag, ending nearly sixty years of naval service.

His rewards for a lifetime of service included promotion to lieutenant-general of the marines in 1799 and general of the marines in 1800, and on 10 June 1801 he was made Viscount Bridport. He died on 2 May 1814, aged eighty-seven, in Cricket St Thomas, Somerset, his wife living on to 18 February 1831. He left no children, and was succeeded as second Baron Bridport by his great-nephew, Samuel, who married Charlotte Mary, only daughter of the Revd William Nelson, first Earl Nelson.

> Lt: 2 December 1746
> M-C: 23 March 1756
> Capt: 10 June 1756
> R-Adm: 26 September 1780
> V-Adm: 24 September 1787
> Adm: 12 April 1794

BRISBANE

REAR-ADMIRAL SIR CHARLES BRISBANE, KCB, is perhaps best known for the plan he conceived as a young man to burn the Brest fleet. It was never to be carried out, but in the planning of it, Brisbane sailed into Brest Roads and had himself rowed around the French ships. The services he performed in the Mediterranean, South Atlantic and Caribbean theatre showed him to be a man of immense resources and moral courage.

He was born in 1769, the fourth son of Admiral John Brisbane of Bishopton, Renfrewshire, and his wife Mary, only daughter of Captain Robert Young, RN. Three uncles were also naval or marine officers, three of his brothers became naval officers, and three of his cousins also became naval officers. So it is of little wonder that he followed the family trade. He was placed on the muster book of *Cerberus* (28) on 7 January 1771 as captain's servant, and after four years 'ashore' did another two months nominal service, in *Flora* (32) in which he was entered on 22 December 1775. His real entry into the navy as an able seaman was on board the *Alcide* (74) on 31 July 1779 under the command of his father. He was rated midshipman on 1 January 1780, and on 12 April 1782 took part in the battle of the Saintes in the *Hercules* (74), when he suffered a severe wound in his back. He returned to active service in *Druid* (32) and *Powerful* (74), and passed his examination on 1 April 1789. [ADM 107.11.217] He was commissioned lieutenant on 18 November 1790. He married Sarah, daughter and coheiress of Sir James Patey of Reading, Berkshire, on 14 June 1792 at St Mary, Reading. The couple had three sons and a daughter.

With the French declaration of war in 1793 Brisbane entered into a period of very active service. He sailed to the Mediterranean in *Meleager* under Admiral Hood, who chose him to command Fort Pomet, an exposed outpost to the British enclave at Toulon. He held his position until the final French assault on the city led him to evacuate and blow up the works. He then took an active part ashore in Corsica, storming the French garrison of

Fornelli. At the siege of Bastia he served under Nelson, and the two men had similar fates, each losing the sight of an eye from the effects of enemy shot. In anticipation of his later feat at Brest, in June 1794, while serving in *Britannia* (100) flying Lord Hood's flag, he put forward a plan for the destruction of a French squadron which had been chased into Gourjon Bay. On 1 July 1794 Lord Hood promoted him commander and gave him temporary appointment to *Tarleton*, sloop, and command over another sloop, both of which were fitted as fireships. The French were found to be too well fortified to be attacked, but his promotion was confirmed all the same. He subsequently took part in the action with the French on 14 March 1795, after which he was ordered to transfer into *Mozelle*, sloop, and proceed to Gibraltar.

In the autumn of 1795 he was ordered to Barbados in convoy of troop ships, but sighting a Dutch squadron he decided to follow it, and then to crowd on all sail for the Cape of Good Hope to warn Vice-Admiral Sir George Elphinstone, Lord Keith, who was in consequence able to capture the entire force in Saldanha Bay on 18 August 1796. The *Naval Chronicle* wrote that:

> The perseverance of Captain Brisbane, upon this occasion, was entitled to much praise. From leaving Gibraltar, till his arrival at the Cape, five months or upwards had elapsed; and during a great part of that time he and his crew were on short allowance of both water and provisions: for a considerable period, indeed, they had only a pint of water a man per day; and must have been reduced to much less, had they not obtained a supply of rain-water on the line. [NC 20.89]

In recognition of his abilities, Brisbane was promoted post captain by Admiral Keith, but his seniority was in fact dated 22 July 1796 because Admiral St Vincent had also given him post rank, although the news was not known at the Cape.

At St Helena on his way home in command of *Oiseau*, schooner, his crew rose in rebellion, hav-

ing heard about the mutiny at Spithead. Brisbane's vigorous personality was enough to put an end to disobedience, and he was then called upon to contain mutiny in *Tremendous* (74), Rear-Admiral Pringle's flagship. In 1798 he returned with Admiral Pringle to England in *Crescent* (36), and then was appointed to the *Doris* (36) under Admiral Cornwallis, who gave him charge of a squadron of frigates watching the motions of the French fleet in Brest. It was then that he performed his celebrated reconnaissance.

Sir Charles Brisbane, Knt.,
engraved by H R Cook after James Northcote, RA,
published by Joyce Gold, 103 Shoe Lane,
31 August 1808.

In July he capped his own success when boats from *Doris* with several from other ships cut out the French corvette *La Chevrette* from Camaret Bay; Captain Keith Maxwell commanded the boats, but it was Brisbane who developed the action plan. This exploit was to become the subject of a painting by the great war artist Philip de Loutherbourg.

Brisbane's fame continued to grow in the new war following the peace of Amiens. He had the misfortune to run *Arethusa* (38) ashore on the

Colorados Rocks north-west of Cuba, and had to lighten ship by throwing overboard her battery of guns. Fortunately this was not evident when he encountered a Spanish ship of the line, which avoided combat and moored close under the guns of Moro Castle at Havana. On 23 August 1806, having refitted at Jamaica, he returned in company with *Anson* and found a Spanish frigate, the *Pomona* (36), moored close under a battery of eleven 36-pounders and protected by twelve gunboats. Not only did he take the frigate by storm, under the red-hot shot from the fort, but he had the satisfaction of seeing the magazine of the fort blowing up.

His reward for bringing *Pomona* into Jamaica was to be put in command of a squadron with orders to reconnoitre Curaçao. He interpreted them as permission to capture the island, which he did by *coup de main* despite the massive batteries guarding the harbour. Reportedly the garrison was incapacitated by the effects of a New Year's Eve party. The governor was given five minutes to surrender, but obtained a full thirty minutes, as he said 'that a shorter time would not save his head in Holland'. When he refused to take an oath to King George, Brisbane declared himself governor, and disarmed the local militia. Vice-Admiral Dacres in his dispatch wrote that he knew 'not how sufficiently to admire the decision of Captain Brisbane in attempting the harbour, and the determined bravery and conduct displayed by himself, the other three Captains, and all the officers and men under his command'. [Marshall 1.741] Brisbane was nominated a KB on 7 April 1807 with a special augmentation and supporters to his badge, and made a KCB on 2 January 1815.

In the autumn of 1808 he was appointed governor of St Vincent, which post he held until his death in December 1829, with the rank of rear-admiral, aged sixty.

Lt: 18 November 1790
Cmdr: 1 July 1794
Capt: 22 July 1796
R-Adm: 12 August 1819

BRISBANE

CAPTAIN SIR JAMES BRISBANE, CB, brother of Rear-Admiral Sir Charles Brisbane, is best known for the part he played as a young commander prior to the battle of Copenhagen of 2 April 1801, when on the nights of 30 and 31 March he was in charge of the boat work sounding and buoying the approaches to Copenhagen.

He was born in 1774, the fifth son of Admiral John Brisbane of Bishopton, Renfrewshire, and his wife, Mary, only daughter of Captain Robert Young, RN. His name was placed on the books of *Powerful* under the command of Captain Thomas Fitzherbert on 28 February 1784, and he entered the navy as a volunteer first class on 16 March 1787 during the Dutch armament, as a midshipman in *Culloden* (74), Captain Thomas Rich. He was rated an able seaman on 3 October, and midshipman on 13 March 1788 when he joined the 12-pounder frigate *Andromeda* (32) under the command of Prince William Henry, later duke of Clarence, under whose command he served at Halifax and in the West Indies. On 3 July 1789 he joined another 12-pounder frigate, *Southampton* (32) commanded by Sir Andrew Snape Douglas, and he followed him into *Goliath* on 10 October, but only for three weeks' work, after which he evidently went ashore. He returned to *Southampton* on 28 January 1791, when he was rated a master's mate by Captain Sir Richard Goodwin Keats, and then in March transferred to *Shark* (14) under Captain Sir Arthur Kaye Legge, with whom he served in the Channel.

On 10 April 1793, following the French declaration of war in February, he joined *London* (90), which was fitting out for the duke of Clarence's flag under his old commander, Captain Keats. But it was decided it was too dangerous for a royal duke to serve at sea where he might be killed or captured, and after a month's leave, Brisbane went on board Admiral Earl Howe's flagship, *Queen Charlotte* (100), in April 1794. Two months later he acted as Howe's signal lieutenant at the battle of the Glorious First of June.

He received his commission as lieutenant on 23

September 1794, and was appointed to *L'Espiegle*, sloop, in the Channel under the command of Captain Bartholomew Roberts; from 21 March 1795 he served in *Sphynx* (20) under Captain George Brisac in Vice-Admiral Sir George Elphinstone's (Lord Keith's) expedition to capture of the Cape of Good Hope; he then joined the flagship, *Monarch* (74), in February 1796. As her first lieutenant he was promoted in June to commander of *Moselle*; then served as acting captain of *Daphne*, a frigate and one of the prizes taken from the Dutch squadron in Saldanha Bay on 18 August 1796. It may have helped that it had been his brother Charles who brought the news of the Dutch squadron to Cape Town.

Daphne was a post command, but he was not confirmed in that rank by the Admiralty, and was for some time unemployed. He was confirmed in the rank of commander on 22 May 1797, and on 17 June 1800 he married Jemima Ann, only daughter of John Ventham and stepdaughter of Vice-Admiral Henry Frankland, at St Peter-the-Less, Chichester, Sussex. The couple were to have one son and two daughters.

In January 1801 he was appointed to command *Cruizer* (18) in the North Sea and at Copenhagen, after which he was taken into Admiral Sir Hyde Parker's flagship, *London*, for a month, and then put successively in acting command of *Alcmene* (32) and *Ganges* (74). In recognition of his service sounding the channel at Copenhagen he was promoted post captain with his commission dating from 2 April 1801, and on 23 May he was appointed to command *Saturn* (74) as flag captain to Rear-Admiral Totty until the admiral's death. When the ship was paid off, he commanded the sea fencibles on the coast of Kent. On 8 September 1805 he was appointed to command the 18-pounder frigate *Alcmene* (32) on the coast of Ireland and in the Channel.

He transferred on 19 March 1808 to the French prize 18-pounder frigate *Belle Poule* (38) for service in the Mediterranean and into the Adriatic. It was while in her command that he made his greatest mark in the service. He was ordered by Lord Collingwood to take command of the squadron

blockading Corfu, and was later employed in the capture of the Ionian Islands and the establishment of the republic of the Seven Islands. He continued in the Adriatic until the summer of 1811, capturing or destroying cruisers, and he was repeatedly engaged with coastal batteries.

He commanded *Cumberland* (74) from 22 April 1811, and *Vengeur* (74) from 13 August 1812, and from 8 September 1812 he commanded the *Pembroke* (74) in the Channel fleet. In the summer of 1813 he returned to the Mediterranean, where he was again actively employed until August 1814. He was appointed flag captain to Admiral Lord Exmouth in *Boyne* (98) in March 1815, transferring with him into *Queen Charlotte* (100) on 3 July 1816 for the expedition against Algiers.

He had been made a CB in 4 June 1815, and following the bombardment of Algiers on 27 August 1816 he was sent home with dispatches, for which he was rewarded on 2 October by nomination as a KB. He died on 19 December 1826, aged fifty-two, in Penang, East Indies, from a disease contracted whilst in command of the naval force during the Burmese war.

Lt: 23 September 1794
Cmdr: 22 May 1797
Capt: 2 April 1801

BROKE

REAR-ADMIRAL SIR PHILIP BOWES VERE BROKE, BARONET, KCB, is best known for the period of his command of the *Shannon* (38) during the war with the United States, and his spectacular success in capturing the USS *Chesapeake* (44), but his most important service to the navy lay in his efforts to improve gunnery by constant drill, and the introduction of gun sights.

He was born on 9 September 1776 at Broke Hall near Ipswich, Suffolk, the first son of Philip Bowes Broke of Nacton near Ipswich and his wife Elizabeth, daughter of the Revd Charles Beaumont, MA, of Witnesham. A descendant of Captain Packington Broke, RN, killed in 1665 at the battle of Solebay, he was sent to the Royal (Naval) Academy, Portsmouth, on 26 January 1789, and entered the navy on 25 June 1792 as volunteer first class, or captain's servant, in the *Bulldog* under the command of Captain George Johnstone Hope. He served with him in the Mediterranean, following him into *Eclair*, ship-sloop, on 5 August 1793, in which ship he was rated as able seaman and midshipman and took part in the occupation of Toulon and the siege of Bastia. Captain George Towry superseded Hope, but Broke followed him in May 1794 to *Romulus* (36) and took part in the action off Toulon on 13–14 March 1795. He had been serving on board *Britannia* (100) flying Vice-

Sir Philip Bowes Vere Broke,
engraved by T Blood with the permission of the
East Anglia Magazine, published by Joyce Gold,
Naval Chronicle Offices, 103 Shoe Lane, London,
31 January 1815.

Admiral Hotham's flag for only five days at the time of the action off Toulon on 13 June 1795. On 18 July he was appointed acting third lieutenant of the 12-pounder frigate *Southampton* (32) under the command of Captain William Shield and later Captain John Macnamara. Actively employed in support of the Austrian army on the coast of Italy, *Southampton* withdrew with the fleet to Lisbon, and took part in the battle of Cape St Vincent on 14 February 1797. Broke's lieutenant's commission was dated 19 August 1797, when he was ap-

pointed to the *Amelia* (48) under the command of Captain the Honourable Charles Hobart in the Channel fleet. In her he took part in the action between Sir John Warren and Rear-Admiral Bompart off the Irish coast on 12 October 1798. He was promoted on 2 January 1799 commander of *Falcon*, brig-sloop (10), at Sheerness, and in the autumn transferred to *Shark*, sloop, engaged in trade protection on the Dutch coast.

He was promoted post captain on 14 February 1801. This, and the peace of Amiens, put him out of employment, but nonetheless he married on 25 November 1802, at Broke Hall, Sarah Louisa, second daughter of Sir William Fowle Middleton, baronet of Shrubland Park near Ipswich. He was not immediately employed on the return to war, and enjoyed a few years of married life. The couple had six sons and one daughter.

Broke was appointed in April 1805 to command *Druid* (32), in which he was employed in the Channel and on the coast of Ireland, and he was transferred to *Shannon* in June 1806, but did not join her in the Downs until 14 September. She was a ship well adapted for his capacity as a gunner, with 32-pounder carronades on the quarterdeck and forecastle and long 18-pounders on the main deck. His first operational cruise took him to Magdalena harbour in Spitzbergen, which he surveyed, and Jan Mayen Island, but there was so much fog that he did not find the whalers he had come to protect. He then took part in the capture of Madeira, and subsequently was employed in the Bay of Biscay until June 1811, when *Shannon* was ordered to fit for service in Halifax under Vice-Admiral Sawyer. Broke acquired such a reputation for gunnery training that the Admiralty regularly drafted away some of *Shannon*'s people to pass on their skills to other ships. During his cruises in defence of British trade, and to destroy the shipping of the United States, he adopted at considerable loss to himself and his ship's company the practice of burning captures rather than deplete his crew in order to take prizes into port for condemnation. It was on 1 June 1813, while senior officer of a squadron watching the American forces at Boston, that

Broke had his famous engagement with USS *Chesapeake.*

USS *President* and *Congress* had both managed to make their escape, and *Chesapeake* and *Constitution* remained, but the last was undergoing repairs. Broke detached the remaining ship under his command, and sent in a challenge to the commanding officer of the *Chesapeake*: 'Sir – As the *Chesapeake* appears now ready for sea, I request you will do me the favor to meet the *Shannon* with her, ship to ship, to try the fortune of our respective flags. To an officer of your character it requires some apology for proceeding to further particulars…' This was sent into the port in the care of a prisoner, but in fact *Chesapeake* weighed before the letter could be delivered. Broke reported:

> The enemy came down in a very handsome manner, having three American ensigns flying; when closing with us he sent down his royal-yards. I kept the *Shannon*'s up, expecting the breeze would die away. At half-past 5 P.M. the enemy hauled up within hail of us on the starboard side, and the battle began, both ships steering full under their topsails: after exchanging between two and three broadsides, the enemy's ship fell on board of us, her mizen-channels locking in with our fore-rigging. I went forward to ascertain her position; and observing that the enemy were flinching from their guns, I gave orders to prepare for boarding. Our gallant bands appointed to that service immediately rushed in, under their respective officers, upon the enemy's decks, driving every thing before them with irresistible fury. The enemy made a desperate but disorderly resistance.
> NC 30.83-4

Broke's unparalleled gunnery, which killed or wounded perhaps 100 of *Chesapeake*'s crew including her captain in the first broadside, and the spirit with which *Shannon*'s ship's company followed him onto *Chesapeake*'s decks, gave him victory in fourteen minutes. *Chesapeake*'s American fans who had come out in boats to watch another American triumph had to return to the now unwanted victory dinner.

However, Broke was himself severely injured by a sabre, and on *Shannon*'s return to England he retired from the sea. He was made a baronet on 25 September 1813 and a KCB on 3 January 1815, and was promoted rear-admiral on 22 July 1830. He died on 2 January 1841, aged sixty-four, at Bayley's Hotel, Berkeley Square, Westminster, where he was undergoing surgery to relieve pressure on his brain. He was buried in the churchyard of St Martin, Nacton, near Ipswich, Suffolk. Sarah Broke died on 20 July 1843, aged sixty-five.

Lt: 19 August 1797
Cmdr: 2 January 1799
Capt: 14 February 1801
R-Adm: 22 July 1830

BROUGHTON

CAPTAIN WILLIAM ROBERT BROUGHTON, CB, was one of the hardy breed of seamen who explored the Pacific in the latter part of the eighteenth century. As a lieutenant he was in 1790 appointed to command the brig *Chatham* forming part of Captain George Vancouver's expedition to the Pacific north-west.

He was born on 22 March 1762, son of Charles Broughton, merchant of Hamburg, and his wife Anne Elizabeth, daughter of Baron de Hertoghe of Hamburg. His name was entered as captain's servant on the books of *Catherine*, yacht, lying in the Thames, by Captain Alexander Hood, later Lord Bridport on 1 May 1774. He was rated able seaman, and later midshipman, when on 18 November he joined *Falcon*, brig-sloop (10), commanded by Captain John Linzee, and proceeded to North America. He served under him until he joined *Harlem* commanded by Lieutenant John Knight on 14 February 1777, continuing in North America, and on 1 July 1778 joined *Eagle* (64). At some time he is supposed to have been taken a prisoner of war. In December 1778 he was rated master's mate when he joined *Superb* (74) commanded by Captain Robert Simenson for service in the East Indies. Captain Stephens succeeded in command, and then on 12 January 1782 Broughton was commissioned lieutenant in *Burford* (68) under Captain Peter Rainier. She was paid off at Woolwich on 19 July 1784, and Broughton was not employed again until 23 June 1788, when he was appointed to *Orestes* (18) under the command of Captain Manley Dixon, with whom he served in the Channel and the Mediterranean. On 13 May 1790 he was appointed to *Victory* (100) under his old commander, now Captain John Knight, with whom he served until his appointment on 28 December to command the storeship *Chatham* 'on a voyage of discovery round the world' as part of Captain George Vancouver's expedition to the Pacific north-west.

He was employed surveying the Columbia river and the adjacent coasts, and in 1793 he was sent home with dispatches, travelling overland to Vera Cruz from San Blas. He was promoted commander on 3 October 1793 of the *Providence* of 400 tons burden, and sent back to rejoin Vancouver. But his departure was delayed until February 1795, and on his arrival he found Vancouver had left. He decided to continue the survey work, and crossing over to the other side, he carried out during the next four years a survey of the coast of Asia, from latitude 35° N to 52° N. On 16 May 1797 the *Providence* struck a coral reef near the coast of Taiwan and was lost, but all the men were saved and taken to Macao in the tender. In it Broughton continued the survey until May 1798. He eventually reached England in February 1799, and in 1804 published *A Voyage of Discovery to the North Pacific Ocean; in which the coast of Asia, from the lat. of 35° north to the lat. of 52° north, the island of the Insu (commonly known under the name of the land of Jesso,) the north, south, and east coasts of Japan, the Lieuchieux and the adjacent isles, as well as the coast of Corea, have been examined and surveyed. Performed in His Majesty's Sloop Providence and her tender, in the years 1795, 1796, 1797, 1798.*

The task of preparing his book for publication necessarily took some time, and kept him from taking part in the war against Revolutionary France. In October 1802 he married his cousin Jemima, fifth and youngest daughter of the Revd Sir Thomas Delves Broughton, baronet of Doddington Hall, Cheshire. The couple were to have one son and three daughters. But he did eventually return to active naval service. He was accorded post rank on 20 January 1797, and appointed to command *Batavier* (50) in the Channel on 23 June 1801. He left her on 27 April 1802 at the time of the ratification of the peace of Amiens, but he did not have to wait long for a ship, being appointed on 17 May to command *Penelope* (44), in which he served in the North Sea and Channel until 28 May 1807. Apparently he had continued to satisfy, for two days later he was appointed to *Illustrious* (74) and served in her in the Mediterranean, the Channel and later the North Sea, and took part in April 1809 in the action against the French Brest fleet in Basque Roads. At the court martial of Lord Gambier he gave evidence which implied a general agreement with Cochrane's charges.

While still commanding *Illustrious* he was present at the capture of Mauritius in December 1810, and was put in charge of the expedition against Java by Vice-Admiral William O'Brien Drury, commander-in-chief East Indies. Drury died on 4 March 1811, but Broughton continued with the plan, sailing from Malacca on 11 June. He made a slow and cautious passage, not arriving at Batavia until a few days before 9 August, when Rear-Admiral the Honourable Robert Stopford arrived, having heard of Drury's death. Despite the fact that he was outside the limits of his station at the Cape of Good Hope, he assumed command. Broughton applied for a court martial of Stopford 'for behaving in a cruel, oppressive, and fraudulent manner, unbecoming the character of an officer, in depriving me of the command of the squadron', but the Admiralty refused the request.

After returning to England he resigned his command on 23 October 1812, but returned to active service on 31 May 1815 when he was appointed to command *Royal Sovereign* (100) in the Channel. On the capture of Napoleon, he was transferred on 30 August to the command of *Spencer,* which was stationary in the Hamoaze. Broughton was made a CB on 4 June 1815, and colonel of the

Royal Marines on 12 August 1819. He died suddenly from angina pectoris in Florence on 12 March 1821, aged fifty-eight, and was buried in the English burial ground at Leghorn. He was survived by his wife, who died on 15 January 1863.

Lt: 12 January 1782
M-C: 3 October 1793
Capt: 20 January 1797

BULLEN

ADMIRAL SIR CHARLES BULLEN, GCB, served in three of the major fleet engagements of the wars against the French Republic and Empire, and had a noose around his neck twice, but was not hanged.

He was born on 10 September 1768 in Newcastle-upon-Tyne to Ruth, daughter of Charles Liddell, and John Bullen of Weymouth, Dorset, who was the Royal Navy's surgeon-general on the coast of North America from 1779 to 1781 during the period of Vice-Admiral Arbuthnot's command. He entered the navy on 16 February 1779 as a volunteer first class on board *Europe* (64) flying Arbuthnot's flag, and crossed the Atlantic with his father, but then transferred into *Renown* (50) under Captain George Dawson, and subsequently was rated midshipman in *Loyalist,* sloop, under Captain John Plummer Ardesoif, with whom he served from October 1779 to May 1781 on the coast of South Carolina, off Charlestown and Savannah. Having returned to Plymouth in *Halifax* (14), a prize from the Americans, he studied ashore until 1786, when he joined *Culloden* (74), Captain Sir Thomas Rich. While she was undergoing a thorough overhaul, he served in different ships, and in May 1788 was accused of striking the first lieutenant, Robert Ratsey, for which he was condemned by court martial to hang. The rope was actually put around his neck before a reprieve was read.

He was promoted lieutenant on 9 August 1791 while serving in *Leander* (50), which was flying the flag of Rear-Admiral Joseph Peyton, and was appointed to a quick succession of ships in the Mediterranean prior to paying off *Eurydice* (24) in December 1791 and marrying on 20 February 1792, in St Marylebone, London, his first cousin, Eleanor Wood.

He returned to *Culloden* under Captain Thomas Rich when his ship was ready for service on 12 January 1793, and in her proceeded to Martinique in March, a month after the outbreak of war. He took part in the actions of 28 and 29 May and the Glorious First of June in 1794 under Captain Sir Henry Harvey on board *Ramillies* (74), to which he had transferred in March, and, after another period of service with Admiral Peyton, was first lieutenant in *Monmouth* (64) under the earl of Northesk during the Nore mutiny, when he was nearly hanged by the crew. He was promoted on 2 January 1798 for his conduct in *Monmouth* (64) at the battle of Camperdown on 11 October 1797, and afterwards he was nearly drowned as prize master of *Delft* when she sank while he was trying to evacuate the wounded Dutch sailors.

Promotion put him out of employment until June 1801, when he was appointed to *Wasp,* sloop, fitting at Plymouth. In the following winter she served as a station ship at Sierra Leone, and on his return to England he found that he had been made post captain on 29 April 1802. On the recommencement of hostilities on 8 March 1803 he was appointed *pro tempore* to command *La Minerve* (38) in the absence of Captain Jahleel Brenton, who had suffered an accident. In July he was put in command of the sea fencibles at Plymouth, where he remained until November; he then took command of the flotilla in the Thames and Medway with responsibilities which in the event of invasion would have been very considerable.

In June 1804 the earl of Northesk asked for him as flag captain of *Britannia* (100), which was then in the Channel fleet but was later detached as a private ship under Sir Robert Calder to reinforce Vice-Admiral Collingwood off Cadiz. For his part in the battle of Trafalgar, in fourth place in the weather line abaft the *Victory* (100), Bullen was awarded a gold medal.

On 7 September 1807 he was appointed to command *Volontaire* (38), transferring on 31 December 1810 to *Cambrian* (32), and served under Collingwood in the Mediterranean. In 1810 and 1811 he commanded a small squadron on the coast of Catalonia co-operating with the Spanish army, coming under the command of Sir Edward Codrington when he arrived with reinforcements in April 1811. When *Cambrian* paid off on 9 December, Bullen went on half pay for reasons of his health until 11 November 1814, when he was put in command of *Akbar* (50), a ship fitted purposely to deal with the American super-frigates. But peace being made with the United States, *Akbar* was ordered to receive the flag of Sir Thomas Byam Martin proceeding to the Scheldt to take charge of the fleet there following the abdication of Emperor Napoleon. Subsequently, *Akbar* was sent as a private ship to Halifax, where Bullen acted as second in command until November 1816.

Akbar was paid off on 1 January 1817, and Bullen went on half pay until he was appointed in December 1823 commodore commanding on the coast of Africa. His career in the later Georgian and Victorian navies was to be long, including civil appointments as resident commissioner of Pembroke dockyard on 16 July 1830, and as superintendent of Chatham dockyard from 1832 to 1837. He had been invested a CB on 4 June 1815, and was to be made a knight commander of the Guelphic order on 13 January 1835 and KB on 25 February 1835 and advanced in chivalry to KCB on 18 April 1839. He received a good service pension on 12 July 1843, was advanced again in chivalry to GCB on 7 April 1852, and was finally promoted admiral on 30 July 1852.

His wife died on 10 July 1842, and he followed on 2 July 1853, aged eighty-four, and was buried at St James's, Shirley, near Southampton.

Lt: 9 August 1791
Cmdr: 2 January 1798
Capt: 29 April 1802
R-Adm: 10 January 1837
V-Adm: 9 November 1846
Adm: 30 July 1852

BULLEN

ADMIRAL JOSEPH BULLEN was a man held in high regard by Admiral Nelson, with whom he served in *Hinchinbrook* and *Agamemnon*, and at the siege of Bastia.

He was born on 14 April 1761, the second son of the Revd John Bullen, rector of Kennett,

Cambridgeshire, and of Rushmoor-cum-Newburn, Suffolk, and entered the navy in November 1774 as a midshipman in *Pallas* (36) under the command of Sir William Cornwallis, with whom he served through most of the American war, in *Isis* (50), *Bristol* (50), *Chatham* (50), and *Lion* (64) (for two periods, in 1778–9 and 1780–1). In between, in 1779, he served in his first acting commission as lieutenant in *Hinchinbrook* (28) under Nelson's command, in the deadly mission to the Mosquito shore, during which all but twenty-seven officers and men died in six weeks. His commission was confirmed on 6 March 1781, and he served as such on board *Prince George* (98) at the battle of the Saintes on 12 April 1782.

During the peace he was employed between 2 May 1785 and 1787 in a succession of guardships at Plymouth, and on 16 June 1790 he joined *Monarch* (74) fitting under Captain Rainier at Spithead for the East Indies. In 1793, just before the French declaration of war, he joined Nelson in *Agamemnon* (64) in the Mediterranean, and on 11 September 1793 he moved into *Victory* (100) flying the flag of Lord Hood.

He was entrusted with the defence of Fort Mulgrave during the occupation of Toulon. Promoted master and commander on 29 November 1793, at the evacuation he acted in command of one of the ships taken at Toulon, *Proselyte* (36), and took the last of the rearguard off the quays. When her captain returned to command of *Proselyte*, Bullen stayed on board as a volunteer, until their ship was burnt by red-hot shot fired from the batteries of Bastia. Bullen subsequently commanded a battery in the siege of Bastia, and after its fall he returned to England and embarked as a volunteer in *Santa Margarita* (44) commanded by Sir Thomas Byam Martin. His last service afloat was in acting command of *Alexander* (74) off Brest. He was promoted post captain on 24 November 1796.

He married on 24 June 1801 Margaret Ann, only daughter of William Seafe (or Scafe), barrister-at-law of The Leazes, county Durham. Following the renewal of war he was appointed to command the sea fencibles at Lyme Regis. On 28 August 1819 he was superannuated, but he continued through ranks until he was promoted admiral on 1 July 1851. He died on 17 July 1857, aged ninety-six, in Bath, Somerset.

Lt: 6 March 1781
M-C: 29 November 1793
Capt: 24 November 1796
Superannuated R-Adm: 28 August 1819
Restored on the Active List
Adm: 23 November 1841
Reserve halfpay
Adm: 1 July 1851

BULLER

VICE-ADMIRAL SIR EDWARD BULLER, BARONET, is best known for his command of *Malta* (74), the last ship in the British line, in Sir Robert Calder's action on 22 July 1805. In patchy but thick fog which effectively isolated *Malta*, he found himself engaging five of the enemy and succeeded in taking two of them prizes.

Buller was born on 24 December 1764 at the Admiralty House, Whitehall, London, the second son of John Buller, member of parliament for East Looe, Cornwall, a lord of the Admiralty and later

Captain Edward Buller,
engraved by H R Cook after M Keeling,
published by Joyce Gold, 103 Shoe Lane,
31 March 1808.

a lord of the Treasury. His mother was Mary, daughter of Sir John St Aubyn, third baronet of Clowance, Devon. In 1774 he was sent to Westminster school, and entered the navy in 1777 as a midshipman under the patronage of Lord Mulgrave, who commanded *Courageux* (74) at the battle of Ushant on 27 July 1778. He was commissioned lieutenant in 1782, and in *Sceptre* (64) he took part in most of Admiral Hughes's actions in the Indian Ocean. On 26 April 1783 he was promoted master and commander of *Chaser,* sloop of war. In her he rode out the great hurricane of November 1783 by good seamanship which enabled him to run through the Manar gulf, which was not considered safe for navigation.

He married on 15 May 1790, in Halifax, Nova Scotia, Gertrude, fifth daughter of Colonel Philip Van Cortlandt, and was posted captain on 19 July 1790. The couple had one son, who died young, and one daughter. Buller made his home at Trenant Park, Cornwall, held the parliamentary seat for East Looe from 1802 to 1820, and was also recorder for East Looe from 1807 until his death.

He had been made colonel of the Royal Marines on 28 April 1805, and the *Naval Chronicle* in its transcription of Admiralty notices of promotions on 9 November 1805 showed Buller as promoted to rear-admiral of the blue, presumably in recognition of his service at Sir Robert Calder's action. In fact, however, he had to wait until 28 April 1808. He was made a baronet on 30 October 1808 and promoted vice-admiral on 12 August 1812, dying on 15 April 1824, aged fifty-nine.

Lt: 1782
M-C: 26 April 1783
Capt: 19 July 1790
R-Adm: 28 April 1808
V-Adm: 12 August 1812

BYRON

REAR-ADMIRAL RICHARD BYRON, CB, is best known for his running fight with an American squadron in June 1812, which signalled the outbreak of war with the United States. The *Naval Chronicle* reported that on the 24th of June, the *Belvidera* frigate, commanded by Captain Richard Byron…, was cruising off Sandy Hook, but not in sight of land, when she fell in with an American squadron, consisting of the *President*, *United States*, *Congress*, and *Essex* frigates, and *Hornet* sloop of war, which ships, as soon as they were within point blank shot, *without previous communication with the Belvidera*, immediately commenced firing upon her. The *Belvidera*, of course, made sail from so very superior a force, and the Americans pursued her, maintaining a running fight with her, as long as she was within reach of shot; in the course of which she had two men killed, and Captain Byron was hurt in the thigh, by a gun falling upon him. The *Belvidera* made her way to Halifax, to acquaint Admiral [Herbert] Sawyer of the transaction, and repair her damages. On her arrival there Admiral Sawyer sent Captain Thompson in the *Colibri* sloop of war, *with a flag of truce*, to New York to request an explanation of the matter. [NC 28.73-4]

A nephew of Vice-Admiral the Honourable John Byron, Richard Byron was born in 1769, the first son of the Revd and Honourable Richard Byron, rector of Haughton, county Durham, and his wife Mary, daughter of Richard Farmer of Leicester. His name was entered as a volunteer in *Proserpine* (42) under Captain George Anson Byron, his first cousin, in October 1781. He was rated an able seaman when he transferred with Byron in January 1782 to *Andromache* (32), in which he served in the West Indies and witnessed the battle of the Saintes and Lord Howe's relief of Gibraltar. He was rated a midshipman on 2 June 1784 when he followed Captain Byron into *Druid* (32), which was employed in customs prevention work between Torbay and Land's End. Captain Byron was succeeded in March 1785 by Captain Joseph Ellison, but on 15 November 1788 Richard Byron again joined his cousin when he was rated able

seaman in *Phoenix* (36) under orders for the East Indies, where on 28 August 1790 he was rated master's mate. The cousins were employed against Tippoo Sahib, but Captain Byron was severely injured in the upset of a boat and returned home to die. Richard Byron, after serving as midshipman in *Crown* (64) flying the flag of Rear-Admiral the Honourable William Cornwallis, and subsequently in *Minerva* (38), to which Cornwallis transferred his flag, was commissioned lieutenant on 1 October 1792 in *Perseverance* (36) under Captain Isaac Smith. Returning home in her and going on leave in July 1793, he was appointed to *Impregnable* (90) flying the flag of Rear-Admiral Caldwell in October 1793. In her he fought in the battle of the Glorious First of June in 1794. He then transferred into *Queen Charlotte* (100) in the Channel fleet flying first the flag of Lord Howe, and then of Lord Bridport, and took part in the action off L'Orient on 23 June 1795. He left her in September 1797 to join *Doris* (36) under Captain the Right Honourable Viscount Ranelagh at Cork. In October 1797 he was appointed flag lieutenant to Sir Hugh Christian, and accompanied him to the Cape of Good Hope in *La Virginie* (38), where he may for a while have joined *Tremendous* (74), and then was put in command of *Cornwallis*, brig, on 22 June 1798. He commanded her for less than a month.

He found employment again in command of the French prize *Rosario* (18) on 12 August 1801, and married on 23 September 1801, in Stoke Damerel, Devon, Sarah, daughter of James Sykes, navy agent and sister of Vice-Admiral John Sykes. His ship was under orders for the West Indies, and he served on the Jamaica station watching the French fleet, which was co-operating with General le Clerc in attempting to recover possession of San Domingo.

Returning in August 1802, he was commissioned post captain on 29 April 1802, and in October 1803 was ordered to fit *Inconstant* (36) for service at Chatham. But when she was ready for sea in December 1803, he was put out of employment, and did not obtain another command until 13 February 1810 when he was appointed to *Belvidera* (42). During his pursuit by the American squadron, which was commanded by Commodore Rogers, Byron led it away from the homebound Jamaica trade which was nearby with a small escort. The following month he came close to capturing USS *Constitution* after a long chase, first under sail, and when becalmed using alternative kedge anchors laid out by the ship's boats. He finally swallowed the anchor on 25 October 1814.

He was made a CB on 4 June 1815, and promoted rear-admiral on 10 January 1837. He died on 2 September 1837, aged sixty-eight, in Leatherhead, Surrey, survived by four sons, and by his wife, who died on 11 August 1861.

Lt: 1 October 1792
Cmdr: 22 June 1798
Capt: 29 April 1802
R-Adm: 10 January 1837

CALDER

ADMIRAL SIR ROBERT CALDER'S action on 22 July 1805 became controversial because it led to his being found guilty at court martial of having failed to do his utmost to defeat the enemy, although it was accepted that his had been an error of judgement. Yet, with inferior forces, in poor visibility and with the threat of the Franco-Spanish squadron being reinforced, he had captured two of the enemy and put an end to the danger that a naval concentration in the Channel would enable the French to invade England.

Robert Calder was born on 2 July 1745 in Park Place, Kent, the fourth and youngest son of Sir James Calder and first wife, Alice, daughter and coheiress of Admiral Robert Hughes. He was educated in Maidstone, was placed on the books in 1757, and entered the navy on 26 December 1758 as a midshipman on board the *Nassau* (70) commanded by his cousin Captain James Sayer. *Nassau* saw service in the American theatre and was dismasted in the storm which struck the British squadron on 24 September. When she reached England she had nine feet of water in her hold. The following spring *Nassau* led a small squadron which succeeded in the capture of Fort St Louis in Senegal. An attempt against the island of Goree was beaten off by the French garrison, but a larger force was then sent from England under Commodore Keppel which succeeded in capturing the fort. *Nassau* also participated in this later operation, and Calder had the misfortune to be severely wounded. He was still on board the *Nassau* the next year, however, when she formed part of the force which took Guadeloupe, Marie Galante and the Saintes.

He was commissioned lieutenant on 31 August 1762 and promoted master and commander on 27 August 1779. On 1 May 1779 he married Amelia, the only daughter of John Mitchell of Bayfield Hall in Norfolk, who had been member of parliament for Boston in Lincolnshire until his death several years before. The step to captain soon followed on 27 August 1780, and a home was purchased at Southwick near Portsmouth, but the marriage proved unhappy because Amelia was mentally unwell. There were to be no children.

During the rest of the American war Calder was employed in the Channel fleet, first in *Buffalo* (50) from 2 August 1780 to 3 January 1781, and then on 30 April 1782 taking command of *Diana* (32), which served as repeating frigate to Lord Howe, and took part in the relief of Gibraltar. He transferred on 24 November 1782 into *Thalia* (36) in the Channel fleet, and served in her until peace was concluded in 1783, when he retired into private life. On 1 May 1789 he was appointed flag captain in *Barfleur* (90), Admiral Barrington's flagship, and he served in her during the Nootka Sound crisis in 1790 until 30 September. After another period ashore, Calder was appointed on 30 August 1791 to *Duke* (90), which was serving as a guardship at Portsmouth and was the flagship of Vice-Admiral Roddam, who had married Calder's sister Alethia. He remained in *Duke* until 31 August 1792.

After the French declaration of war in February 1793 Calder was appointed, on 12 November, to command the *Theseus* (74) in the Channel fleet, and on 2 October 1795 he returned to the *Victory* (100) as Admiral Sir John Jervis's captain of the fleet. As such, he played an important role in preparing the Mediterranean fleet for the battle it fought with the Spanish fleet on 14 February 1797 off Cape St Vincent. Amongst the Calder manuscripts in the

British Library, London, is the order book in which he drew, or likely had drawn for him, in meticulous detail, tactical plans of fleet manoeuvres needed to respond to attempts by the enemy to avoid action, or to defeat him once engaged. It was probably Calder's role in developing the professionalism of the fleet that was to lead Admiral Roddam to write in his defence following his trial that Calder had saved Britain from invasion: 'Sir Robert Calder saved us, and farther, *He*, and *He alone*, laid the entire foundation of every subsequent victory in this war; no victory off Cadiz, no victory in the West Indies, &c. &c. &c.; no honours or rewards in consequence would have taken place *but for him*: and this is the man Englishmen have been taught and permitted to abuse!' [NC 27.451]

Calder received the usual knighthood, KCB, on 3 March 1797, as a reward for carrying Jervis's victory dispatch, and on 22 August 1798 he was granted a patent as baronet with the style of Sir Robert Calder of Southwick. He had to wait two years after the battle before being promoted by seniority to rear-admiral, on 14 February 1799. In 1800 he hoisted his flag in the *Prince of Wales* (98) in the Channel fleet under the command of Jervis, now earl of St Vincent. In February 1801 he was detached with seven ships of the line and three frigates in pursuit of a French squadron which he believed had gone to the West Indies, but in fact entered the Mediterranean. He did not discover his error until he reached Jamaica; he then returned to the Channel fleet, where he arrived in June. Following the peace of Amiens, he was promoted on 23 April 1804 to vice-admiral. In February 1805 Admiral Sir William Cornwallis, who had succeeded to command of the Channel fleet, selected Calder to take charge of the squadron blockading the ports

Sir Robert Calder, Bart.,
Vice Admiral of the White Squadron,
engraved by H R Cooke from
an original painting, published by
Joyce Gold, 103 Shoe Lane,
28 February 1807.

of Ferrol and Corunna. Initially he commanded five ships of the line to watch a Franco-Spanish squadron of ten ships ready for sea, and two more refitting. His force was gradually reinforced, and when joined by the squadron watching Rochefort on 15 July he commanded fifteen ships. His orders then were to stretch to the westward to intercept Vice-Admiral Villeneuve as he returned with the combined Franco-Spanish fleet from the West Indies. This proved to consist of twenty-two ships, and Calder had to deal with the possibility that they would be joined by the five ships of the Rochefort squadron, and that the ships at Ferrol would be able to leave harbour and catch him between two fleets. As a fleet in being, which had just inflicted a sharp defeat on part of the forces it was facing, Calder's force played a major role in deflecting the Franco-Spanish force from concentrating to enter the Channel in support of the invasion flotillas. His censure by the court martial may have had more to do with the public's admiration of Nelson's heroic death than with an honest assessment of Calder's predicament, or his achievement.

Gradually service opinion turned to Calder's support and he was given the step to vice-admiral of the red on 28 May 1808, on 10 June 1810 he was appointed commander-in-chief at Plymouth, and on 31 July he was promoted to vice-admiral of the blue squadron. He died on 31 August 1818, aged seventy-three, in Holt, Hampshire, and the baronetcy became extinct. Amelia died on 1 December 1830, aged seventy-five.

Lt: 31 August 1762
M-C: 27 August 1779
Capt: 27 August 1780
R-Adm: 14 February 1799
V-Adm: 23 April 1804
Adm: 31 July 1810

CAMELFORD – *see* Pitt

CAMPBELL

VICE-ADMIRAL SIR PATRICK CAMPBELL, KCB, established his reputation on the night of 7 July 1800 as commander of *Dart*, an experimental sloop designed by Sir Samuel Bentham, fitted with a dagger-board keel, and armed with thirty 32-pounder carronades. Leading a flotilla including two gun-brigs and four fireships, he entered Dunkirk to destroy four large French frigates, and succeeded in firing into and boarding the *Désirée* (38), bringing her out through the shoals. The other three frigates evaded capture or destruction by running themselves ashore, being refloated by their crews after the British forces retired.

He was born in 1773 a son of Colonel John Campbell of Melfort, Argyllshire, and his wife Colina, daughter of John Campbell of Auchalader. He entered the navy on 24 February 1788 as a volunteer first class in *Astrea* (32) under the command of Captain Peter Rainier, and served on the Jamaica station. He was rated a midshipman when in April 1790 he joined the 12-pounder frigate *Blonde* (32) under the command of Captain William Affleck, with whom he continued on the Jamaica station until July 1792, apparently being lent for a time to *Ambuscade* (32) on 13 January 1791. In September 1792 he was rated midshipman in *Porcupine* (24) under the command of Captain Edward Buller, serving in the Channel and Irish Sea, and in July 1793 he followed Buller into *Adventure* (44), where he was rated master's mate. Between April and September 1794 he served in *Severn* (44) and *Queen* (90), probably as a passed midshipman. He was commissioned on 25 September 1794, and appointed to *Echo*, a carronade-armed ship-sloop, under Captain Temple Hardy, with whom he served in the Channel and at the Cape of Good Hope. In October 1795 he transferred to *Monarch* (74) flying the flag of Admiral Sir George Keith Elphinstone at the Cape of Good Hope and in the East Indies. In August 1796 he returned to *Echo* as her commander, but he was not confirmed in that rank, and within weeks was transferred to a post ship,

Stately (64), but again he was not confirmed in his rank. He remained in her nonetheless until May 1797. His promotion to commander was confirmed on 4 September 1797, and he was appointed to *Firm* (16) at Sheerness, moving in April 1799 to the *Dart*. In her he was employed on the Flemish and Dutch coasts. His action at Dunkirk was rewarded by promotion to post rank on 11 July 1800 and his appointment on the 28th to *Ariadne* (20); he moved in September 1802 to *Doris* (36).

On 12 January 1805 he had the misfortune to lose her when she struck on a rock in Quiberon Bay. She had to be abandoned and burnt a few days later. The officers and men were taken on board the *Tonnant* (80) commanded by Captain William Henry Jervis, and on 26 January, in attempting to go on board the flagship of Admiral Sir William Cornwallis off Brest, Jervis was drowned when the boat carrying the two captains was swamped. Campbell was rescued and served in the Mediterranean in the later years of the war, commanding *Unité* (38), formerly the French *Impérieuse*, in the Adriatic from 19 June 1806 to 11 March 1810, then moving into *Leviathan* (74), where he remained until 11 October 1813.

He was nominated a CB on 4 June 1815, but remained ashore until 1824 when he was appointed to command the teak-built *Ganges* (84) in the Channel. He married in 1825, uniting with Margaret, the youngest daughter of Captain Andrew Wauchope of Niddrie Marischall, Edinburghshire, and sister of Admiral Robert Wauchope. In March 1827 he commissioned *Ocean* (80) for the Mediterranean, but he was unable to complete her manning in time to join the fleet before the battle of Navarino was fought. He was promoted to rear-admiral on 22 July 1830, and served from 1834 to 1837 as commander-in-chief at the Cape of Good Hope, being nominated KCB on 12 April 1836. He died on 13 August 1841, aged sixty-eight, in Edinburgh with the rank of vice-admiral.

Lt: 25 September 1794
Cmdr: 4 September 1797
Capt: 11 July 1800
R-Adm: 22 July 1830
V-Adm: 28 June 1838

CAMPERDOWN – *see* Duncan

CAPEL

ADMIRAL THE HONOURABLE SIR THOMAS BLADEN CAPEL, GCB, served as Nelson's signal lieutenant on board the *Vanguard* at the battle of the Nile on 1 August 1798, following which he was promoted and sent home with a copy of the dispatches. He commanded *Mutine* as far as Naples and then proceeded overland. In consequence of the capture of the *Leander,* which was carrying the originals, he was the first to bring the news of the victory in England.

He was born on 25 August 1776 in Watford, Hertfordshire, the fifth and youngest son of William Anne Holles Capel, fourth earl of Essex, and his second wife, Harriet Isabella, daughter of Colonel Thomas Bladen. His name was entered into the muster book of *Phaeton* (38) on 22 March 1782, but he did not join his ship as a captain's servant until 12 April 1792, when he joined *Assistance* (50) under Captain Mansfield for service at Newfoundland. On 11 July 1792 he was rated an able seaman in *Syren* (32) under Captain John Manley, also on the Newfoundland station, and he continued to be passed back and forth between those ships until 30 September 1794, rating as a midshipman on 1 March 1793 and following Manley into *Apollo* (36), where he served in the North Sea until 23 January 1795. He then joined *Leviathan* (74) under the command of Lord Hugh Seymour, and was serving in *Sans Pareil* (80) when he was commissioned lieutenant on 5 April 1797 and appointed to *Cambrian* (32). In April 1798 he transferred to *Vanguard* (74). In consequence of his battlefield commission on 4 August to command *Mutine*, and his being honoured with carrying home the dispatches, his commander's commission was confirmed and he was made post captain on 27 December 1798, with appointment to command *Arab* (22) on 5 January 1799.

He was appointed on 6 September 1800 to command *Meleager* (32), and was wrecked on the Triangle rocks in the Gulf of Mexico on 9 June 1801, but on 24 August 1802 he was put in command of *Pheobe* (36) and ordered to the Mediterranean. In April 1805, when Nelson sailed in pursuit of the Toulon fleet, Capel was left in command of five frigates and two bombs to cover Sardinia, Sicily and the route to Egypt. He served under Sir Henry Blackwood in the blockade of Cadiz, and following the battle of Trafalgar *Phoebe* saved the prize *Swiftsure* (74) from shipwreck on the Spanish shore, and helped in the rescue of *Bahama* from the same fate.

Capel was a member of the court martial which tried Sir Robert Calder in December 1805, and on 21 August 1806 he was given command of *Endymion* (40) in the Mediterranean. In 1807 he conveyed the British ambassador, the Right Honourable Charles Arbuthnot, to Constantinople, and he later took part in the forced passages of the Dardanelles by the fleet commanded by Sir John Duckworth on 19 February and 3 March. He was put in command of *La Hogue* (74) on 14 December 1811, and following the American declaration of war in 1812 Capel was senior captain in the northern part of the American theatre.

He married on 10 May 1816 Harriet Catherine, only daughter of Francis George Smyth of Upper Brook Street, St George, Hanover Square, Westminster. He was made a CB on 4 June 1815, a KCB on 20 May 1832 and a GCB on 7 April 1852. He had moved through ranks until promoted admiral on 28 April 1847, and died on 4 March 1853, aged seventy-six, in Rutland Gate, London.

Lt: 5 April 1797
Cmdr: 2 October 1798
Capt: 27 December 1798
R-Adm: 27 May 1825
V-Adm: 10 January 1837
Adm: 28 April 1847

CARDEN

ADMIRAL JOHN SURMAN CARDEN is best known as the captain of *Macedonian,* frigate, armed with twenty-eight 18-pounder long guns, sixteen 32-pounder carronades, two long 12-pounders and 2 long, brass 8-pounders and with a total of 297 men, who was defeated by the American super-frigate USS *United States*, which was armed with thirty-two long 24-pounders and twenty-two 42-pounder carronades and had a crew of 509 men.

He was born on 15 August 1771 at Teddington Court near Tewkesbury, Gloucestershire, the second son of Major Carden and his wife, née Surnam. His early prospects were blighted because his mother temporised when ordered to send him as a page to Queen Charlotte's court, and ignored commands that he should muster as an ensign in his father's regiment. It is not clear whether he was as old as eight at the time. She then died at the age of twenty-six, and his father died of wounds in America. Young Carden entered the navy on 28 May 1788 as a captain's servant on board the *Edgar* commanded by Captain Charles Thompson and flying the flag of Rear-Admiral James Gambier. In November, or thereabouts, he transferred to *Perseverance,* commanded by Captain Isaac Smith, for service in the East Indies, and in her was rated midshipman in 1790, apparently remaining with her until 1793 when on the French declaration of war he joined the *Marlborough* (74), commanded by the Honourable George C Berkeley. He served in her until he was commissioned lieutenant on 24 July 1794 following the battle of the Glorious First of June, during which his eyesight was injured by a powder explosion. On 13 March 1795 he transferred with Berkeley to *Formidable* (90), and he continued in Channel service until 1797, when he was appointed to *Barfleur* (90) under Captain James Richard Dacres at Portsmouth. After a week in August 1798 serving on board *Queen Charlotte* (100), in which Vice-Admiral Sir Charles Thompson was flying his flag, he was appointed first lieutenant of *Fisgard* (38). Following conspicuous gallantry in action with *L'Immortalité* (42 or 36) and her capture, Carden was again promoted, to commander, on 25 October 1798.

On 15 July 1799 Carden was appointed to command *Sheerness* (nominally a 44, but with reduced armament) and sent to lead a division of boats in the debarkation of the army at the Helder. He was then employed in support of French royalists on the Vendée coast, before convoying troop ships to the Red Sea to support the British army in Egypt. He was present when the storeship *Bombay* burnt on 17 February 1803 and saved many lives by his leadership in clearing a burning powder magazine. Between 1803 and 1804 he served with the sea fencibles on the Firth of Forth under Captain Isaac (*or* John?) Clements and Captain David Milne, before returning to sea in *Moulle.*

He was posted captain on 22 January 1806, but was not employed in that rank until August 1808, when he was appointed to the first rate *Ville de Paris* (110), in which he served in the Mediterranean and at the evacuation of Sir John Moore's army from Corunna. In April 1809 he transferred to *Ocean* (98) before moving again to *Mars* (74) in June 1810, and to *Macedonian* (38) on 5 April 1811.

At the court martial following the action of 28 October 1812 with the American super-frigate he was criticised for making a tactical mistake in seeking to hold the weather gauge when the better course would have been to close quickly with his enemy, but he was acquitted, and the news of his action and acquittal reached London in time to be used by the ministry to assert in the Commons that there was no defeatism in the navy. Much was also made of the numbers of British seamen, some even of Nelson's barge crew, who were serving on board the *United States.*

When he was married or to whom is not known, but he had one daughter. He was granted a good service pension on 19 May 1837, and died with the rank of admiral on 22 April 1858, aged eighty-six, at Ramcan rectory, Ballycastle, county Antrim.

Lt: 24 July 1794
Cmdr: 25 October 1798
Capt: 22 January 1806
Superannuated
R-Adm: 28 June 1838
He was restored on the Active List
R-Adm: 17 August 1840
V-Adm: 23 March 1848
Reserve half-pay
Adm: 3 July 1855

CARNEGIE – *see* Northesk

CARTERET

CAPTAIN SIR PHILIP CARTERET, BARONET, CB, had the distinction on 20–1 September 1811, when commanding *Naiad* (46), of humiliating Napoleon, who was at Boulogne to observe an exercise by the flotilla still kept there to threaten Britain with invasion. *Naiad*, with three gun-brigs, managed to cut off one of its divisions, which was forced to an action and captured. The rest escaped under the guns of the coastal batteries.

He was born in 1777, the only son of Rear-Admiral Philip Carteret of Trinity Manor, Jersey, and his wife Mary Rachael, only daughter of Sir John Silvester, MD, FRS. On 2 February 1782 his father, who had been one of the circumnavigators of the 1760s, placed his son under the care of his former lieutenant, Captain Erasmus Gower, as a captain's servant in *Medea* (28), and on 8 March 1792 the younger Carteret moved with Gower into *Salisbury* (50). If young Philip had actually been on board, he would have seen service in the East Indies, and at Newfoundland, but his introduction to the service was probably in September 1792, in Gower's next command, *Lion* (64), which was preparing to carry Lord Macartney *en embassy* to China. After returning in October 1794, in the second year of the war with Revolutionary France, he served under Captain James (?) Gower in *Prince George* (90), and then returned to Erasmus Gower in *Triumph* (74), which was part of the Channel fleet. He was slightly wounded in the skirmish with the French fleet on 17 June 1795, and was commissioned lieutenant on 8 October 1795. He was appointed to *L'Imperieuse* (38) under the command of Captain Lord Augustus Fitzroy, and served in the North Sea and Channel.

On 5 December 1796 he was appointed to *Greyhound* (32), which formed part of the western squadron, and also was employed on the Irish station. She was commanded in turn by Captain James Young, Captain Israel Pellew and Captain Richard Lee. On 24 March 1798 he transferred to *Cambrian* (32), under the command of the Honourable Arthur Kaye Legge. With him he continued in the western squadron, and in the Channel fleet, and also made a voyage to St Helena. He was promoted

commander on 7 May 1802, and was appointed to *Bonne Citoyenne* (20) on 17 May, under orders for the Mediterranean. He came ashore in December, and spent the next year and a half on leave before taking command of the brig-sloop *Scorpion* (18) on 11 April 1804, for service in the North Sea and West Indies. He was made post captain on 22 January 1806, but he spent most of 1806 in the West Indies watching the French squadron commanded by Rear-Admiral Willaumez. Only when he returned to England in early 1807 did he learn he had been promoted. He came ashore July 1807, and was not employed in his rank for the next two years.

In 1809 he served in the Scheldt expedition as a volunteer in the *Superb* (74), flagship of Sir Richard Goodwin Keats, and was put in command of a flotilla of gun-brigs, sloops and gunboats. He earned the praise of Sir Richard John Strachan, the commander-in-chief, and Commodore Owen for his work covering the evacuation of Walcheren.

He was appointed to *Naiad* (38) in June 1811, and remained in her, following his triumph off Boulogne, until April 1812, when he was appointed to command *Pomone* (46) in which he was employed at Lisbon and Gibraltar, in the Channel fleet and later on the coast of North America. On 31 December 1813 he was tried by court martial at his own request, to address the criticism directed at him for having let a French frigate escape while he attended to another ship which proved to be a Portuguese galleon. He was acquitted and remained in command of the *Pomone* until the end of the war. On 3 May 1815 he was appointed to the *Désirée* (36), transferring on 19 November to the 18-pounder frigate *Active* (38), in which he served two years on the Jamaica station.

He retired from active service on 9 October 1817, assuming the additional surname of Silvester, on 19 January 1822. Nominated a CB on 4 June 1815, he succeeded his uncle as second baronet on 30 March 1822. He died on 24 August 1828, aged fifty-one, in Leamington, Worcestershire; the baronetcy became extinct.

Lt: 8 October 1795
Cmdr: 7 May 1802
Capt: 22 January 1806

CHRISTIAN

REAR-ADMIRAL SIR HUGH CLOBERRY CHRISTIAN, KB, has the dubious distinction of being known almost exclusively for his misfortune, as rear-admiral commanding the largest troop convoy to have left England to that date, to have had his fleet twice suffer tremendous losses to exceptionally severe storms in the Channel on passage to the West Indies.

The Late Sir Hugh Cloberry Christian, K.B.,
Rear-Admiral of the White Squadron,
engraved by H R Cook after James Northcote, RA,
published by Joyce Gold, 103 Shoe Lane,
31 March 1809.

He was born in 1747 in Buckingham Street, York Buildings, London, the only child of Lieutenant Thomas Christian, RN, and his wife, Ann, daughter of Owen Hughes of Bangor, Caernarvonshire. He entered the navy in 1761 but it is not known who was his service sponsor. It is known that he was examined for competence in naval matters in 1767, but he did not receive his lieutenant's commission until 21 January 1771, when there was an expansion in the fleet due to the Falkland Islands crisis. He married on 6 March 1775 Ann, only daughter of Barnabas Leigh of Thorleigh, Isle of Wight, and had two sons and three daughters, his eldest son becoming Rear-Admiral Hood Hanway Christian. He was promoted master and commander in 1778, and post captain on 8 December 1778. He was appointed flag captain of *Suffolk* (74) flying the broad pendant of Commodore Joshua Rowley commanding seven ships of the line under orders to reinforce the fleet at the Leeward Islands, where he arrived on 12 February 1779. Christian took part in the action off Grenada against the Comte d'Estaing on 6 July 1779, *Suffolk* being the lead ship in the van. He commanded *Fortunée* (40) in the actions off Martinique in April and May 1780, in the battle of the Chesapeake on 5 September 1781, at St Kitts on 26 January 1782, and at Dominica on 12 April 1782.

Following the peace of Versailles in 1783 he was not employed until October 1790, when he was appointed to pay off the *Queen Charlotte* (100) at Portsmouth at the end of the Nootka Sound crisis. He came ashore on 28 December 1790, and resumed command of *Queen Charlotte* on 12 February 1793 following the French declaration of war, joining the fleet at Spithead on 25 March 1793.

In August 1794 he was made a commissioner of the Transport Board, and he was promoted rear-admiral on 1 June 1795, less than six months before he sailed, on 16 November, on the ill-fated expedition.

The fleet he commanded, flying his flag in *Prince George* (90), was to convoy 200 sail of transports and West Indiamen with over 16,000 men embarked. In the storm which struck two days after sailing, several of the transports and merchantmen foundered and were wrecked. Above 200 dead bodies were later found on the coast between Portland and Bridport. Once he had repaired the damage and shifted his flag to *Glory* (90), the fleet set out again on the 9 December, but they were struck a second time by severe weather, and over fifty of the transports and nine of their convoy including *Glory* were forced to turn back. Of the remainder of the dispersed fleet, many were taken by privateers. As a small compensation for his sufferings, not to mention the sufferings of the sailors, Admiral Christian was invested KB on 17 February 1796, and sailed for a third time on 20 March, this time flying his flag in *Thunderer* (74). Third time lucky, he carried his forces successfully to the capture of St Lucia, Grenada and St Vincent.

After returning to England, he sailed in 1797 as second in command of the Cape of Good Hope station, and the following year succeeded to the command, but he died on 23 November 1798, aged fifty-one. The patent of the peerage that had been conferred upon him arrived after his death. His wife died on 22 January 1799 in West Hill, Isle of Wight, without knowing of her husband's death.

Lt: 21 January 1771
M-C: 1778
Capt: 8 December 1778
R-Adm: 1 June 1795

COCHRANE

ADMIRAL THE HONOURABLE SIR ALEXANDER FORRESTER INGLIS COCHRANE, GCB, is well known in the United States for his part in the burning of Washington.

He was born on 23 April 1758, the seventh son of Thomas Cochrane, eighth Earl Dundonald, and his second wife, Jane, eldest daughter of Archibald Stuart of Torrance, Lanarkshire. He received his commission as lieutenant on 19 May 1778, and was wounded in action off Martinique on 17 April 1780 as a junior lieutenant in the *Montagu* (74) under Captain John Houlton. His promotion to master and commander followed on 6 December 1780, and he was made post captain on 17 December 1782. During the peace following the American war, he was unemployed, and he married on 26 April 1788, in New York, Maria, daughter of David Shaw and widow of Captain Sir Jacob Wheate, RN. The couple had four sons and two daughters.

On the French declaration of war in February 1793 Alexander Cochrane was appointed to command *Hind* (24), serving a year in the Channel. He was then transferred to *Thetis* (38) and sailed to America, where he cruised in company with *Hussar* (28) commanded by Captain John Poo Beresford. On 17 May 1795 off Hampton Roads he encoun-

tered a squadron of five French frigates, and immediately closed them to engage, ordering *Hussar* to lie alongside the second ship, which proved to be the commodore's flagship, while he engaged the third and following ships in the French line. Two prizes were taken, both being partly disarmed to enable them to transport naval stores from France to Guadeloupe.

In February 1799 he was appointed to command *Ajax* (80). Initially employed on the coast of France under Sir Edward Pellew and Sir John Borlase Warren in the expeditions to Quiberon Bay and against Ferrol, he then joined Lord Keith in the Mediterranean, and in February and March 1801 took charge of the first wave of the landing operations in Aboukir Bay leading to the capture of Alexandria. He was praised by Keith and General Hutchinson for his work, but Cochrane was to complain of what he considered to be Keith's dishonesty. He was awarded the Turkish gold medal in 1802.

On the recommencement of the war in 1803 he was appointed to command *Northumberland* (74), promoted rear-admiral on 23 April 1804, and dispatched to watch the Spanish coast. The reports that were sent home indicated the extent of French influence over, or more properly coercion of, Spanish policy, and led to the orders on 5 October to intercept Spanish treasure ships off Cape Santa Maria to prevent their cargo passing into French hands. The consequence was that one of the ships blew up with great loss of life, and by the end of the year Spain declared war.

At the beginning of 1805 he sailed in pursuit of Rear-Admiral Missiessy's squadron, which had escaped from Rochefort and was believed to be sailing to the West Indies. Cochrane pursued as far as Barbados, when he found that the French had reached Martinique and were expected at Jamaica, so he proceeded there. On being appointed commander in the Leeward Islands, he left most of his ships at Jamaica and sailed to his command in his flagship. There he met Lord Nelson, who had pursued the Toulon and Cadiz fleets to the West Indies, and cruised with him, prior to Nelson's return to Europe.

In January 1806, following the defeat of the

combined fleet at the battle of Trafalgar, Cochrane was joined by Sir John Duckworth who was pursuing a French squadron, which he eventually encountered off San Domingo. In the action which followed, Cochrane, who was junior to Duckworth and therefore *pro tempore* his subordinate, engaged the *Imperial* (120). The whole of the French squadron was destroyed or captured. In recognition of his services, he was made a KB on 29 March 1806, and with the other captains received a vote of thanks from both houses of parliament, the freedom of the City of London and a sword of honour to the value of 100 guineas.

At the end of June another French squadron, of six ships of the line and four corvettes, arrived at Martinique. Cochrane had at his disposal only four ships of the line and three frigates, but nonetheless sailed to watch the French force, which he followed as far as Porto Rico before returning to escort a convoy.

In 1807 he carried out orders to take possession of the Danish islands, and in 1808 undertook in conjunction with soldiers commanded by General George Beckwith to take Martinique, which eventually surrendered in February 1809. A squadron of three French ships and two frigates arrived too late to affect the outcome, and took refuge in the Saintes sound. Soldiers were sent to flush them out, but there are three exits to the sound, and the French divided to sail from two of them. Cochrane's force managed to intercept the capital ships, one of which, *Le d'Hautpoult* (74), was captured. In the winter of 1810 Cochrane and Beckwith captured Guadeloupe, Cochrane remaining as governor until 1813. He also received the service medals which were struck for the victories at Martinique and Guadeloupe.

Having been promoted to vice-admiral in October 1809, at the end of 1813 he was appointed to command the naval forces operating on the American coast against the United States. He commenced operations against the Chesapeake in August 1814 leading to the successful raid on Washington and the burning of the public buildings. A subsequent attempt against Baltimore was abandoned when the American defences proved to be too strong. The final operations of the war were

in the Gulf of Mexico. Cochrane arrived off New Orleans on 8 December 1814.

This was an exceptionally difficult amphibious operation, owing to the need to keep the frigates sixty miles from the landing beach because of shoal water, the ships of the line being yet further out to sea. Not even gun vessels could provide fire cover at the landing. Strategic warning had been accorded the Americans by the Admiralty's decision that the operational rendezvous should be in Jamaica, and an insufficient number of small craft had been supplied. The defeat, however, occurred to the army after it was ashore, and the navy successfully re-embarked it. The war closed with the successful capture of Fort Boyer at Mobile.

Following the war he was nominated a GCB on 2 January 1815, but he was not made a baronet as his services might have suggested. He held the parliamentary seat for Stirling Burghs, Scotland, from 24 February 1800 to 1802 and from 28 February 1803 to 1806, for Honiton, Devon, from 1806 to 1807 and for Westminster from 23 May 1807 to 5 July 1814, when he was expelled by the house, being reinstated on 16 July and then continuing in his seat to 10 June 1818.

He died on 26 January 1832, aged seventy-three, in Paris, and was buried in Père-Lachaise Cemetery.

Lt: 19 May 1778
M-C: 6 December 1780
Capt: 17 December 1782
R-Adm: 23 April 1804
V-Adm: 25 October 1809
Adm: 12 August 1819

COCHRANE

ADMIRAL SIR THOMAS COCHRANE, EARL OF DUNDONALD, GCB, had a highly volatile personality and a degree of genius which could lead equally to victory or disaster. His disingenuous autobiography adds to the controversy. He became a hero to the radicals of Britain, as he was to the lower deck and to many officers. In the naval war against the French Empire he is as well known for his exploitation of sea power on the French and Spanish coasts, his courage, intemperance and vanity, as he is for his questionable role in the fireship raid on Basque Roads in 1809 and his meteoric fall under the charge of fraud.

He was born on 14 December 1775 in Amisfield, Lanarkshire, the first son of Archibald Cochrane, ninth earl of Dundonald and his first wife Anne, second daughter of Captain James Gilchrist, RN. He was educated at Chauvet's military academy in Kensington, Middlesex, but his name was also placed on the books of the ships commanded by his uncle Admiral the Honourable Sir Alexander Cochrane, and he entered the navy on 27 June 1793 in *Hind* (24), transferred with his uncle into *Thetis* (38), and served on the North American station, where he was ordered to act as lieutenant in January 1795, his commission being confirmed on 27 May 1796. He subsequently served in Admiral Sir George Elphinstone's (Lord Keith's) flagships *Foudroyant* (80) and *Barfleur* (90). He quarrelled with first lieutenant, Philip Beaver, and was court-martialled for disrespect but let off with an admonition. He moved with Keith into *Queen Charlotte* (100) but was away when she burnt at Leghorn. On 18 February 1800 he had been put in charge of *Généreux* as prize master, to take her into Port Mahon despite her battle

The Right Honourable Lord Cochrane, K.B., engraved by H R Cook after Strochling, published by Joyce Gold, 103 Shoe Lane, Fleet Street, 1 August 1809.

damage and weak manning. This led to his being promoted commander on 28 March 1800 in *Speedy*, sloop.

Six weeks later, on 6 May, he further established an already strong reputation through capturing by boarding *El Gamo*, a Spanish frigate of thirty-two guns and 319 men. 'The great disparity of force', Cochrane wrote in his official report, 'rendered it necessary to adopt some measure that might prove decisive.' [NC 22.6] Less than a month later he, with Captain Pulling of the fir-built brig-sloop *Kangaroo* (18), successfully attacked a gun tower, a xebec of twenty guns and three gunboats in an

action which lasted twelve hours and ended with the capture of three brigs. Cochrane, who, the *Naval Chronicle* commented, 'never appears to have been over cautious respecting his person', came out of the affair with a few bruises and a singeing. A few days later Cochrane was forced to surrender *Speedy* to a French squadron, but he was a captive for only a short time, and was exchanged with other British officers captured at the battle of Algeciras Bay, which he had witnessed from the deck of the French battleship *Desaix*. During his period of ten months in command of *Speedy* he had captured thirty-three vessels, and in recognition of his extraordinary abilities he was made post captain in the old French prize frigate *La Raison* (26) on 8 August 1801.

Cochrane was rude to the earl of St Vincent when *Speedy*'s first lieutenant was not promoted, with the result that on the renewal of the war he was able to obtain command of only a scarcely seaworthy prize. And when he complained too much to Lord Keith, he was sent to cruise north-east of the Orkney Islands. Only after St Vincent resigned the Admiralty on the return of Pitt to power did Cochrane get a ship worthy of his talents, *Pallas* (32), and an opportunity to shine in the cruising ground off the Azores. In October 1803 he captured a Spanish galleon freighting £150,000 in gold and other merchandise of a similar value. When the Spanish captain and supercargo expostulated that after a lifetime of labour they were going home with all their wealth, amounting to $30,000 each, and were ruined, Cochrane claimed to have returned $5,000 to each. Cochrane's reputation continued to grow as he conducted a succession of daring raids on the hostile coasts of France and Spain, the latter in support of the Spanish guerillas. On

6 April 1806 he employed his boats to cut out a French sloop from the Garonne and, without waiting to recover his men, pursued three French corvettes and drove them ashore. St Vincent, however, was once more in a position of influence, and Cochrane remained out of favour. On 14 May he engaged and defeated *La Minerve* (40), which was accompanied by three French brigs, but could not take possession because of the appearance of two more French frigates.

He took time in 1806 to campaign for the parliamentary seat for Honiton in Devon. The seat was notorious for its corruption, and he lost in the July election through not paying the usual bribe. But he did pay £10 to every elector who voted for him, and won easily at the general election in October. Reportedly, he appeared in full uniform with an armed boat's crew, which he paraded through the streets. This time, however, he did not pay the electors who had voted him in, nor pay for the customary 'treats'. On 17 November he returned to sea in *Imperieuse* (38), to which the crew of *Pallas* had been turned over, and he served with the squadron blockading Basque Roads, but he was back at Plymouth in February 1807 and took sick-leave to contest the popular seat of Westminster in May 1807. He became closely connected with William Cobbett, the radical, and was elected in tandem with Sir Francis Burdett. He made himself popular by his attacks on the corruption of government, especially at the Admiralty. To get him away from Westminster, he was given orders to join the Mediterranean fleet. He sailed on 12 September 1807, and joined Lord Collingwood's flag off Toulon on 19 November.

An attempt to employ him as senior officer at Corfu, where diplomacy was as much needed as spirit, was quickly brought to an end, and he was sent on detached service to harass the Spanish and French coasts, operating against coastal batteries and signal stations. In June the Spanish rebellion gave the navy the task of providing support along the Spanish coast. Late in 1808 he played an important part in the defence of Rosas by assisting in the defence of Trinity Castle, which was thus able to resist an assault by 1,000 men, although

Rosas later capitulated.

The pinnacle of his achievement, but also the catalyst of his disgrace, occurred when he was placed by Lord Mulgrave, the first lord, in command of a fireship attack on the Brest fleet sheltering in Basque Roads and blockaded there by the Channel fleet commanded by Admiral Gambier. Cochrane was from the Mediterranean fleet, and was resented as an interloper. His attack, which took place on 11 April 1809, was of only limited success, and he conceived that Gambier had been remiss in not heeding his advice to exploit it with the capital ships in time to stop many of the French crossing the bar into the Charente river. As soon as the news of the attack reached London, Cochrane was, on 24 April 1809, nominated a KB. But when he threatened to use his seat in parliament to vote against extending thanks to Admiral Gambier, who asked for and was acquitted by a court martial, the service firmly turned against him. Considering the strength of the tide in Basque Roads, many approved of Gambier's cautious approach, which obtained solid, if limited, results without any loss. In fact, four French ships and an East Indiaman were either driven onto the shore and destroyed, or burnt, and of the rest, several were obliged in their flight across the bar of the Charente to cast their guns overboard to lighten ship.

His career was in tatters, and he was first refused permission to rejoin his ship and then, when his presence in parliament became too obnoxious, ordered to do so, and to join the Mediterranean fleet. He chose to go on half pay, and devoted his energies to attacking the naval administration. In 1811 he made a trip to Italy, and at the copper smelting works at Agrigento in Sicily conceived the idea of using sulphur dioxide gas as a weapon. A committee headed by the duke of York and including Lord Keith, Lord Exmouth and Sir William Congreve rejected his idea only because they considered it unsuitable for a civilised nation, and Cochrane promised to keep it secret from any foreign power.

His private life was as turbulent as was his naval service. He secretly married on 12 August 1812, in Annan, Dumfriesshire, Katherine Frances

Corbett, daughter of Thomas Barnes of Romford, Essex, an orphan who lived under the guardianship of John Simpson of Portland Place, Mile End, London. They were remarried on 22 June 1818 in an Anglican church, and a third time in 1825 according to the forms of the Church of Scotland, and had four sons and a daughter. It was thought that his eldest son, Thomas Barnes Cochrane, who was born in 1814, might be illegitimate owing to the secrecy of the first civil marriage, but the case was proved in his favour in 1863 before a House of Lords committee.

When Cochrane's uncle, Admiral Sir Alexander Cochrane, was appointed in late 1813 to command in North America, he asked his nephew to serve as his flag captain, and left him to prepare his flagship, *Tonnant* (80), for sea, while he himself sailed to the American theatre in a frigate. This chance to recover his reputation, however, was to be lost as a result of his participation or, as he claimed, only his association with the participants, in an attempt to heat the stock market with false news of Napoleon's death. The plot depended on sending a false message by naval telegraph. His name was struck off the navy list on 25 June 1814. He was also fined £1,000 and ordered to stand for one hour in the pillory and to be imprisoned in the King's Bench for one year. He was expelled from the House of Commons on 5 July, and from the chapel of the knights of the Bath. The electors of Westminster promptly returned him to the house, and the hour in the pillory was remitted probably to avoid a riot, but he had to serve his time in prison, in circumstances made more severe by a failed attempt to escape. He blamed John Wilson Croker, the secretary of the Admiralty, for his conviction.

Following his disgrace, he returned to his violent espousal of radical causes in parliament, and was again tripped up by the administration. He was fined, and again imprisoned, but his fine was paid by a penny subscription which was so popular that it also covered the original fine of £1,000 and also a large share of his legal costs. Eventually he was persuaded to embark on a second remarkable career abroad in the navies of newly emerging states. He was in command of the Chilean navy from May 1817 to 29 November 1822. He was in the Brazilian navy from 21 March 1823 to 10 November 1825, and was created marquis of Maranham by Don Pedro of Brazil in 1823, and grand dignitary of the imperial order of the Southern Cross. And under pay from the London Greece Committee he was in command of the Greek navy from March 1827 to December 1828. He was the first to use steam-powered warships and was made a knight of the order of the Redeemer of Greece. So chaotic was the situation in Greece, however, that he was unable to achieve much prior to Sir Edward Codrington's destruction of the Turco-Egyptian fleets at Navarino on 20 October 1827.

He succeeded his father as tenth earl of Dundonald on 1 July 1831, and was restored to the navy list by an order in council of 2 May 1832 with a free pardon, following the coronation of the duke of Clarence, a former naval officer, as William IV. He was also promoted rear-admiral the same day, and received at court. He continued to experiment with the development of steam warships, he registered patents for numerous inventions, he was elevated to GCB on 25 May 1847, and he returned to sea in 1848 as commander-in-chief West Indies. He applied for the post of commander-in-chief in the Baltic during the Russian war, and was turned down, but he was appointed rear-admiral of the United Kingdom on 29 October 1854, and elected an elder brother of the Trinity House. In 1860 he published *The Autobiography of a Seaman* and died with the rank of admiral on 31 October 1860, aged eighty-four, at 12 Prince Albert Road, Kensington, having previously undergone two lithotomies. He was buried on 14 November 1860 in Westminster Abbey. His wife died on 25 January 1865, aged sixty-eight, at Boulogne-sur-Mer, France.

Lt: 27 May 1796
Cmdr: 28 March 1800
Capt: 8 August 1801
Struck off the Navy List: 25 June 1814
Restored to the Navy List by an order in council and promoted
R-Adm: 2 May 1832
V-Adm: 23 November 1841
Adm: 21 March 1851

COCKBURN

ADMIRAL OF THE FLEET THE RIGHT
HONOURABLE SIR GEORGE COCKBURN,
BARONET, GCB, is best known for his part in the
coup de main by sailors, and by soldiers commanded by Major-General Ross, against Washington,
during which the capital of the United States was
burnt. Following the surrender of Napoleon,
Cockburn was given the task of taking him to
prison at St Helena.

He was born on 22 April 1772 in London, the
second son of Sir James Cockburn, eighth baronet
of Langton, Berwickshire, and member of parliament for Peebles. His mother, Sir James's second
wife, Augusta Anne, came from another of the families which served the Church and the navy. Her
father was the Very Revd Francis Ayscough, DD,
dean of Bristol and preceptor of King George III,
and her brother was Commander James Ayscough,
RN. George was entered as captain's servant on the
books of *Resource* (28) when he was nine, on 12
March 1781, and later on those of *William and
Mary,* yacht, but he actually attended the Royal
Navigational School in Old Burlington Street,
London, and did not join a ship until 1786. He
was commissioned lieutenant on 27 January 1793,
five days before the French declaration of war, and
served in the Mediterranean with Vice-Admiral
Hotham in *Britannia* (100) and then in *Victory*
(100) with Lord Hood, who promoted him on 11
October 1793 master and commander of *Speedy*
sloop. After a period in acting command of
Inconstant (36), and *Meleager* (32), he was made
post captain on 20 February 1794 in the latter ship.
Meleager was employed as repeater frigate in
Hotham's two actions off Toulon, on 14 March
and 13 July 1795, and was employed under
Captain Nelson in support of the Austrian and
Piedmontese armies in Italy.

His next appointment was on 25 August 1796
to command *La Minerve* (42), in which Nelson
hoisted his broad pendant on 10 December under
orders to proceed from Gibraltar to evacuate the
British post on Elba. In a remarkable three-hour
engagement he forced *Sabina* (40) to strike and

would have similarly served *Matilda* (34) had not
a battle squadron come onto the scene of action.
After withdrawing the garrison at Porto Ferrajo,
Nelson's squadron sailed to join Vice-Admiral
Jervis before Cadiz and arrived in time for Nelson
to assume command of *Captain* (74) and play a
decisive part in the battle of Cape St Vincent.
Following that action *La Minerve* returned to the
coast of Italy, where it formed part of the force
under Sir Lawrence W Halstead blockading Elba,
which now had a French garrison.

Cockburn married on 28 November 1809 his
cousin Mary, daughter and coheiress of Thomas
Cockburn of Kingston, Jamaica, and sister-in-law
of Vice-Admiral Charles Bayntun Hodgson Ross.
The couple had one daughter.

Following the short peace of Amiens, Cockburn
was appointed in July 1803 to command *Phaeton*
(38), in which he served for two years in the East
Indies; on 18 June 1806 he was appointed to command *Captain* (74), transferring on 31 March 1808
to *Pompée* (80), in which in September he served
in the West Indies. In 1809, with the temporary
rank of commodore, he served under Sir Alexander
Cochrane at the reduction of Martinique. That summer, from 2 July to 7 October, he commanded the
Belleisle (74) in the Scheldt expedition, taking command of a division of the bombs and gun vessels
south-east of Flushing, supporting the landing and
eventual withdrawal. On 7 February 1810
Cockburn was appointed to the *Indefatigable* (64).
After an abortive attempt on 7 March to rescue
the king of Spain from captivity at Valençay,
Indefatigable was ordered to join Sir Richard Keats
in the defence of Cadiz. In August 1812 Cockburn
commanded the boats of the fleet in an amphibious attack on the town of Moguer, and was then
ordered to escort to Havana two Spanish three-
deckers being evacuated from Cadiz to prevent their
falling into the hands of the French; on his return
he was in November 1811 sent to South America
with a temporary rank of commodore to mediate
between the Spanish government and its rebellious
colonies. This objective proved unattainable, and
the commission was dissolved in August 1812.

At the general promotion on 1 August 1811

Cockburn was made a colonel of the Royal Marines, and on 12 August 1812 he was promoted to rear-admiral. He hoisted his flag in *Marlborough* (74) and was given command of the squadron off Cadiz. With the outbreak of war with the United States he was ordered in November to Bermuda to join Sir John Borlase Warren, commander-in-chief North America. He was put in charge of naval operations against the southern American states, which culminated in the battle of Bladensburg and the burning of Washington in August 1814 by Major-General Ross. He also commanded the naval forces at the unsuccessful attack on Baltimore in September 1814, and was at the skirmish on 12 September when Ross was mortally wounded. Sir Alexander Cochrane had succeeded Warren in command of the North American station at the beginning of 1814. When he took direct control of the operations against New Orleans, Cockburn was employed in support, by making diversionary attacks on Georgia.

Following the conclusion of the treaty of Ghent, Cockburn returned to Spithead, where he arrived on 4 May 1815. Emperor Napoleon surrendered on 13 July, throwing himself on the mercy of the prince regent. However, he was not permitted to land in England, where English common law might have permitted him to live in retirement. After he had been kept on board *Bellerophon* (74) in Plymouth harbour, it was determined to send him into exile at St Helena. Cockburn was ordered to hoist his flag in *Northumberland* (74), and after his arrival with his prisoner on 15 October remained at St Helena as governor until the summer of 1816.

After his relief as Napoleon's jailor, Cockburn returned to England. He had been made a KCB on 2 January 1815, and was advanced in chivalry to GCB on 20 February 1818. He embarked on a political career, holding the parliamentary seats in succession for Portsmouth (1818–20), Weobley, Herefordshire (1820 to May 1828), Plymouth (7 June 1828 to 1832) and Ripon (27 September 1841 to 1847). He was a member of the lord high admiral's council from May 1827 to 18 September 1828, and played the major part in persuading the

duke of Clarence to resign when he exceeded the terms of his patent. He was senior naval lord from 19 September 1828 to 25 November 1830; despite his political association with the Tories, he served as commander-in-chief North America and West Indies between March 1833 and May 1836, and he was also first naval lord from December 1834 until April 1835 and from September 1841 to July 1846. In recognition of his services he was promoted to major-general of the Royal Marines on 5 April 1821, rear-admiral of the United Kingdom on 10 August 1847 and finally admiral of the fleet on 1 July 1851. He succeeded his brother as tenth baronet on 26 February 1852, and died on 19 August 1853, aged eighty-one, in Leamington Spa, Worcestershire.

Lt: 27 January 1793
M-C: 11 October 1793
Capt: 20 February 1794
R-Adm: 12 August 1812
V-Adm: 12 August 1819
Adm: 10 January 1837
Adm. of the Fleet: 1 July 1851

CODRINGTON

ADMIRAL SIR EDWARD CODRINGTON, GCB, was one of Nelson's captains at the battle of Trafalgar, but the service for which he is chiefly remembered did not occur until after the end of the war against the French Empire when he commanded the allied fleet at the battle of Navarino Bay, and ensured the independence of Greece.

He was born on 27 April 1770 in London, the third and youngest son of Edward Codrington and his wife, Rebecca, née Le Sturgeon. His father was the second son of Sir William Codrington, first baronet of Dodington Park, Gloucestershire. Edward entered the navy on 18 July 1783 as a midshipman in the *Augusta,* yacht, and acquired the patronage of Commodore Herbert Sawyer serving on the Halifax station, and then of Rear-Admiral Peyton. On the French declaration of war in February 1793 he was moved into Earl Howe's flagship, *Queen Charlotte* (100), and in her he was commissioned lieutenant on 28 May 1793. He served as such in *Margaretta*, frigate, and was transferred by Howe to *Pegasus* (28) so as to have a reliable officer repeating his signals, but he returned to *Queen Charlotte* before the battles of the Glorious First of June to serve as Lord Howe's signal lieutenant. At the action on 1 June he assumed responsibility for the forward division of the lower-deck battery. Howe sent him with the duplicate of the victory dispatch to the Admiralty. In recognition, he was promoted to commander on 7 October 1794 and appointed to the *Comet*, fire vessel, was soon thereafter made post captain, on 6 April 1795, and commanded *Babet* (22) in Lord Bridport's engagement off L'Orient on 23 June 1795. In July 1796 he was transferred to *Druid* (32), in which he served at Lisbon until he brought her home to be paid off in early 1797.

He then came ashore for the next eight years, and married on 27 December 1802, at Old Windsor Church, Jane, daughter of Jasper Hall of Kingston, Jamaica, and of Otterburn, Hexham, and Old Windsor, Berkshire. The couple had three sons and three daughters, amongst whom his third son was to rise to be Admiral of the Fleet Sir Henry John Codrington, KCB. Jane died in 1837.

Edward Codrington did not return to service until 24 May 1805, when he was appointed to command *Orion* (74), in which he fought at Trafalgar in the weather line, engaging *Intrépide* (74), which she forced to strike, and assisting in the defeat of *Swiftsure* (74). He continued in command of *Orion* in the Mediterranean fleet under Lord Collingwood until December 1806, when she was paid off, and he returned to private life.

In November 1808 he was appointed to *Blake* (74) and served in the North Sea under Sir Richard Strachan, and in the following year in the Walcheren expedition, when he agreed to his friend Lord Gardner flying his flag on board. On 17 August *Blake* grounded under fire off Flushing, and engaged the batteries while aground for two hours and three-quarters.

In 1810 he was engaged in the defence of Cadiz, and in August was given the exacting task of escorting four scarcely seaworthy Spanish ships of the line crowded with refugees to Minorca, a passage which took thirty-eight days.

In April 1811 he was entrusted with the detached command on the eastern coast of Spain, and went about his task of bolstering the defence of Tarragona with energy. But the French had the moral upper hand, and when the assault became a rout, Codrington sent in the boats to save as many of the fleeing Spaniards as possible. He continued on that station until the end of the following year, harassing the French and taking station to support Spanish plans to retake Tarragona. He returned to England early in 1813, and on 4 December 1813 he was appointed a colonel of the Royal Marines. After a period on shore he was at the beginning of 1814 appointed to command *Forth* (40) and sent out to the North American station as commodore.

He was promoted rear-admiral on 4 June 1814, and was made captain of the fleet under Sir Alexander Cochrane, serving in the operations around the Chesapeake and being present during the raids on Washington and Baltimore. He flew his flag in *Havannah* (36) at the operation before New Orleans and brought home the dispatches following the capture of the fort at Mobile, and the news of the peace settlement.

He was made a KCB on 2 January 1815 and promoted to major-general of the Royal Marines on 5 April 1821. In December 1826 he was appointed commander-in-chief Mediterranean, and he played a decisive part in the Greek war of independence. He commanded the combined British, French and Russian fleet which on 20 October 1827 moved into Navarino Bay ostensibly to anchor, with the inevitable consequence that fire was opened by the Turkish fleet commanded by Ibrahim Pasha. Maybe 4,000 Turks were killed, and Greek independence became a possibility. The duke of Clarence ensured that Codrington was nominated a GCB on 13 November 1827. France awarded him a grand cross of the military order of St Louis. Russia enrolled him as a knight of the order of St George. He was presented with a gold cross of the order of the Redeemer by Greece, and was made a knight grand cross of St Michael and St George by the Ionian Republic and Malta. But the government in London, while it valued Greek independence, also continued to be opposed to Russia acquiring naval access to the Mediterranean. Turkey was a traditional friend. Codrington was accordingly recalled. He held the parliamentary seat for Devonport from 1832 to 1839, and was appointed groom in waiting in the queen's household in July 1846. He was commander-in-chief Portsmouth from 22 November 1839 to 31 December 1842.

He died with the rank of admiral on 28 April 1851, aged eighty-one, at 110 Eaton Square, Westminster, and was buried in St Peter, Eaton Square. There is a memorial in St Paul's Cathedral.

Lt: 28 May 1793
Cmdr: 7 October 1794
Capt: 6 April 1795
R-Adm: 4 June 1814
V-Adm: 27 May 1825
Adm: 10 January 1837

COFFIN

ADMIRAL SIR ISAAC COFFIN, BARONET, is best known in legal circles for a case which established the absolute power of a court martial, and in naval circles he was also known for his unfortunate encounter with Admiral Rodney in 1782 shortly after he was made post captain in *Shrewsbury*. During the war against revolutionary France, he served ashore.

He was born on 16 May 1759 in Boston, Massachusetts, the fourth and youngest son of Nathaniel Coffin, paymaster of the customs in Boston, and later of Bristol in England, and his wife Elizabeth, daughter of Henry Barnes, merchant of Boston. In October 1771 Isaac was rated an able seaman on the books of *Captain* (74) while she was at Boston under the command of Captain Thomas (?) Symonds, in May 1773 formally transferring to *Gasher*, brig, commanded by Lieutenant Hunter, at Rhode Island. But it is believed he first went to sea in the merchant service, and did not enter the navy until October 1773, with the patronage of George Montagu, then captain of the *Kingsfisher*, and his father Rear-Admiral John Montagu, who was commander-in-chief North America. He was soon given his commission as lieutenant, on 18 August 1776, while serving in *Diligent*, brig, under Lieutenant Edward (?) Dod at Halifax. He was not immediately employed in that rank,

however, being rated midshipman in September 1776 in *Romney* (50) flying Captain John Elliott's broad pendant at Newfoundland, and in June 1778 transferring to *Europa* (50) in the same rate. His first appointment as lieutenant was in October 1778 in *Placentia*, cutter, at which time he was still serving in Newfoundland. In June 1779 he transferred to *Pincon*, armed ship, where he served on the coast of Labrador until his ship was wrecked in August. That November he was appointed to *Adamant* (50) under Captain Gideon Johnstone for service in English and North American waters, where in February 1781 he transferred to *London* (90) flying the flag of Rear-Admiral Thomas Graves, and a month later to *Royal Oak* (74) commanded by Captain Swiney. He acted as Vice-Admiral Marriot Arbuthnot's signal lieutenant at the battle off Cape Henry on 16 March.

As a result he was promoted on 3 July 1781 master and commander of *Avenger*, in charge of an advanced post up the North River. He moved in December into the *Pacahunta* (14), but he and the entire ship's company volunteered for service on board Rear-Admiral Samuel Hood's flagship, *Barfleur* (90), in which he was at the action at Basseterre, St Kitts, on 25 January 1782. Hood saw that he was promoted post captain on 13 June 1782 with appointment to *Shrewsbury* (74), in which he served at Jamaica. It was then that he had his first taste of conflict with naval hierarchy. Rodney ordered him to take as lieutenants three officers with insufficient sea time. When he refused, apparently unaware that the command had come from Rodney himself, he was ordered to stand trial by court martial for disobedience and contempt. He was acquitted, but had to put up with the ill-trained lieutenants. At his request the Admiralty suspended its commissions, but by that time he had been transferred to *Hydra* (20), on 13 December, under orders to return to England. *Hydra* was paid off the following March.

During the peace he had some leave in France, but in May 1786 he was appointed to command *Thisbe* (28) with orders to transport Lord Dorchester and his family to Quebec. As an American loyalist who had lost his patrimony, he was in 1798 to be granted the Magdalen Islands in the Gulf of St Lawrence for his services during the war. His interest in the islands was apparent in 1787 while he was at Quebec. He warned the governor's council that New Englanders were exploiting the fisheries of the gulf and were trading, illegally, with the people on the Magdalen Islands. When eventually he was given his patent he attempted to establish his seigneury, but failed to attract colonists, or to evict the squatters who had migrated from St Pierre and Miquelon.

Sir Isaac Coffin, Bart.,
Rear-Admiral of the White Squadron,
engraved by William Ridley from an original
miniature, published by Joyce Gold,
103 Shoe Lane, 1 August 1804.

He resigned his command of *Thisbe* in May 1788, and he was next employed in the navy following the Nootka Sound crisis, with appointment in April 1791 to command *Alligator* (20), in which he was sent to Canada the following year to bring Lord Dorchester home. While at Halifax he entered four young men into the ship's books as captain's servants, as was the custom, although they were not mustered and were doubtless still at school. This was usual as a means of giving them a false

record of sea time, and to enhance the captain's pay. Almost all naval officers started their careers by being so entered into someone's books. Coffin, however, was brought to trial in 1788 at Halifax for making false musters. Although the charge was malicious, the court had no choice but to find against him. Considering the mitigating circumstances, however, it sentenced him only to be dismissed from his ship, despite the provision in the articles of war which required Coffin to be dismissed from the service. When he returned to England, Lord Howe, who was then first lord, insisted that the full rigour of the statute be enforced. In despair Coffin emigrated to Flanders to serve as a mercenary, apparently travelling through the northern states of Denmark, Sweden and Russia looking for a commission. However, King George, with the approval of the privy council, was persuaded to ask the judicial committee to decide whether the Board of Admiralty had the power to set aside the verdict of a court martial. The judgement was in Coffin's favour and became a frequently cited precedent.

Coffin was also notable for the role he played in Admiral the earl of St Vincent's injudicious efforts at reforming the civil administration of the navy. In April 1793, following the French declaration of war, he was appointed to command the 18-pounder frigate *Melampus* (36) in the Channel. But he was not to be able to serve long at sea because he had suffered an injury while commanding *Alligator* (20), and towards the end of 1794 he found the strenuous life at sea impossible to sustain. He accepted the post of navy commissioner on Corsica during the British occupation from 1794 to 1796, and then transferred to Lisbon, moving on to Minorca in 1798, and in 1799 he was offered the post at Sheerness, but was sent to Halifax for six months before returning to Sheerness. He was influenced by the earl of St Vincent's belief that yard officers were corrupt, and in Halifax and Sheerness acted so forcefully to impose Admiralty regulations that he seriously undermined the effectiveness of the yards. Possibly his earlier unfortunate experience at Halifax, and before that in the West Indies, affected his judgement. Despite the contumely heaped on him at the local level, however, he retained St Vincent's confidence.

Following his years of service as dockyard commissioner, on 23 April 1804 he was promoted rear-admiral, and on 19 May created baronet. He was then appointed admiral-superintendent at Portsmouth. He remained there until he was promoted vice-admiral on 28 April 1808, when he retired; he was not again employed by the navy.

He married on 3 April 1811, in Titley, Elizabeth Browne, only child and heiress of William Greenly of Titley Court, Herefordshire, but the couple had no children. He briefly changed his name to Greenly prior to his marriage, but reverted to his old name after March 1813. He held the parliamentary seat for Ilchester, Somerset, from 1818 to 1826. In 1832 he was appointed knight grand cross of the Guelphic order of Hanover. Elizabeth died on 27 January 1839, and Isaac six months later on 23 July 1839, aged eighty. He was buried in Cheltenham, Gloucestershire.

Lt: 18 August 1776
M-C: 3 July 1781
Capt: 13 June 1782
R-Adm: 23 April 1804
V-Adm: 28 April 1808
Adm: 4 June 1814

COLE

CAPTAIN SIR CHRISTOPHER COLE, KCB, played a major role in Eastern seas, being employed for his diplomatic skills to support a British mission to Persia and to conduct one himself to the Philippines, and as a warrior to end the power of the Netherlands in the Indies. As the prime minister Spencer Perceval saw it, Cole's capture of the Dutch island fortress of Banda Neira 'succeeded in realizing the most romantic daring of the age of chivalry'.

He was born on 10 June 1770 in Marazion, Cornwall, the sixth and youngest son of Humphrey Cole and his wife Phillis, daughter of Francis Maughan. His brother John, who was later to be chaplain to the duke of Clarence, was at the time chaplain in *Royal Oak* (74), under the command of Sir Digby Dent. Christopher joined his ship in May 1780 at the age of ten as midshipman, and proceeded in her to the North American station. Later the same year he followed Dent to

Raisonnable (64), and then in October joined *Russell* (74) flying the flag of Commodore Francis Samuel Drake in the West Indies. In June 1781 he followed Drake into the Dutch prize *Princessa* (70). He saw action with Drake off Martinique on 29 April 1781, at the Chesapeake on 5 September, in the actions at St Kitts in January and February, and in the battles of 9 April and at the Saintes on 12 April 1782.

Following the conclusion of peace, Cole joined *Trepassey* (12) under the command of his brother Captain Francis Cole, in May 1783, serving in the North American station, and at Halifax transferred in July to *Atalante* under the command of Captain Thomas Foley, with whom he served until February 1785. Between June 1786 and January 1789 he served under Captain Edward Pellew in *Winchelsea* (32) at Newfoundland, and then at Drake's recommendation he was taken into *Crown* (64) under Commodore the Honourable William Cornwallis, serving in the East Indies. Cole had passed his lieutenant's examination on 2 January at Somerset House in London, and he blamed Drake's untimely death in November 1789 for his long wait to become a lieutenant. In October 1790 he followed Cornwallis into *Minerva* (38), and in June 1793 he was ordered to act as lieutenant in *Bien Aimé* (20) under the command of Richard King, while continuing in the East Indies.

On 18 September 1793, over six months after the French declaration of war, he was commissioned lieutenant, and in October 1794 he became first lieutenant of *Cerberus* (32) on the Irish station through the direct intervention of the first lord himself, Lord Chatham, who at the request of Captain John Drew appointed two even more junior lieutenants to the ship. Cole transferred on 10 June 1795 to *Sans Pareil* (80), flagship of Lord Hugh Seymour in the Leeward Islands, who eventually promoted him for his activity during the capture of Surinam in 1799, giving him command of the prize corvette *Surinam*. Cole proved to be an energetic and successful cruiser captain, but also an enlightened leader whose efforts kept his crew noticeably healthy in an enervating climate. In 1801 Seymour died of one of the many endemic fevers of the region, but Cole's efforts had caught the attention of Sir John Duckworth, Seymour's successor. Exercising the prerogative of the distant commander-in-chief, he promoted Cole to post rank; he made him flag captain of *Leviathan* (74) on 30 June, and appointed him to *Southampton* (32) on 20 January 1802, both moves being common first steps for promising young post captains. The Admiralty confirmed his post commission on 20 April, but *Southampton* was ordered home with the conclusion of the peace treaty at Amiens, and was paid off in September.

Cole's early service with Cornwallis had been in India, and on 11 May 1804, following the renewal of war, he was again selected as flag captain by one of his old commanders, Sir Edward Pellew, with whom in 1804 he went out to the East Indies in *Culloden* (74). Three strenuous years brought the collapse of his relationship with Pellew. He was appointed on 24 March 1807 to temporary command of *Doris* (36), an 18-pounder armed ship newly built of teak at Bombay. He argued his case for a permanent employment both with Pellew and directly with the Admiralty. In April 1808 he was chosen to convey Colonel John Malcolm on a mission to the Persian court, and with two other frigates remained at Bushehr to protect the embassy, for which he received the thanks of the governor-general in council and a present of £500. Pellew, however, wrote a letter censuring him for leaving the Persian Gulf without orders. For the rest of 1808 and 1809 he was employed cruising in the strait of Malacca, and was sent by Pellew's successor, Rear-Admiral Drury, on a difficult mission to reconcile the Philippine authorities to the new *de facto* alliance between Britain and the colony's Spanish masters. His success was rewarded with the command on 10 April 1810 of *Caroline* (36), the ship in which he was to carry out his most famous exploit.

During the preceding years the strategic aim of the East Indies squadron was principally the steady reduction of enemy (mainly Dutch) colonies in the Asian archipelagos. In the Moluccas, Amboyna had been captured by a British frigate squadron early in 1810, and in May Cole was sent from Madras with *Piedmontaise* (38), the brig-sloop

Barracouta (18) and the transport brig *Mandarin* carrying reinforcements under his command. His orders allowed him considerable discretion to attack likely targets along the way, but his small force carried little more than 100 of the East India Company's European troops. Nevertheless, when he reached Prince of Wales Island on 30 May he decided to attack Banda Neira, a well-fortified island garrisoned by about 700 regular Dutch soldiers and a large force of militia. Approaching by a roundabout route north-east of Borneo – itself an astounding feat of navigation without reliable charts – Cole achieved complete strategic surprise.

The attack itself on 10 August came close to disaster. The defenders were warned by fishing craft, and the British were fired upon by a battery they did not know about. With tactical surprise lost, and a sudden gale which dispersed the landing boats, Cole found himself ashore with only about 180 of his intended force of nearly 400. Nevertheless, a desperate night attack carried the citadel, Fort Belgica, by momentum rather than numbers. The Dutch were expecting an attack from the sea, and were confused when Cole's men, who had been practised in the use of scaling ladders and pikes, assaulted the walls from landward without firing a shot. The ladders had to be hauled over the first wall, and were found to be too short for the second, but the gate of the citadel was opened to let the colonel-commandant in from his residence, and the British rushed it, killing the commandant in his gateway. In the morning the governor in Fort Nassau agreed to capitulation. At a time when the Royal Navy's confidence was unbounded, and small amphibious forces were achieving the apparently impossible, it was still an incredible exploit, worthy of parliamentary praise.

The last remaining significant Dutch holding was Java, and Cole's experience was again called upon for the larger expedition which finally captured the colony in 1811. Because of Admiral Drury's illness, much of the planning fell to Cole, who was also placed in charge of the actual landings. On Drury's death, command of the expedition was taken over by Captain Broughton, but his capacity in this respect was open to question, and he was eventually suceeded by Rear-Admiral Stopford, who arrived at Java just before the landing. Stopford recognised Cole's contribution to the successful outcome, and entrusted him with the victory dispatch, for which he was to receive the usual reward, being nominated a KB on 29 May 1812. He also received a medal for his attack on Banda Neira, Oxford University granted him a doctorate of civil law, and the East India Company presented him with a piece of plate valued at 300 guineas.

At this point his frigate service was over. On 8 March 1813 he was appointed to the *Rippon* (74) for Channel service; but the tedium of blockade duty was relieved in October when his ship secured the capture of the French frigate *Weser*, already battered by two brig-sloops, and by the recapture the following February of an immensely valuable Spanish treasure ship.

When the *Rippon* was decommissioned on 1 September 1814 Cole concluded thirty-four years of almost continuous service. He was promoted to KCB on 2 January 1815, and in the general distribution of orders by the allied monarchs in 1815 the emperor nominated him knight of the military order of Maria Theresa, and the tsar nominated him a knight of the order of St George. He married on 28 April 1815 Mary Lucy, second daughter of Henry Thomas Fox Strangways, second earl of Ilchester, and widow of Thomas Mansel Talbot. They had long been fond of each other, but the only child was from Mary's first marriage. The Talbot connection, and his fame as 'the conqueror of Banda', led to his unopposed election as member of parliament for Glamorgan on 6 December 1817. He held the seat only until 1818, but was elected again on 16 March 1820 and remained in possession for ten years until 1830. In 1828 he was appointed to command the yacht *Royal Sovereign*, and in recognition of his services commanding landing forces he was appointed colonel of the Royal Marines on 22 July 1830. He died on 24 August 1836, aged sixty-six, in Killoy near Cardiff, and his wife survived him to 3 February 1855.

Lt: 18 September 1793
Cmdr: 30 January 1800
Capt: 20 April 1802

COLLIER

CAPTAIN SIR GEORGE RALPH COLLIER, BARONET, KCB, established his reputation by the defeat of a French corvette, *La Flèche* (22), in the Seychelles, but lost it again when trying to bring USS *Constitution* to action.

He was born in London in 1774, the second son of Ralph Collier, chief clerk of the Victualling Board, and his wife, Henrietta Maria. He was first sent to the Chelsea Maritime Academy, and in January 1784 his name was entered in the books of *Triumph* (74) as captain's servant under the command of Captain Robert Faulknor. This was probably a nominal enlistment. Most likely his real entry into the navy was in January 1787 as a midshipman in *Carysfort* (28) under Captain Smith. In June 1790 he joined *Salisbury* (50) under Captain Edward Pellew, and he served on the Newfoundland station until December 1790, when he joined *Victory* (100) under Captain John Knight for Channel service. In March 1791 he transferred to *Juno* (32) under Captain Samuel Hood. Apparently he was not only a good astronomer, marine surveyor and draughtsman, but also a linguist, and passed his examination for lieutenant in 1790, but he was not commissioned until 22 January 1796.

In the précis of his naval service Collier wrote:

> on being discharged from His Majesty's Ship *Juno*, I embarked a passenger onboard the H[onourable] Company's ship *Winchelsea* for the East India station. She was wrecked on a reef of rocks on the Mozambique channel, 8 or 9 miles from the Island of Madagascar on the 3rd of September 1792 – and myself & survivors remained with the natives of the island till May 1792 when a Portuguese ship arriving, we embarked, and after touching at Mozambique, the Brig was captured by a French privateer, by whom we were sent to the Isle of France – where I remained a prisoner till about the end of 1794 – when I sailed for Madras. I mention this to account for my absence from the navy. – So

soon as my health was reestablished, I embarked aboard the flag ship of the commander-in-chief – and served as follows: [etc.]

In June 1795 he was rated midshipman in *Suffolk* (74) under Commodore Peter Rainier, and on 31 July he was appointed lieutenant and commander of *Suffolk Tender*. He wrote:

> The *Suffolk Tender* had been dispatched to the Cape of Good Hope when a survey was held upon her by order of Admiral Pringle, and the vessel being condemned as unseaworthy, I returned to Madras, and at the recommendation of the late Admiral Rainier, embarked for England – at his assurance that my conduct would recommend me for promotion. – arrived in England May 1799 and served, as viz.

On 2 June 1799 he was appointed lieutenant of the Dutch prize *Zealand* (64) under the command of Captain Thomas Parr, and on 29 July he was appointed first lieutenant of *Isis* (50), Vice-Admiral Andrew Mitchell's flagship at the capture of the Dutch squadron at the Texel. He was sent home with the dispatches, perhaps largely because of Mitchell's very great loyalty to his young gentlemen. As was customary, he was promoted on 3 September 1799, and he was given command of *Victor* (18) on 21 October. Mitchell no doubt also saw the potential in the man, which was demonstrated a year later, after troop transports had been escorted into the Red Sea to take part in the defeat of the French in Egypt, when Collier touched at Diego Garcia for turtle and water, and fell in with the French corvette.

After a brief engagement on 1 September 1801, in which *Victor* suffered in her rigging, the French ship made away to windward, and was found on the 5th sheltering in Mahé Roads. Collier wrote in his official letter:

> The extreme narrowness of the channel, added to the wind not being very favourable, compelled me to use warps and the stay-sails only, which exposed the ship to a raking fire for some minutes, till shoaling our water, I was obliged to bring up. Having two springs on the cable, our broadside was soon brought to bear; and at 11h 45' A.M. a well-directed fire was opened, which was kept up incessantly from both vessels till 2h 20' P.M. when I plainly perceived the enemy was going down; in a few minutes her cable was cut, she cast round, and her bows grounded on a coral-reef. Mr. M'Lean, the first Lieutenant, with a party of officers and men, were sent on board; though scarce had they put off, ere we discovered the enemy to be on fire. Lieutenant Smith, and other officers, were then sent with proper assistance; but just as they had succeeded in extinguishing the fire, she fell on her larboard bilge into deeper water and sunk.
> Marshall 3 (Supp) 519

The earl of St Vincent, then the first lord of the Admiralty, was so impressed by Collier's action that he made him post in *Leopard* (50), antedating the commission to 22 April 1802, a week prior to a general promotion that took place following the end of the war.

He was to be ashore for four years, from 1803 to 20 January 1806 commanding the sea fencibles at Liverpool. On 18 May 1805 he married Maria, daughter of John Lyon, MD, of Liverpool. There were to be no children. He amused himself by advancing a plan for blocking the Texel, no doubt in hope of being put in command of the operation. But when in February 1806 he was appointed to *Minerva* (42) he was employed on the north coast of Portugal and Spain, operating against privateers and forts.

On 22 April 1807 he was put in command of the 24-pounder French prize *Surveillante* (38), and he took part in the second Copenhagen operation. Again he found favour with his admiral, being entrusted by Admiral Gambier with his dispatches home, for which he received a knighthood. Later he returned to the Bay of Biscay, and in 1812 to the coast of Spain, where he was employed in support of the guerillas under the command of Admiral Sir Home Popham. On 1 August he was wounded in an attempt against the castle at Santander, which failed but led to the French withdrawing from the exposed position. The following year he was ordered to hoist a broad pendant in *Porcupine* (32), and commanded twelve vessels on the Spanish coast, co-operating with General Wellington and General Sir Thomas Graham in the final reduction in August of San Sebastian, and in the siege of Bayonne.

On 15 March 1814 he was put in command of *Leander*, a large frigate built of pitch pine and mounting fifty guns, intended to deal with the American super-frigates. His particular prey was USS *Constitution*, but she managed to get out of Boston without being brought to action, in circumstances that Admiral William James considered betrayed Collier's incompetence. *Leander* with the fir-built *Newcastle* (60) and *Acasta* (40) nearly caught up with the American squadron at St Jago, but they were frustrated by the weather, or as James would have it, by Collier's mistake in pursuing vaguely seen ships on the horizon rather than the enemy in sight and well within his grasp. In his *Naval History*, James wrote, 'Most sincerely do we regret… that this last and most triumphant escape of the *Constitution*, the first frigate of the United States that had humbled the proud flag of Britain, had not, long ago, been brought under the scrutiny of a court-martial. The blame would then have fallen where it ought to have fallen… The more it is investigated, the more it will show itself to be, the most blundering piece of business recorded in these six volumes.' [James 5.547 *et seq*] Before Collier could recover from his mistake, authentic word was received of the conclusion of peace with the United States.

He was invested a KCB on 2 January 1815, and at some date he was appointed groom of the bedchamber to the duke of Gloucester. In May 1818 he was appointed commodore on the African station, flying his broad pendant in *Creole* (36), where he was employed in the suppression of the slave trade. He was elected an honorary life member of the African Institution on 17 May 1820, but he was to die tragically by his own hand as a result of the publication of James's account in 1823 which suggested that he had been motivated by cowardice. An application to the Admiralty to clear his name was not satisfied, and he cut his throat on 24 March 1824. On his death the baronetcy became extinct.

Lt: 22 January 1796 (1)
Cmdr: 3 September 1799 (1)
Capt: 22 April 1802

COLLINGWOOD

VICE-ADMIRAL CUTHBERT COLLINGWOOD, BARON COLLINGWOOD, when asked to supply the editor of the *Naval Chronicle* with notes for his biography, modestly replied that 'His life had been a continual service at sea, but unmarked by any of those extraordinary events or brilliant scenes which hold men up to particular attention, and distinguish them from those officers who are zealous and anxious for the public service.' That his commitment to his job was total is hardly open to question, but his modesty passes over the signal parts he played in three of the great battles of the wars against the French Republic and Empire.

He was born on 26 September 1748 in Newburn, Northumberland, the first son of Cuthbert Collingwood, a not very prosperous merchant of Newcastle-upon-Tyne, and of his wife Milcah, daughter and coheiress of Reginald Dobson of Barwise near Appleby, Westmorland. After six or seven years' education at Newcastle free school, he entered the navy on 28 August 1761, joining *Shannon* (38) with his brother Wilfred under the command of his maternal uncle, Captain Richard Braithwaite. After returning home when *Shannon* was paid off in February 1763 at the end of the Seven Years War, they rejoined her in October 1764, now under the command of Captain Philip Boteler, and served in west Africa under Commodore Thomas Graves during the Gambian crisis. Graves was a careful man, and war was avoided. Braithwaite resumed his command of *Shannon* in October 1765, and when he was transferred to *Gibraltar* (80) in February 1766 the brothers followed him and served in Newfoundland.

Cuthbert was rated midshipman in 1766 in the *Gibraltar* and master's mate in 1767 in the *Liverpool.* to which the three transferred. They served together again in Newfoundland for eighteen months before receiving orders for the Mediterranean, where they remained for most of the next three and a half years. When *Liverpool* paid off in March 1772 the brothers finally left Braithwaite and joined *Lenox* (74), which was fitted as a guardship at Portsmouth and commanded by Robert Roddam. While serving in her, Cuthbert and Wilfred passed their examinations for lieutenant, but they were to have to wait three and six years respectively before they were commissioned.

Cuthbert spent six months serving in the West Indies in *Portland* (50) and *Princess Amelia* (80) before February 1774, when he joined *Preston* (50) flying the flag of Vice-Admiral Samuel Graves and under orders for Boston. No doubt it was his humble origins which kept him from progressing faster through ranks, but Graves commissioned him lieutenant on 17 June 1775, on the day of the battle of Bunker Hill, with appointment to *Somerset* (74). He returned home in her in February 1776 and in March joined *Hornet,* ship-sloop, as her first lieutenant, sailing for the West Indies in December. *Hornet*'s captain, Robert Haswell, was a flogger, and in September 1777 he had Collingwood tried by court martial for contempt, disobedience to orders and breach of his captain's instructions. He was acquitted, with advice to show more alacrity, but the experience was hardly encouraging.

Fortunately for Collingwood, Rear-Admiral Sir Peter Parker succeeded to command-in-chief at Jamaica. He recognised Collingwood's quality, appointing him second lieutenant of *Lowestoffe* (32) commanded by Captain William Locker. Collingwood had known Nelson since 1773, and his life was to become closely associated with Nelson's from this time on. The appointment to *Lowestoffe* was the first of three rapid moves in succession in which Collingwood was placed in positions vacated by his friend. In June 1779 Parker appointed Collingwood second lieutenant into his flagship, *Bristol* (50), and almost immediately pro-

moted him on 20 June master and commander of *Badger,* brig, again in succession to Nelson. And Collingwood succeeded Nelson a third time when Parker made him post captain on 22 March 1780 with appointment to *Hinchinbrook* (28). He joined his ship at San Juan, Nicaragua, as a result of Nelson's falling ill with fever in an ill-considered expedition against the Spaniards. Nelson was obliged to return to England to save his life. Collingwood had to bury 180 of his crew of 200, but he did not himself fall ill.

In August 1781 while in command of *Pelican* (24) Collingwood had the misfortune to encounter a hurricane near Jamaica, and was driven onto the Morant keys. He and his crew nearly died from hunger and thirst, and the ship was lost, but it was possible to salve her guns and most of her stores, and Collingwood was exonerated at his court martial. He returned to England the following year and remained ashore until he was put in command of *Sampson* (64) at the end of the war, which he paid off in April 1783. Like Nelson, however, he was not long on half pay, and he was appointed to command *Mediator* (44) under orders for the West Indies. The following year Nelson arrived in *Boreas* (28) as senior captain and set about enforcing the navigation acts against the Americans; this created a great deal of ill feeling in the islands. where the pattern of trade with the American colonies was an established fact. Nelson was to suffer for his strict attitude, which was not shared by Rear-Admiral Sir Richard Hughes commanding the station, and some of the taint may have affected Collingwood's prospects. Although the Admiralty approved of the enforcement of the laws, it left Nelson unemployed for five years. Collingwood likewise spent four years 'making my acquaintance with my own family, to whom I had hitherto been as it were a stranger'. [NC 23.381]

He returned to the West Indies in command of the 12-pounder frigate *Mermaid* (32) in July 1790 at the time of the Nootka Sound incident, but he returned home in April 1791, and on 6 June, at St Nicholas, Newcastle-upon-Tyne, married Sarah, daughter of Alderman John Erasmus Blackett. Her father was a coal fitter and four times mayor of

Newcastle. The couple had two daughters, Sarah and Mary Patience, and made a home in Morpeth.

Three weeks following the outbreak of war in 1793, on 22 February, Collingwood was appointed to command *Prince* (90), based at Plymouth. Rear-Admiral George Bowyer hoisted his flag in her in July in the Channel fleet, and at the end of the year they transferred together to *Barfleur* (90). It was while serving in her that they fought in the protracted engagement under Lord Howe from 28 May to the Glorious First of June in 1794. Early in the action of 29 May Bowyer lost his leg, and to Collingwood devolved the command of the sub-division of the fleet. Admiral Howe did not make any specific mention of Collingwood in his action report, and in consequence he did not receive one of the gold medals. This rankled deeply with him, as similar treatment did with several other officers.

In July 1794 Collingwood was put in command of *Hector* (74) as a private ship, and he transferred in December to *Excellent* (74), in which he served a few months off Ushant before joining the Mediterranean fleet off Corsica and Toulon. He was still part of the Mediterranean fleet when Admiral Jervis was ordered to withdraw to Lisbon following the Spanish alliance with France. Fearing a repeat of the crisis in 1779 when a combined Franco-Spanish fleet threatened Britain with invasion, Jervis's victory over the Spanish fleet at the battle of Cape St Vincent was of the greatest strategic importance, even though not many prizes were taken.

Excellent was at the rear of the *ad hoc* line of battle that Admiral Jervis had ordered to meet the rapidly developing threat posed by a significantly superior force, but one which appeared to be divided and attempting to concentrate. To keep the enemy divided, Jervis tacked his fleet at the van, but quickly recognised that he was too late to prevent the enemy closing up, and ordered the rear to meet the threat. Collingwood's friend Commodore Nelson, although not the rear commander, immediately wore out of line and steered into the concentrating mass of the enemy. Jervis signalled for *Excellent* to follow him.

Collingwood had brought her to a high degree of efficiency in gunnery, and this allowed him to direct such a fire at *Salvador del Mundo* (112) that, as he wrote in the log, 'her colours being struck and her fire ceasing, I hailed her, and understanding she surrendered shot ahead under the lee of the next ship in succession.' However, as soon as he moved ahead, 'the former ship rehoisted her colours.' [ADM 51/1193 14.2.1797] By then he was directing a heavy fire against *San Ysidro* (74), which soon struck her colours. Collingwood then braced *Excellent*'s yards to move forward to where Nelson, in *Captain* (74), was isolated and in action with *San Nicolas* (80). *Excellent*'s fire caused the Spanish second rate to collide with *San Josef* (112). Nelson had just followed his boarders into *San Nicolas* and was now able to respond to the small arms fire from *San Josef* by boarding her as well. Collingwood then switched *Excellent*'s target again, and engaged *Santisima Trinidad* (136) for an hour, but had to abandon her when threatened by several Spanish ships. 'My dearest Friend,' Nelson wrote to Collingwood the following day, '"A friend in need is a friend indeed" was never more truly verified than by your most noble and gallant conduct yesterday in sparing the *Captain* from further loss.' [NMM LBK/15]

The battle of the Glorious First of June, and especially that of Cape St Vincent, had identified Collingwood as an officer to watch. When gold medals were being distributed following the latter battle, Collingwood refused to accept his unless he were also sent one for the action in May and June 1794. In due course this was done, by the first lord, Lord Spencer. Collingwood was made colonel of the marines, apparently in 1798, and promoted rear-admiral on 14 February 1799. For a few months in 1797 Jervis, now the earl of St Vincent, ordered him to fly a broad pendant as commodore, but it was Nelson who was detached in the spring to deal with the crisis in the Mediterranean, and eventually to defeat the Toulon fleet at the battle of the Nile. Collingwood paid off *Excellent* at Portsmouth in January 1799, and had four months' leave with his family, the first since his eight-day visit to Morpeth in December 1794.

In May he hoisted his flag in the *Triumph* (74) in the crisis caused by the escape of Vice-Admiral

Bruix with the Brest fleet. Collingwood was ordered to reinforce Lord Keith in the Mediterranean, and participated in the unsuccessful search for the French fleet, which eventually returned with the Spanish Cadiz fleet to Brest with Keith in pursuit. Collingwood then fell into the wearisome routine of the Brest blockade, knowing that the conjunction of the French and Spaniards at Brest posed an overwhelming threat should they be able to get to sea together in the Channel. In January 1800 he transferred his flag to the *Barfleur* (90). After another year of arduous service, on 27 January 1801 his wife, their elder daughter, and her little dog joined him at Plymouth. Within hours of their arrival, he had to sail for Brest and was not able to return for six weeks. He then had only two weeks with his family before he returned to Ushant. It was not until two months after the signature of the peace of Amiens, in May 1802, that Collingwood was permitted to strike his flag and go home to Morpeth.

He had one year of the family life he dearly loved, but on the renewal of war he returned to sea, and although he lived the better part of another seven years, he never saw his family again. He hoisted his flag in *Diamond* (38) and joined Admiral Sir William Cornwallis blockading Brest. His sense of duty was so strong that he repeatedly exchanged flagships at sea, so that ships and crews could be rested and repaired, while he worked on. He was promoted to vice-admiral on 23 April 1804, and on 21 May 1805 he was moved to the blockade of Ferrol and Cadiz. He was watching Cadiz with three ships and a frigate when Vice-Admiral Villeneuve arrived off the harbour on 20 August 1805, and moved aside to let his fleet of

The Right Honourable Lord Collingwood, Vice Admiral of the Red Squadron and Commander in Chief of the Mediterranean Fleet, engraved by William Ridley after Robert Bowyer, published by Joyce Gold, 103 Shoe Lane, 31 May 1806.

thirty-six ships in, without letting it be apparent that he was unsupported. By the end of the month he commanded a fleet of twenty-six ships, and on 29 September Nelson arrived to assume command. Collingwood transferred his flag to *Royal Sovereign* (100) eleven days prior to the battle of Trafalgar.

When the British fleet brought the Franco-Spanish combined fleet to action at Trafalgar on 21 October 1805, Collingwood as second in command to Nelson led the weather column in his flagship, *Royal Sovereign*, in a head-on attack which exposed the leading ships to an exceptionally heavy fire they could not return. Only the moral force of the two admirals leading from the front gave Nelson's highly dangerous tactics the capacity to defeat the enemy. Collingwood was the first into action, engaging the *Santa Ana* (112), the Spanish vice-admiral's flagship, for two hours while sometimes being engaged simultaneously by four other ships. Nearly everyone on *Royal Sovereign*'s quarterdeck was killed or wounded, and by the time *Santa Ana* struck, *Royal Sovereign* had lost two of her masts. Collingwood received a slight wound.

He succeeded Nelson in command following his friend's death in action, transferring his flag into *Euryalus* (36) to deal with securing his fleet and seventeen prizes in the face of imminent storm. When it broke, blowing for five days onto a dangerous coast, many who remembered that day found it more terrifying than had been the battle. Some of the prizes were wrecked, with a loss of life that caused Collingwood great grief, but all of the British ships, with jury rigs and sometimes under tow, were brought into Gibraltar. Collingwood arranged for the Spanish wounded to be sent ashore at Cadiz under parole so that they could be looked after in Spanish hospitals. In recognition of his services he was promoted vice-admiral of the red, created Baron Collingwood of Caldburne and Hethpoole, and awarded a pension of £2,000, half of which would be continued to his widow, and £500 was awarded to each of his daughters. His wish that his title should descend to his daughters, however, was not granted. Collingwood received a third gold medal, an achievement matched only by Nelson and Sir Edward Berry.

The next five years were ones of incessant toil, almost perpetually at sea. Following the collapse of Napoleon's efforts to invade England, the Mediterranean regained its central strategic importance. It was the greatest theatre where sea power could have a decisive influence on events ashore, and Collingwood directed forces from the Levant to the coast of Spain. He had to deal with the conflicts between Turkey and Russia and the efforts of France to use them to its advantage. Following the treaty of Tilsit in July 1807 between France and Russia, he had to ensure that the Russian fleet did not join the French. The Spanish rebellion in May 1808 transformed that reluctant enemy into a determined ally, and opened a new theatre of operations. He immediately sailed to Cadiz, where he was received as a friend, because of his charity after Trafalgar. He provided close support in the local defence of the port, and supported the defence of Catalonia against the French invasion. In 1809 the focus of operations shifted to the Adriatic in support of Austria. He liberated the Ionian Islands of Zante, Cephalonia, Ithaca and Cerigo as insurance against a French invasion of Turkey, and they were to remain a British protectorate until 1864. He controlled as many as eighty ships, including thirty ships of the line, and corresponded with kings, pashas, sultans, ambassadors and generals. To his wife he wrote on 8 November 1808: 'I do everything for myself, and never distract my mind with other people's opinions. To the credit of any good which happens I may lay claim, and I will never shift upon another the discredit when the result is bad. Collingwood (2) 2.286 He was careful of the health of his crews, and insisted that they be treated with re-

spect and with the minimum of flogging.

He was promoted major-general of the Royal Marines on 9 January 1809. But leave he did not have before he died at sea on 7 March 1810, aged sixty-one, in the Mediterranean, having spent sixteen of the preceding seventeen years at sea. His body was brought home to be buried in St Paul's Cathedral near that of Nelson. A monument was erected on Galley Hill, Tynemouth, Northumberland, and another in St Nicholas' Cathedral, Newcastle-upon-Tyne. Sarah outlived him nearly a decade, and died on 17 September 1819.

Lt: 17 June 1775
M-C: 20 June 1779
Capt: 22 March 1780
R-Adm: 14 February 1799
V-Adm: 23 April 1804

COLPOYS

ADMIRAL SIR JOHN COLPOYS, GCB, is best known for the unfortunate part he played in the 1797 mutiny of the Channel fleet at Spithead.

So little is known of Colpoys's early life that it is not known who were his parents or where they lived, although it is believed that he was born in 1742, and that he entered the navy in 1756. He served at the capture of Louisburg in 1758 and of Martinique in 1762, and was commissioned lieutenant on 22 October 1762, just at the end of the Seven Years War. He was not promoted master and commander until 1770, at the time of the Falkland Islands crisis, when he was appointed to command *Lynx,* sloop. In 1773 there was a prospect that Britain might have to resort to naval force to prevent France attacking the Russians in the Baltic, and possibly this was the reason why Colpoys was made post captain on 25 August 1773 with appointment to command *Northumberland* (70). In 1777 he was serving in the West Indies and in 1778 at Jamaica, and in April 1779 he was one of the officers who composed the court martial for Admiral Sir Hugh Palliser following the battle of Ushant. That summer he commanded *Royal George* (100), flagship of Admiral Sir John Lockhart Ross, during the crisis when the Franco-Spanish fleet entered the Channel. Subsequently he commanded *Orpheus* (32) on the North American station, and for a short time in 1783 he commanded *Phaeton* in the Mediterranean.

He was appointed to command the Portsmouth guardship *Hannibal* (74) at the time of the Nootka Sound crisis in 1790. Following the French declaration of war in February 1793 he fitted *Hannibal* for service and was ordered to fly a broad pendant as commodore of a battle squadron sent to secure the Channel Islands. He subsequently sailed to the West Indies, where he served under Rear-Admiral Alan Gardner. He was promoted rear-admiral on 12 April 1794, and hoisted his flag in *London* (90), which had been fitted as a flagship for the duke of Clarence, who it had been decided should not be allowed to serve at sea in wartime. He took part in Bridport's action off L'Orient in July 1795, and was on duty off Ushant when the French made their attempt in December 1796 to invade Ireland. Admiral Morard de Galles managed to evade Colpoys's squadron on the 11th, and it was off station when Sir Edward Pellew discovered on the 16th that the French had sailed. Only the limitations of French training and supplies, and the weather, prevented the landing of the army in Bantry Bay.

The mutiny at Spithead was a tremendous shock to the navy. At Admiral Bridport's insistence, a committee of the Admiralty Board came down to Portsmouth and partly settled the seamen's grievances, but on 6 May the delegates were persuaded by Valentine Joyce, a long-service quartermaster's mate who was evidently the leading figure amongst the mutineers, not to sign without a general pardon to prevent reprisal. On 1 May the Admiralty had issued a general order instructing the officers to suppress any further mutiny. On 7 May, when it was evident that ships brought forward at St Helens for sea were not going to sail, Colpoys, flying his flag at Spithead in *London*, demanded of her crew whether they had any remaining grievances. When they assured him they had none, he ordered them below deck, and tried to seal the ship by closing the gunports. This was a bad mistake. The crew demanded to be allowed on deck and tried to force their way up the hatch-es, at which Colpoys ordered the ship's officers and marines to open fire on them. Many of the marines dropped their weapons, but five men were mortally wounded before Colpoys ordered the officers to cease firing. The crew then set about hanging Lieutenant Peter Bover, who had shot one of the seamen, but were dissuaded by Colpoys, who accepted responsibility, and read aloud the Admiralty order. The seamen then confined their officers in their cabins, and moved their ship to St Helens with

Sir John Colpoys, K.B.,
Admiral of the Blue Squadron,
engraving by William Ridley after
Mather Brown, published by Joyce Gold,
103 Shoe Lane, London, 30 April 1804.

the other mutinous ships. There was discussion of holding a trial of Colpoys and Captain Griffith, who commanded *London*, but instead the officers were sent ashore. When finally the mutiny was settled, by an act of parliament granting the seamen's demands about victuals and pay, and a royal pardon read out by Admiral Howe, who was brought out of retirement, Colpoys was one of the officers whom the delegates refused to readmit to his ship. Bridport respected their decision. In fact, Colpoys had already asked to be relieved, and on 14 May he was ordered to strike his flag. In 1798, as consolation, he was nominated a KB.

Colpoys was unemployed until June 1803, when he was appointed to command-in-chief at Plymouth. He resigned in May 1804 to take a place on the Admiralty Board under Lord Melville, but was not asked to continue on the board when Lord Barham replaced Melville in May 1805. He was, however, appointed treasurer of Greenwich hospital, advanced in chivalry to GCB, and nominated a knight grand cross of the Guelphic order on 2 January 1815. He was governor of Greenwich hospital from 1816 until his death on 4 April 1821, aged seventy-nine. His nephew Admiral Sir Edward Griffith, KCB, inherited his estate.

> Lt: 22 October 1762
> M-C: 1770
> Capt: 25 August 1773
> R-Adm: 12 April 1794
> V-Adm: 1 June 1795
> Adm: 1 January 1801

COOKE

CAPTAIN JOHN COOKE met a heroic death at the battle of Trafalgar, being shot in the right breast while he was reloading his pistols.

His birth date is unknown, but he was baptised on 5 March 1762 at St Mary Whitechapel, London, the second son of Margaret and Francis Cooke. His father was cashier of the navy, and at the age of eleven John went to sea in *Greyhound*, cutter, commanded by Lieutenant Bazely, or Bazeley. He soon returned ashore to Mr Braken's naval academy at Greenwich, but Sir Alexander Hood, later Lord Bridport, arranged for his name to be put on the books of one of the royal yachts. In 1776 he entered the navy, sailing to America in *Eagle* (64), which flew the flag of Lord Howe. Reportedly, his ardour in the assault on the American fort at Rhode Island led Howe to clap him on the back and say, 'Why, young man, you wish to become a Lieutenant before you are of sufficient age.' [NC 17.354] He had to wait until 21 January 1779 to be commissioned to *Superb* (74), and then sailed with Admiral Sir Edward Hughes to the East Indies. Ill health obliged his returning home and deferred his promotion. He spent a year studying in France, and then was appointed to *Duke* (90)

under the command of Captain Alan (later Lord) Gardner, serving in the West Indies and taking part in the action off Dominica on 12 April 1782. He remained with Gardner as first lieutenant of *Europa* (50) after the conclusion of the war, when the latter was ordered to serve as commodore at Jamaica. An injury from a bad fall led to his being again invalided home, but at the time of the Nootka Sound armament, in May 1790, Sir Alexander Hood appointed him third lieutenant of *London* (90), his flagship. On 15 June 1790, at St Leonard, Shoreditch, London, he married Louisa, fourth daughter of Josiah Hardy, governor of the Jerseys in America and later consul at Cadiz, Spain.

Captain John Cooke, who Fell in the Action off Trafalgar, engraved by James Fittler, AS, from an original painting in the possession of Mrs Cooke, published as the Act Directs, 1 May 1807, by Joyce Gold, 103 Shoe Lane.

When Spain and Britain adjusted their difficulties, Cooke again returned ashore, but on the French declaration of war at the beginning of February 1793 Sir Alexander Hood made him first lieutenant of his own ship, the *Royal George* (100), and on 21 February 1794 promoted him commander with appointment to a fireship. Soon thereafter, the captain of *Monarch* (74) suffered an accident, and Cooke was made post captain in *Monarch* on 23 June 1794, the flagship of Sir James Wallace who was bound for Newfoundland. He was too junior an officer, however, to retain command of a 74-gun ship once *Monarch* returned to home waters, and he accepted command of the 9-pounder frigate *Tourterelle* (34). But she was bound for the West Indies, and Admiral Gardner had given him a certificate warning that any return to the tropics was likely to cost him his life, so again he resigned his command, and in the following spring he was placed in command of *Nymph* (36). In company with the *San Fiorenzo* (34) he captured two French frigates on 9 March 1797 after they had landed a group of convicts at Fishguard, and one of them of forty-eight guns was later taken into British service under the name of that port.

The editor of the *Naval Chronicle* wrote that Sir Alexander Hood, now Lord Bridport, 'his zealous and respected friend and patron', always chose Cooke 'for the post of honour or profit', and that Cooke 'through life gloried in asserting, that whatever credit or success he had attained in the service, he owed it all to the example and predilection of his noble friend.' Bridport gave a portrait of himself to Cooke. For his part, Cooke was careful of the education, morals and advancement of the young men who grew up officers on his ships. He regularly took divine service, and had his young gentlemen read passages of the Bible to him in his cabin.

His support for Admiral Colpoys during the 1797 Spithead mutiny, and perhaps his piety, cost him his ship. He was on half pay for two years before he was appointed to *Amethyst* (44) and given orders to carry the duke of York to the Netherlands for the 1799 campaign.

During the period following the peace of Amiens he was unemployed, and was able to purchase a home in southern Wiltshire. The Cookes had a single daughter, born on 26 January 1797 in Stoke Damerel, Devon, and John Cooke was a devoted father whose letters reveal his concern that she be brought up with 'the one thing essential to happiness', religious faith.

In October 1804, after the return to war, he was invited by Admiral Young commanding at Portsmouth to serve under him in command of the guardship on which he flew his flag. Despite the fact that he could live ashore and have his family with him in Portsmouth, after six months Cooke obtained an exchange into a more active command, the *Bellerophon* (74), in which he met his end at Trafalgar.

In the opening minutes of that battle his ship was apparently mistaken by the French for the flagship, and accordingly found herself heavily engaged by four ships of the line, one of which, *L'Aigle*, came into close contact and directed such a withering fire on *Bellerophon*'s poop and quarterdeck that the officers and marines were rapidly reduced. It was pointed out to Cooke that his epaulets were making him a marked man, but he replied, 'It is now too late to take them off, I see my situation. But I will die like a man.' His last order was for the first lieutenant to go below and order the coins to be taken out of the guns to elevate them, so that they would blast through *L'Aigle*'s deck from below. This had the desired effect and she sheered off, followed by three broadsides under her counter, but before that occurred, Cooke was shot. When asked if he wanted to be carried below, he answered, 'No, let me lie quietly one minute, tell Lieutenant Cumby never to strike.' Then he died.

There is a memorial to him in St Paul's Cathedral, and another in St Andrew, Donhead St Andrew, Wiltshire. Louisa died on 5 February 1853, aged ninety-six.

Lt: 21 January 1779
Cmdr: 21 February 1794
Capt: 23 June 1794

CORBET

CAPTAIN ROBERT CORBET had the worst reputation possible with his men. Between August 1806 and March 1807 he ordered 134 floggings of the *Nereide*'s crew in just 211 days, with punishment averaging seventeen lashes. At Bombay in 1808 the crew complained about Corbet's cruelty, and he asked for a court martial. Because there were not enough post captains available, *Nereide* had to be sent to the Cape of Good Hope, but no effort was made to inform the crew that their complaints were being attended to. They mutinied, but the mutiny was suppressed, and at the Cape ten of them were condemned to death, although nine were reprieved. At Corbet's trial it was noted that his seamen deserted even in hostile territory, but he was acquitted of most charges on the usual grounds that he had inherited a badly disciplined crew. In 1810, when he was appointed to command *Africaine*, her crew refused to hear him read out his commission until another ship was brought alongside and ran out her guns.

Paradoxically, Corbet had a good reputation with his superior officers, including Lord Nelson. But he was to be killed in action in circumstances which suggested that his tyranny had not been in the best interest of the service.

Nothing is known of his early career before he was commissioned lieutenant on 22 December 1796. He made a good impression in command of the cutter *Fulminante* during the Egyptian operations in 1801 and was promoted commander on 29 April 1802. On the renewal of war in 1803 Corbet was appointed to command *Bittern,* brig, in the Mediterranean, where in April 1805 Nelson, who remarked on his 'officer-like and regular' conduct, promoted him acting captain of the 9-pounder frigate *Amphitrite* (28). [Nelson 6.363] Four months later Corbet was transferred to *Seahorse* (38), and his rank was finally confirmed on 25 May 1806 when he was serving at Jamaica. Corbet commissioned *Nereide* (38) at Portsmouth in November 1806, and in March 1807 he was employed escorting transports carrying troops to the river Plate. When the British force capitulated, he proceeded with *Nereide* to the Cape of Good Hope station, and thence in August 1808 to Bombay for refit. Apart from his sadistic treatment of his crew, Corbet now began to displease his commander-in-chief, Sir Edward Pellew, who objected to his assuming the duties of a senior officer.

In September 1809, following his court martial, Commodore Josias Rowley gave him responsibility for landing troops during the operations to attack the French cruisers in the harbour of St Paul's in Isle Bourbon, after which Corbet was put in command of one of the prizes with orders to return to England, where he arrived in the spring of 1810. When he completed taking over *Africaine* (44) at Plymouth against the wishes of her people, he was returned to the Indian Ocean, and there, on 12 September 1810 off Isle Bourbon, he met his end. *Africaine,* having surged ahead of her consorts *Boadicea* (38), *Otter*, sloop (16), and the gunbrig *Staunch*, brought to action two French frigates, the *Iphigénie* and *Astrée*. She was badly outmatched. Corbet had his leg shot off, and by 4pm all the others of *Africaine*'s officers were either wounded or dead. She had suffered aloft, there was no wind, she had lost forty-nine dead and 114 wounded out of a crew of 295, and she could man only six of her guns. Her first lieutenant, Joeseph Crew Tullidge, surrendered the ship.

It was widely rumoured that the men had refused to fight, and even that they had inflicted Corbet's wound. This was hotly denied by Captain Jenkin Jones, who had been on board the *Africaine* at the time of Corbet's death. Nevertheless, the circumstances may well have been in mind when in the 1813 edition of the *Naval Chronicle* the reviewer of Lieutenant Thomas Hodgskins's 'An Essay on Naval Discipline' wrote that he had once 'seen an instance of British seamen's backwardness in a time of danger, when they were heartless, pusillanimous, and cowardly'. But, he continued, 'this was in a ship where a severity of flogging, and all the niceties of discipline, were carried to a greater extent than I ever before witnessed: where the captain never permitted any other motive for action but fear of him.' [NC 30.223-4] The high butcher's bill in *Africaine* was consistent with a demoralised crew. Quick and effective firing was the recognised means of disrupting the gun crews in an enemy ship, and once a ship began to take heavy casualties in its gundeck, its firing became ragged and inadequate. Once a ship began to be beaten, its casualties inevitably multiplied.

Lt: 22 December 1796
Cmdr: 29 April 1802
Capt: 24 May 1806

CORNWALLIS

ADMIRAL THE HONOURABLE SIR WILLIAM CORNWALLIS, GCB, after forty years in the navy during which he took part in many hard battles, fought on 17 June 1795 an action which became the talk of the navy. His greatest service to the navy, and to the nation, however, was his command of the Channel fleet between 1801 and 1807, during which years the blockade of Brest was perfected.

He had been born on 20 February 1744, the fourth son of Charles, first Earl Cornwallis, and his wife Elizabeth, eldest daughter of Charles, second Viscount Townshen. From 1753 to 1755 he attended Eton College, and he then entered the navy in *Newark* (80) with the patronage of the duke of Newcastle, sailing with Vice-Admiral Edward Boscawen to North America, where he took part in the capture of Louisburg in 1758. In March 1759, in the year of victories, he fought in the battle of Quiberon Bay. He served under Admiral Charles Saunders, and his commission as lieutenant in *Thunderer* (74) commanded by Captain Charles Proby followed on 5 April 1761, his promotion to master and commander on 12 July 1762. Despite Newcastle's retirement, he stayed in employment following the peace of Paris in 1763, and was made post captain on 20 April 1765. He was one of the first to divide his ship's company into divisions under the particular responsibility of one of the junior officers. He never married, but he had a political life, with the support of his family Whig connections. He held the parliamentary seat for Eye, Suffolk, from 1768 to March 1774.

In that year he was appointed to command *Pallas* (36), and was employed on the west coast of Africa. As one of the first acts of the war against the American rebels, he arrested several colonial ships which were loading gunpowder in African rivers. In the battle fought by Vice-Admiral Byron against D'Estaing off Granada in 1779 Cornwallis commanded the *Lion* (64), which with *Grafton* (70) and *Cornwall* (74) was to leeward of the British line and took the brunt of the enemy fire. When the fleets tacked, *Lion*, which had suffered heavily and had lost most of her spars, was complete-

ly isolated and in danger of capture. Cornwallis took the morally difficult decision to bear away from the action under jury rig, and ran for Jamaica. There he met Horatio Nelson, and established a friendship. The following 21 March, Cornwallis, with a squadron initially of *Lion*, a 50-gun ship and a 44-gun ship, was engaged off Monte Christi by Admiral La Motte Piquet, who commanded three seventy-fours, a sixty-four and a frigate. The British squadron more than held its own, and eventually it was Piquet who broke off the action when

The Honourable William Cornwallis, Admiral of the Blue Squadron, Rear Admiral of England, engraving by William Ridley after D Gardner (1775), published by Burney and Gold, Shoe Lane, 1 February 1802.

British reinforcements arrived, having sailed to the sound of the guns. *Lion* was ordered to England, and Cornwallis took with him as a passenger Nelson, who was being invalided home following the Nicaraguan campaign. *Lion* then served in Vice-Admiral George Darby's relief of Gibraltar.

In June 1781 Cornwallis was appointed to command *Canada* (74), returning in August to the West Indies as part of the fleet under Admiral Sir Samuel

Hood. He fought in the actions at St Kitts on 26 January, and in the battles off Dominica on 9 April and in the Saintes passage on the 12th. Rodney achieved a notable victory at the Saintes, during which the probably accidental cutting of the French battle line became a precedent for innovation in British tactics. But at the end of the action he restrained Cornwallis from pursuit of the fleeing enemy, probably because of his own exhaustion and his unwillingness to trust his subordinates.

Cornwallis's reaction was to express his derision of the Tory Rodney to his Whig friends, and to secure from them an appointment in March 1783, following the conclusion of peace, to the yacht *Royal Charlotte*. From 3 April 1782 to 1784 he was again member of parliament for Eye. He then was put forward by Lord Howe, who was at the time first lord of the Admiralty, for the 'navy' seat of Portsmouth. In effect, accepting the seat was part of his naval career, and he continued to hold Portsmouth to 1790; he then returned to the seat for Eye, which he held from 1790 to January 1807.

Parliamentary duties did not interfere with his service afloat. On 24 September 1787, at the end of his commission to *Royal Charlotte*, he was promoted colonel of the marines, and in October he was promoted commodore. In October of the following year he was given the command-in-chief of the squadron in the East Indies, where his brother Earl Cornwallis was appointed governor-general of Bengal. Following receipt of the news of the French declaration of war on 1 February 1793, on which date he was promoted rear-admiral, he commenced operations against French trade, and supported the military campaigns against the French posts at Chandernagore and Pondicherry. He returned to England in April 1794 and hoisted his flag in May on board the *Excellent* (74). Although he missed the battle of the Glorious First of June, he was again promoted on 4 July 1794, to vice-admiral. In December he moved his flag into *Royal Sovereign* (100), which was a new ship.

In the evening of 16 June 1795, when in command of a squadron of five of the line and two frigates, Cornwallis ran into the Brest fleet commanded by Admiral Villaret-Joyeuse numbering thirteen of the line and fourteen frigates. A fighting retreat was the only option, but the retreat was not a route. Cornwallis ordered the *Brunswick* (74) and *Bellerophon* (74), because they were the slowest sailing ships, to crowd on sail and take the leading positions. *Mars* (74) and *Triumph* (74) were placed in the rear ships. The *Naval Chronicle* reported that 'The [French] line of battle ships came up in succession, and a teazing fire was kept up by them, with intervals, during the whole day, which the English ships returned from their stern chases; the Admiral proportioning his sail to the slowest of the squadron, and edging away to support them when it was requisite.' [NC 7.20-5] The French marine was still in turmoil because of the absenteeism of experienced officers due to the revolution, and Villaret-Joyeuse was contenting himself with a careful 'blooding' of his fleet. He attacked in three divisions, seeking to pick off the slowest sailers by firing into their rigging. When it looked as though *Mars* (74) might be taken, however, Cornwallis wore round in *Royal Sovereign* (100) to come to her defence. In his official report he wrote:

The *Mars* and *Triumph* being the sternmost ships, were of course more exposed to the enemy's fire, and I cannot too much commend the spirited conduct of Sir Charles Cotton, and Sir Erasmus Gower, the captains of those ships. Lord Charles Fitzgerald also in the *Brunswick* kept up a very good fire from the after guns, but that ship was the whole time obliged to carry every sail. The *Bellerophon* being nearly under the same circumstances, I was glad to keep in some measure as a reserve, having reason at first to suppose there would be full occasion for the utmost exertion of us all, and being rather ahead of me was not able to fire much. I considered that ship as a treasure in store, having heard of her former achievements, and observing the spirit manifested by all on board when she past me, joined to the activity and zeal showed by Lord Cranston during the whole cruise. I am also much indebted to Captain Whitby for his activity and unremitting diligence on board the *Royal Sovereign*. The frigates showed the greatest attention and alertness; I kept the *Pallas* near me to repeat signals, which Captain Curzon performed much to my satisfaction. Indeed I shall ever feel the impression which the good conduct of the captains, officers, seamen, marines, and soldiers in the squadron has made on my mind; and it was the greatest pleasure I ever received to see the spirit manifested in the men, who, instead of being cast down at seeing thirty sail of the enemy's ships attacking our little squadron, were in the highest spirits imaginable.

I do not mean the *Royal Sovereign* alone, the same spirit was shewn in all the ships as they came near me; and although (circumstanced as we were) we had no great reason to complain of the conduct of the enemy, yet our men could not help repeatedly expressing their contempt of them. Could common prudence have allowed me to let loose their valour, I hardly know what might not have been accomplished by such men. [NC 7.23]

Cornwallis had given Captain Robert Stopford, the commander of *Phaeton*, instructions early in the day to proceed well ahead of the action, and at 6pm, as ordered, he let fly her sheets, signalling as a *ruse de guerre* the sighting of a fleet. Fearing that the Channel fleet was about to come over the horizon, the French withdrew. The care Cornwallis took in his official report of the retreat action in June 1795 to bestow praise on ships' companies and their captains was in strong contrast with Lord Howe's carelessness in that respect following the Glorious First of June. In recognition of his contribution, in March 1796 he was appointed to the honorary position of rear-admiral of Great Britain.

His relationship with the Admiralty Board was undermined in October when he participated in a protest against orders to exempt embarked soldiers from naval discipline. It suffered a further

blow when he was ordered to escort a convoy to the West Indies and then take the command there in chief. *Royal Sovereign* was damaged in a collision while still in the Channel, and he put back to make repairs once the convoy was safely away from the land. When ordered to proceed in a frigate, he said his health would not endure it, and he was court-martialled for disobedience. He was partly exonerated, but his request for permission to resign his command was accepted.

On 14 February 1799 he was promoted a full admiral, but he was not employed again until Pitt's resignation in 1801. With the appointment by Henry Addington of St Vincent as first lord, Cornwallis succeeded him as Channel fleet commander. His greatest claim to fame rests on his management of the Brest blockade. The structure of the blockade system, developed under Lord Bridport, with Lord Spencer increasingly directing operations from the Admiralty and provided with 'Mediterranean fleet' standards of discipline by St Vincent, reached perfection under Cornwallis's command. He ensured that the Franco-Spanish fleet in Brest was wasted by blockade of supplies and from lack of training, while the British fleet was supplied at sea and kept to the highest state of training by the demands of seamanship off an exposed and hostile coast.

Cornwallis went home following the signing of the peace of Amiens, but he returned to command off Brest on 17 May 1803, the day before the resumption of war. Although relieved by Sir Charles Cotton in July and August 1804, and by Lord Gardner between April and July 1805, he was back in command when he made the dispositions which led to Sir Robert Calder's action on 22 July against the returning Franco-Spanish fleet commanded by Vice-Admiral Villeneuve. On 16 August, after Calder and later Nelson joined his flag, he divided his whole force, sending Calder back to Ferrol with twenty ships. He retained seventeen, including three three-deckers, off Ushant. Admiral Ganteaume made one attempt to leave Brest, on 21 August, with twenty-one battleships, but put about when Cornwallis formed line of battle.

Cornwallis would have preferred to let the French

get to sea where they could be fought, but in the bigger picture it was important that there be no risk of them joining Villeneuve. With the approval of Lord Barham, the first lord of the Admiralty, Cornwallis ordered Calder to pursue Villeneuve if he left Ferrol, and warned Collingwood at Cadiz that he might be caught between Villeneuve's combined fleet, and the ships inside the harbour. Recognising that he had established a moral mastery over the Brest fleet, Cornwallis detached five ships in early September to look for a squadron under Admiral Allemand which was cruizing for trade convoys, and then took his whole force at the end of September. Failing to find his prey, he was back off Ushant on 8 October.

The blockade was inevitably less effective in the winter, because storms forced the fleet to take shelter from time to time. Consequently, late in the year two battle squadrons were able to escape, one of which was eventually destroyed by Sir John Duckworth off San Domingo in January 1806, and Allemand's squadron was able to get into Brest on Christmas Eve. Cornwallis hauled down his flag on 22 February 1806, depressed at the death of his friend Nelson, but having ensured that the French would not be able to invade England or dominate the Mediterranean. He retired from the sea, and in 1807 retired from politics. His flag captain, John Whitby, died on 6 April 1806, and Cornwallis came to spend his time with Whitby's widow. In reward for a lifetime of exertion he was made vice-admiral of the United Kingdom in May 1814, and GCB on 2 January 1815. He died on 5 July 1819, aged seventy-five, and was buried in Milford churchyard, Hampshire, leaving his estate to Mrs Whitby.

Lt: 5 April 1761
M-C: 12 July 1762
Capt: 20 April 1765
R-Adm: 1 February 1793
V-Adm: 4 July 1794
Adm: 14 February 1799

COTTON

ADMIRAL SIR CHARLES COTTON, BARONET, was one of the foremost sailors of his age, and as accomplished a diplomat as he was a warrior. Following the Spanish revolt against Napoleon,

Cotton prevented the French acquiring control of the Russian fleet in the Tagus, and of the Spanish fleet at Cartagena.

He was born in June 1753 in Jermyn Street, Westminster, the third son of Sir John Hynde Cotton, fourth baronet, and his wife Anne, second daughter of Alderman Humphrey Parsons, twice mayor of London. He was educated at Westminster School, and became a member of Lincoln's Inn. But his preference for an active life at sea was strong, and he made a voyage to India in an Indiaman. On his return, he entered the navy as a midshipman in *Deal Castle* (20) on 24 October 1772 under the patronage of the earl of Sandwich, who was a friend of his father and at the time first lord of the Admiralty. The patronage served him well, for he was made acting lieutenant of *Niger* (32) on 24 September 1775 after less than three years in the navy and sailed to America. He served in the evacuation of the army from Boston in March 1776, and in support of the Long Island campaign that August. On 29 April 1777 Admiral Lord Howe confirmed his rank and put him to work in a floating battery, *Vigilant* (16), employed on the Delaware and Chesapeake rivers to guard the landing of troops. With dizzying speed he was promoted master and commander on 3 April 1779 and on 10 August 1779 he was made post captain in *Boyne* (70). As the *Naval Chronicle* remarked, 'so rapidly did he pass through the lower gradations of rank – his name never appeared in the Admiralty Navy List, till it was inserted amongst the post captains!' NC 27.354 His advancement did not stop there. *Boyne* was second abaft Sir George Rodney's flag at the battle of Martinique on 17 April 1780. After returning to England, and paying off *Boyne*, on 21 April 1781 he was put in command of the 12-pounder frigate *Alarm* (32), the first frigate to have her bottom covered with copper sheet antifouling. He was given orders to proceed to the West Indies, where *Alarm* served as a repeating frigate in the battle of the Saintes on 12 April 1782. He brought her home in 1783.

During the subsequent period of peace, Cotton was content to rest on his laurels. On 27 February 1788, in Holles Street, St Marylebone, London, he married Philadelphia, eldest daughter of Vice-Admiral Sir Joshua Rowley, baronet of Tendring Hall, Nayland, Suffolk. The couple had two sons and two daughters.

On the French declaration of war in February 1793 Cotton was given command of *Majestic* (74), in which he took part in the battle of the Glorious First of June in 1794. The close support he provid-

Sir Charles Cotton, Bart., Admiral of the White Squadron engraved by R? Page from a miniature in the possession of Lady Cotton, published by Joyce Gold, 103 Shoe Lane, Fleet Street, 31 May 1812.

ed his divisional commander was noticed by Sir Alexander Hood, Lord Bridport, and later in the action he took possession of the dismasted *Sans Pareil* (80), but Cotton was one of the many officers who felt slighted by Lord Howe's failure to see that one of the medals struck for the occasion was conferred on him. The following year, commanding *Mars* (74), he participated in the remarkable fighting retreat when Rear-Admiral Cornwallis encountered the Brest fleet, which greatly outnumbered his squadron. Because she was one of the cleaner ships, and therefore faster, *Mars* was one of the vessels placed by Cornwallis in the position

of greatest danger, and it was to rescue her that he wore *Royal Sovereign* (100) around to face the enemy, which chose to break off action. 'The *Mars* and *Triumph*,' reported Cornwallis, 'being the sternmost ships, were of course more exposed to the enemy's fire, and I cannot too much commend the spirited conduct of Sir Charles Cotton, and Sir Erasmus Gower, the Captains of those ships.'

On 23 January 1795 Cotton's father had died, and Charles inherited the title. He was promoted rear-admiral on 20 February 1797.

Sir Charles Cotton hoisted his flag in *Prince* (90) as third in command of the Channel fleet in March 1799 under Cornwallis, and in June was detached with twelve ships of the line in pursuit of Vice-Admiral Bruix, who had got the Brest fleet away to sea and on a course for the Mediterranean. Bruix evaded contact, got safely into Toulon, and then returned to Brest on 11 August in company with a Spanish fleet under Admiral Don Gravina. Cotton and Lord Keith were in pursuit. He rose to second in command of the Channel fleet in 1800, still under Cornwallis. Both officers struck their flags on the conclusion of peace, but with the return of war both resumed station. Cotton was promoted vice-admiral on 29 April 1802, and in July and August 1804 he assumed command in the absence of Cornwallis.

In December 1806 he was offered the command of the Newfoundland station, but for personal reasons he resigned that post. Lord Mulgrave, the newly appointed first lord, offered him a position on the Board of Admiralty, but he declined the post and retired for a while into private life. He also refused the Halifax station and command of the expedition against Copenhagen, but eventually he was persuaded to take the command off Lisbon, which he took up in December 1807, succeeding Sir Sidney Smith. There was considerable bad feeling about this, as Smith had just succeeded in persuading the Portuguese court to resist the French and accept the escort of the Royal Navy to Brazil.

Lisbon was a station of particular interest, not only because of its occupation by Marshal Junot with a French army, but also because a Russian squadron commanded by Admiral Siniavin was moored in the Tagus. Cotton imposed a close blockade on Lisbon, to the great distress of the population, but he was not able to force the Russians to sea, because they had taken over the naval provisions of the Portuguese fleet. The most important event of 1808 was the Spanish revolt, which led to revolt in Portugal. Cotton took an active part in encouraging the Portuguese to take up arms. On 21 June, Junot attacked at Vimeiro a British army under Sir Arthur Wellesley, later duke of Wellington, and suffered a signal defeat. But Wellesley was then succeeded by General Sir Hew Dalrymple, the ageing governor of Gibraltar, who agreed to Junot's request for a convention by which the French army would evacuate Portugal, but would not be considered prisoners of war and would be free to carry home their booty. They were even to be provided with transportation by the Royal Navy. The least objectionable part of the convention was that which allowed for the internment of Admiral Siniavin's squadron at Spithead as surety against Russian alliance with France. To Cotton, who three times returned the convention to General Dalrymple for amendment and finally reached an agreement with Admiral Siniavin, must be accorded the principal credit for effecting that outcome. Before returning to England on 20 December 1808 he had organised the facilities at the port of Lisbon for supporting the British army.

Cotton had been promoted a full admiral on 28 April 1808. When Admiral Lord Collingwood died on board the *Ville de Paris* (110) in the Mediterranean on 17 March 1810, Cotton was offered the command-in-chief in the Mediterranean. On that station his achievements were no less great. At a time when Napoleon was making every effort to rebuild his navy, Cotton co-operated with the Spanish officers in Cartagena to evacuate the Spanish fleet there, and the great quantities of naval stores in the Spanish warehouses. Unquestionably these actions were as important as a major victory at sea.

Cotton's command in the Mediterranean was to be unusually short, for in May 1811 he was appointed commander-in-chief of the Channel fleet in succession to Lord Gambier, although he did not hoist his flag at Plymouth until 8 October. During the winter months he resided in Plymouth, where he could proceed to sea on very short notice. On 23 February 1812, however, he died suddenly from a stroke at the age of fifty-eight. After a funeral at which he was accorded full military honours, he was buried at Landwade in Cambridgeshire.

> Lt: 29 April 1777
> M-C: 3 April 1779
> Capt: 10 August 1779
> R-Adm: 20 February 1797
> V-Adm: 29 April 1802
> Adm: 28 April 1808

CUMBY

CAPTAIN WILLIAM PRYCE CUMBY, CB, took command of the *Bellerophon* (74) at the battle of Trafalgar on 21 October 1805, after the death of Captain John Cooke, and was accordingly promoted to post captain rank.

He was born on 20 March 1771 in Dover, the second son of Commander David Pryce Cumby, RN, and his first wife Eleanor, second daughter of William Jepson of Heighington, county Durham. He entered the navy on 20 May 1784 as a lieutenant's servant on board the *Kite*, cutter, commanded by Lieutenant Henry Gunter, and was rated able seaman on 15 February 1785 and midshipman on 5 July 1786 while serving in the North Sea. He then made several voyages in the merchant service, before joining the clinker-built *Brazen*, cutter (10), under Lieutenant James Fegen on 12 October 1789. He served in a succession of ships during the Dutch and Spanish armaments, and acquired the patronage of Lord Mulgrave while serving as master's mate in *Leviathan* (74) in November 1790. His final months before his examination in 1792, and commissioning as lieutenant on 26 October 1793, were spent on board *Hebe* (38) commanded by Captain Alexander Hood. On 27 April 1792 he joined *Assistance* (50) flying the flag of Rear-Admiral Sir Richard King, and he served as a midshipman in Newfoundland, in the Scheldt and at Gibraltar. Lord Mulgrave's death had very serious implications for his career, but the outbreak of war, and the support of Mulgrave's heir, ensured that he had employment. On 20 June 1793 he transferred to *Stately* (64), flying the flag of Vice-Admiral Sir Richard King, and on 26 October 1793 he was commissioned third lieutenant of *Assistance* (50), which was now under the command of Captain Nathan (?) Brenton. In May 1795 he was appointed first lieutenant of *Astraea* (32) commanded by an old shipmate, Lord Henry Paulet, and he continued to serve with him, following him into *Thalia* (36), until Paulet was removed from command of his ship by court martial off Cadiz in June 1798. He then served under Captain Cuthbert Collingwood in *Excellent* (74), and in June 1799 was appointed flag lieutenant to Vice-Admiral Graeme commanding in the Medway, first in *Zealand* (64) and in April 1802 transferring to *Clyde* (38).

During the peace of Amiens he married on 7 July 1801, in Richmond, Yorkshire, Ann Metcalf. The couple had two sons and one daughter.

Following the return to war in May 1803, Cumby was appointed to command the *Swift*, cutter, in the North Sea, and in March 1804 he was given command of the Norfolk district of the sea fencibles. He surrendered that command in November when Captain John Loring asked for him as first lieutenant of *Bellerophon* (74), and when Loring resigned his command Captain Cooke agreed to Cumby retaining his commission. After Cooke's fall in the early part of the battle of Trafalgar, Cumby fought his ship resolutely, losing 150 officers and men killed and wounded.

He was commissioned as commander for rank on 24 December 1805, and as post captain on 1 January 1806. He was one of the followers at Nelson's funeral. His first appointment, on 7 July 1807, was to *Drydon* (36) as a relief for her captain. On 15 May 1808 he was appointed flag captain to Vice-Admiral Bartholomew Samuel Rowley in *Polyphemus* (64) at Jamaica, and in June 1809 Rowley put him in command of a squadron with an embarked military force under Major-General Hugh L Carmichael which was to co-operate with Spanish troops investing San Domingo. He was transferred to command of *Hyperion* (42) on 26 March 1811 prior to Rowley's death on 7 October

1811, after which Cumby bought his ship home for a refit. He was then ordered to the Davis Strait to protect the whale fishery, following which he convoyed trade from Newfoundland to Barbados. His last notable achievement was the capture of the American brig *Rattlesnake* (16) in the Bay of Biscay. *Hyperion* paid off at Portsmouth on 31 August 1815.

Ann died in December 1814, aged forty-six, and Cumby remarried on 29 December 1818, uniting with Elizabeth, eldest daughter of the Revd Thomas Wilson Morley of Eastby House, near Eastby, Yorkshire. Elizabeth was to have one son. Cumby was named a CB on 26 September 1831, and was superintendent of Pembroke dockyard and captain of the *Royal Sovereign,* yacht, when he died on 27 September 1837, aged sixty-six.

Lt: 26 October 1793
Capt: 1 January 1806

CUNNINGHAM

REAR-ADMIRAL SIR CHARLES CUNNINGHAM made his mark as a frigate commander. On 20 August 1799, when in command of the *Clyde* (38), he pursued two French frigates, which fled in different directions. Following the larger, *La Vestale* (36), he brought her to action and captured her. According to Lieutenant Marshall's contemporary biography, King George 'was at one of the theatres when an account of the above event was brought to him. He immediately stood up in the box, and commanded the news to be communicated to the audience; when "Rule Britannia" was loudly called for from every part of the house, and performed with reiterated applause.' Marshall 2.80

Cunningham was born in Eye, Suffolk, a son of Charles Cunningham and his wife, Elizabeth. He first went to sea in the merchant service and entered the navy in 1775, at the outbreak of the American war, as a midshipman in *Aeolus* (32). He served in the West Indies, and was transferred into *Bristol* (50) flying the flag of Sir Peter Parker, who in 1779 ordered him to act as lieutenant. He served for a while as first lieutenant of *Hinchinbrook* (28) commanded by Horatio Nelson, and in September 1782 was appointed to command the brig *Admiral Barrington*, being confirmed in rank on 6 November. Sir Joshua Rowley employed him in defence of Turks Island, but the French were fortunate to find him away reprovisioning in Jamaica when they arrived to seize the island, and subsequent efforts by Captain Nelson to regain possession proved ineffective. Having paid off his ship in Jamaica in May 1783, Cunningham returned to England in *Tremendous* (74).

He appears to have been on half pay for the next five years, but in 1788 was appointed to *Crown* (64) under orders to serve in the East Indies with Commodore William Cornwallis. He was promoted master and commander of *Ariel,* sloop, on 28 October 1790, and was commanding *Speedy* (14) at the time of the outbreak of war in February 1793. He was ordered to carry dispatches to the Mediterranean, and remained there as part of Lord Hood's fleet. On 5 October 1793 *Speedy* accompanied *Bedford* and *Captain* (74s) into Genoa harbour to seize the French frigate *Modeste* and two armed tartans, and then into Especia after *Impérieuse* (40), which was scuttled on the approach of the British. She was salved and taken into British service as *Unité*. Cunningham's promotion to post captain was dated the same day, 12 October 1793, with appointment to the prize. He acted in command of the 12-pounder frigate *Lowestoffe* (32) at the siege of Calvi, and following his return to England overland with dispatches, he was appointed in April 1796 to command *Clyde* (38). She was one of the ships caught up in the mutiny at the Nore, but Cunningham retained enough influence with his crew to be able to detach their loyalties once the mutineers showed a disposition to blockade the Thames. On the night of 29 May *Clyde*'s ship's company took an opportunity to slip away from the mutineers into Sheerness harbour, becoming the first to do so. Many ships followed *Clyde*'s example, and within a week the mutiny was over.

During the summer of 1800, following her triumphant capture of *La Vestale* in 1799, *Clyde* was employed conveying John Thomas Serres, the marine artist, along the coast of France so that he could prepare a series of coastal views as aids to navigation, and to assist the civilians in the Board of Admiralty. These were subsequently published as *The Little Sea Torch*. In May 1801 Cunningham commanded a squadron of frigates and smaller vessels for the defence of the Channel Islands, and in June 1802 *Clyde* was paid off.

In May 1803, after the renewal of the war, he was appointed to the *Prince of Orange* (74). There is a suggestion that he was given command of a squadron watching the Dutch fleet at the Texel, but his days of sea duty soon came to an end. In September he was appointed a commissioner of the Victualling Board by the earl of St Vincent, who later moved him, in 1806, to be resident commissioner of Deptford and Woolwich yards. Before taking up that post he was sent to Falmouth to prepare that port for watering the western frigates. When in 1823 Deptford and Woolwich were reduced, Cunningham was appointed superintendent of Chatham dockyard.

Cunningham was twice married, firstly to the daughter of a clergyman in Norfolk, and then on 10 February 1797, in Chatham, to Beatrice, third daughter of Captain Charles Proby, RN, commissioner of Chatham dockyard, and sister-in-law of Admiral James Pigott. He was again left a widower, and his eldest son died on 11 November 1822, aged twenty, while a midshipman. He was made a KB on 6 November 1832 and on 24 October 1832 a knight commander of the Guelphic order by William IV, who had presumably known him in the West Indies during the American war. He died on 11 March 1834 in Hoxne near Eye, Suffolk. There is a memorial in St Peter and St Paul, Eye.

Lt: 6 November 1782
M-C: 28 October 1790
Capt: 12 October 1793
Superannuated Capt: 1 August 1811
R-Adm: 4 May 1829

CURTIS

ADMIRAL SIR ROGER CURTIS, BARONET, GCB, is best known for his heroic defence of Gibraltar against a force of floating batteries in 1782. This action is dramatically depicted in John Singleton

Copley's gigantic painting now in the London Guildhall Gallery. In the war against Revolutionary France he served as Lord Howe's captain of the fleet in the battle of the Glorious First of June. It is uncertain whether the report should be believed that it was Curtis who urged Howe to be cautious about chasing the defeated French. It certainly appears that the failure to do so was a mistake, and that Howe could have annihilated the Brest fleet if

Sir Roger Curtis, Bart,
Vice Admiral of the Red Squadron,
engraving by William Ridley after Rivers,
published by Burney and Gold, Shoe Lane,
1 November 1801.

he had chased hard, preventing the French from recovering their formation. That might have enabled Rear-Admiral George Montagu's squadron off Ushant to capture isolated fugitives. Curtis was also blamed for Howe's failure to notice the efforts of all his captains in his official report, leading to several complaints from captains who were denied gold medals.

Curtis had been born on 4 June 1746 in Downton, Wiltshire, the only son of a tradesman, Roger Curtis, and his wife Christabella, née Blachford. He entered the navy in 1762 with the patronage of Admiral Barrington in *Royal Sovereign* (100). After the peace of Paris in 1763 he served in *Assistance* (50) on the west coast of Africa, then transferred in succession to the Portsmouth guardship *Augusta* (64), *Gibraltar* (20), in which he served on the Newfoundland station, *Venus* (36) commanded by Samuel Barrington, and in 1770, at the time of the Falkland Islands crisis, *Albion* (74) in the Channel fleet also under Barrington. He was examined in 1769 at the Navy Office, St Mary-le-Strand, Westminster, but not commissioned as lieutenant until 19 January 1771, when he was appointed to *Otter,* sloop, on the Newfoundland station. He made himself such an expert on the fishery that he attracted the attention of the admiral commanding there, Admiral Shuldham, who took Curtis with him when he was appointed in 1775 to the American station. He served as second lieutenant of Shuldham's flagship *Chatham* (50), and was promoted master and commander on 11 July 1776 in the *Senegal*, sloop, remaining on the American station. In the difficult conditions of wartime, when great responsibilities are shouldered early, he attracted the attention of the new commander, Admiral Lord Howe, who made him post captain on 30 April 1777 and appointed him flag captain in the *Eagle.*

Having returned to England with Howe in *Eagle* on 25 October 1778, Curtis refused to proceed in her to the Far East. This put him out of favour with the first lord of the Admiralty, the earl of Sandwich, and he was not employed again until 1780, when he sailed in *Brilliant* (36) with dispatches for Gibraltar. On the first try he was not able to get into the fortress, which was closely besieged. He continued on to Minorca, where he was blockaded by two French frigates, but on 27 April 1781 he was able to get into Gibraltar with twenty-five storeships freighted with much needed supplies. He then played an important part in keeping some communication open with Africa, and in the defence against the floating batteries which the Spaniards had reinforced to withstand intense and heated gunfire. On 13 September 1782 they made their attack on the mole. 'It was on this glorious day,' wrote the *Naval Chronicle*, 'that the marine brigade, under Captain Curtis, gained immortal honour, and no words can do justice to the bravery and humanity of their leader.' [NC 6.258] The floating batteries were at last set on fire, and their magazines began to explode, when Curtis turned from the task of destroying to that of saving the Spanish sailors struggling in the water. Eventually the garrison was relieved by Admiral Howe.

In recognition of his service, Curtis was made a KB on 29 November 1782. Less than two weeks later, 12 December 1778, at St Mary, Portsea, he married Sarah, the youngest daughter and coheiress of Mattich Brady of Gatcombe House, Portsea, Hampshire. He is believed to have offered to serve under Howe on the Board of Admiralty, but instead he was accorded the rank of commodore, and accredited ambassador to Morocco and the Barbary States. And then he was returned to Gibraltar to his old command, where he stayed until the end of 1783. Sarah and Sir Roger Curtis had two sons and one daughter.

From May to December 1787 he commanded a Portsmouth guardship, *Ganges* (74), and he then was on half pay until May 1790. There is a report that he was sent on a secret mission to the northern states in 1789. [Ralfe 2.43] At the time of the Nootka Sound crisis, when Admiral Howe raised his flag in *Queen Charlotte* (100), Curtis was again appointed his flag captain, and later the captain of the fleet. From December to early 1793 he commanded another guardship, *Brunswick* (74), returning then to *Queen Charlotte*. He served for a third time as Howe's captain of the fleet following the declaration of war by France in February 1793.

He was accorded by King George a gold medal following the Glorious First of June in 1794, and a chain such as was given to flag officers. On 4 July he was promoted rear-admiral and colonel of the marines, and on 10 September he was invested a baronet. He served as prosecutor at the court martial of Captain Molloy of *Caesar* (80) for his conduct in the battle, and continued in the Channel fleet, hoisting his flag in *Canada* (74). He transferred to *Powerful* (74) on 18 September 1795, and later to *Invincible* (74), and on 31 March 1796 transferred again, to *Formidable* (90). In early 1797, flying his flag in the *Prince* (90), he was employed in command of a detached squadron off the coast of Ireland. In May 1798 he joined the blockade off Cadiz under the command of the earl of St Vincent, and he was promoted vice-admiral on 14 February 1799.

In May 1800 he was appointed commander-in-chief at the Cape of Good Hope, where he was the first to order a ship repaired in Simon's Bay. He struck his flag on 24 February 1803, in a poor state of health, which required him to endure an operation. He went on half pay, but on 23 April 1804 he was promoted a full admiral, and in January 1805 he was appointed to serve on the commission charged with the revision of the civil affairs of the navy. This kept him busy until the end of 1807. In January 1809 he was appointed commander-in-chief at Portsmouth, and he was president of the court martial of Admiral Gambier following the attack on Basque Roads. The acquittal of Gambier was consistent with Curtis's own careful temperament.

He was invested GCB in 1815 when the order was expanded at the end of the war, and died on 14 November 1816, aged seventy, in Gatcombe near Portsmouth. His wife followed him on 11 April 1817, aged sixty-seven.

Lt: 19 January 1771
M-C: 11 July 1776
Capt: 30 April 1777
R-Adm: 4 July 1794
V-Adm: 14 February 1799
Adm: 23 April 1804

DACRES

VICE-ADMIRAL JAMES RICHARD DACRES'S career took a flying start when *Active* and *Favourite* captured a Spanish register ship from Lima, *Hermione*, the richest prize taken in that war. *Active*'s share was £251,020 12s. An ordinary seaman received £485 3s. 4d. She had sailed from the Caribbean before the British declaration of war, and was freighted with gold coin and ingots of gold, silver and tin, as well as cocoa. When landed at Portsmouth the treasure was carted up to London in twenty wagons decorated with flags and guarded by sailors.

He was born in February 1749 in Gibraltar, the

eldest son of Richard Dacres, secretary of the garrison of Gibraltar, and his wife Mary, daughter of William Bateman of Bury St Edmunds, Suffolk. He had a brother who, most confusingly, was also named Richard, and who also entered the navy and became a vice-admiral. Our hero signed on to the 9-pounder frigate *Active* (28) in February 1762 under the command of Captain Herbert Sawyer, and the capture of the *Hermione* took place on 21 May. He next served in *Aeolus* (32) under the command of Captain, later Admiral, Lord Hotham. In the following years he served in *Thames* (32) with Captain John Elliot, and in *Jersey* (60) under Commodore Richard Spry, who on 17 March 1769 made him lieutenant in *Montreal* (32) under Captain Phillips Cosby.

In the American war he was appointed second lieutenant of the French prize *Blonde* (32), under the command of Captain Philomon Pownall, and went out to Quebec as escort to a troop convoy. At the request of Commodore Sir Charles (?) Douglas, he was selected in June 1776 to lead a detachment to Lake Champlain, where he was appointed to command a schooner, *Carleton* (12), in Captain Pringle's flotilla. On 11 October 1776 he took part in an attack on American naval forces in the passage between Valicour Island and the mainland. The following day the Americans were pursued to Crown Point, where, after two hours' firing, they were routed, and General Waterburgh captured. General Carleton and Captain Douglas sent Dacres home with dispatches, and on his return to England he was made master and commander, on 25 November 1776. He was appointed to *Sylph* (14), and soon afterwards transferred to the larger ship-sloop *Ceres* (18), in which he served in the Leeward Islands.

Back in England again, he was married on 1 August 1777 at Totnes, Devon, to Eleanor Blandford Pearce of Cambridge. The couple were to have two sons, both of whom had successful naval careers, becoming respectively Captain Barrington Dacres, RN, and, to add to the confusion, Vice-Admiral James Richard Dacres.

On 9 March 1778 *Ceres*, in company with *Ariadne* (20), chased two American frigates, one of which, *Alfred* (20), struck. Later that year he

was himself captured by a French frigate, after a chase of forty-eight hours during which he successfully decoyed the enemy away from a troop convoy he was escorting. On his exchange he was made acting captain of *Sultan* (74), and soon afterward transferred to *Maidstone* (28), but he was not confirmed post captain until 13 September 1780, when he was placed in command of *Perseus*

James Richard Dacres, Esq.,
Vice-Admiral of the Red Squadron,
engraved by R? Page, from a painting
by Robert Bowyer.

(20). In this last he served in the Downs until nearly the end of the war, when he briefly commanded the frigates *Orpheus* (32) and *Aurora* (28) before they were paid off in 1783.

He was employed again soon after the French declaration of war in 1793. He served in *Sceptre* (64) in Commodore Ford's squadron, and on 1 June 1793 took part in the bombardment and capture of Fort Bizothen at Port-au-Prince. When his crew became sickly he was sent home in charge of a convoy, and was placed in command of *Barfleur* (90) in the Channel fleet under Lord Bridport. She was at the action on 23 June 1795 when Bridport forced an engagement on the Brest fleet with the capture of three French ships of the line, but *Barfleur* did not fire her guns. Later in the year Vice-Admiral Waldegrave hoisted his flag in *Barfleur* under orders to join Admiral Jervis in the Mediterranean. As his flag captain, Dacres was involved in the mission in the spring of 1796 to the Bay of Tunis to recover *Nemesis* (28), which had been taken into Tunis by her French captors. He was still serving as Waldegrave's flag captain in the Mediterranean fleet when the Spanish fleet from Cartagena was engaged off Cape St Vincent on 14 February 1797, during which *Barfleur* suffered few casualties. Soon afterwards Dacres returned to England in the hired cutter *Flora* (14), and was given command of *Foudroyant* (80), in which he served in the Mediterranean until February 1799, participating in the capture of *Guillaume Tell* on the night of 26 March 1798.

Two years later to the day following the battle, he was promoted rear-admiral of the blue, and he was advanced to the white squadron on 1 January 1801 on the union of Ireland with Great Britain. He was appointed second in command at Plymouth, and assumed the command-in-chief on the conclusion of the peace of Amiens.

On the return to war, he was appointed second in command at Jamaica under Sir John Duckworth, hoisting his flag in *Franchise* (36). This proved a very lucrative posting. In the spring of 1805 he succeeded Duckworth in command at Jamaica, and he remained there until 1809, being promoted vice-admiral. He continued to prosper from the prizes taken on his station, and by the capture of Curaçao, but he did not live long after his retirement to enjoy his wealth. He died on 6 January 1810, aged sixty, owing to a fall from his horse.

Lt: 17 March 1769
M-C: 25 November 1776
Capt: 13 September 1780
R-Adm: 14 February 1799
V-Adm: 9 November 1805

DACRES

VICE-ADMIRAL RICHARD DACRES had a career closely associated with Sir Sidney Smith, who become a personal friend, and with Sir John Colpoys.

Richard Dacres was born in September 1761, younger brother of James Richard and the fifth son of Richard and Mary Dacres. He entered the navy in 1775 in the *Renown* under the command of Captain Francis Banks and took part in the capture of New York under Sir Peter Parker. He was commissioned lieutenant on 28 May 1781 into *Alcide* (74), Captain Charles Thompson, in which he fought in Rear-Admiral Thomas Graves's action off the Chesapeake on 5 September 1781, Rear-Admiral Samuel Hood's actions at St Kitts and Admiral Rodney's at the Saintes on 12 April 1782.

After the French declaration of war in 1793, Dacres was appointed to the *Hannibal* (74) commanded by Captain Colpoys, part of the squadron under the command of Admiral Gardner sent to secure the British islands in the West Indies. On his return to England in late 1793 or early 1794 he was appointed first lieutenant of *Diamond* (32) commanded by Smith, and in October 1794 he joined *London* (90) flying the flag of Rear-Admiral Colpoys. Six months later, on 10 March 1795, he was promoted commander, and another six months later, on 31 October 1795, he was made post captain in *Camilla* (20). About this time he married Martha Phillips Milligan.

Dacres continued to be actively employed in the routine of naval life in wartime until 1806, when Sir Sidney Smith hoisted his flag as rear-admiral in the Mediterranean and asked for Dacres as his flag captain in *Pompée* (80). Dacres was thus heavily involved in the amphibious operations in Calabria and in the assault on the Turkish fleet and the Dardanelles forts as part of Admiral Duckworth's failed attempt at armed diplomacy at Constantinople in February 1807. *Pompée* was then recalled to England, where she arrived in June 1807 and was ordered to form part of a squadron under Vice-Admiral Stanhope for service in the second Copenhagen expedition. In the navy at that date, reassigning a ship to a squadron under another's command was considered an insult to the former squadron commander, in this instance Sir Sidney Smith. In the Copenhagen campaign the navy's job was to provide support for the army besieging the city.

His service in the 1807 Copenhagen campaign

was to be Dacres's last at sea. On his return from Denmark, he was made governor of the Royal Naval Hospital at Greenwich, which position he held from 2 February 1808 to August 1816. He was nominated GCB on 25 January 1836, and died with the rank of vice-admiral on 22 January 1837, aged seventy-five, at Bailbroke Villas near Bath, Somerset.

Lt: 28 May 1781
Cmdr: 10 March 1795
Capt: 31 October 1795
Superannuated Capt: 4 June 1814
R-Adm: 29 March 1817
Restored on the Active List
V-Adm: 22 July 1830

DALRYMPLE

ALEXANDER DALRYMPLE was a man with many faults, but a towering figure nonetheless who was the first Admiralty hydrographer, and the inspiration behind the British colonisation of Australia. His demand that he be permitted to command one of His Majesty King George's ships, however, was firmly turned down.

He was born on 24 July 1737 at Newhailes, near Edinburgh, son of Sir James Dalrymple, second baronet of Hailes in the county of Haddington, and Christian Hamilton, youngest daughter of Thomas, sixth earl of Haddington. After his father's death in 1751 he embarked on an East India Company career, being appointed a writer on 1 November 1752, and was posted to Madras, where he arrived in May 1753. With the support of George Pigot, governor of Madras, of Admiral Hugh Pigot, the governor's brother, and of General St Clair, Dalrymple was promoted to sub-secretary. He became interested in the records of trade to Burma, Indo-China and Borneo, and in February 1759 Pigot freighted the *Cuddalore* with the idea that Dalrymple should attempt to develop new trade routes to China employing Indonesian middlemen. His attempts to establish an entrepôt in the Sulu archipelago became part of the impetus in 1762 to capture Manila from the Spaniards.

Back in London after 1765, he became convinced of the 'counterpoise' argument that there must be a great Pacific continent to counterbalance the Eurasian land mass, and he proposed himself, with the support of the Royal Society, as the leader of an exploratory voyage. But he refused to go as scientific officer in a ship commanded by another, and Lieutenant James Cook was given the job.

In 1766 Thomas Howe, an East India Company captain with whom Dalrymple had sailed, suggested to his brother Lord Howe that a hydrographic office be established by the Admiralty, and that Alexander Dalrymple be appointed to head it, and Lord Howe brought the matter before Lord Egmont, the first lord of the Admiralty. Nothing came of it at the time, but Dalrymple began in 1769 to publish charts and navigational books, and in

Alexander Dalrymple, Esq.,
engraved by T Blood with permission of Mr Asperne,
the proprietor of the *European Magazine*,
published by Joyce Gold, Naval Chronicle Offices,
103 Shoe Lane, London, 30 March 1816.

March 1771 he was elected to the Royal Society. He returned to East India Company employment in 1775, but he was back in London in April 1779, when he persuaded the company to hire him at £500 a year to examine the journals of East India Company ships, which were stored in East India House, with the objective of using the navigational material in them as part of a project to publish charts and sailing directions.

By 1794 he had published almost 550 plans of ports and small-scale charts of parts of the East Indies navigation, with forty-five plates of coastal views, and between fifty and sixty books and pamphlets of sailing directions. Work on larger-scale charts had to await the accumulation of accurate longitude observations. By then he was a considerable figure in London; he was called on to provide the Admiralty with plans and topographical information for Vancouver's voyage, and advised the Colonial Office on routes to supply Nootka Sound after the Spanish controversy in 1790. The post of hydrographer to the Admiralty was created for him by order in council on 13 August 1795 to give official status to the geographical and navigational information he was increasingly asked to provide. He continued at the same time to hold his post at the East India Company.

He sorted and classified the charts held by the Admiralty, and in 1800 hired engravers and a press for the publication of charts. It was at his suggestion that the Admiralty appointed a chart committee of naval officers to advise on charts for fleet use. Home Popham, E H Columbine and Thomas Hurd were appointed, but Dalrymple had worked virtually alone for so long that he had lost the tact to work with a committee. He was dismissed by the Board of Admiralty on 28 May 1808, and his anger led to his death three weeks later, on 19 June 1808, at 57 High Street, Marylebone, at the age of nearly seventy-one. He was buried at St Marylebone parish church. The Admiralty purchased from his estate his collection of accounts of voyages and travels, atlases, charts, maps and nautical papers, which became the core of the Admiralty library and of the hydrographic office collections.

DALYELL

CAPTAIN SIR WILLIAM CUNNINGHAM CAVENDISH DALYELL, BARONET, was one of the young men in Sir Sidney Smith's special forces operating on the coasts of France and the Netherlands.

He was born on 27 April 1784, in Abercorn, Linlithgowshire, the fifth and youngest son of Sir

Robert Dalyell (or Dalziell), fourth (assumed) baronet of Binns, Linlithgow, and his wife Elizabeth, eldest daughter of Nicol Graham of Gartmore, Stirlingshire. His father was an officer in the army, president of the Society for Promoting Useful Arts in Scotland, and vice-president of the Society of Antiquaries of Scotland, and of the African Society of Paris. William Dalyell was first

Captain William Cavendish Cunningham Dalyell, R.N., engraved by T Blood after Douglas of Edinburgh, published by Joyce Gold, Naval Chronicle Offices, 103 Shoe Lane, London, 31 August 1814.

sent to Burney's naval academy at Gosport, and entered the navy in 1793 as a captain's servant or volunteer first class in *Thetis* (38) under the command of Captain the Honourable Alexander Cochrane, with whom he served at Halifax. He was rated midshipman by Captain David Milne when he joined the French prize *Pique* (34) in July 1797 for Channel service, and followed Milne into another French prize, *Seine* (40), in June 1798, proceeding in her to the West Indies. There, as a prize master, he had the ill fortune to have his ship sink under him, which left him and his crew to row all night in a small boat to a barren Cuban coast where they were made prisoner. He was rated midshipman or master's mate in February 1797, and returned to England for his examination in 1802 during the peace of Amiens.

He could not immediately obtain a lieutenant's commission, but with the renewal of the war and with the assistance of Sir Alexander Cochrane he found employment as a passed midshipman under Smith's command in *Antelope* (50), joining her in April 1803. Smith was directing covert operations to monitor naval construction at the Texel and Antwerp and landing intelligence agents, using boat raids to cut out merchant shipping as cover. With a Lieutenant John Martin Hanchett and a Mr Bourne, Dalyell was stranded in the Netherlands in September 1803. They pretended to be Americans who had come to attend school, and, making every mistake in the book which might have compromised those who covertly assisted them, they made their way to Emden and from there to London in a leaking galliot, the deck of which burst from the effects of swelling grain.

On 1 January 1805 he was commissioned lieutenant, and only four days later he was lying badly wounded on the deck of a French privateer while the bodies of the slain were being thrown into the sea. He lived thanks to the charity of a French surgeon and a merchant, but remained a prisoner of war until December 1813. On his exchange he was immediately promoted commander, on 17 February 1814, and on 14 March he was granted a pension for his wounds. On 28 July he was presented at court.

He married on 19 September 1820 Maria, the youngest daughter of Anthony Teixiera Sampayo of Peterborough House, Fulham, Middlesex, and sister of Anthony Sampayo, French minister at Hesse. The couple had two sons and two daughters. He was appointed captain of Greenwich hospital on 27 August 1840, and was promoted to post captain on 1 July 1864, with seniority dated 1860. He succeeded his brother as seventh baronet on 7 June 1851, and died on 16 February 1865, aged eighty, at Greenwich hospital. Maria died on 20 October 1871, aged seventy-two, at 120 Belgrave Road, Pimlico, Middlesex.

Lt: 1 January 1805
Cmdr: 17 February 1814
Retired Capt: 1 July 1864 (seniority 1860)

DANCE

COMMODORE SIR NATHANIEL DANCE, HONOURABLE EAST INDIA COMPANY, distinguished himself in an action fought on 14–16 February 1804, commanding sixteen laden Indiamen and accompanied by eleven country ships, against a French squadron commanded by Vice-Admiral Linois consisting of an 84-gun ship of the line, two heavy frigates of forty-four and thirty-six guns, another lighter ship of twenty guns and a Dutch brig mounting eighteen 32-pounder carronades. Although many a stout defence was made by merchant mariners against attacks by

Nathaniel Dance, Knt., Commodore in the Honourable East India Company's Service, engraved by James Fittler, Associate Engraver, after a drawing by George Dance, Esq., RA, published by Joyce Gold, 103 Shoe Lane, 30 November 1804.

enemy privateers, this action was a nine-days' wonder. The *Naval Chronicle* wrote in glowing words: 'His conduct was worthy of the experience and science of our most approved and veteran Admirals, while the ardour and promptitude with which his orders were obeyed and his plans executed by the several Captains under his command, may have been rivalled, but can scarcely have been exceeded in the most renowned of our naval exploits.' ^{NC 12.137}

Dance was born in London on 20 June 1748, the son of James Dance and his wife Elizabeth, daughter of James Hoper. James Dance had left his family when his son was still very young, leaving his own father, George Dance the City architect, to support his children. With the patronage of Nathaniel Smith, a relative who was in the court of directors of the East India Company, Nathaniel Dance went to sea in 1759. He was on his ninth voyage to India, and his first in command of a ship, when in 1780 the combined fleets of France and Spain captured him, and he spent six months on parole in Spain.

The engagement which made him famous occurred on a voyage begun in January 1803 when he sailed from England in a new ship, the *Earl Camden* of 1,200 tons burthen and armed with thirty-six 18-pounders. On 31 January 1804 the fleet left Canton for the return voyage, and Dance was appointed by right of seniority as commodore of the whole fleet. He was still recovering from an illness on the day of the battle. He reported:

On the 14th of February, at day-break, we saw Pulo Auro, bearing W.S.W. and at eight A.M. the *Royal George* [Indiaman] made the signal for seeing four strange sail in the S.W. I made the signal for the four ships noted in the margin [*Alfred, Royal George, Bombay Castle* and *Hope*] to go down and examine them; and Lieutenant Fowler, of the Royal Navy, late Commander of the *Porpoise*, and passenger with me, having handsomely offered to go in the *Ganges* brig, and inspect them nearly, I afterwards sent her down likewise; and from their signals I perceived it was an enemy's squadron, consisting of a line of battle ship, three frigates, and a brig.

At one P.M. [the 15th by naval usage] I recalled the look-out ships by signal, and formed the line of battle in close order.

As soon as the enemy could fetch in our wake they put about, we kept on our course under an easy sail; at near sun-set they were close in our rear, and I was in momentary expectation of an attack there, and preparing to support them, but at the close of the day we perceived them haul to windward. I sent Lieutenant Fowler, in the *Ganges* brig, to station the country ships on our lee bow, by which means we were between them and the enemy; and having done so, he returned with some volunteers from the country ships.

At nine A.M. [the 15th], finding they would not come down, we formed the order of sailing, and steered our course under an easy sail; the enemy then filled their sails, and edged towards us.

At one P.M. [the 16th], finding they purposed to attack and endeavour to cut off our rear, I made the signal to tack and bear down on him, and engage in succession – the *Royal George* being the leading ship, the *Ganges* next, and then the *Earl Camden*. This manoeuvre was correctly performed, and we stood towards him under a press of sail. The enemy then formed in a very close line, and opened their fire on the headmost ships, which was not returned by us till we approached him nearer. The *Royal George* bore the brunt of the action, and got as near the enemy as he would permit him. The *Ganges* and *Earl Camden* opened their fire as soon as their guns could have effect; but before any other ship could get into action, the enemy hauled their wind, and stood away to the Eastward under all the sail they could set.

At two P.M. I made the signal for general chase, and we pursued them till four P.M.; when fearing that a longer pursuit would carry us too far from the mouth of the Streights, and considering the immense property at stake, I made the signal to tack; and at eight P.M. we anchored in a situation to proceed for the entrance of the Streights in the morning. As long as we could distinguish the enemy, we perceived him steering to the Eastward under a press of sail.

In the Malacca Strait the fleet met two British ships of the line on 28 February, and was given convoy as far as St Helena, where it was the practice to await the arrival of escort into home waters. Dance was rewarded by a present of £5,000 by the Bombay insurance company and a pension of £500 a year from the East India Company, and King George conferred a knighthood on him. He lived the rest of his life in comfortable retirement and died at Enfield on 25 March 1827, aged seventy-eight.

D'AUVERGNE – *see* d'Auvergne

DIGBY

ADMIRAL SIR HENRY DIGBY, GCB, commanded *Africa* (64) at the battle of Trafalgar on 21 October 1805, and owing to accidental circumstances fought almost alone.

Digby was born on 20 January 1770 in Holcombe, Somerset, the eldest son of Charlotte, daughter of Joseph Cox, and the Honourable and Very Revd William Digby, LLD, vicar of Coleshill, Warwickshire, canon of Christ Church, Oxford, dean of Worcester and later of Durham, and chaplain-in-ordinary to George III. These offices were virtually hereditary, as Henry's grandfather was the Venerable William, fifth Lord Digby, dean of Durham, vicar of Coleshill, and chaplain-in-ordinary of George III. But, as in so many church families, there was also a strong connection with the navy. Henry was nephew of Admiral the Honourable Robert Digby, and along with two of his brothers, who were to end as Vice-Admiral Joseph Digby, GCB, and Captain Charles George Digby, RN, and three of his cousins, he was to enter the navy, which he did as a captain's servant in *Vestal* (28), in which he served in North America in 1782 and 1783. He was rated able seaman and midshipman when on 2 April 1783 he joined *Europa* (50) flying the flag of Admiral Innes at Jamaica and in the Gulf of Mexico. In 1786 he served as a supernumerary in *Janus* (32) under Captain Pakenham

in passage to England, and then was rated a midshipman in *Salisbury* (50) in which he served under Sir Erasmus Gower, with the flag of Rear-Admiral John Elliot, commander-in-chief at Newfoundland. He served under Captain Thomas Foley in 1789 on the coast of Scotland in *Racehorse*, ship-sloop, before rejoining Elliot, now flying his flag in *Bellerophon* (74) commanded by Sir Thomas Pasley. When he was commissioned lieutenant on 20 October 1790 he was appointed to *Lion* (64) under Captain the Honourable Seymour Finch, with whom he sailed to the West Indies.

His service following the French declaration of war in February 1793 was active, but not remarkable. He served as lieutenant in *Eurydice* (24) with Captain Thomas (?) Cole in the Channel and Bay of Biscay; in *Pallas* (32) under the Honourable Henry Curzon; and in *Dictator* (64) under Captain Jahleel (Sr.) Brenton at Spithead; and it appears from corrections added to the list supplied to the Admiralty by Digby that he also had periods of service in three other ships. On 11 August 1795 he was promoted commander of *Incendiary*, a fireship, in which he served in Quiberon Bay, on a secret expedition, and off the Texel. The following year he was made post captain on 19 December 1796 with appointment to command *Aurora* (28) on the coast of Spain and Portugal and in the Azores. In 1798 he commanded *Leviathan* (74) flying the broad pendant of Commodore Duckworth in the operations leading to the capture of Minorca, afterwards returning to patrol the coasts of Spain and Portugal. He moved in 1799 to *Alcmene* (32), in which he was employed off Havre de Grace until 1801, when he was appointed to command a new 18-pounder frigate, *Resistance* (36), in which he escorted a convoy to Quebec.

He appears to have spent several years ashore on his return from Canada, until he accepted command of *Africa* (64) and joined the Mediterranean fleet under Lord Nelson off Cadiz. During the night prior to the action *Africa* had become separated from the fleet, and in the morning she was seen by Lord Nelson to be in danger of running without support into the enemy van. *Africa* was accordingly ordered to make all possible sail, but the signal was misinterpreted and Digby cracked on sail while maintaining his course towards the enemy line, which he engaged in sequence while passing. When he reached the *Santisima Trinidad* he found her without flag flying, and not firing, so he sent a lieutenant on board her to enquire whether she had struck. A Spanish officer replied that she had not, and permitted the British officer to return to his ship. Digby then pushed into the thickest of the fight and placed *Africa* alongside the French *Intrépide,* which he engaged for three-quarters of an hour until *Orion* came up and *Intrépide* surrendered. Eighteen of *Africa*'s people were killed, and forty-four wounded. There was a story circulated following the battle of Trafalgar that Lord Nelson had been displeased by *Africa*'s performance, but this Sir Thomas Hardy refuted in no uncertain terms. Nevertheless, Digby fell once more into obscurity.

He married on 17 March 1806 Jane Elizabeth, daughter of Thomas Wenman Coke, first earl of Leicester, member of parliament, and widow of Charles, Viscount Andover. The couple had two sons and one daughter. He was nominated CB on 4 June 1815, KCB on 14 March 1831, and GCB on 23 February 1842, and had the rank of admiral when he died on 13 August 1842, aged seventy-two, at Minterne House, Minterne Magna, Dorset. Jane Elizabeth died on 29 April 1863.

> Lt: 20 October 1790
> Cmdr: 11 August 1795
> Capt: 19 December 1796
> R-Adm: 12 August 1819
> V-Adm: 22 July 1830
> Adm: 23 November 1841

DIXON

ADMIRAL SIR MANLEY DIXON, KCB, was one of Lord Nelson's oldest and closest friends. In 1798 he commanded *Lion* (64), which engaged *Guillaume Tell* (86) and crippled her before bearing away and letting *Foudroyant* (74) take the prize.

He was born on 3 January 1757 in Annapolis Royal, Nova Scotia, the third son of Major-General Matthew Dixon, RE, and his wife Frances. He entered the navy in 1770 as a volunteer in *Royal Oak* at Plymouth under the command of Captain, later Admiral, Shuldham, but was lent to *Kent* (74) and

Egmont (74) before being rated midshipman in 1773 in *Panther* (60) under Captain Cornthwaite Ommanney and proceeding to Newfoundland, where Shuldham was serving as commodore and governor. In 1776 he transferred to *Chatham* (50) and then to *Bristol* (50), and served alongside his father, commanding flat boats attending the army at New York. Before he sailed in February 1777 for England, Sir William Howe is supposed to have offered him an ensign's commission. He was then rated master's mate, and later acting master, in *Badger,* brig of war, under Captain C H E Calmady, and sailed to Jamaica, where Vice-Admiral Clark Gayton commissioned him lieutenant, on 7 September 1777. Apparently he also was put in command of *Badger,* and then served as first lieutenant of *Bristol* under Captain Toby Caulfield in Commodore Cornwallis's defensive actions of 20 March and 20 June 1780. He was appointed on 15 August acting captain of *Ruby* (64), and later of *Janus* (44). He was promoted master and commander on 15 August 1780 with appointment to *Jamaica*, sloop (16), and subsequently of *Jamaica*, brig (18). In April 1783 Sir Joshua Rowley promoted him acting post captain in *Tobago*, sloop, but with the return of peace the Admiralty did not confirm his commission, and he had to wait until 22 November 1790 at the time of the Nootka Sound incident. Prior to that, between 1786 and 1789 he commanded *Orestes* (18).

In 1794 he was appointed to command *Porcupine* (24) as part of the Channel fleet under Lord Howe. On returning from detached service escorting a convoy to Gibraltar, he joined George Montagu's squadron in time to brush with the Brest fleet returning from its encounter with Lord Howe at the battle of the Glorious First of June. He subsequently was appointed to *L'Espion*, in which he served in the North Sea and Channel, and then in 1797 was appointed to command *Lion* (64) following the Nore mutiny. She was severely short of seamen, but he nonetheless joined St Vincent off Cadiz, and from him obtained permission to join Nelson in the Mediterranean. On passage, on 15 July, he encountered four large Spanish frigates each carrying forty-two guns, and despite the condition of his ship he succeeded in beating one of them into submission, in a sinking condition. *Lion*'s people were eager to prove that their quarrel with the navy had had nothing treasonable about it. The prize was towed into Naples, and Dixon set course for Alexandria on 8 August in search of Lord Nelson, learning *en route* that they had missed the battle of the Nile. He remained during the winter blockading Alexandria, and in late December in heavy weather captured *Chasseur,* corvette (10), carrying dispatches, which were thrown overboard before she struck. When he took *Lion* to Cyprus for supplies, the French frigates sailed from Alexandria; Dixon proceeded to Malta to inform Lord Keith, and then joined Nelson at Palermo.

He was back at Malta, lying at anchor in sixty-four fathoms off Valletta harbour and short-handed, when *Guillaume Tell* sailed on the night of 26 March 1798. With eighty-six guns and nearly 1,000 men embarked, she was a formidable foe. She was slowed by Captain Henry Blackwood in *Penelope* (44), and finally engaged by *Lion*. In his account to the French marine, Admiral Decres recalled that

> the *Lion* came up within musket-shot of the *Guillaume Tell*, and during three-quarters of an hour that the *Lion* was close along side, she received from us and returned a very heavy fire; but at last her fire became less, and we were within pistol-shot, when perceiving there was not any person on the poop, I ordered Captain Saunier to seize the first moment and board her. The first attempt made by this officer failed, owing to the care that the *Lion* took to avoid it; but having attempted a second time, he succeeded in getting the *Guillaume Tell*'s bowsprit between the main and mizen rigging of the *Lion*, and the boarding party thereby became inevitable, if our jib-boom had not been carried away at the instant when the sailor was making it fast, and a number of brave fellows had presented themselves to jump on board. This attempt having failed, the *Lion*, with her sails destroyed, and rigging cut, and masts tottering, was obliged to set before the

wind with her sheets flying; and without firing, the *Guillaume Tell* followed her for some minutes, and returned on the larboard tack, to receive the *Foudroyant,* coming to take a part in the battle. [Ralfe 3.26]

Following the action, Dixon joined Nelson at Palermo and was put in command of *Généreux,* which had been captured in February.

On the conclusion of peace, Captain George Martin requested that Dixon be allowed to be the first to go home, as he had been separated for five years from his family. They exchanged, and he returned in *Alexander* (74) to England, where she was paid off. It is not known when Dixon was married, but his wife was Christiana Sophia Hall of Jamaica, and his second son, later Admiral Manley Hall Dixon, had been born on 8 June 1786. Presumably Dixon had never seen him.

On the renewal of the war in 1803 Dixon was appointed to command *Queen* (90) in the Channel fleet, but in 1805 a domestic crisis forced him to return ashore, and for the next three years he commanded the sea fencibles at Swansea, following which he was appointed to command at the Nore. He was promoted rear-admiral on 28 April 1808, and in April 1809 he returned to sea with his flag in *Téméraire* (98) and served under Sir James Saumarez in the Baltic, shifting his flag successively into *Dictator* (64), *Ruby* (64) and *Vigo* (74). Christiana died in March 1810 in Deal, Kent, and Dixon remarried on 21 March 1811 in Fremington, Devon, uniting with Catherine, daughter of Gabriel Jeffreys of Swansea. He hoisted his flag in January 1812 in *Montagu* (74) for service at Brazil, where he was promoted vice-admiral on 4 December 1813. He shifted his flag into *Nereus* (32), *Achilles* (74) and *Valiant* (74) before he returned home in May 1815, when he struck his flag. He was nominated a KCB on 12 August 1819, and died on 8 February 1837, aged eighty, with the rank of admiral.

Lt: 7 September 1777
M-C: 15 August 1780
Capt: 22 November 1790
R-Adm: 28 April 1808
V-Adm: 4 December 1813
Adm: 27 May 1825

DOMETT

ADMIRAL SIR WILLIAM DOMETT, GCB, is remembered in a biographical entry in the *Naval Chronicle* which notes that, although Nelson was dead, 'We feel a cheering consciousness of superiority; satisfied that, from the acknowledged excellence of our naval tactics, and the proved valour of our seamen, we must ever retain that superiority; unless, indeed, for some wise purpose, a higher power than that of man should inflict the stroke of defeat.' [NC 15.1] Domett had been a friend of Nelson's, and God did not see fit to withdraw his bias towards the Royal Navy. Part of the reason was that a man such as Domett, whose parents were not known, could climb the ladder of promotion to the top. His most famous roles were as captain of the fleet to a succession of commanders-in-chief.

Domett had probably been born in 1754, and entered the navy in 1769 as able seaman with the patronage of Captain Alexander Hood, later Lord Bridport, on board the *Quebec* (36) commanded by Captain John Reynolds, who later rated him a midshipman. Throughout his career, his connection with the Hood family was to be important. He served in *Quebec* for three years in the West Indies, and then joined *Scorpion*, sloop, under Captain Elphinstone, and served for two and a half years in the Mediterranean, before returning to England and signing into *Marlborough* (74), where he stayed for only a month. He then sailed in March 1775 as master's mate in the *Surprise* (28) commanded by Captain, later Admiral, Robert Linzee, to relieve the British garrison at Quebec, which was besieged by an American army. She arrived, after lying for three weeks beset with ice in the Gulf of St Lawrence, in time to harry the American retreat. She then was employed for two years on the Newfoundland station. On Linzee's recommendation, Domett was ordered by Admiral John Montagu to serve as lieutenant in *Romney* (50), and returned with him to England four months later at the end of the year. Reverting to midshipman on 5 February 1777, he was appointed to *Robust* (74) commanded by Alexander Hood, and was finally commissioned lieutenant on 27 December 1777, serving as second

lieutenant in *Robust* at the battle of Ushant on 27 July 1778. He remained in *Robust* when Hood resigned following the courts martial of Admirals Keppel and Palliser, being replaced by Captain Cosby. *Robust* was at the head of Admiral Arbuthnot's battle line in the engagement off Cape Henry on 16 March 1781. Domett was also present in the battle of the Chesapeake on 5 September 1781, serving in *Invincible* (74) under the command of Captain Sir Charles Saxton. He was then transferred again into *Barfleur* (90) as signal officer to Alexander Hood's elder brother, Sir Samuel Hood, with whom he served at the remarkable engagement at St Kitts on 25 January 1782, at his engagement with Admiral de Grasse on 9 April 1782 and at the battle of the Saintes three days later, following which he was promoted to first lieutenant. When Samuel Hood captured four enemy ships in the Mona passage on 19 April, Domett was promoted by Admiral Rodney to command one of the prizes, *Ceres* sloop, on 21 August 1782, in which he was sent to England with dispatches.

There his commission was confirmed on 9 September 1782, and he was appointed flag captain of *Queen* (90), flagship of Sir Alexander Hood, who was now rear-admiral. In her he took part in the relief of Gibraltar.

He came ashore at the end of the war, but on 23 June 1786 he was appointed senior officer at Leith and captain of *Champion* (24). On 13 May 1788 he was appointed to *Pomone* (28), in which he served on the west coast of Africa and in the West Indies, returning to England in 1789. He was then transferred at Vice-Admiral Milbanke's request on 9 May to *Salisbury* (50), and served as flag captain on the Newfoundland station. At the time of the Nootka Sound crisis with Spain in 1790 he was appointed flag captain in *London* (90), which was intended for Sir Alexander Hood's flag. When *London* was paid off on 6 December 1790, he was appointed to *Pegasus* (28) and served once again at Newfoundland, returning home at the end of 1791. On 22 March 1792, at the request of Rear-Admiral Goodall, he was appointed flag-captain in *Romney* (50) in the Mediterranean, but with the outbreak of war Sir Alexander Hood asked for him again to be flag captain of *Royal George* (100). In her he saw action at the battles of the Glorious First of June, in recognition of which he was presented by King George with a gold medal. He remained flag captain of *Royal George* when Hood, now Lord Bridport, assumed command of the Channel fleet in 1795, and was entrusted with the despatches telling of the action on 23 June. He was still at that post at the time of the Spithead mutiny.

He was promoted colonel of the marines on 1 January 1801, a month before his appointment as Sir Hyde Parker's captain of the fleet in *London* for the expedition to Copenhagen. This was a highly responsible position, and an anxious one with an admiral who was past his prime. Even before the fleet sailed from Yarmouth, Domett had concluded that Parker was a spent force, and obtained Vice-Admiral Nelson's assistance in getting a stiff letter from the earl of St Vincent, the first lord of the Admiralty. Domett was only with difficulty to get Parker to establish an order of battle, and when it was drawn up, it did not meet contemporary expectations. When on the morning of the 25 March the fleet tacked away from its anchorage and it became apparent that Parker was taking a route through the Belts, instead of past Kronburg, Domett became alarmed. He later wrote to Lord Bridport on 4 May 1801 claiming that he pointed out to Parker that if the fleet did pass through the Belts and reach Kioge Bay, south of Copenhagen, it would be impossible for the larger ships to get north to Copenhagen because southerly gales reduced the depth of water. The attack would have to be made by sixty-fours and smaller, and the Danes would know that under no circumstances could they be reinforced. [Bridport] He credited himself

William Domett, Esq.,
Rear Admiral of the White Squadron,
engraved by William Ridley after a
miniature by Robert Bowyer, published
by Joyce Gold, 103 Shoe Lane,
31 January 1806.

with persuading Parker to change his mind, although *London*'s captain, Robert Waller Otway, later made virtually the same claim, based on the same argument.

When the fleet finally anchored close north of Copenhagen on the night of 30 March, Domett accompanied Parker, Nelson, Rear-Admiral Thomas Graves and Colonel Stewart on board *Amazon* (38), commanded by Captain Riou, to reconnoitre the enemy position. He was also one of Parker's council of war when Nelson obtained an order to command an attack against the southern end of the Danish line. As the youngest officer present, Domett had been the first to speak, and urged the importance of making the attack. Domett of course remained with Parker's flag during the action, and he tried to dissuade Parker from sending his recall order to Nelson, which Nelson famously refused to see.

Following his return with Nelson from the Baltic, Domett was asked for by Admiral Collingwood to be his captain of the fleet in the Channel fleet; he served there until the peace of Amiens, when he apparently was made a commodore on the coast of Ireland. When French troop movements led to a renewal of the war, Collingwood asked Domett to return to the Channel fleet in his old post. There he continued to serve until he was promoted rear-admiral on 23 April 1804 and appointed to the North Sea station, a post he declined on the grounds of ill health.

Apart from his unusually arduous naval service, Domett was a member of parliament from 1795 to 1816. He never married.

About six months after he came ashore he was appointed one of the commissioners for reforming the civil affairs of the navy, and on 9 May 1808 he was appointed to the Board of Admiralty, where he remained until 23 October 1813. He was promoted vice-admiral on 25 October 1809, and on 27 October 1813 he was appointed commander-in-chief at Plymouth in succession to Sir Robert Calder, resigning in March 1814 because of a foot injury. He was nominated KCB on 2 January 1815, and GCB on 16 May 1820. He died with the rank of admiral on 19 May 1828, aged seventy-three, in Hawkchurch, Dorset.

Lt: 27 December 1777
Capt: 9 September 1782
R-Adm: 23 April 1804
V-Adm: 25 October 1809
Adm: 12 August 1819

DONNELLY

ADMIRAL SIR ROSS DONNELLY, KCB, is best remembered as the officer who commanded the inshore frigates which Lord Nelson stationed off Toulon on his return to the Mediterranean station following the peace of Amiens.

He was born about the year 1761, son of Dr Francis Donnelly, MD, and entered the navy in 1776. After service under Vice-Admiral Arbuthnot in the American war, he was commissioned on 27 September 1781 a lieutenant of *Morning Star*, sloop. Being out of employment following the treaty of Versailles, he served as a mate of an East Indiaman from 1785 to the French declaration of war in 1793.

Having returned to the Royal Navy, he served as first lieutenant of *Montagu* (74) in the battle of the Glorious First of June, and assumed command on the death of her captain, James Montagu. By tradition he had a strong claim for promotion to post rank, but this did not happen. Instead, he was promoted commander on 6 July 1794, and did not make the step to post captain until 24 June 1795. Although he applied for one, neither was he given a gold medal, on the grounds that they were being given only to officers of post rank at the time of the action. He commanded in succession *Pegasus* (28), in which he served in the North Sea under Admiral Duncan, and *Maidstone* (32) on the coast of France, in 1801 bringing home a valuable convoy from Oporto, for which he received the usual present of plate from the merchants of that place.

Late in 1801 he was appointed to the *Narcissus* (32) and ordered to transport the ambassador of Algiers to his country, to proceed to the Aegean to undertake astronomical observations, and then to take charge of the embarkation of the British army in Egypt, with the temporary rank of commodore. In Egypt he encountered Colonel Sebastiani from Toulon, whose orders to make a political and military survey of Egypt were to be the final cause of the collapse of the peace of Amiens. He was in Genoa when he learnt of the departure of the British ambassador from Paris, and on his own initiative he evacuated the port of British shipping prior to the arrival of French forces. On the arrival of Lord Nelson to take command of the Mediterranean fleet, Donnelly was put in command of the frigates watching Toulon.

In 1805 *Narcissus* formed part of the naval force under Sir Home Popham which recaptured the Cape of Good Hope, and then proceeded without orders to seize Buenos Aires. Donnelly was entrusted with carrying home the dispatch announcing this development. He was immediately appointed to command *Ardent* (64) and ordered to escort reinforcements of troops to Rio de la Plata. On arrival it was learnt that the Spanish army had successfully driven the British occupying force out of Buenos Aires, and it was decided to seize Montevideo, in which operation Donnelly was put in command of the sailors landed to bring up the artillery. On his return to England he successfully sued Sir Home for his taking a flag officer's part of the prize money when he was entitled to only a temporary commodore's share.

In 1808 he was given command of *Invincible* (74), in which he served under Rear-Admiral Purvis off Cadiz, and successfully undertook the task of hurrying to sea the Spanish ships in the Caracas to prevent their falling to the French. Having proceeded to join Lord Collingwood off Toulon in 1810, he was obliged by a cataract to resign his command, and although he successfully applied two years later for employment as captain of *Devonshire* (74), the end of the war caused his orders to be rescinded, and Donnelly never again served at sea. He was promoted rear-admiral on 4 June 1814 and nominated a KCB on 28 February 1837, dying with the rank of admiral on 30 September 1840, aged seventy-nine, in London. He was a married man, and had several children, but his wife's name and the date of his marriage are not recorded.

Lt: 27 September 1781
Cmdr: 6 July 1794
Capt: 24 June 1795
R-Adm: 4 June 1814
V-Adm: 27 May 1825
Adm: 28 June 1838

DOUGLAS

CAPTAIN SIR ANDREW SNAPE DOUGLAS played notable parts in the American war and in the first years of the war against the French Republic. He is best known through his letters to his maternal uncle Captain Sir Andrew Snape Hamond, RN, baronet, comptroller of the navy.

He was born on 8 October 1761 in Edinburgh, a son of William Douglas of Springfield near Edinburgh, and his wife Lydia, first daughter of Robert Hamond, merchant and shipowner of London. On his father's death in 1770, Captain Hamond entered his name in the books of his ship, *Arethusa* (32), in which they sailed to America and acquainted themselves with its coast and harbours. After service in the West Indies, Douglas rejoined his uncle in 1775 in *Roebuck* (44) at the outbreak of the American war. He was commissioned lieutenant on 23 April 1778, and promoted master and commander on 16 February 1780 with appointment to the armed ship *Germain*, but instead of joining her he took command of a floating battery at the siege of Charlestown. After the fall of that town he was made post captain by being appointed, on 15 May 1780, to the captured American frigate *Providence* (32).

He wrote:

> In July, 1781, the *Roebuck* being ordered to England, I was appointed captain of the *Chatham*, of 54 guns; in command of which ship I continued, during the war, upon the coast of North America. During the first

> part of the time (about three months) I was employed, from my knowledge of the coast, as conductor of the fleet under Admiral Graves, in a cruise to the Bay of Boston, which was at that time the rendezvous of the French fleet: and during the latter part of the same period, (about two years) I was commander of a squadron of frigates, and senior officer upon the northern coast of North America: having taken or destroyed in the last 20 months, 50 sail of vessels from the enemy, one French frigate, of 36 guns, the *Magicienne*, and several stout privateers.
>
> NC 25.354

By his capture of *Magicienne* he thwarted a French plan to attack British mast ships in the St John river.

During the peace he first studied naval architecture at Chatham dockyard, and then served afloat, mostly in the Mediterranean, but latterly in the Channel, when his command, the 12-pounder frigate *Southampton* (32), was appointed guardship at Weymouth and he had the honour of taking King George for his first voyage in a warship. Afterwards the king appointed Douglas a knight bachelor on 13 September 1789. He married Anne Burgess of New York, and the couple had one son and two daughters.

On the French declaration of war in February 1793 he was appointed to command the *Phaeton* (38) in which he captured a French privateer and her prize, the Spanish galleon *St Jago*, for which Douglas could claim prize salvage. Lord Howe made him commodore in charge of the fleet frigates, which was a hitherto unknown appointment; he sometimes served on detached cruises but mostly worked with the fleet. On 8 April 1794 he was moved into *Queen Charlotte* (100) as flag captain, and wrote to his uncle asking him to convey his thanks to Lord Chatham, the first lord. As Howe's flag captain he fought in the engagements of the Glorious First of June in 1794, and remained on deck even after receiving what was eventually to prove a mortal wound in the head. He was appointed colonel of the Marines on 1 June 1795, and, continuing as *Queen Charlotte*'s captain after

Lord Howe struck his flag, he fought with Lord Bridport on 23 June 1795 off L'Orient. This was to be his last action, and to him should have come what honours were earned on that day.

A brother officer wrote:

> By watching every breath of wind that blew from the Heavens, and trimming incessantly to give it with the best advantage to the sails, Sir Andrew Douglas, soon after the morning broke on the 23rd, had the satisfaction to find himself within two miles of the enemy's rear. Undismayed by the fire which they soon poured upon the *Queen Charlotte*, and the slender prospect of an essential support, he appeared willing, if necessary, to sacrifice his ship for the public benefit. She was seen to approach the enemy with a silent intrepidity, that at least deserved a pointed notice; and with even royals and steering sails set, she dashed amidst the thickest of the enemy. Sir A. Douglas thus received the broadsides of 5 or 6 of their ships, and the stern chasers of 3 of them at the same time; but closing with the nearest, four of them were brought into one point, by which the effect of their guns was greatly diminished.
>
> Close as the French were to the shelter of their own coasts, it was only on such a display of gallantry that the British admiral could build a hope of checking their retreat... *NC 25.365*

Bridport apparently greeted Douglas with the warmest thanks for bringing the French to action, but in his public letter he was more guarded, much to the disgust of th e editor of the *Naval Chronicle*. He did not receive any particular recognition from government or the court.

His persistent headaches and declining health eventually forced him to come ashore, and on 4 June 1797 he died. An autopsy revealed a brain tumour.

Lt: 23 April 1778
M-C: 16 February 1780
Capt: 15 May 1780

DOWNMAN

ADMIRAL HUGH DOWNMAN was another sailor who progressed from humble birth to the highest ranks in the navy, but only because of his longevity. His most notable services were as flag captain.

He was born on 29 October 1765 in Plympton near Plymouth, Devon, and a few weeks short of eleven years of age entered the navy on 10 October 1776, as an able seaman on board *Thetis* (32), Captain Michael Graham. On 14 August 1778 he joined *Arethusa* (32) under the command of Captain Samuel Marshall, and he was rated midshipman a few days before his ship was cast away on the coast of France when in pursuit of the enemy. The crew were made prisoners of war, but apparently Downman was well treated, and he was exchanged in January 1780, at which time Captain Marshall was appointed to command the 12-pounder frigate *Emerald* (32) and took Downman with him. He served on board *Edgar* (74) commanded by Commodore Hotham during the relief of Gibraltar in 1782, and was examined in nautical knowledge in 1783, but he was not commissioned lieutenant until 5 March 1790 in the appropriately named *Perseverance* (36), during the Nootka Sound crisis. In the meantime he had served in *Queen* (90), *Triumph* (74), *Barfleur* (90) and *Crown* (64), which were respectively flying the flags of Admiral John Montagu and Vice-Admiral Lord Hood, and Commodore the Honourable William Cornwallis's broad pendant. He served in the East Indies in *Crown*, and then in *Perseverance* under Captain Isaac Smith, finally returning to England in May 1792 in *Crown* with Captain Robert Manners Sutton.

Shortly before the outbreak of war in 1793 he was appointed fourth lieutenant of *Alcide* (74) under the command of Captain Robert Linzee, and went to the Mediterranean, where Linzee was made a commodore and was sent to Corsica to assist General Paoli in the defeat of the French garrisons. When Linzee was promoted rear-admiral and hoisted his flag in *Windsor Castle* (90) in June 1794, Downman accompanied him as second lieutenant. In October he was appointed to *Victory* (100) flying Admiral Sir John Jervis's flag, and was still serving in her during the action off Cape St Vincent on 14 February 1797. When Jervis moved into the *Ville de Paris* (110) a few weeks after the battle, Downman accompanied him as first lieutenant. On 16 July 1797, or 26 July according to the Admiralty clerk's correction of his record of service, he was promoted commander of *Speedy*, sloop, stationed at Oporto, and in her fought a hard and

Captain Hugh Downman,
engraved by H R Cook from an original painting,
published by Joyce Gold, 103 Shoe Lane,
31 January 1809.

drawn battle with a French privateer, *Le Papillon*. As reward he was made post captain on 1 September 1798, seniority dating from his confirmation in rank on 26 December.

In the spring of 1800 Downman was employed on detached service in company with *Chamelion* and the Neapolitan brig *Strombolo* to blockade the fortress of Savona. Famine brought its surrender on 16 May, and Downman signed the articles of capitulation. The French victory at Marengo led to the occupation of Tuscany, and Downman was sent to destroy the fortifications at La Spezia. He also took charge of the art treasures in the Uffizi

Gallery in Florence and transported them to Palermo. He commanded the 12-pounder French prize *Santa Dorothea* (42) from September 1798 until April 1801 or more likely 1802, and was subsequently awarded the Turkish gold medal for distinguished services on the coast of Egypt. He succeeded Jahleel Brenton as flag captain to Rear-Admiral Sir James Saumarez in *Caesar* (80) and returned to the coast of Portugal and the Gibraltar station.

He married on 23 June 1803, at St Thomas Portsmouth, Dorothea Marie, daughter of Peter Palmer of Portsmouth. The couple had one son and two daughters.

On 3 January 1804, following the renewal of war, Downman was again appointed flag captain to Saumarez, now promoted to vice-admiral and flying his flag in *Diomede* (50) at Guernsey and later in the North Sea. In November 1805 he transferred to *Diadem* (64) as flag captain to Commodore Sir Home Popham during the expedition to capture the Cape of Good Hope. He was entrusted with bringing home Popham's dispatches, after which he rejoined *Diomede* in the river Plate in October 1806 following the unauthorised capture of Montevideo. Perhaps some of the taint from that failed expedition rubbed off on him. When *Diomede* paid off on 22 June 1807 Downman's next appointments were to command *Assistance* (formerly *Royal Oak,* 74) and *Vengeance* (formerly a French prize, 52), prison ships at Portsmouth. His last command was to be the Danish prize *Princess Carolina* (74), to which he was appointed on 23 January 1811 and served off Cherbourg, in the Baltic and then in Greenland waters, the North Sea and finally Madeira. He swallowed the anchor on 28 September 1811, and although he reached flag rank in 1825 he never was given a command.

He died with the rank of admiral on 4 January 1858, aged ninety-two, at Hambledon, Hampshire.

Lt: 5 March 1790
Cmdr: 16 (or 26) July 1797
Capt: 26 December 1798
R-Adm: 27 May 1825
V-Adm: 10 January 1837
Adm: 24 April 1847

DUCKWORTH

ADMIRAL SIR JOHN THOMAS DUCKWORTH, BARONET, GCB, is best known for fighting five ships of the line off San Domingo in 1806 with a more capable but only slightly larger force and capturing or destroying the entire enemy squadron. As the squadrons were coming into firing range he signalled his ships, 'This is Glorious' and 'Engage the Enemy more Closely'. He also has some notoriety for the futile raid he was ordered to mount on Constantinople the following year, and a great deal more for the lengths to which he went to enrich himself. But he acquired the respect of Admirals Howe and Jervis for his careful attention to the education and training of the young men who were introduced by him into the navy, and was kept in employment despite his grumbles.

He was born on 9 February 1748 in Leatherhead, Surrey, a son of the Revd Henry Duckworth, curate and afterwards vicar of Stoke Poges, rector of Fulmer, Buckinghamshire, and canon of Windsor, and his wife Sarah, née Johnson, of Ickenham, Uxbridge, Middlesex. He was sent to Eton College in 1757 when only nine years old, and entered the navy on 22 February 1759 as a captain's servant in *Namur* (90) with the patronage of Admiral Edward Boscawen. He was at the destruction of de la Clue's squadron in Lagos bay, and after Boscawen left *Namur* was at the battle of Quiberon Bay in 1759. He next served in *Prince of Orange* (70) under Captain Samuel Wallis, and then in *Guernsey* (48) under Captain Hugh Palliser, commander of the Newfoundland station. He passed his lieutenant's examination in 1766, and served several months as acting lieutenant, but was not confirmed in his rank until 14 November 1771 with appointment to *Rainbow* (44) under Captain Charles Fielding. They moved together to *Kent* (74), and both survived the explosion which destroyed her quarterdeck in Plymouth Sound. Early in 1776 he was made first lieutenant in the 12-pounder frigate *Diamond* (32), still under Feilding's command. Soon after their arrival in Rhode Island the accidental discharge of a gun, which killed five men on board a transport, led to his being tried by

court martial along with the gunner, gunner's mate and gun crew. They were exonerated, but the trial had been flawed because neither the men's names, nor the fact that it was a capital charge of murder they were facing, had been included in the warrant. Admiral Hawke insisted on a retrial to preempt any civil proceedings, and the new court merely confirmed the findings of the first court.

He married on 16 July 1776, in Stoke Damerel, Devon, Anne, daughter and heiress of John Wallis of Fentonwoonwith near Camelford, Cornwall. But he did not long remain in England. The couple had one son and one daughter, born in June 1782 and September 1784.

In March 1779 Duckworth was transferred to Admiral Byron's flagship, *Princess Royal* (90). When he was sent to look into Port Royal, Martinique, to assess the strength of the enemy fleet, he sent in an exaggerated estimate because he did not come close enough to see that some of the ships were armed *en flute*. But he did well in the action off Granada on 6 July, and ten days later, on 21 July 1779, he was promoted master and commander of *Rover*, sloop. Less than a year later, on 16 June 1780, he was posted into *Terrible* (74). Soon afterwards he returned to *Princess Royal* as flag captain to Sir Joshua Rowley, and served at Jamaica in 1781 before bringing a convoy home. After making three cruises in the Channel, he went on half pay on 7 April 1783 until the Nootka Sound crisis in 1790 when he was appointed to command *Bombay Castle* (74).

With the outbreak of war in 1793 Duckworth was transferred to *Orion* (74) in the Channel fleet under Admiral Lord Howe, and took part in the battles of the Glorious First of June in 1794. He was one of the few Howe mentioned in dispatches, which led to his receiving from King George a gold medal. Early in 1794 he was transferred into *Leviathan* (74) and served in the Leeward Islands under Admiral William Parker, who suddenly fell ill and departed for England, leaving Duckworth somewhat to his dismay in command, with orders to act as commodore.

He returned home in April 1797 to find that his wife was dying. To add to his troubles, *Leviathan* was almost immediately caught up in the mutiny at Plymouth. He was soon restored to command, and was made colonel of the marines on 8 June 1797, but his wife died in August. Still in *Leviathan* he served in the blockade of Brest until in November he was detached to the Irish station as senior captain under Vice-Admiral Kingsmill. He then joined the Mediterranean fleet in Rear-Admiral Sir Roger Curtis's squadron under Admiral the earl of St Vincent. In November 1798 he was again ordered to fly a broad pendant and sent to cover landing operations at Minorca. When the general commanding, the Honourable Charles Stuart, was nominated a KB, Duckworth thought he should receive the same, or be awarded a baronetcy, but he failed to convince St Vincent or Lord Spencer. He was, however, promoted to rear-admiral on 14 February 1799 and ordered to hoist his flag in his own ship, which was considered an honour. He took part in the pursuit of Vice-Admiral Bruix, spent some time serving under Nelson at Naples and in the defence of Minorca, and then assumed command of the blockade of Cadiz.

His wealth was to be increased considerably when on 5 April 1800 he had the good fortune to intercept a Spanish convoy from Peru which was mostly captured, yielding him perhaps as much as £75,000. His fortune was again increased when in March and April 1801 he was commander-in-chief of the Leeward Islands station. On the formation of the Armed Neutrality he and General Trigge captured the Swedish and Danish islands, which were almost immediately returned following the battle of Copenhagen and the dissolution of the northern alliance. This time he was made a KB, on 6 June 1801. But he did not get any leave to return home

Sir John Thomas Duckworth, K.B., Vice Admiral of the White Squadron, engraved by H R Cook after Robert Bowyer, published by Joyce Gold, 103 Shoe Lane, 30 April 1807.

and see his daughter during the peace. His son came out to the West Indies as an aid to General Trigge, and Duckworth succeeded to the command-in-chief at Jamaica in 1803 at the death of Lord Hugh Seymour. Following the renewal of war, Duckworth directed the operations which led to the defeat of the French in San Domingo. He was promoted vice-admiral on 23 April 1804.

On his supersession he returned to England in *Acasta* (40) laded with booty, removing Captain James Wood from command, allegedly because he would not countenance violating the article of war that forbade warships carrying merchandise. On Wood's complaint, Duckworth was court-martialled, but, when he claimed the booty was all gifts, and the teak planks intended for his house, he was acquitted of the charges, which were termed 'gross, scandalous, malicious, shameful and highly subversive of the discipline and good government of His Majesty's service'. He was 'fully and honourably' acquitted. When Wood's brother made a motion in the House of Commons that the proceedings of the court martial, and the customs record of duty paid on imports in the *Acasta*, should be laid on the table, it failed to be carried.

The Admiralty expressed its approval of Duckworth by appointing him to succeed Lord Northesk as third in command under Nelson, but he missed taking part in the battle of Trafalgar because his flagship was not ready in time, and also because he insisted on waiting for his own officers to join him, and for his quartet of fiddlers.

In September 1806 Duckworth was ordered to join the blockade of Cadiz, flying his flag in *Superb* (74). He arrived on 15 November, and assumed command from Lord Collingwood. Two weeks later he raised the blockade to chase a squadron believed to have got out of Rochefort, and on his way back to his station he encountered a French squadron of equal force which he pursued, coming within seven hours' sailing of the enemy but turning back because he had so outsailed the rest of the squadron that he did not think they would be able to join him should he risk an unequal contest with six French ships. After detaching the *Powerful* to reinforce the squadron in the East Indies should that be the destination of the French, he ran to the Leeward Islands in order to replenish with water.

He might well have been court-martialled for lifting the blockade of Cadiz, or for abandoning his chase of a flying enemy, but he was to be more fortunate. At St Christopher's, known as St Kitts, he was joined by Rear-Admiral Alexander Cochrane with two 74-gun ships, and with this addition of force Duckworth, with seven of the line, encountered on 6 February a French squadron of five ships of the line, of which one was of 120 guns, and two frigates under Vice-Admiral Leissègues. At the battle of San Domingo he captured three of the enemy and drove the other two ashore and burnt them. The frigates escaped, but this was the most nearly complete victory of the age of sail, if one of relatively small proportions. All the flag officers, of whom there were three, and all the captains were awarded gold medals and the subordinate admirals were given honours, but Duckworth thought he had been ill used in being given only a pension of £1,000 a year, and loudly complained that he should have had an Irish peerage. He did have some right to complain, as he had not seen his daughter since 1797 and she was now twenty-two years old and married.

Later that year he rejoined the Mediterranean fleet under Collingwood's command, flying his flag in *Royal George* (100), and was given orders to proceed to Constantinople to provide for the safety of the British ambassador, Charles Arbuthnot. The operation was a fiasco, because the ambassador had already made a safe exit from Constantinople. With the help of French engineers the fortifications of the Dardanelles forts had been strengthened to a for-

midable degree. Nevertheless he ran them, on 19 February 1807, and made his way to the Bosporus, but there he was becalmed and could not raise anchor because of the currents. Moored eight miles from the walls of Constantinople, his threats were without force. It remained only to run the forts again outbound. He was subjected to considerable criticism, but perhaps unfairly.

Nevertheless, his honour reasonably intact, his wealth legendary, and ten years after Anne's death, Duckworth married for a second time on 14 May 1807 in Crediton, Devon, uniting with Susannah Catherine, second daughter of the Right Revd Dr William Buller, bishop of Exeter. She gave him three more sons. He was appointed second in command in the Channel, and even pursued an imaginary French squadron around the Atlantic. He was promoted admiral on 31 July 1810. From 1810 to 1813 he was governor of Newfoundland, and on his return he at last received his baronetcy, on 2 November 1813. He was member of parliament for the Admiralty seat of New Romney, Kent, from 1812 to 31 August 1817. He was nominated a GCB on 2 January 1815, and was appointed commander-in-chief Plymouth. Here he distinguished himself by refusing to receive a social call from General Napoleon, sometime emperor. He oversaw the preparations for Sir Israel Pellew's expedition to Algiers in 1816, and died on 31 August 1817, aged sixty-nine, being buried with great pomp at Topsham near Exeter. Susannah lived on to 27 April 1840.

Lt: 14 November 1771
M-C: 21 July 1779
Capt: 16 June 1780
R-Adm: 14 February 1799
V-Adm: 23 April 1804
Adm: 31 July 1810

DUFF

CAPTAIN GEORGE DUFF is best known for the series of letters he wrote to his wife in the last months before his death at the battle of Trafalgar. On 23 September he wrote that their son Norwich, who was a midshipman, had joined him, having arrived on *Aurora* (28). A week later, on 1 October 1805, less than three weeks before the action, he

The Late Captain George Duff,
engraved by William Ridley from a painting
by Geroff of Edinburgh, published by
Joyce Gold, 103 Shoe Lane,
30 April 1806.

wrote that 'On Saturday night we were joined by Lord Nelson with the *Victory*, *Ajax*, *Thunderer*, and the *Euryalus*; when I had the happiness of receiving yours, my ever dearest wife, of the 8th September, and the papers up to the 7th. Many, many thanks! I dined with his Lordship yesterday, and had a very merry dinner; he certainly is the pleasantest Admiral I ever served under. I hope the Austrians and Russians will make quick work with Buonapart, and let us get to our homes once more; when I expect to be an Admiral before I am called upon again.' On the 10th he wrote to complain about the rain which he was afraid would 'spoil my fine work, having been employed for this week past to paint the ship... *a la Nelson*, which most of the fleet are doing. He is so good and pleasant a man, that we all wish to do what he likes, without any kind of orders. I have been myself very lucky with most of my Admirals; but I really think the present the pleasantest I have met with.' Finally, on the morning of the 21st, he wrote: 'My Dearest Sophia, I have just time to tell you we are going into action with the combined fleet. I hope and

trust in God that we shall all behave as becomes us, and that I may yet have the happiness of taking my beloved wife and children in my arms. Norwich is quite well, and happy. I have however, ordered him off the quarter-deck. Yours ever, and most truly, George Duff. NC 15.289–93

The date of Duff's birth is not known, but he was born in Banff, and baptised on 22 February 1764. He was the youngest son of James Duff, who was a relative of the earl of Fife. The name of his mother, who died six weeks after George was born, is not known, but she was a Skene of Rubislaw, Aberdeenshire. George entered the navy in November 1777 but little is known about his early years at sea. He was commissioned lieutenant on 15 September 1779. Reportedly he had been in thirteen engagements before he was sixteen years of age, and was a lieutenant in *Montagu* (74) when she weathered the great hurricane of 1780, totally dismasted and thrown on her beam ends. How to get promotion was the great problem, and in Jamaica he was introduced in 1782 to Admiral Rodney, who was willing to put forward the great-nephew of Vice-Admiral Robert Duff, but Rodney had been recalled before news of the battle of the Saintes reached England, and had no time to deliver on his undertaking. Finally in 1787 Duff had to return to Scotland to recover his health, and there he was befriended by the duke and duchess of Gordon, who pressed his name upon the Right Honourable Henry Dundas, minister for Scotland and at the time treasurer of the navy. Dundas made a strong representation to the Admiralty Board, and Duff was promoted master and commander on 21 September 1790 during the Nootka Sound crisis, being given command of *Martin*, sloop.

This preferment enabled him to marry, on 6 May 1791 at Fintry House, Monifieth near Forfar, Angus, his childhood friend Sophia, second daughter of Alexander Dirom of Muiresh, Aberdeenshire, Scotland. The couple made their home in Edinburgh, and had two sons and three daughters, the eldest son, Norwich, eventually reaching the rank of vice-admiral.

On 9 February 1793, days after the outbreak of war with France, Duff was made post captain by the earl of Chatham, the first lord, whom he had met in the previous war. He was first appointed to a frigate in which he had good chances of prize money, but he was persuaded to relinquish that prospect in order to take command of *Duke* (90) flying the broad pendant of the Honourable Commodore John Murray. *Duke* led the attack on the batteries at Martinique, and her magazine had just been secured when she was struck by lightning and so badly damaged that she had to return to England. Duff was then appointed to the *Ambuscade* (32) and served in her and in the fir-built 18-pounder frigate *Glenmore* (36) in the North Sea and on the Irish coast. In 1801 he was appointed to the *Vengeance* (74), part of the Channel fleet. She was detached to reinforce the fleet sent to Copenhagen and then sent to Bantry Bay. There her crew refused to join in the mutiny being hatched, and when they returned to Portsmouth they alone were trusted with shore leave.

On the conclusion of peace, instead of returning to his family, he and the crew of *Vengeance* were ordered to proceed to Jamaica to watch the actions of the French fleet, which had been sent to recover San Domingo from the former black slaves who had established an independent government. He was back in home waters long enough to have eighteen months' leave with his family before war broke out again. His friends again solicited for him an appointment, and while waiting for one to be offered he helped in the preparation of the Firth of Forth to resist any invasion attempt.

In April 1804 he was appointed to command the *Mars* (74), which he joined at sea off Ferrol. For the next year *Mars* was part of the Channel fleet blockading Brest, and then in May 1805 she was sent as part of a detachment under Vice-Admiral Collingwood to watch Cadiz. When Vice-Admiral Lord Nelson arrived to assume command, Duff was appointed to command the advanced or inshore squadron stationed midway between the frigates watching the harbour entrance and the battle fleet, which kept as much as possible out of sight over the horizon. During the manoeuvre period of the battle of Trafalgar, Duff had the responsibility for relaying signals from the frigates to the flag-

ship. Then *Mars* was ordered to lead the lee division in the head-on attack on the Franco-Spanish line, but as she was a slow sailer she was passed by the *Royal Sovereign* (100) with Collingwood's flag, and by *Belleisle*. The ships were heavily engaged when Duff was decapitated by a cannonball.

Soon after the battle, Admiral Collingwood moved Norwich Duff to *Euryalus* (36) commanded by the Honourable Captain Henry Blackwood, who undertook to take charge of his friend's son. Norwich wrote home:

> My Dear Mamma,
> You cannot possibly imagine how unwilling I am to begin this melancholy letter. However, as you must unavoidably hear of the fate of dear Papa, I write you these few lines to request you to bear it as patiently as you can. He died like a Hero, having gallantly led his ship into action, and his memory will ever be dear to his King and Country, and his Friends... [NC 15.293]

Captain Richard Dudley Oliver, who had arrived at Trafalgar the day after the battle in the French prize *Melpomene* (46) and took part in the work of securing the prizes and damaged ships, assumed command of *Mars*. A monument to Duff's memory was erected in St Paul's Cathedral.

Lt: 15 September 1779
M-C: 21 September 1790
Capt: 9 February 1793

DUNCAN

ADMIRAL ADAM DUNCAN, VISCOUNT DUNCAN, BARON OF CAMPERDOWN, a gigantic and handsome man, and a deeply religious one who was greatly respected by his crew, was a late bloomer. Although Admiral Keppel recognised his quiet qualities, it was not until his appointment to command in the North Sea in 1795 after years of unemployment that he showed that his abilities matched his stature.

He was born on 1 July 1731 in Dundee, Angus, the third son of Alexander Duncan of Lundie, Forfarshire, provost of Dundee from 1744 to 1746.

His mother was Helen, the youngest daughter of John Haldane of Gleneagles, Perthshire, member of parliament. He is believed to have entered the navy on 10 April 1746 on board *Trial* (10) under the command of his cousin, Lieutenant Robert Haldane, and transferred with him to *Shoreham* (24) in February 1748. In 1749 he was transferred to *Centurion* (50) under the command of Captain, later Admiral, Keppel, who rated him midshipman. Duncan served with him for three years, eventually becoming a close friend. His examination occurred on 4 October 1752, but he was not commissioned until 10 January 1755 when Keppel was put in command of the naval force carrying General Braddock to America, when Keppel strongly supported his appointment to *Norwich* (50). Once in North America, he was returned by Keppel into his flagship, *Centurion*, in August transferred with him into *Swiftsure*, and in January 1756 moved again into *Torbay* (74). In 1758 he took part in Keppel's attack on the French fort at Goree, when he was slightly wounded, and soon afterwards was appointed first lieutenant of *Torbay* (74). He was promoted on 21 September 1759 master and commander of a hired ship, *Royal Exchange*, and was made post captain on 25 February 1761 when he was appointed to command *Valiant* (74) flying Keppel's broad pennant as commodore under Sir George Pocock in the expedition to capture Belleisle. This successful amphibious operation led to Keppel's being sent to command a division of the ships employed covering the landing of the troops for an assault on Havana. Duncan was put in command of the assault boats. He also, apparently, speeded the signing of the Spanish capitulation by setting fire to the ships of the line on the stocks in Havana dockyard,

The Right Honourable Lord Viscount Duncan, Admiral of the Blue Squadron, engraving by William Ridley after Lemuel F Abbot, published by Burney and Gold, Shoe Lane, 1 September 1800.

thus removing an issue that was delaying the Spanish signature and also, incidentally, reducing the prize money. For the latter reason the matter was kept quiet.

He was unemployed during the years of peace, living for several years in Bath and Cheltenham to recover his health after service in the tropics, and then returning to Dundee. Nor was he immediately employed on the outbreak of civil war in the American colonies. He married on 6 June 1777 Henrietta, third daughter of Robert Dundas, president of the Court of Session and member of parliament for Edinburghshire, and niece of Henry Dundas, first Lord Melville. It was only when the war spread back to Europe that he was appointed, in May 1778, to command *Suffolk* (74). She formed part of the Channel fleet commanded by Admiral Keppel. The only notable part he played in the opening years of the American war was to participate in both the courts martial following the battle of Ushant on 27 July 1778, first on his friend Keppel and afterwards on Sir Hugh Palliser, who was the second in command. Evidently neither party found fault with him. In December he had been moved into *Monarch* (74) and, to prevent him taking part in Palliser's trial, the Admiralty had ordered her to move from Portsmouth to St Helens. The first lord, the earl of Sandwich, was not a neutral in the admiral's quarrels, because Keppel was an adherent of the marquis of Rockingham's opposition, which was posing as a party in favour of the aspirations of the American colonists. *Monarch*'s crew, however, had refused to weigh anchor until they were paid, with the result that Duncan was at Palliser's trial.

In the summer of 1779, when the combined Franco-Spanish fleet dominated the Channel and invasion was feared, *Monarch* was part of Sir Charles Hardy's fleet. In December she formed part of Sir George Rodney's force intended to break the siege of Gibraltar. On 16 January 1780 she was the first to get into action in the 'Moonlight Battle' against the Spanish squadron under Don Juan de Langara. Duncan obliged *San Augustin* (70) to strike her colours, although he was unable to take possession of her, and she eventually made it into Cadiz. *Monarch* returned to England with Robert Digby, and when she was ordered to join Rodney in the West Indies in 1781 Duncan resigned his command for reasons of health.

When in March 1782 Rockingham came to power, and Keppel was appointed first lord of the Admiralty, Duncan was appointed to command *Blenheim* (90). He served in Lord Howe's relief of Gibraltar, but again left his ship when she was ordered to the West Indies. He returned to England and was appointed to command *Foudroyant* (84), and after the peace he commanded a guardship, *Edgar*, for three years. He was promoted rear-admiral on 24 September 1787, and to vice-admiral on 1 February 1793 on the French declaration of war, but was unemployed until February 1795.

His appointment as commander-in-chief North Sea was providential for his country. Apparently it was made, by Lord Spencer, only as a result of a conversation with Henry Dundas, whose niece Duncan had married, and whose Edinburgh house he had purchased. Duncan was duly ordered to hoist his flag on 11 March in *Prince George* (98), from which he soon moved to *Venerable* (74), which was more suitable for the shallow Dutch coast. He was promoted a full admiral on 1 June 1795. For five years he was charged with watching the Dutch fleet at the Texel. From July he also had within his station a strong Russian squadron, commanded by Vice-Admiral Hanickoff. Tsar Paul was to appoint him to the imperial order of Alexander Nevski for his effective relationship with the allied commander. He became a close associate of Spencer and of William Pitt, who, as lord warden of the Cinque Ports, resided at Walmer Castle at the Downs, where Duncan visited from time to time.

The violent sequel to the mutiny at Spithead which broke out at the Nore on 12 May 1797 and spread to the North Sea squadron at Yarmouth fully tested Duncan's abilities at a time when the Dutch were expected to sortie in support of an invasion. The mutineers stopped merchant shipping entering or leaving the Thames in the hope of forcing the government's hand. Eventually the supply of victuals to the fleet was cut off, and the forts at Tilbury, Gravesend and Sheerness were prepared to fire red-hot shot. The buoyage in the Thames estuary was removed to deter attempts by the mutineers to surrender to the Dutch, and the Revolutionary French, at the Texel. Duncan was reduced to keeping up the appearance of a blockade of the Dutch fleet using only his own *Venerable*, and *Adamant* (52) in which Vice-Admiral Richard Onslow flew his flag. Duncan, and Captain William Hotham of *Adamant*, persuaded, and perhaps intimidated, their crews into continuing their duty.

Gradually the ships' companies turned against their leaders, fights broke out, and finally one by one the ships sailed away to surrender. Richard Parker, who had allowed himself to be identified as leader of the mutineers was hanged with twenty-eight delegates, and others were flogged round the fleet.

Despite the bitterness left behind by the mutiny, when the Dutch sailed in October under Admiral de Winter, too late to support the attempted invasion of Ireland, the crews of the Nore ships delivered a stunning and hard-fought victory at the battle of Camperdown. Duncan's tactics, an attack in two divisions in a ragged line abreast on the enemy van and rear, seeking to cut through the Dutch to prevent their withdrawal to leeward, was a logical development of those employed by Howe at the First of June, and was a foreshadowing of those used by Nelson at Trafalgar. His intention had been to comb the Dutch line simultaneously, but he recognised that any delay to re-form his own line would allow the Dutch to adopt a defensive position in water too shallow for the heavier British ships to follow. *Venerable* was herself heavily engaged and was surrounded by enemy ships. Duncan later said that only he and the ship's pilot were left alive on the quarterdeck. When eventually the

Dutch flagship, *Vrijheid*, surrendered, only Admiral de Winter was unhurt on his own quarterdeck. Nine Dutch ships were captured, having been severely damaged. The rest escaped, taking advantage of a gale. No sooner had the firing ceased than Duncan called for the chaplain, and dropped to his knees in unfeigned thanks to God for their victory and deliverance.

Duncan was created Baron Duncan of Lundie and Viscount Duncan of Camperdown on 21 October 1797, and granted a pension of £2,000 per annum for himself and his two succeeding heirs. He was also granted freedoms and pieces of plate by the City of London and many English and Scottish towns. The surrender of the remaining Dutch ships at the Helder and the Texel in September 1799 to Vice-Admiral Mitchell, serving under Duncan, put an end to any possibility of further action in that quarter, but Duncan remained in his command until he struck his flag on 28 April 1800. He offered his services on the renewal of the war in 1803, but his age was considered too great, and in fact he died of the gout in the stomach on 4 August 1804, aged seventy-three, in Corn Hill near Edinburgh, on his return journey from London. A monument to his memory was erected in St Paul's Cathedral. Henrietta died on 8 December 1832 in Edinburgh.

> Lt: 10 January 1755
> M-C: 21 September 1759
> Capt: 25 February 1761
> R-Adm: 24 September 1787
> V-Adm: 1 February 1793
> Adm: 1 June 1795

DUNCAN

CAPTAIN THE HONOURABLE SIR HENRY DUNCAN, CB, was a fighting captain whose most interesting memorial is perhaps a letter he received from the crew of *Imperieuse* when in early 1813 it was learnt that he was to be transferred to another ship:

> Being informed you are going to leave us, we have taken the liberty at the unanimous request of all hands, to return you our most grateful thanks for your continued

goodness and indulgence to us since we have had the happiness of being under your command. Your continued attention to our comforts is more than we ever experienced in any ship, and more than we pasably can do with any other Captain – from gratitude for your past goodness to us, we humbly hope our best services will still be exerted under your command, and hope you will not lave us. Every one is praying for your continuance with us... Marshall 2.997

Adam and Henrietta Duncan's fourth and youngest son, Henry, was born on 27 April 1786 in Gosport near Portsmouth harbour, where at the time his father commanded a guardship. In 1796 his name was put on the books of his father's flagship, *Venerable* (74), as a volunteer or admiral's retinue, and he may actually have served in her in the North Sea until the end of 1797, when he followed his father to *Kent* (74). He joined *Maidstone* (32) on 6 April 1800 under the command of Captain Ross Donnelly, with whom he was employed in escorting convoys to North America and to Lisbon, and served in the Channel. He had been intended to sail in the *Lutine*, frigate, carrying specie for the British army in the Netherlands, but at the last minute his father changed his mind, and thus saved his son from death when the *Lutine* was wrecked on 9 October 1799 with all hands near the Texel. He followed Captain Donnelly to *Narcissus* (32) at the peace of Amiens. During the peace and in the following year she served in the Mediterranean until ordered home in September 1804. Duncan had been acting in the rank of lieutenant from July 1802, and was commissioned on 21 April 1803. On his return to home waters he transferred into *Royal Sovereign* (100) as junior lieutenant. Following his father's death on 4 August 1804, Lord Nelson offered Duncan temporary command of *Martin* as a means of promoting him, but that scheme fell through, and he returned to *Royal Sovereign* as a volunteer. His rank of commander was confirmed, and he commissioned *Minorca* (18) at Chatham on 21 August 1805, and was made post captain by Lord Collingwood on 18 January

1806, retaining command of *Minorca* until April.

He was unemployed for a while, but was made a CB on 4 June 1805; he was appointed in 1807 to command *Porcupine* (24), which had recently been launched. He sailed to the Mediterranean on 10 July, joined Collingwood off the Dardanelles on 2 September 1807. He served in the Adriatic to enforce the blockade of the French garrisons of Ragusa and Cataro, and in the Mediterranean. Marshall records that Duncan was surprised, and alarmed, when an accident led to *Porcupine*'s full broadside being discharged when close alongside an American merchant vessel – surprised and alarmed that the gunnery was so poor that not a shot went home. Accordingly he paid particular attention to drilling the crew to conduct aimed fire. He never encountered a French frigate during his tour of duty, but the fire from *Porcupine* and from the ships he subsequently commanded proved devastating against shore batteries. Between September 1807 and January 1814, in *Porcupine* and subsequently in *Mercury* (28) and from June 1811 in *Imperieuse* (38), he captured at sea or under enemy batteries fifteen gunboats, one schooner, three armed transports, two privateers, three letters of marque and upwards of 200 merchantmen, with the recapture of six British merchant ships.

He was not happy when ordered to transfer from *Porcupine* into *Mercury* because she was in very poor condition. He was to have transferred a third time, to *Resistance* (38), but refused her after receiving the letter from his crew, and remained in command of *Imperieuse* until she returned home in July 1814. He was then placed in command of *Glasgow*. Following the conclusion of the war he was in June 1818 given command of the *Liffy* (50).

Duncan married on 22 April 1823 Mary Simpson, only daughter of Captain James Coutts Crawford, RN, and granddaughter of Alexander Duncan of Restalig House near Edinburgh. The couple had one son and one daughter. He was appointed naval aide-de-camp to William IV on 4 August 1830 and storekeeper of the Ordnance on 30 December 1830. He was made a KB, and on 13 January 1835 he was made a knight commander of the Guelphic order. He died on 1 November 1835, aged forty-nine, his wife surviving him until 7 April 1885.

Lt: 21 April 1803
Cmdr: 6 November 1804
Capt: 18 January 1806

DUNDONALD – *see* Cochrane

DURHAM

Admiral Sir Philip Charles Henderson Calderwood Durham, GCB, should have borne the responsibility for the sinking of the *Royal George* at Spithead, but escaped punishment. The navy knew what it was doing, for he went on to become a successful frigate captain in the French Revolutionary War, to command *Anson* in the capture of *Hoche* in October 1798, and *Defiance* (74) in two fleet actions in 1805, under Sir Robert Calder and Lord Nelson.

He was baptised on 29 July 1763 in Largo, Fife, the third son of James Durham and his wife Anne, daughter and heiress of Thomas Calderwood of Polton, Edinburghshire. He entered the navy in July 1777 as a captain's servant in *Trident* (64) under Captain John Elliot, who later rated him midshipman. In *Trident* he served in the Downs, North America and the West Indies, but Elliot returned home a few weeks after his arrival at New York, and the nineteenth-century historian J K Laughton wrote that Durham subsequently spent a year enduring the tyrannical regime of Captain Malloy on the North American station before getting his discharge in June 1779, and returning to England as a passenger. DNB Durham's own précis of naval service makes no mention of this. Instead, he says he moved from *Trident* into the storeship *Supply* (26), under the command of Captain John Lockhart Nasmith. *Supply* was eventually burnt, and he came home in *Snake*, sloop, with Captain Douglas. In any event, he was then able to follow Captain Elliot into *Edgar* (74). He continued with him until July 1781, taking part in the defeat of Langara and the relief of Gibraltar, and then was appointed acting lieutenant and signals officer of the *Victory* (100) flying the flag of Rear-Admiral Kempenfelt, whom he followed in May 1782 to the *Royal George* (100).

When on 29 August she sank at Spithead, Durham was officer of the watch. Although the subsequent court martial laid the blame to decay in the ship, the real reason was that water had been allowed to accumulate on her gundeck while the ship was taking on stores. The free liquid eventually compromised the ship's stability. An alert officer of the watch would have prevented the tragedy in which Kempenfelt, amongst hundreds of others, lost his life. Durham was one of those picked up from the water, and was tried for the loss of the ship, but instead of being discharged from the service he returned to *Victory*. He was transferred in September into *Unicorn* (90) under Captain John Dalrymple, in which he was at Lord Howe's relief of Gibraltar, and then proceeded to the West Indies. His commission was confirmed on 26 December 1782.

He returned to England in *Raisonnable* (64) on the conclusion of the peace, and rejoined *Unicorn* when she arrived in Plymouth in October 1783, but for reasons of his health he resigned his position when it was discovered that she was to be employed on the coast of Africa. Instead, he spent two years ashore in France, and then was asked for by Captain Elliot going out in *Salisbury* as commodore to command at Newfoundland. In June or July 1790, at the time of the Nootka Sound incident which might have led to war with Spain, he was appointed signal lieutenant of *Barfleur* (90) by Elliot, who had been promoted rear-admiral in September 1787. When that crisis was settled, he was promoted on 12 November master and commander under orders to take *Daphne* (20) to the West Indies, and return with *Cygnet*, sloop.

About the time of the French declaration of war on 1 February 1793 he was appointed to command *Spitfire*, sloop (20). His précis of service indicates that he took command on the 12th, but if so he put to sea immediately, and the following day made the first prize of the war, a French privateer. He was made post captain on 24 June 1793, and left *Spitfire*. It is believed he was appointed to *Narcissus* (36), and transferred on 26 October to *Hind* (24). Following a successful convoy operation escorting 157 ships, he was transferred again to *Anson*, a sixty-four cut down and armed with forty-six long 12-pounders for her main batteries and 42-pounder carronades on the quarterdeck and forecastle. In her he was employed on the coasts of France, mostly under the orders of Sir John Borlase Warren. He was at Lord Bridport's action on 23 June 1795, and the following month *Anson* was part of the armament sent against Quiberon. Durham was still serving in *Anson* in September and October 1798 when he sighted, and for three weeks kept in contact with, a French squadron consisting of *Hoche* (80) and several large frigates carrying soldiers intent on making a landing in northern Ireland. He finally delivered them to Sir Borlase Warren, and took part in their defeat and capture off Tory Island on 12 October. With the other captains present, he received the thanks of parliament and a gold medal. On 28 March 1799 he married Lady Charlotte Matilda, only surviving daughter of Charles Bruce, ninth earl of Elgin.

On 26 February 1801 he transferred into *Endymion* (40), and was employed at Lisbon, in the South Seas and at St Helena, coming ashore in April 1802 following the signing of the peace of Amiens.

On 10 April 1803, on the renewal of the war, he was appointed to command *Windsor Castle* (90) lying in Portsmouth harbour, but he was moved on 28 May into *Defiance* (74). She was considered the fastest third rate in the fleet, and she was employed in the Channel, off Cadiz and at Gibraltar. Late in 1803 he was so fortunate as to capture the *Flying Fish* loaded with ivory and gold-dust from Africa. *Defiance* formed part of Sir Robert Calder's reinforced squadron on 22 July 1805 when it engaged the combined French and Spanish fleet on its return from the West Indies. When the fog hid the enemy, Calder sent the frigates and *Defiance* to report its number and disposition, and Durham reported that the allied force contained twenty battleships instead of the sixteen that Calder had expected. In the subsequent action *Defiance* lost her mizzen topsail yard, and her mainmast, foreyard and driver-boom were damaged. She was sent home for repairs, and then Durham was ordered to join Lord Nelson's force before Cadiz. Durham refused Calder's request that he return to England as a witness at his court martial, because he was determined not to miss the battle which was fought on 21 October off Cape Trafalgar. He was wounded in that action, and in the storm following was exhausted by the efforts to save *L'Aigle* from being wrecked on the coast of Spain. He then returned to England in time to be a witness at Calder's trial, and carried the banner as KB at Nelson's funeral.

He was appointed in January 1806 to command *Renown* (74) in the Channel fleet, and for a time was St Vincent's flag captain, before being sent to join the Mediterranean fleet under Lord Collingwood. He remained there until 1810, and was ordered to hoist a commodore's broad pendant towards the end of his commission. On 26 October 1809, while in company with Rear-Admiral George Martin, he engaged and destroyed two French ships near Cette.

He was promoted rear-admiral on 31 July 1810, and in 1811 he commanded a division of the North Sea fleet, sailing into the Baltic and off the Texel, hoisting his flag on 14 April in *Ardent* (64), and subsequently shifting in succession into *Hannibal* (74), the Danish prize *Christian VII* (80) and *Venerable* (74). Hardly had he struck his flag, when an emergency occurred. A French squadron sailed from L'Orient and Durham was ordered to collect every available ship at Portsmouth, and sailed in pursuit, flying his flag in *Bulwark* (74). But the French soon returned to their harbour, and Durham brought his squadron back to Portsmouth and struck his flag for a second time. Subsequently he was given command of a squadron watching Basque Roads, and then on 13 December 1813 he was appointed commander-in-chief at the Leeward Islands, flying his flag in *Venerable*. He captured two French frigates on his way out, and operated effectively against American cruisers, ending his tour of duty by co-operating in the reduction of Martinique and Guadeloupe.

On 2 January 1815 he was nominated a KCB, and following the peace he received the unusual distinction for a British officer of the cross of the order of Military Merit of France for his part in reducing Guadeloupe to obedience to Louis XVIII. On 17 November 1830 he was advanced in chivalry to GCB.

His wife having died on 21 February 1816 leaving no children, he remarried on 16 October 1817, taking as his second wife Anne Isabella, only daughter and heiress of Sir John Henderson, baronet of Fife. He assumed the additional surname of Henderson on his second marriage, and assumed the additional surname of Calderwood on inheriting the Polton estate at the death of his elder brother, Lieutenant-General James Durham, on 6 February 1840. Again the marriage produced no children, and his wife died in November 1844. He embarked on a political career, holding the parliamentary seat for Queensborough in 1830 and for Devizes from 1834 to 1836. He was forced to resign his seat, however, on his appointment in March 1836 as commander-in-chief at Portsmouth. He ended his tour by commanding a squadron off Brighton during Queen Victoria's visit in 1837. Durham died on 2 April 1845 in Naples with the rank of a full admiral.

Lt: 26 December 1782
M-C: 12 November 1790
Capt: 24 June 1793
R-Adm: 31 July 1810
V-Adm: 12 August 1819
Adm: 22 July 1830

EKINS

ADMIRAL SIR CHARLES EKINS, GCB, is best known for his scholarship, publishing in 1824 *Naval Battles from 1744 to the Peace in 1814, Critically Reviewed and Illustrated*, and in 1837 *Naval and Universal Signals, in Symbols of Black and White; Forming a Numerical Code of Signals by Day, for Her Majesty's Fleets*. In 1824 he also contributed to the debate about ship design with *A Reply to the letter of Sir R. Seppings,... Surveyor of H.M. Navy, on the Round Bows and Circular Sterns*. As a serving officer, he had a successful, if not spectacular, career, which culminated in his taking a part in the 1816 Algiers campaign.

He was born at Quainton rectory, Buckinghamshire, the second son of the Right Revd Dr Jeffery Ekins, DD, dean of Carlisle and bishop of Dromore, county Down, and his wife Anne, daughter of Philip Baker of the War Office, from Colston, Wiltshire.

He was baptised on 16 October 1768, and attended the public school at Newcastle, but because of an impediment in his speech he was then sent to Edinburgh, under the care of a Mr Braidwood. He entered the navy on 20 March 1781 as a captain's servant on board the *Brunswick* (74) under the temporary command of Captain Cromwell. Following the return to duty of the Honourable Keith Stuart, Ekins had his first taste of action in the battle of the Dogger Bank on 5 August. Stuart was later succeeded by Captain John Ferguson, but in 1782 Ekins followed Stuart into *Cambridge* (80) and in her took part in Lord Howe's relief of Gibraltar. He was rated midshipman on 11 September 1782 while serving in *Marquis de Seignally*, sloop, under Captain John Hunter. For a few months in 1785 'to serve out my time' before he could sit his examination, he moved into a guardship at Chatham, *Irresistible* (74) under the command of Sir Andrew Snape Hamond. He passed at the Navy Office on 2 May 1786, but then returned to sea as a passed midshipman, and later acting lieutenant, in *Pearl* (32) under the command of Captain the Honourable Seymour Finch, with whom he served in the Mediterranean until 1789; he then followed Finch into *Lion* (64) and made a voyage to Barbados. His lieutenant's commission is dated 20 October 1790, and he was appointed to *Flirt* (14), brig, under the command of James Nicoll Morris, and later to *Alarm* (32) under Captain Lewis Robertson and Captain James Carpenter, before joining *Boyne* (98) bearing the flag of Sir John Jervis following the outbreak of war. He was still serving in her when she was burnt at Spithead on 1 May 1795.

This brought a change in his fortunes. He was briefly put in command of *Pilote* (12), cutter, at Spithead, and then was promoted on 18 June 1795 commander of *Ferret*, sloop, in the North Sea, following which he was ordered to travel to the Cape of Good Hope to take command of *Echo* (24), only to discover on his arrival that she had been broken up as unserviceable. However, he was put in command of *America*, one of the Dutch prizes taken in Saldanha Bay, and was promoted post captain on 22 December 1796. He was appointed in August 1797 to command the 9-pounder frigate *Amphitrite* (28). Serving in the West Indies, he was a successful frigate captain, and participated in the capture of Surinam and of Devil's Island at Cayenne. In March 1801 *Amphitrite* formed part of the force under Sir John Duckworth when he captured the Danish islands. Ill health had obliged Ekins to remain at Barbados, but he was able to rejoin in time to take charge of landing the men at St Martin. A return of the yellow fever later led to his being sent home with dispatches, arriving in May 1801.

On 16 April 1804 he was appointed to *Beaulieu* (40), and after serving again in the West Indies, and paying her off in March or April 1806, he took command of *Defence* (74) on 10 November. The following year he took a part in the second Copenhagen operation, and later he was sent to the force off Lisbon under Sir Charles Cotton's command. Learning of the escape of the Rochefort squadron, and believing it was heading for the West Indies, he proceeded there and at Martinique joined Sir Alexander Cochrane. The Rochefort squadron had in fact gone to the Mediterranean, and when that was learnt, Ekins was sent home as an escort to a convoy. He next served in the Baltic under Sir James Saumarez, and in 1809 was detached to blockade the Russian army in Sweden.

He married on 27 February 1810, at St George, East Stonehouse, near Plymouth, uniting with Priscilla, daughter of Thomas Parlby of Stone Hall, Devon. A year later he resigned his command and came ashore.

Following the end of the war, Ekins served in the *Superb* (74) under Lord Exmouth, and suffered ninety-two killed and wounded at the attack on Algiers in 1816. He was subsequently made a CB on 19 September 1816 and a KWN, a knight of the Netherlands military order of Wilhelm. He became a KCB on 8 June 1831, and a GCB on 6 April 1852. He was promoted rear-admiral on 12 August 1819, and died with the rank of admiral on 2 July 1855, aged eighty-seven, at 69 Cadogan Place, Chelsea, Middlesex.

Lt: 20 October 1790
Cmdr: 18 June 1795
Capt: 22 December 1796
R-Adm: 12 August 1819
V-Adm: 22 July 1830
Adm: 23 November 1841

ELLISON

CAPTAIN JOSEPH ELLISON's career exemplifies the strength of the eighteenth-century Royal Navy, which ensured that competent men of all classes were brought forward by senior officers who recognised the importance of doing so, sometimes finding suitable appointments for the deserving when wounded and not fully fit. Ellison was apparently an effective administrator, and a captain of men who could be ruthless with those who departed from the code of naval discipline. He is probably best known for his quelling of mutiny in *Marlborough* (74).

Captain Joseph Ellison,
engraved by H R Cook from a miniature
in the possession of Mrs Ellison,
published by Joyce Gold, 103 Shoe Lane,
31 December 1807.

Ellison was born in Newcastle-upon-Tyne, a son of Joseph Ellison, who died when his son was only six months old. The young Joseph was adopted by an aunt who had no children of her own, moved to Portsmouth, and first went to sea when only nine years old with Admiral Sir Edward Hawke. He served in many different ships, and was in action repeatedly during the American war; like Manley Dixon, he was reportedly offered a commission in the army by Sir William Howe. Later he saw active service in the East Indies under Sir Edward Vernon in August 1778, at the capture of Pondicherry. He was commissioned lieutenant on 29 July 1778, and was serving on board *Queen* (90) in the Channel fleet when it was chased by the combined French and Spanish fleets in the summer of 1779. He married Esther Collis on 6 November 1779 in Alverstoke, Hampshire.

On 4 July 1780 while serving in *La Prudente* (36), Captain Waldegrave, Ellison was hit in the arm by an 18-pounder ball in a protracted gunnery fight with two French frigates in the dark, one of which, *La Capricieuse*, struck her colours. The French surgeon then amputated Ellison's shattered arm. On his recovery Ellison asked Lord Sandwich, the first lord, for a sea appointment. Because of his injury he had to make do with the impress service, in which he did so well that Admiral Keppel, who succeeded Sandwich at the head of the Admiralty Board, promoted him master and commander on 6 June 1782 but left him in the impress service. On 21 January 1783 he was promoted post captain in *Panther* (60), but again left in the impress. At some time before 1795 he was awarded a pension of five shillings for his wound.

With the signing of the treaty of Versailles he was sent to northern Ireland to conduct fishery research. He retired for a while from the service because of his injury, but was able to return to sea in February 1785 in command of *Druid* (32). On his return in her from the West Indies in September 1792 he spotted the royal standard flying in Portland Road and went ashore to pay his respects. On hearing how long he had commanded *Druid* King George allegedly said: 'Do you never mean to give her up?' – 'No, please your Majesty,' Ellison replied, 'if you will have the goodness to make me a present of her.' [NC 19.15] Following the French declaration of war in February 1793 Ellison continued in command of *Druid*, and in the spring of 1794 was part of a frigate squadron commanded by Sir James Saumarez that was chased by a greatly superior French force off Guernsey. Saumarez was in his home waters, and extricated his command by exploiting local knowledge to navigate in waters the French could not risk.

In June 1795 Ellison was transferred to the *Standard* (64) and permitted to bring with him all his officers and fifty of *Druid*'s crew. In *Standard*, Ellison participated in Sir John Warren's operations in Quiberon Bay in support of the French royalists. The garrison of Belleisle refused his invitation to surrender, and showered the British with equal measures of fresh provisions and cannon shot. Eventually *Standard*'s men were so affected by scurvy that they were landed on the island of Hedic, where Ellison blew up the forts and pitched tents for a hospital. Early in 1796 he sailed to St Helena to bring home a convoy of East Indiamen, and in the Downs on his return was ordered, by the new telegraph, to proceed to Sheerness to refit; he was permitted to leave his ship there in the care of an acting captain for four months while he recovered his health.

He did not return to her, and instead accepted command of *Marlborough* (74), the crew of which had been in the forefront of the mutiny at Spithead in April 1797. Her captain, Nicholls, had been obliged to go ashore. The *Naval Chronicle* says that 'when Captain Ellison took the command, he was received by them with marked approbation. They gave him three cheers; said they had heard that he was the seaman's friend; and that they would go round the world with him.' Not all was entirely well, however, and in passage to join Admiral the earl of St Vincent off Cadiz Ellison was awakened in the middle of the night by a sailor: 'For God's sake, Captain Ellison, get up. The ship is in a state of mutiny; you and your officers are to have your throats cut, and the ship is to be taken possession of!' Ellison immediately went on deck, when he found more than the watch on the poop. His prompt action put an end to the mutiny, and eventually the ringleaders were betrayed. When *Marlborough* reached the fleet, the two were hanged.

Ellison's health continuing to be precarious, he was asked to resume his place in the impress service, in which he served until the peace of Amiens in 1801. He was then made third captain at Greenwich hospital. In 1805 he was promoted to second captain and director of the chest. He died on 1 October 1816, aged sixty-three.

Lt: 29 July 1778
M-C: 6 June 1782
Capt: 21 January 1783
Superannuated Capt: 9 November 1805

ELPHINSTONE – *see* Keith
EXMOUTH – *see* Pellew

FAIRFAX

VICE-ADMIRAL SIR WILLIAM GEORGE FAIRFAX had an ancestry dating back to the reign of Henry VI, and his father had been an officer in the Horse Guards, but this did not ensure him rapid promotion. When put to the test he proved a resolute officer, but his years of employment were relatively few.

He was born on 8 March 1738, son of Joseph Fairfax of Bagshot, Surrey, and his wife, Mary. He entered the navy in 1750 in the *Centurion* (50) under Augustus Keppel, and served in the Mediterranean. He subsequently served in *Mars* (64) and *Garland* (24) under Marriot Arbuthnot and was commissioned lieutenant on 20 December 1757 in *Duke* (90). He served in the St Lawrence from 1758 to 1760 in a French prize privateer corvette, *Eurus* (24), under Captain John Elphinston . For the next six years he was unemployed, following which he was appointed in June 1766 to *Greyhound* (20). Nothing is known of his service in her, and he returned to half pay in June 1769. He first married on 23 July 1767, in Burntisland, Fife, uniting with Hannah, daughter of the Revd Robert Spears. That lady died in 1770 leaving no children. He married for a second time in April 1772, in Burntisland, uniting with Margaret, daughter of Samuel Charters, solicitor of customs for Scotland, and cousin of Admiral Sir Samuel Carlovich Greig of the Russian navy. Margaret gave birth to four sons and three daughters.

Apparently he returned to service in September 1776, but nothing is known of it prior to his promotion on 13 May 1778 as master and commander of *Alert,* cutter, following the withdrawal of the

British ambassador from Paris as a result of French intervention in the American revolution. In the first encounter of the Channel fleet with the French on 17 June prior to the declaration of war, Fairfax brought to the French lugger *Coureur*. When the French opened fire, he returned it so effectively that they struck their colours. This, and other local engagements, became the official pretext for war. After *Alert* was repaired and put back in service, she encountered a heavy French frigate, *Junon* (40),

Sir W. G. Fairfax, Knt., Rear Admiral of the Blue,
drawn and engraved by William Ridley,
published by Burney and Gold, Shoe Lane,
1 July 1801.

and Fairfax was captured. He was not immediately exchanged, and does not appear to have been employed again until 12 January 1782, when he was made post in *Tartar* (28) at the end of the American war, serving in the West Indies until the signing of the treaty of Versailles in 1783.

He was not then employed again until he was appointed to the *Sheerness* (44) upon the French declaration of war in 1793. After the French occupation of the Netherlands, Fairfax was appointed in May 1795 into *Repulse* (64), and then moved in October 1796 into *Venerable* (74) to be Admiral Duncan's flag captain. He was very senior for such

an appointment, but he accepted it, and accounted well for himself during the Nore mutiny in May and June 1797 and at the battle of Camperdown the following October. He was entrusted with carrying Duncan's dispatches, for which he was rewarded with a knighthood, and on 14 February 1799 a colonelcy of marines. He was ashore while *Venerable* had a long refit after Camperdown, and returned to her in April 1799, when he was ordered to join the Channel fleet.

He was promoted rear-admiral on 1 January 1801, but was not employed in that rank. He died with the rank of vice-admiral on 17 November 1813, aged seventy-five, in Edinburgh.

Lt: 20 December 1757
M-C: 13 May 1778
Capt: 12 January 1782
R-Adm: 1 January 1801
V-Adm: 13 December 1806

FAULKNOR

CAPTAIN ROBERT FAULKNOR was the iconic naval hero of the turn of the nineteenth century. 'It is to be hoped,' wrote the *Naval Chronicle*'s memoir of the late captain, 'that whenever this honourable Board [of Admiralty] shall be pleased to abandon the blasphemous deities and monsters of Pagan history, and the names of brutes, for some titles more in character with the patriotism and heroic valour of the British Navy, they will select other names, besides that of our ever to be lamented Hero, Admiral Lord Nelson, wherewith to denominate the wooden bulwarks of our country.' [NC 16.27] But the fleet had to wait until the flotilla leader of 1914 before a warship was named after Robert Faulknor.

A member of the fourth generation of Faulknors in the Royal Navy, he was probably born in 1763 in Northampton, the first son of Captain Robert Faulknor, RN, and his wife Elizabeth, née Ashe, from Dijon in France. When his father died in 1769, at Dijon, his mother returned to Northampton and was awarded a small pension through the intercession of the duke of Cumberland. He was sent to the Royal (Naval) Academy in Portsmouth on 21 January 1774, and

Captain Robert Faulknor,
engraved by William Ridley from a miniature
in the possession of the
Honourable Elizabeth Stanhope.

joined the *Isis* (50) on 9 March 1777 as a midshipman under the command of Captain the Honourable William Cornwallis serving in the North American station as part of Lord Howe's fleet. He followed Cornwallis into *Bristol* (50) and later *Lion* (64), serving in the action off Grenada in January 1779 under Admiral Byron, and the following year in the actions with M. de la Motte Piquet and M. de Ternay. He received his lieutenant's commission on 20 December 1780 on board the *Princess Royal* (90) commanded by Captain Sir Thomas Rich, baronet, and flying the flag of Rear-Admiral Josias Rowley. On 7 April 1782, after a year ashore, he joined *Britannia* (100) flying the flag of Vice-Admiral Barrington, and was part of Lord Howe's force in the relief of Gibraltar.

His ship was paid off on 13 March 1783 following the signing of the treaty of Versailles, but he was soon employed again in a succession of ships. On 22 November 1790 he was promoted master and commander, but he was not appointed to command *Pluto*, fireship, until 2 April 1791. In the interval, however, he was fortunate to be employed

in the rank of lieutenant in a succession of ships. He retained *Pluto* only until September, and then went on half pay until 12 June 1793, when he was appointed to command the *Zebra,* sloop (16), in the Channel. Soon afterwards, Lord Chatham, the first lord of the Admiralty, wrote to his mother to say 'That her son should be sent, according to her wishes, to the West Indies, under the protection of Sir John Jervis'. No doubt her concern was that her son should establish his fortune in rich, if unhealthy, cruising grounds.

At the assault on the Martinique forts, as Jervis wrote in his dispatch, Faulknor ran 'the *Zebra* close to the wall of the fort, and leaping overboard, at the head of his sloop's company, assailed and took this important post before the boats could get on shore, although they rowed with all the force and animation which characterize English seamen in the face of an enemy.' The only man killed in *Zebra* was the pilot, who had been rendered incapable of effective action by a premonition of his death. Faulknor relieved him of the helm. 'The poor fellow,' wrote Commodore Charles Thompson, 'panick struck, went away; and overcome with shame, sat down upon the arm chest; whilst Captain Faulknor seized the helm, and with his own hand laid the *Zebra* close to the walls of the fort: but before he had got upon them, at the head of his gallant followers, a cannon ball struck the arm chest, and blew the Pilot to atoms.' To his mother, Faulknor wrote, 'As the *Zebra* came close to the fort, a grape shot struck, or rather grazed my right hand knuckle, and shattered the cartouch in the centre of my body: had it not miraculously been there, I must have been killed on the spot. – Thanks to Almighty God for his kind preservation of me in the day of battle!'

In recognition of his quality, he was made post captain on 20 March 1794, and put in command of the *Blanche* (32). But there was a degree of insanity, or at least excitability, about him. In the subsequent action on Guadeloupe, during which he was nearly killed in the attack on Fort Fleur d'Epée, he became so outraged by an army quartermaster during a quarrel over the siting of a battery that he killed him with a single thrust of his sword. He was exonerated by a court martial, but he was not able to forgive himself for 'being accessory to the death of any human being not the natural enemy of myself or my country . . . the hasty and sudden punishment I unhappily inflicted on the spot will be a source of lasting affliction to my mind.' ^{Ralfe 3.314} He became depressed and restless, but this did not reduce his courage when on 4 January 1795 *Blanche* pursued a French frigate, *Pique* (34), off Pointe à Pitre, Guadeloupe. Early the following morning Faulknor was able to open fire, and when after an hour and three-quarters the *Pique* ran her bow on board the *Blanche*, which had lost her main and mizzen masts, Faulknor lashed the French ship's bowsprit to the remains of the *Blanche*'s main mast. Faulknor was wounded, and was subsequently killed by two musket shot, but two hours later the *Pique* hauled down her colours to Lieutenant Frederick Watkins, who had assumed command.

Faulknor was buried on the Isles des Saintes, and a monument to his memory was erected in St Paul's Cathedral.

Lt: 20 December 1780
M-C: 22 November 1790
Capt: 20 March 1794

FITTON

LIEUTENANT MICHAEL FITTON never rose above that rank, despite proving himself a brilliant and courageous frigate captain. This was almost certainly the result of a youthful mistake in jumping ship when he found naval service irksome.

He was born in Gawsworth, Cheshire, a son of Henry Fitton and his second wife, Ann, née Kelsal, and was baptised on 29 December 1765. He entered the navy in January 1780 as a captain's servant to George Keppel in *Vestal* (28), serving at Newfoundland. He made a good impression on his captain when, *Vestal* having stopped an American privateer, he noticed a bag being thrown overboard. It was recovered and proved to contain a copy of a secret treaty between the American revolutionaries and the Netherlands government. It was used to justify declaring war on the Dutch before they could join the Russo-Swedish League of Armed Neutrality. Keppel was praised in par-

liament, and Fitton served with him to 1784 in a succession of five ships, being rated in 1783 master's mate in *Hebe* (38). But when Keppel was succeeded by Edward Thornbrough, Fitton became disgusted and deserted. On the French declaration of war in February 1793 Keppel evidently decided to give Fitton another chance, and signed him on as an able seaman in *Defiance* on 25 September 1794. However, in June 1795 Keppel was promoted to flag rank and went on half pay. Fitton, no doubt having discovered that he had little chance of obtaining a commission with his patron sidelined, on 11 January 1797 accepted the position of purser in the sloop *Stork* (16).

She sailed from the Nore for the West Indies in May or June 1797 at the height of the mutiny, with Fitton allegedly threatening to return the fire of any ship which fired at *Stork*. After two years Fitton managed to obtain an appointment as acting third lieutenant in a former Indiaman, *Abergavenny* (56). As flagship of the Jamaica station she spent most of her time in fever-ridden Port Royal, but Fitton was give command of a tender, and between 1799 and the peace of Amiens in 1802 he demonstrated a remarkable ability in commerce warfare. At the peace, however, he was out of employment, and although he returned to the West Indies after the renewal of war he was not to have his lieutenant's commission confirmed until 9 March 1804 following his participation in the failed attempt to capture Curaçao.

Possibly his most remarkable success was against a powerful privateer, the *Superbe*, which he caught up with after a sixty-seven-hour chase, forced ashore, captured and then burnt. That notwithstanding, he was soon afterwards superseded by an Admiralty nominee on the orders of the commander-in-chief of the Leeward Islands. Keppel had died, Thornbrough was an influential admiral, and Fitton's desertion of the latter may not have been forgotten. He did not get employment until 1811, when he was appointed about 15 April to the command of a brig, the *Archer*, subsequently shifting on 6 February 1812 into another brig, the *Cracker*, on the Channel and Baltic stations. With the conclusion of peace, he was again unemployed until on 20 April 1835 he was appointed lieutenant of Greenwich hospital.

He had married on 15 November 1812, in Gawsworth, Mary Stanway. The couple had at least one son, Michael, who was born on 24 June 1814, was a clerk in the Royal Navy and died in the West Indies. Michael senior died on 31 December 1852 in New Peckham, Surrey, leaving the little property he had to his wife, in trust for his daughter Emily Mary Ann Michael.

Lt: 9 March 1804

FLINDERS

CAPTAIN MATTHEW FLINDERS is well known as the first person to circumnavigate Australia.

He was born on 16 March 1774 in Donington-in-Holland near Boston, Lincolnshire, the eldest son of Matthew Flinders, surgeon apothecary, and his wife Susanna, née Ward. His education began at Donington free school in 1780 and continued at John Shinglar's grammar school at Horbling, Lincolnshire, with the intention that he should enter the medical profession, but he was determined to join the navy. The advice of his cousin John Flinders, who had served eleven years in the navy under Admirals Gardner and Affleck without much hope of a lieutenant's commission, was that without powerful friends no one should risk undertaking a naval career, but Matthew's fancy had been caught by reading *Robinson Crusoe* and he was determined. He taught himself trigonometry and navigation with some help from his father. At the late age of sixteen and with the patronage of Captain Thomas Pasley, whose daughters were being taught by Matthew's cousin Henrietta, he entered the navy in 1789 as a lieutenant's servant on board *Scipio* (64) and later on board *Bellerophon* (74). He was rated midshipman or master's mate in May 1790, but the settlement of the Nootka Sound dispute made his prospects slim, and in 1791 he accepted an appointment on board the *Providence* being fitted out by Captain William Bligh in the second attempt, following the *Bounty* voyage which had ended in mutiny, at collecting breadfruit from the Friendly Islands for planting in the West Indies.

On his return to England in 1793, Flinders rejoined *Bellerophon,* which was now flying Rear-Admiral Pasley's flag, and in her took part in the battle of the Glorious First of June in 1794. But he preferred voyages to battles, and joined the *Reliance* (10) under the command of one of *Bellerophon*'s former lieutenants, Captain Henry Waterhouse. They sailed on 15 February 1795 for

Captain Mathew Flinders, R.N., engraved by T Blood from a miniature in the possession of Mrs Flinders, published by Joyce Gold, Naval Chronicle Offices, 103 Shoe Lane, London, 30 September 1814.

Port Jackson, New South Wales, carrying Captain John Hunter to be the governor of the young settlement. In Australia, Flinders undertook many voyages of discovery in small boats, surveyed the Furneaux Islands, and circumnavigated Van Diemen's Land (Tasmania). He was examined for nautical knowledge in 1797, and commissioned lieutenant on 31 January 1798.

When he returned to England, Sir Joseph Banks, president of the Royal Society, was so impressed by the hydrographic work Flinders had done that he recommended him to the Admiralty as the appropriate leader of another expedition. He was accordingly appointed to the *Xenophon* (8) fitting for foreign service, now renamed *Investigator*. Flinders was promoted commander on 16 February 1801, and on 17 April 1801 at St Nicholas Partney, Lincolnshire, he married Ann Chappelle of Partney. Her father had been a master mariner who died at sea and she was stepdaughter of the Revd William Tyler, rector of Bratoff, Lincolnshire.

In July 1801 *Investigator* sailed, by way of the Cape of Good Hope, and Flinders made a remarkably accurate running survey of the south coast of Australia, the name being coined by him in preference to Terra Australis. To increase accuracy, he experimented with the use of soft iron bars for reducing deviation in magnetic compasses; these became known as Flinders Bars. After surveying the Gulf of Carpentaria, *Investigator* returned on 9 June 1803 to Port Jackson and was condemned as unseaworthy. Flinders decided to return with most of his crew and the scientific officers to England as passengers in *Porpoise*, a Spanish prize that had become a station ship. She was wrecked on a coral reef, along with an East India Company ship, *Cato*. Another Indiaman, *Bridgewater*, avoided the reef but sailed off without offering assistance. Flinders made his way back to Port Jackson in a boat to obtain a relief ship capable of taking his people as far as Canton. He himself started his return voyage to England in a 29-ton schooner, *Cumberland*, completing his survey by passing through the Torres Strait. But despite his passport from the French government indicating that he was on a scientific voyage, he was arrested by General Decaen, governor of Isle de France, when he called at Port Louis. He remained there for six and a half years, part of the time in close confinement. *Cumberland* was not the ship indicated in the passport, and nor had he been given clearance to go to the Isle de France, which was a restricted military area. Flinders was also rather tactless. Decaen was sent instructions from Paris to release Flinders, but refused to carry them out.

He was finally released on 7 June 1810, and reached England on 24 October, when he was made post captain with his commission dated 7 May, the first possible date following that of the patent making Charles Philip Yorke first lord of the Admiralty. Flinders then set about writing the report of his voyage, but his health never recovered from his imprisonment, and he died in London on the day following the publication of *Voyage to Terra-Australis* on 19 July 1814, when he was aged forty. One daughter, Anne, had been born to him, on 1 April 1812, and his grandson was to be Professor Sir William Matthew Flinders Petrie (1853–1942), the noted Egyptologist.

Lt: 31 January 1798
Cmdr: 16 February 1801
Capt: 7 May 1810

FOLEY

ADMIRAL SIR THOMAS FOLEY, GCB, became a close friend of Lord Nelson, having played leading roles in the battles of the Nile and Copenhagen.

He was born in 1756 in Ridgeway near Narbeth, Pembrokeshire, the second son of John Foley of Ridgeway, whose brother Thomas had gone round the world with Captain Anson. Young Thomas entered the navy in April 1771 as a captain's servant in *Otter*, sloop, and served under the command of Commander John Morris on the Newfoundland station. In November 1773 he transferred to *Egmont* (74), which was serving as a guardship at Spithead under Captain Edward Jekyll. In March 1774 he was rated a midshipman in *Antelope* (50) under Rear-Admiral Clark Gayton. At Jamaica in August 1775 he transferred again into *Racehorse* (18) under Lieutenant Charles Holmes Everitt Calmady, serving in the Windward Passage protecting trade against American privateers and in the Windward Islands. In April 1776 he was ordered to act as lieutenant in *Atalanta*, sloop, under Commander Thomas Lloyd, serving in Pensacola and the Mississippi. There he transferred in April 1777 to *Lord Amherst*, under Commander Francis Hartwell, before rejoining *Antelope* the following month. He left her at Spithead in May 1778, received his commission on 25 May, and was appointed to *America* (64) under Lord Longford. With him he fought the battle of Ushant on 27 July and served in the dangerous summer of 1779 when the combined Franco-Spanish fleet was in the

Channel with overwhelming numbers.

He transferred to *Prince George* (98) in September 1779 and returned in 1781 to North America and the West Indies. There he fought in Rear-Admiral Sir Samuel Hood's actions at Basseterre Roads, St Kitts, on 25 and 26 January 1782, and in the engagements with de Grasse off Dominica and the Saintes on 9 and 12 April 1782. He was promoted on 1 December 1782 master and commander of *Otter*, in which he was employed at Long Island and New York. In January 1783 he transferred briefly to *Britannia*, armed ship, and then was put in command of another of his old ships, *Atalanta*, in which he proceeded to the Bay of Fundy, *en route* to Quebec. He left her in March 1785, and had two and a half years unemployed, before being appointed to a third of his old ships, *Racehorse*, in which he served on the north-east coast of England. He made the next step, to post captain, on 21 September 1790, and from then was unemployed until the declaration of war by the French Republic on 1 February 1793.

Foley was appointed flag captain of *St George* (98) under Rear-Admiral John Gell, who was to join Vice-Admiral Lord Hood's fleet in the Mediterranean. In their passage, Gell's squadron captured the French privateer *Général Dumourier* and her Spanish prize, the *San Iago*. They were found to be carrying a cargo of such value that Foley was to be able to purchase an estate in Wales. When Gell was succeeded by Rear-Admiral Hyde Parker, Foley continued to serve as flagcaptain of the *St George* (90). In March 1795 she was part of Admiral William Hotham's fleet during an engagement with the French fleet off Toulon. Foley then was appointed to command *Britannia* (100), and on 14 February 1797 took part in the battle of Cape St Vincent as flag captain to Vice-Admiral Sir Charles Thompson.

The next month he was appointed to command *Goliath* (74), and in May 1798 he was sent to join the small squadron under Rear-Admiral Nelson's command in the Mediterranean to deal with the armament that General Buonaparte had assembled for the conquest of Egypt. Nelson found the Toulon fleet in Aboukir Bay late in the day on 1 August,

and *Goliath* led the attack. Foley had managed to get into the leading position by having his studding sails hoisted and ready to break out when Nelson made his signal, and he was better equipped to pioneer the route because he had an atlas which showed the bay and which was based on a survey done within the last forty years. It was he who noticed that the French ships were spaced at 500 feet, and who judged that it should be possible to pass inshore of the head of their line. He was heard to say he should not be surprised to find the Frenchmen unprepared for action on the inner side, as proved to be the case.

Following the battle he remained in the Mediterranean until the end of 1799, when he was sent home. On 6 January 1800 he was appointed to command the *Elephant* (74) and was employed blockading Brest, before being attached to the fleet being prepared in early 1801 under Admiral Sir Hyde Parker and Vice-Admiral Nelson to deal with the threat of an armed and pro-French northern coalition. Because *Elephant* was lighter and more manoeuvrable than was Nelson's *St George*, he transferred his flag to her prior to the attack. Before the battle, Foley and Edward Riou dined with Nelson and spent the night writing Nelson's detailed battle orders for each of the ships.

On 31 July 1802, during the peace of Amiens, Foley married Lady Lucy Anne Fitzgerald, youngest daughter of the duke of Leinster and granddaughter of the duke of Richmond. He was nominated colonel of the Royal Marines on 2 October 1807, which sinecure provided an increase of income, and he was promoted rear-admiral on 28 April 1808, but ill health prevented his again serving at sea. In March 1811 he accepted appointment as commander-in-chief of the Downs station, nominally flying his flag in the former Indiaman *Monmouth* (64) but in reality based ashore at Deal. At the end of the war he was nominated KCB on 2 January 1815, and GCB on 16 May 1820, and he was appointed rear-admiral of the United Kingdom on 14 June 1831. He died with the rank of admiral on 9 January 1833, aged seventy-six, in Portsmouth, and was buried in a coffin made of the wood of the *Elephant* at the Garrison Chapel in

Portsmouth. Lucy Anne survived him to 1851, when she died aged eighty.

Lt: 25 May 1778
M-C: 1 December 1782
Capt: 21 September 1790
R-Adm: 28 April 1808
V-Adm: 12 August 1812
Adm: 27 May 1825

FOOTE

VICE-ADMIRAL SIR EDWARD JAMES FOOTE, KCB, is best known for the charges he laid against Nelson for the inhumanity of his actions during the reconquest of Naples in 1799. Foote had been put in command of the force blockading Naples, and negotiated a capitulation with Cardinal Ruffo, but Nelson, on his arrival, declared the treaty annulled and participated in the repression of those Neapolitans who had co-operated with the French to put an end to despotic government.

Foote was born on 20 April 1767 in Bishopsbourne near Canterbury, the fourth and youngest son of the Revd Francis Hender Foote, a barrister who had taken holy orders and purchased Charlton Place from his relatives. His mother, Catherine, was a daughter of Robert Mann of Linton House, Kent, who was a contractor for clothing the army. Young Foote was sent as a scholar to the Royal (Naval) Academy at Portsmouth in February 1779 before he entered the navy in May 1780 in the *Dublin* (74) as a captain's servant under the command of Captain Samuel Wallis, the circumnavigator. In February 1781 he transferred into the French prize *Belle Poule* (36) under the command of Captain Philip Patton, and he was present at the battle of Dogger Bank on 5 August 1781. In December he transferred again, and was rated midshipman in *Endymion* under the command of Captain James Gambier, with whom he fought in the battle of the Saintes on 12 April 1782. After the treaty of Versailles he followed Gambier into *Europa* (50), in which his uncle Vice-Admiral Gambier was ordered to fly his flag as commander-in-chief at Jamaica. Foote was ordered to act as lieutenant, and subsequently served as acting lieutenant in *Swan* (10), and possibly *Antelope* (50), before his commission was confirmed on 12 August

1785 and he was appointed to *Janus* (44) under Captain John Pakenham. Between September and December 1787 he served again under Vice-Admiral Gambier's nephew James in *Royal Sovereign* (100), which was being fitted at Plymouth for Admiral Pigot's flag. He was transferred in September 1788 into *Crown* (64), in which Commodore William Cornwallis flew his broad pendant as commander in the East Indies. Cornwallis promoted him on 1 October 1791 master and commander of *Atalanta,* sloop, and later he was transferred into another sloop, *Ariel*, which he brought home and paid off in October 1792.

He was unemployed during the first year of the war declared by the French Republic on 1 February 1793, but was promoted to post captain on 7 June 1794 and in September was appointed to command *Niger* (32), in which he served on the coast of France, before being ordered to join the Mediterranean fleet under Sir John Jervis's command. He brought Jervis the first positive news of the approach of the Spanish fleet, and was present at the battle of Cape St Vincent on 14 February 1797. On returning to England in the autumn, *Niger* was stationed at Weymouth to guard the king at his seaside retreat. Apparently Foote was well received, for the king requested that when *Niger* was paid off at Spithead in September 1797, Foote be appointed to *Seahorse* (38) and sent to rejoin the Mediterranean fleet.

Circumstances led to his being the first in the service to know that the military expedition commanded by General Buonaparte in the summer of 1798 was heading for Egypt. He had searched without success for the detachment of the Mediterranean fleet sent from off Cadiz under Rear-Admiral Nelson's command, and then encountered off Sicily on 26 June the French *Sensible* (36), which he succeeded in capturing. On board were General Baraquay d'Hilliers and his staff, and Foote learnt from them their destination. He immediately sailed for Alexandria in company with *Terpsichore*, and arrived on 20 July, twelve days before the battle of the Nile. The Toulon fleet was in Aboukir Bay, and Foote set out to find Nelson, but their courses did not cross and by the time

Foote returned to the coast of Egypt on 17 August Nelson had fought his battle.

It was in the spring of 1799, when the appearance of the Brest fleet under Vice-Admiral Bruix in the Mediterranean obliged Nelson to join Vice-Admiral Keith's flag, that Foote was left in command of the blockade of the French army in Naples, and concluded the capitulation with the Neapolitan collaborators. Foote did not formally protest to Nelson about his disregard for the capitulation, and they were to remain on good terms until he was ordered home in September. But on proceeding to Palermo to convey the Sicilian court to Naples, he personally appealed to the prime minister, Sir John Action, to honour the terms of the convention which had obviated the need to take the forts of Revigliano and Castel-à-Maré by storm. He published in 1807 a pamphlet entitled 'Captain Foote's Vindication of his Conduct, &c'.

In October 1799, following the grounding of *Seahorse* at Leghorn on 29 July, Foote sailed to England, where his ship could be properly repaired. He returned to the Mediterranean in May 1800 to convey Rear-Admiral Sir Richard Bickerton and General Sir Ralph Abercromby to Alexandria. Subsequently, he again provided the guard at the royal residence at Weymouth, before sailing to Calcutta, where he arrived at the end of January 1802 with an East India Company convoy. There he succeeded in the difficult job of salving his former prize, *Sensible*, which had been wrecked close off shore, but in water deep enough to flood the gundeck.

Seahorse was paid off in October 1802, and again the king saw that Foote was looked after. He was not, however, given another warship to command. Instead, he was appointed to *Princess Augusta*, yacht, in which he returned to Weymouth, and then *Royal Charlotte*, yacht, in the Thames, from which he commanded the force organised for the protection of the capital. He was promoted rear-admiral on 12 August 1812, and in December hoisted his flag as second in command at Portsmouth, which appointment he retained until February 1815.

Foote's first wife was Nina, daughter of Sir Robert Herries, who was a banker. Neither the date of their marriage nor that of Nina's death is recorded, nor the number of their children. On 24 August 1803 he married for a second time, but the name of his second wife is not recorded. She was the eldest daughter of Admiral Philip Patton, and she died at Nice in December 1816, aged thirty-two. Again, there is no record of any children's names.

Foote was promoted vice-admiral on 19 July 1821, and nominated KCB on 19 May 1831. He died on 23 July 1833, aged sixty-six, at his house near Southampton, Hampshire.

Lt: 12 August 1785
M-C: 1 October 1791
Capt: 7 June 1794
R-Adm: 12 August 1812
V-Adm: 19 July 1821

FRASER

VICE-ADMIRAL ALEXANDER FRASER, although of an ancient family, had little in the way of connections which could ensure promotion through the higher ranks.

He was born in 1748, in Lerwick, Orkney, the eldest surviving son of Hugh Fraser, surveyor of the customs in Lerwick, and his wife Jane, daughter of the Revd Thomas Linning of Waterstein, Scotland. He entered the navy in June 1760 when only eleven years old in the *Fly*, sloop, commanded by Captain, later Admiral, George Gayton. On the conclusion of peace in 1763 he is supposed to have returned to his education in Edinburgh, but his précis of service indicates that he was also rated as a midshipman in the *Adventure*, cutter, and served at Leith. This may have been some approach at an officer training programme. At any rate, he began his naval service in earnest in 1768 when he joined *Mermaid* (28) as midshipman under Captain James Smith for service in North America, and in 1770 he was made acting lieutenant in *Bonetta* sloop under the command of Lieutenant Matthew Squire. Having returned to home waters, he passed his examination in March 1773, but he was not immediately commissioned, and joined *Royal Oak* (74) at Spithead as a passed midshipman under Captain George Balfour. The following year he returned to North America as

*Alexander Fraser, Esq.,
Rear Admiral of the White Squadron,*
engraved by T Blood, published by
Joyce Gold, Naval Chronicle Offices,
103 Shoe Lane, London,
30 April 1814.

acting lieutenant in *Scarborough* (20) commanded by Andrew Baulay. The active part he took in
the American war, notably at the burning of
Falmouth, finally led to his being commissioned
lieutenant on 18 July 1777 by the earl of Sandwich,
who was remarkable for his determination to promote only men of professional merit.

Fraser was appointed to the *Hector* (74) under
the command of Sir John Hamilton, and in the skir-
mishing leading to the declaration of war with
France in 1778 he was put in charge of the French
frigate *La Licorne* (32) detained by the *Hector*. He
continued to serve in *Hector* at the battle of Ushant
on 27 July, and in 1779 in the West Indies when
Captain Cornwallis engaged Admiral de Ternay.
He was first lieutenant of *Conqueror* (74) at the
time when she encountered a hurricane in 1780 in
passage to England, and continued in active service until the end of the war.

He continued in employment during the peace,
until he was finally promoted master and commander
on 1 December 1787. He was then unemployed until
the Nootka Sound crisis in 1790, when he was given

command of the *Savage*, sloop, stationed at
Greenock. He married on 6 April 1788 Helen, eldest daughter of John Bruce, advocate and collector
of the customs in Sumburgh in the Shetlands. The
couple had three sons and two daughters.

On the outbreak of war with the French
Republic, Fraser was ordered to take the *Ferret*,
sloop, and several cutters under his command and
to proceed to Ostend, to keep open communications with the duke of York's army in Flanders.
There he received a request from Baron de Mylius
to land and take possession of the town and garrison, to which he agreed, landing 500 men and
taking *Savage* into the harbour. In recognition of
his services he was promoted post captain on 1
July 1793 in the *Redoubt*, armed with twenty 68-
pounder carronades, to which the crew of *Savage*
was turned over. Fraser continued on the same station and was employed in support of the army in
the defence of Nieuport.

In 1799, when in command of *Diana* (38), he escorted a large convoy to the West Indies, but two
attacks of yellow fever obliged him to return to home
waters. He was then appointed to the *Berschermer*
(54) employed as a guardship in the Swin until the
end of the Revolutionary war. In command of
Hindostan (54) he spent 1804 to 1806 in the East
Indies. In command of *Vanguard* (74) he took part
in the 1807 operations against Copenhagen, after
which he took charge of the blockade of Zealand
and the protection of Baltic trade. This proved a demanding task as the Danes fitted out scores of gunboats. On his return to England he was accused
of neglect of duty by the Baltic merchants, but was
able to satisfy the Admiralty.

His health having been affected by his duty, he
resigned from sea service in 1810 and accepted command of the sea fencibles at Dundee until they were
disbanded later in the year, when he was appointed an equerry to the duke of Cambridge. He was
promoted rear-admiral on 1 August 1811, and vice-
admiral on 12 August 1819, in which year he died.

Lt: 18 July 1777
M-C: 1 December 1787
Capt: 1 July 1793
R-Adm: 1 August 1811
V-Adm: 12 August 1819

FREDERICK

REAR-ADMIRAL THOMAS LENOX FREDERICK is perhaps best known for the loss of his ship.

He had been born on 25 March 1750 in London, the second son of Sir Charles Frederick, KB, member of parliament for Queenborough and surveyor-general of the Ordnance. His mother was Lucy, ninth daughter of Hugh Boscawen, first Lord Falmouth, and sister of Admiral the Honourable Edward Boscawen. He entered the navy in 1768, and with the patronage of Captains John Montagu and Sir Peter Parker was commissioned lieutenant on 12 March 1770 and master and commander on 11 October 1776. He was then appointed to command the *Spy,* sloop (14), on the Newfoundland station, where Vice-Admiral John Montagu flew his flag. For a few months he was transferred to *Swift,* sloop (14), on the North American station under Rear-Admiral Richard Howe. Unfortunately, *Spy* was wrecked on the coast of Newfoundland, but Frederick was exonerated at the subsequent court martial, and on 14 July 1779 was made post captain in *Unicorn* (20), in which he was captured in the summer of 1780 and taken prisoner to Martinique. He was soon exchanged, again acquitted by a court martial, and employed in Channel service, but in the autumn went on half pay. He had married on 2 June 1773, in Stoke Damerel, Devon, Annie Greigson, but had been almost constantly on service.

In 1782 he at last was given command of a large new frigate, *Diomede* (44), in which he proceeded to the North American station. On 19 December he had the good fortune to capture after a long chase and a stiff fight the powerful American frigate *South Carolina,* which was armed with forty guns, of which twenty-eight were 42-pounders. On the conclusion of peace *Diomede* was paid off in November 1783 and Frederick returned to half pay.

On the outbreak of war in 1793 Frederick was placed in command of *Illustrious* (74) and served with Admiral Lord Hood in the Mediterranean. In the action fought by Vice-Admiral Hotham on 13 March 1795 *Illustrious* led the centre squadron and was hotly engaged, having twenty men killed, and being reduced to a wreck which had to be taken in tow in extreme conditions. In his report, Frederick wrote that

after having parted from the fleet on the beginning of the night of the 17th, about 1 o'clock the hawser, by which the *Meleager* (Captain George Cockburne) had us in tow, gave away, and it was impossible, from the very great sea that was then running (it blowing hard and the gale increasing), for us to recover it, or make it fast again; I therefore brought-to. The gale increased very much towards day-light in the morning of the 18th, at which time the ship laboured very much, and shipped a great deal of water at the lower-deck ports; some of them having been much damaged in the action of the 14th. When the day appeared, we saw the land, but from the thickness of the weather we could not make out what part of the coast it was... At noon a heavy squall came on, in which the foresail split, and went in pieces; and at the same time the jury-mizen-mast went by the board... On the 18th, at ½ past 1 P.M. and 19th per log, the third gun from forward on the larboard side of the lower-deck went off, from the friction of the shot in the gun, burst off the port, and carried away part of the upper cell of the port; when I was obliged to wear the ship, to prevent her from filling, before the carpenters could secure the port. [NC 37.355]

A seaman who believed he knew the coast was employed as a pilot, but nonetheless *Illustrious* was embayed. When her anchor cable parted, she went on the rocks. It was impossible to get a hawser ashore to raft the men in, but the ship did not break up, and eventually her people were saved. The wreck Frederick burnt.

Following his acquittal at the inevitable court martial for the loss of *Illustrious,* Frederick continued to play an active part in the war against Revolutionary France. He returned to England by land, but on the general promotion on 1 June 1796 he was appointed to command the *Blenheim* (90) in Hotham's fleet, returning to the Mediterranean by the way he had come. When Vice-Admiral Sir Hyde Parker succeeded to command, Frederick was ordered to wear a commodore's broad pendant. After service in Corsica, Frederick joined Admiral Sir John Jervis off Cadiz in time to take an active part in the battle of Cape St Vincent on 14 February 1797.

He was promoted rear-admiral in the general promotion on 20 February 1797, but at the end of November 1797 he began to experience the effects of disease. Dr Harness was able to ease it for the moment, but in September 1799 he was forced to strike his flag and he died on 7 November 1799, aged forty-nine, in Nottingham Place, London.

> Lt: 12 March 1770
> M-C: 11 October 1776
> Capt: 14 July 1779
> R-Adm: 20 February 1797

FREMANTLE

VICE-ADMIRAL SIR THOMAS FRANCIS FREMANTLE, GCB, first made his mark and cemented an already strong connection with Horatio Nelson in the action off Toulon on 13 March 1795, when commanding *Inconstant* (36).

He was born on 20 November 1765 in Aston Abbots, Buckinghamshire, the third son of John Fremantle and his wife Frances, daughter and coheiress of John Edwards of Bristol. He entered the navy in 1778 on *Hussar* (28), joined *Jupiter* (50) two years later, and soon thereafter moved to *Phoenix* (44) commanded by Sir Hyde Parker. He served in many different ships on the Jamaica station, and on 13 March 1782 was commissioned lieutenant. He remained at Jamaica until December 1787, and during the Nootka Sound crisis in 1790 again served with Parker, in the *Brunswick*. On 3 November he was promoted master and commander of *Spitfire*, sloop.

At the time of the French declaration of war in February 1793 Fremantle commanded the *Conflagration* (14), and on 16 May he was made post with an appointment to command *Tartar* (28) preparing to sail with Lord Hood for the

Mediterranean. He led the way into Toulon when Hood occupied it on 27 August 1793, and in 1794 served under Nelson in the capture of Bastia.

In the action on 13 March 1795 he spotted the vulnerability of the French third rate *Ça Ira* (80). Skilfully weaving across her stern, he winged her enough that Nelson was able to bring *Agamemnon* (64) into action and capture her. He subsequently served in the squadron Nelson commanded on the coast of Genoa, and he continued to serve with Nelson when *Inconstant* was ordered home, exchanging on 1 July 1797 into *Seahorse* (38), one of the inshore squadron off Cadiz. Fremantle was with Nelson during a bombardment of the city when his barge was attacked by a Spanish boat. *Seahorse* was one of the ships detached with Nelson to Tenerife, and Fremantle was severely wounded in the attack on Santa Cruz on the morning of the 25th. Nelson, who had himself lost an arm, hoisted his flag on *Seahorse*, and the two wounded officers made the passage to England under the care of Fremantle's wife Betsy. The two were to serve together again at the battle of Copenhagen on 2 April 1801, when Fremantle commanded *Ganges* (74), and for a last time at the battle of Trafalgar on 21 October 1805, in which Fremantle commanded *Neptune* (98), which was placed the second astern of Nelson's flagship *Victory* (100).

Sir John Jervis officially recognised his 'unparalleled exertions' during the evacuation of Leghorn on 27 June 1796. He was at the capture of Elba on 10 July 1796, was sent to Algiers to negotiate with the dey and to Smyrna in charge of a convoy, and on his return assisted in the capture of Piombino on 7 November. He was left as senior officer in the Mediterranean when Jervis concentrated his forces west of Gibraltar.

His marriage to the diarist Elizabeth (Betsy) Wynne, daughter and coheiress of Richard Wynne of Falkingham, Lincolnshire, had taken place on 12 January 1797 when she and her family were refugees from the French army of Italy, and Naples was being evacuated. Hence it was that against the usual Admiralty regulations, she was on board her husband's ship during the boat and landing actions at Cadiz and Santa Cruz, and available to nurse his and Nelson's wounds. She was to give birth to six sons and four daughters, and outlived her husband to 2 November 1857, dying at the age of eighty.

Fremantle was well enough in August 1800 to take command of *Ganges* (74), in which he fought at Copenhagen, and he returned to her following the peace of Amiens, taking command of *Neptune* in May 1805. After Trafalgar, Fremantle remained under the command of Collingwood until December 1806. He was a commissioner of the Admiralty from October 1806 to March 1807 when he was appointed to the yacht *William and Mary*. He was also member of parliament for Sandwich, Kent, from 1806 to 1807.

He was promoted rear-admiral on 31 July 1810, and a month later was appointed commander-in-chief Mediterranean. In June 1812 was sent into the Adriatic in charge of the squadron there, and in the course of the next two years he cleared the French from the coasts of Dalmatia, Croatia, Istria and Friuli, capturing Fiume on 3 July 1813 and Trieste on 8 March 1814.

At the end of the war he was nominated KCB on 2 January 1815, GCB on 20 February 1818 and GCH in 1818. The Spanish court nominated him a knight of the royal and military order of San Fernando, the Austrian court made him a knight of the military order of Maria Theresa and a baron on 26 November 1816, and the Ionian Republic and Malta made him a knight grand cross of St Michael and St George. He was promoted vice-admiral on 12 August 1819, but he was not to enjoy his honours for long, dying of an inflammation in the bowels on 19 December 1819, aged fifty-four, in Naples, while commander-in-chief in the Mediterranean. His eldest son, Thomas Francis, was created a baronet on 14 August 1821 in posthumous recognition of the services of his father, and several of his children and grandchildren were to continue the family commitment to naval service.

Lt: 13 March 1782
M-C: 3 November 1790
Capt: 16 May 1793
R-Adm: 31 July 1810
V-Adm: 12 August 1819

GAMBIER

ADMIRAL OF THE FLEET SIR JAMES GAMBIER, BARON GAMBIER, GCB, was thirty-eight when he established a reputation as a fighting captain in the battles collectively known as the Glorious First of June in 1794. His reputation, however, was to diminish in the course of the war, and his piety came to irritate his brother officers.

He had been born on 13 October 1756 in New Providence, Bahamas, the second son of John Gambier, lieutenant-governor of the Bahamas, and his wife, Deborah, née Stiles, of Bermuda. He was a nephew of Vice-Admiral James Gambier and, more importantly, of Admiral Sir Charles Middleton, Lord Barham, whose wife took charge of him as a child. He joined the navy in 1767 as a midshipman in *Yarmouth* (60) which was serving as a guardship in the Medway under his uncle James's command, and followed him to the *Salisbury* (50) in 1769 and served in the North American station. In 1772 he transferred to *Chatham* (50) flying the flag of Rear-Admiral Thomas (*or* William ?) Parry in the Leeward Islands; Parry placed him in *Spy*, sloop, under Captain Thomas Dumaresque. Having returned to England, later in the year he joined *Royal Oak*, (74) which was serving as a guardship at Spithead under Captain Joseph Deane.

In 1774 he returned to the Leeward Islands in *Portland* (50) again under Dumaresque's command and flying the flag of Rear-Admiral James Young. He had passed his examination for nautical knowledge at the Navy Office in St Mary-le-Strand, Westminster, prior to sailing. He was not commissioned lieutenant until 12 February 1777, but he served as a lieutenant in *Shark*, sloop, under Commander John Chapman, in *Hind* (24) under Captain H Boyne in 1776, in *Sultan* flying the flag of Vice-Admiral Lord Shuldham in 1777, and in *Ardent* (64) flying the flag of his uncle Rear-Admiral Gambier in 1778. Lord Howe promoted him on 9 March 1778 master and commander of *Thunder,* bomb, but he was obliged to surrender her to the fleet under d'Estaing owing to her having been dismasted the previous day. When exchanged he was promoted post captain, on 9 October 1778, and appointed to *Raleigh* (32), in which he served under his father and under Vice-Admiral Arbuthnot. He served ashore in the expedition to Charlestown, and then was employed in cruising. In 1780 he was appointed to command *Endymion* by Admiralty order, and served in home waters.

On the conclusion of the American war he went ashore, and did not return to sea duty until the French declaration of war. He married in July 1788 Louisa, second daughter of Daniel Mathew of Felix Hall, Essex, and of Pennytinney, Cornwall, high sheriff of Essex in 1769. The couple were to have no children.

In February 1793 following the French declaration of war he was appointed to command *Defence* (74) in the Channel fleet. In the battle of the Glorious First of June he was the first to obey Lord Howe's signal to cut the enemy line, passing between the seventh and eighth ships of the French fleet and engaging them from leeward. He had to deal with as many as four of the enemy at one time. All *Defence*'s masts were shot away, the main falling on board and putting out of action the forecastle guns, and fifty-seven of her crew were killed or wounded. Howe was so impressed by Gambier's conduct that he was one of the very few commanders singled out in his dispatch; as a result he was awarded a gold medal, and on 4 July was nominated a colonel of marines. He was transferred into *Prince George* (98), and on 7 March 1795 he was appointed to the Admiralty Board, where he served until 19 February 1801. He was promoted rear-admiral on the anniversary of the battle, and without ever hoisting his flag in that rank was promoted again to vice-admiral on 14 February 1799. In 1801 he served with his flag in *Neptune* (90) under Admiral the Honourable William Cornwallis in the Channel fleet, and the following year shifted his flag into *Isis* (50) as commander-in-chief Newfoundland.

He was to return to the Board twice, to serve on it from 15 May 1804 to 10 February 1806 and from 6 April 1807 to 9 May 1808, and he was promoted vice-admiral on 14 February 1799, and admiral on 9 November 1805. He took particular interest in improving ship construction, tactical signals, and shipboard discipline. The last included careful attention to divine services on board ship. Gambier's reputation for religious convictions eventually became more firmly established in the navy than was that for resolute action in the face of the enemy. A fellow officer wrote that Gambier was generous with his personal charity to wounded sailors, and continued:

> To the idle and dissolute his punishments were with vigilance directed, but in no instance were they attended with cruel severity: the old but now obsolete custom of the wooden collar and fine for swearing was invariably adhered to; and no women were allowed to remain on board without possessing marriage certificates. The chaplain's attendance likewise on Sundays was never dispensed with, unless prevented by absolute necessity. This steady adherence to the instruction and laudable endeavours to improve the morals of the seamen were the only complaints I every heard alleged against him. [Ralfe 2.89]

Gambier attracted some odium for being willing to command the naval forces sent as part of the 1807 campaign against Copenhagen, an operation which some felt accorded imperfectly with the religious discipline he imposed on the service. The attack on the Danish fleet in 1801 had been unpopular enough, but that in 1807 which extended to the bombardment of Copenhagen met so much criticism in England that there were votes cast in parliament against the speech from the throne. Nevertheless, it was held by the Admiralty Board to be essential to prevent the Danish fleet falling into the hands of Napoleon, and when the Board had difficulty in finding a commander willing to undertake the unpleasant action it was natural enough that one of its members should take it on.

The first division of the fleet of twenty-five ships of the line sailed from Yarmouth on 26 July 1807, the bombardment of Copenhagen began on 2 September employing Congreve rockets, and three days later the Danes capitulated. The prizes included eighteen ships of the line, two of which had to be destroyed, twenty-one frigates and brigs and twenty-five gunboats, together with an immense quantity of naval stores. In recognition of his services Gambier was raised to the peerage as Baron Gambier of Iver, Buckinghamshire, on 9 November 1807.

The following year he was appointed to command the Channel fleet, and in April 1809 he chased into Basque Roads a French squadron which had escaped from Brest but, instead of heading for the West Indies, had found shelter behind the shoals, islands, forts and boom in the estuary. Several officers made proposals for an incendiary attack, which was eventually carried out by Lord Cochrane. Explosion vessels were used to intimidate the French so that the fireships could get in amongst them, after which ships of the fleet under the immediate orders of Rear-Admiral Stopford were to finish the job. On the news that Cochrane had been appointed by the Admiralty to command the flotilla, and that in consequence Gambier rejected Admiral Eliab Harvey's offer of his own services, the latter 'is stated to have expressed the greatest dissatisfaction, and to have bestowed upon Lord Gambier himself, epithets descriptive of other qualities than those which he has evinced in his profession, such as *Jesuit*, *Methodist*, and *Psalm-singer*'. NC 21.315-16; 348-9 Cochrane carried out his part of the operation, with limited success, followed up with the two frigates under his command, and signalled to Gambier that an immediate movement of the capital ships could destroy the enemy. Gambier was not stimulated by the advice of the young captain, and was content with the more restricted part played by the ships under Stopford's command when the tide permitted their movement with safety. Four French ships and an East Indiaman were either driven onto the shore and destroyed, or burnt, and of those ships which succeeded in making their way across the bar of the Charente, the larger ones were obliged to cast their guns overboard to lighten ship.

These events led to a major row. Cochrane threatened to use his vote in parliament against a

resolution to thank Gambier, and the latter applied for a court martial, at which he was exonerated. Admiral Harvey was less fortunate, being dismissed from the service, but he was later to be reinstated.

Gambier continued in command of the Channel fleet until 1811, and then left the sea. In 1814 he was one of the commissioners who negotiated peace with the United States at Ghent. He was nominated KCB on 2 January 1815 and GCB on 7 June 1815, and promoted admiral of the fleet on 23 July 1830. He died on 19 April 1833, aged seventy-six.

Lt: 12 February 1777
M-C: 9 March 1778
Capt: 9 October 1778
R-Adm: 1 June 1795
V-Adm: 14 February 1799
Adm: 9 November 1805
Admiral of the Fleet: 23 July 1830

GARDNER

ADMIRAL SIR ALAN GARDNER, BARONET, later Baron Gardner, served in three wars, taking part in the battle of Quiberon Bay in 1759, the battle of the Saintes in 1782 and the battle of the Glorious First of June in 1794.

He was born on 12 April 1742 in Uttoxeter, Staffordshire, the fourth son of Lieutenant-Colonel William Gardner of the 11th Dragoon Guards, and his wife Elizabeth, eldest daughter and coheiress of Valentine Farrington, MD, of Preston, Lancashire. He was only five years old when entered on the books, and seven years old when he entered the navy on 1 May 1755 on board *Medway* (60) commanded by Captain Peter Denis, who had been one of the lieutenants on *Centurion* (50) when Captain Anson circumnavigated the world. Gardner saw very active service in the following years. In January 1758 he followed Denis on board *Dorsetshire* (70), and he was serving in her at the battle of Quiberon Bay on 20 November 1759. He received his commission as lieutenant on 7 March 1760, when he was appointed to the *Bellona* (74) commanded by Captain Denis. He remained in her when Denis was succeeded by Captain Robert Faulknor, father of the hero of 1793-5. On 14 August 1761 *Bellona* was in action with *Le*

Courageux (74), which may have contributed to Gardner's promotion on 12 April 1762 to master and commander of *Raven,* fireship.

Within six months the preliminary articles of peace were signed, but nonetheless Gardner was promoted post captain on 19 May 1766 and appointed to command the *Preston* (50) on the Jamaica and Windward Islands station as Rear-Admiral William (?) Parry's flag captain. He was transferred into *Levant* in 1768, and commanded her until 1771. While serving in Kingston, Jamaica, he married on 20 May 1769 Susanna Hyde, only daughter and heiress of Francis Gale of Liguana, Jamaica, and widow of Sabine (or Samuel) Turner. The couple were to have nine sons and one daughter. His eldest son was Admiral Sir Alan Hyde, second Lord Gardner, KCB.

On the outbreak of civil war in the American colonies in 1775, Gardner was appointed to *Maidstone* (28) and sent to Jamaica for another tour of duty. Early in 1778 he was entrusted with carrying warning of the arrival of the French fleet to Lord Howe on the American station. Back on station on 3 November, *Maidstone* engaged a large French merchantman, *Lion,* armed with forty guns and freighted with tobacco. This Gardner carried into Antigua, where he was promoted by Vice-Admiral Byron to command *Sultan* (74). In her he was at the action off Grenada on 6 July 1779, serving as one of the seconds of the admiral. In 1780 he was sent home in charge of a convoy, and in December 1781 he was appointed to commission *Duke* (90) with orders to join Sir George Rodney in the West Indies, which he did in time to fight in the battle of the Saintes on 12 April 1782. *Duke* was the first to break the enemy line.

On 8 September 1785 Gardner was appointed commander-in-chief on the Jamaica station, with the temporary rank of commodore and flying his flag in *Europa* (50). He served there for the usual term of three years. On returning home, he was appointed to command *Courageux* (74) at the time of the Nootka Sound incident in 1790. When the crisis was resolved, *Courageux* was paid off. Gardner had been appointed to the Admiralty Board on 19 January 1790 and served there until

7 March 1795. He also held the parliamentary seat for Plymouth from 1 February 1790 until 1796. He contested the 1796 election in Westminster, to keep out the radical Charles James Fox, and held that seat to 1806.

At the general promotion which took place at the outbreak of war, Gardner was promoted rear-admiral on 1 February 1793, and was given command of a squadron, flying his flag on *Queen* (90).

The Right Honourable Lord Gardner, Vice Admiral of the Blue Squadron, and Major General of the Marines, engraving by William Ridley from a painting in the possession of Dobree Esq., 1782, published by Joyce Gold, Shoe Lane, 1 October 1802.

This force arrived at Barbados on 27 April, and at the end of the season, having been unable to achieve anything against the French establishments with his limited resources, he returned to join the Channel fleet, and to fight in the battles before and on the Glorious First of June in 1794. In the fighting on 29 May the *Queen* suffered heavily, and was only saved from destruction or capture by the actions of Admiral Thomas Graves in *Royal Sovereign* (100) and an impromptu line of battle that he formed between *Queen* and the enemy.

In recognition of the part he had played in the action, Gardner, who had been appointed colonel of the marines probably in 1792, was promoted on 28 June 1794 major-general of the Royal Marines, and was awarded a gold medal and chain by King George. On 4 July he was promoted vice-admiral and invested a baronet. On the anniversary of the battle, at the memorial service, he was promoted to vice-admiral of the white squadron, and on 23 June 1795 he was at the action off Port L'Orient under Admiral Lord Bridport, although he played little part.

He was also unavoidably involved in the Spithead mutiny in 1797, and was with Admirals Colpoys and Pole when they met the delegates. Gardner had a rope shaken over his head by one of them, and according to his kinsman Joseph Farington RA, 'such was His mortification and despair that He told them they had better hang him at once. This struck them a little and they replied, "They did not mean to hurt his honour."' Farington (2) 3. 938–9

He was promoted admiral on 14 February 1799, and on 30 August 1800 put in command of the Irish station. This was a bitter blow to him, as he thought he should have succeeded Lord Bridport in command of the Channel fleet. No doubt to ease his feelings, on 29 December he was created Baron Gardner in the Irish peerage. When he hauled down his flag in 1805 he was advanced in the English peerage to Baron Gardner of Uttoxeter, Staffordshire, on 27 November 1806. He had, in fact, made a very good impression in his command, and in 1807 was finally appointed commander-in-chief of the Channel fleet. However, he was obliged to resign the following year owing to declining health. He died on 1 January 1809, aged sixty-six, in Bath, Somerset, his wife surviving to 1823.

Lt: 7 March 1760
M-C: 12 April 1762
Capt: 19 May 1766
R-Adm: 1 February 1793
V-Adm: 4 July 1794
Adm: 14 February 1799

GARDNER

VICE-ADMIRAL SIR ALAN HYDE GARDNER, BARON GARDNER, KCB, pursued a career which exemplifies the working of naval dynasties, but he was to prove his worth in action. Following the peace of Amiens and the renewal of war, Gardner was given command of *Hero* (74) in the Channel fleet, and served under Vice-Admiral Sir Robert Calder in the engagement of 22 July 1805, when he led the van squadron into action against superior numbers in poor visibility. Later *Hero* was detached to serve under Captain Sir Richard Strachan in the action of 4 November 1805.

He was born on 6 February 1770, the eldest son of Admiral Sir Alan Gardner, baronet, later first Baron Gardner of Uttoxeter, Staffordshire, and his wife Susanna Hyde, only daughter of Francis Gale of Liguana, Jamaica, and widow of Sabine Turner. He entered the navy in 1781 and served as midshipman on board *Duke* (90), under his father's command, at the battle of the Saintes on 12 April 1782. He was still only a little over twelve years old and served as his father's aid. He was wounded, and the *Naval Chronicle* commented that 'though it might have been thought lightly of by a veteran, [the wound] must have been sufficiently alarming to a boy'. NC 21.357 He was promoted lieutenant in 1787, master and commander on 1 December 1788 and post captain on 12 November 1790.

At the time of the French declaration of war in February 1793 he commanded *Heroine* (32), and was ordered to join the squadron under his father's command which was sent to secure the British West Indian islands at the beginning of the war. He was then ordered to proceed to India where *Heroine* formed part of the force under Commodore Peter Rainier. When it was known that war had been declared against the Netherlands, Rainier set about the conquest of Ceylon and the Dutch settlements in the East Indies. Gardner was entrusted with the command of the naval forces operating against Colombo. He married on 9 March 1796, in Madras, Maria Elizabeth, only daughter of Thomas Adderley of Innishannon, county Cork, but the marriage was to be dissolved by an act of parliament in 1805. In 1797 he returned to England and, in command of *Ruby* (64) and later *Resolution* (74), served in the Channel fleet.

For his service in Calder's and Strachan's actions, he was awarded a gold medal, and a sword was awarded to him by Lloyd's Patriotic Fund. In

1807 he was appointed captain of the Channel fleet, which was then commanded by his father, and remained in that position until ill health obliged his father's retirement. On 28 April 1808 he was promoted rear-admiral and hoisted his flag on board *Bellerophon* (74). On his father's death on 1 January 1809 he succeeded to the barony of Uttoxeter. He was nominated a KCB on 2 January 1815.

The Right Honourable Alan Hyde Lord Gardner,
Rear-Admiral of the Blue Squadron,
engraved by H R Cook after Henry Edridge,
published by Joyce Gold, 103 Shoe Lane,
Fleet Street, 31 May 1809.

He remarried on 10 April 1809 in Whitehall, London, uniting with Charlotte, third daughter of Robert Smith, Lord Carrington. The couple had one son and one daughter before Charlotte died on 27 March 1811. He died on 27 December 1815, aged forty-five, in Berkeley Square, Westminster.

Lt: 1787
M-C: 1 December 1788
Capt: 12 November 1790
R-Adm: 28 April 1808
V-Adm: 4 December 1813

GORDON

ADMIRAL OF THE FLEET SIR JAMES ALEXANDER GORDON, GCB, had a long and distinguished career, serving as a midshipman in *Goliath* in the battles of Cape St Vincent and the Nile and as captain of the *Active* in the action near Lissa on 13 March 1811, and losing a leg shot off at the knee in the capture of the *Pomone* on 29 November. In the war with the United States he acted in August 1814 as senior officer in command of the squadron which forced the Potomac and captured Fort Washington, its supporting batteries, and the city of Alexandria. Twenty-one laden prizes were taken away. Although the losses in the expedition were small, the labour was extreme. Reportedly the crews were able to swing their hammocks on only two out of twenty-three days. Gordon also served in the unsuccessful expedition against New Orleans.

He was born in 1782 in Kildrummie Castle, Aberdeenshire, the eldest son of Charles Gordon of Wardhouse and his second wife, who was a daughter of Major James Mercer of Auchnacant. He entered the navy on 25 November 1793 as a captain's servant in *Arrogant* (74) under the command of Captain James Hawkins Whitshed. Seven years of very active service followed, including serving in three fleet actions – the action off L'Orient on 23 June 1795 in the French prize *Révolutionnaire* (38) under the command of Captain Francis Cole, and the battles of Cape St Vincent and the Nile in *Goliath* (74) under Captain Thomas Foley. After a period of service in *Royal William* (100) flying the flag of Admiral Milbank at Spithead, he was commissioned lieutenant on 27 January 1800 in another French prize, *Bordelais* (24), under the command of Captain Thomas (?) Manley, and later Captain John Hayes. His promotion to commander came as a result of actions on 11 July and 17 August 1803 when he was first lieutenant of *Racoon* (18). *Lodi,* brig, was captured and another brig, the *Mutine*, was stranded near Santiago de Cuba. In recognition of his achievement, *Racoon*'s captain, Austin Bissel, was promoted to another ship, and Gordon was promoted on 4 March 1804 to commander of *Racoon*. After more than a year of successful operations against privateers he was posted to the Spanish prize *Diligentia*, renamed *Ligera* (22), on 16 May 1805, and then in June 1807 to *Mercury* (28) in which he served at Newfoundland, and later off Cadiz. There he participated in the capture or destruction of a Spanish convoy and gunboats off Rota. In June 1808 he was appointed to the 18-pounder frigate *Active* (38), in which he served in the Adriatic, fighting in the action off Lissa, participating in many boat actions, and going home at the end of 1811 to recover from his injury in the action against *Pomone* (38). He was granted an honorary medal for the action off Lissa on 13 March 1811, and a pension for wounds on 31 July 1812.

While in England he took the opportunity to get married, on 7 August 1812. The name of his wife is unknown, but she was the youngest daughter of John Ward of Malborough. The couple had seven daughters and one son.

Soon after his wedding he was appointed to *Seahorse* (38), on approximately 14 September, and late in 1813 he was attached to the force commanded by Sir Alexander Cochrane in North America, for which service he was nominated a KCB on 2 January 1815 and a knight bachelor on 29 June 1815. He had a few weeks' home leave in late September and October 1815, and then was appointed to *Madagascar* at Sheerness. He transferred on 24 October 1816 to *Meander,* which on 19 December he had the misfortune to put on the Orford Ness in a gale, but the ship and her people survived when she drove over the shoal. He remained in his command, still based at Sheerness, until January 1817, when he returned to command of *Active*. In her he was employed in the North American and Mediterranean stations.

That was his last seagoing command, but in 1828 he was appointed superintendent of Plymouth hospital, and in 1832 he transferred to Chatham dockyard. He was promoted rear-admiral on 10 January 1837 at the end of his term at Chatham, when he was appointed lieutenant-governor of the Royal Hospital, Greenwich. On 28 October 1853 he succeeded Sir Charles Adam as governor. He was advanced in chivalry to GCB on 5 July 1855,

and died at Greenwich on 8 January 1869, aged eighty-six, with the rank of admiral of the fleet.

Lt: 27 January 1800
Cmdr: 3 March 1804
Capt: 16 May 1805
R-Adm: 10 January 1837
V-Adm: 8 January 1848
Adm: 21 January 1854
Retired Adm. of the Fleet: 30 January 1868

GORE

VICE-ADMIRAL SIR JOHN GORE, KCB, was flag captain to Vice-Admiral Nelson during the abortive attack on Boulogne in 1801, but his main claim to fame is that he became immensely rich through luck in prize money. He continued to serve, nonetheless.

He was born on 9 February 1772 in Kilkenny, the third son of Colonel John Gore of the 33rd regiment, lieutenant-governor of the Tower of London in 1776 and a distant relative of the earls of Arran. His mother's name is not known. Young John entered the navy in May 1781 as a captain's servant in *Canada* under the command of the Honourable William Cornwallis, and took part in the battles of 1782 in the West Indies. He served in the Channel fleet in *Dragon* from November 1782 to January 1783, and then served in the West Indies under Captain James Cornwallis, son of William Cornwallis, in the *Iphigenia* (32), to November 1786. He then was taken in by William Cornwallis, who was commanding *Royal Charlotte,* yacht, at Deptford. In September 1787 he was ordered to act in the capacity of lieutenant in *Robust* (74) which was fitting at Chatham. When she was paid off in November, he reverted to midshipman in *Hake* under Captain Edward Thornbrough, with whom he served in the Channel until September 1788. William Cornwallis had been promoted to commodore and commander-in-chief East Indies station, and was ordered to fly his broad pendant on *Crown* (64), which was under the command of his son James. Gore was rated a midshipman, and Cornwallis senior commissioned him lieutenant on 26 November 1789. While in the Indies, Gore fell seriously ill, and when he returned home in October 1791 he was entered in *Crown*'s muster as an invalid lieutenant. In November 1792, prior to the French declaration of war on 1 February 1793, Gore was appointed to *Lowestoffe* (32) commanded by Captain William Wolseley under orders to join the Mediterranean fleet. From her he was transferred in July to *Britannia* (100), flying Vice-Admiral Hotham's flag, and in September transferred again to *Victory* (100) flying Admiral Lord Hood's flag. He was on board her at the occupation of Toulon. He made a mark for himself in the defence of Fort Mulgrave, and was badly burnt during the destruction of the French fleet, when Toulon had to be evacuated. He served at the siege of Bastia, and two days after it surrendered, on 24 May 1794, he was promoted commander, with appointment to *La Fleche* (14), and again was wounded. In November he was made post captain in *Windsor Castle* (90) flying the flag of Rear-Admiral Linzee, his promotion being confirmed and dated on 12 November 1794. In her he took part in the skirmishes with the French fleet on 14 March and 13 July 1795.

On 7 October, when in command of one of the prizes, *Le Censeur* (74), and escorting a convoy, he was captured by a French squadron owing to his foreyard rolling out of its slings while wearing. After his exchange he was appointed successively to command *Robust* (74 guns) in March 1797, and the 32-pounder frigate *Alcmene* (36) in June, and in October 1797 he was appointed to command *Triton* (32). He was employed in the Channel for nearly five years, and had his first great stroke of luck, assisting on 18 October in the capture of two heavy Spanish frigates, *Santa Brigida* (36) and *Thetis* (36), laden with treasure from Vera Cruz. In his eagerness to take the prize, Gore ran *Triton* onto rocks at the rate of seven knots, but his share of the prize money exceeded £40,000 sterling.

He was injured by a gun exploding in March 1801, and came ashore, but two months later he was appointed to command another 32-pounder frigate, *Medusa* (36). It was in her that Nelson flew his flag during the attack on Boulogne. Gore remained in her during the peace of Amiens in customs prevention work, and then proceeded to the Mediterranean. He was employed in attendance

on the British ambassador in Constantinople when he learnt that the peace was not likely to survive much longer. Without waiting for orders, he sailed to rejoin Rear-Admiral Sir Richard Hussey Bickerton. He was senior officer of the frigates watching Toulon until Nelson arrived with the fleet in July 1803. He was then employed as senior officer at Gibraltar commanding a small squadron in the straits.

It was after his joining Captain Moore off Cadiz that he completed his fortune. *Medusa* was one of the ships which on 5 October 1804 intercepted four Spanish treasure ships to prevent their cargo reaching the French. It was necessary to fire into the Spaniards to bring them to, with the unfortunate result that one blew up, and a few weeks later Spain declared war. What was disaster for hundreds of Spanish families returning home, and helped stoke the flames of war, was extremely profitable to Gore. The cargo was valued at $811,000, and Gore's share cannot have been less than £40,000. Nor was that all. The following month Gore intercepted *Matilda* (38) carrying a cargo of quicksilver.

Probably largely in recognition of his very great wealth he was nominated a knight bachelor on 21 February 1805. He was then employed in taking Marquis Cornwallis, brother of his old commander, to India, returning in the record time of eighty-four days for the 13,831-mile voyage.

In February 1808 Gore was transferred into *Revenge* (74) commanding the advanced squadron of the Channel fleet under the command of his old friend, Admiral Cornwallis. In June 1808 he was entrusted with conveying from Cadiz the commissioners sent by the Council of Seville to arrange peace with Britain. He found time on 15 August 1808 to marry at St George Hanover Square, Westminster, Georgiana, eldest daughter of Admiral Sir George Montagu and Queen Adelaide's lady of the bedchamber. Money married rank, and the couple had one son and six daughters.

He commanded *Tonnant* (80) from 10 September 1810 to July 1812 in the Bay of Biscay and was stationed in the Tagus to co-operate with the army. In October 1812 he returned to *Revenge* to serve in the Mediterranean, where in the summer of 1813 he commanded the inshore squadron off Toulon.

He was promoted rear-admiral on 4 December 1813, commanding a detached squadron in the Adriatic with his flag in *Revenge*. On 2 January 1815, following the end of the war, he was nominated KCB. He was promoted vice-admiral on 27 May 1825, and nominated knight grand cross of the Guelphic order of Hanover in 1835. From 31 March 1818 to 24 June 1821 he was commander-in-chief at Chatham and the Nore, with his flag in *Bulwark* (74). Following the battle of Navarino on 20 October 1827, he was sent by the duke of Clarence, during his cameo appearance as lord high admiral, to report on Codrington's actions. From December 1831 to 1835 he was commander-in-chief of the East Indies station.

His life was saddened by the death in 1835 of his only son, Lieutenant John Gore, who was drowned trying to save a sailor. Gore senior died on 21 August 1836, aged sixty-four, in Datchet, Buckinghamshire.

> Lt: 26 November 1789
> Cmdr: 24 May 1794
> Capt: 12 November 1794
> R-Adm: 4 December 1813
> V-Adm: 27 May 1825

GOWER

ADMIRAL SIR ERASMUS GOWER played prominent parts in the establishment of British interest in the Pacific, served in the naval operations of the wars against the French Republic and Empire, and ended his career contributing to the establishment of a permanent settlement in Newfoundland.

He was born on 3 December 1742 in Pembroke, Wales, the first son of Abel Gower of Glandowen and his wife, Laetitia or Lettice Lewes, daughter of the Revd Doctor Erasmus Gower, DD. He entered the navy in 1755 as a captain's servant in *Brilliant*, hired ship, commanded by his uncle Captain John Donkley, who died at sea the following year. After serving in several different ships, being rated midshipman in *Superb* (74), he was examined for nautical knowledge in August 1762,

but he was not commissioned. Instead, apparently after serving two years in the Portuguese navy, he joined in 1764 the *Dolphin* (20) as able seaman for a voyage round the world under the command of Commodore Byron. The service was considered so severe that the government allowed the officers and men double pay and additional clothing. 'This circumstance deserved to be particularly noticed,' wrote the *Naval Chronicle*, 'as there is no instance, on record, of any such reward having been given before, or since, on any occasion whatever.' [NC 30.266]

Following their return, Gower was commissioned lieutenant on 9 July 1766 in *Swallow* (16), to which Philip Carteret, who had been Byron's lieutenant, had been appointed to command. She was an old ship which had lain in ordinary in the River Medway for nearly twenty years and then been given a copper bottom. Carteret protested that she was not seaworthy, but was sent to sea anyway with sealed orders. Only at Madeira was it found that their destination was the other side of the world in company with *Dolphin* commanded by Captain Samuel Wallis. Protest was in vain. After getting both ships through the Straits of Magellan, with great difficulty, Wallis abandoned Carteret without leaving any orders as to his further proceeding. Nevertheless, Carteret and Gower navigated *Swallow* across the Pacific, making many new discoveries, including Pitcairn Island, on which the *Bounty* mutineers later established themselves.

In 1770 Lieutenant Gower was appointed to *Swift* (16) commanded by Captain Farmer, which was sent with *Favourite* (16) to the Falkland Islands. On 13 March *Swift* was wrecked on the coast of Patagonia. Subsequently Gower was appointed second lieutenant of *Princess Amelia* (80) commanded by Captain Samuel Marshall on the Jamaica station and flying the flag of Admiral Sir George Rodney. Promotion continued to be slow. He was transferred to *Portland* (50) as first lieutenant in May 1773, and returned to England the following year. In March 1775 he was appointed to *Levant* (28) under orders for the Mediterranean. In 1779 Rodney appointed him first lieutenant of his flagship, *Sandwich* (90).

On 9 January 1780 he was promoted post captain in *Prince William* (64) without previously serving in the rank of master and commander. This was a very rare proceeding, but it was justified by the arduous experience Gower had acquired. He briefly served as flag captain to Commodore Elliot in *Edgar* (74) at Gibraltar, and then was appointed to *Medea* (28), in which he served in the East Indies under Admiral Sir Edward Hughes; there he captured *Chaser* (20) and *Vrijheid*, Dutch East Indiaman (32). He returned to England in January 1784 with £5,000 in prize money. He was then unemployed for two years, and was disappointed in a promise which was not kept to give him command of a squadron in the East Indies, but instead he was asked to serve again as Commodore Elliot's flag captain, in *Salisbury* (50), in Newfoundland. This caused him to miss command of *Vestal* (28), which was to have carried a diplomatic mission to China, but that voyage was cut short by storms and disease. He was available when the plan was again put into operation two years later.

On 1 August 1792 Gower was nominated a knight bachelor and later that year sailed in *Lion* (64) to China, carrying Lord Macartney on his embassy, returning two years later. This was an exceedingly difficult command, but Gower carried it off successfully, if with the loss of large numbers from disease. There was also another disappointment; the *Naval Chronicle* wrote:

> We must, as honest Chroniclers, express our astonishment at the conduct of government towards this most excellent officer. It had long been the practice to present captains of men of war, who were employed in conveying ministers or general officers abroad, with a certain extra allowance, to assist in the equipment of their ships. Sir Erasmus Gower spared no expense, in making the different apartments on board the *Lion*, for Lord Macartney and his numerous suite, as comfortable as possible; and he besides gave up all his own cabins, reducing himself to a small place usually allotted to a servant. Yet no consideration was in consequence given him. [NC 30.207]

Sir Erasmus Gower, Kt.,
Rear Admiral of the White Squadron,
engraving by William Ridley after Richard Livesey,
published by Burney and Gold, Shoe Lane,
1 November 1800.

In November 1794 he was appointed to command the *Triumph* (74), which was one of the ships under the command of Vice-Admiral Cornwallis during his famous fighting retreat on 17 June 1795. *Triumph* was one of the two ships placed in the rear because their faster rate of sailing made it easier for them to weave round to fire on the pursuing French ships. At the time of the mutiny at the Nore in 1797 Gower was very disappointed that his men, whom he thought he had treated well, joined the mutineers. Driven ashore, he was appointed to command *Neptune* (98) fitting to act against the chief mutineers, as commodore with command over all ships between London Bridges and the Nore. Fortunately the mutiny collapsed before it was necessary to use fratricidal violence. He remained in *Neptune* as a private ship under Admiral Sir Thomas Pasley until he was promoted rear-admiral on 14 February 1799. On 9 February 1801 he hoisted his flag on board *Princess Royal* (90) and joined the Channel fleet, but when the preliminaries of the peace of Amiens were signed he struck his flag on 13 February 1802.

He was appointed vice-admiral on 23 April 1804, over a year after the renewal of war, and on 21 May hoisted his flag on *Isis* (50) as commander-in-chief and governor of Newfoundland. There he raised a subscription amongst the naval, military and law officers with which to endow the first school in St John's, in which the boys 'are taught to read and write; to make and repair all descriptions of nets that are used in either the salmon, mackerel, herring, or other fisheries. When thoroughly educated, they are employed at sea with the fishermen, and are thus trained up to be excellent sailors. A finer nursery for seamen cannot be devised.' This was to be his last command, but he was promoted admiral on 25 October 1809. He died a bachelor on 21 June 1814, aged seventy-one, in Hambledon, Hampshire.

Lt: 9 July 1766
Capt: 9 January 1780
R-Adm: 14 February 1799
V-Adm: 23 April 1804
Adm: 25 October 1809

GRAHAM

CAPTAIN EDWARDS LLOYD GRAHAM was a good-natured fighting captain.

He was born in London, son of Aaron Graham, police magistrate in London, and his wife, who was a daughter of Admiral Richard Edwards, after whom, and Captain Thomas Lloyd, they named their baby. He first went to sea on 10 April 1789 in *Salisbury* (50) flying the flag of Vice-Admiral Milbanke, with Captain William Domett and later Captain Edward Pellew. He was initially rated as 'Admiral's Retinue' but this was not a nominal placement on the ship's books, as she was employed in Newfoundland, where Milbanke, was governor and commander-in-chief, until 20 July 1791. Graham progressed during that period to able seaman, and then to midshipman. On 25 June 1795 he joined *Triumph* (74) under the command of Captain Erasmus Gower, eight days after that ship had been in action in Admiral Cornwallis's famous retreat.

He returned ashore on 31 December 1796, and apparently was prepared to pass his examination by Captain Sir Edward Pellew. On 17 February 1797 he was commissioned lieutenant in Pellew's ship *Indefatigable* (64). This was a real professional challenge. Pellew was a thrusting commander who provided plenty of excitement for his officers and men, and had just fought a remarkable action in a full gale on the French coast which ended in the wreck of *Droits de l'Homme* (74) and the British frigate *Amazon* (38). Graham left *Indefatigable* on 6 December 1800, and after a period of recuperation ashore, on 10 February 1801 he joined *Windsor Castle* (90) commanded by Captain Oughton and flying Admiral Sir Andrew Mitchell's flag. Ill health returned, and he had to be invalided ashore.

Admiral the earl of St Vincent recognised Graham's abilities, and on 29 April 1802, when he was first lord, he promoted Graham to the rank of commander. But it was peacetime, and Graham's next ship was the *Princess Royal* (90) flying Sir Erasmus Gower's flag, which he joined on 15 June as a lieutenant. He had to wait until 29 November 1803 before he was appointed to the *Zephyr,* brig (10). His service was first at Margate to guard against invasion, and then *Zephyr* was sent cruising in defence of trade.

On 8 May 1804 St Vincent, on his leaving office, again ensured Graham's promotion, to post captain's rank. Graham was unemployed in his new rank until 1 July 1806, when he was appointed by the Honourable Charles Grey, the first lord, to the *Vestal* (28). He was then placed under the command of Commodore E W C R Owen in *Clyde* with orders to watch the French flotilla at Boulogne and endeavour to 'annoy' it. In 1806 the annoyances included Congreve's rockets and the most implacable foe was the weather.

The *Naval Chronicle* reports:

In February [1807], during the severe gale of wind, when so many of our ships and brave mariners were lost, Captain Graham experienced a most miraculous deliverance. On the 18th of that month, when at his station off Dungeness, about four A.M. whilst the weather which had been previously serene, was extremely severe from cold wind at N.N.E. and a very heavy snow; a most tremendous gale came on. The cold was so intense, that several of the crew, who had been sent up aloft to furl the topsails, became benumbed, and were obliged to be lowered down, in that state, by ropes. After repeated efforts, the sails of the *Vestal* were at length furled, except the main-top-sail which was blown to atoms. The *Vestal* was then brought to; and such continued the violence of the gale, that at eight P.M. finding they could not weather the French shore, no alternative was left to save their lives, but to risk their immediately anchoring the ship within only three miles of the town of Dieppe. The gale afterwards continued with unabated fury during all the night; and the ensuing break of day displayed one of the most awful and tremendous sights, that was ever beheld by those 'who go down to the sea in ships, and see the works of the Lord and his wonders on the deep.' As the morning

broke, around the *Vestal* were at first indistinctly discerned through the haze, between 20 and 30 sail of British merchant ships, which had been blown out of the Downs. Some already wrecked on the enemy's shore, others driving bodily on the French coast, with signals of distress flying; many without masts, and the greater part with their sails split. NC 29.359

From the Downs, *Vestal* was deployed into the North Sea, and then, according to the *Naval Chronicle*, to Newfoundland, but time was found for a visit to the Azores to purchase wine for the garrison, and to sightsee amongst the hot pools of São Miguel. On the last leg of the voyage, *Vestal* was beat to quarters expecting immediate action with what turned out to be an iceberg. In July the following year it was found to be necessary to visit the Azores again, this time for beef, and yet another visit was made in 1809, when *Vestal* was detained there a full three months. The contrast with the winter gales in the Channel, the North Sea and Newfoundland must have been hard to resist. In his précis of his service record, however, Graham did not admit to having been to Newfoundland, let alone the Azores.

He left the *Vestal* in May 1810 and immediately assumed command of the 12-pounder frigate *Pallas* (32), in which he served in the North Sea until November, when he was appointed to command another 12-pounder frigate, *Southampton* (32) at Portsmouth. On 30 January he took command of the *Alcmene* (32), in which he served in the Adriatic; reportedly Graham was then made governor of the captured island of Lissa, and then stationed off Sardinia. He transferred on 1 February 1814 to *Caledonia* (120) as flag captain to Pellew, who was now vice-admiral and commander-in-chief Mediterranean, and on 18 April 1814 he moved into his last command, *Apollo* (38). He left her in July, and died on 1 June 1820 in Cheltenham, Gloucestershire.

Captain Edward Lloyd Graham, R.N.,
engraved by T Blood from a miniature in the
possession of Mrs Graham, published
by Joyce Gold, Naval Chronicle Offices,
103 Shoe Lane, London,
31 May 1813.

Lt: 17 February 1797
Cmdr: 29 April 1802
Capt: 8 May 1804

GRAVES

ADMIRAL SIR THOMAS GRAVES, KB, was part of one of the Royal Navy's largest dynasties. He was a kinsman of Admiral the Right Honourable Thomas Lord Graves, and nephew of Admiral Samuel Graves, his brothers Samuel, John and Richard were all to become rear-admirals, and his cousin Thomas was, like himself, to become a full admiral. His career exemplifies the incestuous society of the Royal Navy, which ensured promotion for the well-connected, and thereby ensured that young officers were effectively mentored by senior officers whom they would be very reluctant to disappoint.

He was born in January 1747 in county Londonderry, the fourth son of the Revd John Graves of Castle Dawson and his wife Jane, daughter of John Hudson. It is believed that at an early age he entered the navy in his uncle's ship as a midshipman, and served during the Seven Years War on board the *Scorpion* (10), *Duke* (90) and *Venus* (36). After the conclusion of peace in 1763, he was placed under the charge of his kinsman Captain Thomas, later Lord Graves, serving first in the *Antelope* (50) and following him to the *Edgar* (74). In 1765 Captain Graves was dispatched to the coast of Africa to prevent the French recovering their former possessions on the river Gambia, and on 30 October 1765 young Thomas was given a lieutenant's commission on board *Shannon* (38), continuing as her first lieutenant on her return to Portsmouth. There was a tradition that, in the sickly climate of West Africa, commanders had a right to promote anyone to fill the place of officers who died there, and this may have been the reason why there is no record of young Graves

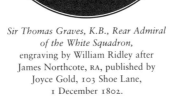

Sir Thomas Graves, K.B., Rear Admiral of the White Squadron, engraving by William Ridley after James Northcote, RA, published by Joyce Gold, 103 Shoe Lane, 1 December 1802.

being formally examined and why he was under the requisite twenty years old. Reportedly his enthusiasm for the dangers of the mission in the Gambia had been manifest to his kinsman. All the same, he remained unemployed after returning to Portsmouth until the Falkland Islands crisis in 1770, when apparently he was in the impress service, and had to deal tactfully but forcefully with angry crowds. He may also have served as lieutenant of *Arethusa* (32).

He was selected in 1773 by Captain Phipps, later Lord Mulgrave, as one of his lieutenants on board *Racehorse* for the expedition towards the North Pole, after which his uncle, Admiral Samuel Graves, gave him command of *Diana*, schooner (4), at Boston. This put him into the firing line at the outset of the American rebellion. After an intense skirmish, General Putnam succeeded in burning the schooner at Winnisimmet Ferry, and while evacuating his men, Thomas and his brother John, who had come to render assistance from his ship the *Preston*, were badly burnt. He was soon in action again in the fighting around Boston and Rhode Island. When the Admiralty recalled his uncle, young Thomas also returned to England as lieutenant of the *Preston*, but he returned in her with Commodore Hotham and was in the fighting at Rhode Island, New York and the Chesapeake.

Captain Thomas Graves was promoted rear-admiral on 15 March 1779 and given command of the West Indies station, and young Thomas was promoted master and commander the same day and given command of *Savage*, sloop, in which he served under his kinsman's command. He soon returned to the American station carrying dispatches to Vice-Admiral Arbuthnot, and was given the task of controlling the Potomac river to prevent the French army under Marquis de La Fayette effecting a crossing. On 5 May 1781 Arbuthnot made Graves post captain in the *Bedford* (74) during the absence of Commodore Edmund Affleck. He took a part in Admiral Thomas Graves's tactically careful and strategically disastrous action with the Comte de Grasse off the Chesapeake on 5 September 1781. Young Graves was again in action in *Bedford* as Commodore Affleck's flag captain under Admiral Sir Samuel Hood against de Grasse on 25 January 1782 in Basseterre Road, St Kitts, and in the actions on 9 April and the battle of the Saintes on 12 April.

Graves had been promised a frigate fitting out at Halifax by Vice-Admiral Arbuthnot, and had delayed his acceptance because he deemed the immediate prospect of action against the French fleet more important, but eventually late in 1782 he took command of *Magicienne* (32). He was kept employed in convoy work, but in January 1783 had a stiff fight with a French frigate which left *Magicienne* dismasted.

Graves was not employed during the peace, much of which he spent in France, nor was he employed at the beginning of the war with the French Republic, but at last in 1800 he was put in command of *Cumberland* (74) in the Channel fleet under Admiral the earl of St Vincent. At the great promotion which occurred on 1 January 1801 in honour of the union of Ireland with Britain, Graves was advanced to rear-admiral, and in March he hoisted his flag in *Polyphemus* (64) with orders to place himself under the command of Admiral Sir Hyde Parker for the expedition to Copenhagen and the Baltic. He shifted his flag into *Defiance* (74) and on 2 April served as second in command to Vice-Admiral Nelson in the attack on the Danish line of defence before the city and naval arsenal. Nelson, in his official letter to Hyde Parker, called attention to 'the high and distinguished merit and gallantry of Rear-Admiral Graves', and in recognition he was made KB on 14 May 1801. The investiture took place on board *St George* (90) in Kioge Bay near the scene of the battle. His health was poor, but nevertheless he shifted his flag back to the *Polyphemus* and then to the *Monarch* (74),

in which he continued to serve until January 1802.

Continued deterioration in his health led to his retirement, but he did return briefly to service between October 1804 and February 1805, when he served in the Bay of Biscay, usually flying his flag in *Foudroyant* (80). His decision to take his squadron to Quiberon Bay to water in January 1805 was the beginning of the chain of events which led to the battle of Trafalgar because it allowed Rear-Admiral Missiessy to sail from Rochefort under orders to meet Vice-Admiral Villeneuve at Martinique. In effect this mistake also led to Graves's dismissal. He was promoted vice-admiral on 9 November 1805, and was not employed in the new rank. He retired to Woodbine Hill, Honiton, Devon.

His first marriage was to Miss Bacon, sister of Colonel Philip Bacon, and by that lady he had one daughter, Mary. He married again on 20 August 1808, uniting with Susanna Blacknell of Packham, Suffolk. There were no children from the second marriage, and Graves, having been promoted admiral on 12 August 1812, died on 29 March 1814, aged sixty-seven. His wife survived him until 31 January 1816.

Lt: 30 October 1765
M-C: 15 March 1779
Capt: 5 May 1781
R-Adm: 1 January 1801
V-Adm: 9 November 1805
Adm: 12 August 1812

GRAVES

ADMIRAL THOMAS, LORD GRAVES, BARON OF GRAVESEND, had the misfortune to be the man who commanded in the decisive battle that led to the defeat of the Loyalist cause in the American colonies. His last service was as a subordinate to Lord Howe at the battle of the Glorious First of June in 1794.

He was born on 23 October 1725 in Thanckes, Cornwall, the second son of Rear-Admiral Thomas Graves, and his second wife Elizabeth, eldest daughter of the Revd Dr Giles Budgell, DD, rector of St Thomas's, Exeter. He first went to sea when quite young, with the patronage of Commodore Henry Medley, who at the time was governor of

Newfoundland. He served with his father in *Norfolk* (80) at the unsuccessful expedition against Cartagena in 1741, and afterwards in the Mediterranean. He was promoted lieutenant in *Romney* (50) on 25 June 1743 by Admiral Matthews, and served in her at the battle of Toulon on 11 February 1744. In 1746 he served under Admiral Richard Lestock as lieutenant in the Spanish prize *Princessa* (70) in the expedition against L'Orient. When Lestock died, Graves was appointed to the *Monmouth* (70) with Captain Harrison, and was present at the first and second battles of Cape Finisterre on 3 May and 14 October 1747. In 1751 he served as first lieutenant of the *Assistance* (50) on the coast of Africa under Commodore Matthew Buckle, and later Commodore George Stepney. He was promoted on 12 March 1754 master and commander of *Hazard*, sloop, and was made post captain on 8 July 1755 in *Sheerness* (20); but he was court-martialled and censured in 1757 for being too cautious when he encountered a ship which he thought was a ship of the line, but was in fact a French East Indiaman. Nevertheless, he continued to be employed. In January 1758 he was appointed to command *Unicorn* (28) in the Channel fleet under Admiral Anson, and served the following year under Rear-Admiral George Rodney. He was put in temporary command of *Oxford* (?) from September 1760 to May 1761, and then appointed to *Antelope* (50) under orders to command at Newfoundland. When he arrived on 5 July he found himself faced with a superior force under Admiral de Ternay at St John's. He sheltered in Placentia Bay, putting men ashore to repair the fortifications and sending to Halifax to request reinforcements from Rear-Admiral Lord Colvill and General Amherst. He remained at Newfoundland until 21 November 1762.

Graves held the parliamentary seat for East Looe, Cornwall, from 2 January 1755 to May 1775.

In November 1764 he was given command of a guardship at Plymouth, *Temeraire* (74), and in 1765 he was dispatched in *Edgar* (74) flying a broad pendant to the coast of Africa to put a stop to the evident intentions of the French governor of Senegal to recover the former French possessions on the river Gambia. The Grenville cabinet's handling of this crisis might have had serious consequences, but Graves's circumspect character here proved its value. He then returned to command of *Temeraire* until the end of the usual three-year appointment. At the time of the Falkland Islands crisis in 1770 he was given command of *Cambridge* (80). He married on 22 June 1771 Elizabeth, daughter and coheiress of William Peere Williams of Cadnay, Devon. She presented him with two sons and three daughters.

In 1773 at the time of the Swedish crisis he was

The Right Honourable Thomas Lord Graves,
Admiral of the White,
engraving by William Ridley after
James Northcote, RA, published by
Burney and Gold, Shoe Lane,
1 June 1801.

appointed to *Raisonnable* (64). He was appointed colonel of the marines on 31 March 1775 and with the outbreak of hostilities in America he was appointed in 1776 to *Nonsuch* (64). In 1777 he moved into *Conqueror* (74) under the command of Vice-Admiral John Byron, serving in North America and the West Indies, but he returned to England when he was promoted to rear-admiral of the blue on 19 March 1779, hoisting his flag on *London* (90) in the Channel fleet under Sir Charles Hardy. While in home waters he took part in rear-admiral Kempenfelt's experiments with tactical signals.

The following March he was put in command of a squadron to reinforce Vice-Admiral Arbuthnot on the North American station, where he arrived on 13 July, and fought in the engagement off the Chesapeake on 16 March 1781. He succeeded to command on the North American station on 4 July 1781, and on 5 September he brought the reinforced French fleet to action off the Chesapeake. The outcome was a tactical draw, and a strategic defeat of the first order. Admirals de Grasse and Barras were able to repass the capes with thirty-six ships, to Graves's eighteen. Graves had no choice but to withdraw to New York, and the surrender of the British army at Yorktown under Lord Cornwallis followed on 19 October, the day Graves sailed again from New York hoping he might yet parry the French attack. Graves then handed over his command to Rear-Admiral R Digby, according to previous order, and sailed to the West Indies.

Sir Samuel Hood, who served under Graves at the Chesapeake, blamed Graves for failing to catch the French as they passed out of the roads, and bring about a mêlée in which they could not deploy their superior force. Whether that would in fact have been possible is uncertain, and the blame may have lain more with Rodney in the West Indies for letting de Grasse proceed to the Chesapeake with overwhelming force. In order to address the criticism, Graves obtained leave to return to England. *En route* in command of a convoy he was to suffer severe losses to a hurricane, including the foundering of his flagship, *Ramillies* (74). He and his entire crew, however, survived by being taken on board a merchant ship.

He was promoted vice-admiral on 24 September 1787, and the following year was appointed to command at Portsmouth. With the French declaration of war in 1793 he was appointed second in command of the Channel fleet under Admiral Lord Howe, and promoted admiral on 12 April 1794. He played a prominent part in the battle of the Glorious First of June in 1794, flying his flag in

Royal Sovereign (100). This, however, was to be the end of his service life; he was so badly wounded in the arm that he had to retire. He was awarded a gold medal and chain, and was made baron of Gravesend of county Londonderry on the Irish establishment on 12 August 1794. He died on 1 February 1802, aged seventy-six, in Cadhay near Ottery, Devon.

Lt: 25 June 1743
M-C: 12 March 1754
Capt: 8 July 1755
R-Adm: 19 March 1779
V-Adm: 24 September 1787
Adm: 12 April 1794

GREY

CAPTAIN EDWARD GREY'S was a story of merit scarcely rewarded, probably because he had few friends great enough to secure him promotion.

Nothing is known of his parents, but he was probably born in 1765, and it is known that he entered the navy on 29 September 1778 as an able seaman on board the *Alexander* (74), or perhaps the *Adventure*, under the command of Captain, later Admiral, Richard Kempenfelt. He served in the Channel fleet, and was rated master's mate on 1 July 1779; he transferred into *Britannia* (100) flying the flag of Vice-Admiral George Darby, and was rated midshipman when he transferred into *Prothee* (64) under Captain Charles Buckner. He served in *Victory* (100) flying the flag of Rear-Admiral Kempenfelt, *Ocean* (90) under Captain Edgar and *Alexander* (74) under Captains Lord Longford and Thomas Fitzherbert, and, when she paid off in 1783 after the peace, joined *Powerful* (74). She was a guardship at Plymouth under Captain Thomas Fitch, and just launched.

Admiral Kempenfelt's death in 1782 when the *Royal George* sank doubtless had serious consequences for his followers. Accordingly Grey obtained permission to quit the service, became a part-owner and master of a merchant vessel, and traded for seven years between London and Bordeaux. He returned to naval service only after the French declaration of war on 1 February 1793.

He had been examined on 14 July 1785, but he was rated master's mate when in March he joined

Edward Grey, Commander R.N.,
engraved by R? Page, published by Joyce Gold,
103 Shoe Lane, Fleet Street, London,
31 August 1811.

Britannia (100), under the command of John Holloway and flying the flag of Vice-Admiral Hotham, second in command in the Mediterranean fleet. In September, Grey shifted into *Victory*, flying the flag of Admiral Lord Hood, the commander-in-chief, who commissioned him lieutenant on 29 September 1793 in *Windsor Castle* (90), which was flying the flag of Vice-Admiral Crosby. Later he was appointed to *Eclair,* sloop, and after Admiral Hotham succeeded Lord Hood, Grey was commissioned first lieutenant of *Romulus* (36), commanded by Captain George Johnstone Hope.

In *Romulus* he was present at Hotham's engagement off Genoa on 13 March 1795, when Captain Fremantle in *Inconstant* (36), supported by Captain Nelson in *Agamemnon* (64), attacked *Ça Ira* (80), which struck. The next morning it was found that *Ça Ira* had been abandoned by the prize crew and was sinking.

> Captain Hope, with the utmost promptitude, ordered the stern-boat to be lowered, and despatched Lieutenant Grey,

and Mr. Anderson (the carpenter of the *Romulus*) to inspect and ascertain the real state of the ship. When the boat approached the *Ça Ira*, the number of Frenchmen who pressed forward to jump into her was so great, that it was not safe to venture alongside. Lieutenant Grey, therefore, went under the counter, got on board by the rudder pendants, and ordered the boat to lie off on her oars.... On sounding the well, there appeared seven feet water in the hold. The first step, therefore, that Lieutenant Grey took was, to set all the pumps to work – seven in number; an object which he accomplished, with considerable difficulty, chiefly by French soldiers, as the seamen, on the plea of being prisoners, would not work. The French officers declined all exertion of their influence, on the same ground. With the assistance of his own carpenter, and the carpenter and gunner of the *Ça Ira*, who rendered every assistance in their power, Lieutenant Grey then inspected the ship, with all the minuteness of which his time would allow. She was in a most alarming state. The water was forcing its way in, through the shot-holes under water, fore and aft; several of the lower ports, in the gun-room, rendered useless in the action, were obliged to be filled up with deal plank; many of the bolts in the sides, for securing the lower-deck guns, had been shot away, and others so much damaged as to render it scarcely possible to secure the guns, which were French 36-pounders. [NC 26.185]

With the assistance of carpenters sent from the fleet, Grey managed to control the leaks and secure the guns, and to bring *Ça Ira* into port under tow by *Romulus*. Later *Romulus* was dispatched to the assistance of *Illustrious* (74), which had been driven ashore and in the end had to be burnt.

These services led Captain Hope to recommend Grey for promotion, and he was taken into *Britannia* (100), the flagship. Later he was given charge of the transports at Leghorn, and in 1796 he commanded a division of transports at the navy's evacuation of Leghorn, re-entering the harbour after the French occupation to bring out the last ship loaded with timber, which was unrigged and lying on an inside berth within the mole. For this service he was mentioned in dispatches. The convoy of transports was nearly taken by the Spanish fleet off Gibraltar just before the battle of Cape St Vincent, but got safely past and into the Tagus.

He spent the last four years of the war as first lieutenant of *Adamant* (50), commanded by Captain William Hotham, mostly at the Cape of Good Hope station. There Grey distinguished himself by leading three boat loads of marines to destroy a French frigate, *La Preneuse*, which was aground on Isle de France and guarded by her landed batteries. Hotham recommended Grey for promotion, without any immediate result. Grey next distinguished himself by cutting a ship out of Port Louis harbour in September 1800, and again Hotham recommended him for promotion. But it was not until 29 April 1802 that he was finally promoted commander by the earl of St Vincent.

He was to remain in that rank for a long time. His employment on the resumption of hostilities was in the impress service, in which he worked until August 1810, raising and sending to the Nore 2,305 men and 200 artificers to the dockyards. After the surrender of Copenhagen in 1807 he recruited the voluntary services of 245 seamen mostly from the Danish Greenland ships, and several pilots, to help navigate the captured Danish warships back to England. He also superintended the equipment of the armed ships and transports hired at Hull.

The *Naval Chronicle* in its biographical memoir of Edward Grey published in 1811, commented that 'when Captain Grey received his appointment, in 1803, the apprehension that he should stand a worse chance of promotion, than if afloat in the command of a ship, was removed, by an intimation, that a successful rendezvous was, of all others, a situation the most likely to lead to promotion. Unfortunately, however, he has been disappointed in his hopes...' NC 26.194

He was not immediately employed after leaving the impress service, but he was finally made post captain on 4 December 1813. There is no record that he ever married. He became a Greenwich hospital out-pensioner on 14 October 1815, and died on 1 November 1825 in Holy Island, Northumberland.

Lt: 29 September 1793
Cmdr: 29 April 1802
Capt: 4 December 1813

HALLOWELL

ADMIRAL SIR BENJAMIN HALLOWELL, GCB, having learnt his trade in five battles during the American war, fought in Corsica, at Cape St Vincent and at the Nile, as well as participating in numerous other important but lesser actions.

He was born on 1 January 1761 in Boston, Massachusetts, a son of Benjamin Hallowell, who was captain of a privateer, then collector and later controller of the customs in Boston. His mother was Mary, née Boylston. He entered the navy as a midshipman in *Sandwich* (90) under the command of Captain Richard Edwards on 11 May 1777. His ship was lying at Spithead, and he was lent into several different cruisers. On 22 April 1778 he transferred to *Asia* (64) under Captain Vandeput for service in the East Indies; he returned home to transfer again on 26 April 1781 into *Fortunée* (40) under Captain Hugh Cloberry Christian, for service in the West Indies. He was rated an able seaman, and transferred on 31 July to *Barfleur* (90) flying the flag of Rear-Admiral Sir Samuel Hood, who gave him an order to act as lieutenant in *Alcide* (74), which he joined on 31 August, five days before the battle of the Chesapeake. On 5 November he joined *Alfred* (74), and he was still serving in her at the time of the two actions in Basseterre Road, St Kitts, on 25 and 26 January 1782, and at the actions near Dominica and the Saintes on 9 and 12 April. His commission was confirmed on 25 April 1783.

With the conclusion of peace, Hallowell came ashore on 26 July, but he obtained command of *Falcon*, brig-sloop (10), on 1 May 1784, and served in the West Indies until his return to Portsmouth on 25 July 1786. On 3 October 1787 he was appointed to *Barfleur* flying Hood's flag, and he remained on board until 15 May 1790, when he followed Captain John Knight to *Victory* (100) for service in the Channel fleet at the time of the Nootka Sound crisis. He was promoted master and commander on 22 November 1790, and appointed on 5 December to *Scorpion,* sloop, in which he was ordered to the coast of Africa. He remained on board until 1 October 1792, and then had a year and a half's leave ashore.

On 21 February 1793, three weeks after the French declaration of war, he was appointed to the storeship *Camel,* under orders for Mediterranean service. There he was promoted post captain on 30 August 1793, and made acting captain of *Robust* (74) on 11 September in the place of Captain Elphinstone, later Lord Keith, who had been made governor of Fort la Malgue during the occupation of Toulon. When it was found necessary to evacuate Toulon, Hallowell was entrusted with the embarkation of part of the army, and then was appointed on 23 December to command *Courageux* (74) in the place of Captain Waldegrave who had been sent to England with dispatches. He returned to *Victory* as a volunteer on 1 May 1794, served at the reduction of Bastia in command of the flotilla of gunboats and launches, and afterwards landed with a party of seamen to serve as a volunteer with Captain Nelson at the siege of Calvi. He subsequently served under Admiral Hotham and under Jervis, in command of *Lowestoffe* (32), which he joined on 11 August. On 17 June 1795 he transferred to *Courageux,* but was so unfortunate as to be ashore as part of a court martial when she dragged her anchors in Gibraltar Bay during a heavy gale. Not being released from his duty to return to his ship, he suffered the agony of learning she had been wrecked with the loss of most of her people on the coast of Africa.

He was taken into *Victory* flying Jervis's flag, and served in her during the battle of Cape St Vincent on 14 February 1797. He was then charged with carrying duplicate dispatches home, and on 15 March was given command of *Lively* (26).

On 25 October he was moved into the *Swiftsure* (74), which formed part of the inshore squadron off Cadiz. The news of the mutinies in the home ports led to expressions of discontent on board her, but Hallowell was an intimidating figure who took forceful, but unofficial, action to restore discipline. In May 1798 he was ordered to form part of the squadron under Rear-Admiral Nelson's command and entrusted with defeating the French armament which succeeded in taking Malta and Egypt, but which Nelson defeated at the battle of the Nile on 1 August 1799. *Swiftsure* was last into action, because earlier in the day Nelson had ordered her and *Alexander* (74) to look into Alexandria. Hallowell had to find his way into the firing line through smoke and the gathering darkness. He very nearly fired into *Bellerophon* (74), which was retiring so badly damaged as not to be able to show her recognition lights, but he had determined not to fire before his anchors were down. He put *Swiftsure* where she lay across the bows of *L'Orient* flying Vice-Admiral Bruey's flag, and across *Franklin*'s quarter. When *L'Orient* caught fire he focused his gunnery on her until she blew up, when he redirected his guns towards *Franklin,* which was forced to surrender.

After Nelson left the coast of Egypt, Hallowell remained under the command of Captain Samuel Hood, attempting to concert a common defence with the Turkish navy. When Sir Sidney Smith assumed command, Hallowell joined Nelson at Palermo. It was there that he gave Nelson his famous gift of a coffin made from *L'Orient*'s mainmast, evidently with the hope that it would cool his commander's inflated ego. During the following three months he served on the coast of Italy under Thomas Troubridge, taking part in the capture of Fort St Elmo, Capua and Civitavecchia. The king of Naples appointed him to the order of St Ferdinand and of Merit, and awarded him one of the customary gifts of kings, a snuffbox emblazoned with diamonds in the form of the royal cipher. *Swiftsure* was then ordered to join Rear-Admiral Duckworth at Minorca, and under his command proceeded to Lisbon.

He married on 17 February 1800, in Gibraltar. His wife's name is not recorded, but she was of a naval family, being a daughter of Captain John Nicholson Inglefield, RN, commissioner of the dockyard and sister of Rear-Admiral Samuel Hood Inglefield and sister-in-law of Captain Henry Whitby, RN.

Hallowell subsequently served for a while on the coast of Spain off Cadiz as flag captain to Sir Richard Bickerton, before proceeding with him to Egypt. During the operations there he briefly exchanged into *Kent* (74). Following the defeat of the French at Alexandria, and having returned to *Swiftsure*, he was detached for Malta, eighty-six men short of complement and with fifty-nine sick on board. He was charged with the escort of a convoy, but when he learnt that a greatly superior French force under Rear-Admiral Ganteaume was attempting to land troops near Tripoli, he felt his duty lay in abandoning the convoy and joining Sir John Borlase Warren off the African coast. The outcome was that he encountered the enemy alone on 24 June 1801 and was captured after a stout resistance. Following his release on parole, he was on 18 August acquitted by a court martial of the charges of deserting his charge and subsequently surrendering his ship.

For these services he was nominated a knight of the royal and military order of San Fernando of Spain in 1800, and awarded a Turkish gold medal for distinguished services on the coast of Egypt in 1802.

On 12 August 1802, during the peace of Amiens, he was given command on the coast of Africa, flying a broad pendant in *Argo* (44). Touching at Barbados on his return voyage to England, he learnt from Sir Samuel Hood that renewal of the war was expected, and decided to assist his old chief in the reduction of St Lucia and Tobago, after which he was sent home with dispatches: 'The royal marines and a body of seamen were landed to co-operate with the army, under the command of Captain Hallowell; and it is scarcely necessary for me to add, his zeal and exertions were equally conspicuous as on the late expedition to St. Lucia. He is charged with this despatch...' Marshall 1.465

In early 1804 he was ordered to carry the Mammluk Elfi Bey back to Egypt, and Hallowell wrote a detailed account to St Vincent describing the failings and deceits of that gentleman.

On 18 August he was appointed to command of *Tigre* (80) in the Mediterranean fleet, in which he took part in Nelson's pursuit of Villeneuve and the combined Franco-Spanish fleet from Toulon and Cadiz to the West Indies in the summer of 1805. He was still under Nelson's command before the battle of Trafalgar, but *Tigre* was one of the ships detached under Rear-Admiral Louis on 3 October to take on water at Gibraltar. In the spring of 1807 he commanded the naval forces which carried an army under Major-General Fraser to take possession of Alexandria. He then served in the eastern Mediterranean, and subsequently in the force watching Toulon and the coast of Spain.

At the general promotion on 31 July 1810 he was made a colonel of marines, and he continued to command *Tigre* until he was promoted rear-admiral on 1 August 1811, when he hoisted his flag in *Elephant*, subsequently shifting to *Malta* (84). In January 1812 he returned to the Mediterranean where he remained until after the end of the war, striking his flag on 23 December 1814. He was nominated a KCB on 2 January 1815, commanded in Plymouth Sound from 28 April to 16 August 1815, with his flag flying in *Royal Sovereign* (100), and then transferred to *Tonnant* as commander-in-chief Cork harbour, where he remained until 28 October 1818. He was promoted vice-admiral on 12 August 1819. From 1 July 1821 to 31 July 1824 he commanded at the Nore with his flag flying in *Bulwark* (74) and later in *Gloucester*, and he finally shifted to *Prince Regent*. He was advanced in chivalry to GCB on 6 June 1831.

He assumed the additional surname of Carew on inheriting the estates of the Carews in Beddington, Surrey, at the death of his cousin, Mrs Anne Paston Gee, on 28 March 1828. He died with the rank of admiral on 12 September 1834, aged seventy-three, at Beddington Park, Surrey. A monument to his memory was erected in St Mary-the-Virgin, Beddington. His wife survived until 1839.

Lt: 25 April 1783
M-C: 22 November 1790 (21)
Capt: 30 August 1793
R-Adm: 1 August 1811
V-Adm: 12 August 1819
Adm: 22 July 1830

HAMILTON

ADMIRAL SIR EDWARD HAMILTON, BARONET, KCB, is equally well known for his valour in cutting His Majesty's former ship *Hermione* out of Puerto Cabello, Venezuela, and for his mental imbalance. The navy cherished him for the achievement, and took care to protect the service from his weakness.

He was born on 12 March 1772, the second and youngest son of Captain Sir John Hamilton, RN, who had been created baronet of Marlborough House, Northamptonshire, on 6 July 1776 for his services at the siege of Quebec while in command of the *Lizard* (28). His mother was Cassandra Agnes, daughter of Edward Chamberlayne of Maugersbury, Gloucestershire, and sister of Admiral Charles Chamberlayne. His name was entered on the muster book of his father's ship *Hector* (74) in 1777 when he was five, and he joined the ship as a midshipman on 21 May 1779 when he was seven years old. He served on the Jamaica station both in this own ship and in *Ramillies* (74), to which he was lent, and experienced one general action and the great hurricane of 1780. On the return of peace he went ashore to the Royal Grammar School at Guildford, returning to sea in 1787 in the *Standard* (74) under Captain Chamberlayne to serve the remainder of his seven years before being examined in 1790. He then served as a passed midshipman in the 18-pounder frigate *Melamphus* (36) under Captain Charles Morice Pole, and in 1791 joined *Victory* (100) flying the flag of Vice-Admiral Lord Hood. When the threat of war as a result of the Nootka Sound incident passed, he spent some time as a student at the University of Caen in Normandy and afterwards travelled in France and Portugal.

On the declaration of war in February 1793 he joined *Queen Charlotte* (100), Admiral Howe's flagship, and in July joined *Dido* (28) commanded by his brother Sir Charles Hamilton, being commissioned one of her lieutenants on 29 October. He established his reputation for courage when with a boat crew of only eight he captured a grounded privateer, put out the combustibles placed

to set her on fire, and then went ashore to make the crew prisoners of war. The *Naval Chronicle* commented that 'he could not resist giving way to that manly impulse of vengeance which the base attempt of burning a vessel subdued, had excited in his mind.' [NC 5.1] Later he served at the siege of Bastia in Corsica, and commanded 100 British and 300 Corsican soldiers at Girolate, where he constructed batteries on a commanding height within pistol shot of the enemy battery. After thirteen days of fire they were obliged to surrender. On 10 July 1794 he was appointed ninth lieutenant of

Sir Edward Hamilton, Kt.,
engraving by William Ridley after [William?]
Thompson, published by
Burney and Gold, Shoe Lane,
1 February 1800.

Victory, but on 7 October Admiral Hood exercised the right of flag officers to promote whom they wished, and Hamilton advanced to first lieutenant. When Hood was ordered home soon afterwards, however, and went ashore for the winter, Hamilton found himself serving in a private ship and was reduced again to junior lieutenant.

The following spring *Victory* returned to the Mediterranean, and Hamilton fought in the action of 13 July. Admiral Jervis succeeded to the command late in the year, and promoted him commander on 11 February 1796 in *Comet,* fireship, ordering him to the West Indies. On his return to Lisbon with dispatches he was promoted post captain on 3 June 1797 in the *San Josef* (110), one of the prizes from the battle of Cape St Vincent. From her Hamilton transferred into *Surprise* (24), in which he sailed to Newfoundland. Between October 1798 and January 1800 he served on the Jamaica station under Sir Hyde Parker, and reportedly made both their fortunes by bringing in, or destroying, more than eighty privateers, armed vessels and merchant ships, yielding £200,000 prize money. It was during that time that he undertook the action which made him famous, cutting out on 25 October 1799 *Hermione* (32) from inside the enemy harbour although she was moored between two batteries mounting 200 guns.

He conceived that the honour of the Royal Navy depended on the recovery of the *Hermione,* which had been taken by her crew in a bloody mutiny on 22 September 1797 and delivered to the enemy. In overcoming a very stiff Spanish resistance he was badly wounded with a blow to the head from a musket, and with cuts from sabre, pike and grape shot. The Spaniards suffered 119 killed and ninety-seven wounded, but, remarkably, the British lost only twelve men. In recognition of his merits he was awarded a 300 guinea sword by the House of Assembly in Spanish Town, Jamaica. King George created him knight bachelor on 1 February 1800 and conferred on him a naval gold medal for gallantry. While travelling home to recover from his wounds he was captured, and spent six months as a prisoner of war in Paris, where Buonaparte is supposed to have taken notice of him before he was exchanged for four French midshipmen. The Court of Common Council of the City of London awarded him 50 guineas, and on the anniversary of the retaking of the *Hermione* he was dined at the Mansion House, where he was given the freedom of the city in a gold box. But he refused an offer of a pension of £300 for his wounds, believing it would be used as an excuse for not employing him again. In any case, he had acquired suffi-

cient riches from prize money to be able to be indifferent about the proffered pension.

It may be that the blow to his head occasioned his fall from fortune, or perhaps the 'manly impulse of vengeance' early displayed, and the fearlessness shown in action, betrayed a degree of insanity not improved by the lionising he received. He was tried by court martial on 22 January 1802 for having strung his gunner and the gunner's mates in the rigging for a trivial offence. The punishment was both excessive and illegal, and Hamilton was dismissed from the service. It is possible that the navy had learnt something about the consequences of turning a blind eye to the eccentricities of captains from the sequence of brutalities which led to the murder of *Hermione*'s former captain, Hugh Pigot.

Hamilton was restored in June 1802 by order in council, but was never again employed in an operational role. He married on 1 November 1804, at St George, Hanover Square, Westminster, uniting with Frances, daughter of John Macnamara of Llangoed Castle, Brecknockshire, and of Baker Street, London. In June 1806 he was appointed to the royal yacht *Mary*, and later he moved to the *Prince Regent,* which he commanded until his resignation on 7 January 1819. He was nominated KCB on 2 January 1815 and created a baronet on 26 January 1819, and he was appointed deputy lieutenant for Brecknockshire. He continued to be promoted through ranks, and when he died on 21 March 1851, aged seventy-nine, at 17 Cumberland Terrace, Regent's Park, London, he had the rank of admiral. His wife had predeceased him on 27 March 1840.

Lt: 29 October 1793
Cmdr: 11 February 1796
Capt: 3 June 1797
R-Adm: 19 July 1821
V-Adm: 10 January 1837
Adm: 9 November 1846

HARDINGE

CAPTAIN GEORGE NICHOLAS HARDINGE was a man who could have shone in the law or been a scholar, but his heart was in the navy, and he died a hero's death in action. Someone, whom the *Naval Chronicle* simply describes as 'a lady... than whom none of her sex was ever more accomplished, and more acute in the discernment of character...', described him in August 1808: 'I had the good fortune (and I call it still by that name), to pass a week in his charming society, and was much alone with him: I discovered in him then, as far as I could presume to judge, a depth of solid understanding,... engaging manners – a high sense of honour in every thing – a noble way of thinking, and principles of gratitude, beyond any which I had ever observed in a human creature, especially at his age. His excellent capacity had been improved by a fund of general knowledge, very singular I believe in his profession. His temper was gentle, and his heart was no less affectionate than it was elevated by the heroism of public spirit.' Could that have been Jane Austen writing, the sister of naval officers and certainly an acute judge of character? [NC 20.265–7]

He was born on 11 April 1781 in Kingston-upon-Thames, Surrey, the second son of the Revd Henry Hardinge, rector of Stanhope, county Durham, and vicar of Kingston-upon-Thames. His mother was Frances, daughter of James Best of Boxley and of Chatham. His uncle George Hardinge, a Welsh judge and the attorney-general, undertook George's education at Eton with the intention he should go into the law, but he did not do well, and expressed a determination to go to sea, perhaps in emulation of his uncle Sir Richard Hardinge, baronet, captain of an East Indiaman. He was sent in 1793 to join the *Meleager* (32) as a midshipman under the command of Captain Charles Tyler, seeing service in Toulon and Corsica. When the French frigate *La Minerve* (34) was captured, sunk, salved and put into service as *San Fiorenzo*, Captain Tyler was put in her command and took Hardinge with him. He served in *Diomede* (50) at the time of Admiral Hotham's action off Hyères, and while he was subsequently employed on the coast of Italy, Sir William Hamilton, British envoy to the court of Naples, took an interest in him and introduced him to the study of history and the arts.

In 1798, after a few months at home, he returned to sea in the *Aigle* (38), again under Captain Tyler, and on 18 July had the ill fortune to be wrecked on the Isle of Planes off the African coast. After his rescue, he came to the attention of the earl of St Vincent, who was much taken by his good appearance and intellect. He was placed in the *Theseus* (74) under the command of Captain Ralph Willett Miller, and was still on board when Miller was killed by shells fired into *Theseus* off Acre in May 1799. He was then ordered home, and put into *Foudroyant* (80) as a supernumerary lieutenant, and was in her at the action with the *Guillaume Tell* on 29 March 1800. He then returned to the Egyptian theatre, in *Tigre* (80), Captain Sir Sidney Smith, and was

The Late Captain George Nicholas Hardinge, engraved by H R Cook after Lethbridge, published by Joyce Gold, 103 Shoe Lane, 31 October 1808.

promoted lieutenant on 15 October 1800. He was subsequently awarded a Turkish gold medal.

The earl of St Vincent when he was first lord promoted Hardinge commander, on 29 April 1802, and gave him command in March 1803 of *Terror*, bomb, in which he served first under Captain E W C R Owen off Boulogne and then under Admiral Sir James Saumarez. His most notable action was during the attack on Granville in which *Terror* was reduced to a wreck. He was then appointed to the *Scorpion* (18) with orders to serve in the North

Sea, where he captured a Dutch sloop, *Atalante*, in Vlie Roads, Texel, on 31 March 1804. He led a boarding party from *Scorpion*'s boats and came close to losing his life when the Dutch captain disarmed him. 'At this time,' he wrote to a friend, 'all the men were come from the boats, and were in possession of the deck. Two were going to fall upon the captain at once. I ran up – held them back – and then adjured him to accept quarter. With inflexible heroism, he disdained the gift, kept us at bay, and compelled us to kill him. He fell, covered with honourable wounds.'

In recognition of his victory, Hardinge was made post captain on 10 April 1804, and was presented by the committee of Lloyd's with a sword of 300 guineas' value. He was three times disappointed in ships he was offered, which turned out to be either beyond repair or, in the case of one he sailed to Bombay to join, only just building on the ways. He had to make do with the now ancient and crazy *San Fiorenzo* (34), and in her was killed on 8 March 1808, aged 26, towards the end of a three-day action with a powerful French privateer, *Piémontaise*, off Ceylon, which ended in the capture of the enemy. He was buried at Colombo, and a monument to his memory was erected in St Paul's Cathedral, and another in Bombay.

> Lt: 15 October 1800
> Cmdr: 29 April 1802
> Capt: 10 April 1804

HARDY

VICE-ADMIRAL SIR THOMAS MASTERMAN HARDY, BARONET, GCB, served as flag captain to Nelson in seven ships, including *Elephant* at Copenhagen and *Victory* at Trafalgar.

He was born on 5 April 1769 at Kingston Russell House near Portisham, Dorset, the second son of Joseph Hardy of Portisham, Dorset, and his wife Nanny, daughter and coheiress of Thomas Masterman of Kingston Russell and Winterbourne St Martin. He entered the navy on 30 November 1781 as a captain's servant in the brig *Helena*, but left her in April 1782 and was sent to Crewkerne grammar school, although he remained on the books of the guardships *Seaford* (20) and *Carnatic*

(74). He then served for several years in the merchant service, before joining the *Hebe* (38) on 5 February 1790, being rated midshipman, and on 1 March 1791 master's mate. He later joined *Tisiphone*, sloop, under Captain Anthony Hunt. In May 1793 he followed Hunt to *Amphitrite* (24), where he was rated an able seaman, and in her proceeded to the Mediterranean. He was commissioned lieutenant of *Meleager* (32) under the command of Captain Charles Tyler on 10 November 1793, and served in the squadron commanded by Horatio Nelson off Genoa. In June 1794 his old messmate Captain Sir George Cockburn succeeded to command of *Meleager*, and when in August 1796 he transferred to *La Minerve* (40) Hardy accompanied him. Hardy was still serving in *La Minerve* in December 1796, when Nelson hoisted his broad pendant on her to undertake his orders to withdraw the garrison on Elba. *En route* he encountered during the night and engaged the *Santa Sabina*, which surrendered, and Lieutenants Culverhouse and Hardy were sent to her with the prize crew. The night did not end there, however, for Nelson ran into the Spanish fleet, and only managed to get *La Minerve* away because Culverhouse and Hardy drew the Spanish squadron away from her, defending the prize until dismasted. They became prisoners of war, but were almost immediately exchanged, rejoining *La Minerve* at Gibraltar. Hardy was again in the news on 10 February 1797, as the frigate was passing through the straits with the Spanish fleet in chase. When a man fell overboard, Hardy jumped into the jolly boat to save him, and Nelson instantly backed the mizzen topsail to wait for him. The manoeuvre disconcerted the Spaniards enough to allow time to recover the boat.

Three days later *Minerve* rejoined the fleet off Cadiz and took part in the battle of Cape St Vincent on the 14th.

Following that action, Hardy commanded a boat force which on 29 May cut out of Santa Cruz de Tenerife Road a French brig of war, *La Mutine*. She was taken into British service, and St Vincent promoted Hardy to be her commander on 10 July. The following year, when a detachment of the

Mediterranean fleet under Nelson, now a rear-admiral, was sent into the Mediterranean under orders to investigate the French armament which captured Malta and Egypt, Hardy was sent in chase to advise him of the approach of reinforcements under Captain Thomas Troubridge. They joined off Elba on 5 June 1798.

Following the battle of the Nile when Captain Berry took passage home with the victory dispatch, Hardy was made post captain on 2 October 1798 in Nelson's flagship, *Vanguard* (74). Nelson shifted his flag into *Foudroyant* (80) in June 1799, and Hardy accompanied him. He served with Nelson at Naples and Palermo until October 1799, and then was appointed in November to the frigate *Princess Charlotte*, in which he returned to England. He served as Nelson's flag captain in *Namur* (90) and *San Josef* (110), and then in *St George* (90) during the 1801 Copenhagen campaign. In the night prior to the battle of Copenhagen, Hardy sounded the middle and eastern grounds in Copenhagen Sound, and the channel up to the Danish battle line. Hardy returned to England in *St George* when Nelson was relieved by Vice-Admiral Charles Morice Pole, and was subsequently appointed to the *Isis* (50) flying Commodore John Sutton's broad pendant.

When Nelson was put in command of the Mediterranean fleet on the renewal of war in May 1803, Hardy carried him from off Brest to Toulon in the 32-pounder frigate *Amphion* (36), and moved with him into *Victory* (100) when she arrived in July or August to serve as his flagship. Hardy continued to serve as Nelson's flag captain and companion on his last campaign, sailing from Portsmouth on 14 September 1805. When at the battle of Trafalgar on 21 October 1805, Nelson was shot on the quarterdeck of *Victory*, Hardy was at his side. Nelson was carried below, and Hardy, besides fighting his ship, had to take on some of the duties of higher tactical command which would usually have been undertaken by the captain of the fleet. When the French van tacked and seemed intent on threatening the British rear, Hardy organised the response. It was an hour before he could attend to Nelson's request that he come to the orlop deck where he lay dying. Hardy came again when the battle was nearly over, and Nelson told him to 'bring the fleet to anchor'. Hardy suggested that command should devolve on Vice-Admiral Collingwood, but Nelson replied, 'not whilst I live, I hope, Hardy ... Do you bring the fleet to anchor.' He then desired Hardy to kiss him farewell. Nelson's body was taken back to England on board *Victory* under Hardy's command, and at his funeral Hardy bore the banner of Emblems before Nelson's relatives.

Hardy was created a baronet on 4 February 1806, and was later appointed to command *Triumph* (74) at Halifax, where in 1807 he married Anne Louisa Berkeley, elder daughter of his admiral, the Honourable Sir George Cranfield Berkeley, GCB. She was niece of the duke of Richmond and of Admiral Sir Eliab Harvey, and sister-in-law of Admiral of the Fleet Sir George Francis Seymour, GCB. The couple had three daughters. In May 1809 he was appointed Admiral the Honourable George Cranfield Berkeley's flag captain in *Barfleur* (90) at Lisbon, and in 1811 the Portuguese government gave him the rank of chief-of-division in the Portuguese Royal Armada. In September 1812 he was appointed to command *Ramillies* (74), and later in the year he was ordered to North America, where in the summer of 1813 he commanded a blockade force off New London. On 25 June *Ramillies* captured a schooner which was packed with gunpowder and a timed igniter under a layer of fresh provisions. But Hardy had the presence of mind to order her moved from alongside *Ramillies*, to lie against another prize ship, which was destroyed by her explosion. Later he took possession of the islands in Passamaquoddy Bay.

Following the end of the war, Hardy was on 2 January 1815 made a KCB, and on 29 June 1815 a knight bachelor. In 1816 he was given command of the yacht *Princess Augusta*, but he did not stay in this inactive ship for long, and on 30 November 1818 he was given command of *Superb* (78). In the following year he hoisted a broad pendant as commodore of the squadron on the coasts of South America, where he was employed in dealing with the new governments of the former Spanish imperial provinces. On 27 May 1825 he was promoted rear-admiral, and in December 1826, with his flag in the *Wellesley*, he commanded the escort for the expeditionary force to Lisbon. Subsequently he commanded an experimental squadron, and finally struck his flag on 21 October 1827. He was not employed again at sea, but he was briefly the first sea lord in November 1830, then master and governor of Greenwich hospital from April 1834 until his death. He became an elder brother of the Trinity House in 1837.

The honours had continued to accumulate. He was made colonel of the Royal Marines on 19 July 1821, GCB on 13 September 1831 and GCH in April 1834. He died on 20 September 1839, aged seventy, with the rank of vice-admiral, at Greenwich hospital and was buried in the mausoleum of the hospital's burial ground. A monument to his memory was erected at Blackdown Hill, Portesham, in 1846. The baronetcy became extinguished.

Lt: 10 November 1793
Cmdr: 10 July 1797
Capt: 2 October 1798
R-Adm: 27 May 1825
V-Adm: 10 January 1837

HARNESS

DR JOHN HARNESS, by his attention to the medical needs of the fleet, did as much to bring victory as any admiral in the Royal Navy.

He was born on 15 November 1754 in London, but little is known about his family. He was educated by the Revd Mr Birkhead at Watlington, in Oxfordshire, and by his grandfather John Foote Harness, who was a physician and cousin of Dr Frank Nicholls, professor of anatomy at Oxford University and physician to King George II. John Harness later studied at the schools in London, and Lord Charles Spencer, who was on the Board of Admiralty, persuaded him to join *Sylph* (14), Captain James Richard Dacres, in December 1776 as assistant surgeon. In Antigua he was appointed to assist at the naval hospital, and in May 1778 he was promoted by Admiral James Young to the rank of surgeon. While there he formed an opinion about

John Harness, Esq., M.D., F.L.S., Medical Commissioner of his Majesty's Navy, engraved by T Blood, published by Joyce Gold, Naval Chronicle Offices, 103 Shoe Lane, London, 30 April 1816.

the nature of scurvy which lacked the modern knowledge of vitamins, but was functionally correct.

At the French declaration of war in 1793 he was serving as surgeon at the Royal Naval Hospital at Haslar, and was asked to accept the appointment of physician to the Mediterranean fleet. Eight years later, on 2 November 1805, he described his accomplishment while on that station to Lord Barham, then first lord of the Admiralty:

> During the blockade of Toulon in the summer of 1793, many of the ship's companies were afflicted with symptoms of scurvy; and as the object Lord Hood (then commander in chief in the Mediterranean) had in view, would not allow of the ships, whose companies were so afflicted, to be detached into port, to obtain the necessary refreshment, I was induced to propose to his lordship the sending a vessel into port for the express purpose of obtaining lemons for the use of the fleet; with which

his lordship most cheerfully complied; and the good effects of its use were so evident to every commander employed on the station, that an order was soon obtained from the commander in chief, that no ship under his lordship's command should leave port without being previously furnished with an ample supply of lemons. [NC 18.386–8]

After six years of service in the Mediterranean, Harness returned to England and in January 1800 was appointed by Earl Spencer a commissioner of the Sick and Hurt Board, being appointed to the chair on 5 May 1802 by the earl of St Vincent. In September 1804 he successfully petitioned Lord Melville for improvement in the pay of naval surgeons so that better-qualified men would be encouraged to join the service. In January 1806, when the duties of the Sick and Hurt Board were consolidated with those of the Transport Service, Dr Harness was appointed the sole medical member of the board.

His claim to have originated the regular and preventative use of antiscorbutics in the navy was disputed by Sir Gilbert Blaine, who had taken charge of the health of the West Indian fleet under Admiral Rodney during the American war and whose appointment in 1795 to the Sick and Hurt Board enabled him to make lemon juice regular issue to the whole navy. Dr Thomas Trotter, appointed by Lord Howe physician of the fleet, also claimed credit. All three played important parts in this victory. Unfortunately, professional jealousy led to disputes. The date of Dr Harness's death is not known.

HARVEY

ADMIRAL SIR ELIAB HARVEY, GCB, had his finest hour at the battle of Trafalgar on 21 October 1805, when he commanded *Téméraire* (98), second ship of the weather column and next astern of the *Victory*. For 'more than three hours,' he wrote to his wife on 23 October, 'two of the enemy's line of battleships were lashed to her, one on each side.' [Jackson 2.223] *Téméraire* came to symbolise the wooden walls of Britain. Although she took a tremendous beating, the two French ships were

obliged to strike their colours.

Less attractive was Harvey's bragging about his victory, but it was consistent with his intemperate character. As a young man he lost £100,000 gaming, although his opponent let him off most of it. And in April 1809 Harvey, by then a rear-admiral, expressed his contempt so violently for his commander-in-chief, Lord Gambier, after he learnt that Lord Cochrane was to command the fireship attack at Basque Roads, that he was court-martialled and dismissed from the service. 'His intemperate manner is such', wrote Lord Gardner to Joseph Farington the Royal Academician on 26 May 1809, 'that, had I been told the circumstance without a name being given, I should have supposed it to be Admiral Harvey.' [Farington 5.173]

Harvey was born on 5 December 1758 at Rolls Park near Chigwell, Essex, the fourth son of William Harvey, member of parliament for Essex, and his wife Emma, daughter and coheiress of Stephen Skynner of Walthamstow. He was educated at Westminster school in 1768–9 and at Harrow school for most of 1770–4, his name was put on the books of the yacht *Mary* under Captain Richard (?) Edwards at Deptford in 1771, and he also got some experience of naval service during the summer of 1773 in the *Orpheus* (32) under Captain John MacBride. His real entry into the navy was in May 1774 when he went to the Leeward Islands in *Lynx*, sloop, under the command of Captain A Scott. In September 1776 he returned to North America in the *Mermaid* (28), and he transferred in July 1777 to *Eagle* (64), Lord Howe's flagship. In February 1778 he suffered shipwreck in the *Liverpool* (28), to which he had been lent, and he returned to England in *Eagle* in October. He was then ashore for three years. On 25 February 1779 Harvey was commissioned lieutenant of *Resolution*, but he did not join his ship. Perhaps he was anticipating the death of his elder brother, William, knowing he would succeeded to the family property. From May 1780 to 1784 Harvey was the elected member of parliament for Maldon, Essex, returning to sea in September 1781 for four months as lieutenant of *Dolphin* (44) in the Downs. He was promoted on 21 March 1782 commander of *Otter,* sloop, and on 20 January 1783 was promoted again to post captain; he remained in employment until 1790, when he was appointed to the *Hussar* (28) during the Nootka Sound crisis.

On 15 May 1784 he married at St George, Hanover Square, Westminster, Louisa, second and youngest daughter of Robert Nugent, first Earl Nugent, by his third wife. The couple had three sons and six daughters.

On the French declaration of war in February 1793 he was appointed to the *Santa Margaretta* (38), in which he served under Sir John Jervis in the capture of Martinique and Guadeloupe in March and April 1794, and then under Sir John Borlase Warren in the Channel fleet. In August 1795 he was appointed to *Valiant* (74) as part of the squadron dispatched to the West Indies under the orders of Sir Hyde Parker. Returning home in February 1797 because of ill health, he took command of the sea fencibles in Essex. In 1800 he returned to sea in *Triumph* (74), serving in the Channel and off Brest. He came ashore at the conclusion of the peace of Amiens and was elected member of parliament for Essex in June 1802.

He continued to hold the seat until 1812, but with the renewal of war he returned to sea. In November 1803 he commissioned the *Téméraire,* and after fifteen months off Brest and in the Bay of Biscay he received orders to join the fleet under Lord Nelson's command off Cadiz. Following Trafalgar, on 9 November he was promoted rear-admiral of the blue, and in March 1806 he hoisted his flag in *Tonnant* (80) serving under Jervis, now the earl of St Vincent, in the Channel and off Finisterre. In 1808 he hoisted it again when Admiral Lord Gambier assumed command of the Channel fleet, and served until he was informed that Cochrane had been appointed by the Admiralty to command the fireship flotilla to be used against the French squadron sheltering in Basque Roads, and that in consequence Gambier rejected Admiral Harvey's offer of his own services. This led to the disastrous outburst, court martial and dismissal. Harvey, as it will be recalled, 'is stated to have expressed the greatest dissatisfaction, and to have bestowed upon Lord Gambier

himself, epithets descriptive of other qualities than those which he has evinced in his profession, such as *Jesuit, Methodist,* and *Psalm-singer*; and all this', continued the *Naval Chronicle,* 'in the presence of Captain Bedford, of the *Caledonia,* who desired to know if it were meant, that this reply should be conveyed to the commander-in-chief: to which the other answering, in the heat of passion, in the affirmative, the communication accordingly took place, and the letter for a court martial was the result.' [NC 21.315–16; 348–9] In his defence he claimed that his breach of discipline had occurred only in private, with only senior officers present, and that he had subsequently expressed his regret to Gambier. This consideration may have influenced the Admiralty Board. On 21 March 1810 he was reinstated in his rank and seniority, out of consideration for his years of service. That ensured he would receive half pay, but he was never again employed.

He was nominated KCB in January 1815 and GCB in 1825, and in 1820 he was again elected member of parliament for Essex, holding the seat until his death on 20 February 1830 at his home. He was buried on 27 February in Hempstead.

> Lt: 25 February 1779
> M-C: 21 March 1782
> Capt: 20 January 1783
> R-Adm: 9 November 1805
> V-Adm: 31 July 1810
> Adm: 12 August 1819

HARVEY

ADMIRAL SIR HENRY HARVEY, KB, is best known for the part he played at the battle of the Glorious First of June.

Henry had been born in July 1737 in Elmton, Kent, the second son of Richard Harvey of Barfreston and his wife, Elizabeth, daughter of Henry Nicholls of Barham. Quite unusually, as a child he was sent to the École Royale de la Marine in Calais. He first went to sea in the merchant service before entering the navy in May 1751 as a captain's servant on board the *Centaur* (24) commanded by Captain Cosby. He was rated midshipman or master's mate on 16 April 1753, and part of his time in the merchant service was allowed to count as sea time for his examination, allowing him to be commissioned lieutenant on 10 March 1757 and appointed to *Hampshire* (50). While in passage back from the West Indies in the summer of 1762 he became a friend of the Honourable Constantine Phipps, later Lord Mulgrave; the latter was subsequently appointed in 1773 to command an expedition as far as possible towards the North Pole by way of Spitzbergen, and he asked for Harvey as first lieutenant of the *Racehorse* (18). This was the same expedition in which Horatio Nelson served as a midshipman in the consort ship, *Carcus*. On Harvey's return, *Racehorse* was immediately paid off, and he was promoted master and commander, on 15 October 1773, with an appointment to recommission his old ship.

In January 1776 he was appointed to *Martin*, sloop, and sailed to Quebec, where he played an active part in defeating the American attack. He was promoted to post captain on 9 May 1777, was actively employed throughout the American war, and continued to be employed in the following peace. In March 1786 he was appointed to command the *Rose* (28) fitting for the Newfoundland station, but soon thereafter, in a most unusual development, he was ordered to leave his lieutenant to complete her commissioning, and to take charge of fitting *Pegasus* (28) for the same command. He was thus commanding two ships. The first lieutenant of *Pegasus* was Prince William Henry, later the duke of Clarence, and he was to have command of the ship once she had been properly fitted out by a professional seaman. Evidently Harvey's tact was adequate to the occasion. The two ships proceeded in company to their station, and shortly after the French declaration of war he was put in command of a 74-gun ship of the line, *Ramillies* in the Channel fleet.

During the battle on 1 June 1794 he noticed that his brother's ship, *Brunswick* (74), was heavily engaged with *Le Vengeur* and went to her assistance. As he later wrote:

> The *Ramillies*, being on their weather quarter at a little distance, bore up to give any assistance that was possible to the *Brunswick*, and passing close under the quarter of *Le Vengeur*, then lying to

windward of the *Brunswick*, had an opportunity of giving her a raking fire; and going to leeward of both ships, wore, and stood back on the other tack, when having passed the *Brunswick*, and opening the quarter of *Le Vengeur*, repeated the same raking fire as before. At this time the main and fore-masts of the *Le Vengeur* fell, and almost immediately after the *Brunswick* dropped clear of her opponent, with the loss of her mizen-mast, and the *Vengeur* was left dismasted. [Ralfe 2.105]

She subsequently sank, and John Harvey died of his wounds following his return to Portsmouth.

A month following the battle, on 4 July, Henry Harvey was promoted rear-admiral. After service in the North Sea, he hoisted his flag on board *Prince of Wales* (98) in January 1795 in the Channel fleet, and fought under Lord Bridport in the action off L'Orient on 23 June. In April 1796 he was appointed commander-in-chief of the Leeward Islands station, with orders to support Sir Ralph Abercromby in an expedition to capture Trinidad, which was accomplished the following January. They were less successful in an attempt to capture Porto Rico. He was promoted vice-admiral on 14 February 1799, and at his request he was succeeded in July 1799 by Lord Hugh Seymour. On 8 January 1800 he was nominated KB. He then hoisted his flag as second in command of the Channel fleet under the earl of St Vincent, and remained at that post until the conclusion of peace. He did not seek employment on the renewal of the war, but was promoted admiral on 23 April 1804.

It is not recorded when he married Elizabeth, daughter of Captain William Boys, RN, lieutenant-governor of Greenwich hospital. The couple had three sons and one daughter. Harvey died on 28 December 1810, aged seventy-three, in Walmer, Kent, and Elizabeth followed in March 1823, aged eighty-three.

Lt: 10 March 1757
M-C: 15 October 1773
Capt: 9 May 1777
R-Adm: 4 July 1794
V-Adm: 14 February 1799
Adm: 23 April 1804

HARVEY

CAPTAIN JOHN HARVEY was certainly the great-est hero of the battle of the Glorious First of June in 1794, and died from the wounds he received in action.

He was born on 9 July 1740 in Elmton, Kent, the third son of Richard Harvey of Barfreston, and his wife, Elizabeth, daughter of Henry Nicholls of Barham. Like his elder brother Henry, he was ed-ucated at the École Royale de la Marine in Calais, but he then went into the navy at the age of fifteen, in 1755, going to sea in *Falmouth* (50) with Captain Sir Piercy Brett, RN, who was a relative of his mother. On 13 January 1759 he left the *Falmouth*, and Admiral Francis Holbourne com-manding at Portsmouth gave him an order to act in the rank of lieutenant. He was confirmed in rank on 18 September 1759, and appointed to *Hornet,* sloop, but soon moved to the *Arethusa* (32), com-manded by the Honourable Raby Vane.

Following the conclusion of peace with France and Spain, Harvey married on 27 September 1763 Judith, daughter of Henry Wise of Sandwich, Kent. The couple had four sons and four daughters. Two of their sons, John and Edward, were to follow their father into the navy, and both became admirals.

Harvey was lucky enough to get command of the cutter *Alarm* in November 1766, and stayed in her for two years, until he was promoted mas-ter and commander on 26 May 1768. He then ap-pears to have remained ashore until January 1777, when he was given command of *Speedwell* sloop. On 16 September 1777, during the armament in-tended to meet the threat of French intervention in the American revolution, he was made post cap-tain and given command of *Panther* (60), which became Vice-Admiral Robert Duff's flagship in the Mediterranean. Harvey found himself at the cen-tre of action when Spain declared war in 1779 and laid siege to Gibraltar. On 6 June 1780 he was in command of the naval forces there when the Spaniards launched a fireship attack on the moored squadron, which he defeated by towing the blaz-ing ships clear of their targets. In July 1780 the *Panther* returned to England, and in November

was sent to the West Indies as part of the squadron under Sir Samuel Hood. On her return again to England the following summer, Harvey was trans-ferred to *Sampson* (64) and ordered to form part of Admiral Lord Howe's force which sailed in 1782 to relieve Gibraltar. During the subsequent peace, Harvey continued to be employed, serving in 1787 as regulating captain at Deal. Between 1788 and 1792 he commanded *Arrogant* (74), fitted as a guardship at Sheerness.

On the outbreak of war in 1793 Harvey was ap-pointed to command the *Magnificent* (74), but Lord Howe decided he should provide for the pos-sibility he might need to shift his flag into a small-er ship, and requested that Harvey transfer into *Brunswick* (74) so that he could have a captain he knew in command of one of the most powerful two-deckers. It also put Harvey next astern of the *Queen Charlotte* (100) in the battle line, where he could be relied on to second his chief.

During the action on 29 May 1794 Harvey was unable to get into his proper place in the order of battle, found a place further back in the line, and from there bore down to provide assistance for his friend John Bazeley in the *Alfred* (74), which was heavily engaged by a French 80-gun ship. On 1 June he was able to keep his position, and on the signal being given to bear down together and close with the enemy, *Brunswick* and *Queen Charlotte* raced each other close aboard to cover the danger-ous distance when they were being fired on, but could not reply. The *Naval Chronicle* reports that *Brunswick*'s cockpit was filled with wounded men before a single shot was fired. Harvey was unable to find a gap in the well-formed French line, and putting his helm hard a-port laid alongside *Le Vengeur*, hooking onto her chains. The crews of some of the guns were obliged to fire through their ports because there was not room to open them. Hotly engaged, the antagonists ran off large for about an hour and ten minutes, by which time they were about a mile to leeward of the French fleet. At that point another French line of battle ship was seen manoeuvring to put boarders across, with her nets rigged and decks covered with men in arms, but Harvey ordered double-headed shot to be added to the 32-pounder ball in the larboard batteries, and all the masts of the new assailant were shot down before she could close.

Relief was at hand, and from the *Ramillies* (74) commanded by Henry Harvey, John Harvey's brother. 'This dreadful conflict had now continued for two hours, and an half,' wrote the editor of the *Naval Chronicle*, 'the crew of the *Brunswick* with the greatest coolness, at one time driving home the coins, watching attentively the rising of the enemy's ship to fire below the water line; and at another withdrawing the coins to elevate the muzzles of their guns, and rip up the decks of *Le Vengeur*.' That ship had lost her masts, and was sinking. Finally her crew was forced to hoist a British Jack, but as *Brunswick*'s boats had all been shot to pieces, only 200 of her crew were saved. *Brunswick* was herself so badly damaged that there was no option but to bear away for an English harbour.

Early in the engagement Harvey had been severely and repeatedly wounded, and when his arm was shattered he had to leave the deck from loss of blood. The amputation did not serve to save his life, and he died on 30 June 1794, aged fifty-three, in Portsmouth. A monument to his memory was erected in Westminster Abbey, and there is a memorial in St Mary-the-Virgin, Eastry, Kent. Judith died on 4 September 1817, aged seventy-four, at Sandwich, Kent.

> Lt: 18 September 1759
> M-C: 26 May 1768
> Capt: 16 September 177

HARVEY

ADMIRAL SIR JOHN HARVEY, KCB, was a son of the hero, and fought in Sir Robert Calder's action.

He was the second son of Captain John Harvey who commanded *Brunswick* (74) at the battle of the Glorious First of June in 1794, and subsequently died of his wounds. His mother was Judith, daughter of Henry Wise of Sandwich, Kent, and he was baptised on 12 March 1769, at St Peter-the-Apostle in Sandwich. He entered the navy on board the *Agamemnon* (64) at a date now forgotten, was rated midshipman in the frigate *Rose* commanded by his uncle, Sir Henry Harvey, and was

commissioned lieutenant on 3 November 1790. His father lived to see him promoted commander on 9 May 1794, but not to hear of his command, *L'Actif*, sloop, foundering off Bermuda on 26 November. Young John survived, and as a compliment to his late father was made post captain on 16 December with appointment as flag captain of *Prince of Wales* (98) flying the flag of his uncle Sir Henry Harvey. He served in that ship in the action off L'Orient, on the coast of Brittany, the following winter, and during the capture of Trinidad in February 1797, being sent home with dispatches. Subsequently he commanded the 12-pounder frigate *Southampton* (32) and 9-pounder frigate *Amphitrite* (28), in the Leeward Islands, and in March 1801 he assisted in the capture of the Virgin Islands under Rear-Admiral Duckworth.

He married in 1797 his cousin Elizabeth, daughter of William Wyborn Bradley of Sandwich, Kent. The couple had one daughter.

In August 1804 he was appointed to recommission *Agamemnon* following the peace of Amiens, and on 1 November he sailed for the Mediterranean in a squadron commanded by Sir John Orde. On 18 November he was ordered to chase a Spanish frigate, and it turned out that she was sailing to the Spanish colonies to warn of the declaration of war against Britain, but Orde instructed Harvey to escort her back to Cadiz without taking her as prize. On receipt of orders on 27 December to detain Spanish shipping, Harvey soon compensated for his disappointment.

Agamemnon was at Gibraltar during a violent storm on 31 January 1805, and was lying at St Lucar making repairs when the Toulon fleet under Vice-Admiral Villeneuve appeared before Cadiz. Orde was obliged to raise the blockade, and the Spanish fleet was able to join the French and proceed to the West Indies. On the return of the combined fleet to Ferrol, *Agamemnon* formed one of the squadron commanded by Sir Robert Calder which brought them to action on 22 July.

In September Harvey was appointed to *Canada* (74) fitting for the Leeward Islands. He paid her off at Chatham in January 1808, and subsequently commanded *Leviathan* (74) in June 1809 and

Royal Sovereign (100) in October 1810, and on 12 August 1812 he was given command of one of the royal yachts. He was promoted rear-admiral on 4 December 1813, and in August 1815 hoisted his flag as commander-in-chief of the Leeward Islands.

He was nominated KCB on 1 June 1833, and died with the rank of admiral on 17 February 1837 at his residence of The Oaks, Upper Deal, Kent. Elizabeth died on 17 August 1853, aged seventy-six.

Lt: 3 November 1790
Cmdr: 9 May 1794
Capt: 16 December 1794
R-Adm: 4 December 1813
V-Adm: 27 May 1825
Adm: 10 January 1837

HAYES

REAR-ADMIRAL JOHN HAYES, CB, made little mark on his profession until 17 December 1812, when he was in command of *Magnificent* (74) and saved his ship through an astonishing piece of seamanship. He went on to show how to defeat American super-frigates.

He was born in 1767, and all that is known of his parentage is that his great-uncle, Adam Hayes, who was master shipwright of Deptford dockyard, decided to bring him up as a shipwright with the hope he would eventually be surveyor of the navy. Young John bore with this until Adam died in 1787, but he had been put on the books of a warship in 1774, and when free to do so in October he joined *Orion* (74) as a volunteer first class under the command of Sir Hyde Parker. The following year he joined the *Scout* commanded by Captain Charles Cobb, with whom he served in the Channel, and in 1790 he was rated as midshipman and acting master of the 12-pounder frigate *Pearl* (32) under the command of Captain George William Augustus Courtenay. On the outbreak of war in 1793 Hayes followed Courtenay into *Boston* (32), in which he served as an acting lieutenant on the Newfoundland station. A French frigate, *L'Ambuscade* (36), was at New York, and Hayes was sent in with a challenge, which was accepted. The action which ensued on 31 July was indecisive, but the butcher's bill on both sides was

high and included Captain Courtenay. In recognition of Hayes's part in the action, the Admiralty commissioned him lieutenant on 7 October 1793 despite the fact that he had not served enough time as a rated midshipman, and appointed him to the *Dido* (28) under the command of Sir Charles Hamilton, whom he followed on 12 July 1794 to the frigate *San Fiorenzo* (34) in the Mediterranean. Hamilton was succeeded in command by Harry Inman, and then by Lord Lecale.

On 2 November 1794 he was appointed to *Brunswick* flying the flag of Admiral Sir Richard Rodney Bligh in the North Sea, and subsequently to *Queen* (90) bearing Sir Hyde Parker's flag in the West Indies. While serving in the West Indies he was promoted commander on 1 March 1799, and on 3 September he was appointed to command *Lark*, a ship-sloop of 16 guns. He transferred on 13 April 1799 to *Swallow,* which was a fir-built brig-sloop, to *Tisiphone* (14) on 25 April 1801, and finally to the French prize privateer *Bourdelois* (22) on 17 December, all in the West Indies. He was appointed for post rank to the 12-pounder frigate *Pearl* (32) by the Admiralty on 29 April 1802.

He was not employed in that rank until 1 December 1808, when he was appointed to command *Alfred* (74) in the Channel fleet and on the coast of Spain, taking charge of the embarkation of troops after the battle of Corunna. He commanded *Achille* (74) in the Walcheren expedition, following which he was appointed to the former Danish frigate *Freya* (42) on 5 September 1809, and served under Sir Alexander Cochrane at the capture of Guadeloupe in January 1810. He returned to England in the following autumn, and on 7 August 1812 was appointed to temporary command of the *Magnificent.*

His remarkable feat of seamanship, which saved his own life and the lives of all the crew, occurred when *Magnificent* was anchored in an exceptionally dangerous position in Basque Roads, in a full gale, with rocks on every side and a reef immediately to leeward, over which the sea was breaking violently. Her topmasts had been struck, in a seamanlike manner, in order to reduce her windage, but that precaution added to the difficulties of getting her under sail when her anchors began to drag, and her cables threatened to break. An attempt to cast her head off with a spring failed when the cable broke, but by an astounding piece of seamanship he got her under sail with the fore and main yards swayed two-thirds of the way up outside the topmasts, and the courses and topsails stopped only with spun yarn so they could be broken out in a moment.

The men were strictly enjoined to be quick in obeying the commands given them, and to be extremely cautious not to let a sail fall, unless it was particularly named; as any mistake in that respect would occasion the loss of the ship. The yards were all braced sharp up for casting from the reef, and making sail on the starboard tack. The tacks and sheets, top-sail sheets, and main and mizen stay-sail halyards, were manned, and the spring hove taut: Captain Hayes now told his crew that they were going to work for life or death; if they were attentive to his orders, and executed them properly, the ship would be saved; if not, the whole of them would be drowned in a few minutes. Things being in this state of preparation, a little more of the spring was hove in, the quarter-masters at the wheel received their instructions, and the cables were instantly cut; but the heavy sea on the larboard bow would not let her cast that away, the spring broke, and her head paid in towards the reef. The oldest seaman in the ship at that moment thought all lost; but the probability of her casting to starboard had happily been foreseen by Captain Hayes, who now, in the coolest manner, gave orders 'to put the helm hard a-starboard; sheet home the fore-top-sail; haul on board the fore-tack, and aft fore-sheet; keep all other others sails fast; square the main, mizen-top-sail, and cross jack yards; and keep the main-yard as it was.' The moment the wind came abaft the beam, he ordered the mizen-top-sail to be sheeted home, and then the helm to be put

hard a-port – when the wind was nearly aft, to haul on board the main-tack; aft main-sheet; sheet home the main-top-sail; and brace the cross-jack-yard up. When this was done, (the whole of which took only two minutes to perform,) the ship absolutely flew round from the reef, like a thing scared at the frightful spectacle. The quarter-masters were ordered to keep her South, and Captain Hayes declared aloud, 'The ship is safe.' [Marshall 2.678]

Despite the exceptional reputation this event gave him, Hayes is better known for the suggestion he made to the Admiralty on his return to port, that ships of the line be cut down and fitted expressly to deal with the American super-frigates. His idea was accepted and he was put in command in January 1813 of *Majestic*, a third rate cut down and armed with twenty-eight 32-pounders and the same number of 42-pounder carronades, with a long 12-pounder chase gun. On 5 February 1814 he brought to action a French 44-gun frigate, *Terpsichore*, which struck and then sank in heavy weather. On 15 January 1815, with *Endymion* and *Pomone* under his command, he caught up with USS *President* commanded by Commodore Decatur and a brig, and after a prolonged chase and an action of two and a half hours, she was forced to strike her colours.

Following this triumph, he was made a CB on 4 June 1815, and came ashore on 24 June 1815. On 15 March 1819 he was appointed port captain at Portsmouth. In 1829–30 he commanded the teak-built *Ganges* (84) at Portsmouth; and from 1830 to 1832 was commodore on the west coast of Africa, flying a broad pendant on board *Dryad* (42).

He did not become surveyor of the navy, but he did publish a treatise on naval construction which may have influenced Sir Robert Seppings, and in 1836 he signed as chairman of an Admiralty commission struck to consider 'Mr. Kyan's patent for the prevention of dry rot in timber'. Hayes was married and his eldest son, named Courtenay Osborne Hayes, was to become an admiral, and another son, John Montagu Hayes, became a vice-admiral. He was promoted rear-admiral on 10 January 1837, and died on 7 April 1838, aged seventy, at Southsea.

Lt: 7 October 1793 (4)
Cmdr: 1 March 1799 (2)
Capt: 29 April 1802 (67)
R-Adm: 10 January 1837

HEYWOOD

CAPTAIN PETER HEYWOOD's name had been put by Captain A Sutherland on the books of his ship, *Powerful*, as a captain's servant on 4 October 1786, and he may actually have had eleven months sea time to justify his being rated able seaman when on 11 October 1786 he made the momentous step of signing in the *Bounty* under the command of Lieutenant William Bligh, who was about to depart on his first voyage to collect breadfruit from Tahiti for transplanting in the West Indies.

Heywood had been born on 5 June 1772 in the Nunnery, Isle of Man, to Elizabeth, née Spedding, and Peter John Heywood, deemster of the Isle of Man and seneschal to the duke of Atholl. Young Peter was sent to school in Cheshire and Westmorland, but there was a naval connection through his uncle, Captain Thomas Pasley, and his parents were friends of Richard Betham, William Bligh's father-in-law. He undertook to persuade Bligh to take young Heywood into the *Bounty* (4) as an able seaman.

Bligh's character and actions were such that he experienced two mutinies in his service life, the second as governor of Port Jackson. Heywood's part in the more famous mutiny on the *Bounty* may not have been more than guilt by association, and because Bligh when he returned to England made no attempt to distinguish between the real mutineers and those who were left in the *Bounty* because the launch was too small to accommodate all the loyal hands. In any event, Heywood's age of fifteen should, and eventually did, plead for him.

He was one of those who refused to accompany Lieutenant Fletcher Christian to Pitcairn Island, and when Captain Edward Edwards came to Tahiti looking for the mutineers in HMS *Pandora*, Heywood immediately went on board to report

for duty. He was clapped in irons, and confined in the notorious '*Pandora*'s Box' with the other mutineers who had remained on Tahiti. The conditions of the following eighteen months were brutal in the extreme, and when *Pandora* sank in a storm only the unofficial charity of the master at arms in dropping the keys to the lock-up through the grille before he left the ship saved the lives of the prisoners. With the help of the Dutch at Batavia, who treated them with greater humanity, they were all transported back to England, stood trial and were condemned to death.

The court which condemned Heywood also recommended him to the royal mercy, and he was reprieved on 24 October 1792, by the king's grace. Marshall's *Naval Biography*, which, primed by Heywood's notes, first published an account of the mutiny showing Bligh's actions in a negative light, commented that 'the misfortunes of his [Heywood's] youth proved highly beneficial to him. The greater part of those distinguished officers who had sat as members of the court-martial, justly considering him much more unfortunate than criminal, extended their patronage to him immediately after his release.' Lord Hood, who had presided at the trial, offered to take him into *Victory* (100) as a midshipman, but Heywood's uncle, Commodore Pasley, thought it better that he should serve under him in *Bellerophon* (74), which he joined on 17 May 1793. Pasley later arranged for him to join the 12-pounder frigate *Niger* (32) under the Honourable Captain Legge, in which he was rated master's mate on 9 July. On 24 September he joined *Queen Charlotte* (100) flying the flag of Admiral Lord Howe commanding the Channel fleet, in which ship he served as able seaman and signal midshipman. On board were also Sir Roger Curtis, the captain of the fleet, Captain Sir Andrew Snape Douglas and Captain Sir Hugh C Christian, all of whom had served on his court martial. In the actions of 28 and 29 May and 1 June 1794 Heywood served as aide-de-camp to Captain Douglas, and during the Spithead fleet review he was employed attending on Queen Charlotte.

His career was otherwise not remarkable. Lord Howe gave him an acting commission as lieutenant in the *Robust* (74) on 24 August 1794. On 10 October he returned to *Queen Charlotte* as midshipman and master's mate, and on 9 March 1795 his commission was confirmed and he was appointed to the fireship *Incendiary*. He served as a lieutenant of the *Nymphe* (36) under the command of Captain George Murray in the action off L'Orient on 23 June. Early in 1796 he joined the cutter *Fox* (10) under Captain Pultney Malcolm and served in the East India station. On 17 June 1798 he was moved into the *Suffolk* (74), flagship of Vice-Admiral Peter Rainier, on Earl Spencer's recommendation. On 17 May 1799 he was put into command of the *Amboina*, brig, to carry the earl of Mornington's dispatches after the surrender of Seringapatam, rejoining the *Suffolk* at Madras in June. In August 1800 he was promoted acting commander of the bomb-vessel *Vulcan*, and on 11 June 1801 appointed to *Trident* (64), which he in fact did not join, but instead took acting command of *Leopard* (50) flying the flag of Vice-Admiral Rainier on 15 May 1802. When he was appointed on 30 September to command *Le Dedaigneuse* (32) he described himself as a post captain, but he was not in fact confirmed in post rank until 5 April 1803. While in the East Indies he undertook a survey of the east coast of Ceylon and the coast of Coromandel.

Returning home in January 1805, as a result of ill health and the death of his eldest brother, on 20 October 1806 he was appointed flag captain to Rear-Admiral George Murray in the *Polyphemus* (64). He served with him at the Cape of Good Hope and later in the river Plate, which he also surveyed. On 5 November 1808 he was appointed to *Donegal* (76), in which he served off Brest and in the Bay of Biscay. On 27 May 1809, after a few weeks' leave, he transferred to the *Nereus* (32), in which he proceeded to the Mediterranean. He was entrusted with returning Lord Collingwood's body to England in April 1810, and then was employed on the east coast of South America. He returned to England in October 1813 in the *Montagu* (74) and served in the North Sea until April 1814.

It was a remarkable turn of fortune which then brought the reprieved mutineer to accompany Louis XVIII to France, after which he evacuated part of the British army from Bordeaux. At the Spithead naval review in honour of the allied monarchs, the *Montagu*, wearing the flag of Sir Thomas Byam Martin, led the fleet.

When Napoleon left his exile at Elba, *Montagu* was sent to the Mediterranean, and served under Lord Exmouth transporting British and Austrian troops from Naples to Genoa and Marseilles. Heywood subsequently served as senior officer at Gibraltar. His career ended, appropriately, with participation in Lord Exmouth's mission to the Barbary states in February 1816, in which some 1,800 'poor wretches who had been dragged into the most miserable and revolting state of slavery' were freed.

The dreadful experience he had had nurtured his humane instincts, as Marshall observed: 'The young men who have had the honour of serving under him, many of whom now enjoy commissions, will readily and gratefully acknowledge that, both by precept and his own example, he invariably endeavoured to form their characters, as men and officers, on the solid principles of religion and virtue.' On his resigning his command on 16 July the seamen of *Montagu* wrote a song which includes a verse: 'Farewell to thee, Heywood! A truer one never Exercis'd rule o'er the sons of the wave; The seamen who served thee, would serve *thee* for ever, Who sway'd, but ne'er fetter'd, the hearts of the brave.' Marshall 2.747

Two weeks later he married Frances, only daughter of Colonel Francis Simpson of Plean House, Falkirk, Stirlingshire, and widow of an M. Jolliffe. She was a niece of Aaron Graham, who had defended Heywood at his court martial, but she probably met him through her scientific and literary salons. He was not again employed, but he was offered the command on the Canadian lakes and, when he refused, the post of Admiralty hydrographer, which he also refused. He died on 10 February 1831, aged fifty-eight, in London at 26 Cumberland Terrace, and was buried at St Michael's Church, Highgate.

Lt: 9 March 1795
Cmdr: August 1801
Capt: 5 April 1803

HILLYAR

REAR-ADMIRAL SIR JAMES HILLYAR, KCB, is best known for his five-month pursuit of USS *Essex* in the Pacific ending in her capture on 28 March 1814.

He was born on 29 October 1769 at Portsea, Hampshire, the eldest son of James Hillyar, surgeon, RN, and entered the navy on 27 January 1779 as a surgeon's servant on board the *Chatham* (50) under the command of Captain William Owen, although he later described himself as having been a 'boy doing duty as a midshipman'. Owen was later succeeded by Captain John Orde. Hillyar was rated a midshipman or master's mate on 1 February 1781, fought in the action which ended in the capture of *Magicienne* off Boston on 2 September, and when *Chatham* was paid off at the peace, remained in employment in the North American station and at home, serving in *Presilyce, Ardens, Fortune, Bellona, Princess Royal* (90) flying the flag of Admiral Hotham at Portsmouth, and *Alcide* under Captain Sir Andrew Snape Douglas. As that ship was stationary at Portsmouth, he was lent to *Bedford* (74) cruising in the Channel under the command of Sir Andrew Snape Hamond.

On the French declaration of war in February 1793 Hillyar was appointed to *Britannia* (100) flying Vice-Admiral Hotham's flag, and then transferred into *Victory* (100) flying Lord Hood's flag. Following service at Toulon and Corsica he was commissioned lieutenant on 8 March 1794, with appointment to *Aquilon* (32) under Captain Robert Stopford. In her he saw action in the battles of the Glorious First of June in 1794, and then transferred with Stopford into *Phaeton* (38) prior to the action on 17 June 1794 as part of William Cornwallis's squadron. He remained in the Channel fleet until June 1799, and then transferred again with Stopford into *Excellent* (74). In April 1800 he was given command of *Niger*, flute, under orders to transport troops to the Mediterranean.

On 3 September 1800 he, and Lieutenant Charles Marsh Schomberg, led *Niger*'s boats in support of those of *Minotaur* (74) to capture two Spanish corvettes in Barcelona Road. He also took a leading role in the boat work required to land Sir Ralph Abercromby's army in Aboukir Bay on 8 and 13 March 1801.

His promotion to post rank was by the direct intervention of Vice-Admiral Lord Nelson, who on 20 January 1804 wrote to the first lord, the earl of St Vincent, urging his merits:

> At twenty-four years of age, when I made him a Lieutenant for his bravery, he maintained his mother, sisters, and a brother. For these reasons he declined the *Ambuscade* (32) which was offered him; because, although he might thus get his rank, yet, if he were put upon half-pay, his family would be the sufferers. From all these circumstances, so honourable to Captain Hillyar, independent of his services, which every one thought would have obtained him promotion in the later war, I beg leave to submit, as an act of the greatest kindness, that as the *Niger* is a very fast sailing frigate, well manned, and in most excellent condition, she may be fitted with the *Madras*'s 32 carronades, which are not so heavy as her present 9-pounders, and that your Lordship would recommend her being considered as a post-ship. Captain Hillyar's activity would soon complete the additional numbers of men, and she would be an efficient frigate. MARSHALL 2(Supp).857

St Vincent did as he was asked on 29 February, and with the increase in pay Hillyar was able, on 14 July 1805, to marry Mary, daughter of Nathaniel Taylor, naval storekeeper at Malta dockyard.

On 29 February 1809 he was appointed to command *St George* (90) as flag captain to Rear-Admiral Sir Eliab Harvey. Subsequently he was ordered to the Baltic with Rear-Admiral Francis Pickmore's flag, and there was transferred by Sir James Saumarez to the *Phoebe* (36). The following spring he was put under orders to join the East Indies squadron. He took part in the reduction of Isle de France (Mauritius) in December 1810, and in the action against the French squadron near Madagascar, before proceeding to Batavia. He served there under Rear-Admiral Stopford in support of Sir Samuel Auchmuty's campaign to take from the Dutch their establishments in Indonesia in August 1811.

Hillyar's presence on the Pacific coast of South America in 1813 was the result of orders to destroy the American fur stations on the Columbia river, but at Juan Fernandez he heard that the *Essex* (46), Captain David Porter, was cruising against British trade and arming her prizes to increase her force. He detached *Racoon* to the Columbia, and retained *Cherub*, sloop of war, to help track down the American raider. She was found at Valparaiso. Given the disparity of force, Hillyar had every reason to respect Chilean neutrality, but he anchored his squadron close to the Americans, and when, nearly six weeks later, Porter attempted to slip out of the harbour, Hillyar pressed *Essex* so hard that her fore-topmast broke from carrying too much sail to windward. Porter then ran into shallow water and anchored, but cut *Essex's* cable when she saw that *Phoebe* was preparing to anchor and commence a methodical bombardment at a range which would favour her long 18-pounders over the American's 32-pounder carronades. After a running fight, hampered by her broken spar, *Essex* struck.

Hillyar was made a CB on 4 June 1815 when that order was created, and was made a KCH on 1 January 1834. He was advanced in chivalry on 4 July 1840 to KCB, and he was eventually promoted rear-admiral on 10 January 1837. Two of his sons entered the navy and became admirals. He died on 10 July 1843, aged seventy-three, at Torpoint House, Cornwall, and his wife died in 1884, aged ninety-six.

Lt: 8 March 1794
Cmdr: 16 April 1800
Capt: 29 February 1804
R-Adm: 10 January 1837

HOLLOWAY

ADMIRAL JOHN HOLLOWAY. In 1808 the *Naval Chronicle* wrote that 'by plain sailing, and keeping a steady course, Holloway had gained a high character in his profession, and preserved the confidence of government, amidst the vicissitudes and

John Holloway, Esq.,
Vice Admiral of the Red Squadron, &c.,
drawn and engraved by H R Cook,
published by Joyce Gold, 103 Shoe Lane,
31 May 1808.

cabals of party. Truer than the compass, he has throughout life displayed no variation.' [NC 19.373]

He was born on 25 January 1747 in Wells, Somerset, son of M Holloway of Wells, Somerset, and his wife, née Lyons. He entered the navy in 1760 on board the *Antelope* (50) Captain Webb, and the following year sailed in her to Newfoundland with Captain Thomas, later Lord Graves, who had been appointed governor. Holloway continued in Newfoundland when Graves was replaced by Sir Hugh Palliser. His examination took place in 1766, but he was not promoted lieutenant until 19 January 1771. He had served under Captain Samuel Hood at Halifax, and on Hood being relieved there and appointed to the *Marlborough* (74), guardship at Portsmouth, he invited Holloway to fill a vacancy on board.

Holloway had an active life during the American war, serving under Commodore Hotham and later under Admiral Parker, who promoted him master and commander in 1780, and a few days later, on 17 January 1780, made him post captain and flag captain to his friend Hotham in *Vengeance*

(74). Hotham was left in charge of the West Indies station during the hurricane season, and, so great was the storm that struck St Lucia that *Vengeance* was driven from her mooring within the careenage onto the rocks and saved only by cutting away her masts. Many ships were lost.

He married in 1781 Elizabeth, first daughter of Main Swete Walrond of Antigua, Philadelphia, and Montrath, Devon. The couple were to have one son and three daughters. His son entered the Royal Navy and died in August 1802, aged thirteen, while on board the *Narcissus* (32) on her passage from Leghorn to Palermo. His eldest daughter, Clementina, married Admiral Sir Robert Waller Otway, baronet, GCB.

In September 1782 in command of *Buffalo* (60), perhaps the least serviceable ship in the navy, Holloway took part in the relief of Gibraltar. When the combined fleets stood out of Algeciras, Lord Howe called Holloway on board the *Victory* (100) and gave him verbal orders to take charge of the storeships which had been unable to get into the anchorage.

During the peace Holloway was unemployed until 1787, when he was appointed to command the *Solebay* (32) in the Leeward Islands, where Captain Nelson was senior officer, and where they both became acquainted with the duke of Clarence, who was then commanding *Pegasus* (28). During the Russian and Spanish armaments Holloway rejoined Admiral Hotham as his flag captain, and after the declaration of war in 1793 went with Admiral Lord Hood to the Mediterranean in the same capacity. When Hotham succeeded Hood, Holloway became captain of the fleet from the end of 1794 to November 1795, during which period there were two fleet engagements, on 14 March 1795 and 13 July. He was promoted rear-admiral on 14 February 1799, and appointed second in command at Portsmouth, where he stayed until the peace of Amiens, and returned on the renewal of the war until he was promoted vice-admiral on 23 April 1804. He then hoisted his flag in the Downs, and in 1807 was made governor of Newfoundland.

He died with the rank of admiral on 26 June 1826, aged seventy-nine, in Wells, Somerset.

Lt: 19 January 1771
M-C: 1780
Capt: 17 January 1780
R-Adm: 14 February 1799
V-Adm: 23 April 1804
Adm: 25 October 1809

HOOD

CAPTAIN ALEXANDER HOOD started his naval career with the greatest adventure of them all, and ended it in victorious action.

He was born on 23 April 1758 at Netherbury in Kingsland, Dorset, the second son of Mr Samuel Hood, purser in the Royal Navy, and first cousin of Admiral Sir Samuel Hood, Viscount Hood, and of Admiral Sir Alexander Arthur Hood, Lord Bridport. His name was entered in the muster of two ships simultaneously, one commanded by his cousin and the other by his father, in 1767 or 1768, but it was his father's command, the yacht *Katherine*, which appeared on his passing certificate, and it was from that ship he was discharged in 1772 into *Resolution* (12) under the command of Lieutenant James Cook for his second voyage around the world. Nothing is recorded about his experiences. At the beginning of the American war he served with Lord Howe in the North American station, and was commissioned lieutenant in the *Raisonnable* (64) on 18 July 1777. In March 1780 he was put in command of *Ranger*, cutter, in which he served the following year in the West Indies. Sir George Rodney there promoted him on 17 May 1781 master and commander, and with breathtaking speed made him post captain on 27 July with appointment to *Barfleur* (90) as flag captain to his cousin Sir Samuel Hood. He served as such in the action off Cape Henry on 5 September 1781, and in the actions at Basseterre Road, St Kitts, on 25 and 26 January 1782. He was then appointed to a private ship, in command of *Champion* (24), which acted as a repeating frigate in the action on 9 April and the battle of the Saintes on 12 April, and took part in the pursuit into the Mona passage of the French survivors.

One of the prisoners captured by his cousin was the Baron de Parois, nephew to the Marquis de

Vaudreuil. A friendship developed, and following his return to England in command of *Aimable* (32), a prize, and the conclusion of peace, Alexander Hood visited the Vaudreuil family. Shortly afterwards, in 1784, he married Elizabeth, only child of John Periam of the Middle Temple, of Wooton, Somerset. The couple had one son and one daughter, the former inheriting the baronetcy of his uncle, Vice-Admiral Sir Samuel Hood.

In 1790 at the time of the Nootka Sound incident, Hood was appointed to command *Hebe* (38), remaining in command of her until she was paid off in 1792, and then returning to her at the outbreak of war in 1793. He moved to the *Audacious* (74) on 15 July 1794, but ill health obliged him to give up his command for several years, until on 7 January 1797 he was appointed to command *Ville de Paris* (110) and then, a month later, *Mars* (74), which formed part of the Channel fleet then under Lord Bridport's command. He was one of the officers sent ashore by the Spithead mutineers, but he was permitted to return to his command. On 21 April 1798 *Mars* encountered *L'Hercule* (74), which, in the words of Lieutenant William Butterfield of the *Mars*,

> endeavoured to escape through the Passage du Raz, but the tide proving contrary, and the wind easterly, obliged her to anchor at the mouth of that passage, which afforded Captain Hood the opportunity of attacking her by laying her so close alongside as to unhinge some of the lower-deck ports, continuing a very bloody action for an hour and a half, when she surrendered. I lament being under the necessity of informing your Lordship, that His Majesty has on this occasion lost that truly brave man Captain Hood, who was wounded in the thigh late in the conflict, and expired just as the enemy's ship had struck her colours.

Hood was buried in Wooton, Somerset. There is a memorial in St Mary, Netherbury, Dorset.

Lt: 18 July 1777
M-C: 17 May 1781
Capt: 27 July 1781 (2)

HOOD

ADMIRAL SIR SAMUEL HOOD, VISCOUNT HOOD, GCB, exhibited his capacity in the American war as a tactical commander, and in the French Revolutionary War he faced unparalleled politico-military challenges when he persuaded Toulon to declare for the royalist cause.

He was born on 12 December 1724 in Butleigh, Somerset, the eldest son of the Revd Samuel Hood who was vicar of Butleigh, later of Thorncombe, Devon, and prebendary of Wells. His mother was Mary, daughter of Richard Hoskins of Beaminster, Dorset. He was seventeen when he entered the navy on 6 May 1741 as a captain's servant on board *Romney* (50) commanded by Captain Thomas Smith, and served on the Newfoundland station. In 1742 Smith was succeeded by Captain Thomas Grenville while *Romney* was in the Mediterranean, and in April 1743 Hood followed Grenville to the *Garland* (24). In November, Captain George Bridges Rodney rated Hood a midshipman while the young man was serving under him in the *Sheerness* (20). Hood subsequently moved with Rodney to the *Ludlow Castle* (24). On 23 January 1746, at the time of the Jacobite rebellion when Commodore Smith commanded a squadron on the coast of Scotland, Hood returned to service with his first captain, who appointed him acting lieutenant of the *Winchelsea* (20) on 17 May. The promotion, seconded by her captain, Henry Dyve, was confirmed by the Admiralty a month later, on 17 June 1746. He was wounded in the hand in an action near the Isles of Scilly, was transferred into *Greenwich* (50) under Captain John Montagu in March 1748, and then was transferred again into the flagship of Rear-Admiral Charles Watson, *Lyon* (60). In her he made a voyage to North America, before his ship paid off.

He married on 25 August 1749, at St Thomas, Portsmouth, Susannah daughter of Edward Lindzee, surgeon and apothecary, nine times mayor of Portsmouth. She was also sister of Admiral Robert Lindzee and of Captain John Lindzee, RN. The couple were to have three sons.

In 1753 Hood was able to obtain appointments

on guardships at Portsmouth with the help of Admiral Smith. When his father heard of the failing health of a captain on the North American station, he was hurried out to Jamaica, apparently with the help of Admiral Anson, and bitterly regretting the parting from his wife. This stratagem served, and Hood was promoted master and commander on 10 May 1754. After distinguishing himself in action with a French squadron off Louisburg on 27 July 1756, he was made post captain by Commodore Charles Holmes, and flag captain of *Grafton* (70). As it happened, five days earlier the Admiralty had posted him captain of *Lively* (20).

While in temporary command of *Antelope* (50) in 1757 he engaged a French ship of equal force off Brest, and drove it ashore, where it was totally destroyed. He was then given permanent command of *Bideford* (20) in the Channel fleet under the command of Sir Edward Hawke. On 7 February 1758 Hood was given command of the *Vestal* (32) and on 21 February 1759 he defeated a French ship of equal force off Cape Finisterre. Following his return to Portsmouth he was presented to the king by Lord Anson. *Vestal* was then employed in operations against an invasion flotilla, under Rodney's command. In the spring of 1760 he asked to be sent to the Mediterranean, for reasons of his health.

Following the conclusion of peace, and despite Admiral Smith's death, he was able to find appointment to command *Thunderer*, fitted as a guardship at Portsmouth. In the summer of 1765 he was employed carrying troops from Ireland to Halifax, and in April 1767 he was appointed commander-in-chief of the North American station. This put him into the centre of resistance at Boston to the stamp act, and Hood came to consider it necessary to conciliate colonial feeling. In 1768 he wrote a series of letters to ministers which described the ferment and discontent that pervaded North America, and predicted the revolt (*Letters to the Ministry from Governor Bernard, General Gage, and Commodore Hood. And also memorials to the Lords of the Treasury, from the Commissioners of the Customs. With Sundry Letters and Papers Annexed to the Said Memorials*, Boston, 1769).

From January 1771, during the mobilisation occasioned by the Falkland Islands crisis, he was appointed to command *Royal William* (100), which was later reduced to a guardship at Portsmouth. He remained in her until November 1773, and soon afterwards he was appointed to *Marlborough* (74), another guardship. He was able to live ashore at Catherington, near Horndean. On 5 July 1776 *Marlborough* was damaged by a powder explo-

*The Right Honourable
Samuel Lord Viscount Hood,
Admiral of the White Squadron,*
and Governor of Greenwich Hospital, engraving by
William Ridley after Hickel, published by
Joyce Gold, 103 Shoe Lane,
1 June 1804.

sion which killed twenty people and wounded another fifty, and her complement was turned over to *Courageux* (74), which saw active service in the Channel, rebellion having turned to war in America.

Hood accepted a civil appointment as resident commissioner at Portsmouth, and governor of the Royal (Naval) Academy, in February 1778. He was created a baronet on 20 May 1778, following the king's visit to Portsmouth. He watched from ashore the naval crises of 1778 and 1779 following the

French alliance with the American colonists, but he urged the first lord, Lord Sandwich, to give him a seagoing appointment, and finally he was ordered to hoist his flag as rear-admiral on 26 September 1780 on board *Barfleur* (90) to serve as second in command in the West Indies under Admiral Rodney. He had initially rejected the offer, because of concerns about his health, but finally persuaded himself to agree; perhaps this was a result of Sandwich agreeing to salvage his brother Alexander's career following the latter's alteration of his logbook before the Keppel court martial. Both brothers were promoted at the same time.

Samuel Hood's record as a flag officer began badly. He was so hampered by Rodney's tactical instructions to cruise to leeward of Martinique that he was unable to bring Admiral de Grasse to action before he could unite with the ships blockaded there. This was to prove disastrous, as de Grasse pressed on to the Chesapeake. Rodney having returned to England with the loot from St Eustatius, Hood followed the French, and joined Rear-Admiral Thomas Graves at New York. But by the time the British force was back at the Chesapeake, de Grasse had been reinforced by the French ships at Rhode Island. Following the battle of the Chesapeake on 5 September 1781 Hood was critical of Graves's tactical caution, which proved so disastrous strategically because it led to the surrender of General Cornwallis at Yorktown, and thence to the loss of thirteen of the American colonies. But Hood must take a large measure of responsibility for his remaining in line ahead out of range, until nightfall ended the engagement.

Thereafter, Hood's career took a better turn. He persuaded Graves's successor, Rear-Admiral Robert Digby, to release four additional ships of the line for Caribbean service by offering to share prize money. With this reinforced squadron, on 25 January 1782 he performed a remarkable battle manoeuvre against de Grasse's still superior French fleet anchored in Basseterre Road, St Kitts, in support of an army which was fighting to take the island. By offering battle, he induced de Grasse to leave the anchorage so as to be able to exploit his numerical superiority, and then, having previous-

ly carefully explained his intentions to his captains, Hood deployed the British fleet into the anchorage vacated by the French and moored his ships under fire in a strong defensive position between the French fleet and the French army. Two fleet attacks by the French were fought off, but on 13 February the Marquis de Bouille obliged the garrison at Brimstone Hill to capitulate. This put Hood's fleet in a dangerous position as the French could command the anchorage from the land, and in the night the fleet, having synchronised their watches, simultaneously cut their cables and slipped past de Grasse.

Hood joined Admiral Rodney, who arrived from Europe on 19 February. On 9 April Hood's squadron was brought to action by de Grasse off Dominica when the British centre and rear squadrons were respectively four and twelve miles distant, but they fought off the assault and inflicted such damage on the French that two ships had to be detached from de Grasse's battle line. Three days later, de Grasse was defeated by Rodney, who employed, by design or accident, the tactic of cutting through the French line. *Barfleur* was closely engaged with *Ville de Paris*, and it was to Hood that de Grasse surrendered his sword. On 17 April, after repeated requests, Hood was then detached from Rodney's fleet and on 19 April captured four enemy ships in the Mona passage. He was scathing in his criticism of Rodney, however, for the delay which prevented the annihilation of the shattered enemy fleet. In recognition of his qualities and service, he was created Baron Hood of Catherington in Ireland on 12 September 1782. Hood spent the last months of the war in Jamaica, repairing the fleet, and in New York, and during that time provided tutelage for Horatio Nelson and the duke of Clarence.

Following the end of the war Hood devoted his energies to civil life. In the election of 4 March 1785 he was returned for the parliamentary seat for Westminster, which he held until 16 July 1788. He then held the seat for Reigate, Surrey, from 18 August 1789 to 1790, when he regained the seat for Westminster, which he held until 1796. During the debate on the impeachment of Warren

Hastings on 2 March 1787 he made an effective defence of the need to grant a degree of consideration to commanders on detached service:

> Should the fear of an impeachment by Parliament, said his Lordship, be hung out to every commander, in whose hands was placed the defence of our national possessions, it must necessarily operate as a dangerous restraint to their exertions; when it was considered that no general, or admiral, had scarcely ever been fortunate enough to conduct himself in the performance of his duty, without occasionally falling into circumstances, in which the public service compelled him to do things, in themselves not pleasing to his feelings, nor strictly legal, but from the indispensable necessities of their situation perfectly justifiable. NC 2.23

Hood's political expenses were difficult for him to meet, but in his contesting the seat for Westminster he was doing a service for the king in keeping out Charles James Fox, and to help him he was appointed commander-in-chief at Portsmouth for the years 1786 to 1788 and again for 1791 to 1793. On the appointment of Lord Chatham as first lord, he was also given a seat on the Admiralty Board, which he occupied from 16 July 1788 to 7 March 1795. He was promoted vice-admiral on 24 September 1787.

Following the outbreak of war in February 1793 Hood was appointed to command in the Mediterranean. He hoisted his flag in *Victory* (100) on 6 May, and the fleet sailed at the end of the month to Minorca, where it was to co-operate with a Spanish fleet commanded by Admiral Don Juan de Langara. The prospect of a Hispano-British fleet engaging the French Toulon fleet, however, was short-lived. To reassert their authority in Toulon after the local overthrow of the Jacobins, the government in Paris sent an army south, and the Toulonese, out of desperation, invited Hood on 23 August to occupy the port. He landed two regiments of British infantry and 200 marines, and a Spanish army was rushed across the frontier to provide its landward defence. Small contingents were also sent by Naples, Piedmont and Sardinia. The French fleet moved into the inner harbour and landed its gunpowder, and about 5,000 of their crews were put on board four disarmed and unserviceable seventy-fours which sailed under passport to the Atlantic ports. This was an unprecedented situation for a British commander, who had to establish a landward defence against a revolutionary army with the artillery commanded by Napoleon Buonaparte, and maintain close liaison with Spanish officers who had once been enemies, and who began to see that their interests might still lie with the French. In the middle of December, Toulon's defences were overrun, and the British had to withdraw, bringing with them those Toulonese whose fate for their treachery would be the guillotine.

Even before the evacuation of Toulon, Hood had set about driving the French from their garrisons in Corsica, with the help of Pasquale Paoli's Corsican insurgents. The variety of operations he set in motion had the unfortunate effect of weakening the defence of Toulon, and his optimism that Toulon could be held delayed preparations to evacuate or destroy the Toulon fleet until it was too late to remove more than three French ships, or to burn more than nine ships of the line, three frigates and two sloops. He was promoted admiral on 12 April 1794, but his health was so much affected by the strain of his work that he was obliged in December 1794 to return to England. His demands to the government, over the head of the Admiralty, that he be provided with additional ships was viewed by Earl Spencer, the first lord, as a threat to discipline. The following May, when he was preparing to return to the Mediterranean, he was, unexpectedly, ordered to strike his flag.

Unusually, he was rewarded for his services by the creation of his much loved wife Susannah as baroness on 25 March 1795. On 1 June 1796 he was created Viscount Hood of Whitley, Warwickshire, and on 2 January 1815 he was nominated GCB. He held the office of governor of Greenwich hospital from 1796 until his death, and was an elder brother of the Trinity House.

Baroness Hood died on 25 May 1806, and her husband died on 27 January 1816, aged ninety-one, in Bath, Somerset. He was buried in Greenwich hospital cemetery, Kent, and a monument to his memory was erected in Butleigh, Somerset.

Lt: 17 June 1746
M-C: 10 May 1754
Capt: 22 July 1756
R-Adm: 26 September 1780
V-Adm: 24 September 1787
Adm: 12 April 1794

HOOD – *see* Bridport

HOPE

ADMIRAL SIR HENRY HOPE, KCB, is best known for the engagement he fought while commanding *Endymion* (48) on 15 January 1815, ending in the capture of the American super-frigate USS *President* (52).

He was the eldest son of Captain Charles Hope, RN, commissioner at Chatham dockyard, and his wife Susan Anne, daughter of Admiral Herbert Sawyer and sister of Admiral Sir Herbert Sawyer. His father's brother was Rear-Admiral Sir George Johnstone Hope, KCB. He was probably born in 1787, and entered the navy on 2 April 1798 as a volunteer first class on board the *Princess Augusta*, yacht, in the Thames river. He was rated midshipman or master's mate on 14 May 1800 on the *Kent* (74), commanded by his cousin, William Johnston Hope, and served in the Channel and off the Egyptian coast. On 31 May 1801 he moved into the *Swiftsure* (74) commanded by Captain Benjamin Hallowell, and he was made prisoner when she was captured on 24 June 1801. After his exchange he served in *Leda* (38) and *Defence* (74) under the command of his uncle George, and was commissioned lieutenant on 3 May 1804 in *Adamant* (50) commanded by Sir George Burton. On 15 March 1805 he was appointed to *Narcissus* (32) flying the flag of Admiral Donnelly on the Irish station, and at the capture of the Cape of Good Hope. He was promoted commander of *Espoir*, sloop, in the Mediterranean on 22 January 1806,

and made post captain on 24 May 1808 with appointment to the converted Indiaman *Glatton* (56). Subsequently he commanded in the Mediterranean the 18-pounder frigate *Leonidas* (38), the 12-pounder French prize frigate *Topaze* (38), and the 18-pounder frigate *Salsette* (38), being in 1811 senior officer in the Greek archipelago. His appointment to command the 24-pounder frigate *Endymion* (48) was made on 25 May 1813, and his encounter with *President* occurred on 15 January 1815 off Sandy Hook, New Jersey.

The capture of one of the American super-frigates was, for the Royal Navy, a satisfactory conclusion of the naval war against the United States. The *Naval Chronicle* calculated that the *President* could deliver 1,688 pounds of shot in a single discharge, both broadsides simultaneously, while the *Endymion*, an exceptionally strong frigate by Royal Navy standards, could deliver only 1,324 pounds. *Endymion*, however, was part of a strong squadron which considerably outnumbered the American. The *President* arrived at Spithead on 28 March and was taken into the Royal Navy, mostly as a trophy because she was too old and had suffered too much damage for her to be of much use to the peacetime fleet.

Hope was awarded a gold medal by the Admiralty, the merchants of Bermuda presented him with a silver cup, and another for the ship, and on 4 June 1815 he was made a CB, but he then went on half pay. He married on 21 July 1828 his first cousin, Jane Sophia, the youngest daughter of Admiral Sir Herbert Sawyer and sister of Lieutenant John Jervis Sawyer, RN. In just over a year's time she was dead, and there were no children. Hope continued to be promoted, eventually reaching the rank of admiral on 20 January 1858; he was naval aide-de-camp from 1831 to 1846, was advanced to KCB on 5 July 1855, and died on 23 September 1863, aged seventy-six, in Holly Hill, Hampshire.

Lt: 3 May 1804
Cmdr: 22 January 1806
Capt: 24 May 1808
R-Adm: 9 November 1846
V-Adm: 2 April 1853
Adm: 20 January 1858

HOPE

VICE-ADMIRAL THE RIGHT HONOURABLE SIR WILLIAM JOHNSTONE HOPE, GCB, is not particularly well known for any single naval action, but he had a long and active career.

He was born on 16 August 1766 in Finchley, Middlesex, the third and youngest son of John Hope Vere, merchant of London, and his first wife Catharine, only child and heiress of Sir William Weir, baronet, of Blackwood, Lanarkshire. Three of his uncles were senior officers in the Royal Navy, and in 1776 one of them, Captain, later Rear-Admiral, Sir George Johnstone Hope, entered him as a captain's servant into the books of his ship *Weazle* (14), which he joined on 10 January 1777 for service on the Guinea coast. He served in several different ships with his uncle, following him into *Hind* (24) on 3 December for service at Jamaica, then into *Crescent* (36) on 10 October 1778 for service at Guernsey, Ireland and Lisbon, during which he was rated midshipman and mate, into *Iphigenia* (32) on 3 January 1781 for service in the North Sea, and finally into the Spanish prize *Leocadia* (36) on 14 December of that year for service at Lisbon and at Newfoundland, with a rating of master's mate. On 26 September 1782 he spent a few months serving in *Portland* (50) with Vice-Admiral Campbell at Newfoundland, before he was commissioned lieutenant on 10 November 1782 in *Daedalus* (32) under Captain Thomas Pringle, with whom he continued at Newfoundland, and then served in the North Sea until 3 July 1784, when he came ashore. But he did not languish during the peace. Between 31 January 1785 and 19 March 1786 he had an appointment to *Sampson* (64), which was a guardship at Portsmouth, and it is believed that he served as flag lieutenant to Admiral Milbanke, commander-in-chief Portsmouth. He was next appointed lieutenant of *Pegasus* (28), at the request of Prince William Henry, who had recently been posted as her commander. Hope sailed with him to Newfoundland, Halifax and the West Indies, where the officers of *Pegasus* fell out with the prince, and Hope obtained a transfer on 9 May

1787 to *Boreas* (28) commanded by Captain Nelson. Having returned with him to England, he joined *Adamant* (50) commanded by Sir Richard Hughes on 10 February 1789, and went out with him to Newfoundland and Nova Scotia. In June 1790, when at Halifax, he was ordered to act in the place of Captain Knox of *Adamant*, who was ill, and shortly afterwards to command *Penelope* (44) because her commander had resigned from the service. But the Admiralty did not confirm the appointment, and Hope brought *Adamant* back to Plymouth, where she was paid off.

Captain William Johnstone Hope,
engraved by H R Cook after a miniature in
the possession of Lady Ann Hope, published
by Joyce Gold, 103 Shoe Lane,
31 October 1807.

He was promoted master and commander on 4 April 1791, and on 8 July 1792 he married his cousin, Anne Johnstone, eldest daughter of James Hope, third earl of Hopetoun, and sister-in-law of his uncle Rear-Admiral Sir George Johnstone Hope, KCB. Apparently the engagement had been a long one. His promotion seems finally to have settled the matter.

On 9 February 1793, only a week following the French declaration of war, he was appointed to command *Incendiary,* fireship, in the Channel. He was promoted to post captain on 9 January 1794 and was appointed on 21 May to command *Bellerophon* (74) flying the broad pendant, and later the flag, of Rear-Admiral Sir Thomas Pasley. *Bellerophon* was one of the ships which succeeded in carrying out Admiral Lord Howe's tactical manoeuvre in the battle of the Glorious First of June of cutting through the French line in line abreast, and Hope was rewarded by King George with a gold medal.

He left *Bellerophon* on 30 November, and on 24 January 1795 he was appointed to command *Tremendous* (74), but did not remain in her long. In March 1795 Admiral Adam Duncan asked Hope to be his flag captain in *Venerable* (74) in the North Sea station, to which he agreed. He took no part in the action off Camperdown bank in October 1797, however, because he had been forced to go ashore in September after receiving a concussion when on board one of the Russian men of war attached to Duncan's command. He was unable to return to sea until 5 March 1798, when he was appointed to command *Kent* (74). Admiral Duncan subsequently also transferred to the *Kent,* and in the summer of 1799 Hope was at the capture of the Dutch fleet in the Texel, following which he was sent home the bearer of dispatches. The king honoured him with £500 to purchase a sword, and shortly afterwards the tsar sent him the ribbon and cross of a commander of the order of Malta.

In June 1800, when Duncan hauled down his flag, Hope was ordered to join the Mediterranean fleet. He was detailed to command a company of sailors in the operation to capture Cadiz which was cancelled owing to the pestilence in the city, and later participated in landing General Abercromby and his army at Aboukir, and in the blockade of Alexandria. He resigned his command and returned to England, after which *Kent* was chosen by Sir Richard Bickerton as his flagship. The sultan awarded him a Turkish gold medal for distinguished services on the coast of Egypt in 1802.

During a very active career, his life ashore had not been entirely neglected. Anne had four sons, three of whom became senior naval officers, and two daughters. In 1800, with the patronage of Henry Dundas, Lord Melville, the electors for Dumfries Boroughs returned him to parliament while he was away at sea, and he continued to hold that seat until 1802. With the peace of Amiens in 1802 Hope went on half pay until 22 March 1804, when he was appointed to command the *Atlas* (90), but on 29 August poor health obliged him to come ashore. In that year he was elected to the parliamentary seat for Dumfries County, again with Melville's patronage, and he held that seat until 1830. He was a commissioner of the Admiralty from 6 April 1807 until 30 March 1809 and from 13 March 1820 to 2 May 1827, and he was a commissioner of the Board of Longitude. He was appointed colonel of the Royal Marines on 1 August 1811, and was eventually promoted vice-admiral on 12 August 1819. From 1813 to 1819 he served as commander-in-chief Leith. He was made a KCB on 2 January 1815, and promoted to GCB on 4 October 1825. He was a fellow of the Royal Society, king's counsel and privy councillor.

Anne died on 28 August 1819 in Rosehill, Aberdeenshire, and a little over two years later, on 30 October 1821, he married Maria, second daughter of Sir John Eden, fourth baronet, and widow of Frederick Willem van Reede, seventh earl of Athlone. In 1828 he was appointed treasurer of Greenwich hospital, and when that post was abolished he was made one of the five commissioners overseeing the hospital. He had no children in his second marriage, and died on 2 May 1831, aged sixty-four, in London. Maria died on 4 March 1851.

Lt: 10 November 1782
M-C: 4 April 1791
Capt: 9 January 1794
R-A: 12 August 1812
V-Adm: 12 August 1819

HOSTE

CAPTAIN SIR WILLIAM HOSTE, BARONET, KCB, one of Nelson's protégés, is best known for his victory over a greatly superior combined French and Italian squadron near the island of Lissa in the

Adriatic on 13 March 1811. As he manoeuvred to engage, he signalled 'Remember Nelson' to inspire his squadron.

He was born on 26 August 1780, the second son of the Revd Dixon Hoste, rector of Tittleshall, Norfolk, and his wife Margaret, daughter of Henry Stanforth of Salhouse. His name was entered on the books of *Europa* (50) by Admiral Hotham on 25 June 1785 when he was under five years old, but his real entry into the navy was as a captain's servant in *Agamemnon* (64) commanded by Horatio Nelson, which he joined on 15 April 1793. Nelson rated him a midshipman, and took him with him into *Captain* (74) when he transferred into her on 11 June 1795, and again when he moved into *Theseus* (74) on 27 May 1797. Hoste was present at the two actions off Toulon on 14 March and 13 July 1795, the battle off Cape St Vincent, and witnessed the disastrous raid on Tenerife in which Nelson lost an arm, although he did not himself go ashore. When Nelson went home to recover from his wound, Hoste continued in *Theseus* as acting lieutenant under the command of Captain Ralph Willett Miller. His commission was confirmed on 8 February 1798, and following the battle of the Nile he succeeded Captain Capel on 26 September 1798 in command of *La Mutine*. His promotion to commander was dated 3 December.

He continued to command the *Mutine* for the next three years under Nelson and Lord Keith. When he fell ill with malaria at Alexandria, and suffered permanent damage to his lungs, Lord and Lady Elgin provided a home for him in Athens where he could convalesce, and also set about his education in Greek antiquities. After he received his orders to take acting command of *Greyhound* (32) at Malta, which he did on 5 February 1802, and was employed on the coast of Italy, he was able to continue his classical education with Sir Francis Drake, the envoy at Florence. The earl of St Vincent had promoted him to the rank of post captain on 7 January but news of his advance did not reach him until May. He returned in *Greyhound* to England in April 1803, and came ashore in May for a year and a half.

On 14 November 1804 he was appointed to the *Eurydice* (24), and on 13 October 1805 Nelson moved him into the 32-pounder frigate *Amphion* (36). He was not present at the battle of Trafalgar, however, and when he learnt of it on 9 November he wrote to his father that 'Not to have been in it is enough to make one mad; but to have lost such a friend besides is really sufficient to almost overwhelm me.' [Hoste 1.251]

Hoste's service in the Mediterranean during the following years was to be very active indeed. From 23 June 1808 to Christmas Day 1809 the *Amphion* took or destroyed 218 of the enemy's vessels. At the beginning of 1809 he was senior officer in the Adriatic, and Admiral Collingwood regarded his abilities highly: 'I have on many occasions had to represent the zeal, the bravery, and the nice concert of measures that are necessary to success, which have distinguished the services of Captain Hoste; and this late attack of the enemy is not inferior to those many instances which have before obtained for him praise and admiration.' [Marshal 2.471] The Franco-Italian force Hoste engaged at Lissa in March 1811 consisted of five frigates, one corvette, one brig, two schooners, one gunboat and one xebec, which he opposed with four frigates, with a combined force of 156 guns compared with the 284 on the enemy ships. Two French ships were captured, *Bellona* and *Cerberus*, and a third ran ashore and blew up. Hoste was severely wounded by an explosion and by a musket shot in his right arm, and the total British losses were 190 killed and wounded. As was generally the case, casualties amongst the defeated far exceeded those of the conqueror, and at Lissa the Franco-Italian enemy suffered over 700 killed or wounded. After refitting at Malta, Hoste took his prizes home in triumph. He and his brother captains received gold medals.

Late in 1811 he was appointed to command *Bacchante* (38) but she was not ready for service until March or July 1812. Returning to the Mediterranean, Hoste continued his active service against enemy shipping in the Adriatic and along the Dalmatian shore, leading to the capture of Ragusa and Cattaro. In March 1814 the residents of Parga in Albania requested his assistance in driving out the French garrison. Repeatedly the navy demonstrated its ability to hoist heavy guns to elevations thought by enemy garrisons to be inaccessible.

Soon afterwards ill health led to his return to England. He was invested with the Austrian honour of a knight of the order of Maria Theresa on 23 May 1814, and was made a baronet on 21 September 1814 with an augmentation to his arms of 'Lissa' and 'Cattaro', made a KCB on 2 January 1815, and made a knight bachelor on 8 June 1815.

He had two daughters from a first marriage to Anne, daughter of Robert Glover, but she had evidently died, and on 17 April 1817 he remarried, uniting with Harriet, daughter of Horatio Walpole, second earl of Orford, and sister of Captain the Honourable William Walpole, RN. His health prevented his returning to sea, and it was not until 1 June 1822 that he accepted the command of a guardship, *Albion*, lying at Portsmouth. On 27 May 1825 he was appointed to command the yacht *Royal Sovereign* at Deptford.

Harriet gave birth to three sons and three daughters before Hoste died in London of consumption on 6 December 1828. He was buried in St John's Wood Chapel, Westminster, and a statue was placed in St Paul's Cathedral. Harriet survived him until 18 April 1875.

> Lt: 8 February 1798
> Cmdr: 3 December 1798
> Capt: 7 January 1802

HOTHAM

VICE-ADMIRAL THE HONOURABLE SIR HENRY HOTHAM, KCB, was a highly successful commander of frigates and third rates. His most remarkable action took place on 22 May 1812 when he brought *Northumberland* (74) so close to the rocks off Isle Groais [Groix] south of L'Orient that two French frigates and a brig running home after a successful cruise against British shipping were obliged to attempt an inshore passage which proved too shallow. All three ran aground on the rapidly falling tide. *Northumberland* had been engaged by three batteries in beating up the Channel

and was much damaged aloft, but after effecting repairs Hotham returned under fire from one of the batteries to anchor where he could bring his broadsides to bear on the stranded wrecks, which he holed repeatedly in their copper bottoms and finally set on fire. They blew up as the fire reached their magazines.

He was born on 19 February 1777, the third and youngest son of Sir Beaumont Hotham, second Baron Hotham of South Dalton, Yorkshire, and his wife Susanna, second daughter of Sir Thomas Hankey of Fetcham Park, Surrey, and widow of James Norman. He was a nephew of Admiral Lord William Hotham, and first cousin of Admiral Sir William Hotham. Educated at the Royal (Naval) Academy at Portsmouth, where he arrived on 31 May 1788, he entered the navy in January 1791 as a midshipman on the *Princess Royal* (90) flying his uncle's flag, but almost immediately transferred into the *Lizard* (28) in the Channel under the command of Captain John Hutt. In July he transferred again into the *Lapwing* (28) and served in the Mediterranean under the Honourable Henry Curzon before the outbreak of war in 1793. In April he was moved into the *Victory* (100), Lord Hood's flagship. In her he served in the occupation of Toulon and the operations in Corsica. Following the capture of Bastia, he was commissioned lieutenant on 6 June 1794 in the *Aigle* (38) under the command of Captain Samuel Hood, and moved back to *Victory* following the capture of Calvi. When Lord Hood returned to England at the end of the summer, Hotham was taken into his uncle's flagship, *Britannia* (100), and was promoted by him on 12 November to command of *La Fleche*, sloop. He was commissioned post captain on 13 January 1795 and appointed to command *Mignone* (32), a prize taken at Calvi which soon proved to be unfit for service, when he was taken into *Egmont* (74) as a volunteer. He was serving in her as such at the time of the action off Hyères on 13 July. Finally he was found a ship when he was appointed on 19 July to *Dido* (28).

He acquired such a reputation that when on 7 January 1797 he was transferred to *Blanche*, her crew refused to hear him read his commission, saying they had heard from the *Dido* that 'he was a dam'd tartar'. When threatened with punishment for mutiny, they trained the forecastle guns on the quarterdeck. Eventually they were persuaded by Commodore Nelson to return to their duty by a promise: 'If Captain Hotham ill treats you, give me a letter and I will support you.' [Nagle 209] He remained in the Mediterranean fleet until he returned home in August 1798 in charge of a convoy.

He began to attract more favourable attention in September 1800 when in command of the French prize *Immortalité* (36), and following the renewal of war in 1803 in command of *Imperieuse* (40) and *Revolutionnaire* (44). In the last, he served on the North American station during 1804, returning home in 1805. On 4 November 1805 he was serving under Rear-Admiral Sir Richard Strachan when four French ships of the line that had escaped from the battle of Trafalgar were put in the bag.

He was put in command of *Defiance* (74) in March 1806, and commanded the squadron watching L'Orient. In 1808 he commanded a squadron on the coast of Spain, and was under Rear-Admiral Robert Stopford's orders on 23 February 1809 when he had a taste of the sort of close inshore action which he was to repeat three years later. Stopford's squadron chased three French frigates into Sable d'Olonne and anchored within half a mile of them on a falling tide under fire from shore batteries. The enemy, on that occasion, were left rolled on their sides by the ebb. During the rest of the year and the following summer Hotham was employed on the coast of Spain in co-operation with the Spanish resistance. He assumed command of *Northumberland* (74) on 1 August 1810, and in recognition for his brilliant action off L'Orient in May 1812, he was, at the general promotion of 4 December 1813, nominated a colonel of Royal Marines.

On 22 February 1813 he was appointed captain of the fleet to Sir John Borlase Warren, in *St Domingo* (74), and in May 1814 he assumed the same duties on board *Asia* (50) for Sir Alexander Cochrane, commander-in-chief on the American station. He was ordered to hoist a commodore's broad pendant on *Superb* (74) in August 1814 as

second-in-command, and continued on that station after he received notice of his promotion to rear-admiral on 4 June 1814. At the termination of the war he was nominated KCB on 2 January 1815.

He was back in England when Napoleon returned to France for the campaign ending at the field of Waterloo, and he was given command of a squadron in the Biscay. His dispositions effectively prevented Napoleon making his planned escape to America, and led to his surrendering to *Bellerophon* (74).

Hotham struck his flag on 31 August 1815, and he married on 29 June 1816 Frances Anne Juliana, the eldest daughter of John Rous, first earl of Stradbroke, and half-sister of Admiral the Honourable Henry John Rous. The couple had three sons.

He was promoted vice-admiral on 7 May 1825 and nominated knight grand cross of the Guelphic order of Hanover on 4 July 1831. He served as a commissioner of the Admiralty from 2 April 1818 to 23 March 1822 and from 19 September 1828 to 25 November 1830. He died on 19 April 1833, aged fifty-six, in Malta, while commander-in-chief of the Mediterranean station.

Lt: 6 June 1794
Capt: 13 January 1795
R-Adm: 4 June 1814
V-Adm: 7 May 1825

HOTHAM

ADMIRAL SIR WILLIAM HOTHAM, GCB, commanded the only two-decked ship on the North Sea station, *Adamant* (50), that did not join the mutiny at the Nore in May 1797. Until support arrived from the Russian squadron at Harwich, and later from ships deserting the mutiny, she was the only capital ship that was available to support Admiral Lord Duncan's blockade of the Texel, by means of careful manoeuvre and false signals.

William Hotham was born on 12 February 1772, the second son of General George Hotham and his wife Diana, the youngest daughter of Sir Warton Pennyman Warton, baronet. Admiral Lord Hotham was his uncle, and Vice-Admiral the

Honourable Sir Henry Hotham, KCB, was a first cousin. William was first educated at Winchester school, but from 21 December 1779 was borne on the books of *William and Mary,* yacht, commanded by Captain Vandeput, and he is believed to have attended the Royal (Naval) Academy at Portsmouth. In his précis of naval service, he recorded that in January 1786 he was rated as captain's servant and ordinary seaman when he joined *Grampus* (50), under the command of Captain Edward Thompson, who was commanding with a broad pendant on the coast of Africa. He was rated able seaman when he joined *Ardent* (64) at Portsmouth on 17 June 1786, and midshipman on 20 September when he transferred to *Solebay* (32) under the command of Captain John Holloway, with whom he proceeded to the Leeward Islands, where he was again rated an able seaman on 30 September 1788. A year later, on 11 September, he was rated midshipman when he joined *Royal Charlotte,* yacht, under the command of Sir Hyde Parker. He transferred into *Hebe* (38) under Captain Alexander Hood on 20 January 1790 for Channel service, and on 2 June transferred again into *Princess Royal* (90) under Captain Holloway and flying the flag of his uncle, Rear-Admiral Hotham. He was commissioned lieutenant on 27 October 1790, and remained in his uncle's flagship until 26 January 1791, when he was appointed to *Alligator* (20) commanded by Captain Isaac Coffin, and served at Halifax until 20 October. He then had a few months ashore before being appointed on 18 February 1792 to *Winchelsea* (32) under Captain Richard Fisher for service at Halifax and in the Leeward Islands.

There, following the French declaration of war, he transferred on 29 May 1793 into *Duke* (90), flying the broad pendant of Commodore John Murray. On 11 October he transferred into *Inconstant* (36) under Captain Augustus Montgomery, with whom he served in the Mediterranean. On 13 January 1794 he was appointed to *Victory* (100), flying Lord Hood's flag in the Mediterranean. After the evacuation of Toulon he served on shore at the siege of Bastia under Nelson, and on 12 August was promoted to the command of the sloop *Eclair.* On 7 October he made post rank in the 9-pounder frigate *Cyclops* (28). He continued to serve in the Mediterranean fleet until the beginning of 1796, when he was sent home in her with dispatches.

Cyclops was paid off 8 March 1796, and Hotham was appointed on 11 January 1797 to command of *Adamant* (50), only a few months prior to the Nore mutiny. He fought in the battle of Camperdown, and then *Adamant* was attached to the squadron off Le Havre, under Sir Richard Strachan. Late in 1798 Hotham was ordered to proceed to the Cape of Good Hope, where he served for three years, until 14 December 1801.

Following the peace of Amiens he was appointed on 14 March 1803 to command *Raisonnable* (64) in the North Sea, but he resigned on 8 September, for reasons of health. On 12 June 1804 he married Anne, daughter of Sir Edward Jeynes of Gloucester and sister-in-law of Admiral Sir Edward Thornbrough, GCB. The couple had four sons and one daughter. He returned to semi-active service commanding the sea fencibles at Liverpool from 25 May 1808 to 28 February 1810, and then went into semi-retirement in command of the *Royal Sovereign,* yacht, from 31 August 1812 to 2 April 1814, retaining her even after his promotion to rear-admiral on 4 December 1813.

In his précis of service, Hotham noted:

> Finding his health impaired in the North Sea, Captain Hotham applied for a survey to be held upon him; the captains and surgeons composing it, judged it necessary for him to retire for a time from active service. Dr. Frazer his physician in London also certifying the same, he enclosed that certificate to the late Lord Melville. He occasionally made application for employment, when he found himself equal with [that prospect].

He added, 'I declined one or two offers of dock yards with the hope of being employed afloat.' ADM9/2/97 But nothing to his satisfaction was found.

He was nominated KCB on 2 January 1815, was promoted vice-admiral on 19 July 1821, was appointed a gentleman-in-waiting at court, and wrote a manuscript book, 'Characters, Principally Professional'. His wife died in 1827, and eight years later he married Jane Seymour, daughter and co-heiress of Francis Colman of Hillersdon, Devon, and widow of Roger Pettiward of Great Finborough, Suffolk. He was promoted to admiral on 10 January 1837, advanced in chivalry to GCB on 4 July 1840, and died on 31 May 1848, aged seventy-six, in New Windsor, Berkshire. There is a memorial in All Saints, Binfield.

Lt: 27 October 1790
Cmdr: 1794
Capt: 7 October 1794
R-Adm: 4 December 1813
V-Adm: 19 July 1821
Adm: 10 January 1837

HOTHAM

ADMIRAL WILLIAM HOTHAM, BARON HOTHAM, is known for his two partial engagements with the Toulon fleet in March and July 1796, and for Nelson's disgust that he was content with limited success.

He was born on 8 April 1736 in York, the third son of Sir Beaumont Hotham, seventh baronet of South Dalton, commissioner of the customs. His mother was Frances, daughter of the Revd Stephen Thompson of Thornthorpe, Yorkshire. He was sent to Westminster school, and then to the Royal (Naval) Academy Portsmouth on 6 August 1748, at a date when its reputation was not very high, and entered the navy on 30 July 1751 as a volunteer per order in *Gosport* (40) on the North American station. He passed his examination on 7 August 1754 after serving in *Advice* (50) in the West Indies, and in *Swan*, sloop, in the North American station, and received his commission on 28 January 1755 with appointment to *St George* (98), flagship of Sir Edward Hawke. He followed Hawke into *Namur* (90), *Antelope* (50) and *Ramillies* (74), and was promoted by him to the command, in succession, of a 10-gun polacre and *Fortune,* sloop. As the latter was at sea, he was placed in temporary command of *Syren* (20). In

her he was in action with *Télémaque* (26), and *Fortune* captured a large French privateer by boarding. In recognition of his abilities, he was made post captain on 17 August 1757 with appointment to *Gibraltar* (20), being transferred in November to *Squirrel* (20) and on 17 April 1758 to *Melampe* (36) in the North Sea. He continued to enjoy success, mostly in independent cruises, moving to the Channel. In April 1761 he was attached to a squadron under Augustus Keppel during the operations to capture Belle isle, following which, on 20 May, he was moved into *Aeolus* (32).

Following the peace of Paris, Hotham was appointed in 1766 to the *Hero* (74), a guardship at Plymouth, and was employed in 1769 in transporting soldiers to relieve the garrison at Minorca. At the time of the Falkland Islands crisis in 1770 he was appointed to *Resolution* (74), which had just been launched at Portsmouth, and in 1773 took part in King George's fleet review at Spithead, which was staged to restrain French adventures in the Baltic. In 1776 with the outbreak of serious hostilities in America he was appointed to *Preston* (50) and ordered to hoist a commodore's broad pendant. He sailed from Spithead on 6 May to escort a convoy of transports with a corps of Hessian soldiers and a detachment of Guards embarked. At Long Island they were put ashore, and Hotham was moved into *Phoenix* (44) to continue in close support of the army. In November 1778 he escorted a convoy of 5,000 soldiers to Barbados, where he joined the squadron under Rear-Admiral Barrington for an assault on St Lucia. When Admiral Sir George Rodney arrived in late March 1780 Hotham shifted his broad pendant into *Vengeance* (74) and was stationed to lead the line in Rear-Admiral Rowley's division, taking part in the three engagements with the French fleet commanded by the Comte de Guichen in April and May. He was anchored in the careenage at St Lucia when the hurricane struck on 10 October 1780, and escaped total loss only by cutting away *Vengeance*'s masts and jettisoning her guns. In the spring of 1781 he returned to England escorting the West Indies trade, and ran into a greatly superior French squadron under Admiral de la Motte

Piquet, which captured a number of trade ships.

The following year, with the fall of Lord North's administration and Rockingham's appointment of Admiral Keppel to first lord of the Admiralty, Hotham was ordered to hoist a broad pendant in *Edgar* (74) and in her participated in Admiral Lord Howe's relief of Gibraltar.

He had been honoured with a commission as colonel of the marines on 19 March 1779, and was promoted rear-admiral on 24 September 1787 and vice-admiral on 21 September 1790 at the time of the Nootka Sound crisis, hoisting his flag in *Princess Royal* (90) as commander of the rear division of the Channel fleet.

In April 1793, two months subsequent to the French declaration of war, he was appointed second in command under Vice-Admiral Lord Hood in the Mediterranean, hoisting his flag on *Britannia* (100). In November 1794 the crew of the 90-gun *Windsor Castle* demanded the removal of all their senior officers, including Rear-Admiral Lindzee and the boatswain. In the climate of fear brought to aristocratic Europe by the French Revolution, Hotham, perhaps unwisely, complied in part with the demands of the mutineers, and pardoned them.

Hood returned home in late 1794 to recover his health, leaving Hotham in temporary command, and without even an adequate base or stores. In March of the following year he had an encounter with the Toulon fleet, when on both sides together over 1,000 men were killed or wounded in passing actions on the 12th and 14th. Two French ships, the *Ça Ira* and *Censeur*, were cut off and winged by *Inconstant*, frigate, and eventually captured by Nelson in *Agamemnon*. Hotham refused to allow a pursuit in which his fleet would lose formation in the fitful wind, and in any event be unlikely to overhaul the clean-hulled French. Nelson went so far as to have himself rowed to the flagship to express his wish to harry the foe.

Hotham was thanked by both houses of parliament for his command in the battle, and he found himself placed in absolute command when Hood was ordered to strike his flag. This brought on a nervous breakdown on the part of the overburdened Hotham.

He again brought his fleet to action in July when he was surprised watering at San Fiorenzo, Corsica.

> Finding they had no other view than that of endeavouring to get from us, I made the signal for a general chase, and for the ships to take suitable stations for their mutual support, and to engage the enemy as arriving up with them, in succession, but the baffling winds and vexatious calms, which render every naval operation in this country doubtful, soon afterwards took place, and allowed only a few of our van ships to get up with the enemy's rear about noon, which they attacked so warmly, that, in the course of an hour after, we had the satisfaction to find one of their sternmost ships viz. *l'Alcide* of 74 guns, had struck.
> NC 9.356

The rest got away, and *L'Alcide* caught fire and blew up. The relative failure of the July encounter was to be an important factor contributing to the defeat of the Austrian army on the Riviera.

In November Hotham was relieved by Sir John Jervis, and resigned his command. As a reward for his services he was on 17 March 1797 created Baron Hotham of South Dalton on the Irish establishment, and was promoted admiral on 14 February 1799, but he remained in retirement. He died on 2 May 1813, aged seventy-seven, at his seat in South Dalton, Yorkshire, and was succeeded by his brother Beaumont Hotham.

Lt: 28 January 1755 (1)
M-C: 19 November 1756
Capt: 17 August 1757 (1)
R-Adm: 24 September 1787
V-Adm: 21 September 1790
Adm: 14 February 1799

HOWE

ADMIRAL OF THE FLEET THE RIGHT HONOURABLE SIR RICHARD HOWE, EARL HOWE, KG, was a towering figure in the Royal Navy, who fought in four wars, and won the first great victory in the war against the French Republic. He was a central figure in the development of naval tactics, and was so popular with the sailors that he was called out of retirement to settle the 1797 naval mutiny at Spithead.

He was born on 22 January 1726 in London, the second son of Sir Emanuel Scrope, second Viscount Howe of Langar, Nottinghamshire, who died on 29 March 1735 as governor of Barbados when his son was nine years old. His mother was Maria Sophia Charlotte, natural daughter of George I and his mistress Madame de Platen, countess of Darlington. Howe was educated at Westminster school, and possibly also at Eton college. He first went to sea in the merchant service, and formally entered the navy on 16 July 1739 when he was placed on the book of *Pearl* (40) commanded by Captain Edward Legge. If he actually joined his ship, he would have sailed on 23 July with Edward Vernon's squadron to Lisbon, but he may have spent that year at Eton. On 2 July 1740 he followed Legge to the *Severn* (50), which formed part of Commodore Anson's squadron under orders to proceed via Cape Horn into the Pacific. Anson, flying his broad pendant in *Centurion* (50), captured a Manila galleon and returned home via Canton and the Cape of Good Hope, but it took *Centurion* months to round Cape Horn sailing east to west, and hundreds of her crew died of scurvy. *Severn* did not make it past Tierra del Fuego, and returned to England in April 1742. Howe then served in *Burford* (70) under Captain Franklin Lushington in the West Indies in Charles Knowles's squadron, and after Lushington was killed in action he was moved into Knowles's own ship, the *Suffolk* (70). He was given an acting commission to serve as lieutenant in *Eltham* (44) on 10 July, but on 8 October returned to *Suffolk* as midshipman.

He was commissioned lieutenant on 25 May 1744, this time having his acting order confirmed 8 August, and made such a good impression during the Jacobite rebellion, serving in a succession of ships, that he was promoted master and commander on 5 November 1745, and postcaptain on 10 April 1746. In March 1747 he made a cruise to the west African coast, in temporary command of *Poole* (44). He then joined Knowles at Barbados, where he arrived on 23 January 1748,

and was appointed flag captain of *Cornwall* (70). She was paid off in July 1749 following the conclusion of peace, but Howe managed to keep in employment, and he had the dubious distinction of firing the first shots in the Seven Years War.

On 20 January 1755 he was appointed to command *Dunkirk* (60) and sailed as part of a fleet commanded by Edward Boscawen to North America. Off Louisburg on 7 June he captured *Alcide*, a French frigate loaded with soldiers for

The Honourable Richard Earl Howe, K.C.,
drawn and engraving by
William Ridley, published by
Joyce Gold, 103 Shoe Lane,
31 May 1803.

the garrison. Having made inevitable the conflict which soon grew into the first truly world war, Boscawen then returned to England, accompanied by Howe in *Dunkirk*. Howe spent most of the war in the Channel, in command of *Dunkirk* and later *Magnanime* (74), in which latter ship in September 1757 he took a prominent part in the expedition to Isle d'Aix and Rochefort. In June 1758 in the *Essex* (64) he led the first British fleet ever to sail through the tidal race between the French coast and Alderney, in order to attack shipping at St Malo and Granville. The following year, on 20

November 1759, he led Admiral Hawke's fleet into the confined waters of Quiberon Bay in a full gale to defeat Admiral Conflans. In recognition of his services he was given the rank of colonel of the marines on 4 February 1760. He spent the last two years of the war watching the coast of France, and served as commodore of the force in Basque Roads watching Rochefort. In June 1762 he was flag captain to the duke of York, and he hoisted his flag on board *Princess Amelia* (80).

On 10 March 1758 Howe had married Mary, daughter of Colonel Chiverton Hartopp of Welby, Leicestershire. The couple were to have three daughters. Four months after his marriage he succeeded his brother, who had been killed in action on 5 July 1758 at Ticonderoga, becoming the fourth viscount. He was member of parliament for Dartmouth, Devon, from 23 May 1757 to 20 April 1782, and occupied a seat on the Admiralty Board from 20 April 1763 to 31 July 1765, when he became treasurer of the navy, which office he held to 1770. On 18 October 1770 at the time of the Falkland Islands crisis he was promoted rear-admiral.

With the outbreak of the American revolution, Howe returned to active service at sea, hoisting his flag in *Eagle* (64) as vice-admiral, to which rank he had been promoted on 5 February 1776, and proceeding to Halifax. He and his brother, who commanded the army, combined the roles of peacemaker and aggressive war maker during the period of transition from civil war to international conflict, but they did not have enough to offer the belligerent Americans. On 22 August 1776 they moved against New York, which they established as the *place des armes*. A close blockade was attempted of the middle colonies, but it proved impossible to prevent the importation by the continental army of gunpowder from the French West Indian islands. The failure of the 1777 campaign to defeat the revolution, and the failure of renewed efforts to negotiate a settlement, made the French decision to conclude a treaty with the Americans the strategic focus for the remainder of the war.

The arrival in 1778 of a French fleet under Admiral D'Estaing forced Howe, outnumbered in ships of the line, to shelter inside Sandy Hook, where the water was too shallow for the larger French ships. He had already requested supersession in command, and within days the first of Vice-Admiral John Byron's ships began to arrive, but they were storm-damaged, and the French retained their naval superiority in American waters. Howe nonetheless acted offensively against the French, who made Rhode Island their fleet rendezvous, but was unable to bring them to battle. When six more of Byron's squadron arrived under Rear-Admiral Hyde Parker, Howe decided to hand over command to Vice-Admiral James Gambier, and return to England.

As part of his preparation of the fleet for action, he had distributed on 12 July 1776 a *Signal Book for the Ships of War*, which was to be an important part of the process by which the Royal Navy acquired the tactics and communications needed to deploy its force while engaged with the enemy. By the time he was superseded in command in 1778 he had practically created the system which he was to use in the operations of the Channel fleet in 1782.

He remained ashore during the three and a half years following his return to England, and became active in parliament, defending his conduct in America and demanding a parliamentary investigation, which started work on 29 April 1779. He became increasingly critical of the administration of Lord North. When it fell in March 1782 he was made commander-in-chief of the Channel fleet by the Rockingham ministry, promoted to a full admiral on 8 April 1782, and advanced in the peerage to Viscount Howe on 10 April 1782. On 11 October he broke the siege of Gibraltar, and the corporation of London commissioned John Singleton Copley to paint a gigantic picture to commemorate the event.

On 28 January 1783 he was made first lord of the Admiralty. He resigned on 8 April on the formation of the duke of Portland's administration, but returned to the office on 30 December on Portland's replacement by William Pitt and continued in office until 24 September 1787, when he resigned and was advanced again in the peerage to Earl Howe of Great Britain. His period at the head of the Admiralty was marked by his unco-operative attitude to the controller of the navy, Charles Middleton, later Lord Barham. He resigned when Pitt insisted on breaking with tradition and promoted Middleton to rear-admiral. After he left the government, Howe was appointed vice-admiral of Great Britain, in June 1792, and he was also made an elder brother of the Trinity House.

His departure from the Admiralty was far from being the end of his active career at sea. At the time of the Nootka Sound crisis in 1790 he hoisted his flag on board *Victory* (100) in command of the Channel fleet, with six subordinate flag officers – Samuel Barrington, Samuel and Alexander Hood, John Jervis, Richard Bickerton and William Lord Hotham. He returned to that duty on the outbreak of war in February 1793, this time hoisting his flag in the new first rate *Queen Charlotte* (100) with Vice-Admiral Thomas Graves and Alexander Hood as his flag officers. In her he undertook the arduous task of blockading the French Brest fleet, which he finally brought to battle on 29 May and 1 June 1794, in engagements collectively known as the battle of the Glorious First of June.

Admiral the earl of St Vincent succinctly described the action in a letter written in 1806:

> On the 29th May a manoeuvre, by which Lord Howe proposed to cut off the rear of the enemy, by passing through his line, failed in its effect, owing to the mistake or disobedience of signals; the only advantage gained was the weather gage, which he preserved to the first of June, when he ran down in a line abreast, nearly at right angles with the enemy's line, until he brought every ship of his fleet on a diagonal point of bearing to its opponent, then steering on an angle to preserve that bearing until he arrived on the weather quarter, and close to the centre ship of the enemy, when the *Queen Charlotte* altered her course, and steered at right angles through the enemy's line, raking their ships on both sides as she crossed, and then luffing up and engaging to Leeward.

Tucker 281–3

Howe's tactics were successful because they made the best use of British superiority in gunnery, putting captains in a position where they could overwhelm individual French ships by their superior rate of fire. The *Naval Chronicle* commented that: 'During the action the sailors' wives, who were in board some of the English ships, fought with the most determined valour, at the guns; encouraging and assisting their husbands. After the action, seven ships of the line were in possession of the English; one of which, the *Vengeur*, sunk almost immediately on being taken.' [NC 1.21]

On Howe's return to Spithead, King George reviewed the fleet, and distributed gold medals and chains to the flag officers and some of the captains, but Howe's failure to provide detailed mention in dispatches of many of his captains' exploits created a great deal of discontent. It was also felt that he should have pursued the defeated fleet and added to the captures. He was probably so exhausted after the days of anxiety and work that he was incapable of continuing. Nonetheless, he commanded the Channel fleet until April 1797, although he resided ashore from May 1795, leaving the daily routine to Admiral Lord Bridport. His final service was his recall to Portsmouth in May 1797 during the great mutiny because 'Black Dick' Howe was such a favourite with the seamen that his presence served as a guarantee of good faith on the part of the administration.

He had been promoted admiral of the fleet and general of the marines on 12 March 1796, and received his final honour on 2 June 1797, being created a knight of the Garter. He died of the gout in the head on 5 August 1799, aged seventy-three, in Grafton Street, Piccadilly, Middlesex, and was buried in Langar, Nottinghamshire, a monument to his memory being erected in St Paul's Cathedral. His wife died on 9 August 1800.

Lt: 25 May 1744
M-C: 5 November 1745
Capt: 10 April 1746
R-Adm: 18 October 1770
V-Adm: 5 February 1776
Adm: 8 April 1782
Adm. of the Fleet: 12 March 1796

HUMPHREYS

REAR-ADMIRAL SIR SALUSBURY PRYCE
HUMPHREYS, CB. The *Naval Chronicle* in 1812
noted that: 'Captain Humphreys was the officer
who commanded HMS *Leopard*, of 50 guns, at the
time of her encounter with the U.S. frigate
Chesapeake, in the month of June, 1807. The ex-
isting political differences with America – differences which, in some measure, have arisen from
that encounter – therefore, render his services a
subject of considerable interest to the British public.' NC 28.353

He was born on 24 November 1778 at
Clungunford rectory near Ludlow, the third son of
the Revd Evan Humphreys, rector of Montgomery,
Wales, and of Clungunford, and of his wife Mary,
eldest daughter and coheiress of the Revd Salusbury
Pryce, DD. Entering the navy on 1 July 1790 as a
volunteer in *Ardent* (64) under the command of
Captain James Vashon, he moved in quick succession first to *Trusty* (50) flying the flag of Rear-
Admiral Sir John Laforey; then to the 12-pounder
frigate *Solebay* (32) commanded by Captain
Mathew Squire, in which he was rated an able seaman; to *Fairy* (14) commanded by Captain Francis
Laforey; and, at the time of the French declaration
of war in February 1793, he was rated a midshipman in *Severn* (50) under the command of Captain
Paul Minchin. With Minchin he sailed to Quebec,
following him into *Hebe* (38) in 1794 while serving in the West Indies. He was ordered to act as
lieutenant in *Fury* (14) under the command of
Captain Henry Evans in 1796, and was promoted
lieutenant on 27 January 1797 with an appointment to *Sally,* armed ship, commanded by Captain
George Wolfe, under whom he served in the North
Sea. In 1798 he was appointed to *Juno* (32) under
Captain George Dundas, continuing in the North
Sea, and moving the following year into *Isis* (50)
flying the flag of Vice-Admiral Sir Andrew Mitchell
in the Channel fleet, following him in 1800 into
Windsor Castle (90).

He was promoted commander on 29 April 1802,
but was not appointed to a ship until 1804 when
he took command of *Prospero*, bomb-vessel, at

Portsmouth. On 8 May of that year he was promoted to post captain, and in March 1805 he married Jane Elizabeth, eldest daughter and coheiress
of John Tirel Morin of Weedon Lodge,
Buckinghamshire, and of St George, Hanover
Square, Westminster. This was the high point in
his life. His wife gave him a son, and in 1806, while
serving at Halifax, he was given command of the
Leopard (50), which was intended as Vice-Admiral
George Berkeley's flagship. As the admiral preferred to live ashore, *Leopard* was generally employed as a private ship.

Captain Salusbury Pryce Humphreys, R.N.,
engraved by R? Page from an original miniature,
published by Joyce Gold, Shoe Lane, Fleet Street,
30 November 1812.

It was Humphreys's misfortune that it fell to his
lot to enforce the orders Berkeley issued on 1 June
1807 requiring his captains to stop USS *Chesapeake*
(44) at sea to recover deserters, by force if necessary. *Leopard* did so off Cape Henry on 22 June,
and Humphreys fired a few shot into her when her
captain, Commodore Barron, rejected his demand.
This obtained his objective, but it also led to a
major crisis in Anglo-American affairs, and a
British order in council banning the use of force
against foreign warships. Eventually it was to be

the major pretext for the American declaration of war in 1812.

Humphreys had attracted too much American anger to continue in employment, however justified he had been by his orders. He returned to England in 1808 and, in the words of Marshall's *Naval Biography*, 'has ever since been on half-pay; his sword converted into a ploughshare, and his naval uniform exchanged for a magisterial gown, serving as Justice of the Peace for Buckingham, Chester and Lancaster.' [Marshall 2.897] Adding tragedy to disappointment, Jane Elizabeth died in September. He married for a second time on 31 May 1810, taking for his wife Maria, daughter and heiress of William Davenport of Bramall Hall near Stockport, Cheshire. She was to increase his family by five sons and two daughters.

At the end of the war he was put on the list of superannuated captains, but he was made a CB on 26 September 1831, nominated a knight commander of the Guelphic order of Hanover in February 1834, and promoted rear-admiral on 10 January 1837. He assumed the surname of Davenport when his wife inherited the Davenport estates of Bramall, Cheshire, in 1838. He was restored on the active list on 17 August 1840, and died on 17 November 1845, aged sixty-six.

Lt: 27 January 1797
Cmdr: 29 April 1802
Capt: 8 May 1804
Superannuated R-Adm: 10 January 1837
Restored on the Active List: 17 August 1840

HURD

CAPTAIN THOMAS HANNAFORD HURD spent a lifetime in hydrographic survey work, and succeeded Alexander Dalrymple as Admiralty hydrographer.

He had been born in Plymouth, was baptised on 30 January 1747, the son of Edward and Jane Hurd, and entered the navy on 1 September 1768 as an able seaman in *Cornwall* under the command of Captain Molyneux Shuldham. He began a life career in hydrography as a young man on the Newfoundland and North American stations during the years 1771 and 1774, learning his trade under Samuel Holland in the armed vessel *Canceaux* commanded by Lieutenant Henry Mowatt. He passed his examination for lieutenant on 1 March 1775, joined *Eagle* (64) flying the flag of Lord Howe in January 1776, and on 31 January 1777 was appointed by Howe as first lieutenant of the *Unicorn*, a copper-bottomed ship under the command of Captain John Ford. He was second lieutenant of *Hercules*, under the command of Captain Savage, in the battle of the Saintes, 12 April 1782, following which he was appointed first lieutenant of a prize, *Ardent* (64) commanded by Captain Richard (?) Lucas. She formed part of the convoy battered by the hurricane of 17 September 1782 in her passage to England.

At that point, however, his hydrographic service came to dominate his career. In 1785 Lord Howe obtained for Hurd appointment as surveyor-general of Cape Breton, but he was dismissed the following year by J F W Des Barres, who was the province's lieutenant-governor and was conducting his own hydrographic survey of Nova Scotia. In 1789 Hurd was ordered to conduct a hydrographic survey of Bermuda. He was at this work for nine years, and a further three years' work followed in London preparing charts. He was promoted commander on 18 August 1795 and captain on 29 April 1802, but he did not again serve in a combat role. His marriage to Elizabeth probably took place while he was working on the Bermuda survey.

In 1802 he was given command of *Glatton*, which had played an important part in the battle of Copenhagen under the command of Captain William Bligh, but Hurd's appointment was not regarded primarily as in the light of a Channel fleet captain. The blockade of Brest had been sustained by then for ten years, with a break during the peace of Amiens. This was difficult and dangerous work, made all the more so by the inadequacy of British charts. Accordingly Hurd was ordered, rather belatedly, to conduct a hydrographic survey of the Brest approaches, which he undertook between 1804 and 1806, publishing the results in two charts and sailing directions. He also carried out a detailed survey of Falmouth harbour and its approaches so that it could be used in greater safety as a forward base for frigates.

In November 1807, having left the *Glatton*, he was appointed to a committee to advise Alexander Dalrymple, hydrographer to the Admiralty, on the selection of charts for issue to the navy. Dalrymple reacted badly to the interference of the committee, and on his dismissal Hurd was appointed in May 1808 to replace him. He was given authority to commission surveys by specialist naval officers in command of ships specially allocated for their use, and in 1821 he persuaded the Admiralty to place Admiralty charts on sale to the public.

When he died on 29 April 1823 Hurd had created the hydrographic branch of the navy, and was also superintendent of chronometers and a commissioner for the discovery of longitude. He was survived by his wife.

> Lt: 31 January 1777
> Cmdr: 18 August 1795
> Capt: 29 April 1802

INGLEFIELD

CAPTAIN JOHN NICHOLSON INGLEFIELD was a follower of Sir Samuel, Viscount Hood, and captain of the Mediterranean fleet in 1794. He retired from the sea when his patron was ordered to haul down his flag. Thereafter he served ashore. His experience in the great hurricane of 1780 was certainly enough to last any man a lifetime.

Nothing appears to be known about this officer's parentage. He was born in 1748, entered the navy in 1759, and passed his examination in April 1766, but at a time of settled peace he was able to get employment only as an able seaman in *Launceston* (40), Vice-Admiral Philip Durell's flagship in the North American station. Two years later, on 26 May 1768, he was commissioned lieutenant in *Romney* (50), on which Commodore Samuel Hood was flying a broad pendant. He returned to *Launceston* in October, but then reverted to *Romney* the following July and became one of Hood's followers, transferring with him in December 1770 to *Marlborough* (74) and then to *Courageux* (74).

About the year 1775 he married a daughter of Sir Thomas Slade, the naval constructor. The couple had several children, of whom one son was to be Rear-Admiral Samuel Hood Inglefield. One of his daughters married Admiral Sir Benjamin Hallowell Carew, GCB. His youngest daughter, Catherine Dorothea, married Captain Henry Whitby, RN.

In 1778 he was moved to *Robust* (74) under the command of Hood's brother Alexander, and fought in the battle of Ushant on 27 July. The following June he was promoted to command of *Lively*, sloop, and after a little over a year in that rank he was made post captain on 7 October 1780 and captain of *Barfleur* (90), on which Sir Samuel Hood flew his flag in the actions in the West Indies and in American waters at the close of the American war. Inglefield was in command of *Centaur* (74) at the battle of the Saintes on 12 April 1782, and it was on his passage home in her, with a convoy under the command of Rear-Admiral Thomas Graves, that he encountered the great hurricane on 16 September.

Centaur was laid

> so much on her beam ends, that the water burst through from the hold between decks; she lay motionless, and seemed irrecoverably overset. Her masts falling overboard, she in some degree righted, with the loss of her rudder, and such extreme violence as caused unspeakable mischief and confusion. The guns broke loose, the shot were thrown out of the lockers, and the water that came from the hold swept away every thing between decks, as effectually as the waves had from the upper. The officers, when the ship overset, ran up from their beds naked; neither could they get at a single article of clothes to put on in the morning, nor receive any assistance from those who were upon deck, they themselves having no other but what they had on. Marshall 2.66

The storm raged unabated, and at last all hope was gone. Each thought how he should meet his end.

But a few decided to launch the pinnace into the raging sea, and Inglefield jumped into the boat. Others, less fortunate, fell into the sea and were drowned. The twelve survivors sailed, with virtually no supplies, nearly 800 miles to the Azores. Inglefield was acquitted at the court martial, and almost immediately appointed to command another ship. But the circumstances occasioned enough controversy that in 1783 he published *Capt. Inglefield's Narrative, Concerning the Loss of His Majesty's Ship the Centaur, etc.* Pamphlets were anonymously published attacking him, and he defended himself by publishing more of his own.

He was appointed to command of a guardship, *Scipio* (64), in the Medway, and between 1788 and 1792 he served on the west coast of Africa in command of *Adventure* (44) and, from 1790, *Medusa* (44). Shortly before the outbreak of the French Revolutionary War he was appointed to command *L'Aigle* (36) in the Mediterranean, and served at the siege of Bastia. In 1794 he succeeded Sir Hyde Parker as Lord Hood's captain of the fleet, and returned with him in the *Victory* (100) at the end of the year.

When Hood was ordered to haul down his flag Inglefield left the sea. From then, until 1811, he served ashore as resident commissioner of the navy at Corsica, Malta, Gibraltar and finally Halifax. In order to retain these civil appointments, he refused promotion to rear-admiral, and instead was on 21 February 1799 put on the list of superannuated captains He was the inventor of the Inglefield clip still in use to secure flags to halyards, and was the author of *A View of the Naval Force of Great Britain* published in 1791, which appeared under the name of Admiral John Borlase Warren. He died on 30 January 1828, aged seventy-nine.

Lt: 26 May 1768
M-C: 7 June 1779
Capt: 7 October 1780
Superannuated Capt: 21 February 1799

INMAN

CAPTAIN HENRY INMAN's experience of naval service was that it was 'a bitch' ending in an untimely death. Three times during his early years of service he lost his ship, once to the enemy, once to grounding and once to a hurricane, twice he had to deal with a murderous crew, and he fought in two major fleet actions.

He was born in 1762, son of the Revd George Inman, vicar of Burrington near Bristol, Somerset. The *Naval Chronicle* remarked that 'we have frequently had occasion to remark, that England is more particularly indebted to the clergy, than to any other class or description of men, for her heroes both by sea and land.' [NC 25.1] He entered the

The late Captain Henry Inman, R.N., engraved by H R Cook from a painting in possession of the family, published by Joyce Gold, 103 Shoe Lane, Fleet Street, 31 January 1811.

navy in 1776 in *Barfleur* (90) commanded by Captain Sir Samuel Hood, later Lord Hood, who continued to provide patronage and friendship throughout Inman's life. He was transferred to *Lark* (32), Captain Smith, in 1778 and was serving in her as part of a squadron commanded by Captain Brisbane at Rhode Island when Admiral d'Estaing put in his appearance. *Lark* had to be run ashore and burnt, and her crew set to man the shore batteries, which eventually drove off the French. Inman lost all his possessions, and the navy did not recognise any obligation to help him, even with the cost of a new uniform. He received his lieutenant's commission on 14 June 1780, and while serving in the West Indies he, for a second time, lost all his possessions when *Santa Monica* (36) was wrecked off Tortola.

In passage back to England in September 1782 on board *Hector* as first lieutenant he had to deal both with enemy action and the great hurricane. Nominally a seventy-four, *Hector* was in such a shattered state after the battle of the Saintes that twenty-two of her guns had been removed, and smaller spars put into her. Her crew was mostly made up of invalids who were unable to keep her in station with the fleet. When attacked by two French 44-gun frigates, Captain John Bourchier was so severely wounded early in the fight, and the other officers so ill, that only Inman stayed on deck to work the ship and repel boarders. Gunshot damage, added to *Hector*'s already unfit condition, made her hardly capable of weathering a hurricane, which dismasted her and caused such leaks that the hold was filled, the provisions and fresh water spoiled, and the ship was in immediate danger of sinking without fit men to man the pumps.

> Lieutenant Inman, for the safety of the whole, was under the necessity of resorting to pistols to enforce his commands, which, at this time, were more dreadful than death itself. Numbers of the crew were so exhausted, so completely worn out by incessant fatigue, that they dropped from their severe labours into the arms of death; while others, on being relieved, lay down amidst the torrent of water which was thrown up, till they were again aroused to their duty.

Fortunately the *Hawke*, snow, a little letter of marque trader commanded by Captain John Hill, came by and without hesitation jettisoned his own cargo overboard in order to accommodate *Hector*'s people. Inman was the last man across, and *Hector* sank within ten minutes. In the voyage to St John's, Newfoundland, all were on short rations, and the

last water was consumed the day they arrived.

For Inman, a period of peace at his father's home was very welcome, but he was employed again at the time of the Nootka Sound incident in 1790. He married in 1791 a sister of Commander Thomas Dalby, RN. The couple had one son and one daughter.

On 11 September 1793, six months after the French declaration of war, he was promoted master and commander of *Pigmy*, cutter (14), stationed at the Isle of Man. He next served in *Victory* (100) in the Mediterranean, and then was made post captain on 9 October 1794. He was appointed to command of *L'Aurore* (32), which was stationed during the British occupation of Toulon near Hyères island in support of one of the batteries, firing 8,000 rounds against the Republican army the first month, and 12,000 the next. After the fall of Toulon, Inman, again with a weakened crew, had to deal with a rising of the prisoners he was transporting, who holed the bottom. At Malta he moored his ship under the guns of the battery, leaving on board only the prisoners, who had the choice of pumping her out and repairing the leak, or drowning.

On his return to England he was put in command of a succession of ships, and once again had the experience of taking an ageing vessel through a storm which he only just weathered, this time with his wife and children on board.

Late in 1797, after the mutiny at the Nore, he was put in command of *Belliqueux* (64). Three of her crew were condemned to be hanged and six others punished. The remainder were in such an angry state that Inman did not go to his bed for six months without a brace of pistols in his pocket and another under his pillow.

Following a period of service in the Brest blockade Inman was put in command of a beautiful frigate, *Andromeda* (32). Towards the end of 1799 he was ordered to participate in the evacuation of the duke of York's army, which had failed to restore the Dutch monarch to his throne.

> To those who are acquainted with the dislike which the officers of the navy

entertain to the reception of troops on board – a dislike not to be wondered at, from the want of room for their accommodation, without interfering with the seamen, already sufficiently limited, and in a great degree, preventing that discipline and cleanliness which constitute the very life and soul of the service – it will be pleasing to learn [NC 25.1]

that Inman's treatment of the soldiers was such as to earn their thanks.

On 7 July 1780 he commanded a fireship attack on Dunkirk, which failed to set fire to the two frigates at which they were launched. However, part of the plan was to cut out two other French frigates, and in that objective he enjoyed partial success. Only just avoiding death by friendly fire, he brought *Désirée* (36) out of the harbour, and when she was refitted he was put in her command, with orders to form part of the fleet under Admiral Hyde Parker sent at the end of the winter in 1801 to deal with the crisis in the Baltic. At the battle of Copenhagen on 2 April *Désirée* followed the ships of the line into action and engaged the second ship in the moored line of Danish ships and floating batteries. This was a very hard-fought battle but *Désirée* was fortunate in having only four men wounded. After the firing ceased, however, she had the misfortune to go aground, and only with great difficulty was she got off two days later.

Inman was in command of *Triumph* (74) at Sir Robert Calder's action on 22 July 1805, and when asked at Calder's court martial why he had not informed his admiral of the damage sustained by his ship, he answered, 'I did not think that a proper time to trouble the admiral with my complaints.' Not long after this, ill health obliged him to leave the sea. After a period in command of the sea fencibles at Lynn, Lord Mulgrave appointed him the Admiralty commissioner at Madras, where he died on 15 July 1809, aged forty-seven, ten days after his arrival.

Lt: 14 June 1780
M-C: 11 September 1793
Capt: 9 October 1794

IRBY

REAR-ADMIRAL THE HONOURABLE FREDERICK PAUL IRBY, CB, is known for his period in command of *Amelia* (38) from late 1807 to 1813.

Irby was born on 18 April 1779, the second son of Frederick Irby, second baron of Boston, Lincolnshire, and his wife Christian, only daughter of Paul Methuen of Corsham House, Wiltshire, member of parliament for Great Bedwyn. He was educated at Eton College, and entered the navy in December 1790 as a captain's servant on the *Catherine*, yacht, at Deptford, under the command of Sir George Young. In February 1792 he joined the 12-pounder frigate *Winchelsea* (32) under the command of Captain Richard Fisher, and served at Halifax and in the West Indies. In May 1793 he was rated midshipman in *Hannibal* (74) commanded by John Colpoys in the West Indies and before Cadiz, and he served in *Montagu* (74) at the battle of the Glorious First of June in 1794, during which his captain, James Montagu, was killed. When she was put out of commission late in 1795 he joined *London* (90) flying the flag of Rear-Admiral Colpoys.

He was commissioned lieutenant on 6 January 1797 and appointed to *Circe* (28), which was employed as a repeating frigate at the battle of Camperdown. He subsequently followed her captain, Peter Halkett, into *Apollo* (36), which was wrecked near the Texel on 7 January 1799. He was promoted commander on 22 April 1800, when he was appointed to *Volcano*, bomb, which formed part of Vice-Admiral Archibald Dickson's force deployed to Copenhagen to support the diplomacy of Lord Whitworth. The next year he was moved into *Jalouse* (18) in the North Sea, and finally was promoted post captain on 14 April 1802, when he went on half pay. On 1 December 1803 he married Emily Ives, the youngest daughter and coheiress of William Drake of Amersham, Buckinghamshire, and in 1805 he was appointed to command the sea fencibles on the Essex coast. The couple had a single son, but Emily died on 7 August 1807, a few months before Irby obtained command of the *Amelia* (38) in October.

On 24 February 1809, when part of the Channel

fleet under Lord Gambier and commanded by Rear-Admiral Robert Stopford, Irby assisted in the destruction of a part of a French squadron near the batteries of Sable d'Olonne. In May he was ordered to co-operate with guerrilla forces on the north coast of Spain, but he was again employed on the coast of France when on 24 March 1811 *Amelia* attacked *L'Amazon*, frigate, in a bay near Cap Barfleur. The action ended with the French frigate being destroyed by her own crew.

Late in 1811 Irby was made senior officer of a squadron employed in suppression of the slave trade on the coast of Africa. One of his less glorious deeds occurred when he exacted collective punishment on the town of Winnebah for the murder of the governor of Fort Winnebah, burning the town and then demolishing the fort which had been erected to provide protection against slavers.

At the end of the tour of duty, on 6 February 1813, the sickly crew of *Amelia* engaged *L'Aréthuse* (40) off the coast of Sierra Leone:

> At 7:45, being within pistol-shot on his weather-bow, both ships commenced firing nearly at the same time, which continued (remaining nearly in the same situation,) until twenty-one minutes past eleven, when the enemy bore up, having the advantage of being able so to do, leaving us in an ungovernable state, with our sails, standing and running rigging cut to pieces, and masts injured. During the action, we twice fell on board the enemy, in attempting to thwart his hawse, when he attempted to board, but was repulsed by the marines... and the boarders. Though I most sincerely lament the numerous list of killed and wounded, which amounted to 141; yet it is the greatest consolation in reflecting, that we were never once exposed to a raking shot, or the slightest accident occurred; all fell by fair fighting. Marshall 2.495

He was able to avoid action with another French 40-gun frigate, *Rubis*.

Following her years in commission in a hot cli-

mate, *Amelia* was paid off in May 1813, when Irby's health obliged him to leave active service. He married for a second time on 23 January 1816, uniting with Frances, second daughter of Ichabod Wright of Mapperley Hall, Nottinghamshire. He settled in Norfolk, at Boyland Hall, near Norwich, where the couple had three sons and three daughters. He was made a CB on 26 September 1831, was promoted rear-admiral on 10 January 1837, and died on 24 April 1844, aged sixty-five, in Morningthorpe, Norfolk. Frances survived him to 16 January 1852.

Lt: 6 January 1797
Cmdr: 22 April 1800
Capt: 14 April 1802
R-Adm: 10 January 1837

JERVIS

CAPTAIN WILLIAM HENRY JERVIS (RICKETTS) was very well connected, but had a career made memorable only by a shipwreck and by being drowned.

He was born on 4 November 1764 in Park Street, Grosvenor Square, Westminster, Middlesex, the first son of William Henry Ricketts of Canaan, Jamaica, and of Longwood, Hampshire, who was a bencher of Gray's Inn. His mother Mary was the third daughter of John Swynfen Jervis, and sister of Admiral of the Fleet Sir John Jervis, the earl of St Vincent. In 1801 Ricketts was to assume her maiden name. After studying at the grammar school at Odiham and Winchester College, he entered the navy in 1781 in his uncle's ship, *Foudroyant* (80). He was commissioned lieutenant on 5 September 1782 in *Success* (32), and promoted master and commander on 17 March 1783 when he was appointed to command the *Shrewsbury* (74), later moving to the sloop *Bonetta* (16). He was made post captain on 22 November 1790 and appointed to command the 12-pounder frigate *Hermione* (32), and then the *Magicienne* (32), which formed part of the squadron commanded by Sir Sidney Smith on the coast of France following the French declaration of war in 1793. He then served on the Jamaica station, and, after the renewal of war following the peace of Amiens, in the Channel.

He had married on 9 November 1793 Elizabeth

Captain William Henry Jervis,
engraved by H R Cook from a painting by
Lubersac, in the possession of Mrs Ricketts,
published by Joyce Gold, 103 Shoe Lane,
31 July 1808.

Jane, daughter of Richard Lambert, sixth earl of Cavan. The couple had two daughters, but the marriage was dissolved by an act of parliament in 1799. His civil appointments included those of verdurer of the New Forest and treasurer of Greenwich hospital.

On 25 March 1801 he had the misfortune to wreck his ship, the *Magnificent* (74), on the Black Rocks. 'Events of this nature', notes the *Naval Chronicle*, 'are always distressing in their immediate consequences,' but, it added, 'it is gratifying to reflect upon the good order, fortitude, and determination preserved by Captain Jervis.' He was acquitted by the inevitable court martial, and in May 1804 he succeeded Sir Edward Pellew in command of *Tonnant* (80). On 26 January 1805 he was overturned and drowned, aged forty, when being transferred in his gig to the flagship of Vice-Admiral Sir Charles Cotton, *San Josef* (110), to inform him of the sailing of Rear-Admiral Missiessy's squadron from Rochefort.

Lt: 5 September 1782
M-C: 17 March 1783
Capt: 22 November 1790

JERVIS – *see* St Vincent

KEATS

ADMIRAL SIR RICHARD GOODWIN KEATS, GCB, whom Nelson described to the duke of Clarence as 'a treasure to the service', is especially remembered for his daring part in Sir James Saumarez's night attack in the Straits of Gibraltar in 1801, and for his part in the repatriation of the Spanish army in Denmark in 1808. ^{Nelson 5.302}

He was born on 16 January 1757 in Chalton, Hampshire, the elder son of Elizabeth and the Revd Richard Keats, who was rector of Shipton under Wychwood, Oxfordshire, later rector of Bideford and King's Nympton, Devon, and headmaster of Blundell's free grammar school in Tiverton, Devon. Intended for the priesthood, Richard was educated at New College school, Oxford, in 1766, and received into Winchester College in 1768. But the academic life did not suit him, and he entered the navy on 25 November 1770 at the time of the Falkland Islands mobilisation as an able seaman in *Bellona* (74), Captain John Montagu, under the patronage of the earl of Halifax. *Bellona* was a guardship at Portsea, but Keats rapidly moved on to *Yarmouth* (60) under the command of Weston Varlo, and then to *Cambridge* (80), which was serving as a guardship at Plymouth. Keats rejoined Montagu in 1771 in *Captain* (74), after Montagu had been promoted a rear-admiral and appointed commander-in-chief of the North American station. He was transferred on 16 December 1772 to *Halifax*, schooner, rejoined *Captain* on 10 April 1773 with the rating of midshipman, and on 2 May 1774 joined *Kingfisher*, commanded by Montagu's son James. Subsequently they both transferred to *Mercury* (20 guns), at which time Keats was rated master's mate. After the conquest of Rhode Island in December 1776, Keats returned to Rear-Admiral Montagu, now a rear-admiral and flying his flag in the *Romney* (50) as commander-in-chief at Newfoundland, with his son George in command of the ship. In *Romney*, Keats was again rated an able seaman.

Following his return to England he was commissioned lieutenant on 7 April 1777 by the Admiralty and appointed to the *Ramillies* (74) under the command of Captain Robert Digby. He served in the battle of Ushant on 27 July 1778. Digby was made a rear-admiral in March 1779, and on 18 May Keats followed Digby into *Prince George* (98). He served in her for the next three years with Thomas Foley a fellow lieutenant, and with Prince William Henry, the future duke of Clarence, as midshipman in the same watch. *Prince George* took part in Admiral Rodney's relief of Gibraltar, the capture of the Caracas fleet and the defeat of Langara. Rodney then sailed to the West Indies and Digby returned to the Channel to join Sir Charles Hardy's fleet of only thirty-eight sail of the line which was obliged to avoid action with a combined Franco-Spanish fleet of sixty-seven.

In 1781 Digby was appointed commander-in-chief in North America. Keats was again actively employed against the rebels, and was promoted on 18 January 1782 master and commander of *Rhinoceros*, a floating battery at New York. He was transferred on 31 July to *Bonetta* (16). Following the conclusion of the war, Keats was employed bringing loyalist refugees down the Hudson to New York, and settling them at Port Mouton in Nova Scotia, coming ashore on 3 January 1785.

Between 1785 and 1789 Keats was unemployed, and spent much of his time on the Continent, but the influence of the duke of Clarence led to his being promoted post captain on 24 June 1789 and appointed on 22 October to command *Southampton* (32), where he served until 14 February 1791. He then had six months' leave, after which on 29 August he was appointed to the 12-pounder frigate *Niger* (32). At some unremembered date Clarence also appointed Keats's father his domestic chaplain.

On 11 April 1793, following the French declaration of war in February, Keats was appointed flag captain to the duke of Clarence in *London* (90). The duke, however, was never permitted to hoist his flag, and *London* was paid off in March 1794. Keats was then appointed to *Galatea* (36) on 24 May and was employed under Sir John Warren and Sir Edward Pellew in operations to support the French royalists. On 15 June 1795 he fell in with the Brest fleet at sea, and was the means of ensuring that Lord Bridport, on station with the Channel fleet off Brest, and Sir John Warren, were warned. He was given responsibility for landing the army at Carnac, and was actively employed in the operations on Quiberon, Noirmoutier and Isle d'Yeu. On 23 August 1796 he disregarded his pilot's advice and gave chase to a larger French frigate, *Andromaque*, driving her into the shoals near Arcachon, where she ran aground and surrendered.

Following the Spithead mutiny he suffered the humiliation of being turned out of his ship on 28 May 1797 when the discontent spread to Plymouth, but he was appointed on 19 June to command the 18-pounder frigate *Boadicea* (38), in which he also had to deal with discontent. He served very actively in the Brest blockade, at one time taking his ship and a consort through the Passage du Raz in the dark without a pilot in pursuit of an enemy. This turned out to be the Spanish fleet seeking to get into Brest, but unable to do so, and making instead into Basque Roads. In September he was instrumental in warning Sir John Warren on the Irish station of the approach of a French troop convoy under Rear-Admiral Bompart. When in 1800 St Vincent assumed command of the Channel fleet, Keats was released from the arduous work of the inshore squadron, and detached to cruise against enemy trade.

On 16 March 1801 he was transferred to the *Superb* (74), and in June was placed under the command of Sir James Saumarez, who on 5 July learnt that three French ships of the line on passage out of the Mediterranean under the command of Vice-Admiral Linois had anchored in Algeciras Bay. Keats was at that time off San Lucar, and believed the six ships with Saumarez were more than capable of undertaking the attack. Accordingly, *Superb* remained watching Cadiz. But the attack against the anchored ship and the batteries of Algeciras miscarried, with the British squadron badly damaged, and *Hannibal* (74) surrendered to the enemy. The Spanish squadron at Cadiz commanded by

Admiral Don de Moreno now sailed to support its French allies. Keats followed, and when the Franco-Spanish force of ten ships and three frigates sailed from Algeciras, *Superb* was able to join the remnant of Saumarez's squadron in a night attack. Moreno adopted a defensive line abreast, with the three French in a second line ahead of the Spaniards. Saumarez exploited this weak formation by sending Captain Keats in *Superb*, in the dark, to engage from the landward side. This confused two Spanish ships, which began to fire on each other. *Real Carlos* caught fire. *San Hermenegildo*, thinking she was an enemy, tried to capture her and also caught fire. Both blew up in the dark with the loss of nearly all hands. Keats was thanked by parliament, and his first lieutenant was promoted.

Superb continued in service in the Mediterranean during the peace of Amiens, and when on the renewal of war Lord Nelson was appointed to command the Mediterranean fleet, Keats became one of his captains, meeting him for the first time. He was three times entrusted with 'gunboat' diplomatic missions to the dey of Algiers: to compel him to release Maltese sailors, to compensate merchants for losses to Algerian raiders, and to make amends for having expelled the British consul. Despite *Superb*'s need for dockyard repair, Keats was part of Nelson's pursuit of the Toulon fleet to the West Indies and back to England. Her bottom had become so foul that Keats had to keep his studding sails set all the way.

In Portsmouth *Superb* was cleaned, repaired and fitted to take on board Sir John Duckworth. Keats, having been ashore only one night between 19 March 1801 and 22 August 1805, now visited Nelson at Merton, and from him heard his tactical plans for the battle which was fought off Cape Trafalgar on 21 October. He was nominated colonel of the Royal Marines on 9 November 1805.

It took so long to fit *Superb* for service that Keats was not present at the battle of Trafalgar. Sir John Duckworth, who was to travel on board at least as far as Cadiz, was more interested in waiting for his followers and his string quartet to join him than he was to get to sea. Keats, however, was at the centre of Duckworth's action at San Domingo in 1806 in which the entire French battle squadron was captured or destroyed. At the commencement of the action, Keats hung a portrait of Nelson in the rigging. All of the San Domingo captains received a gold medal and the thanks of parliament, and Keats was awarded a 100-guinea sword from the patriotic fund.

Having returned Duckworth to England, Keats was then ordered to join the Channel fleet under St Vincent, made a commodore, and given charge of a flying squadron of five to six sail of the line.

In April 1807 he was relieved by Sir Richard Strachan, and ordered to Portsmouth to command a secret service, which, however, was later cancelled. He had a few weeks' leave, then hoisted his broad pendant in *Ganges* (74), with Captain Peter Halkett in command of the ship, to take part in the second Copenhagen campaign. His employment was to secure the Great Belt to prevent Danish reinforcements reaching Zealand. As a compliment to him, the Admiralty sent *Superb* to join him, and he shifted his pendant into her. Following the highly unpopular Danish campaign, Keats was promoted rear-admiral on 2 October 1807, and flew his flag in *Superb*. He took charge of the passage of the captured Danish ships to Portsmouth, where they arrived on 15 November and became the subject of one of J M W Turner's greatest marine paintings.

After another period ashore, Keats was given charge in April 1808 of a fleet of transports carrying 5,000 soldiers under Lieutenant-General Sir John Moore to Göteborg, and then resumed his command of the squadron in the Great Belt. While there, he established contact with the Marquis de la Romana commanding Spanish soldiers serving Napoleon in Denmark. Together they arranged for repatriation of the Spanish regiments to join the war in Spain against the French. Between 6,000 and 7,000 men undertook a forced march to the port of Nyborg, which Keats occupied. Seizing fifty-seven merchant ships and fitting them for sea in forty-three hours, the entire force was embarked before the French could interfere, and then the town was returned to the Danish governor. Unfortunately, a regiment of cavalry failed to make the rendevous, and two regiments of infantry stationed at Copenhagen were surrounded by Danish soldiers who prevented their embarkation. Two thousand more men were collected at Langland, and eventually the whole force was landed at Göteborg, then transported to England and finally landed in Spain. In recognition of this remarkable service, Keats was nominated a KB.

On the return of Sir James Saumarez from the Baltic at the end of the season, Keats was left in command with instructions to keep open the trade until the upper parts of the Baltic were frozen. But it proved an early and a severe winter, and several of his ships, including *Superb,* were frozen in and had great difficulty reaching a port of safety.

The following year he brought home a convoy of 400 ships, and commanded a part of the force employed under Sir Richard Strachan in the Scheldt. On 5 November 1809 *Superb* was paid off, and Keats spent a winter recovering his health. He was appointed governor of Malta, but soon resigned, and in July 1810 hoisted his flag in *Implacable* (74) to be employed in support of the Spanish garrison of Cadiz. He proceeded there with a squadron of eight ships of the line, and a company of shipwrights to assist in the construction of gunboats for defence of the city. The shipwrights were also employed in making older Spanish ships fit for sea so that they could be evacuated to Cartagena or Havana. With the help of the ships under Keats's command, the garrison of Cadiz was able actively to harass the flanks of the French army. He was promoted vice-admiral on 1 August 1811, and accepted the post of second-in-command of the Mediterranean fleet under Sir Charles Cotton, but was invalided home in 1812, coming ashore on 7 December.

On 10 February 1813 Keats was given a post of semi-retirement commanding the Newfoundland station, with his flag first in *Bellerophon* (74) and later in *Salisbury* (50). He was nominated GCB on 2 January 1815. On his return from Newfoundland on 16 April 1816 he retired to north Devon, and on 27 June 1820 he married Mary, eldest daughter of Francis Hurt of Alderwasley and Castern, Derbyshire. He was promoted to major-general of

the Royal Marines on 7 May 1818, was appointed a commissioner of the Board of Longitude, and in 1821 was appointed governor of the royal hospital at Greenwich. He lived there until his death on 5 April 1834, with the rank of admiral, aged seventy-seven. He calculated on his précis of naval service provided to the Admiralty in 1828 that he had been employed at sea fifty-seven years, nine months, two weeks and three days.

Lt: 7 April 1777
M-C: 18 January 1782
Capt: 24 June 1789
R-Adm: 2 October 1807
V-Adm: 1 August 1811
Adm: 27 May 1825X

KEITH

ADMIRAL SIR GEORGE KEITH ELPHINSTONE KEITH, VISCOUNT KEITH, GCB, was described by the nineteenth-century naval historian John Knox Laughton: 'The numerous appointments of the first importance which during his long service Keith held, and the many tangled and difficult affairs with which his name is connected, give his career an interest far above what his character seems to warrant. Steady, persevering, and cautious, equal to the necessities of the moment, but in no instance towering above them, he made few serious mistakes, he carried out satisfactorily the various operations entrusted to him, and left behind him the reputation of a good rather than a great commander.' DNB 634 The modern scholar Brian Lavery writes that 'his historical reputation rests on his meticulous organisation of complex fleets, such as the North Sea fleet in 1803–07, and in his expertise in amphibious warfare.' Le Fevre and Harding 399

He was born on 7 January 1746 at Elphinstone Tower, Airth, near Stirling, the fifth son of Charles, tenth Baron Elphinstone. His mother was Clementina, only daughter and heiress of John Fleeming, sixth earl of Wigtoun. Two of the Elphinstone boys joined the navy, but his brother William soon resigned to enter the service of the East India Company. George was educated at Glasgow and entered the navy with £5 to his name on 4 November 1761 as an able seaman on board *Royal Sovereign* (100). As she was confined to harbour service he obtained a berth in a smaller ship, and on 1 January 1762 he was rated midshipman or master's mate in *Gosport* (44) commanded by Captain John Jervis, later Admiral the earl of St Vincent. He saw action at the close of the Seven Years War when the French were driven out of Newfoundland, and at Halifax, Nova Scotia. In March 1763 he transferred to *Juno* (32), and two months later transferred again to *Lively* (20) commanded by the Honourable Keith Stewart. The peace of Paris having been concluded, he was lucky to have employment, and served in the Mediterranean from July to January 1765. He then had a short period at home before joining the 9-pounder frigate *Emerald* (32) in August 1766, under the command of Charles Douglas, but he soon requested a discharge so that he could join his brother William's East Indiaman, *Tryton*, for a voyage which established his financial independence. He returned from the East Indies in 1768 and in August rejoined *Emerald*, transferring in September 1769 to *Stag* (32) under the command of Commodore Sir John Lindsay, who was proceeding to Madras. On the voyage he was ordered to act as lieutenant on 21 December 1769, which commission was confirmed on 28 June 1770. He did not stay long in India, however, because illness obliged him to return home, where he arrived in March 1771. He was appointed second lieutenant of *Trident* (64), flagship of Sir Peter Denis going out as commander-in-chief Mediterranean. On 18 September 1772 he was promoted master and commander of a recently purchased merchant ship-sloop, *Scorpion* (14), and he served in her in the Mediterranean for the next two years. Denis entrusted him with the armed diplomacy needed when the dey of Algiers expelled the British consul, and then sent him home overland with dispatches reporting the outcome. In March 1775 at the outbreak of the American rebellion he transferred into *Romney* (50) with an acting rank of post captain, which was confirmed on 11 May 1775. He was to play an active part in the war, beginning with escorting a troop convoy to Newfoundland, during which he provided passage for Rear-Admiral Robert Duff, who was going out

to be governor. On his return home, he transferred to *Perseus* (20) to escort a convoy to New York, sailing in July 1776. In February while at Antigua he transferred temporarily to *Pearl* (32) when her captain died, but he was back in *Perseus* in May, cruising off the Delaware. In early 1779 he was in the West Indies, and in the spring of 1780 he was put in charge of landing General George Clinton's army near Charlestown, after which he command-

The Right Honourable Lord Keith, K.B.,
Vice Admiral of the Red Squadron,
engraving by William Ridley after
John Hoppner, RA, published by
Joyce Gold, 103 Shoe Lane,
31 July 1801.

ed the sailors who had been landed to storm the town. He was then sent home with dispatches, and was given command of *Warwick* (50), in which he cruised in the Channel, and then returned with a convoy to the Delaware. With him sailed Prince William Henry, later duke of Clarence, in the gun-room. In September he captured *Aigle* (44) and all but one of her convoy. And in November 1782 he transferred into *Carysfort* (28) to return home, in poor health.

He spent the next ten years on half pay, but he had by then become reasonably wealthy. He had already embarked on a nominal life as a parliamentarian, more as a means to promote his naval career than because of any great political ambition. He occupied the seat for Southwark, Surrey, from 1768 to 1775, and he was returned by the electors for Dunbarton in 1781. He retained his place in the Commons until 1790, and on 10 April 1787 he married Jane, daughter and heiress of Colonel William Mercer of Aldie and Meekelem, Perthshire. She gave birth to one daughter, Margaret Mercer, born at London on 12 June 1788, before she died on 12 December 1789 at Scarthing Moor, Yorkshire. Keith was appointed a keeper of the signet in Scotland, and was a fellow of the Royal Society. On the French declaration of war in February 1793 he was appointed to command the *Robust* (74), but nonetheless he was elected the member for Stirling in 1796, and held the seat until 1801.

Robust was one of the ships which made up Vice-Admiral Lord Hood's fleet under orders to proceed to the Mediterranean at the outbreak of war, and when Toulon surrendered, Elphinstone was given command of 1,500 men to take possession of Fort La Malgue, protecting the eastern side of the harbour. He demonstrated an unusual ability in military tactics when in command of British and Spanish soldiers, and he was entrusted with the evacuation of British forces and French royalists on 17 December 1793. On his return to England he was made a KB, on 13 April 1794.

He had been promoted rear-admiral on 12 April 1794 and hoisted his flag on *Barfleur* (90) under Admiral Lord Howe in the Channel fleet on 24 July, but he served there for a few months only. In March 1795 he was selected to command the East Indies squadron, and he sailed on 4 April in *Monarch* (74) under orders to persuade the Dutch at the Cape of Good Hope to declare their loyalty to the exiled prince of Orange, the Stadtholder. It proved necessary to employ force, and the outcome was for a long time uncertain. Following the capitulation of Cape Town, Elphinstone, who had proceeded to India, obtained warning of the approach of a Dutch relief force in time to hurry back, and captured the entire Dutch squadron in

Saldanah Bay. Ultimately he was to receive £64,000 in prize money from his period in command in the East Indies. He was promoted vice-admiral on 1 June 1795.

On his return to Crookhaven in Ireland on 23 December 1796 he learnt that the Brest fleet with an army embarked was in Bantry Bay attempting invasion, but his own ships had been battered by gales and all that he could do was obtain intelligence for Lord Bridport, the Channel fleet commander. Once back in England, in ill health, he received notice of his creation as Baron Keith of Stonehaven Marischal in the Irish peerage, on 7 March 1797.

Because his good reputation with the sailors was thought to equip him to deal with the mutiny in May 1791 of the ships at the Nore, Lord Keith was appointed admiral commanding at Sheerness. He wrote to the seamen urging them to

> be not too long misled by designing men; but return to your old friends, who like myself have spent their days among you, and can defy the world to say they ever did you an injury.... While your respected Admiral [Duncan] is off the Texel unreinforced, blocking up the Dutch, you are idle at the Nore, under wicked influence... I bid farewell, until we can meet as before, like men and friends, when you will find me, with true affection, Yours etc., Keith. Allardyce 144–5

Within a week ships began to desert the conspiracy, and within three weeks the mutiny was over. He was then appointed second in command in the Channel, and again his reputation helped to quell the disaffection in the ships at Plymouth.

In December 1798 he was sent to the Mediterranean as second in command to Admiral the earl of St Vincent, and in February 1799 he assumed the command before Cadiz with fifteen ships and flying his flag in *Barfleur*, St Vincent remaining in Gibraltar with his flagship. The rest of the Mediterranean fleet was scattered from Minorca to Naples and Malta, and found itself in difficulties when on 25 April Vice-Admiral Bruix took the Brest fleet to sea and headed for Cadiz with twenty-five ships of the line. Keith's fifteen were between them and the twenty-two Spanish ships of the line under Admiral Gravina inside the harbour. The weather was so violent, however, that Bruix felt he had no choice but to continue towards Toulon, where he arrived on 14 May. The blockade having been raised at Cadiz, the Spaniards sailed, but were badly damaged by weather and put into Cartagena.

St Vincent and Keith were able to leave Gibraltar only on the 12th, without any knowledge of where Bruix or the Cadiz fleet had gone. On 2 June St Vincent was obliged by deteriorating health to leave the fleet again at Minorca, but he continued to exercise a distant and ill-judged command. Rear-Admiral Nelson, for his part, refused to obey Keith's orders to join him. Finally St Vincent resigned and turned over his authority to Keith in mid-July. Meanwhile Bruix had joined the Spaniards at Cartagena, and the combined Franco-Spanish fleet sailed to Brest with Keith in pursuit three weeks behind, having waited to provide the cover for the British station at Minorca which Nelson ought to have supplied. This was the last great opportunity for the allies to seize command of the Channel preparatory to an invasion of England, but in fact they disappeared into Brest and remained there until the end of the war.

Keith was then ordered to return to the Mediterranean to assume command, much to the disappointment of Nelson, who thought he should have succeeded St Vincent. On 17 March 1800 he suffered the loss of his flagship *Queen Charlotte* (100), with 690 of her people, when she caught fire while he was ashore at Leghorn. His first task was to support the Austrian reconquest of Genoa, which fell on 5 June 1800, opening the port to British ships. Buonaparte's crushing victory at Marengo on the 14th, however, reversed the situation, Genoa being restored to French control. The next order of business was to finish the defeat of the French in Egypt. Admiral Sir Sidney Smith had negotiated a convention with General Kleber by which the French were to be allowed transport to France with the honours of war. Keith suspended this, pending approval from London. When it arrived he reopened negotiations with Kleber, but the latter was assassinated before the convention was agreed. As a result, it was necessary to land an army in Egypt under General Abercromby.

The event did not take place until 2 March 1801 because the force was first directed at the more important objective of seizing control of Cadiz. Only when the troops were actually in their boats, on 4 October 1800, was that operation cancelled upon learning of the pestilence in the town which would have been far more dangerous than was the Spanish army. This may have been the lowest point in Keith's career, as he did not co-operate well with the soldiers in an operation which he believed to be unsound. He insisted that the Spaniards surrender their ships to him, but when they refused, he nonetheless cancelled the attack.

The Egyptian operation was more successful, although General Abercromby was killed. The landing operation, involving five ships of the line, two frigates, twelve smaller vessels, 100 troopships carrying 16,150 soldiers and fifty-seven Turkish vessels, was carefully rehearsed in the sheltered harbour of Marmorice Bay in south-west Turkey. Keith appointed to command the armed boats Captain Alexander Cochrane, who made meticulous plans for ferrying the men ashore, and for support of the army as it advanced from Aboukir Bay to Alexandria. This left Keith free to concentrate on the threat posed by a sortie from Toulon. Keith, however, affected to regard Cochrane as unreliable, and also quarrelled with Benjamin Hallowell, and with Abercromby's successor, General Hely Hutchinson, whom he regarded as indolent.

He had been promoted admiral on 1 January 1801, and on his return to England at the conclusion of the peace of Amiens he was made Baron Keith of Stonehaven Marischal, Kincardineshire, on 15 December 1801, on the English establishment. For his work in driving the French from Egypt, the sultan appointed him to the order of the Crescent. On 17 September 1803 he was made Baron Keith of Banheath, Dunbarton, with a dispensation for the title passing to his daughter.

Following the renewal of the war, Keith assumed command of the North Sea station and of all inshore operations against the threat of French invasion. This was a demanding job which he continued to carry out until the spring of 1807, commanding from a house at Ramsgate where he could see both the Downs and the Thames estuary. His relations with his subordinate commanders, Sir Sidney Smith and Sir Home Popham, were difficult, because both were creative geniuses, and because Smith's loyalties were divided by his secret intelligence work, in which he reported to William Pitt at Walmer Castle. Both were inclined to throw experimental forces against the French defences at Boulogne, whereas Keith regarded the fleet at Flushing as the key to French ability to invade, and wanted to conserve his forces for what could be the decisive battle. Following the battle of Trafalgar, when invasion was no longer a threat, Napoleon issued his Berlin Decrees forbidding trade with Britain, and Keith's job became that of blockading any port along the enemy-controlled coast which complied with the demand of their imperial master. In May, 1807, exhausted, he struck his flag and came ashore.

On 12 December 1808 he remarried in Ramsgate, taking for his wife Hester Maria, known as Queeney, eldest daughter and coheiress of Henry Thrale, brewer of Streatham, Surrey, and member of parliament for Southwark. Thrale had been a close friend of Dr Samuel Johnson, and his daughter was an intelligent 'blue stocking' woman. Although aged forty-six when she married, she and Keith had a daughter.

In February 1812 Keith was appointed commander-in-chief of the Channel fleet, and raised in the peerage to Viscount Keith on 1 June 1814. Because of his age and concerns about his health, and the impossibility of fleet action, he mostly commanded from a house ashore in Plymouth. He struck his flag in July 1814, but returned to service following Napoleon's return from exile in Elba. He organised his ships into small squadrons around the coast of France, controlling every harbour. After the battle of Waterloo one of them, *Bellerophon*

(74), was in position to accept the surrender of Napoleon Buonaparte and prevent his fleeing to the United States.

At the conclusion of peace Keith resigned from the service. In 1821 the king of Sardinia appointed him to the order of St Maurice and St Lazarus in recognition of his services at Genoa. He died on 10 March 1823, aged seventy-seven, in Tulliallan, Firth of Forth, Fife. Hester Maria died on 31 March 1857, aged ninety-five.

Lt: 28 June 1770
M-C: 18 September 1772
Capt: 11 May 1775
R-Adm: 12 April 1794
V-Adm: 1 June 1795
Adm: 1 January 1801

KERR

VICE-ADMIRAL LORD MARK ROBERT KERR was to play a minor role in the campaign leading to Trafalgar. He had been put in command of *Fisgard* (38) on the renewal of war in 1803, and was cruising in the Straits of Gibraltar in early 1805 when the Toulon fleet sailed. It was he who reported its passage to the Atlantic, leading to Lord Nelson's pursuit to the West Indies and the concentration of forces for the defence of the Channel.

Kerr was born on 12 November 1776, the third son of General William John Kerr, fifth marquis of Lothian, and his wife Elizabeth, only daughter of Chichester Fortescue of Dromisken, county Louth. He entered the navy in May 1790 as a midshipman in *Canada* (74) at Spithead under the command of Lord Hugh Seymour. In 1791 he joined *Lion* (64) under the command of the Honourable Seymour Finch, but was lent to *Bonetta* (16). In 1792 he joined *Shark* under the Honourable Anthony Kaye Legge for Channel service, but in August he returned to the *Lion* under the command of Sir Erasmus Gower, and served in her during the passage to Canton conveying Lord Macartney *en embassy* to the emperor of China. *Lion* returned to England on 6 September 1794, and Kerr was commissioned lieutenant on 1 November, being posted first to *Pylades,* which was wrecked in the North Sea before he could join, then to *Triumph* (74), and in May to *Sans Pareil* (80) flying the flag of Lord

Hugh Seymour. In her he fought in the action off L'Orient on 23 June 1795. He was promoted commander in September 1796, and appointed to *Fortune* (12) in the Mediterranean under Sir John Jervis. Following the battle of Cape St Vincent, Jervis put him in command one of the prizes, *San Ysidro* (74), on 18 February 1797. He was confirmed as post captain on 7 March 1797 and appointed to *Danae* for rank, and on 17 October to *Cormorant* (20), in which he took part in the capture of Minorca by Sir John Duckworth.

He married on 18 July 1799 Charlotte, third daughter of Randall William Macdonnell, marquis of Antrim, niece of the marquis of Lothian and in her own right countess of Antrim. The couple had three sons and six daughters. His appointment to command *Fisgard* was dated 15 July 1803 and he remained in her until September 1805.

During the war that was declared by the United States against Britain in 1812 he was put in command of *Acasta* (40). The *Naval Chronicle* published an anecdote about him in 1813:

> On receiving the accounts of the capture of the *Guerriere*, Captain Kerr assembled his crew, and addressed them as follows: – 'My Lads, it is with a distress which I cannot sufficiently depict to you, that I inform you of the capture of the *Guerriere*, by the *Constitution* American frigate. We are going to sea, and in the largest and best armed frigate in the service. Hear my determination – *I am determined never to strike the colours of the Acasta* – My mind is made up – What say you, my boys?' The exclamation of – 'To the bottom!' and three truly British cheers, followed his words, and the anchor was weighed. – From the excellent equipment of the *Acasta*, her great size, weight of metal, and number of men, we are confident that with her there will be no desecration of the seaman's religion – the Flag! The *Acasta* has taken on board 24-pounders on her maindeck – and we may cheerfully trust the national honour to her efforts. *NC 29.189*

Kerr was promoted rear-admiral on 19 July 1821, and died with the rank of vice-admiral on 9 September 1840, aged sixty-three. His wife predeceased him on 26 October 1835.

Lt: 1 November 1794
Cmdr: September 1796
Capt: 7 March 1797
R-Adm: 19 July 1821
V-Adm: 10 January 1837

KING

VICE-ADMIRAL SIR RICHARD KING, BARONET, KCB, was another Trafalgar captain.

He was born on 28 November 1774, the first son of Admiral Sir Richard King, first baronet of Bellevue, Kent, member of parliament, and of his wife, Susannah Margaret, daughter of William Coker of Maypowder, Dorset. His father had had the good fortune in 1762 of participating with Hyde Parker in the capture of an Acapulco galleon, his share of which was reputed to have been worth £30,000. Young Richard first had his name placed on the books of his father's ship, *Exeter* (64), on 25 January 1780, rated as a clerk and supposedly serving in the East Indies. He was also placed on the books of his father's next two ships, *Hero* (74), and *Crown* (64), but it is believed that he actually joined *Crown* as an able seaman and midshipman on 18 January 1789, and served in the East Indies under Commodore the Honourable William Cornwallis. He then followed Cornwallis into *Minerva* (38) on 9 March 1791, and was commissioned by him lieutenant on 14 November 1791. That was probably four years short of his six and a half years' required sea time and three years short of the required twenty years of age. His rate of promotion continued to be meteoric. He was appointed to *Phoenix* (36) under Captain Sir Robert Strachan, and was promoted master and commander on 20 September 1793 and made post captain on 14 May 1794. On 1 November, after his return to England, he was appointed to command *Aurora* (28) in the North Sea. On 28 July 1795 he was transferred into *Druid* (32) in the Channel, and he was transferred on 2 March 1797 into *Sirius*

(36), which was employed in the North Sea under Admiral Duncan. In June he served as a member of the court martial which tried Richard Parker, the Nore mutineer, and was appointed to command *Sirius* in the North Sea. There, and later on the coast of France, he made a succession of captures, and during the peace of Amiens he was employed in customs prevention work until 3 August 1802.

On 29 November 1803, in Stoke, Devon, he married Sarah Anne, only daughter of Admiral Sir John Thomas Duckworth; the couple were to have four sons and one daughter.

He briefly commanded *Veteran* (64) in the Downs and on the coast of France between 8 February 1804 and 26 June. Two years after the renewal of the war, on 27 March 1805, he was appointed to command the *Achille* (74), which formed part of Nelson's fleet at Trafalgar on 21 October 1805. Subsequently King was employed on the west coasts of France and Spain, having succeeded his father as second baronet on 27 November 1806. In 1808 he was employed in the blockade of Cherbourg, then served in the defence of Cadiz. On 2 March 1811 he joined *San Josef* (110) as captain of the Mediterranean fleet, under the command of Sir Charles Cotton, whom he later followed to the Channel fleet. He was promoted rear-admiral on 12 August 1812 and hoisted his flag in *Mulgrave* (74), then *Royal George* (100), and finally returned to the *San Josef* off Toulon as second in command to Sir Edward Pellew.

He was nominated KCB on 2 January 1815, and served as commander-in-chief in the East Indies from 6 February 1816 to 20 October 1820, flying his flag in *Magnificent* (74) and then in *London* (90). His wife died on 20 March 1819, on board his flagship at the time, the teak-built *Minden* (74), on her passage to Bombay. Three years later, on 16 May 1822, he married Maria Susanna, daughter of his old chief, Sir Charles Cotton. His second marriage produced another four sons and four daughters. He was promoted vice-admiral on 19 July 1821, and in July 1833 he was appointed commander-in-chief at the Nore. He died of the cholera on 4 August 1834, aged fifty-nine, at the Admiralty House, Sheerness. He was buried in Eastchurch, Sheppey, Kent.

Lt: 14 November 1791
M-C: 20 Sept 1793
Capt: 14 May 1794
R-Adm: 12 August 1812
V-Adm: 19 July 1821

KING

LIEUTENANT WILLIAM ELLETSON KING was a worthy son of Neptune without enough influence to rise above the rank of lieutenant despite a promising early start and the advantages of 'a sickly season' on the coast of Africa.

He was born in 1776, in Portsmouth, the third son of Matthew King, transport storekeeper at Portsmouth dockyard, and was godson of Commander William Elletson, RN. His naval education began at the Chelsea Naval Academy in 1788. The *Naval Chronicle* tells us that at that date it was considered

> one of the best institutions for a maritime education. The novelty of having a ship built on the play-ground of this seminary, completely rigged, with sails bent, and of capacity sufficient to admit of twenty-four of the young gentlemen going aloft at one time, attracted general notice, and formed a strong inducement for parents to send their sons thither for naval instruction. This ship moved round on swivels, which enabled her to represent the evolutions of tacking or wearing. She was under the care of an old naval lieutenant, and a superannuated boatswain, and was named the *Cumberland*. [NC 30.449]

The school also contained an observatory, a rope-house and a battery of two six-pounders. King would have received instruction in drawing from John Thomas Serres, who was to be employed by the Admiralty in 1800 to make sketches of the entire Atlantic coast of France. King was entered on the muster book of *Goliath* (74) in June 1789 and in 1790 obtained a midshipman's berth in the

Dover (44), commanded by Lieutenant John Drummond.

King's career was in most ways quite usual, apart from the fact that there were so many William Kings in the service that he persuaded the Admiralty to change his records to include his middle name after he was superseded in command of *La Legere,* sloop, in December 1797 as a result of an order meant for someone else. Also unusual were the circumstances of his promotion to first lieutenant of *Sheerness* (44) in 1798. The *Naval Chronicle* observed in its biography of King:

> Before we proceed any farther, it will be proper to state; that, in the case of promotion, there is a privilege existing, from time immemorial which is not enjoyed on any other station than that of the coast of Africa; it is that of the next officer giving himself the rank of his superior in the event of his decease; and which self-appointments have even been held good by the Admiralty. NC 30.455

But the exceptional provision was no longer common, and the only recent example was that occasioned by the death of Commodore (James) Cornwallis, *Sheerness*'s commander, which led Lieutenant William Hanwell to promote himself to post captain, with King succeeding as lieutenant. 'We know of no other living instance of such a fortunate advancement in the navy. The present Naval Instructions, established by his Majesty's order in council, dated January 25, 1806, appears to abrogate this regulation so far as concerns post rank.'

It was as third lieutenant of *Ardent* (64), Captain Thomas Bertie, that King took part in the battle of Copenhagen on 2 April 1801, commanding the main gundeck of twenty-eight 42-pounder carronades. Nearly all the guns were disabled in the action, and *Ardent* suffered 93 men killed and wounded. Following the peace of Amiens, King was appointed lieutenant of *Venerable* (74), and thus was one who endured the horrors of her wreck in the Torbay storm of 24 November 1804. The officers subsequently petitioned the Admiralty for compensation for the loss of their property, but it was refused as unprecedented. On 9 October 1812 he again had the disappointment of being shipwrecked, this time in command of a brig, *Sentinel*, in a Baltic fog on the island of Rugen, when he had to destroy his ship while under fire. Again, he lost all his possessions, and applied for compensation in vain.

A lieutenant, even one commanding his own ships, was not a good catch for a respectable girl, and King died a bachelor, on 8 March 1829, aged fifty-two.

Lt: 22 March 1797

KINGSMILL

ADMIRAL SIR ROBERT BRICE KINGSMILL, BARONET, was an oddity, as circumstances conspired to make him a gentleman who had only one notable operational command.

He was born in 1730 in Belfast, the second son of Captain Charles Brice of Castle Chichester near Kilroot, who was a naval officer, and his wife Jane, daughter of William Robinson of Newtownards, county Down, who was a captain in the army. He entered the navy on 29 October 1746 as an able seaman on board the *Speedwell,* sloop, and rated midshipman or master's mate on 3 October 1748. He passed his examination on 5 July 1754, but was not commissioned lieutenant until 29 April 1756. In February 1761 he was promoted master and commander of *Swallow,* sloop, being confirmed in that rank on 3 July following his capture of a French privateer, *Sultan* (10). When in command of a bomb-vessel, *Basilisk*, he was wounded at the capture of Martinique and St Lucia in 1762. He was made post captain on 26 May 1762 with an appointment to command *Crescent* (28), and returned to England in 1764 following the end of the Seven Years War.

He married Elizabeth, daughter of Hugh Corry of Newtownards, about 1766, and through her succeeded to the Kingsmill estates when her uncle, William Kingsmill, died on 8 January 1766. Her husband assumed the surname Kingsmill by act of parliament. She died in 1783 and there were no children.

Very content to spend the years of peace enjoying his new wealth, he apparently was equally willing on the outbreak of hostilities with France in 1778 to accept command of *Vigilant* (64), in which he took part in the battle of Ushant on 27 July, after which his prospects were touched by the political storm following the unsatisfactory outcome of the battle. Rather than accept service in the West Indies, he resigned his ship and was not offered another until April 1782. At that time, *Elizabeth* (74) was just fitting out after a major repair, but was

Sir Robert Kingsmill, Bart., Admiral of the Blue Squadron, engraving by William Ridley after Lemuel F Abbot, published by Burney and Gold, Shoe Lane, 31 March 1801.

not ready to take part in Admiral Lord Howe's relief of Gibraltar. Kingsmill was willing to accept command of a reinforcement squadron intended for the East Indies, but it was badly damaged in a Biscay storm, *Elizabeth* being dismasted. On putting back to Spithead for repair the expedition was cancelled on news of the preliminaries of peace. Kingsmill spent the next three years in command of *Elizabeth* reduced to a guardship.

He had been elected member of parliament for Yarmouth, Isle of Wight, in 1779, which he held

only until 1780. In 1784 he was elected the member for Tregony, Cornwall, which seat he held until 1790. He is not known to have ever spoken in parliament, but he voted for Pitt's parliamentary reform bill in 1785, against Richmond's fortification plans in 1786 and against Pitt in the Regency crises of 1788 and 1789.

It was not until the Nootka Sound crisis in 1790 that Kingsmill was again employed, taking command of *Duke* (90). But she was decommissioned on the settlement of the dispute, and thus it was that when he was promoted rear-admiral on 1 February 1793, at the general promotion made on the French declaration of war, he had remarkably little experience at sea. Nevertheless, he was put in command of the Irish station, which in the circumstance of the outbreak of hostilities was well suited to the rapid refreshment of his already great wealth. His resources were limited to two ships of the line, seven frigates and four smaller vessels, and the area was infested with enemy cruisers, against which Kingsmill acted vigorously. The recapture of British ships taken by the enemy was a useful supplement to the income from the capture of enemy ships. He was also necessarily involved in the critical events at the end of 1796 when the French, in conjunction with the United Irishmen led by Lord Edward Fitzgerald, attempted the invasion of Ireland.

It was intended by the French naval ministry that the Brest fleet should avoid an engagement. It was to escort an army to Bantry Bay in south-west Ireland, from whence it was to make a quick movement to Cork where the Royal Navy victualling stores would have been taken easily. There was next to no British military force ashore in Ireland. Admiral Morard de Galles was able to sail his fleet of seventeen of the line, and nineteen light craft with seven transports and a powder ship, from Brest without opposition because Vice-Admiral Colpoys commanding a squadron of the Channel fleet was not on station. But the inadequacy of French seamanship in the wake of the revolution, and the fact that the ships were supplied for only a few weeks, were to defeat the expedition. The fleeting opportunities which occurred to put the army ashore were missed by General Grouchy. The continued easterly wind and shortage of supplies made it unhealthy to remain long in the bay when Admiral Lord Bridport could be expected to appear with the Channel fleet.

Kingsmill was given additional resources in the autumn, and was directly involved in the sequel sixteen months later when an army of 5,000 solders was sent to northern Ireland transported by *Hoche* (84), eight frigates, a schooner and a brig. But it was Commodore Sir Borlase Warren who brought the squadron to action, capturing the *Hoche* after three hours' action, and four of the frigates. Three of the remaining frigates landed soldiers in Lough Swilly, but they were soon swept up.

Kingsmill had been promoted vice-admiral on 4 July 1794, and admiral on 14 February 1799. Having asked Lord Spencer in February 1798 for leave to retire, towards the end of 1800 he was superseded by Admiral Sir Alan, later Lord, Gardner. On 4 November 1800 he was created a baronet. He died on 23 November 1805, aged seventy-five, in Sidmonton Place, Newbury, Berkshire.

Lt: 29 April 1756
M-C: 3 July 1761
Capt: 26 May 1762
R-Adm: 1 February 1793
V-Adm: 4 July 1794
Adm: 14 February 1799

KNOWLES

ADMIRAL SIR CHARLES HENRY KNOWLES, BARONET, GCB, was a naval intellectual of the highest order. In 1777, when only a lieutenant, he published *A Set of Signals for a Fleet on a Plan Entirely New*. This was important both for its innovative use of numerical signals which could be flown where they could best be seen, and for the tactics which he envisaged being employed. Most interesting are his ideas that the line of battle should be abandoned once fleets were engaged, each captain being free to pursue the ship it was his lot to fight. He later claimed that he had communicated his work with Lord Howe, whose tactics at the battle of the Glorious First of June had reflected his thinking. In 1798 he printed another signal book incorporating his revisions of 1780, 1787 and 1794.

The published account of his seamanship, and especially his ship handling at the battle of Cape St Vincent on 14 February 1797, indicates that his intellect was such that he could put his ideas into practice. But his history was also to show how such brilliance could blight an officer's career.

He was born on 24 August 1754 in Kingston, Jamaica, the second son of Admiral Sir Charles Knowles, first baronet of Lovell Hill near Windsor, and at the time of his son's birth the governor of Jamaica. His mother was Maria Magdalena Theresa, daughter of Henry François, Comte de Bouget, of Aix-la-Chapelle, councillor of the elector of Cologne. Educated at Eton College about 1764–6, and in Glasgow and Edinburgh, he entered the navy in 1768 as a midshipman in the *Venus* (36) under the command of Captain the Honourable Samuel Barrington, and served in the Channel. He then joined *Lenox* (74) serving under Captain Robert Roddam as a guardship at Spithead, and in December 1771 joined *Southampton* (32) commanded by Captain John MacBride in the Channel and at Plymouth. In 1773 Sir George Rodney appointed him acting lieutenant of *Diligence*, sloop, without pay. He subsequently served in the same capacity in *Princess Amelia* (90), *Portland* (50), *Guadeloupe* (28) under the Honourable Captain William Cornwallis at Pensacola and cruising from Jamaica, *Seaford* (20) under Captain Collins at Cap François and San Domingo, *Antelope* (50) flying the flag of Rear-Admiral Clark Gayton at Port Royal in 1774 to May 1776, and *Squirrel* (20) under the command of Captain Stair Douglas at Jamaica, the Mosquito shore, the Bay of Honduras and Port Royal, Jamaica. His commission was confirmed on 28 May 1776 with an appointment as second lieutenant of *Boreas* (28) under Captain Charles Thompson at Port Royal, and later in the North American station following the battle of Bunker Hill, when he progressed to first lieutenant. He was then moved into *Chatham* (50) flying the flag of Vice-Admiral Shuldham at New York and Barbados in 1776, and he served in the flat boats at New York, where he arrived in August, and Rhode Island.

He returned to Britain in January 1777 to be with his ailing father, during which time he also prepared his first signal book for publication. He returned to North America that summer, though he left for England again when his father died on 9 December, whereupon he became second baronet. He returned to active service in the summer of 1778, joining the fleet in the Leeward Islands. He was in the action in the Cul-de-Sac off St Lucia on 15 December while serving in the large ship-sloop *Ceres* (18) under Commander James Richard Dacres. He was briefly a prisoner when she was captured by Comte d'Estaing's squadron, but was exchanged and acquitted by the court martial for loss of his ship. He was subsequently second lieutenant by seniority, but fifth by duty, in *Prince of Wales* (74) flying the flag of Vice-Admiral the Honourable Samuel Barrington. In May 1779 he was ordered to act in the rank of master and commander of the storeship *Supply*, but he was serving again in *Prince of Wales* on 6 July when he was slightly wounded in action off Grenada.

He returned to England at the end of October, and in December was fit to sail with Admiral Sir George Rodney, who was flying his flag in *Sandwich* (90) in the relief of Gibraltar. Rodney promoted him to command the xebec *Minorca* (18) at the end of January 1780, and again to post captain on 2 February, with appointment to *Porcupine* (24). His service in the Mediterranean was to be exciting, in defence of British trade. He was briefly blockaded into Minorca, where he fell ill. In January 1781 he got away to sea, and was employed at Gibraltar until his return to England in April 1782, when he found himself accused of piracy and murder. Having cleared his name, he returned to Gibraltar as senior naval officer until April 1783, and returned to England in a Spanish ship of the line, *San Miguel* (74), which he had captured.

During the years of peace he continued with his scholarship, and in 1788 made a tour of France. When the French declared war in February 1793, Knowles was appointed to command the *Daedalus* (32) with written orders to proceed to Halifax, but with a verbal *carte blanche* to make his way to the Chesapeake, where it was believed a French con-

voy was preparing to sail. He left Portsmouth with only twelve seamen, and fewer than a total of thirty who had ever been to sea before. It took this crew four hours to furl the main course, a task requiring three minutes on a fully worked-up seventy-four. By the time he had reached Hampton Roads, however, his crew were fully trained. Soon thereafter the French escort arrived. They sailed again on 15 April with the convoy, and thus set in motion the sequence of events that led to the sortie of the Brest fleet under Admiral Villaret-Joyeuse, the movement of the Channel fleet under Lord Howe, who had been alerted by Knowles, and the subsequent series of engagements known as the battle of the Glorious First of June. The attitude to the British ship by the mob at Norfolk was distinctly hostile.

Daedalus sailed in May to Halifax, and thence to England, where in August Knowles was appointed to *Edgar* (74). So desperate was the problem of manning his ship that he sailed from the Nore with soldiers from twenty-three different regiments, commanded by officers from still other regiments, and all infected with jail-fever and the itch. The disease spread throughout the ship and was not eradicated until return to port, when the ship was scrubbed with lime water and fumigated with vinegar, 100 men being sent to the hospital. She returned to the Nore under tow, having lost her masts off the Texel when returning from a cruise to Norway.

While at Lisbon in command of *Goliath* (74) in 1796 Knowles was tried by court martial on a charge by no less a man than Sir John Jervis of not obeying a verbal order. Jervis's captain of the fleet, Robert Calder, swore that no order was ever given, and the lieutenant who was supposed to have transmitted the order swore he had not received one, so the charge was dismissed. But there was to be a sequel.

At the battle of Cape St Vincent, on 14 February 1797, Jervis ordered the fleet to tack in succession while in close action with the enemy. When Jervis's flagship *Victory* (100) tacked, *Edgar* (74), the next astern, protected her during the vulnerable turn by passing on the engaged side. When *Edgar* tacked, Knowles passed close under her lee and threaten to rake any ship threatening *Edgar*. When *Goliath* herself tacked, her next astern apparently was not close enough to provide effective cover, but she had the good luck to fire a double-headed shot which split the backed main topsail of a three-decker trying to manoeuvre to rake her stern. That caused her assailant to shoot forward and discharge her broadside into the sea. Another Spanish first rate, however, and three 74-gun ships luffed into the wind to present their broadsides to *Goliath*. Under a hail of great shot she completed her turn without many of her sheets, but then had to lay by for five minutes while they were knotted.

Coming back into action, Knowles saw an opportunity to pass to windward of *Santisima Trinidad*, becalm her and take her. This was consistent with his published attitude to the line of battle, but Jervis signalled using *Goliath*'s number, to stop the movement. The next morning both Knowles and Captain Whitshed of *Namur* (90) signalled to report the continued vulnerability of *Santisima Trinidad*, but got no reply. The next day when the fleet anchored in Lagos Bay, Knowles placed *Goliath* where she could provide flanking cover for the line, but on going on board *Victory* to congratulate Jervis he was informed that his ship was vulnerable where she lay. With scarce tact Knowles replied that the Spaniards were hardly likely to attack in the condition they were in.

Inevitably Jervis had the last word. When Knowles was dining with Admiral Waldegrave, Jervis sent the *Victory*'s master, Mr Jackson, to move *Goliath*. This was about as great an insult as could have been offered, although not untypical of Jervis's manner. Soon thereafter Knowles found means to return to England.

He took part in the service at St Paul's on 19 December 1797 in thanks for the victories of Cape St Vincent and Camperdown, and then retired into private life. He was offered command of *Britannia* (100) but declined, on the grounds of his health. In the next decade and a half he printed seven books of professional studies, but did not publish his 1798 code of signals for security reasons. In 1803 he suggested the use of balloons to observe Brest. His last book was his semi-autobiographic

Observations on Naval Tactics of 1830. He married on 10 September 1800, uniting with Charlotte, daughter of Charles Johnstone of Ludlow. The couple had three sons and four daughters. Knowles was nominated GCB on 16 May 1820 at the accession of George IV, and died on 28 November 1831, aged seventy-seven, with the rank of admiral.

Lt: 28 May 1776
Cmdr: date unknown
Capt: 2 February 1780
R-Adm: 14 February 1799
V-Adm: 23 April 1804
Adm: 31 July 1810

LAFOREY

ADMIRAL SIR JOHN LAFOREY, BARONET, was a controversial character who suffered for his loyalties, and transformed a local following into public hostility.

He was born about 1729, the second son of Lieutenant-Colonel John Laforey, governor of Pendennis Castle. His mother Mary was daughter and heiress of Lieutenant-General Jasper Clayton. Nothing is known of his entry into the navy, but he received a lieutenant's commission on 12 April 1748, and was promoted by Commodore Augustus Keppel master and commander on 24 May 1755, when he was appointed to a sloop built on the Canadian lakes, appropriately named *Ontario*, and which was captured by the French at Oswego on 14 August 1756. He served in *Hunter*, sloop, under Admiral Edward Boscawen at the reduction of Louisburg, and commanded one of the boat assaults on the moored French line of battle ships during which *Prudent* was burnt and *Bienfaisant* captured, for which Boscawen made him post captain the following day, on 26 July 1758, in a captured French privateer, *Le Maréchal de Richelieu*, which was renamed *Echo* (24). Subsequently, he took part in the capture of Quebec in 1759, and then served in the West Indies, taking part in the capture of Martinique by Rodney in 1762.

He married in 1763, while serving in Antigua, uniting with Eleanor, only surviving daughter of Colonel Francis Farley, RE, member of the council and one of the judges of Antigua. The couple had one son and two daughters.

Laforey served in *Ocean* (90) at the divisive battle of Ushant on 27 July 1778 as one of Admiral Sir Hugh Palliser's seconds, which made his testimony in support of his old friend Admiral Keppel all the more significant. It also threw a shadow over his career. In November 1779 he was appointed commissioner at the Leeward Islands station, and to enhance his authority Rodney made him a commodore in August 1780. Laforey later quarrelled with Rodney over the purchase of naval stores captured at St Eustatius in 1781. Laforey also had disagreements with Rodney's successor, Admiral Hugh Pigot, about the purchase and commissioning of prizes.

After the conclusion of the peace of Paris in 1783, Laforey returned to England and became naval commissioner at Plymouth dockyard. He was passed over in the promotion of 24 September 1787 on the grounds of having accepted a civil office as resident commissioner. This was the contemporary practice, but the *Naval Chronicle* believed that the real reason was that his support of Admiral Keppel was unacceptable to the administration. So much pressure was brought in his defence that by special order in council he was promoted to rear-admiral of the white in 1789 with seniority consistent with his commission to post captain. This precedent, it believed, prevented 'private attachments and connexions, however hostile they may be meanly deemed to the interests of men in power, from ever again interfering with that just, and regular promotion, which officers have to look up to as the certain reward of a long, and meritorious service.' [NC 25.182] On 3 November 1789 he was made a baronet, and immediately after his promotion he hoisted his flag on *Trusty* (50) as commander-in-chief of the Leeward Islands station.

He was just at the end of his appointment when in February 1793 France declared war. An attack on Tobago was immediately planned and successfully carried out in April, shortly before Laforey's supersession by Rear-Admiral Gardner. He had been promoted vice-admiral on 1 February 1793, and was again promoted, to admiral, on 1 June 1795, when he was ordered back to resume his command at the Leeward Islands, travelling out as

a passenger in *Aimable* (32) commanded by his son, Captain Francis Laforey. His main job on arrival was to support the army, which, with only the small forces of the island garrisons, was engaged in the suppression of slave revolts in St Vincent, Grenada and Dominica. He was less successful in dealing with the swarms of French privateers which were pillaging British trade, and John Charnock in his *Biographia Navalis* suggests that Laforey was hampered by the unsuitability of his ships. The failure of his efforts led the local people to such hostility that he in turn lost any enthusiasm for the task beyond the bare minimum required of him. As a result, 'This gentleman' was 'a strong instance how possible it is for an officer to outlive the popularity he had once attained.'

His last act as commander was to organise the naval operations leading to the capture of Demerara and Berbice. He then, well before the usual term, resigned to his successor, Rear-Admiral Sir Hugh Cloberry Christian. He departed for England in *Majestic* (74), but died in passage of yellow fever on 14 June 1796, aged sixty-seven. He was buried in Portsmouth.

Lt: 12 April 1748
M-C: 24 May 1755
Capt: 26 July 1758
Superannuated Capt: 24 September 1787
R-Adm (White): 11 October 1789
V-Adm: 1 February 1793
Adm: 1 June 1795

LAMBERT

CAPTAIN HENRY LAMBERT had the misfortune of twice losing his ship to superior enemy force. The second time, when he commanded *Java* (38) and engaged with the American super-frigate *Constitution* (44), he also lost his life.

The date of his birth is not recorded, but it is known that he was the third son of Captain Robert Alexander Lambert, RN, and Catherine, daughter of Thomas Byndloss of Jamaica. He entered the navy in 1795 on the *Cumberland* (74), and was present in the action off Toulon on 13 July 1795. Later he served on the East India station in the *Virginie* (38) and *Suffolk* (74), being commissioned lieutenant on 15 April 1801. He was transferred in October to the *Victorious* (74) and one year later to the *Centurion* (50), promoted commander of the troop ship *Wilhelmina* on 5 April 1803, and locally promoted captain of the *San Fiorenzo* (34) on 9 December 1804. In February 1805 he distinguished himself by the capture of the French frigate *Psyche* commanded by Captain Bergeret, and as a result he was confirmed in his rank on 10 April 1805. In June 1806 he returned to England, and after more than a year ashore, in May 1808 he was appointed to the *Iphigenia* (32), which he took first to Quebec and afterwards to India.

There Lambert's luck ran out. *Iphigenia* was one of the squadron under Captain Samuel Pym which attempted the disastrous attack on the French squadron in Grand Port, Isle de France (Mauritius), during 22–7 August 1810, in which three of the four frigates engaged were lost or destroyed. On the afternoon of 27 August *Iphigenia*, with the men of two of the other frigates on board and with little or no ammunition remaining, was attempting to warp out of the bay against a contrary wind when three other French frigates appeared off the entrance. Resistance was useless. Lambert surrendered, on an agreement that he, the officers and the crew should be sent on parole to the Cape of Good Hope or to England within a month. But the capitulation was not respected, and the prisoners were detained in Isle de France until the island was captured by the British on 3 December. *Iphigenia*, which had been taken into French service, was then recovered, and Lambert was acquitted when tried by court martial for the loss of his ship.

On 27 August 1811 he married Caroline, second daughter of Nicholas Hall of Truleigh, Hampshire. She gave birth to his only child, who died before 1813.

In August 1812 Lambert was appointed to commission *Java* (38), the French prize *Renommée*, captured off Tamatave on 21 May 1811 and taken into British service. When she was ready, he was ordered to return to the East Indies. On the voyage south, poorly manned and heavily laden with stores, she encountered the *Constitution* off the coast of Brazil on 29 December. Although Lambert could have avoided action, he did not do so. No doubt he was still influenced by the anger and shame of his surrender at Isle de France, and he chose to fight in the hope that he could inflict so much damage on the *Constitution* that her commander, Commodore Bainbridge, would be obliged to abandon his cruise. Lambert was fatally wounded by a musket shot in the breast, but *Java* did not strike until she was close to sinking and was so heavily damaged that the Americans burnt her the following day. The prisoners were landed at San Salvador on 3 January 1813 and Lambert died the following day.

Caroline remarried on 28 July 1814; her second husband was a Captain Gwern.

> Lt: 15 April 1801
> Cmdr: 5 April 1803
> Capt: 10 April 1805

LAPÉNOTIÈRE

CAPTAIN JOHN RICHARDS LAPÉNOTIÈRE commanded the schooner *Pickle* at the battle of Trafalgar on 21 October 1805, and afterwards carried Lord Collingwood's victory dispatch home to England.

He was a son of Lieutenant Frederick Lapénotière, RN, and his wife, Mary, who baptised him on 22 June 1770, in Ilfracombe, Devon. He first went to sea on 8 June 1780 as a lieutenant's servant on board the *Three Sisters*, hired armed ship, commanded by his father. He entered the navy in May 1785. His first voyage was a long one, for he sailed with Lieutenant Portlock from Gravesend on 30 August 1785 on a commercial voyage to develop for the King George's Sound Company the seal fishery of north-west America. Portlock had sailed with Cook. Some time after Lapénotière's return to England on 24 August 1788, Captain William Bligh reached England following the mutiny on the *Bounty* and was ordered back to the Pacific to continue the collection of breadfruit for use in the West Indies plantations. Portlock was given command of a tender to accompany him, the *Assistance* 110 tons, and Lapénotière sailed again from England with him on 2 August 1791.

His examination in sea knowledge took place on 2 October 1793 at Somerset House, Westminster, and he was commissioned lieutenant on 29 April 1794 by Sir John Jervis after serving in the capture of the French islands in the West Indies. He was appointed to command the *Berbice,* schooner, and returned home as first lieutenant of *Resource* (28). He then seems to have been unemployed for some time, until in 1800 he was appointed to command the *Joseph,* hired cutter, in which he continued to gather the good opinion of Jervis, now the earl of St Vincent. When *Joseph* was paid off in the spring of 1803, Lapénotière soon gained command of *Pickle,* mounting ten guns and with a complement of thirty-five men.

On 25 March 1804 the *Magnificent* (74) was wrecked near Brest, and Lapénotière was one of those who were engaged in the dangerous work of rescuing her crew. At Trafalgar, he undertook the even more dangerous work of rescuing French seamen from the burning *Achille* (74), the guns of which were cooking off, and then accommodated 100 prisoners of war and two women who were overheard planning to take over the vessel.

As reward for bringing home Collingwood's dispatches, Lapénotière was promoted commander on 6 November 1805, and appointed to command the *Orestes,* brig (16). He also married in 1805, uniting with Mary Ann, daughter of Commander John Graves, RN. The couple were to have seven children.

In *Orestes* he served in the North Sea, and at the 1807 Copenhagen operation, after which he had the misfortune to be very badly burnt in the face by an exploding small-arms magazine. He was finally promoted post captain on 1 August 1811 but does not appear to have been appointed to command a ship. He died in 1834 in Fanny Vale, Menheniot, near Liskeard, Cornwall, and was buried in Menheniot churchyard.

> Lt: 29 April 1794
> Cmdr: 6 November 1805
> Capt: 1 August 1811

LEGGE

ADMIRAL THE HONOURABLE SIR ARTHUR KAYE LEGGE, KCB, fought in four of the major actions of the wars against the French Republic and Empire.

He was born on 25 October 1766, the sixth son of William, second earl of Dartmouth, and his wife Frances Catharine, only daughter of Sir Charles Gunter Nicholl, KB. His name was entered into the muster book of *Diamond* (32) as a captain's servant on 16 December 1779, and he then is supposed to have transferred to *Duke* (90) on 25 January 1780. Whether he ever entered either ship is uncertain. Most probably he entered the navy on 9 April when he was rated a landsman in *Prince George* (98) flying the flag of Rear-Admiral Digby, for service in the Channel, North America and the West Indies. He was accommodated for a few weeks in a purchased armed vessel, *Rhinoceros* (10), in November 1782, and was then rated midshipman in *Aigle* (38) on 13 December, only to rejoin *Rhinoceros* on 17 June 1783 for another month's accommodation, before being rated a master's mate in *Bonetta* (16) under Captain Richard Goodwin Keats on 18 July. He served in her for two years, during which he was ordered to act as lieutenant, then transferred on 22 June 1784 to *Ariadne* (20) under the command of Captain Samuel Osborn, for service at Nova Scotia and in the Bay of Fundy. He left her on 1 July 1786, and had three years ashore.

He was commissioned lieutenant on 3 August 1789 and appointed to *Salisbury* (50) flying the flag of Admiral Mark Millbanke as commander-in-chief Newfoundland, with Captain William Domett in command. On 10 May 1790 he transferred to *Valiant* (74) under the command of the duke of Clarence, for service in the Channel, following which he was promoted master and commander on 19 November 1790, with appointment to command *Atalante.* On 25 February 1791 he transferred to *Shark,* sloop, and a few days after the French declaration of war he was promoted post captain, on 6 February 1793, and appointed to *Niger* (32), which served as one of Lord Howe's repeaters at the battle of the Glorious First of June in 1794. He was transferred to *Latona* (38) in July following that battle, and in May 1797 to *Cambrian* (40), in which he was employed in the Channel, and in a voyage to St Helena. He left her in October 1801, and was ashore for nearly two years following the negotiation of peace at Amiens.

On the renewal of hostilities he was appointed in August 1803 to command *Repulse* (74) and in her participated in Sir Robert Calder's action against the Franco-Spanish fleet on 22 July 1805 following its return from the West Indies with Nelson in pursuit. After the battle of Trafalgar, Legge was ordered to the Mediterranean, and in 1807 *Repulse* formed part of Sir John Duckworth's squadrons which forced the Dardanelles. In 1809 he participated in the Scheldt operations under Sir Richard Strachan, and became infected with Walcheren fever, which obliged him to resign his command.

He was promoted to rear-admiral on 31 July 1810, and hoisted his flag in the spring of 1811 on board *Revenge* (74) in command of the forces at Cadiz. At the end of the war he was commanding in the river Thames, flying his flag from *Thisbe* (28) lying off Greenwich. He was made a KCB on 2 January 1815, and served as groom of the bedchamber to George IV and as vice-president of the Naval Charitable Society. He was finally promoted admiral on 22 July 1830, and died on 21 May 1835, aged sixty-eight, in Blackheath, Kent.

Lt: 3 August 1789
M-C: 19 November 1790
Capt: 6 February 1793
R-Adm: 31 July 1810
V-Adm: 4 June 1814
Adm: 22 July 1830

LIND

CAPTAIN SIR JAMES LIND, KCB, was given his knighthood for a notable defensive action against the squadron of Rear-Admiral Linois at Vizagapatam Road, nearly 500 miles north of Madras.

He was the second son of Dr James Lind, MD, physician of the Royal Naval Hospital in Haslar, Portsmouth, and one of the pioneers of the use of lemon juice to cure scurvy. His mother was Isabel, daughter of John Dickie of Corstorphine Hill, accountant-general of excise in Scotland. James entered the navy as an able seaman in *Rippon* (54) under the command of Captain

Samuel Thompson on 1 August 1765, and served in North American waters. On 20 September 1769 he transferred to *Dorsetshire* (70) under Captain Michael (?) Clements, in the home station, and was rated a midshipman. After a few months in *Carysfort* (28) in the spring of 1770 he joined *Dolphin* (20) under Captain Digby Dent and later Captain Henry Lloyd for service in the East Indies, transferring on 10 March 1772 to *Northumberland* (68) flying the flag of Admiral Sir Robert Harland. He served in her until 29 May 1775, and then had a few weeks of home leave before joining *Arethusa* (32), once more under Dent, with whom he served in the Channel. On 13 February 1776 he transferred to *Worcester* (64) under Captain Mark Robinson, and on 21 April he transferred again to *Preston* flying the broad pendant of Commodore Sir William Hotham, with whom he served on the North American station. In her he was rated a master's mate. On 25 or 26 January 1778 he was ordered to act as lieutenant in *Perseus* (20) under Captain the Honourable George Keith Elphinstone, moving in the same capacity into *Monmouth*; his commission having been confirmed, he was appointed to *Alfred* (74) under the command of Captain William (?) Baines on 31 October 1780.

He was unemployed between 26 July 1783 and 13 May 1790, when he was appointed to *Gibraltar* (80) under Captain Samuel Goodall during the Nootka Sound crisis. In October he followed Goodall when the latter was promoted to rear-admiral and ordered to raise his flag on *London* (90); he moved with him into *Romney* (50) on 22 March 1792, and into *Princess Royal* (98) on 24 May 1793, by which time he had risen to second lieutenant. *Princess Royal* was part of the Mediterranean fleet.

Lind was promoted commander on 2 November 1795, but for rank only, and it was not until 26 August 1800 that he was appointed to command the *Wilhelmina*, troop ship, in the force under Sir Home Popham sent to take the French position in Egypt in the rear, from the Red Sea. He then served in the East Indies, and on 16 March 1803 transferred to *Sheerness* (44). He was made post captain on 6 March 1804 but remained in command of *Sheerness* and on 5 May made a notable capture of a fast French privateer, by stratagem. As Marshall's *Naval Biography* described it:

> Observing *l'Alfred* in chase of the *Sheerness*, he disguised her as much as possible, and by standing away from his pursuer, and setting and taking in sail in the style of a merchantman, completed the deception, and ensured the capture of the enemy. After a short chase, the privateer ranged upon his quarter, fired a broadside, and commanded him to strike. Her summons was answered by a fire which killed 3 and wounded 6 of *l'Alfred*'s crew, when the astonished Frenchmen immediately hauled down their colours.

The action at Vizagapatam Road took place because Linois had received intelligence that an Indiaman was expected under a light escort. At the last minute Vice-Admiral Rainier had substituted *Centurion* (50) and on 9 September 1804 put her under Lind's temporary command. The latter was ashore when the French line of battle ship and two frigates appeared, and his lieutenant, James Robert Phillips, cut *Centurion*'s cable and opened fire, while ordering the convoy to close the shore to avoid capture. Lind was not able to persuade his Indian boatmen to put him on board until the French stood off. He found *Centurion*'s rigging too badly cut to pursue them, and came to anchor just inside the line of surf. This put him too far offshore to get support from the guns of a battery. He returned ashore to try and arrange for guns to be brought down to the beach, but that was found to be impracticable. He wrote in his report:

> We prepared again for action; and whilst thus employed, the enemy wore and stood towards us: the *Marengo*, after having repeatedly tried the range of her guns, came to an anchor abreast of us, and about a mile distant; clewed up her top-sails, furled her courses, and commenced cannonading. This threatening appearance of being

determined to persevere and to succeed, only served to animate the officers and men of H.M. ship to greater exertions of defence with the lower-deck guns, the only ones that would reach the enemy, for she was too far distant for the carronades; but all the enemy's shot reached us. In the mean time one of the frigates kept under sail on our quarter, nearer than the *Marengo*, and annoyed us much by her fire; the other frigate carried off the Indiaman from her anchorage in the road. ^{Marshall 2.873}

Another merchant ship had got too far into the inner line of surf, and been wrecked. Having achieved his objective, Linois made off.

That appears to have been Lind's last command, and how he returned to England is not known. His nomination as a knight bachelor was made on 5 April 1805. He was advanced in chivalry to KCB on 2 January 1815 at the end of the war, and died on 12 June 1823 in Southampton.

Lt: 25 January 1778
Cmdr: 2 November 1795
Capt: 6 March 1804

LOUIS

REAR-ADMIRAL SIR THOMAS LOUIS, BARONET, is best known for his support of Rear-Admiral Nelson at the battle of the Nile, but should be no less respected for his service under Vice-Admiral Duckworth.

The date of Louis's birth is unknown, but he was baptised at Holy Trinity Church, Exeter, on 11 May 1758, the third son of John Louis of Alphington Cross near Exeter, a schoolteacher or dancing master who was a grandson of King Louis XIV. His mother was Elizabeth, daughter of Ensign Atkinson. He entered the navy in November 1769, when aged eleven years, and served in home waters in *Fly*, sloop, under the command of Captain Mitchell Graham. In 1771 he moved to *Southampton* (32), frigate, commanded by John MacBride, and he was on board in 1772 when *Southampton* formed part of the squadron which transported King George's sister Caroline Matilda, the disgraced queen of

Denmark, to virtual imprisonment at Stadt. With MacBride he moved to the frigate *Orpheus* (32) in April 1773 and followed him again to the *Kent* (74 guns). In June 1775 he joined *Martin*, sloop, under the command of Captain William Parker, and served in the Newfoundland station. He returned home in January 1776 and joined *Thetis* (38) under the command of his old chief Graham, visiting Ascension Island and St Helena. He was commissioned lieutenant on 18 July 1777 in *Bienfaisant* (64) commanded by Captain MacBride, and in her took part in the battle of Ushant on 27 July 1778. He was promoted to first lieutenant the following year and took part in Admiral Rodney's relief of Gibraltar in 1780, the capture of the fleet of Royal Caracas company ships, and the engagement with the Spanish fleet commanded by Don Juan de Langara on 16 January, during which the *San Domingo* blew up while firing at *Bienfaisant* from her quarter guns. One of *Bienfaisant*'s officers wrote:

> Had this awful event taken place a few minutes later, we must have shared her fate: it was impossible to avoid the wreck, great part falling athwart us; but we passed through it without any damage. Many small pieces fell on board, which wounded three men. The sails and rigging being wet with the rain, and at the instant a shower coming on, it prevent the fiery matter that hung upon them taking effect: the sea was so agitated that it filled the decks with water. As the ship sailed into the chaos at the rate of nine knots an hour, it was impossible to distinguish if any of the unfortunate people were upon the wreck.
> NC 16.177

Later, *Bienfaisant* engaged the *Phoenix*, forcing its surrender, upon which Louis was appointed prize master despite a gale blowing so hard that the boat used to board the prize was swamped, the night dark, and the passage to Gibraltar along a lee shore. Rodney recommended him for promotion, but he did not become a master and commander until 9 April 1781. In January 1781 he followed

MacBride to *Artois* (38), a recently captured French frigate, and on 9 April he was appointed to command the armed vessel *Mackworth*, convoying the trade between Milford Haven and Plymouth. Fifteen months later he again followed MacBride, joining the impress service at Sligo and Cork.

Admiral Keppel made him post captain on 20 January 1783 at the very end of the American war; this at least allowed him a captain's half pay, on which, with the help of prize money, he survived until the French declaration of war in 1793. He

Sir Thomas Louis, Bart., K.M.T. and K.S.F.,
Rear Admiral of the White Squadron,
engraved by William Ridley after Freese,
published by Joyce Gold, 103 Shoe Lane,
30 September 1806.

married in 1784 Jacquette, daughter of Samuel Belfield, of Primley House, Paignton, Devon. The couple lived in Torbay and had four sons and three daughters.

On the French declaration of war in February 1793 Admiral MacBride asked Louis to be his flag captain in *Quebec* (32) in the Downs. With him he brought his son, who was to die an admiral in 1863. Louis was soon transferred into *Cumberland* (74), which he was able to man almost entirely with volunteers from Torbay, but it is not known whether they were allowed to follow him to *Minotaur* (74) in the spring of 1794. He missed the battle of the Glorious First of June by being placed in Rear-Admiral George Montagu's squadron, which was detached to find the French convoy. Later, Admiral MacBride shifted his flag into *Minotaur*. In 1796 Louis escorted a convoy to the West Indies and back, and in 1797 he joined the Mediterranean fleet.

In the spring of 1798 *Minotaur* was one of the squadron detached under Captain Troubridge from the Mediterranean fleet cruising before Cadiz and sent to join Nelson watching the French armament at Toulon and the coast of Italy. At a critical moment during the battle of the Nile on 1 August, Louis interposed *Minotaur* between the flagship and *L'Aiquilon*, which was raking her and had killed or injured sixty men in ten minutes. *L'Aiquilon* was forced to strike to *Minotaur*. When, later, Nelson was wounded and thought himself likely to die, he begged that Louis come to him so that he could personally thank him: 'this is the hundred and twenty-fourth time I have been engaged, but I believe it is now nearly over with me.' 'Farewell, dear Louis, I shall never forget the obligation I am under to you for your brave and generous conduct; and now, whatever may become of me, my mind is at peace.'

In the summer of 1799, Louis and Thomas Troubridge liberated Civitavecchia from the French, and then Louis was ordered by Nelson to take possession of the territory of Rome. Both officers were afterwards appointed to the Sicilian order of St Ferdinand and of Merit. In 1800 when Vice-Admiral Keith's flagship *Queen Charlotte* (100) was burnt, Keith shifted his flag for a while into *Minotaur* during the siege of Genoa. After Keith had again shifted his flag, Louis was ordered to take part in the campaign to drive the French from Egypt. In 1802 the Austrian emperor made Louis a knight of the military order of Maria Theresa, and the sultan awarded him the Turkish gold medal.

On half pay during the peace of Amiens, Louis was in 1803 appointed to *Conqueror* (74) and put in command off Boulogne until he was promoted rear-admiral on 23 April 1804. He then shifted into *Leopard* (50) with Francis Austen his flag captain. He had under his authority some forty ships and vessels operating against the French invasion force. In January 1805 he and Austen sailed to the Mediterranean to join *Canopus* (80), one of the Nile prizes, to serve under Nelson. They shared with him the chase to the West Indies and back, but *Canopus* was detached from the force gathered off Cadiz on 11 October, shortly before the battle of Trafalgar.

Louis was serving with Vice-Admiral Duckworth at the time of the battle of San Domingo in 1806 when five French ships were captured or destroyed in less than two hours. All the admirals and captains were given gold medals, and on 1 April 1806 he was created baronet. He was then sent by Vice-Admiral Collingwood to undertake a preliminary survey of the Dardanelles fortifications prior to Duckworth forcing a passage through to the Bosporus and back.

Louis was Duckworth's second in command for that futile operation. Duckworth later reported that on 17 February 1807,

> At half past nine o'clock, the *Canopus*, which, on account of Sir Thomas Louis's knowledge of the channel, joined to the steady gallantry which I had before experienced, had been appointed to lead, entered the narrow passage of Sestos and Abydos, and sustained a very heavy cannonade from both castles, within point-blank shot of each. They opened their fire upon our ships as they continued to pass in succession, although I was happy in observing that the very spirited return it met with had so considerably diminished its force, that the effect on the sternmost ships could not have been so severe.

One of *Canopus*'s officers wrote to his wife about the cannonade on the return passage:

> You will be astonished, my dear Mary, to hear what unmerciful stone shot they fire from their forts; had I not witnessed it

myself, I could not have given credit to it. We received one shot, which is now in my storeroom, that weighs 546 lbs., is 23 inches diameter, or five feet nine inches in circumference. Another of the same size broke in the forecastle; we have got some others something smaller. [NC 17.421–40, 463–72]

Louis accompanied Duckworth to Alexandria, and remained there in command until he died on 17 May 1807, aged forty-eight. He was buried on 8 June 1807 in Manoel Island, in the middle of Marsamxett harbour, Sliema, Malta. The chief mourner was the British governor, Rear-Admiral Sir Alexander John Ball. Jacquette survived him until 13 October 1824 when she died, aged seventy-two, at Cadewell House near Torquay, Devon.

Lt: 18 July 1777
M-C: 9 April 1781 (1)
Capt: 20 January 1783 (1)
R-Adm: 23 April 1804

LYDIARD

CAPTAIN CHARLES LYDIARD was a humble man, and a true hero.

Nothing is known about this officer's family, but it is known that he entered the navy on 13 May 1780 as a captain's servant in *Britannia* (100), the flagship of Vice-Admiral George Darby. He was rated an able seaman on 25 July 1781 and was transferred in that rate on 27 May 1782 into *Resistance* (44), being made a midshipman on 12 October. Subsequently he served in *Bombay Castle* (74) and *Edgar* (74) before he passed for lieutenant on 27 May 1791.[ADM 107.15.200] He was not commissioned until 25 November 1793 after a period of the most arduous service ashore in defence of Fort Mulgrave at Toulon during Admiral Lord Hood's occupation of the port. In July 1795 he was appointed first lieutenant of *Southampton* (32), which won a remarkable victory over *La Vestal* and *Le Brun* off Genoa. This should have ensured Lydiard his promotion, but before possession could be taken of *La Vestal*, *Southampton*'s mast went by the board, and the French took the opportunity to get away. Another spectacular triumph, this time

before the eyes of the Mediterranean fleet and Vice-Admiral Jervis, was required. This took place in June 1796 in the approaches to Toulon and under the fire of its batteries, when Lydiard led the boarders to capture a French corvette, which was then taken out to sea under fire. He was promoted commander of the prize, the commission being confirmed on 22 July 1796.

After another four and a half years of service he was promoted post captain on 1 January 1801, but he was not immediately employed, and the preliminaries of the peace of Amiens soon put an end

Captain Charles Lydiard,
engraved by H R Cook after Richard Livesay,
published by Joyce Gold,
103 Shoe Lane, Fleet Street,
1 July 1808.

———

to that hope. He took the opportunity to marry 'an amiable and accomplished woman, and retired to an estate upon the borders of Surrey'. [NC 19.416] The couple were to have three sons.

It was not until the end of 1805 that he obtained employment in command of a 64-gun ship which had been cut down in 1794 into a frigate, *Anson* (38). He sailed on 24 March 1806 to the West Indies where on 14 August, in company with *Arethusa* (32) commanded by Captain Charles Brisbane, he captured a Spanish frigate, *Pomona* (38), guarded by a battery and twelve gunboats, of which three were blown up, six sunk and the remaining three badly damaged. On 15 September Lydiard engaged a French 84-gun ship without any support, but lost it when it passed into Havana harbour. *Anson* formed part of Commodore Brisbane's expedition to Curaçao which against the odds was taken by storm on 1 January 1807. Lydiard was sent to Jamaica with the prisoners, and then entrusted with dispatches to the Admiralty. All the captains were to be awarded a gold medal to commemorate the event.

Anson was ordered home, and Lydiard rejoined her in Plymouth. After refit, she was ordered to join the Channel fleet, to be stationed off the Black Rocks, with Falmouth as her rendezvous. This was not good use of the ship, which rolled deeply because she had retained her original spars intended for a 64-gun ship. On 27 December a south-western gale forced Lydiard to leave his station and in very heavy weather try and make Falmouth, but *Anson* came onto the wrong side of the Lizard Point, and when breakers were sighted, with the land in sight ahead, there was no choice in such an unweatherly ship but to anchor. The top-gallant-masts were struck to reduce the windage, but one by one the anchor cables parted.

The *Naval Chronicle* pieced together an account of her last hours by talking to survivors:

> At daylight the other cable parted, and we were then so close to the land, that we had no alternative but to go on shore, when Captain L. desired the master to run the ship in the best situation for saving the lives of the people, and fortunately a fine beach presented, upon which the ship was run.... It was the captain's great wish to save the lives of the ship's company, and he was employed in directing them the whole of the time. He had placed himself by the wheel, holding by the spokes, where he was exposed to the violence of the sea, which broke tremendously over him, and from continuing in this situation too long, waiting to see the people out of the ship, he

became so weak, that, upon attempting to leave the ship himself, and being impeded by a boy who was in his way, and whom he endeavoured to assist, he was washed away, and drowned. [NC 19.453]

He was buried in the family vault in Haslemere, Surrey.

Lt: 25 November 1793 (1)
Cmdr: 22 July 1796
Capt: 1 January 1801

MACBRIDE

ADMIRAL JOHN MACBRIDE's naval career was relatively commonplace, although there is some notoriety in his having been dispatched in 1766 to establish a British colony on the Falkland Islands, which four years later Spanish forces evicted, bringing about a crisis in European affairs that nearly ended in war.

He was born in Scotland, the second son of Robert MacBride, Presbyterian minister of Ballymoney, county Antrim, and his wife, née Boyd.

John MacBride, Esq., Admiral of the Blue Squadron,
engraved by H R Cook after
John Smart, 1780, published by
Joyce Gold, 103 Shoe Lane,
30 April 1808.

He first went to sea in the merchant service in 1751, entered the navy in 1754 as an able seaman, served in *Garland* (24) in the West Indies, and was commissioned lieutenant on 27 October 1758. In August 1761, while in command of *Grace*, cutter, he commanded a boat attack at Dunkirk which succeeded in cutting out a French privateer. On 7 April 1762 he was promoted master and commander of *Grampus*, fireship, and after several successful actions he was made post captain on 20 June 1765. He was in command of the 12-pounder frigate *Jason* (32) when he was sent on the mission to the Falkland Islands, and after his return, probably in 1770, he published a thirteen-page monograph, 'A Journal of the Winds and Weather... at Falkland Islands from 1 February 1766 to 19 January 1767'. In May 1772 he commanded the *Southampton* (32) in the mission to transport the king's sister Caroline Matilda to Stadt.

When it was that he married a woman who is only remembered to have been the daughter of a naval officer is not known, nor is it known how many children they may have had. However, his first wife evidently died, and on 14 July 1774 he married Ursula, eldest daughter of William Folkes of Hillington Hall, Norfolk. His son by this marriage, John David MacBride, was born in 1778 and became the principal of Magdalen Hall, Oxford. His daughter, Charlotte, married in 1795 Admiral Sir Willoughby Thomas Lake, KCB.

In 1777 he was appointed to *Bienfaisant* (64), in which ship he took part in the battle of Ushant on 27 July 1778, but did not ever become closely engaged. His evidence in support of Admiral Keppel, however, was important in the latter's acquittal following the trial for his conduct during the action. MacBride was less supportive of Sir Hugh Palliser.

In December *Bienfaisant* sailed as part of Sir George Rodney's relief force for Gibraltar, and took a major role in the capture of the convoy from San Sabastian to Cadiz laden with naval stores. The Spanish flagship, *Guipuscoana* (64), surrendered to her. MacBride was also closely involved in Rodney's action against Admiral Langara on 16 January 1780, *Bienfaisant* having a close call with

disaster when the *San Domingo* blew up. He then captured *Phoenix*, Langara's flagship. He did not take prisoners into *Bienfaisant* because the ship was infected with smallpox. Instead he put Lieutenant Louis on board as a prize master and obtained Langara's parole not to interfere with the running or defence of the ship. He was then sent home with Rodney's dispatches, and resumed command of *Bienfaisant* in March 1780. On 13 August he took a prominent part in the capture of *Comte d'Artois* (64), and in January 1781 following, confusingly he was appointed to command a prize frigate, confusingly called *Artois* (40).

In *Artois* MacBride served in the North Sea under Sir Hyde Parker and took part in the Dogger Bank action against the Dutch fleet on 5 August. On the death of Captain Macartney, MacBride was moved into the *Princess Amelia* (90), but soon returned to *Artois*. While cruising in the Channel in April 1782 he sighted a French fleet steering a course for the West Indies, and was able to get the intelligence to the Channel fleet in time for it to make an interception and capture half of the French ships. In June he was employed in Ireland, in the impress service.

At the beginning of the subsequent peace he appears to have been unemployed, and in 1784 he was returned as member of parliament for Plymouth, holding that seat to 1790. He spoke several times on naval questions, and he served on the duke of Richmond's commission in 1785–6 investigating the defences of Portsmouth and Plymouth. He voted against the proposed measures. In 1788 he was appointed to command a guardship at Plymouth, *Cumberland* (74).

He was promoted rear-admiral on 1 February 1793 in the general promotion at the outset of the war with Revolutionary France, and hoisted his flag in the *Cumberland* as commander-in-chief of a frigate squadron based in the Downs. Later he was transferred into *Quebec* (32) and continued in the Downs station, during which time he took possession of Ostend on the retreat of the French, and transported troops for the defence of Dunkirk. Having transferred again to the 18-pounder frigate *Flora* (36), he sailed on 1 December from Portsmouth carrying an army commanded by Earl

Moira to support the French royalists in Brittany and Normandy. In 1794 he was put in command of a small squadron in the western Channel, and was promoted vice-admiral on 4 July, but after service in the North Sea he left the navy and was not again employed.

Following his retirement he was promoted admiral on 14 February 1799, but died of a paralytic seizure on 17 February 1800 at the Spring Garden Coffee House, London.

> Lt: 27 October 1758
> M-C: 7 April 1762
> Capt: 20 June 1765
> R-Adm: 1 February 1793
> V-Adm: 4 July 1794
> Adm: 14 February 1799

MACKENZIE

ADMIRAL THOMAS MACKENZIE was one of Admiral Lord Howe's captains at the Glorious First of June.

He was born in 1753, a son of Vice-Admiral George Mackenzie, who died in 1780, and entered the navy on board *Montreal* (32) under the command of Captain Cosby. In 1771, after being examined at the Navy Office, St Mary-le-Strand, Westminster, he sailed to Jamaica, where he was soon given a lieutenant's commission and appointed to the *Tryal,* sloop. On 15 April he was again promoted, to master and commander, and, in recognition for his services ashore at the American siege of Quebec in the winter of 1775–6, he was made post captain on 12 June 1776 at the age of twenty-three. On 10 September the ship he commanded, *Ariel* (20), was captured by a French frigate, *L'Amazone* (36), off Charlestown bar, and he remained on board as a prisoner of war during Admiral d'Estaing's abortive attack on Savannah in October. In Cadiz he was set free, and he made his way back to England, where he arrived at the end of December. After his acquittal at court martial, he was, in September, appointed to command the 9-pounder frigate *Active* (28), which was not yet launched. When she was ready for sea, she was attached to a squadron commanded by Sir Thomas Pye.

In 1781 *Active* formed part of a squadron under Commodore Johnston with orders to attempt to capture the Dutch station on the Cape of Good Hope. Word of the expedition had reached the French, who sent a squadron of their own under Admiral Suffren to reinforce the Dutch. At Porto Prayo in St Jago the two squadrons met, and Suffren, disregarding Portuguese neutrality, attacked the British ships. They managed to beat off their assailants, but the French reached Cape Town first.

Mackenzie had orders to continue on to the East Indies, and to place himself under the command of Vice-Admiral Sir Edward Hughes. He was there

The Late Thomas Mackenzie, Esq.,
Rear-Admiral of the Blue Squadron,
engraved by T Blood after Robert Bowyer, published
by Joyce Gold, Naval Chronicle Offices,
103 Shoe Lane, London, 31 May 1815.

employed in blockade of Hyder Ali's ports on the Malabar coast, and commanded the seamen employed in the reduction of the Dutch fort of Negapatam. But he failed to show up for the attack on Trincomalee in northern Ceylon in January 1782 because he had obeyed the request of the supreme council at Calcutta to escort a supply ship to the Hoochly to break the blockade by a privateer, and was further delayed when damaged grounding on a coral head. It took the intervention of Lord Macartney, governor of Fort St

George, Madras, to placate the irate admiral. Soon after that, the preliminaries of peace were concluded, and Mackenzie was ordered home as part of a squadron commanded by Captain Sir Richard King. There he went on half pay.

On the outbreak of war in February 1793 he was appointed to command the *Gibraltar* (80) with a crew of raw recruits, and so far succeeded in training them to their job that they were able to account well for themselves in the battles of 28 and 29 May 1794. In the action of 1 June *Gibraltar* forced the French *Northumberland* to strike her colours. However, Mackenzie was not one of the few singled out for mention in Admiral Howe's dispatches, and, like many of the commanders in the battles of the Glorious First of June, he felt badly used. He was promoted rear-admiral with the commission dating from 4 July, and he continued to be promoted until eventually he ranked as admiral on 23 April 1804, but for some reason he was never ordered to hoist his flag.

He was married, but nothing is known of his wife, and he left no children when he died a disappointed man on 20 September 1813, aged sixty.

Lt: 1771
M-C: 15 April 1771
Capt: 12 June 1776
R-Adm: 4 July 1794
V-Adm: 14 February 1799
Adm: 23 April 1804

MACNAMARA

REAR-ADMIRAL JAMES MACNAMARA is best known for a remarkable action of daring on 9 June 1796 when commanding the 12-pounder frigate *Southampton* (32). Without written orders from Admiral Jervis, who simply asked him to 'bring out the enemy's ship if you can', he entered Hyères Bay under the guns of the French batteries guarding Toulon, and captured *L'Utile,* corvette (24). 'Sir,' wrote Macnamara reporting his triumph, 'In obedience to the orders I received from you on the *Victory*'s quarter-deck last evening, I pushed through the Grande Passe, and hauled up under the batteries on the N.E. of Porguerol with an easy sail, in hopes I should be taken for a French or neutral frigate, which I have great reason to believe

succeeded, as I got within pistol-shot of the enemy's ship before I was discovered, and cautioned the Captain through a trumpet not to make a fruitless resistance, when he immediately snapped his pistol at me, and fired a broadside. At this period, being very near the heavy battery of Fort Breganson, I laid him instantly on board, and Lieutenant Lydiard at the head of the boarders, with an intrepidity no words can describe, entered and carried her in about ten minutes, although he met with a spirited resistance from the Captain, (who fell) and a hundred men under arms to receive him.... After lashing the two ships together, I found some difficulty in getting from under the battery, which kept up a very heavy fire, and was not able to return through the Grande Passe before half after one o'clock this morning…' [Marshall 1.684] *Southampton*'s first lieutenant, Charles Lydiard, was promoted commander of the prize.

Macnamara's parentage is unknown, but he is believed to have been born in 1768, in county Clare. He entered the navy in 1782 on board the *Gibraltar* (80) flying the broad pendant of Sir Richard Bickerton, sailing to the East Indies. There he served in *Superb* (74) flying Sir Edward Hughes's flag, and fought in the action against M. de Suffren off Cuddalore on 20 June 1783, after which he was given the acting rank of lieutenant in the Spanish prize taken by Rodney in the 'Moonlight Battle' in 1780, *Monarca* (68). On his return to Europe in her he reverted to the rank of midshipman and served in *Europa* (50) flying Admiral Innes's flag at Jamaica. His lieutenant's commission was dated 1 December 1788. He served during the Russian and Spanish armaments in *Excellent* (74) and *Victory* (100), the latter flying Lord Hood's flag. On the outbreak of war in 1793 he again served under Lord Hood, and by him was promoted master and commander on 22 October 1793.

His commission as post captain was mistakenly dated 6 October 1795, but prior to that he had been in acting command of *Bombay Castle* (74) and of *Southampton,* frigate. This second ship formed part of the squadron under Commodore Nelson co-operating with the Austrian army in Genoa. Subsequent to his capture of *L'Utile* he was employed by Commodore Nelson in taking possession of Porto Ferrajo, evacuating Capreja and Corsica, in the expedition against Piombino and at the siege of Castiglione, sustaining his reputation for intrepidity to the point of recklessness. In the battle of Cape St Vincent on 14 February 1797 *Southampton* was the repeating frigate of the centre of the line. When a few months later she returned to England and was paid off, Macnamara was appointed to command *Cerberus* (32), in which he served on the coast of Ireland, in the Bay of Biscay and in the West Indies. After the peace of Amiens the *Cerberus* was for some time employed on the coast of San Domingo, and was paid off in February 1803.

He may indeed have been a little mad. He shot Colonel Montgomery on 6 April 1803 in a duel arising out of a fight between their dogs in Hyde Park. He was tried for murder at the Old Bailey but asked for Nelson and Hood to vouch that 'he was the reverse of quarrelsome', and was acquitted.

On the renewal of the war Macnamara commanded *Dictator* (64) in the North Sea for two years, and *Edgar* (74) in the Baltic and in the Great Belt with Sir Richard Goodwin Keats in 1808, and he was appointed in 1809 to the *Berwick* (74) in the North Sea and on the north coast of France. He was promoted rear-admiral on 4 June 1814, but never hoisted his flag.

He married on 26 January 1818 Henrietta, daughter of Henry King of Askham Hall, Nottinghamshire, and widow of Lieutenant-Colonel the Honourable George Carleton. He died on 15 January 1826, aged fifty-seven.

Lt: 1 December 1788
M-C: 22 October 1793
Capt: 6 October 1795

MAITLAND

REAR-ADMIRAL SIR FREDERICK LEWIS MAITLAND, KCB, was a star frigate captain who got lucky at the end of his career and was in the right place at the right time to take Napoleon Buonaparte prisoner.

He was born on 7 September 1777 in Rankeillour near Cupar, Fife, the third son of Captain the Honourable Frederick Lewis Maitland, RN, and his wife Margaret, daughter of James Dick Macgill, heiress of Rankeillour and Lindores. His was a naval family. A brother Robert was a midshipman who died at Malta on 2 July 1801, and three first cousins became admirals. Frederick Lewis junior was borne on the books of *Princess Augusta*, yacht, at Deptford as a volunteer first class under the command of his father in May 1784 when he was not yet seven, and subsequently on the books of *Goliath* (74) at Portsmouth when she was in ordinary and commanded by her master. His real entry into the navy was in April 1792 as an able seaman in *Martin,* sloop, under Captain George Duff, with whom he served at Leith and in the North Sea. He followed Duff into *Nemesis* (28) in January 1793 for a voyage from the Nore to Portsmouth, and there joined *Royal William* (100) under Captain George Gayton, but he did not stay with her long. With the outbreak of war there was turmoil, and men were turned over as ships needed men to help fit them for sea. He was rated midshipman when he joined *Falcon*, brig-sloop (10), in March, and on 4 May he joined *Southampton* (32) under the Honourable Robert Forbes. This was to be his ship for nearly a year, serving in the Channel.

On 3 April 1795 he was commissioned lieutenant in *Andromeda* (32), but was moved on 7 September into *Venerable* (74), flying the flag of Admiral Duncan in the North Sea. He served with him until April 1797, just before the mutiny at the Nore, when he left *Venerable* and joined Admiral the earl of St Vincent, who had promised him promotion out of respect for his father, who had died on 16 December 1786. He was appointed first lieutenant of *Kingfisher,* sloop, under the command of Captain the Honourable Charles Herbert Pierrepont, and her ship's company were so impressed by his officer-like qualities that they subscribed £50 from their prize money to purchase him a sword. On 3 December 1798, *Kingfisher*, while temporarily under Maitland's command, was wrecked in the Tagus, but he was acquitted by a court martial. St Vincent appointed him his flag lieutenant in *Ville de Paris* (110) the next day, at the time when he was commanding from Gibraltar. When reconnoitring the combined French and Spanish fleets passing into the Mediterranean on 7 July 1799, Maitland, in temporary command of a hired cutter, *Penelope*, came too close and was captured. Blame for this failure was attached to the hired crew, who were accused of cowardice and disobedience. Admiral Gravina ordered Maitland's release without exchange out of compliment to St Vincent.

Almost the last act of that admiral as commander-in-chief Mediterranean was to make Maitland commander, backdating the promotion to 14 June 1799 and appointing him to *Camelion,* sloop. He joined Sir Sidney Smith's squadron off El Arish in time to be present at the signing of the convention on 24 January 1800. Maitland was then sent overland home to deliver a copy to London, before rejoining his ship. On 10 December 1800 Lord Keith appointed him acting captain of a storeship, *Wassenaar*, but she was at Malta unfit for service and Maitland obtained permission to accompany General Abercromby's invasion force to Egypt. He commanded the armed launches which supported the landing at Aboukir in March 1801 and, with Captain James Hillyar, who provided armed support from the lakes inland of the Alexandria Road, continued to support the flanks of the army as it advanced, providing fire-power in the actions of 13 and 21 March 1801. By a coincidence, the Admiralty confirmed Maitland's commission as post captain on 21 March 1801. He was awarded the Turkish gold medal for distinguished services on the coast of Egypt.

He served in the Mediterranean until the peace of Amiens, in temporary command of *Dragon* (74), moving in August or September to the 12-pounder frigate *Carrère* (44), which had recently been captured from the French, who had themselves taken her from the Venetians. He took her back to England to pay her off in October 1802. On 15 October St Vincent, who was then first lord of the Admiralty, appointed him to command the 18-pounder frigate *Loire* (46).

In her he had a very active career on the west coast of France and the north coast of Spain following the recommencement of war, acting vigorously against enemy privateers. He earned the thanks of the City of London, the freedom of Cork and a sword from the Patriotic Fund for an action in Muros Bay, south of Cape Finisterre, on 4 June 1805. Six months later he assisted in the capture of a French frigate, *Libre*, on 24 December. He was transferred into the 18-pounder frigate *Emerald* (36) on 27 November 1806, and continued his employment in the Bay of Biscay. In April 1809 she was one of the fleet under Lord Gambier at Basque Roads, and on the 12th was one of the ships which entered the roads following the fireship attack.

In April 1804, in Cork, he married Catherine, second daughter of Daniel Conner of Ballybricken and sister of Captain Richard Conner, RN.

On 3 June 1813 Maitland was appointed to *Goliath* (58). This was the same ship he had nominally served in as a nine-year-old. She was now a cut-down seventy-four intended to meet the American super-frigates on equal terms, but in fact a defective ship. After twelve months on the Halifax station, she was paid off, and Maitland was appointed on 15 November 1814 to *Boyne* (98). He was at Cork making up a convoy of transports and merchant ships under orders for North America when Napoleon escaped his exile at Elba. Maitland's orders were immediately cancelled, and he was moved into *Bellerophon* (74) and sailed from Plymouth on 24 May under the orders of Sir Henry Hotham. He was senior officer of a squadron off Rochefort when Napoleon, defeated at Waterloo and fearing retribution from the French, failed in an attempt to get away to the United States. In desperation he resolved to entrust himself to 'the most powerful, the most constant, and the most generous of his enemies'. He surrendered unconditionally to Captain Maitland on 15 July 1815, and was taken to Plymouth Sound.

Maitland wrote to the *Edinburgh Annual Register*:

> I must say that Buonaparte never conducted himself with arrogance whilst he was on board the ship which I commanded. He knew the world too well, and was aware he could not have adopted a measure more likely to defeat any wish he might have

entertained, of being considered as a crowned head; but, in fact, he never attempted to exact such respect; and so far from its being shewn to him, he had not even the honours due to a General-Officer paid on his coming on board the *Bellerophon*.

Moored at Plymouth, *Bellerophon* became the centre of intense curiosity and was surrounded day and night by people in small boats come to catch a glimpse of the fallen tyrant.

Maitland was, with so many, appointed a CB on 4 June 1815. In June 1819, while in command of *Vengeur* (74), he was directed to form part of the squadron commanded by Sir Thomas Hardy on the South American coast, and in 1820 while still in command of *Vengeur* he conveyed the king of the Two Sicilies from Naples to Leghorn to attend the congress of Laybach, upon which occasion he was appointed knight commander of the Sicilian order of St Ferdinand and of Merit. In the spring of 1821 he returned to England, and then was appointed to *Genoa* (74), which was serving as a guardship at Portsmouth. He remained with her for the usual term of three years. In 1827 he was appointed to command the teak-built *Wellesley* (74) in the Mediterranean, and again retained his command for the usual three years.

He was promoted rear-admiral on 22 July 1830, and advanced in chivalry to KCB on 17 November 1830. He was superintendent of Portsmouth dockyard from June 1832 until July 1837, and commander-in-chief East Indies when he died at sea on board the *Wellesley* off Bombay on 30 November 1839, aged sixty-two. He had no surviving children, and his wife died on 6 March 1865.

Lt: 3 April 1795
Cmdr: 14 June 1799
Capt: 21 March 1801
R-Adm: 22 July 1830

MAITLAND

REAR-ADMIRAL JOHN MAITLAND, nephew of Captain the Honourable Frederick Lewis Maitland and first cousin of Rear-Admiral Sir Frederick Lewis Maitland, made his reputation early in his career when midshipman, and later acting lieutenant of *Boyne* (98), serving on shore in the 1793–4 campaign to capture Martinique and Guadeloupe. At the storming of Fort Fleur d'Epée on 12 April 1794, he was the first person to mount the rampart, and assisted Faulknor and others up before rushing the fort, when he saved Faulknor's life. In the attack on Pointe à Pitre on Guadeloupe he succeeded to battlefield command when all the more senior officers were killed, wounded or exhausted.

He was born in 1771 in Scotland, the third son of Colonel the Honourable Richard Maitland, uncle of the earl of Lauderdale, and his wife, Mary, née McAdam, of New York. He was commissioned lieutenant on 20 July 1794 and served in home waters in temporary command of *Lively* (26), then in her in the Mediterranean, where Sir John Jervis promoted him commander on 23 December 1796. His gallantry continued to impress his superior, and he was promoted again to post captain on 11 August 1797 following his violent repression of a mutiny on board *Kingsfisher*. The Admiralty confirmed the promotion, and he returned home in command of the *San Nicolas*, prize. He married on 22 April 1799 Elizabeth, daughter of Archibald Ogilvy of Inchmurrin, Dunbarton, Scotland.

From 1800 to 1803 he commanded the fir-built 18-pounder frigate *Glenmore* (36), and after the renewal of the war he was put in command of the 18-pounder frigate *Boadicea* (38). He chased a French seventy-four, *Duguay-Trouin*, and *La Guerrière* (38) for twenty-four hours, thinking they were armed *en flute* as troopers, but in the end was forced to haul off when finally they turned to fight and revealed full broadsides. Later when serving off Brest *Boadicea* struck the Bas de Lis rock and was holed so badly that it was necessary to depart with an escort for repairs in Portsmouth. He was back on station in eight days, three of which had been in dock. In 1804 he was employed in watching Rochefort, and at times was left alone and threatened by a ship of the line and a frigate, which he kept just out of range. In 1805 he served in the North Sea and on the Irish station. On 2 November he encountered off Cape Finisterre the four French ships of the line under Rear-Admiral Dumanoir le Pelley which had escaped from the battle of Trafalgar, and led Sir Richard Strachan's squadron onto them. A little later, he chased a French frigate for two days, but on the evening of the second day the closeness of the shore forced him to haul off. Later it was learnt that the French frigate had run onto the Isle de Groais [Groix] near L'Orient with all sails set. In 1807 *Boadicea* was dispatched in such haste to the Davis Strait that there was no opportunity for her people to purchase warm clothing.

Towards the end of 1813 he was appointed to command *Barfleur* (90), in which ship he served in the Mediterranean until the end of the war. He married for a second time on 8 January 1820, uniting with Dora, eldest daughter of Colthurst Bateman of Bedford, county Kerry, and widow of George Augustus Simson. He was promoted rear-admiral on 19 July 1821, and died on 20 October 1836, aged sixty-five.

Lt: 20 July 1794
Cmdr: 23 December 1796
Capt: 11 August 1797
R-Adm: 19 July 1821

MALCOLM

ADMIRAL SIR PULTENEY MALCOLM, GCB, was the genius behind a remarkable coup at Cavite, the naval port for Manila, on 5 January 1798 when he managed to convince a succession of Spanish officers sent out to his becalmed frigate that his was a French ship. When his senior captain, Edward Cooke commanding the French prize *Sybille* (40), came on board he was introduced as Commodore Citoyen la Tour. Together they employed the deception to take control of three armed vessels lying just outside the bar of the river, and then released their captives.

In the scale of war, however, his more important services were in command of *Donegal* (74) and as a flag officer in the Peninsular and American wars.

He was born on 20 February 1768, in Douglan near Langholm, Dumfriesshire, the third son of George Malcolm of Burnfoot and his wife, Margaret, daughter of James Pasley of Craig,

Dumfriesshire, who was the father of Admiral Sir Thomas Pasley, baronet. Vice-Admiral Sir Charles Malcolm and Lieutenant George Malcolm, RN, were his brothers. According to Marshall's *Naval Biography*, Pulteney entered the navy on 20 October 1778 as a midshipman in *Sybil* (28) commanded by his uncle, but that ship was not launched until January 1779. He then is supposed to have followed Captain Pasley to *Jupiter* (50), which was one of the ships in Commodore George Johnstone's squadron which fought the action in Porto Praya and later captured a fleet of Dutch Indiamen in Saldanha Bay. *Jupiter* later carried Admiral Hugh Pigot to the West Indies, where Malcolm was taken into his flagship. Pigot commissioned him one of *Jupiter*'s lieutenants on 3 March 1783, and he remained in employment during the subsequent ten years of peace. At the French declaration of war in February 1793 he was serving as first lieutenant of *Penelope* (32) in the Jamaica station under the command of Captain Bartholomew Rowley.

After a few months serving in the squadron flagship *Europa* (50), he was promoted commander on 3 April 1794 by Rear-Admiral Ford, and appointed to the French prize *Jack Tar*, brig. On the French royalists at Cape Nicholas Mole inviting the British to garrison the post, he was given its command.

Having returned to England in *Jack Tar*, he was made post captain on 22 October 1794 with command of a cutter, *Fox* (10). He escorted a convoy to the Mediterranean, sailed thence to Quebec, then served in the North Sea, and escorted another convoy to the East Indies, where he captured *La Modeste* (20), and eventually proceeded to Macao and Cavite in company with *Sybille*. Following the coup at the last port, the two ships attempted to reduce the fortress at Sambangen on Mindanao, but were beaten off and later lost two boat's crews to a Filipino raid, although most of the men were eventually recovered.

On 18 June 1798 he was appointed to command *Suffolk* (74) flying the flag of Vice-Admiral Rainier, commander-in-chief East Indies, and he later shifted with him into *Victorious* (74). On returning to Europe in 1803, his ship, which was crazy from long service in Asian waters, was so badly damaged by a gale in the Bay of Biscay that it was only just able to retrace its route to the Tagus, where it was run ashore and broke up.

In January 1804 he was appointed to command *Royal Sovereign* (100) proceeding to the Mediterranean, and then moved into a succession of third rates before being given command of *Donegal*. She took part in Vice-Admiral Nelson's pursuit of the Toulon fleet to the West Indies, and then joined Sir Robert Calder's squadron sent to reinforce Vice-Admiral Collingwood before Cadiz. She was one of the ships Nelson detached to Gibraltar on 17 October 1805 to take on water, and thus Malcolm missed the battle of Trafalgar. After prodigious exertions he managed to sail from Gibraltar, towing *Donegal*'s fore yard because there was not time to get it on board and slung, and to join Collingwood on 23 October. He took possession of *El Rayo*, one of the Spanish ships which sortied from Cadiz in an attempt to recapture some of the prizes taken at the end of the battle of Trafalgar. When on the night of the 24th some of the prisoners on the French *Berwick* cut her cable and she almost immediately broke up on the shore, the *Donegal*'s boats succeeded in saving a considerable number of her men. She later brought *Bahama* into Gibraltar.

Donegal remained off Cadiz under the orders of Sir John Duckworth until late in 1805, when she accompanied him to the West Indies; she there fought at the battle of San Domingo on 6 February 1806. While escorting the captured ships home, a gale was encountered which dismasted one of them, *Le Brave*, and put her at immediate risk of foundering. But Malcolm had anticipated that danger, and kept close to her. Despite a heavy sea he was able to take all the men out of her before she sank. As did all the captains, he received a gold medal for the action at San Domingo, and the Patriotic Fund presented him with a vase valued at £100 guineas.

In 1808 Malcolm escorted the transports carrying Sir Arthur Wellesley from Cork to Mondego Bay in Portugal, and secured their safe disembarkation. He was then attached to the Channel fleet under Lord Gambier's command. Taking his chance on 18 January 1809, in St Marylebone, London,

he married Clementina, eldest daughter of the Honourable William Fullarton Elphinstone, a director of the East India Company and niece of Admiral Keith, GCB.

Donegal was paid off in 1811 and Malcolm was transferred to *Royal Oak* (74), and then on 1 March 1812 to *San Josef* (110) as captain of the Channel fleet under Lord Keith. He was promoted colonel of the Royal Marines on 12 August 1812 and rear-admiral on 4 December 1813, and on 1 June 1814 hoisted his flag in *Royal Oak* with orders to transport a body of soldiers commanded by Brigadier-General Ross from Bordeaux to North America. There Malcolm supported Sir Alexander Cochrane in the expedition to the Chesapeake, leading to the raids on Washington and Baltimore. He also served in the abortive New Orleans expedition, in which he was responsible for the disembarkation of the army, and served at the reduction of Fort Boyer on Mobile Point, which was the last action of the war.

He was nominated a KCB on 2 January 1815, and on Napoleon's returning to France from Elba he was put in command of the naval forces appointed to support the duke of Wellington and the allied armies. He struck his flag on 26 September 1815, but was subsequently appointed to command at St Helena, where Napoleon was held prisoner, remaining there until the spring of 1816.

He served as commander-in-chief in the Mediterranean between 1828 and 1831, and as was then the practice, was nominated a knight grand cross of St Michael and St George by the Ionian Republic on 21 January 1829. During the Dutch crisis in 1832 he commanded a combined British, French and Spanish fleet on the coast of the Netherlands, and was subsequently nominated a GCB on 24 April 1833. He had a last tour of duty as commander-in-chief Mediterranean from May 1833 to April 1834, dying on 28 June 1838, aged seventy, in Langholm.

Lt: 3 March 1783
Cmdr: 3 April 1794
Capt: 22 October 1794
R-Adm: 4 December 1813
V-Adm: 19 July 1821
Adm: January 1837

MARTIN

ADMIRAL OF THE FLEET SIR GEORGE MARTIN, GCB, was a capable commander who died as admiral of the fleet, covered with honours.

He was probably born in 1764, the third and youngest son of Captain William Martin, RN, and his wife Arabella, daughter of Admiral of the Fleet Sir William Rowley. He was borne on books of *Mary*, yacht, on 13 December 1771 and entered the navy on 20 November 1776 as a captain's servant in the *Monarch* (74) commanded by his uncle, Captain, later Vice-Admiral, Sir Joshua Rowley. He was progressively rated ordinary seaman and midshipman, and served with him at the battle of Ushant on 27 July 1778. He transferred on 8 December 1778 to *Suffolk* (74) under the command of Hugh Cloberry Christian, with whom he served in the West Indies in Admiral Byron's action at Grenada on 6 July 1779. He subsequently served in the 18-pounder frigate *Actaeon* (44), and in the ship-sloop *Camelion* (14) under Commander Thomas Watson. He was rated second master's mate and midshipman in *Rover*, sloop, by Captain John Thomas Duckworth, with whom he served between 29 January and 17 June 1780, taking part in Admiral Rodney's engagements off Martinique in April and May. He then served in *Hart* under James (?) Vashon until 15 July. He was ordered to act as lieutenant of *Russell* (74) under Robert Hanwell on 16 July 1780; he served with Duckworth again in *Princess Royal* (98) at Jamaica until he transferred with him to *Ulysses* (44) on 26 June 1781, by which time his commission had been confirmed; he then served in *Sandwich* (90) under Silverius Moriarty until he came ashore on 30 September 1781. On 9 March 1782 he was promoted commander of *Tobago*, sloop; he was posted captain of *Preston* (50) on 17 March 1783, leaving her in England on 2 April 1784.

He was unemployed during the peace until appointed to command the *Porcupine* (24) on 9 July 1789, and served in her on the coast of Ireland until 21 August 1792. After the French declaration of war on 1 February 1793 he was appointed to *Magicienne* (32) on 12 March, and served under Commodore Ford at Jamaica. Returning to England, he transferred to *Irresistible* (74) on 8 November 1795 and served in her at the battle of Cape St Vincent on 14 February 1797. At the end of the battle, Commodore Nelson transferred his broad pendant to *Irresistible* for a few days because of the damage suffered by his own ship. On 26 April Martin made a good impression when he, in company with an 18-pounder frigate, *Emerald* (36), chased two Spanish frigates into the reefs of Conil Bay, driving one of them ashore and capturing the other.

After a period of service with Lord Bridport in the Channel fleet, he transferred on 14 July 1798 to *Northumberland* (74) and served in the Mediterranean, where he assisted in the capture of *Le Généreux* (74) on 18 February 1800, and in May succeeded to command of the squadron blockading Malta. Years later, on 17 May 1837, the Ionian Republic and Malta appointed him knight grand cross of the order of St Michael and St George. After the capitulation of the French garrison of Valletta to him in September, he was employed under Lord Keith in the Egyptian campaign. He was awarded the Turkish gold medal in 1802, and came ashore on 21 September following the signing of the peace of Amiens.

With the renewal of the war in 1803 he was appointed on 22 May to the new *Colossus* (74) in the Channel fleet. After transferring to *Glory* (90) on 24 April 1804, the day after his nomination as colonel of the Royal Marines, and then to *Barfleur* (90) on 21 November, he fought in Sir Robert Calder's action of 22 July 1805. He resigned his command on 16 September, and was promoted rear-admiral on 9 November 1805. He served between 17 January and 9 November 1806 as second in command at Portsmouth, but soon returned to sea, watching Cadiz and then on the coast of Italy.

In June 1809 he took possession of Ischia and Procida, and in October, while flying his flag in the French prize *Franklin*, captured at the Nile and renamed *Canopus* (80), he was ordered to pursue several ships under Rear-Admiral Baudin that had come out of Toulon. His squadron succeeded in driving two of them ashore, where their own crews set them on fire, another ship of the line and a frigate got into Cette harbour, and a second frigate escaped.

> *Canopus, at Sea, October* 27, 1809. My Lord. In obedience to the signal for the *Canopus* to chase E.N.E. I stood that way the whole of the night of the 23d, and the following day, in company with the *Renown, Tigre, Sultan, Leviathan,* and *Cumberland.* In the evening four sail were seen, to which we immediately gave chase, and pursued them till after dark; when, from shoal water, and the wind being direct on the shore, near the entrance of the Rhone, it became necessary to keep to the wind during the night. The following morning (the 25th) the same ships were again seen and chased between Cette and Frontignan, where they ran on shore – two of them (an 80-gun ship, bearing a rear-admiral's flag, and a 74) at the latter place, and one ship of the line and a frigate at the former. From the shoal water and intricacy of the navigation, it was impossible to get close enough to the enemy's two line-of-battle ships near Frontignan, to attack them when on shore; for in attempting to do so, one of his Majesty's ships was under five fathoms water, and another in less than six. On the 26th, I sent the boats to sound; meaning, if possible, to buoy the channel (if any had been found) by which the enemy's ships could be attacked; but at night we had the satisfaction to see them set on fire.
>
> NC 22.501–2

After his promotion to vice-admiral on 31 July 1810, Martin commanded at Palermo, providing support for the army in Calabria under Sir John Stuart, for which he was appointed to the order of St Januarius by the king of Naples on 6 July 1811. Having returned to England and struck his flag on 14 October 1810, and hoisted his flag in *Impetueux* (78) in 1812, he commanded at Lisbon until the end of the war, hauling down his flag on 24 June 1814.

He was nominated a knight bachelor on 25 June when the prince regent visited the fleet at Spithead, a KCB on 2 January 1815 and a GCB on 23 February 1821. He was commander-in-chief at Portsmouth, with his flag in the *Victory* (100), from 27 March 1824 to 30 April 1827. He was appointed rear-admiral of the United Kingdom in February 1833, and was vice-admiral of the United Kingdom from April 1834 to November 1846 and again in July 1847 until his death. He was also elected vice-president of the Naval Charitable Society.

He was married twice. On 3 April 1804, in St Marylebone, he was united to Harriet, the youngest daughter of Captain John Albert Bentinck, RN, and sister of Vice-Admiral William Bentinck. She died on 15 October 1806 in Hampton Court, and he married for a second time on 2 June 1815, uniting with Ann, daughter of William Locke of Norbury Park, Surrey. She, too, predeceased him, dying on 1 March 1842. There had been no children, and he died on 28 July 1847, aged eighty-three, at Berkeley Square, Westminster.

Lt: 16 July 1780
M-C: 9 March 1782
Capt: 17 March 1783
R-Adm: 9 November 1805
V-Adm: 31 July 1810
Adm: 19 July 1821
Adm. of the Fleet: 9 November 1846

MARTIN

ADMIRAL OF THE FLEET SIR THOMAS BYAM MARTIN, GCB, is best known for his very long service in the post-war navy, but he should be as well known as a star frigate captain during the French Revolutionary War and the war against the French Empire.

He was born on 25 July 1773 at Ashtead House, Surrey, the fourth and youngest son of Captain Sir Henry Martin, RN, first baronet of Lockynge, Berkshire, who was the comptroller of the navy and member of parliament for Southampton. His mother was Eliza Anne, daughter of Harding Parker of Hilbrook, county Cork, and widow of St Leger Hayward Gillman of Gillmanville. He began his education privately at Freshford near Bath in 1780, was sent to Southampton grammar school in 1781, and then spent three years at Mr Cole's boarding school in Guildford between 1782 and 1785. Reportedly, his name was placed on the muster books of *Canada* (74) in 1780, *Foudroyant* (80) in 1782 and *Orpheus* (32) in 1783, but in his summary of naval service he mentions only being rated a captain's servant in *Foudroyant* on 23 June 1782 under Captain John Jervis, with whom he remained until 31 December 1782. He was sent on 11 August 1785 to study at the Royal (Naval) Academy, Portsmouth, and entered, or returned to, the navy in April 1786, as a captain's servant in *Pegasus* (28) under the command of Prince William Henry, later duke of Clarence, with whom he served at Newfoundland, on the North American station and in the West Indies. He following the prince on 11 March 1788 to the *Andromeda* (32), where he was rated a midshipman, and served with him in the Channel, North America and West Indies. He afterwards served for a few months each in a succession of ships: he was in *Southampton* (32) under Captain Richard Goodwin Keats; he returned on 19 May 1790 to the prince, now duke, in *Valiant* (74); in June he joined *Barfleur* (90) flying the flag of Admiral Barrington; in August he moved with him to *Royal Sovereign* (100), in which his first commander, Jervis, was captain of the fleet; and on 21 October he joined *Canada* (74), where on 22 November 1790 he was commissioned lieutenant but then came ashore in December. In April 1791 he was appointed to *Inconstant* (36) under Captain George Wilson, and he remained with him until September, when he was transferred to *Juno* (32) under Captain Samuel Hood.

Soon after the outbreak of war with France, on 22 May 1793, he was promoted master and commander of *Tisiphone*, sloop, which formed part of the Mediterranean fleet under Lord Hood. Six months later he made the step to post captain, on 5 November 1793, with an appointment to command *Modeste* (36), a French frigate which had been cut out of Genoa on 17 October. His battle honours were to increase rapidly. After service at the siege of Bastia, he was appointed on 4 July 1794 to command *Santa Margarita* (40) on the Irish station, where in 1795 he captured a French corvette, *Le Jean Bart*, and on 8 July 1796 a frigate, the *Tamise* (42), which had been captured from the British two years previously. In October of that year his tally was increased by the capture of two French privateers. In December 1796 he was appointed to command a fir-built 18-pounder frigate, *Tamar* (38), in the West Indies, where he captured nine privateers before returning to England in command of the *Dictator* (64). In command of *Fisgard* (38) on 20 October 1798 he captured *L'Immortalité* (36 or 42) after a long engagement during which *Fisgard* was at one point so damaged as to be immobilised. *L'Immortalité* had formed part of Rear-Admiral Bompart's squadron during the failed operation to land an invasion force in Loch Swilly, and had 250 soldiers on board at the time. This action considerably enhanced Martin's reputation.

Subsequently *Fisgard* formed part of the force commanded by Sir John Borlase Warren on the coast of France. In a remarkable operation on 1 July 1800 Martin sent a force of men ashore at Noirmoutier under Lieutenant Burke to burn a warship, four armed vessels and fifteen merchantmen. The landing party were then beached under a very heavy fire on the fall of the tide, and secured the retreat of over half the men only by capturing another French ship, dragging her two miles over the sands, and launching her while up to their necks in water. He came ashore on 6 December 1801, and remained ashore for the next year and a half following the peace of Amiens.

Martin married on 9 August 1798 Catherine, daughter of Captain Robert Fanshawe, resident commissioner at Plymouth. His wife's brothers included the younger Captain Robert Fanshawe and Admiral Sir Arthur Fanshawe, and she was sister-in-law of Vice-Admirals William Bedford and Sir John Chambers White, and of Admiral the Honourable Sir Robert Stopford. The couple had three sons and three daughters, of whom their eldest son was to be Admiral Sir William Fanshawe Martin, fourth baronet and their second son Admiral Sir Henry Byam Martin.

Following the renewal of the war in 1803 Martin

was put in command of ships of the line, being appointed in March 1803 to *Impetueux* (74). On 24 November 1804 while in the Channel he helped save many lives from the wreck of *Venerable* (74) in Tor Bay, Devon. On 22 December 1805 he transferred to *Prince of Wales* (98), serving in the Channel and North Sea, and in July 1807 he transferred to *Implacable* (74), which he took to the Baltic as part of the force under Sir James Saumarez and Sir Samuel Hood co-operating with the Swedes. On 26 August 1808 he attacked the Russian *Sewolod* (74) and silenced her guns in twenty minutes' firing, but was prevented from taking possession by the approach of the Russian fleet. For this service the Swedish court awarded him the insignia of a knight of the order of the Sword. In September 1808 he was appointed by Saumarez his captain of the fleet, and moved into *Victory* (100), but before the end of the year he returned to *Implacable*, where he remained until 1810. There followed a period of comfortable retirement in the *Royal Sovereign,* yacht, from August of that year to September 1811. He was promoted to rear-admiral on 1 August 1811 and returned to the Baltic between April and November 1812 with his flag flying on *Aboukir* (74), taking part in the defence of Riga against a French army commanded by Marshal Davoust. In September 1813 he was sent to Wellington's headquarters in Spain to resolve a problem with transport, flying his flag in *Creole*; and in 1814 he commanded for a while in the Scheldt with his flag in *Akbar*, before being appointed second-in-command at Plymouth.

He was made a knight bachelor in 1814, and advanced in chivalry to KCB on 2 January 1815. Following in his father's footsteps, he was appointed deputy comptroller of the navy in 1815, and held the office of comptroller of the navy from 24 February 1816 to 9 November 1831. He held the parliamentary seat for Plymouth from 1818 to 1832, and was again advanced, to GCB, on 3 March 1830. But he was dismissed from the Navy Board by King William IV, his old shipmate Prince William Henry, duke of Clarence, because he attacked from his seat in the Commons the policy of retrenchment adopted by the Whig administration.

The following year the Navy Board was abolished. Subsequently, Martin was twice offered the command-in-chief in the Mediterranean, but he declined because of his wife's health, and also because his substantial pension made further employment unnecessary. He continued to be called on to advise governments until his death, and was eventually promoted to admiral of the fleet on 13 October 1849. He died on 21 October 1854, aged eighty-one, in Portsmouth dockyard.

Lt: 22 October 1790
M-C: 22 May 1793
Capt: 5 November 1793
R-Adm: 1 August 1811
V-Adm: 12 August 1819
Adm: 22 July 1830
Admiral of the Fleet: 13 October 1849

MAURICE

VICE-ADMIRAL JAMES WILKES MAURICE made a remarkable reputation for himself through the initiative he showed in carrying out Commodore Sir Samuel Hood's plan to establish batteries on the all but inaccessible Diamond rock, close to Martinique Roads. He became identified in the official mind with garrison duties, and subsequently took command of a succession of island fortresses.

Nothing is known of Maurice's early life and parentage, apart from the fact that he was born on 10 February 1775 in Devonport. His name was entered in the books of *Monkey*, as a boy, under the command of Lieutenant James Glassford as a boy in 1783, but his real entry into the navy took place in August 1789, when he was rated an able seaman on joining the sloop *Inspector* (14) under the command of Captain Alexander Mackey. In December 1792 he joined the *Powerful* (74) as a midshipman, under the command of Captain Thomas Hicks, and sailed to the Cape of Good Hope as escort to a fleet of Indiamen, Hicks later being succeeded by Captain William Albany Otway. Maurice left his ship before she sailed to the Jamaica station because he had been subpoenaed to give evidence against a warrant officer accused of embezzling the king's stores. Unable to regain his ship, he was given a rating on board *Cambridge* (80) under the command of Captain

Richard Boyer in January 1794, at Plymouth. In May he transferred to *La Concorde* (32) commanded by Captain Sir Richard Strachan, who was later succeeded by Captain Anthony Hunt, and served in the western squadron based on Falmouth. On 23 June 1795 he was present at the capture of *Tigre*, *Alexander* and *Formidable*, ships of the line, off L'Orient, and later at the Quiberon operation commanded by Commodore Sir John Borlase Warren, who gave him in August an acting commission as lieutenant in *Thunderer* (74) under Captain Albemarle Bertie. He returned to *La Concorde* in January 1796, remaining in her when Hunt was succeeded by Captain Richard Bagot. In February 1797 he served for three weeks in Lord Bridport's flagship, *Royal George* (100), and was then again given an acting commission, in *Glory* (90), which this time the Admiralty confirmed. From 17 January 1799 to May 1802 he served as a lieutenant in *Canada* (74), in which Sir Borlase Warren was flying his broad pendant in the Channel and at Minorca, and in the late summer of 1802 he was appointed first lieutenant of *Centaur* (74), on which Sir Samuel Hood was flying his broad pendant, under orders for the West Indies. He was present at the capture of St Lucia, Tobago, Demerara and Essequibo. He was severely wounded by the explosion of the magazine during the destruction of a battery at Petite Anse d'Arlet on Martinique on 26 November 1803, and later was awarded a sword valued at £50 by the Patriotic Society.

On 8 January 1804 *Centaur* (74) was anchored close to the south side of Diamond rock, and Maurice led a party of men ashore. Three 24-pounder guns were hoisted up the precipitous and overhanging slopes and placed to command all approaches to the rock, and two long 18-pounders were taken right to the top, where a platform was created, and the rocks drilled for the ring bolts needed so that the recoil of the guns could be checked. Marshall's *Naval Biography* notes:

> Lieutenant Maurice having succeeded in scrambling up the side of the rock, and fastened one end of an 8-inch hawser to a pinnacle, the viol-block was converted into a traveller, with a purchase block lashed thereto, and the other end of the hawser set up, as a jack-stay, round the *Centaur*'s main-mast. The gun being slung to the viol, the purchase-fall was brought to the capstern. In this manner the desired object was effected in the course of a week, during which time lieutenant Maurice and the working party on shore suffered most dreadfully from excessive heat and fatigue, being constantly exposed to the sun, and frequently obliged to lower themselves down over immense precipices to attend the ascent of the guns, and bear them off from the innumerable projections against which they swung whenever the ship took a shear... Marshall 3 (Supp) 437

When ready for service, the establishment was commissioned as HM sloop *Diamond Rock* and the Admiralty confirmed Maurice's promotion and appointment to command.

For the next year he maintained his station, and supplied intelligence of the movements of the fleet under Rear-Admiral Missiessy, but there was no natural water supply on the rock, and this was to prove fatal. In May 1805 *Diamond Rock* was attacked by a force of two ships of the line, a frigate, a brig, a schooner, eleven gunboats and about 1,500 soldiers, and after a three-day resistance Maurice was obliged to surrender, owing to shortages of water and ammunition. Having surrendered his 'ship' he had to face a court martial, but was unanimously and honourably acquitted.

Nelson apologised to him for being too late in his pursuit of the Toulon fleet to Martinique to have averted the attack on *Diamond Rock*, and he arranged for him to take command on 20 August of a new brig, *Savage* (18). She was to have sailed with Nelson to Cadiz before the battle of Trafalgar, but she could not be manned in time. With Nelson's death died Maurice's hope for immediate promotion, but in July 1808 he joined the flag of Sir Alexander Cochrane at Barbados with a strong recommendation from the Admiralty that he be made post. Cochrane appointed him governor of Marie Galante on 1 October, and his commission was dated 18 January 1809.

The situation at Mariegalante was extremely difficult, on a captured island with only 400 soldiers, most of whom were dangerously ill. A black regiment greatly outnumbering the British soldiery was raised to preserve order, but there was no confidence in its loyalty. No attack was made on the island, however, before Maurice was obliged by ill health to resign his office and return to England.

In August 1810 he was appointed governor of Anholt in the Kattegat. He was given a garrison of 400 marines, and British cruisers made any attempt by the Danes to land a force on the island possible only for the few weeks at the beginning and end of the winter freeze, when the cruisers would be off station. On 27 March 1811 he reported that he had received warning of an impending Danish attack, but:

> as every exertion had been made to complete the works as well as our materials would allow, and as picquets were nightly stationed from one extreme of the island to the other, in order to prevent surprise, I awaited with confidence the meditated attack.... The enemy's flotilla and army, consisting in all of nearly four thousand men, have this day, after a close combat of four hours and a half, received a most complete and decisive defeat, and are fled back to their ports, with the loss of three pieces of cannon, and upwards of five hundred prisoners: a number greater by one hundred and fifty men than the garrison I command.

The editor of the *Naval Chronicle* commented:

> It is proper to mention, that the assailing force consisted of a Danish flotilla, of 33 sail, amongst which, according to our Gazette account, were 18 heavy gun-boats, carrying nearly 3,000 men. Our little garrison, including officers, seamen, marines, &c, amounted to only 350 men;

yet, with the loss of only two killed and 30 wounded, we killed the Danish commander, three other officers, and 50 men; and took prisoners, besides the wounded, five captains, nine lieutenants, and 504 rank and file! Three pieces of artillery, 500 muskets, and 16,000 rounds of cartridge, also fell into our possession; and two gun-boats, and 250 more prisoners, were taken by his Majesty's ships *Sheldrake* and *Tartar*, in their retreat! [NC 25.343–9.]

These ships had just arrived, and their presence was unknown to the Danes at the time they made their attempt.

The garrison of Anholt presented Maurice with a sword in recognition of his achievement, and he remained there in command until September or October 1812. That ended his active service. On 5 October 1814 he married Sarah Lyne of Plymouth, but, alas, she died of the typhus fever in June 1815, aged twenty-one. Maurice did not remarry, and lived on until 4 September 1857, when he died, aged eighty-two, in East Emma Place, East Stonehouse, Plymouth, Devon.

Lt: 3 April 1797
Cmdr: 7 May 1804
Capt: 18 January 1809
Retired R-Adm: 1 October 1846
V-Adm: 28 May 1853

MIDDLETON – *see* Barham

MILLER

CAPTAIN RALPH WILLETT MILLER was a heroic leader and a humane commander, whose reputation was such that in August 1796 Nelson, as a commodore, selected Miller to be his captain in HMS *Captain*. Together they fought at the battle of Cape St Vincent on 14 February 1797. Miller was an amateur artist, and recorded Nelson's tactical initiative at Cape St Vincent when he ordered *Captain* to wear out of the line to prevent the junction of two parts of the Spanish fleet, thus exposing his ship unsupported to greatly unequal odds. Miller was in the habit of sending such sketches to his wife Ann (known as Nancy), along with long descriptive letters of his actions. In May he transferred with Nelson to *Theseus* (74), and transformed a mutinous crew into a loyal and determined one which fought at the battle of the Nile, and later at Acre. There, while engaged in intercepting a French squadron, he was killed by the accidental explosion of a quantity of French shells with faulty fuses which had been collected to fire back at the enemy. In his will he left a moving testimony to his love for his wife and his two daughters Charlotte Sophia (born 1791) and Maria Elizabeth (born 1792).

He had been born on 24 January 1762 in New York, a son of a Mr Miller and his wife Maria, née Willett, who was of the family of the first English mayor of Manhattan. They were loyalists, and were to lose all their property to the American rebels. Ralph was educated at the Royal (Naval) Academy at Portsmouth by his grandfather, and it was the daughter of his master, George Witchell, whom he eventually took to wife. He went to sea in 1778 in *Ardent* (64) flying the flag of Rear-Admiral James Gambier, and served in all the major actions of the American war, being wounded three times. He was commissioned lieutenant on 25 May 1781.

At the time of the French declaration of war in February 1793 he was serving in *Windsor Castle* (90). He was nearly drowned twice during the evacuation from Toulon on 18 December, but he acquired a great respect for Captain Sir Sidney Smith, who had been put in charge of the destruction of the French fleet and arsenal. He was subsequently transferred to *Victory* (100) as third lieutenant, and was employed in the boats and on shore in the sieges of San Fiorenzo, Bastia and Calvi. It was at Calvi that he first met Nelson. He disappointed the commander-in-chief, Lord Hotham, when he volunteered to make a fireship attack against some French ships, for which purpose he was promoted commander on 1 July 1794. Five attempts were frustrated by the wind. He subsequently learnt that his name was on a confidential list of officers not recommended for promotion, but he was able to make his number with Sir John Jervis when he assumed command. On 12 January 1796 he was made post captain, and he was appointed to *Mignonne* and then to *Unité*, both frigates. In the latter he was employed in the Adriatic, where he helped to stabilise Austrian resistance to the French. He made a strong impression with his fellow captains, and with Jervis.

At Cape St Vincent, Santa Cruz de Tenerife, the Nile and Acre, he demonstrated that his gentle and humane parts were linked with great fortitude. His death at the age of thirty-seven was a great loss to the navy. The government granted pensions of £100 a year for life to his widow, and £25 each to his daughters until such time as they should marry. His brother officers jointly subscribed the sum of £500 for a memorial sculpted by Flaxman, which was erected in St Paul's Cathedral. Ann remarried, uniting with Captain Edward Kittoe, RN, and died in May 1808 in Bath, Somerset.

Lt: 25 May 1781
Cmdr: 1 July 1794
Capt: 12 January 1796

MILNE

ADMIRAL SIR DAVID MILNE, GCB, was a daring and successful frigate captain in the wars against Revolutionary and imperial France.

He was born on 25 May 1763 in Musselburgh, Edinburghshire, the first son of David Milne, merchant of Cample House, Musselburgh, and his wife Susan, daughter of Robert Vernor. He entered the navy on 26 May 1779 as a midshipman in *Canada* (74) and served in the American war under the command of Captain Hugh Dalrymple, and later of the Honourable George Falconar, who in turn was replaced by Sir George Collier. Milne stayed with her when *Canada* was paid off and recommissioned on 6 July 1779 under the command of the Honourable Captain William Cornwallis. In *Canada* he saw action during the relief of Gibraltar in 1780, at Sir Samuel Hood's actions at Basseterre, St Kitts, on 25–7 January 1782, at Dominica on 9 April and at the battle of the Saintes on 12 April 1782, following which he was rated master's mate. He weathered the hurricane of 17 September during the return passage to England, and *Canada* was finally paid off on 27 October.

He was appointed to the *Elizabeth* (74) under the command of Captain Robert Kingsmill the following day, but she was paid off on 29 March 1783 at the peace, and Milne found employment in the East India Company. He did not return to the navy until the Nootka Sound crisis in 1790, when on 6 July he was rated an able seaman in *Eurydice* (24) under the command of Captain George Lumsdaine. She was paid off on 17 December 1791, and he was again unemployed by the navy until 14 September, when, for six weeks, he joined *Aurora*, before being rated a master's mate on 31 October in *Boyne* (98) flying the flag of Vice-Admiral Sir John Jervis as commander-in-chief in the West Indies.

Jervis commissioned Milne lieutenant on 13 January 1794 and appointed him in June to *Blanche*, frigate, and he was still serving in her when she engaged *Le Pique* on 5 January 1795, at which time she was commanded by Captain Robert Faulknor, who was killed during action. Following the enemy's striking their colours, Milne distinguished himself by swimming with some seamen to take possession. As a result he was promoted commander of *Inspector* (14), on 26 April 1795, and after serving successfully as superintendent of transports, he was on 2 October made post captain with appointment to command *Matilda* (28), but told to continue his work with the transports while his lieutenant cruised for prizes.

In January 1796 he was appoint to command *Pique* (34), and while employed in protection of trade at Demerara he undertook, on his own authority, to escort trade to join convoy at St Kitts. When it was discovered that the convoy had sailed, he further extended his instructions by escorting the Demerara ships all the way to England, arriving at Spithead on 10 October. His conduct was approved, and he was ordered to join the Channel fleet. He was necessarily involved in the Spithead mutiny in May 1797, and when that was settled, he was employed on the coast of France. He lost his ship in action with the enemy on 29 June 1798 when *Pique*, the 18-pounder frigate *Jason* (38) and the French frigate *Seine* all went aground. *Pique* was bilged, and had to be abandoned and burnt.

Seine had been obliged to surrender, and when she was brought into British service Milne was appointed to command her, bringing with him all the officers and men from *Pique*.

He was employed in October 1799 in a voyage to west Africa, and then in convoying the African trade to the West Indies. On 20 August 1800 he engaged *Vengeance* (52) in the Mona passage. Milne chased her for two days and nights, occasionally engaging, and finally brought her to close action. The *Naval Chronicle* wrote that 'This action was justly considered by naval men, as one of the most brilliant fought during the war between single ships, an uncommon degree of skill, and indefatigable exertion, being necessary, to keep sight of, as well as conquer, a very superior ship.' [NC 36.364]

La Seine was paid off at the conclusion of peace, but on the renewal of war Milne was reappointed to her, only to lose her on 23 June 1803 by grounding near the Texel. 'There are few circumstances in the life of a naval commander', observed the *Naval Chronicle*, 'which gives so much pain and vexation to him as the loss of his ship.' The court martial laid the blame entirely on the ship's pilots, who were ordered to serve two years' penal servitude. Milne was himself exonerated, but his attempt to protect the pilots at the trial, and his contemptuous observations about the board, led to his being obliged to make do with command of the sea fencibles on the Firth of Forth until that force was disbanded in 1811. He married on 16 April 1804, in Inverness, Grace, daughter of Sir Alexander Purves, baronet, of Purves Hall. The couple had two sons, the youngest of whom was to grow to be Admiral of the Fleet Sir Alexander Milne, GCB.

Milne returned to sea duty in 1811, with command of a succession of ships of the line. He served in *Impétueux* (74) off Cherbourg and on the Lisbon station, was then appointed to the *Dublin*, and from her was transferred to *Venerable* (74), reportedly one of the poorest sailing ships in the service, but Milne was able to transform her into a flyer by a readjustment of her stowage. He afterwards commanded the *Bulwark* (74) on the coast of North America, participating in the capture of Castine on the Penobscot.

He was promoted rear-admiral on 4 June 1814, and returned to England in November as a passenger. His wife died on 4 October 1814 in Bordeaux, France, during the period of Napoleon's exile at Elba.

Following the conclusion of the war, in May 1816, Milne was appointed commander-in-chief on the North American station, flying his flag in the 24-pounder *Leander* (50), but his sailing was delayed to permit his serving as second-in-command to Admiral Lord Exmouth at Algiers. He was moved into *Impregnable* (100), and during the action she suffered the loss of 210 men killed and wounded. This heavy butcher's bill was a result of Milne's failure to ensure that his flag captain complied with instructions to moor close under the walls of the batteries. He was nevertheless invested KCB on 19 September 1816, and received knighthoods from the Netherlands and Sicily.

He proceeded to his command in North American waters in 1817, staying there until 1819, and on 19 September, shortly before he returned home, he married for a second time, taking for his wife Agnes, daughter of George Stephen of Grenada. He was elected to parliament for Berwick-upon-Tweed in 1820. He was promoted vice-admiral on 27 May 1825, and nominated GCB on 4 July 1840. He returned to active service late in life, as commander-in-chief Plymouth from April 1842 to April 1845, accepting the command so as to be able to provide preferment for his son Alexander. His health soon made him wish to retire, and he died with the rank of admiral on 5 May 1845, aged eighty-one, on his passage from London to Granton Pier, Scotland, in the *Clarence*, steamer. Agnes died on 27 January 1862.

> Lt: 13 January 1794
> Cmdr: 26 April 1795
> Capt: 2 October 1795
> R-Adm: 4 June 1814
> V-Adm: 27 May 1825
> Adm: 23 November 1841

MITCHELL

ADMIRAL SIR ANDREW MITCHELL, KB, was described by the editor of the *Naval Chronicle* in 1806: 'No one, better than Sir Andrew Mitchell,

knew how to preserve that spirit of subordination which is essential to the interests of the Navy; yet no one lived on better terms with, or was more beloved by, his officers. Like a father among his children, his sole care seemed centred in the wish to make them happy. Sir Andrew was extremely fond of music; and, being generally provided with an excellent band, it was his custom, every evening, when professional duties did not interfere, to assemble such of his officers who were not on duty, in the great cabin, there to enjoy the concert which he provided. When obliged to part with his officers, several of whom were educated on his quarter-deck, and are now post captains, he could scarcely refrain from tears.' [NC 16.89]

He was born in 1757, the second son of Charles Mitchell of Pittedie and later of Baldridge near Dunfermline, Fife. His mother, who raised him on her own, following her husband's death two years after Andrew's birth, was Margaret, daughter of William Forbes, Writer to the Signet. He was educated at the High School in Edinburgh, and entered the navy in 1771 on the *Deal Castle* (20). In 1776 he sailed to the East Indies as a midshipman on board *Rippon* (54) commanded by Commodore, later Admiral, Sir Edward Vernon. Mitchell was commissioned lieutenant on 11 October 1777 in *Coventry* (28), and first experienced action off the coast of Coromandel against a French squadron commanded by M. Tranjolly, after which he was made post captain in *Coventry*, with his rank confirmed on 25 October 1778. Vernon was succeeded in 1779 by Rear-Admiral Sir Edward Hughes, but *Coventry* did not return to England at that time. On 12 August 1782 Mitchell had a notable action against a French frigate of superior force, and although he did not succeed in taking her, he did bring intelligence of the arrival of the French fleet commanded by Admiral de Suffren at Ceylon. This led to his being promoted to *Sultan* (74), and after the fleet was hit by a hurricane off Madras, Hughes shifted his flag into her. Mitchell remained on the station following the conclusion of the peace of Paris as commodore of a small squadron flying his broad pendant in the *Defence* (74), and returning to England

Sir Andrew Mitchell, K.B.,
Admiral of the Blue Squadron,
engraved by H R Cook after Robert Bowyer,
published by Joyce Gold, 103 Shoe Lane,
30 August 1806.

in 1786. He acquired a great deal of prize money during his ten years in Asian waters, but it was all lost when his agent declared bankruptcy. He was appointed to command the *Asia* (74) at the time of the Nootka Sound incident in 1790, but she was paid off on the resolution of the dispute.

The French declaration of war in February 1793 did not immediately bring Mitchell employment. He waited two years until he was appointed to command *Impregnable* (90), and then almost immediately afterwards he was promoted rear-admiral, on 1 June 1795. He was promoted again to vice-admiral on 14 February 1799, but did not hoist his flag until April 1799 on *Zealand* (64) at the Nore.

He was then moved to *Isis* (50) in the Downs to take command under Admiral Duncan of the naval part of the operations in August to restore the Stadtholder to the throne of the Netherlands, supported by a Russian squadron. Having successfully landed the duke of York's army, he received the surrender of the Dutch fleet at the Helder and Texel from Admiral Storey, who hoisted the colours of the house of Orange because his crews would not fight.

The capture of twenty-five ships of the line and three Indiamen effectively eliminated the Dutch threat, and completed the work begun by Duncan at the battle of Camperdown in October 1797. Following the duke of York's request for an armistice, Mitchell had to withdraw his ships from the Zuyder Zee.

In proposing a vote of thanks in parliament, Dundas, later Lord Melville, recorded that:

> The armament, destined for Holland, sailed with very fair weather which continued for two or three days; but early on the morning of the third day, there arose a very heavy, and, for the time of the year, a very uncommon storm. In this storm this gallant Admiral had the conduct of an armament of two hundred transports of various descriptions, subject to no military discipline, from the nature of things; and in this condition that Admiral conducted the whole of this mass for ten or twelve days; he kept them together, immense as they were, and brought them in safety to their place of landing; an event that could not have taken place, but from consummate skill, unremitting perseverance, and great exertion.

He was inducted into the order of the Bath on 8 January 1800, and presented by the City of London with a sword valued at 100 guineas.

He was promoted admiral on 9 November 1805, and died on 26 February 1806, aged forty-eight, in Bermuda, while commander-in-chief of the Halifax station, Nova Scotia.

When it was he married is not known, but he had three sons, all of whom became captains in the Royal Navy. His wife died in 1803 when Mitchell was at Bermuda, and when he was commanding at Halifax he married again, taking as his wife the daughter of the judge-advocate of Nova Scotia. His second wife gave him a daughter, Martha Maria, who married a captain in the navy.

Lt: 11 October 1777
Capt: 25 October 1778
R-Adm: 1 June 1795
V-Adm: 14 February 1799
Adm: 9 November 1805

MONTAGU

ADMIRAL SIR GEORGE MONTAGU, GCB, has the misfortune to be known as the man who failed to intercept the grain convoy bound for Brest which was the occasion for the battle of the Glorious First of June in 1794, and subsequently failed to bring the defeated and retreating Brest fleet to action.

He was born on 12 December 1750, the second son of Admiral John Montagu and his wife Sophia, daughter and coheiress of James Wroughton of Wilcot, Wiltshire. He was sent in 1763 to be educated at the Royal (Naval) Academy, Portsmouth, and entered the navy in 1766 as a midshipman in *Preston* (50) under the command of Captain Alan Gardner and flying the flag of Rear-Admiral William (?) Parry, commander-in-chief at Jamaica. He was rated master's mate when he followed Gardner to *Levant* (28) in 1769, and returned to England as a midshipman in *Bellona* (74) under the command of his father. In 1771 he joined *Namur* (90) under the command of Captain Griffiths, and served in her under Captain Bickerton after he was commissioned lieutenant on 14 January 1771. He was soon afterwards appointed to the *Captain* (60) flying his father's flag as a rear-admiral and together they served in the American theatre. He was promoted master and commander on 9 April 1773 with an appointment to the ship-sloop *Kingsfisher* (14), and post captain on 15 April 1774 in *Fowey* (20). He had a very active service during the early part of the American war, especially in the embarkation of the army at Boston in March and in the occupation of New York in October 1776. He was then obliged for reasons of his health to return to England, and from 1777 to 1779 he served as flag captain of *Romney* (50) under his father at Newfoundland. Afterwards he was appointed to command *Pearl* (32) and was actively employed in European and North American waters, returning to England in 1782.

During the Nootka Sound crisis of 1790 Montagu was appointed to the *Hector* (74), which was kept in commission and was ordered out to the Leeward Islands with Rear-Admiral Gardner following the French declaration of war in February 1793. From there Montagu continued to Jamaica to convoy the homeward-bound trade, after which he served with the squadron in the Downs under Rear-Admiral John MacBride. On 12 April 1794 he was promoted to rear-admiral, hoisting his flag in the *Hector* (74) as part of the Channel fleet under Lord Howe.

His part in the operations before and after the battle of the Glorious First of June began on 4 May when he was detached with a squadron of six sail of the line to convoy a large fleet of merchant ships as far as Cape Finisterre, and then to cruise to the west until 20 May in the hope of meeting the French convoy daily expected from Norfolk, Virginia. Failing to make the interception, despite remaining at sea several days beyond his orders, he returned to Plymouth on 30 May. By then Howe was at sea looking for the Brest fleet, which had sailed to meet the convoy from Norfolk, and on 2 June he received orders from the Admiralty to sail again to look for the convoy off Brest. Before he left on the 4th, word arrived of the action on 28 May, but there was no change in Montagu's orders. He had been able to gather nine ships, and with them he chased a French squadron of eight ships into Brest on the evening of the 8th. Next morning at dawn, nineteen of the Brest fleet were sighted to the west, with some ships in tow and others under jury masts, but he judged them still a greatly superior force and contented himself with trying to draw them away from their harbour in hope that Howe would arrive to complete their destruction. This might have served, but Howe had not been in a physical state after four days of action to make or even order a vigorous pursuit. After a brief show of chasing Montagu's force, the French admiral Villaret-Joyeuse entered Brest.

Although he was subsequently promoted vice-admiral on 1 June 1795 and admiral on 1 January 1801, Montagu was never again employed in an operational command. Howe and the Admiralty had both expressed their approval of his strategic decision. However, he had sought leave for health reasons after the action, perhaps in part because of the death of his brother James in the action on 1 June, and by the time he was feeling like returning to work, the mud had stuck. In 1803 he was appointed commander at Portsmouth, and in that capacity, ironically, he had the duty in 1806 of presiding at the court martial of Sir Robert Calder, who was tried for making a similar difficult decision to avoid action with a superior enemy. He was nominated GCB on 2 January 1815.

He married in 1783 his first cousin, Charlotte, daughter and coheiress of George Wroughton of Wilcot. The couple had three sons and two daughters. He died on 24 December 1829, aged seventy-nine, at Stowell Lodge, Wiltshire.

> Lt: 14 January 1771
> M-C: 9 April 1773
> Capt: 15 April 1774
> R-Adm: 12 April 1794
> V-Adm: 1 June 1795
> Adm: 1 January 1801

MONTAGU

CAPTAIN JAMES MONTAGU, born on 12 August 1752, the third son of Admiral John Montagu and his wife, Sophia, and brother of Admiral George Montagu, had seen service in North America and the East Indies in the American war. On the French declaration of war in 1793 he requested appointment to the *Montagu* (74) because of her name. Following his death in action at the age of forty-one at the battle of the Glorious First of June in 1794, he was buried at sea. A monument was commissioned, by Flaxman, which was placed in Westminster Abbey. There is another memorial in St Cyriac, Lacock, Wiltshire.

> Lt: 18 October 1771
> Cmdr: 11 September 1773
> Capt: 14 November 1775

MOORE

ADMIRAL SIR GRAHAM MOORE, GCB, is best known for his command of the frigates sent to intercept Spanish treasure ships in October 1804 to prevent their cargoes reaching the French. Britain was not at war with Spain at the time, and by a disastrous oversight Moore was given only four frigates to stop four Spanish frigates. Lacking a decisive and apparent superiority of force, he was not able to bring to the Spanish ships without firing into them, and the consequence was that one of them blew up, killing 240 people, many of whom were women and children. The prize money made Moore a very wealthy man.

A brother of Lieutenant-General Sir John Moore, baronet, who was killed in the heroic stand on the beach at Corunna on 16 January 1809, Graham Moore was born in 1764 in Glasgow, the third son of Dr John Moore, MD, of Dovehill, and his wife Jane, the youngest daughter of the Revd James Simpson, professor of divinity in the University of Glasgow. He entered the navy in June or July 1777 as captain's servant in *Prince George* (98), a guardship at Spithead commanded by Captain Middleton. In August or September he transferred to *Trident* (64) under the command of Captain John Elliot, with whom he served in the Channel, in the North American station and in the West Indies until April 1780, when he joined *Pegasus* (28) under Captain Bazeley as a supernumerary midshipman for passage home. He then joined *Champion* (24) under Captain Charles Hamilton, and served in the Channel fleet until the end of the year. He then joined *Romney* (50) flying Commodore Johnston's broad pendant, and served in the expedition to capture the Dutch settlement at the Cape of Good Hope.

He received his lieutenant's commission on 8 March 1782 in the *Crown* (64), in which he served under Lord Howe in the relief of Gibraltar, and with the engagement with the Franco-Spanish fleet off Cape Spartel in October 1782.

With the conclusion of the peace of Paris, like so many naval officers in the period, he spent time in France studying the language. However, he soon found employment, being appointed to *Perseus* (20) in which he served under Captain George Palmer in the Irish Channel until 1787, when he transferred to *Dido* (28) lying at Spithead under Captain Charles Sandys, and later that year followed him to *Adamant* (50), on which Sir Richard Hughes flew his flag as commander-in-chief at Halifax. On 22 November 1790 he was promoted master and commander, and he was appointed on 3 June to a sloop, *Bonetta* (16). Again he returned to the Newfoundland station, and later to the West Indies; he returned in her to England in

1793 at the time of the French declaration of war.

He continued in her until he was made post captain on 2 April 1794, but before then he had served during the winter of 1792–3 as acting captain of *Assistance* (44) flying Commodore the Honourable George Murray's broad pendant in the Scheldt. On 8 June he was appointed to command the *Syren* (32) in the North Sea, and subsequently on the coast of France in the squadron under the command of Sir Richard Strachan. In her and later in command of the 18-pounder frigate *Melampus* (36) he proved a successful frigate captain. In the summer of 1798 he served in Sir John Borlase Warren's squadron on the coast of Ireland, and took part in the action against Rear-Admiral Bompart's invasion force on 12–14 October, taking the surrender of *La Résolue* (40), which had a crew strengthened to 500 with embarked soldiers. He was ordered out to the West Indies in February 1800, but his health collapsed and he was invalided home in August 1801.

He was fit to return to duty on the renewal of the war following the peace of Amiens, and appointed in July 1804 to command *Indefatigable* (46) for Channel service. The action against the Spanish frigates in 1804 did not immediately lead to a Spanish declaration of war, because there was little enthusiasm in Spain for Napoleon. It was not until December that Madrid felt it had no option, and not until 24 January 1805 that Britain reciprocated with a declaration of its own. Moore used his share of the prize money to acquire the estate of Brook Farm at Cobham in Surrey.

He commanded *Fame* from 29 October 1805 to May 1806. He then had over a year ashore before he was appointed to command *Marlborough* (74) in August 1807. He was employed serving in Tagus station, and in the winter of 1808 Sir Sidney Smith detached him with a squadron, flying a commodore's broad pendant, to escort the Portuguese fleet to Brazil. They arrived at Rio de Janeiro on 7 March, and the prince regent invested Moore with the insignia of the order of the Tower and the Sword.

In the autumn of 1809 Moore was employed under Sir Richard Strachan at Flushing, taking charge, during the evacuation of the port, of the destruction of its basin, arsenal and defences. In August 1811 he declined an offer to command the yacht *Royal Sovereign*, and on 3 March 1812 he was appointed to *Chatham* (74). Following his promotion to rear-admiral on 12 August 1812 Moore hoisted his flag in *Vigo* (74) as commander-in-chief in the Baltic, where he remained until 12 April 1814. Between 5 May 1815 and 23 June he served in command of *Ville de Paris* (110) under Lord Keith in the Channel fleet.

He was forty-eight when on 9 March 1812 he married Dora, eldest daughter of Thomas Eden, deputy auditor of Greenwich hospital, and sister of Admiral Henry Eden. The couple lived at Hill Street, Westminster, and had one son. Moore was made a KCB on 2 January 1815, and was ordered to serve as second-in-command in the Mediterranean at the time of Napoleon's escape from Elba, shifting his flag into *Caledonia*, but the orders were cancelled. Instead, he served as commissioner of the Admiralty from 24 May 1816 until 13 March 1820 when, having been promoted vice-admiral on 12 August 1819, he shifted into *Rochford* to command in the Mediterranean, replacing Sir Thomas Fremantle on the latter's sudden death. On 28 September 1820 the Ionian Republic nominated him a knight grand cross of the order of St Michael and St George, and he was advanced in British chivalry to GCB on 11 March 1836. He was promoted to admiral on 10 January 1837, and served as commander-in-chief Plymouth between 1839 and 1842. He died on 25 November 1843, aged seventy-nine, at Brook Farm.

> Lt: 8 March 1782
> M-C: 22 November 1790
> Capt: 2 April 1794
> R-Adm: 12 August 1812
> V-Adm: 12 August 1819
> Adm: 10 January 1837

MORRIS

VICE-ADMIRAL SIR JAMES NICOLL MORRIS, KCB, commanded *Colossus* (74) at the battle of Trafalgar on 21 October 1805, and was wounded. His ship suffered more than any other in the British fleet, losing forty killed and 160 wounded.

He was born in 1763, the only child of Captain

John Morris, RN, under whose patronage he entered the navy. On 19 January 1772 he was put into the books of the ship-sloop *Otter* (14) as captain's servant, or 'quarterdeck youngster', under his father's command while he was serving in Newfoundland and on the Labrador coast. With scarcely a break, he was then transferred to *Resolution* (74) serving as a guardship at Portsmouth under the command of Captain Hallowell, coming ashore on 13 July 1775. Young Morris may have spent the next years at school. His father was mortally wounded at the attack on Sullivan's Island on 2 July 1776, but nearly two years later, on 31 March 1778, James Nicoll was rated midshipman when he joined *Prince of Wales* (74), flagship of Rear-Admiral Samuel Barrington in the West Indies. He transferred to *Ariadne* (20) in October and served under Captain Thomas King in the Leeward Islands, in the capture of St Lucia, in two defensive actions against the Comte de Grasse and in the battle off Grenada, during which *Ariadne* served as repeating frigate. On 27 November 1779 he transferred to a sloop, *Fortune* (10), under the command of Lewis Robinson. She was fitting for service in the West Indies, and Morris sailed as far as Cork, but then returned to Portsmouth in the 9-pounder frigate *Amphitrite* (24), where on 12 January 1780 he joined *Barfleur* (90), in which Barrington was now flying his flag in the Channel fleet.

Commissioned lieutenant on 14 September 1780 when he transferred into *Queen* (90), he subsequently transferred again into *Namur* (90) under the command of Captain Herbert Sawyer and later Captain Robert Fanshaw. He served in her in the Channel fleet and at the relief of Gibraltar. Crossing the Atlantic, he fought under Admiral Sir George Rodney in the battle of the Saintes on 12 April 1782. He came ashore on 6 June 1783 following the conclusion of peace.

During the peace, he was continuously employed from the time he was appointed to *Leander* (50) on 23 August 1786, moving in sequence into *Orion* (74), *Arrogant* (74), *Barfleur* and *Royal George* (100), the last-named ships serving as Barrington's flagship during the 1790 Nootka Sound crisis. On

21 September of that year he was promoted commander for rank, and on 2 January 1791 he was appointed to a brig, *Flirt* (14), in which he served in the Channel and in the West Indies. He left his ship on 28 November, and was appointed on 26 December to *Pluto* (14), on which he served in the Newfoundland station under Rear-Admiral Richard King.

There, following the French declaration of war in February 1793, he captured a privateer, *Lutine* (16). In recognition of his achievement, he was made post captain on 7 October 1793 in a 12-pounder frigate, *Boston* (32), in which he continued to capture privateers. In 1798, when in command of *Lively* (26), he had the misfortune to be wrecked near Cadiz, but on 14 July 1799 he was nevertheless appointed to command the 18-pounder frigate *Phaeton* (38). On 4 September at Portsmouth the earl of Elgin came on board *en embassy* to the Porte. *Phaeton* arrived at the Dardanelles on 2 November and thence proceeded to Constantinople. In the spring of 1800 she was employed on the coast of Genoa in support of General Ott.

In the spring of 1802 Morris returned home with Lord Keith's dispatches. He resigned his command on 27 February, and married on 25 October Margaretta Sarah, second daughter of Thomas Somers Cocks of Downing Street, Westminster, who was a banker at Charing Cross. She was a niece of Charles Cocks, first Lord Somers, and sister-in-law of Admiral Sir William Hargood.

Following the renewal of the war, Morris was on 12 July 1803 put in command of the sea fencibles between Blackwater and the Stour, but he did not stay there long. On 10 October he was put in command of *Leopard* (50), and he then moved on 11 May 1804 into *Colossus*, a new seventy-four. He was employed for eighteen months in the blockade of Brest under Admiral Cornwallis before being ordered in October 1805 to join the fleet under Lord Nelson off Cadiz. At the battle of Trafalgar, *Colossus* was the sixth ship in the lee line, following Collingwood. Morris was severely wounded in the thigh but was able to remain on deck until the close of the action, using a tourniquet to control the bleeding. After the battle,

Colossus was paid off on 29 December, but on 5 July 1806 Morris recommissioned her and joined St Vincent at Lisbon. Later he was employed under Rear-Admirals the Honourable Michael De Courcy and Eliab Harvey off Ferrol, and in the Channel fleet under Admiral Lord Gardner. Then he joined Rear-Admiral Sir Richard Strachan in pursuit of a French squadron to the Mediterranean, where he joined Lord Collingwood. He left his ship again on 9 August 1808 and was then ashore until 1 April 1810, when he was appointed to *Formidable* (98) and employed in the Baltic under Vice-Admiral Sir James Saumarez. He was nominated colonel of the Royal Marines on 31 July 1810, was promoted rear-admiral on 1 August 1811, and in 1812, at the request of Sir James Saumarez, was appointed third in command in the Baltic with his flag in *Vigo* (74). In his summary of services, he wrote that he was employed 'escorting the Russian fleet through the Great Belt to Wango sound, and then under Rear-Admiral Sir George Johnstone Hope to Houley Bay', and subsequently 'passed the great convoy which had wintered at Carlscrona through the sound to Wango, and then returned home'.

Following the end of the war he was nominated KCB on 2 January 1815. He was promoted vice-admiral on 12 August 1819, and died on 15 April 1830, aged sixty-six, at his house in Marlow, Buckinghamshire. He was buried in Marlow church, where there is a memorial. His wife died in January 1842.

Lt: 14 September 1780
M-C: 21 September 1790
Capt: 7 October 1793
R-Adm: 1 August 1811
V-Adm: 12 August 1819

MOUNSEY

CAPTAIN WILLIAM MOUNSEY, CB, was a forty-three-year-old commander when he fought an epic battle that not only made his reputation, but led to general promotion throughout his ship. On 18 April 1809 he was appointed to command *Bonne Citoyenne* mounting eighteen 32-pounder carronades and two long 9-pounders. Despite this force, she was not rated as a 'post' ship, but after a seven-hour engagement with *La Furieuse*, a frigate armed *en flute*, the first lord of the Admiralty, Lord Mulgrave, notified him of the award of a medal and promotion to post rank with appointment to command his prize. He went on to advise him that his lieutenant, Symes, was being promoted to commander, requesting that Mounsey supply him with 'the names of the warrant officers of the *Bonne Citoyenne*, with a view to their promotion in their several ranks; together with the name of the mate, or midshipman, whom you shall recommend for the rank of lieutenant, and the names of any very meritorious petty officers severally under the boatswain, gunner, and carpenter, who may be deserving of promotion, and qualified to receive it. I trust', he added, 'that this general promotion, through every rank serving in the *Bonne Citoyenne*, may be a satisfactory testimony of my estimation of the action which has been achieved; and may operate as an incentive to others, to emulate an example so worthy of imitation and applause.' Marshall 2 (Supp) 26

Mounsey was born in 1766, the fifth son of George Mounsey of Carlisle and his wife Margaret, daughter of John Stephenson. He entered the navy on 23 February 1780 as a midshipman on *Royal Oak* (74) and sailed in May under the command of Captain Digby Dent to reinforce Vice-Admiral Arbuthnot in North America. He followed Dent into *Raisonnable* (64), which was so much battered by a hurricane while making a return voyage to England that she was immediately paid off. He then followed Dent into *Repulse* (64) and *Cumberland* (74), in which last he served in the East Indies and took part in the action against M. de Suffren off Cuddalore on 20 June 1783. He returned to England in May 1784 and served in *Orestes* (18) under Captain Manley Dixon. He was rated master's mate when he joined *Arethusa* (32) under Captain John Stanhope in 1789, and then served successively in *Duke* (90), *Juno* (32) and *Victory* (100), until the last ship, flying the flag of Lord Hood, sailed for the Mediterranean following the French declaration of war on 1 February 1793.

He had passed his examination on 3 December 1788, and now received his lieutenant's commission on 22 May and appointment to the *Ardent* (64), under Captain Robert Manners Sutton, which was to form part of the Mediterranean fleet. In July, at Gibraltar, he again transferred, into the 12-pounder frigate *Lowestoffe* (32) commanded by Captain William Wolseley, under whose orders he played a very active part in the occupation of Toulon, the attack on Fornelli in Corsica and the capture of San Fiorenzo, Bastia and Calvi. He then returned to home waters and served in *L'Imperieuse* (40), *Trident* (64) and *Impregnable* (90), returned to *Duke*, and served in *Defiance* (74) and finally *Clyde* (38) under Captain Charles Cunningham, with whom he remained until 29 April 1802; he was then promoted to commander of *Rosario,* sloop, in which he served in the Channel, the Irish station and the West Indies until 5 September 1808. His appointment to *Bonne Citoyenne* was dated 19 April 1809, and his post captain's commission was dated 6 July 1809, the date of the action between *Bonne Citoyenne* and *Furieuse*. The repairs needed on the prize were so extensive, however, that it was not before November 1811 that Mounsey was able to commission her.

He was then actively engaged in the Mediterranean for the remainder of the war, most particularly in the capture of Ponza on 26 February 1813 under the command of Captain Charles Napier, and under Sir Josias Rowley in the capture of Via Reggio, the unsuccessful attack on Leghorn in December 1813, the occupation of Santa Maria and other forts in the Gulf of Spezia and the capture of Genoa and its dependencies in March and April 1814. After the conclusion of peace in Europe, he was employed in transporting the 62nd Regiment to Halifax, after which he was engaged in the operations in the Penobscot river. Following the peace with the United States he commanded a small naval force left to help in the fortification of the Castine peninsula.

With the final defeat of Napoleon, Mounsey retired from active service. He was nominated a CB on 4 June 1815, and died on 25 September 1830, aged sixty-four.

Lt: 22 May 1793
Capt: 6 July 1809

MURRAY

VICE-ADMIRAL SIR GEORGE MURRAY, KCB, is perhaps most interesting for what his life tells about the patronage needed for promotion, and the responsibilities borne in this respect by senior officers. But he is best known for his special relationship with Nelson.

He was born in January 1759, in Chichester, son of Alderman Gideon Murray, who was a justice of the peace. His mother's name is not known, but he had a grandfather who was an officer of the marines and had settled in Chichester. In 1770 he entered the navy as a captain's servant in the *Niger* (32) commanded by Captain Francis Banks, when he was only eleven years old, and he had his baptism of fire when he sailed in *Bristol* (50) in December 1775 in the squadron commanded by Commodore Sir Peter Parker with orders to capture Charlestown, North Carolina. During that operation *Bristol* was so heavily exposed to red-hot shot from the American batteries that she was on fire twice, and only the commodore survived on the upper deck without injury. During operations against the French fleet Murray made such a good impression on Vice-Admiral Lord Howe that he was persuaded to accept a transfer to Howe's flagship.

This ought to have been a good career move, but, in the words of the *Naval Chronicle,*

> it is certain that Lord Howe returned to England in great disgust; and, what was deeply to be regretted, as casting a shade upon his lordship's character, notwithstanding the recommendations which he had had of young Murray, notwithstanding the assurances of promotion which he had given to his friend, Sir Peter Parker, (who afterwards possessed the means of promoting him [i.e. Murray], had he remained in the *Bristol*) he [Howe] returned, leaving several vacancies in America, which he had a right to fill up. He brought home the subject of this memoir, with several other gentlemen on

his quarter-deck, who equally looked to him for promotion; and unjustly, as well as unnecessarily, left them to shift for themselves, without assigning to them a reason, or even offering them an apology, for such extraordinary conduct. NC 18.180

Captain George Montagu, who was a friend of Murray's father, asked young Murray 'to draw up a memorial of his service; which, with certificates of his good conduct, particularly one from the captain of the *Eagle* (64), was transmitted to Lord Sandwich, then at the head of the Admiralty. The consequence was, that a lieutenant's commission was forwarded to him, almost by the return of post.' Sandwich was given a reputation for cynically using his patronage powers for political purposes, but modern research has shown that to be false, and that to the contrary he was remarkable for his determination to reject the applications from the rich and powerful, in order to be able to provide for the truly deserving. Murray's examination took place on 19 November 1778, and he was commissioned second lieutenant on 31 December in *Arethusa* (32), in which he remained until February 1779, when she was wrecked near Ushant during pursuit of a French frigate. Whilst in captivity Murray studied French and the regulations of the French navy, but he was exchanged when he came to the attention of the French police as a result of an encounter with an American privateersman who was improperly wearing a British uniform.

In the spring of 1781, as first lieutenant of *Monmouth* (64), he took part in the expedition under Commodore George Johnstone to the Cape of Good Hope, and the ineffectual action against Admiral Pierre André de Suffren at the Cape Verde Islands. Continuing to the East Indies, *Monmouth* joined Rear-Admiral Sir Edward Hughes in time to take part in the action against Suffren off Madras on 15 February 1782. Following the battle of Providien on 12 April 1782 Murray was appointed second lieutenant in Hughes's flagship, *Superb* (74). A little over a month after the battle of Trincomalee, in which Murray was wounded, he was promoted master and commander, on 9 October 1782, and promoted again to post captain three days later with command of a captured Spanish privateer, *San Carlos* (22).

The peace of Paris enabled Murray to take leave from naval service, in which he had fought his way from midshipman to post captain by the age of twenty-four, and return to his studies, possibly going to France for two years to study French and literature. In June 1790, during the Nootka Sound incident he returned to naval service, being ordered to commission the frigate *Triton* (32). The following April he was employed in surveying the Great Belt and the approaches to Copenhagen. This work was to equip him well for his service in the 1801 campaign. After service at Halifax and Jamaica he returned home in June 1793. He was appointed in December to command the 12-pounder frigate *Nymphe* (36), which had been captured from the French in June, and took part in the action by Sir John Borlase Warren's squadron on 23 April 1794 in which *La Pomone* (44) was captured, and in the fleet action under Lord Bridport off L'Orient on 23 June 1795. On 15 September 1795 he married Ann, daughter of Colonel Christopher Teesdale, returning to sea two weeks later to take command of *Formidable* (90).

In 1796 Murray was appointed to *Colossus* (74) and ordered to join Admiral Sir John Jervis in the Mediterranean. The story goes that while Murray was in command of the inshore squadron at Cadiz, the Spanish admiral extended to him an invitation to attend a bullfight, offering to leave his nephew as surety. *Colossus* should have led the fleet in the battle of Cape St Vincent on 14 February 1797, but accidental damage to the fore-topsail yard caused her to drop away to leeward. The following year Jervis sent Murray to join Nelson in the Mediterranean, but *Colossus* proved to be so much in need of repair that as soon as possible she had to be sent back to England. On her entering the chops of the Channel a north-east gale obliged Murray to make a course for Scilly. Once she had anchored in the landlocked road, the wind blew up to such an extent that *Colossus*'s anchors dragged, and she was wrecked, although only one of her people was killed. With her went down a treasure of antique vases which had been collected by Sir William Hamilton while envoy to the court of Naples.

Murray was acquitted of blame, and almost immediately appointed to the *Achille* (84) in the Channel fleet. He was transferred in March 1801 to the *Edgar* (74), which was more suitable for service in the Baltic, and because of his experience with the difficult navigation at Copenhagen, *Edgar* led the fleet into action on 2 April. She had to pass

George Murray Esq.,
Rear Admiral of the White Squadron,
engraved by H R Cook after an original drawing,
published by Joyce Gold, 103 Shoe Lane,
30 September 1807.

---

four Danish ships before reaching her assigned position opposite the *Jylland*, which she engaged for four hours until the truce. The Danes were able to bring reinforcements to take the place of fallen men, and *Edgar* was heavily damaged, losing thirty-one men killed and 104 wounded. Then, and during the subsequent operations to watch the Swedish fleet in Karlscrona, he established a strong rapport with Nelson, who succeeded Sir Hyde Parker as commander-in-chief.

On the resumption of hostilities in 1804 after the peace of Amiens, Nelson was appointed to command the Mediterranean fleet, and Murray was asked for as captain of the fleet. Murray hesitated:

> On his lordship asking the reason, he answered, by observing, that the nature of the service was such, as very frequently terminated in disagreement between the admiral and the captain; and he should be extremely unwilling to hazard any possible thing that should diminish the regard and respect which he should ever entertain for his lordship. Lord Nelson coincided in opinion with Captain Murray; but assured him, that, on whatever service he might be called, or whatever measure he might be directed to carry into execution, he never should forget the intimacy which subsisted between them; and even, should any thing go contrary to his wishes, he would wave the rank of admiral, and explain, or expostulate with him, as his friend, Murray.

'Indeed,' noted the editor of the *Naval Chronicle*,

> 'Admiral Murray's disposition is so gentle, and his manners are so mild, that but few men are equally well beloved in the navy; while few possess the facility of commanding with such ease, and, at the same time, with such energy and effect.' NC 18.177

He was promoted rear-admiral on 23 April 1804, but chose not to hoist his flag in order to continue with Nelson. He took part in the chase of the Toulon fleet to the West Indies, and back to European waters. But he then went ashore for a while to settle his father's estate, and Nelson sailed for his final rendezvous off Cape Trafalgar without any captain of the fleet. None but Murray would do.

His last operational command was in November 1806 when he was appointed commander-in-chief of operations against Buenos Aires, returning home in January 1808 after the collapse of General Whitlocke's assault and the capitulation of the army. He was promoted vice-admiral on 25 October 1809 and nominated KCB on 2 January 1815. He died on 28 February 1819, aged sixty, in Chichester. Ann died in Boulogne in 1859, aged ninety-five.

Lt: 31 December 1778
M-C: 9 October 1782
Capt: 12 October 1782
R-Adm: 23 April 1804
V-Adm: 25 October 1809

NAPIER

ADMIRAL SIR CHARLES JOHN NAPIER, KCB, is best known for his second career following the end of the war against the French Empire. In the dynastic conflict in Portugal, he was appointed vice-admiral and major-general of the Portuguese navy, and from 8 June 1833 to 15 October 1833 served as commander-in-chief of the fleet loyal to Donna Maria and Dom Pedro. After the defeat of the squadron of Dom Miguel off Cape St Vincent, on 3 July 1833, he had every honour bestowed on him. He was promoted admiral and created Viscount Cape St Vincent in the peerage of Portugal, then nominated knight grand cross of the orders of St Bento D'Avis and of the Tower and Sword, and finally created Count Cape St Vincent.

Napier's foreign service, however, came as a sequel to a stellar career as a frigate captain late in the war against the French Empire, and as a curtain-raiser to his success as a captain with forty years' seniority in the 1840s and as fleet commander in the Baltic in the first year of the Russian war.

He was born on 3 June 1787 at Merchistoun Hall near Falkirk, Stirlingshire, the second son of Captain the Honourable Charles Napier, RN, and his second wife, Christian, daughter of Gabriel Hamilton of Westburn, Lanarkshire. He was educated at Edinburgh high school, and entered the navy on 1 November 1799 on board the Martin with the patronage of Henry Dundas, treasurer of the navy. In 1800 he was rated midshipman or master's mate in *Renown* (74), flying the flag of Sir

John Borlase Warren in the Channel and the Mediterranean. In November 1802 he joined *Greyhound* (32) under the command of Captain William Hoste; while serving in the 24-pounder frigate *Egyptienne* (38) he made a voyage to St Helena; he then served in the converted Indiaman *Mediator* (44) and the former French *Renommée* (44) in the Downs, during which time his part in actions against the Boulogne invasion flotilla in 1804 and 1805 was noted. This led on 24 April 1805 to his being given command of *Starling*, gunbrig, in which he captured seven heavily armed coasters off Cap Gris Nez. He was commissioned lieutenant on 30 November 1805 in *Courageux* (74), and served under Admiral Warren at the capture of *Marengo* and *Belle Poule* under the command of Rear-Admiral Linois on 13 March 1806.

While serving in the West Indies under Admiral Sir Alexander Cochrane, and with the continued support of Dundas, he was promoted commander on 30 November 1807. He served in the occupation of the Danish islands of St Thomas and Santa Cruz in December, and was transferred to the brig *Recruit* (18) in April 1808. He was wounded with a compound fracture to the thigh when in action on 6 September 1808 with a French corvette, *Diligente*, that brought down *Recruit*'s mast and then disengaged. The good impression he had made on Cochrane was confirmed the following year during the capture of Martinique when he harassed the rear of a French battle squadron during the action, engaging a French 74-gun ship until the heavy ships of Cochrane's squadron were able to join and capture her. In recognition of his courage and skill Cochrane promoted him post captain with command of a prize, his commission being confirmed on 22 May 1809. He was then moved into the 12-pounder frigate *Jason* (32) and sent home with a convoy; after this he was unemployed for two years, during which time he visited his brother and cousins in Portugal serving with General Wellington. He was slightly wounded at the battle of Busaco, accompanied the army in the retreat to Torres Vedras, and in November 1810 moved into Cadiz.

During the remainder of the war he commanded in succession the 12-pounder frigate *Thames* (32) and the *Euryalus* (32) in the Mediterranean. In the summer of 1811 he was engaged under the orders of the Honourable Henry Duncan in the close support of the army in Calabria, on 21 July leading the brig *Cephalus* (18) into Porto Infreschi, where the force captured naval stores, eleven gunboats and fifteen coasters. He assumed the command of the naval squadron in early 1812, and on 26 February 1813 he carried out the capture of Ponza with *Thames, Furieuse,* frigate, commanded by Captain William Mounsey, and soldiers of the 2nd battalion of the 10th Regiment commanded by Lieutenant-Colonel Coffin.

Marshall became lyrical in its description of Napier's attack on that island.

> A more beautiful marine subject never presented itself to the imagination of a [Nicholas] Pocock than the advance of the British to the attack: the troops being ordered below, both ships rapidly closed the mole, shortened sail, and anchored, with the coolness of a common manoeuvre: the boats pulled so closely under the cliffs on which the batteries were constructed, as to elude their fire; and the battalion having landed in a small sandy bay, soon gained the heights in the rear of and above the enemy, who being then placed between two fires, immediately surrendered. Marshall 2 (Supp) 6

In March, Napier transferred into *Euryalus* (32) and was employed in watching Toulon under the orders of Captain Thomas Ussher. On one occasion when hazy weather was obscuring Ussher's order of recall, Napier chased two French ships as far as Calvi, driving one of them ashore, where she was bilged. The following year *Euryalus* was ordered to Bermuda as part of a squadron under Captain Andrew King, escorting a fleet of transports carrying part of the army which had been serving in the siege of Genoa. She was then placed under Sir Alexander Cochrane's orders, and Napier served in the naval operations against Alexandria and Virginia and in support of the raid on Baltimore. Napier, serving under Captain James Alexander Gordon, received the surrender of Alexandria, and then oversaw the salving of the shipping scuttled in the harbour. They were then freighted with the valuables taken in the town, and brought downriver through fire from batteries and fire rafts. Napier was slightly wounded, but was fit enough to command the rocket boats in the bombardment of Baltimore, and to volunteer to lay *Euryalus* alongside Fort McHenry. Subsequently he was employed blockading USS *Constellation* at Norfolk, Virginia. *Euryalus* was sent home for repairs after the conclusion of the treaty of Ghent. During Napoleon's last campaign, the second Lord Melville selected Napier to command a detachment of sailors building bridges for Wellington's army in Belgium, but he was rejected for the post because he outranked the army's chief engineer.

He was nominated a CB on 4 June 1815, and that same month he married Eliza (Frances Elizabeth), daughter of Lieutenant George Younghusband, RN, and widow of Lieutenant Edward Elers, RN. He thereby acquired several stepchildren, and Eliza also gave him a son, who died in infancy, and one daughter. He lost his fortune in an attempt to promote iron steamers on the Seine between 1819 and 1827, and hence the need to seek employment, first returning to active service in the West Indies in command of the 18-pounder frigate *Galatea* (36) from January 1829 to the end of 1831, and in February 1833 entering the service of the Portuguese constitutional government. In order to maintain a fiction that he was not breaking the Foreign Enlistment Act, he adopted the *nom de guerre* of Dom Carlos de Ponza when appointed to command the constitutional fleet. Nonetheless, his name was struck from the navy list in 1833 and was restored only in 1840.

Returning to the Royal Navy, in January 1839 he was appointed to command a battleship, the Calcutta-built *Powerful* (84) under Admiral Sir Robert Stopford, and in June 1840 he hoisted his pendant as commodore of a small squadron ordered to watch events in the Levant. He was joined by the Mediterranean fleet in September, and took a prominent part in littoral operations leading to the capture of Beirut and Acre and the capitulation of Mehmet Ali. In recognition, he was nominated KCB by the British court, knight of the military order of Maria Theresa by Austria, knight of the order of the Red Eagle by Prussia, and knight of the order of St George by Russia. He was presented with the freedom of the City of London on 23 September 1841, and his popularity was such that he at last succeeded in entering politics, having earlier stood unsuccessfully for Portsmouth. He now won and held the popular parliamentary seat for St Marylebone, London, from 1841 to 1847, and for Southwark from 1855 to 1860.

He also served as naval aide-de-camp to Queen Victoria from 30 November 1841 to 9 November 1846, but this was not the end of his naval career. The Admiralty commissioned him in 1845 to design a first-class steam frigate, which reflected his career in littoral operations, being built with shallow draught, a heavy armament and accommodation for 1,000 embarked soldiers. On 9 November 1846 he finally received promotion to rear-admiral, having worked his way up the navy list. And in May 1848 he was given command of the western squadron, which was employed in ship and steam trials. He hauled down his flag in April 1849, but was employed again in the Russian war, in command of the Baltic fleet in 1854. In 1851 he published *The Navy: Its Past and Present State in a Series of Letters*, and in 1857 *The History of the Baltic Campaign of 1854*.

He died on 6 November 1860, aged seventy-three, at Merchistoun Hall, Horndean, Hampshire, with the rank of admiral, and was buried in Catherington. His wife had predeceased him on 19 December 1857.

> Lt: 30 November 1805
> Cmdr: 30 November 1807
> Capt: 22 May 1809
> R-Adm: 9 November 1846
> V-Adm: 28 May 1853
> Adm: 6 March 1858

NEALE

ADMIRAL SIR HARRY BURRARD NEALE, BARONET, GCB, had as one of his strongest claims to fame the fact that the people of *San Fiorenzo*

(34), which he commanded, refused to take part in the Nore mutiny.

He was born on 16 September 1765 in Lymington, the eldest son of Colonel William Burrard, governor of Yarmouth Castle, Isle of Wight, and his second wife, Mary, daughter of Joseph Pearce, MD. Educated at Christchurch, London, he entered the navy on 4 March 1778 as a captain's servant on board the *Roebuck* (44) commanded by Sir Andrew Snape Hamond, and was at the capture of Charlestown in April 1780. When Hamond was succeeded by his nephew Captain Andrew Douglas on 15 May, Neale was given the rating of midshipman. On 3 July 1781 he followed Captain Douglas into *Chatham* (50), on 2 September 1781 taking part in the capture of the French frigate *Magicienne* off Boston. He returned to England in 1783 as acting lieutenant of the *Perseverance* (36), and was transferred on 24 November to *Hector* (74) under Sir John Hamilton, serving as a midshipman. On 13 November 1784 he joined *Europa* (50) flying the flag of Rear-Admiral Innes in the West Indies, being rated as able seaman and later as acting lieutenant. On 24 May 1786 he was ordered again to act as lieutenant in the 18-pounder frigate *Flora* (36) under a Captain Stoney, and on 2 January 1787 he joined the 12-pounder frigate *Astria* (32) under Captain Peter Rainier, being rated as able seaman and later ordered to act as lieutenant. On 29 September 1787 he was finally commissioned lieutenant of the cutter *Expedition* (10) under Captain the Honourable John Chetwyn. During all this time he had continued in West Indies service, until 21 May 1789.

He had one year of unemployment, but on 1 June 1790, at the time of the Nootka Sound crisis, he was appointed to *Southampton* (32) under the command of Captain Richard Goodwin Keats, transferring on 22 October to *Victory* (100), Lord Hood's flagship. On 3 November he was promoted commander, with appointment on the 18th to *Orestes* (18), in which he was employed in customs preventive service until 24 December 1792. In 1790 he was also returned to parliament for the family seat of Lymington, which he represented until 1802, again in 1806–7, from 1812 to 1823, and from 1832 to 1834. He succeeded to his uncle's baronetcy on 12 April 1791, and was made post on the day war was declared, 1 February 1793, with appointment on the 7th to command *L'Aimable* (32), in which he served under Lord Hood in the Mediterranean.

By royal licence dated 8 April 1795, he assumed the name and arms of Neale on his marriage on 15 April to Grace Elizabeth, the daughter and co-heir of Robert Neale of Shaw House, Wiltshire.

On 15 June he was appointed to command the *San Fiorenzo* (34) in the Channel fleet under Lord Howe and Lord Bridport. She was stationed for some time at Weymouth, in attendance on the king. When caught up in the Nore mutiny, she was ordered to lie under the stern of *Sandwich* (90), which was firmly in the hands of the mutineers. A few days later, however, she escaped, although she was fired on. This was a major blow to the mutineers, and on 7 June 1797 Neale and his ship's company were honoured by a vote of thanks by a meeting of London merchants and shipowners at the Royal Exchange. In 1801 he may have been appointed briefly to *Centaur* (74), but on 12 May he was transferred to the royal yacht *Royal Charlotte*, from which he commanded a flotilla of frigates in the mouth of the Thames. In the season he attended the king at Weymouth. It is a moot point whether to give more importance to the effect that attendance on the king had on the loyalty of *San Fiorenzo*'s people, or to the effect of Neale's leadership. In either case, Neale profited from the confidence the king had in him.

He served as an Admiralty commissioner under the earl of St Vincent from 17 January to 13 September 1804, and after another period in command of a yacht, *Royal Sovereign*, was on 28 November 1805 appointed to *London* (90) flying the flag of Sir John Borlase Warren at the Cape Verde Islands. On 13 March 1806 he took a notable part in the action by a small squadron which captured the *Belle Poule* and *Marengo* commanded by Rear-Admiral Linois returning from the East Indies. Neale returned to the Board of Admiralty from 10 February 1806 to 6 April 1807 during the

'Ministry of all the Talents'. On 18 May 1808 he was appointed Lord Gambier's captain of the fleet in *Ville de Paris* (110), and was serving with him during the attack on the Brest fleet in Basque Roads the following year.

Following his promotion to rear-admiral on 31 July 1810 he hoisted his flag in 1811 in *Caledonia* (120) commanding a squadron of the Channel fleet on the coast of France, then shifted to *Boyne* (98), and again to the *Ville de Paris*. He remained in that station, often acting for Lord Keith when he was ashore, until the end of the war in 1814, hauling down his flag on 15 June. He also served as groom of the king's bedchamber at Windsor to 1812. He was promoted on 4 June 1814 to vice-admiral, on 2 January 1815 nominated KCB, and on 14 September 1822 nominated GCB. He was riding forester of the New Forest from 1813 to 1820, and returned to sea as commander-in-chief Mediterranean from 31 July 1823 to 26 April 1826, flying his flag in *Revenge* (74), but he refused the offer to command at Portsmouth when a condition was attached that he should resign his seat in the Commons. On 14 January 1824 he was nominated knight grand cross of the order of St Michael and St George in the heraldry of the Maltese and Ionian Republic, as was customary at the time for commanders-in-chief Mediterranean. In his retirement he was elected mayor of Christchurch, Dorset.

He died in Brighton on 7 February 1840 with the rank of admiral, and was buried at Walhampton, near Lymington. An obelisk was erected on Mount Pleasant near the town.

> Lt: 29 September 1787
> M-C: 3 November 1790
> Capt: 1 February 1793
> R-Adm: 31 July 1810
> V-Adm: 4 June 1814
> Adm: 22 July 1830

NELSON

VICE-ADMIRAL SIR HORATIO NELSON, VISCOUNT NELSON, KB, wrote in an application for the receipt of a pension in 1797: 'That, during the present war, your Memoralist has been in four actions with the fleets of the enemy, viz. on the 13th and 14th of March 1795; on the 13th July 1795; and on the 14th of February 1797; in three actions with frigates; in six engagements against batteries; in ten actions in boats employed in cutting out of harbours; in destroying vessels, and in taking three towns. Your Memorialist has also served on shore with the army four months, and commanded the batteries at the sieges of Bastia and Calvi. That during the war, he has assisted at the capture of seven sail of the line, six frigates, four corvettes, and eleven privateers of different sizes; and taken and destroyed near fifty sail of merchant vessels; and your Memorialist has actually been engaged against the enemy upwards of ONE HUNDRED AND TWENTY TIMES. In which service your Memorialist has lost his right eye and arm, and been severely wounded and bruised in his body. All of which services and wounds your memorialist must humbly submit to your Majesty's most gracious consideration.' NC 1.29 Far from that being the end of his career, in the next eight years he was to fight and win his three great victories at the Nile, Copenhagen and Trafalgar.

Nelson was born on 29 September 1758, the third son of the Revd Edmund Nelson, MA, rector of Burnham Thorpe, Norfolk. His mother was Catherine, first daughter of the Revd Maurice Suckling, DD, prebendary of Westminster, and sister of Captain Maurice Suckling, RN. She died when Horatio was young, leaving him with the chief recollection that she 'hated the French', and a great sense of loss he was never able to resolve. He entered the navy in 1770 in *Raisonnable* (64) under the command of Captain Suckling, when the fleet was mobilised during the Falkland Islands crisis. When that dispute was settled, *Raisonnable* was paid off and Suckling appointed to a guardship in the Thames, the *Triumph* (74). He took Nelson with him, and then sent him on a voyage in a merchant ship to the West Indies to learn seamanship. After Nelson's return, Suckling had enough influence to get him a place on the *Carcus*, a survey vessel commanded by Captain Skeffington Lutwidge in an expedition led by Captain Phipps, Lord Mulgrave, which penetrated the ice fields north of Spitzbergen. Reputedly, Nelson had to be

rescued from a youthful effort to kill a polar bear, and endured the danger and hardship when his ship was iced into the floe and it appeared necessary to drag the ship's boats five miles to the edge of open water. He then made a voyage in *Seahorse* (24) under Captain Farmer to the East Indies, returning home in *Dolphin* (20) after a serious illness in 1775. His promotions came fast, helped by Suckling's appointment as comptroller and head of the Navy Board in 1775. He was ordered to act as lieutenant in *Worcester* (64), and with Suckling as comptroller presiding at the examination for lieutenant, Nelson passed at the early age of eighteen on 9 April 1777. His commission was confirmed the next day with an appointment to the 12-pounder frigate *Lowestoffe* (32) under Captain William Locker. He served with Locker in the West Indies, and became a close friend.

At the outbreak of war with France in February 1778 Nelson was taken into the flagship of Sir Peter Parker, who put him in command of *Badger*, brig, serving on the Mosquito coast. Following the Spanish alliance with France, Parker promoted Nelson again on 11 June 1779, to post captain of *Hinchinbrook* (28), in which he returned to the Mosquito coast as part of an expedition to attack the Spanish possessions in Central America.

His first active service in a land operation was against San Juan de Nicaragua, and he nearly died there of fever. He recovered when he was invalided home, and received an appointment to command the French prize frigate *Albermarle* (28). After a period in the North Sea, his duty took him to the healthier climate of Canada, which completed the cure. In Quebec he fell in love with the daughter of an army officer and was with difficulty restrained from matrimony. At New York he met Prince William Henry, then a midshipman. He then returned to the West Indies, and came home to England on the conclusion of peace.

During a period in France studying French he again fell in love, only this time it was he who was rejected.

Nelson was fortunate enough to obtain appointment in March 1784 to the *Boreas* (28), frigate, in which he sailed to the West Indies; there he made many enemies because he insisted on enforcing the Navigation Acts against the king's former American citizens who were attempting to continue their trade with the islands. Despite the reputation this gave him in the planter community, which needed the American trade, his offer of marriage was accepted by Frances (Fanny) Nisbet, daughter and only child of William Woolward, senior judge of Nevis. They were married on 11 March 1787 and Prince William Henry insisted on giving away the bride.

Nelson's disproportionate deference to the wayward prince was to cause his temporary fall from favour at the Admiralty, and did him more lasting damage at court. His patron Viscount Samuel Hood wrote to him in 1798 that he had 'often heard you mentioned for the advice you gave' the prince 'which is on record at the Admiralty' to refuse to submit his muster book to the dockyard officers, and for encouraging his resentment at the more experienced officers who had been placed under him to ensure he learnt his job.[Mon E540] Nelson went so far as to exceed his authority, by sending the prince out of his station to Jamaica, where a court could be assembled to try his first lieutenant, Isaac Schomberg.

As a result, he was not employed again until just before the French declaration of war in 1793, when he was given command of *Agamemnon* (64) and ordered to join Vice-Admiral Hood's fleet destined for the Mediterranean. When Toulon invited Hood to occupy the town, Nelson was sent to Naples to obtain military support from King Ferdinand IV, and was in action on 22 October off Sardinia with a squadron of French frigates. In January 1794, following the evacuation of Toulon, Hood put him in charge of the blockade of Corsica. On 4 April

The Right Honourable Lord Nelson K.B., Rear Admiral of the Red, Duke of Bronti &c, engraving by P Roberts after Lemuel F Abbot, published by Burney and Gold, Shoe Lane, 1 April 1800.

he landed to take command of the siege of Bastia, which surrendered on 23 May. In June he was put in command of the naval forces co-operating with the army siege of Calvi, and on 12 July he was wounded, losing the sight of his right eye. Nelson returned to sea after the surrender of Calvi on 10 August, and was employed cruising on the Italian and French coasts. After Vice-Admiral Hotham succeeded Hood in command, Nelson fought in three fleet engagements, in March and July 1795. During the March encounter, Captain Freeman in *Inconstant* (36) crippled the 80-gun ship *Ça Ira*, enabling Nelson to finish her off. He was forced by her effective use of stern chasers to open fire earlier than he wished, but thereafter he kept *Agamemnon* weaving across the stern of his enemy so that he could repeatedly rake her, suffer no damage himself, and finally take her.

When Admiral Sir John Jervis assumed command in the Mediterranean in January 1796 the French had so far prevailed that in the autumn the government felt compelled to withdraw British resources to the blockade position off Cadiz. Nelson, who was ordered on 4 April 1796 to assume the rank of commodore first class flying his broad pendant on *Captain* (74), was employed in evacuating the British garrisons on Corsica and the British viceroy there, Sir Gilbert Elliot. They were all removed successfully to Elba, and following the withdrawal of the fleet, Nelson returned to Elba with two frigates to carry the soldiers to Gibraltar. Without orders, however, they refused to move, and Nelson succeeded only in recovering the naval stores and the viceroy.

He rejoined Jervis just in time to play a notable part in the battle of Cape St Vincent on 14 February

1797, when he was again flying his broad pendant on *Captain*. When it appeared that the Spanish van was going to double the British van, which Jervis had ordered to tack, Nelson had the moral and physical courage to leave his station in the rear of the line of battle, and steer to contain the threat, coming into action ahead of the British van lead by *Culloden*. In doing so he exposed *Captain* for some time to fire unsupported. With the help of Captain Cuthbert Collingwood in *Excellent* (74), also of the rear squadron, he captured two ships, of which one was the first rate *San José*. He took them by boarding and, in an unheard-of move, was himself the first to enter the *San José*.

These events catapulted him into a fame he was careful to cultivate by briefing Colonel John Drinkwater, who wrote an account of the action, and by himself writing a narrative of the action for Locker to publish. Rear-Admiral William Parker protested that Nelson had deliberately obscured the part played by other ships, and in particular by Parker's ship *Prince George,* which he believed had already beaten the *San José* into submission. Nelson had been made colonel of the Royal Marines on 1 June 1795, and was promoted rear-admiral on 20 February 1797. For this action he was made a KB on 27 May 1797, preferring an order with a sash and star, which would attract attention, to a baronetcy, which he could not support.

Following the action, Nelson took a leading part in the close blockade of Cadiz, and in the containment of disaffection following the mutinies at Spithead, the Nore and Plymouth in May and June 1797. Discontent in *Theseus* (74) was dealt with by Jervis, now the earl of St Vincent, by appointing Ralph Willett Miller to her command, and by Nelson moving his flag into her. On the night of 3–4 July, although now a flag officer, he personally commanded a boat force which came into close action with Spanish gunboats. He would have been killed but for his coxswain John Sykes, who interposed his arm to ward off a cutlass blow. By exposing his own life, Nelson helped repair the morale of the fleet.

He was less fortunate in July 1797 when he attempted to seize the Spanish fortress of Santa Cruz de Tenerife and was repelled with heavy losses, having his right arm shot off. He was obliged to spend the winter in England, where he had his last good days with his wife, and then returned to the fleet off Cadiz on 10 April 1798. Despite his injury, he was the man Lord Spencer, the first lord, and St Vincent agreed they needed to take a force into the Mediterranean in early 1798 to meet the threat being prepared at Toulon and the occupied coast of Italy which might be intended for invasion of England, but which in fact was intended for the conquest of Egypt. After months spent looking for the French, complicated by the dismasting of his flagship, *Vanguard* (74), owing to the inexperience of Edward Berry, his flag captain, the French were found on 1 August in Aboukir Bay, where Vice-Admiral Bruey had moored following the disembarkation of the army under General Buonaparte at Alexandria. Attacking immediately at the end of day, Nelson won the most decisive victory of the age of sail, only two enemy ships of the line escaping. He became the hero of Europe. For this action he was made Baron Nelson of the Nile and of Burnham Thorpe, Norfolk, on 6 November 1798, and the sultan made him knight of the order of the Crescent.

He had been wounded in the head at the battle, and together with the adulation he received everywhere he went, this appears to have unbalanced him. It cost him his marriage when he fell under the spell of Emma Hamilton, and the respect of his superiors when he uncritically threw his energy behind the ambitious plans of Queen Maria Carolina, who dominated the court of Naples. Disregarding King Ferdinand's concern about the quality of his army, Nelson transported it to Leghorn on 28 November, and occupied Rome. But this greatly overstretched resources, the French counterattacked a week later, and Nelson on 23 December had to evacuate to Palermo the Neapolitan royal family, secretly and at night because it was known the citizens of Naples would try to prevent their leader's desertion. Subsequently, in May 1799, he disregarded orders to join the fleet seeking the Brest fleet which had entered the Mediterranean, because he believed his first duty was to support the royalist reconquest of Naples, for which service he was made commander-in-chief of the Neapolitan navy. He risked the defeat in detail of the small British squadrons in the Mediterranean, and was deservedly admonished by the Admiralty. Fortunately, the French returned to Brest without bringing any of the British fleet to battle. Nelson was implicated in the brutality of the counter-revolution, which extended to the execution of republican leaders who believed they had capitulated on terms, but he was rewarded by King Ferdinand with nomination as knight grand cross of the royal order of St Ferdinand and of Merit, and the Sicilian dukedom of Bronte. His attention to duty was seriously undermined by his growing devotion to Emma, and finally he was all but ordered to strike his flag and return to England, which he did overland and to hero's welcomes everywhere. Everywhere, that is, except in the British court, where George III viewed his desertion of his wife as disgraceful.

He was promoted vice-admiral on 1 January 1801, and hoisted his flag in the Channel fleet on the *San Joseph* (110), which he had captured at Cape St Vincent. On the day Emma gave birth to his daughter Horatia in great secrecy, he was also ordered to take part in a planned operation to prevent the union of Denmark, Sweden and Russia adding their fleets to those of France. But he was appointed only as second in command under Admiral Sir Hyde Parker. He suspected that he was being deliberately taken away from Emma by his fellow officers, who believed he was making a fool of himself.

He more than recovered his reputation by his leadership in the campaign leading to, and at, the battle of Copenhagen on 2 April 1801. Hyde Parker had lost to age and comfort the aggressive edge needed for the expedition, and Nelson's tact was essential in persuading him to brave the dangers of the passage of the batteries at Elsinore, and to delegate the conduct of the attack on the Danish defence line. Nelson was put in charge, and it was by his plan that he outflanked the Danes, who had failed to provide their ships and batteries with the means to warp across the approach along the King's Deep channel.

Cuthbert Collingwood was Nelson's friend from the time they served together as lieutenants in the West Indies, although their personalities were very different. In comments to Dr Alexander Carlyle on 24 August 1801 about Nelson's method, he expressed a belief that it was not a matter of careful planning in a narrow sense. In Collingwood's opinion, it was Nelson's habit of tactical analysis, flexibility of mind and rapport with his officers, which enabled him to make deft responses. 'Without much previous preparation or plan,' Collingwood wrote, 'he has the facility of discovering advantages as they arise, and the good judgment to turn them to his use. An enemy that commits a false step in his view is ruined, and it comes on him with an impetuosity that gives him no time to recover.' [Collingwood no 69.130] The situation of the Danish fleet, and that of the French at Aboukir Bay, led Nelson to adopt similar tactics, but the greater time he had to prepare for the attack at Copenhagen led him to provide captains with detailed tactical instructions. The accidental grounding of some of his ships in the approach then led him to shout extemporised revised orders to each captain as he passed the disengaged side of *Elephant* (74), on which Nelson was flying his flag.

When Hyde Parker considered that Nelson might be in trouble, he sent a flag signal ordering him to discontinue action. To have done so in the circumstances of close action in a confined channel and after battle damage to spars would have been fatal. Notoriously, Nelson turned his blind eye to the signal. Parker had made it a 'general' one which each and every captain should have obeyed, but only the most junior of them did so. The rest continued to obey Nelson's signal for close action. When Danish fire began to slacken, he entered into a convention with Commodore Olfert Fischer, commanding the Danish defences, and the Danish crown prince. Hyde Parker subsequently concluded a truce, which freed the British fleet to act against Russia, but the Admiralty ordered his supersession, and it was Nelson who conducted the negotiations with the Russian government which ensured the end of the threat of armed intervention in British Baltic trade in naval stores. He was advanced in the peerage to viscount on 22 May.

On his return from the Baltic, Nelson was put

in command of the seaward defences of England against invasion, as much to keep him away from Emma as to reassure a frightened population. With the ratification of the peace of Amiens in 1802, however, he was able to have nineteen months' leave, and settled to a comfortable *maison à trois* with the Hamiltons. Sir Gilbert Elliot wrote of this period that Emma 'goes on cramming Nelson with trowelfuls of flattery, which he goes on taking as quietly as a child does pap. The love she makes to him is not only ridiculous, but disgusting.' [Elliot 3.242] Nelson did not attend his father's funeral because he knew he would meet his wife, who had continued to support her father-in-law in his old age.

On 14 May 1803, on the eve of the renewal of war, Nelson was given command of the Mediterranean fleet, with his flag on the *Victory* (100). When the Toulon fleet sailed on 30 March 1805 Nelson thought it was again going to Egypt, but eventually discovered it had sailed to the West Indies. He followed it to Martinique, and then followed its return to Europe, where it was under orders to join the fleet at Brest to command the Channel for the few days required to effect an invasion of England. Vice-Admiral Villeneuve encountered Vice-Admiral Calder off Finisterre on 22 July, put into Vigo after suffering the loss of two Spanish ships, and eventually sailed south to Cadiz *en route* to returning to the Mediterranean. After a short final period at home in England, Nelson took command off Cadiz, and on 21 October he fought and won the battle of Trafalgar, which cost the combined fleet Franco-Spanish fleet the loss of eighteen ships, and put an end to France's being able to make more than fleeting use of the sea. It also cost Nelson his life. This was the first fleet action he commanded which did not take place while the enemy were at anchor.

His tactics were a radical and extemporised development of those used by successive commanders in the previous twelve years of war, but were intended, as had been Howe's at the Glorious First of June and Duncan's at Camperdown, to prevent the enemy fleeing before they could be defeated. Instead of the tried method of a close-hauled line ahead working its way progressively into action, Nelson ordered a head-on attack in two columns.

'I think it will surprise and confuse the enemy. They won't know what I am about. It will bring forward a pell-mell battle, and that is what I want.' [Nelson 7.241] If he intended that the columns should pay off on a course parallel to the enemy, he abandoned that plan when Villeneuve ordered the combined fleet to wear about onto a reciprocal course. As the enemy bunched into a crescent shape, Nelson held his course to cut through, and engage to leeward. The danger was very great, and indeed Nelson was surprised by the vigour of the Franco-Spanish response, and it is probable that the British fleet prevailed only because Nelson, and his second in command, Vice-Admiral Collingwood, led the two columns in their flagships. As in the actions at Cadiz in 1797, Nelson knew the effect his fully sharing the dangers would have on British morale. His famous signal to the fleet, that 'England Expects that Every Man will do his Duty', was also intended to stimulate enthusiasm on the part of the men, and achieved all that he could have asked for. There were twenty-seven British ships of the line against the enemies' thirty-three, of which seventeen were taken as prize and another burnt.

As he was dying in *Victory*'s cockpit, he told his flag captain, Thomas Hardy, that the fleet should anchor. But with all the battle damage the ships had suffered, that was not a viable option, and Collingwood found the terrors of the storm which followed the battle worse even than those of the battle itself.

Nelson was buried in St Paul's Cathedral after a period of lying in state at Greenwich and a procession up the Thames. Monuments were erected all over Britain and in Canada. He had left his mistress Emma Hamilton and their child Horatia as a charge on the nation, but their status was not recognised, and instead a pension was paid to his widow, and his quite undeserving brother was made an earl. Fanny Nelson died on 4 May 1831, aged seventy, at 26 Baker Street, London, and was buried in Littleham near Exmouth, Devon.

Lt: 10 April 1777
M-C: 8 December 1778
Capt: 11 June 1779
R-Adm: 20 February 1797
V-Adm: 1 January 1801

NEWMAN

CAPTAIN JAMES NEWMAN's brief life was marked by his great success as a frigate captain.

He was born on 10 January 1767 in Scaldwell, Northamptonshire, the eldest son of Charles Toll, of Preston Deanery, Northampton, and his wife, Hester, daughter of Herbert Langham of Cottesbroke, Northamptonshire. In 1775 Charles Toll changed his surname to Newman on inheriting the estate of Sir Richard Newman, baronet. Young James Newman was a great-nephew of Rear-Admiral Edmund Toll, and entered the navy on 6 September 1782 as an ordinary seaman on board the *Queen* (90) under the patronage of Rear-Admiral Alexander Hood, Lord Bridport. He was promoted midshipman or master's mate on 27 November 1782, and the following April he moved into *Iphigenia* (32), Captain James Cornwallis, sailing to the West Indies. He saw service in many different ships, was commissioned lieutenant in *Ariel*, sloop, on 26 February 1790 while in the East Indies, and travelled home as an invalid in the early summer of 1792.

In January 1793, shortly before the outbreak of war, Newman was appointed to *Venus* (36), and in March was made fourth lieutenant in *Royal George* (100) commanded by Captain Domett and flying the flag of Vice-Admiral Sir Alexander Hood, who was then second in command of the Channel fleet. His promotion to commander came on 24 May 1794 when he was at sea, and he did not learn of it until the return of the fleet to Spithead after the battles of the Glorious First of June. He had influence enough to participate in the general promotion which followed that battle, and was made post captain on 1 August 1794 in *Vestal* (28).

He married on 11 March 1798 Ann, third daughter of Francis Brace of Stagbatch, Herefordshire, and sister of Vice-Admiral Sir Edward Brace, KCB. The couple were to have no children.

On 15 October 1798, when in command of the 12-pounder frigate *Mermaid* (36), he engaged *La Loire* (44) in a hard-fought action, in which his ship was eventually made unmanoeuvrable so that the enemy could make off. Six days later, he engaged

The late Captain James Newman, R.N., engraved by Scriven, Historical Engraver to the Prince Regent, after A J Oliver, ARA, published by Joyce Gold, Naval Chronicle Offices, 103 Shoe Lane, London, 31 December 1813.

a damaged French frigate and forced it to surrender. Two days after her action with *Mermaid*, *La Loire* had fallen to *Anson*, a 64-gun ship of the line cut down to a frigate of thirty-eight guns, and when *Loire* was refitted, Newman was given her to command. In her he continued the active life of a frigate captain until the peace of Amiens, when, almost for the first time since his marriage, he enjoyed time ashore with his wife. On 27 June 1804, however, with the return to war, he was appointed to command *Veteran* (64) in the Downs under the command of Rear-Admiral Louis. In October, *Veteran* was placed under Admiral Cornwallis's command at Portsmouth, and in February detached to form part of a squadron under Rear-Admiral the Honourable Alexander Cochrane off Ferrol, whence they pursued a French squadron to Barbados and through the West Indies to Jamaica. Newman exchanged into *Vanguard* (74) under orders for England so as to avoid a prolonged stay in the West Indies, which threatened a renewal of his yellow fever. He was then unemployed until 12 April 1808, when he was appointed to *Hero* (74); she served in the Baltic and North Sea escorting the trade until 24 December 1811, when she was wrecked with all hands on the Haak sands, off the Texel. The ship was not in the best of condition at the time, and December was very late in the year for a ship of the line to be required to escort the trade. It was speculated that she lost her mast in a sharp gale and was unable to keep off the bank.

Lt: 26 February 1790
Cmdr: 24 May 1794
Capt: 1 August 1794

NISBET

CAPTAIN JOSIAH NISBET was Nelson's stepson, and saved his life at the abortive raid on Tenerife, but fell out with him when Nelson deserted his mother.

He was born in May 1780 in Salisbury, Wiltshire, the only son of Josiah Nisbet, apothecary in Coventry and physician in Nevis who died in 1781, and his wife Frances Herbert. His mother was daughter of William Woolward, senior judge of Nevis, niece of John Richardson Herbert, president of the council of Nevis, and granddaughter of Captain William Woolward, a sea captain. Her second husband was Captain Horatio Nelson, later Vice-Admiral Viscount Nelson, KB, who became Josiah's legal guardian.

Nelson entered Nisbet's name as a volunteer first class in the books of *Boreas* (28) in October 1785, but his real entry into the navy was in March or April 1793 as a midshipman on board *Agamemnon* (64) under Nelson's command. Nelson kept him with him in *Captain* (74) and *Theseus* (74), and he was commissioned lieutenant in 1797. On the night of 24 July 1797, when Nelson was preparing to go ashore at Santa Cruz de Tenerife, he begged Nisbet to remain behind: 'Should we both fall, Josiah, what would become of your poor mother!' But Nisbet insisted, and when Nelson's arm was shot through as he tried to step ashore, Nisbet applied a tourniquet and got him back to his ship.

At Nelson's wish, Nisbet was immediately promoted commander, on 18 September 1797, and

put in charge of *Dolphin*, hospital ship, off Cadiz. He was moved into *La Bonne Citoyenne* (20) on 3 July 1798, and Nelson praised his abilities to Admiral the earl of St Vincent. With astounding lack of tact, he wrote to Fanny 11 December 1798 that 'The improvement made in Josiah by Lady Hamilton is wonderful; your obligation and mine are infinite on that score; not but Josiah's heart is as good and as humane as ever was covered by a human breast. God bless him, I love him dearly with all his roughness.' [Marshall 2.184] To make matters worse, Emma Hamilton had herself written to Fanny a few days before in almost the same words.

Nisbet was promoted post captain on 24 December 1798 in *Thalia* (36) and served in the Mediterranean until October or November 1800, but he fell out with Nelson when he remonstrated about his infatuation with Emma. He retired from active service, and was superannuated as a captain in 1825.

He married on 31 March 1819 Frances Herbert Evans, and by that lady he had seven children, of whom four died in infancy. He died of a pleurisy on 9 July 1830, during the revolution of 1830, aged fifty, at his house in Quay d'Orsay, Paris, and was buried near his mother at St Margaret, Littleham, near Exmouth. His widow died on 15 January 1864, aged seventy-two, in Cheltenham, Gloucestershire.

Lt: 1797
Cmdr: 18 September 1797
Capt: 24 December 1798
Superannuated Capt: 1825

NORTHESK

ADMIRAL SIR WILLIAM CARNEGIE, EARL OF NORTHESK, GCB, was described by the editor of the *Naval Chronicle*: 'If he has not displayed the dazzling coruscations of a comet, he has at least moved with mild, equable, unsullied lustre, through his prescribed orbit.' [NC 15.441]

He was born on 10 April 1756, the second son of Admiral George Carnegie, sixth earl of Northesk, and his wife Anne Leslie, eldest daughter of Alexander, fifth earl of Leven. He entered the navy in 1771 as a captain's servant in *Albion* (74), a guardship at Plymouth commanded by the Honourable Captain Barrington, and the following year joined *Otter* (14) for service at Newfoundland. Later that year he was rated a midshipman in *Southampton* (32) under the command of Captain John MacBride, with whom he served in the Baltic. In 1774 he served under Captain Stair Douglas in *Squirrel* (24), in which he proceeded to the Jamaica station, and the following year he moved to *Eagle* (64) under Captain Duncan in the North American station, where he was ordered to act as lieutenant in *Nonsuch* (64) under Commander Griffiths. He was commissioned lieutenant on 7 December 1777 by Admiral Lord Howe, and appointed to *Apollo* (32) under the command of Captain Philemon (?) Pownoll. Returning to England in 1778 or 1779, he was appointed to *Royal George* (100) in the Channel fleet, flying the flag of Admiral Sir John Lockhart Ross, and later in 1779 transferred to *Sandwich* (90) flying Admiral Lord Rodney's flag. With Rodney he served at the relief of Gibraltar, and then proceeded to the West Indies, where Rodney promoted him master and commander with appointment on 17 April 1780 to *Blast* (16), his commission being confirmed on 10 September. He continued in command of *Blast* until he was made post captain on 10 April 1782, and appointed to command the Dutch prize *St Eustatius* (20) under Admiral Hugh Pigot at Jamaica. In the latter part of 1782 he was transferred into the 9-pounder frigate *Enterprise* (28).

He was mostly unemployed during the subsequent decade of peace. He married on 9 December 1788 Mary, only daughter of William Henry Ricketts of Longwood, Hampshire, niece of Sir John Jervis, later earl of St Vincent, KB, and sister of Captain William Henry Ricketts, RN. In due course the couple had four sons and five daughters. He succeeded his father as seventh earl on 22 January 1792.

In January 1793, just prior to the outbreak of war, he commissioned *Beaulieu* (40) and brought home a convoy from the Leeward Islands, returning in *Andromeda* (32). In 1796 he was elected one of the representative peers of Scotland, and governor of the British Linen Company, but this did

Rear Admiral the Earl of Northesk,
engraved by William Ridley, published by
Joyce Gold, 103 Shoe Lane,
30 June 1806.

not prevent his returning to active service. From 1795 he commanded *Monmouth* (64) in the North Sea fleet under Admiral Adam Duncan, but she was one of the ships brought in May 1797 by its mutinous crew to the Nore buoy, and Northesk was prevailed upon to carry a list of grievances to London, as 'one who was known to be the seaman's friend'. ^{Marshall 1 (Supp i) 200} He was required to bring an answer within fifty-four hours from 3pm on 6 June, and in London the first lord, Lord Spencer, took him to the king. The demands were rejected. A message was sent to Richard Parker and the delegates at the Nore, but Northesk did not himself return there. On the collapse of the mutiny and after the completion of the trials, he retired from the sea until 1800, when he was appointed to command *Prince* (98) in the Channel fleet.

He again retired from sea during the peace of Amiens, but returned to service in 1803 in command of *Britannia* (100), in which he served under Vice-Admiral the Honourable William Cornwallis in the Channel. When he was promoted rear-admiral on 23 April 1804 he hoisted his flag in the same ship and continued his service in the blockade of Brest until August. *Britannia* was then ordered to form part of a squadron under Vice-Admiral Sir Robert Calder to reinforce Collingwood off Cadiz. At the battle of Trafalgar, on 21 October, she was fourth or sixth ship in the van division to break through the enemy line, and Northesk provided close support to the *Victory* (100) flying Vice-Admiral Lord Nelson's flag. *Britannia* suffered fifty-two casualties. Northesk transferred to *Dreadnought* (98) and continued off Trafalgar until March 1806, when he hauled down his flag.

He was created a knight of the Bath on 29 January 1806 and GCB on 2 January 1815, and appointed rear-admiral of the United Kingdom in December 1821. However, he never again chose to serve at sea, although from 1827 to 1830 he was commander-in-chief Portsmouth. He served in parliament in 1802, 1806 and 1830. He died with the rank of admiral after a short illness, aged seventy-five, in Albemarle Street, London, on 28 May 1831, and was buried on 8 June in the crypt of St Paul's Cathedral.

Lt: 7 December 1777
M-C: 10 September 1780
Capt: 10 April 1782
R-Adm: 23 April 1804
V-Adm: 28 April 1808
Adm: 4 June 1814

ONSLOW

ADMIRAL SIR RICHARD ONSLOW, BARONET, GCB, made a cameo appearance in the war against Revolutionary France during the Nore mutiny, and subsequently as Duncan's vice-admiral at the battle of Camperdown. His achievement was all the more impressive as he was known as the convivial founder in 1765 of the Naval Society dining club. It was his daughter Frances, known as 'Batter Pudding' in the fleet, who in 1801 married Admiral Sir Hyde Parker when he was forty-three years older than she.

Onslow was born on 23 June 1741, the second son of Lieutenant-General Richard Onslow, member of parliament, governor of Plymouth, and his second wife, Pooley, daughter of Charles Walton of Little Bursted, Essex, and niece of Admiral Sir

George Walton. Arthur Onslow, the speaker of the House of Commons, was an uncle. This connection ensured for Richard rapid promotion. He was commissioned lieutenant on 17 December 1758 when only seventeen. Shortly after, he was made post captain on 14 April 1762 in the 18-pounder frigate *Humber* (44). He had the misfortune to run her on Haysborough sands, where she was a total loss, but he was exonerated at the court martial, the blame being laid to the pilot.

He continued in active employment during the years of peace following the Seven Years war, and in June 1773 he married Anne, daughter of Captain Matthew Mitchell, RN, of Chitterne All Saints, Wiltshire. The couple had three sons and four daughters.

After three years ashore, he returned to sea and served in the American and West Indian theatres, in the Mediterranean and in the Channel during the American war. He took command of *St Albans* (64) on 31 October 1776, joining Lord Howe at New York prior to the confrontation with d'Estaing at Sandy Hook on 22 July. Later he joined Commodore William Hotham in the West Indies and served at the capture of St Lucia and in the later action against d'Estaing in the Cul-de-Sac between 15 and 29 December. Returning to England in August 1779, in February 1780 he took command of *Bellona* (74) as part of the Channel fleet under the command of Admiral Francis Geary, and took part in the two reliefs of Gibraltar, by Vice-Admiral George Darby in April 1781 and by Lord Howe in October 1782, during which he fought in the night action of the 21st. Subsequently he served again in the West Indies, returning home in June 1783 at the conclusion of the war. He was on half pay for most of the following thirteen years, apart from the first half of 1789, when he was appointed to *Magnificent* (74) at Portsmouth. As a reward for his services he was appointed colonel of the marines on 21 September 1790, and was advanced to rear-admiral on 1 February 1793 in the general promotion on the French declaration of war. He was promoted again to vice-admiral on 4 July 1794. He was out of employment, however, until 1796, when for a short while he was put in command at Plymouth, and then was ordered to hoist his flag in *Nassau* (64) as second in command under Admiral Duncan in the North Sea.

During the mutinies of 1797 Onslow had to deal repeatedly with trouble in his ship. When on 26 May 1797 *Nassau*'s people refused to sail, he shifted his flag to *Adamant* (50). Until 17 June, when the mutiny at the Nore ended, the two flagships, *Adamant* and Duncan's ship *Venerable* (74), alone kept up the appearance of a blockade of the Dutch fleet at the Texel. On 25 July Onslow moved to the *Monarch* (74), in which he fought in the battle of Camperdown on 11 October. The Dutch were

struck to *Monarch*. In appreciation, Onslow was created a baronet on 30 October 1797. He was promoted admiral on 14 February 1799 when he resigned his command, and was not again employed at sea.

He was promoted lieutenant-general of the Royal Marines on 7 May 1814 and created GCB on 2 January 1815. He died on 27 December 1817, aged seventy-six, in Southampton, his wife living until 31 January 1837. Reportedly he left directions that no more than £20 was to be spent on his funeral to prevent any unnecessary ostentation; 'the funeral of a brave and honest sailor costs a much less sum.'

Lt: 17 December 1758
M-C: 11 February 1761
Capt: 14 April 1762
R-Adm: 1 February 1793
V-Adm: 4 July 1794
Adm: 14 February 1799

Admiral Sir Richard Onslow, Bart.,
engraved by Daniel Orme, engraver to
His Majesty, published by Joyce Gold,
103 Shoe Lane, Fleet Street,
30 April 1805.

in close order, but Duncan signalled his fleet to repeat Howe's tactic of the Glorious First of June, cutting through the enemy in line abreast, then luffing to leeward and engaging. *Monarch* was the first to effect the order, as Onslow is reported to have said, by 'making a passage' through the tight Dutch formation. He took a position alongside the *Jupiter* (72), flagship of Vice-Admiral Reyntjes, which

ORDE

ADMIRAL SIR JOHN ORDE, BARONET, is best known for challenging his superior officer, the earl of St Vincent, to a duel. When Rear-Admiral Nelson was sent with a detachment of the Mediterranean fleet to arrest Buonaparte's amphibious operation in early 1798, Orde conceived that he ought to have been sent because of his senior rank. Soon after the departure of Nelson's ships, Sir Roger Curtis arrived on 24 May, relegating Orde to fourth in command. And then St Vincent received a letter of complaint which he thought Orde might have written, and acted with typical roughness. This led Orde to write to the Admiralty requesting St Vincent's court martial for what he considered a succession of slights he had received. The first lord, Earl Spencer, refused, and St Vincent considered this letter in the same light as the seamen's mutinies. He was not at liberty to hang his insubordinate vice-admiral, but he did send him home. For this he was reprimanded, and Orde was offered a command in the Channel fleet, but he felt he could not accept: 'I must confess that I was influenced in my decision by the well-weighed reflection on my very peculiar predicament, which did seem to me to require even for my justification, not less than for retribution to me after the disgracing insults and hardships I had experienced, some more distinguished token of approbation and confidence.' *NC 11.198* He waited until St Vincent returned to England, and then he acted. On 4 October 1799, reported the *Naval Chronicle*, 'about three o'clock

Sir John Orde,
Vice Admiral of the White Squadron,
engraving by William Ridley after George Romney,
published by Joyce Gold, 103 Shoe Lane,
1 April 1804.

this morning, Admiral Sir John Orde was taken into custody, at Dorant's Hotel, in Jermyn Street, on a charge of sending a challenge to Admiral Earl of St. Vincent, whom he was to have met at six o'clock yesterday morning.' *NC 2.440*

In 1802, soon after the signing of the definitive treaty of peace at Amiens, Orde published an account of his dispute with St Vincent: 'The right of remonstrating should certainly be exercised in military service with great prudence; but Lord St. Vincent, both in the case of Sir John Orde's first letter to Lord Spencer, and that of the 31st of August to his Commander in Chief, would appear to have deemed the most respectful use of that privilege, a crime to be followed with immediate punishment and disgrace…' *NC 11.205* On King George's

making it clear that he forbade them to fight, the matter was allowed to drop.

Orde had been born on 22 December 1751 in Morpeth, Northumberland, the third and youngest son of John Orde of East Orde and Morpeth, justice of the peace and deputy lieutenant for Northumberland, and of his second wife Anne, daughter of Ralph Marr of Morpeth and widow of the Revd William Pye, clerk. He was educated at the grammar school at Morpeth, and entered the navy in 1766 on board *Jersey* (60) commanded by Captain William Dickson, the flagship of Commodore Sir Richard Spry, who was appointed to command in the Mediterranean. In the following years he served with Captain George Gayton, Commodore Byron when he was commander-in-chief Newfoundland, Sir Andrew Snape Hamond, Captain Samuel Marshall and Admiral Sir George Rodney, who commissioned him lieutenant on 7 April 1774. He returned to England as third lieutenant in *Rainbow* (44), Commodore Collingwood, and then travelled to France to improve his French. On the outbreak of hostilities in America, he was appointed second lieutenant in *Roebuck* (44) commanded by Snape Hamond, with whom he served until 1777, when he joined Vice-Admiral Lord Howe's flagship *Eagle* (64) as first lieutenant. In early 1776 Orde had been captured while carrying a flag of truce during the evacuation of the governor of Virginia, the earl of Dunmore, to Gwynn Island, but he was held for only a short period. He was promoted master and commander on 26 September 1777 in *Zebra*, in which he assisted in the reduction of Philadelphia and the forts of the Delaware. This service led to his being made post captain on 19 May 1778 in *Virginia* (32), which ship was a recent prize from the young American navy. In the autumn of 1779 he led a small British squadron up the Penobscot, driving the American warships on shore, where their crews burnt them.

In 1780 Orde participated in the capture of Charlestown, seizing control of Mount Pleasant, overlooking Fort Moultrie, and thus opening the approaches to the city. As a reward he was put in command of *Chatham* (50), and on 8 February

1781, in Charlestown, Orde married Margaret Emma, daughter and heiress of Richard Stephens of Beaufort, St Helena, South Carolina. The couple were to have one son, who died in infancy, before Margaret Emma herself died in 1790.

In February 1783, with the return of peace, Orde was appointed governor of Dominica, where he stayed until 1789. He was created a baronet on 9 August 1790, and then lived in Dominica again until 1794. The *Naval Chronicle* was enthusiastic about the measures he took against slaves who had attempted to liberate themselves following the edict by the French National Convention ending slavery throughout the French Empire.

He returned to naval service in 1794, was promoted rear-admiral on 1 June 1795, and was in command at Plymouth during the mutinies, when he proved himself no less effective in the measures he took against disobedient seamen: so much so that in June 1797 he was put in command at Portsmouth so that he would preside at the courts martial of the Nore mutineers. Finally he was sent to sea, flying his flag on *Princess Royal* (98), and joined St Vincent on the Mediterranean station.

Surprisingly, after the challenge to St Vincent, Orde was employed again on the resumption of hostilities, but only after St Vincent resigned as first lord of the Admiralty. In the autumn of 1804, following the Spanish declaration of war, he was given command of a squadron watching Cadiz. He mounted a most efficient blockade which kept the Spanish fleet in harbour throughout that winter, but Nelson, who commanded in the Mediterranean, thought Orde was trespassing in his actions against enemy trade, taking what might have been Nelson's prizes. Finally disgusted, Orde made a written request that he should be allowed to return home. Before any action could follow his request, however, the French Toulon fleet commanded by Vice-Admiral Villeneuve escaped through the Straits of Gibraltar and sailed for Cadiz, where Orde's squadron lay at anchor. Outnumbered, and caught between the French and Spaniards, Orde complied with standing orders and withdrew to join the Channel fleet off Ushant. His dispatches to London were the first warning of Napoleon's plan that Villeneuve should draw off the Channel fleet by sailing to the west and then concentrate naval resources in the Channel for the short time needed by the French army of England to cross the Straits of Dover.

He served as a pall-bearer at Nelson's funeral. Retiring from active service, he entered politics, holding the parliamentary seat for Yarmouth, Isle of Wight, from 14 August 1807 until 1812. He was also vice-president of the Naval Charitable Society. At some date not recorded Orde remarried, uniting with Jane, daughter of John Frere. The couple had five children. He died on 19 February 1824, aged seventy-two, at his house in Gloucester Place, Portman Square, St Marylebone, London.

Lt: 1 April 1774
M-C: 26 September 1777
Capt: 19 May 1778
R-Adm: 1 June 1795
V-Adm: 14 February 1799
Adm: 9 November 1805

OTWAY

ADMIRAL SIR ROBERT WALLER OTWAY, BARONET, GCB, is almost certainly best known for his part in the 1801 Copenhagen campaign and the subsequent battle, but those who served with him reported on his merits on many other occasions. In particular, Captain Ussher wrote in November 1826 that he remembered Otway as 'one of the best seamen in the service, certainly that I ever sailed under, and as undoubtedly the most active. It is also most true of him, that he had courage to execute whatever his head planned, however daring might be the attempt. There was also so much method in his manner of carrying on the service, that his officers and men, though in a constant state of activity, had perhaps as much leisure as any other ship's company, and no one was more attentive to the comforts of both officers and men. I may also mention that the *Trent* [which Otway commanded in 1797] was considered the most perfect man-of-war in the West Indies, and always ready to go into action in five minutes: there was no unnecessary display on board of polished bolts or nail-heads; but every rope and spar was in its place, and the decks constantly kept clear. When at sea, and after the men had been exercised at quarters, the captain visited every gun, and saw that it was ready and in order; after which inspection not a rope-yarn or chip was to be seen at or near any of the guns.... He always set a noble example himself; and it was a matter of perfect indifference to him whether it was a lee or weather shore; wherever the enemy was expected there was the *Trent*, with leads-man in the chains and anchors ready. With regard to sending boats on service, if the duty to be performed was considered dangerous, he generally went himself (as a volunteer), unless the situation of the ship required him to remain on board; and he several times did me the honor to come in the boat, advising, but not commanding.' Marshall 4.429

He was born on 26 April 1770, the second son of Cooke Otway, who was an officer in the army at Castle Otway, county Tipperary, and his wife Elizabeth, daughter of Samuel Waller of Lisbrian. He entered the navy on 15 April 1784 as a captain's servant in *Elizabeth* (74), which was a guardship at Plymouth and commanded by Captain Robert Kingsmill. In September 1785 he was rated a midshipman in *Phaeton* (38) under Captain Dawson, with whom he served in the Mediterranean until she was paid off in August 1786. He then joined *Southampton* (32) under Captain Andrew Douglas at Spithead for the passage back to the Mediterranean, where in November he joined *Trusty* (50), which was flying the broad pendant of Commodore Cosby as station commander. *Trusty* was paid off in February 1789, and he immediately joined the 12-pounder frigate *Blonde* (32) under the command of Captain William Affleck, with whom he went out to the West Indies, and he continued in her until January 1792 when he followed Affleck, who had been promoted to rear-admiral and was flying his flag on *Centurion* (50) commanded by Captain William Albany Otway, who was not a close relative of Robert Waller. When she was paid off in August, our hero joined the powerful 18-pounder frigate *Charon* (44) under Commodore Edmund (?) Dod commanding on the coast of Guinea. He remained in her until after the French declaration of war on 1 February 1793.

He was commissioned lieutenant on 8 August 1793 and was appointed to *Falcon*, brig-sloop (10), under the command of Commander James Bissett, and served in the Channel fleet. In December he was appointed to *Impregnable* (90) flying the flag of Rear-Admiral Benjamin Caldwell, and he served as her junior lieutenant in the actions of the Glorious First of June in 1794. There he established his reputation by lashing the fore-topsail yard to the cap at a critical moment, thus enabling the ship to wear. He was offered immediate promotion, but declined because he did not want to displace senior lieutenants. In September, however, he was transferred as first lieutenant into *Majestic* (74), in which Caldwell hoisted his flag as commander-in-chief West Indies. He served at Martinique in command of *Thorn*, ship-sloop (14), against the French nationalists and freed slaves led by Victor Hughes, and in the Carib war on St Vincent. He attracted the attention of Sir John Laforey, who promoted him to post rank and command of the recent French prize 9-pounder frigate *Le Jacobin* (28), which was renamed *Matilda*. The Admiralty confirmed the promotion to master in April, but did not confirm this second step. Laforey, however, was able to convince the incoming first lord, Earl Spencer, who appointed Otway on 30 October 1795 to the 12-pounder frigate *Mermaid* (32). At a critical moment in the fighting ashore, Otway went so far as to refuse to re-embark the soldiers, and then helped them drive off a threatened flank attack.

He was transferred into the 12-pounder frigate *Ceres* (32) in April 1797, and then into *Trent* in August 1798. This latter was one of the first fir-built frigates, and carried thirty-six 18-pounders on her main deck. In July 1799 he attempted to cut *Hermione* (32) out of a Cuban harbour where she had been taken by her mutineers, but after a nine-hour row, *Trent*'s people found that she had been moved. Instead they managed to capture a small Spanish ship, but although they got clear of the shore batteries, the wind then failed. They would have been taken by Spanish gunboats but for Otway's decision to scuttle the ship by firing

12-pounders triply shotted into her hold and making off in the boats. The Spaniards were kept too busy rescuing their own people from the sinking ship to pursue the British any further.

Otway returned to England in November 1800 in *Royal George* (100) as flag captain to Sir Hyde Parker, who was returning from command at Jamaica. The relationship was evidently a comfortable one, and Otway was asked to serve as his flag captain in *London* (90) in the 1801 Baltic expedition. This circumstance enabled him to be influential at a critical point in the Copenhagen campaign. The decision had been made to make a roundabout passage through the Great Belt, which would have required lightening the ships of the line to enable them to approach Copenhagen Road from the south. According to his own report, Otway, who was very junior to be interfering in matters of grand tactics, used his diplomatic skills to persuade Hyde Parker to change his plan.

He had the frustration of having to watch the battle of Copenhagen from afar, but when Hyde Parker made his famous signal to Lord Nelson to discontinue action, Otway obtained permission to row over and tell Nelson that the signal might be ignored if in his judgement that was the right course to take. In fact, Nelson had already done so. The following day, Otway's diplomacy again came into play when he convinced the Danish commodore, with the help of a sailor who quietly removed a pendant left flying on the *Holstein* after she had struck her colours, that indeed she had surrendered.

Immediately after returning from the Baltic, he married on 15 August 1801, in Kingston, Somerset; his wife was Clementina, eldest daughter and co-heiress of Admiral John Holloway of Wells. The couple were to have five sons and seven daughters.

In the last year of the war he commanded *Edgar* (74) in the Channel fleet and later in the West Indies. She was paid off in July, and a domestic crisis prevented his returning to service immediately after the renewal of the war. That apparently resolved, in December 1804 he was appointed to *Montagu*, in which he served in Charles Cornwallis's squadron off Brest. He engaged *Alexandre* in the skirmish with the French fleet on 22 August 1805; in the spring of 1806 he took part in Sir Richard Strachan's pursuit of the French squadron under the command of Admiral Willaumez; and in 1807 he was employed on the coast of Calabria, moving in 1808 to the coast of Catalonia, where he co-operated with the Spanish patriots. In August 1808 he was transferred to *Malta* (80), which was paid off in December. In May 1809 he was appointed to *Ajax* (74), and he continued in her until August 1811, when he transferred to *Cumberland* (74), in which he was employed in the blockade of Toulon and the French coast. He left her in December, and after a period ashore to recover his health, he was able to return to the Channel fleet on 13 May 1813, when he was reappointed to *Ajax*. In June 1814 he escorted an army of 5,000 from Bordeaux to Quebec; he stayed there to assist in the equipping of the flotilla on Lake Champlain, where he stayed until November.

Following the end of the war he served from August 1818 to December 1821 as commander-in-chief at Leith, Scotland, with his flag in *Phaeton* (38). On 8 June 1826 he was made a KCB and appointed commander-in-chief in South America during the transition from Spanish imperial authority to independence. The Brazilian government appointed him to its order of the Southern Cross. On his return he was appointed groom of the bedchamber to William IV on 23 December 1830, created a baronet on 15 September 1831 and nominated GCB on 8 May 1845. He held the rank of admiral when he died on 12 May 1846, aged seventy-six, in London.

Lt: 8 August 1793
Cmdr: April 1795
Capt: 30 October 1795
R-Adm: 4 June 1814
V-Adm: 22 July 1830
Adm: 23 November 1841

OWEN

ADMIRAL SIR EDWARD WILLIAM CAMPBELL RICH OWEN, GCB, is best known for his energy as inshore commander of *Immortalité* (36), attacking the French invasion flotilla sheltering in the Channel ports or working its way in small groups along the coast. In September 1803 Dieppe and St

Valery en Caux were bombarded, and on 20 July 1804, when a division of the flotilla was ordered out of Boulogne by Buonaparte to demonstrate its ability to carry out an invasion, it was engaged and suffered heavily, although mostly from the weather. In October 1804 a number of praams trying to round Cap Gris Nez were engaged, and in July 1805 Owen again engaged a part of the Boulogne flotilla. He was moved into *Clyde* (38), with orders to act as commodore, and in October 1806 he commanded a force attacking Boulogne with Congreve rockets.

He was born in June 1771 in Wales, a son of Captain William Owen, RN, who was accidentally killed in 1778 at Madras on passage to England with dispatches, and a brother of Vice-Admiral William Fitzwilliam Owen. Who his mother was is not known. On 11 August 1775, when he was little more than four years old, Edward Owen was entered as captain's servant of *Enterprise* (28) under the command of his godfather, Sir Thomas Rich, and he continued on the musters of Rich's subsequent three commands in the West Indies. In fact he was sent as a scholar to the maritime school at Chelsea, and finally entered the navy in July 1786 as a midshipman in *Culloden* (74), which was a guardship at Plymouth. He noted in the précis of his services that he spent much of his time working in unfinished ships, preparing them for service. But this servitude did not last long, for in August he was lent to *Fairy* (14) under the command of Captain Sir George Manley, and moved in October to *Leander* (50) flying the broad pendant of Commodore Herbert Sawyer in Nova Scotia. In January 1788 to joined the 12-pounder frigate *Lowestoffe* (32) under Captain E. Dod, and he served in the Channel and Mediterranean prior to passing his examination in 1790. In April, as a passed midshipman and master's mate with charge of a watch, he joined *Thisbe* (28) under Captain Rupert George, and returned to Nova Scotia. He returned again to England as a supernumerary in *Dido* in November 1790 and the next month joined *Vengeance* (74) under Sir Thomas Rich for service at Plymouth and Spithead; in December 1791 he got a berth as able seaman in

Hannibal (74) commanded by Sir John Colpoys in a squadron of observation in the Channel; in September 1792 he joined *Porcupine* (24) under Captain Edward Buller as an additional midshipman in charge of a watch; and in January 1793, just before the French declaration of war, he joined *Culloden* (74), again under Sir Thomas Rich's command. With him he made a voyage to the West Indies, leaving her at Plymouth on 5 November.

His lieutenant's commission was dated the following day, when he joined *Fortune* commanded by Captain Wooldridge. Between December and May 1794 he served again in *Hannibal* under Colpoys, during which time he moved from fifth to fourth lieutenant while serving off Cadiz, then returned as second lieutenant to *Culloden,* which was now flying the flag of Sir Thomas Rich, who had been promoted to rear-admiral but permitted to remain in his ship. Rich hauled down his flag in October, and command was assumed by Captain Thomas Troubridge, who presumably brought his first lieutenant with him, relegating Owen to third lieutenant. The following January, he moved into *London* (90) flying the flag of Rear-Admiral Sir John Colpoys, dropping again to fifth lieutenant, but by August 1796 he had risen to being her first lieutenant, and had acted as temporary captain of *Impregnable* (90) in March and April, and of *Queen Charlotte* (100) from May to July. He was then promoted for rank to commander, but remained in *London* as a volunteer until May 1797, when he was appointed to command a number of gun-brigs under Sir Erasmus Gower at the Nore during the mutiny.

He was promoted to post captain on 23 April 1798 and appointed to *Northumberland* (74), then to *Irresistible* (74) based on the Medway, and then moved to the operational area in which he made his mark, the North Sea and off Dunkirk and Boulogne with command of the 9-pounder frigate *Nemesis* (28). He described his employment as 'commanding a detachment off the Scheldt, east of Dunkirk'. [ADM9 f72] In May 1802 he was appointed to the French prize *Immortalité* (36), in which he returned to the Channel coast of France on the renewal of the war, 'commanding a guard of frigates held ready in the Downs'. *Immortalité* was paid off in March 1803, but immediately returned to service with the renewal of the war, and Owen again commanded 'inshore, [a] detach[ment] off Boulogne and command[ed] also a squad[ron] in the rivers Elb and Weser to bring off Lord Cathcart's army'. On 21 March 1806 he transferred into *Clyde*, but his work remained as before, except that the threat of invasion was past, and instead attention had to be paid to naval construction at Antwerp. He played a part in the siege of Flushing in August 1809.

In December 1810 he took command of *Inconstant* (36), and in 1811 he commanded in the Gulf of Mexico flying a broad pendant as commodore. In February 1813 he was appointed to command the *Cornwall* (74) in the North Sea, and at the end of 1813 he commanded the Royal Marines landed in South Beveland to co-operate with the Dutch royalists. In the second half of 1814 he was given a well-earned holiday, commanding the yacht *Dorset* at Deptford, but in December he was put in command of naval forces on the Canadian lakes. In February 1816 he returned to his rest, commanding the yacht *Royal Sovereign* at Deptford.

He first married on 19 December 1802, a daughter of John Cannon of Middle Deal, Kent, and was married a second time in 1829, to Selina, daughter of Captain John Baker Hay, RN.

Following the war he was made a KCB on 2 January 1815, nominated a knight bachelor on 14 June 1816, promoted colonel of the Royal Marines on 19 July 1821 and to rear-admiral on 27 May 1825, installed as a knight grand cross of the Guelphic order on 24 October 1832, and advanced in chivalry to GCB on 8 May 1845. He was member of parliament for Sandwich, Kent, between 1826 and 1827, and a member of the council of the Royal Astronomical Society. He was appointed surveyor-general of the Ordnance in 1827, and in March 1828 a member of the lord high admiral's council. From December 1828 to 1832 he served as commander-in-chief in the East Indies, in 1834 he was appointed to the Board of Ordnance, and from 1841 to 1845 he was commander-in-chief

in the Mediterranean. He eventually was promoted to admiral on 11 December 1846, and died on 8 October 1849, aged seventy-eight.

> Lt: 6 November 1793
> Cmdr: 19 September 1796
> Capt: 23 April 1798
> R-Adm: 27 May 1825
> V-Adm: 10 January 1837
> Adm: 11 December 1846

PALMER

CAPTAIN EDMUND PALMER, CB, earned an honorary medal in 1814 in command of *Hebrus* (42), when after a long chase and violent engagement, he captured the French frigate *L'Etoile* (44), and he was made a CB in 1815 for services during Buonaparte's One Hundred Days.

The date of his birth is unknown, as is his mother's name. His father was John Palmer of Bath, member of parliament and controller-general of the Post Office. Edmund entered the navy as a volunteer first class in *Gibraltar* (80) under Captain John Pakenham on 31 July 1794, and served in the Channel and Mediterranean. He was rated a midshipman before he left her in 1796 to join the French prize *L'Aigle* (36) under Captain Charles Tyler, with whom he continued in Mediterranean service, in the Adriatic and on the coasts of Spain and Portugal. In 1798 he joined the *Ville de Paris* (110) flying the earl of St Vincent's flag off Cadiz, and the following year he joined the *Royal William* (100) at Spithead, but he returned in 1800 to *Ville de Paris*, which was now St Vincent's flagship in the Channel fleet. That same year he was made an acting lieutenant in *Princess Royal* (98) flying the flag of Rear-Admiral Sir Erasmus Gower in the Channel fleet, with his commission confirmed and dated 3 April 1801. He later served in *Triton* (32) and *Childers,* brig-sloop (10), and was promoted commander on 8 May 1804, with appointment on 20 September 1805 to the not-yet-launched *Wizard,* brig (16). He served at the reduction of Alexandria in March 1807, and was promoted to post rank on 10 October 1807, which put him out of a job. It appears that his first command was the yellow-pine-built 18-pounder frigate *Hebrus* (36), which was launched on 13 September 1813.

In his official letter of 27 March 1814, Captain Palmer described his action against *L'Etoile*:

> ... we continued in pursuit... the whole day, with all our canvas spread. About midnight she reached the Race of Alderney, and the wind scanting, we began to gain upon her fast; by the time she had run the length of Point Jobourg, leading into the bay of la Hague, she was obliged to attempt rounding it almost within the wash of the breakers; and here, after an anxious chase of 15 hours, and running him upwards of 120 miles, we were fortunate enough, between one and two A.M., to bring the enemy to battle; we crossed his stern, our jib-boom passing over his taffrail, and shot in between him and the shore, in eight fathoms water; and it falling nearly calm about this time, the ships continued nearly in the same spot until the conclusion of the action. At its commencement we suffered severely in our rigging; the enemy firing high, he shot away our fore-top-mast and fore-yard, crippled our main-mast and bowsprit, and cut away almost every shroud, stay, and brace we had. Our fire from the first, and throughout, was directed at our opponent's hull; and the ships being as close together as they could be without touching, he suffered most severely, every shot which struck passing through him. About four o'clock his mizzen-mast fell by the board, and his fire ceased; when after an obstinate contest of two hours and a quarter, he hailed us, to say that he had struck his colours. The moment we could get possession, it became necessary to put the heads of both ships off shore, as well from the apprehension of grounding, as to get them clear from a battery which had been firing at both of us during the whole action, those on shore not being able from the darkness to distinguish one from the other...

Hebrus was then ordered to the American theatre, where Palmer served under Sir Alexander Cochrane on the Patuxent, and ashore under Major-General Ross at the battle of Bladensburgh on 24 August 1814. In the summer of 1815 *Hebrus* was one of the squadron sent to Bordeaux to arm and equip the Bordelais against Buonaparte, during which service the forts at the river entrance had to be destroyed to ensure the possibility of retreat. Fortunately the battle of Waterloo and the subsequent armistice averted the threat of civil war. The following year *Hebrus* was employed in the fleet under Lord Exmouth at Algiers.

Palmer married Henrietta Elizabeth Mary, daughter of Captain William Henry Ricketts Jervis, RN, on 27 November 1817. She gave birth to a large family, one of whom, John Jervis Palmer, entered the Royal Navy. Palmer died on 19 September 1834.

> Lt: 3 April 1801
> Cmdr: 8 May 1804
> Capt: 10 October 1807

PARKER

ADMIRAL SIR HYDE PARKER is best known for the ineffectual part he took in the 1801 Baltic expedition, but he had by that time had a long and successful career.

Probably born in 1739, he was the second son of Admiral Sir Hyde Parker, known as 'Vinegar Parker', fifth baronet of Melford Hall, Suffolk, and his wife Sarah, daughter of Hugh Smithson of Northumberland. Young Hyde entered the navy when he was twelve years old in November 1751 in his father's ship *Vanguard* (74), and later was a midshipman in *Cruiser*, sloop. His examination took place on 7 November 1757, and he was commissioned lieutenant on 25 January 1758. He was then appointed to his father's ship *Brilliant* (36), which was launched on 27 October 1759. In 1760 both Parkers were appointed to the *Norfolk* (74) with orders to join the East Indies squadron. Later transferring first to *Grafton* (70) and then to *Panther* (60), they were so fortunate as to capture a galleon freighted for Acapulco during the Manila campaign.

Confiding to the strength and thickness of their ship's sides, which the shot even of the *Panther* were unable to penetrate, except in the upper works, they lay almost without returning a shot, and patiently endured a cannonade of more than two hours continuance, as though they hoped to foil the attempts of their assailant rather by their obstinacy, than by their prowess. Finding, nevertheless, that all hope of escape was fruitless, they were at length content to surrender. [NC 5.283]

The younger Hyde Parker was made post captain on 18 July 1763 at the end of the Seven Years War, and was continuously employed from December 1766. He was appointed to command the *Boston* (32) in September 1770 at the time of the Falkland Islands crisis, and the *Phoenix* (44) in July 1775. With the outbreak of civil war in the American colonies he made a controversial decision not to take action against a rebel army occupying New York, for fear of the injury which the citizens would suffer, but in October 1776 he made a good impression when Lord Howe sent him to force the passage of the North river above New York. The river was defended by gunboats and shore batteries, but Parker destroyed two of the gunboats and ran the remainder ashore. The *Phoenix* continued in American waters and conveyed troops to Savannah in January 1779. When she returned home for dockyard repair, Parker was, on 21 April 1779, created a knight bachelor. In 1780 he was ordered to the Jamaica station, sailing as part of Admiral Sir George Rodney's relief of Gibraltar, but on 4 October *Phoenix* was struck by the great hurricane, and was wrecked on the Cuban coast east of Cape Cruz. 'According to Sir Hyde Parker's representation,' wrote the station commander, Admiral Sir Peter Parker, 'if she had not been driven on shore she must soon have foundered. All the ship's company were happily saved except twenty, the greater part of whom were lost with the mainmast, and washed overboard.'

When he returned to England he was appointed to the 18-pounder frigate *Latona* (38) and served in the North Sea squadron, fighting in the battle of Dogger Bank under his father's command. In October 1781 he was appointed to command *Goliath* (74), and he served in Lord Howe's relief of Gibraltar the following year. He continued to be employed during the years of peace until 1790, when he was appointed colonel of the marines.

It is not recorded when he married Anne, daughter of John Palmer Boteler of Henley, Suffolk. The couple had three sons, of whom his eldest was to join the navy and become the third Hyde Parker to reach flag rank.

Parker was appointed to the *Orion* (74) during the French crisis in 1787, and to the *Brunswick* during the Nootka Sound crisis with Spain in 1790; and at the time of the Russia crisis in 1791, when preparations were made to deploy a Baltic fleet commanded by Lord Hood, Parker was appointed captain of the fleet. On the declaration of war by France on 1 February 1793 he was promoted rear-admiral and again accepted the post of captain of the fleet to Lord Hood, who was to command in the Mediterranean. He continued in the post under Admiral Lord Hotham. The job of captain of the fleet, especially when the fleet was involved in such complicated operations as the defence of Toulon, requiring liaison with the Toulon corporation and the land and naval forces of Spain, was both highly demanding and generally unrecognised. At the same time, it is a very different job from that of commander-in-chief. Possibly the long years of serving in ships commanded by 'Vinegar Parker' had fitted him more for staff work than for command.

On his promotion to vice-admiral on 4 July 1794 he was appointed commander of a division of the fleet, and as such took part in Hotham's two skirmishes with the Toulon fleet on 13 March and 13 July 1795. Parker returned to England early in 1796, but the probability that Spain would change sides led to his being sent back with a squadron to join Sir John Jervis in the Mediterranean. He was given unusually complicated orders, to avoid action with the French if they were in company with a Spanish force, and to pursue the squadron under Rear-Admiral Richery if he had managed to elude the squadron under Rear-Admiral Robert Man stationed off Cadiz. This latter proved to be the case. Richery had gone to Newfoundland, but Parker concluded he would be bound for the West Indies, and chased as far as Martinique, where he arrived in September 1796. Richery did great damage in the Newfoundland fishery, but Parker's decision was approved by the Admiralty nevertheless, and he was appointed commander at the Jamaica station. The Jamaica command was a plum which usually meant riches from the captures made by cruisers. Parker may have made as much as £200,000 before he returned home in 1800. Cupidity may have been a factor in the quarrel he had with his second in command, Vice-Admiral Richard Bligh, over the pardoning of some of the *Hermione* mutineers. Quite against regulations, Parker sent him home.

On his own return to England, Parker was given a command in the Channel fleet under the earl of St Vincent, who found him wanting, but nonetheless recognised that his experience in the Baltic made him the man to send to Copenhagen to deal with the situation created by Tsar Paul's new friendship with France, and the renewal of the alliance amongst the northern powers. Parker had been promoted admiral on 14 February 1799, and he was given the more thrusting Nelson for his vice-admiral.

To all appearances, Parker was not, in fact, so very interested in the job. It is not recorded when Anne died, but on 23 January 1801 Parker remarried. He chose for his wife Frances, youngest daughter of Admiral Sir Richard Onslow, baronet, GCB, a girl of eighteen who was referred to unkindly in the fleet as 'Batter Pudding'. The difference of their ages was forty-three years. The comforts of home contrasted strongly with the nervous strain of commanding a battle fleet in the still ice-strewn Baltic, although his experience as captain of the fleet had given him experience of dealing with complex diplomacy.

His flag captain, Sir Robert Waller Otway, and Nelson managed to get him into station before Copenhagen, and Nelson assumed responsibility for carrying out the attack. Parker was clearly too old for the command he held. When he thought Nelson too heavily engaged and likely to get into

trouble, he went so far as to signal his recall. The consequences could have been disastrous, as it would have required the damaged fleet to work its way out through the shoals under a very heavy fire, but Nelson ignored the signal. After Nelson had made the initial contact with the Danish government, Parker was needed to conclude the truce which ended the fighting.

When the proceedings at Copenhagen were known in London, Parker was ordered home and Nelson was left to command in chief. Parker then retired into private life with his new wife. She gave him another son, Charles, who eventually entered the navy and reached the rank of captain, and two daughters. Parker died on 16 March 1807, aged sixty-seven, in Bentwell Lodge, Suffolk. There is a memorial in the Holy Trinity, Long Melford, Suffolk. Frances Parker died in March 1844.

Lt: 25 January 1758
Capt: 18 July 1763
R-Adm: 1 February 1793
V-Adm: 4 July 1794
Adm: 14 February 1799

PARKER

CAPTAIN SIR PETER PARKER, BARONET, derives his claim to fame from his role in the battle of Trafalgar when in command of the brig-sloop *Weazle* (18), which on the evening of 19 October 1805 was stationed close inshore, not more than four miles from Cadiz lighthouse, where Parker could watch the combined fleet in Cadiz. At six o'clock on the morning of the 20th she saw the enemy's fleet getting under way. Parker signalled this intelligence to Captain Blackwood commanding the inshore frigate force in *Euryalus* (32), and was ordered by him to carry the warning to the ships at Gibraltar and to Rear-Admiral Louis, who had been sent there to complete stores. Parker accordingly missed being at the battle, but Vice-Admiral Collingwood was so pleased with the promptness of his actions that he promoted Parker, with appointment to command *Melpomene* (38). He took rank from 22 October 1805, the day after the battle, and was sent to cruise in the Mediterranean.

Parker had been born on 18 April 1786, in St

Marylebone, London, the eldest son of Vice-Admiral Christopher Parker and his wife, Augusta Barbara Charlotte, daughter of Admiral the Honourable John Byron. The Navy Office credited him with joining the naval service on 6 January 1793 as a captain's servant in *Blanche* (32), where he remained until 4 April 1794. On 22 November 1795 he joined the *Royal William* (100) as a volunteer, but was rated an ordinary seaman on 5 Janaury 1796, and a midshipman on 10 September. On 23 April 1799 he was transferred to the former Indiaman *Pigot*, renamed *Lancaster* (64) and commanded by Sir Roger Curtis at the Cape of Good Hope. Rated a midshipman and able seaman, he passed his examination on 4 May 1801. ADM 107.25.286 His lieutenant's commission was dated 21 October 1801, four years to the day before the battle of Trafalgar. After service in several ships in the Mediterranean, he was appointed on 7 October 1803 to *Victory* (100) flying the flag of Lord Nelson, who promoted him on 8 May 1804 to the rank of commander. From October 1804 to April 1805 he commanded the hired ship *John*, after which he was transferred into the *Weazle*.

His service during the four years following his promotion to command *Melpomene* was in the Mediterranean, until the summer of 1808, when he was employed in transporting $3 million from Vera Cruz to Cadiz for the Spanish government, now in alliance with Britain. Parker would have received a very substantial fee for this service, but he and many of his crew also contracted yellow fever. *Melpomene* was ordered to Portsmouth, and Parker recovered quickly enough that on 11 February 1809 he married Marianne, daughter of Sir George Dallas, baronet of Petsall, Staffordshire. The couple were to have one son. Parker also ran for, and won, the parliamentary seat for Wexford, which he held from 3 March 1810 to June 1811. On 21 December 1810 he succeeded his grandfather and became second baronet.

He continued to serve at sea, although he was still troubled with his health. In May 1810 he was appointed to the *Menelaus* (38). Having been sent in July to St Helena to convoy home the East India fleet he heard about the loss of the frigate squadron

at Isle de France. He sailed at once for Bourbon to reinforce Commodore Rowley, joining in time to take part in the capture of the island. In October 1811 he was employed in transporting Lord William Bentinck as ambassador to the king of Sicily, and in January 1812 he joined Sir Edward Pellew at Port Mahon. He served there for the greater part of the year, employed in the inshore squadron before Toulon, before returning home in charge of a convoy. He was then employed as a cruiser and in the Channel until the spring of 1814, when he was ordered to the North American station.

He was twenty-eight when he lost his life while serving in the Chesapeake. Displaying more gallantry than wisdom, he rashly pursued an American militia force in the dark, four miles into their own familiar territory. Mortally wounded by buckshot, he was carried by his men back to his ship, where he died. His body, brought home, was buried in St Margaret, Westminster.

> Lt: 21 October 1801
> Cmdr: 8 May 1804
> Capt: 22 October 1805

PARKER

RICHARD PARKER, seaman and Nore mutineer, was not a hero to aristocratic Britain or to the naval command. Nor was he a hero to the nameless delegates of the earlier Spithead mutiny, who saw the excesses and violence of the Nore mutiny as undermining the position they had gained through more effective and less violent action. But he was certainly a martyr in the repressive world of the last decade of the eighteenth century, when the example of the French Revolution, and fear that it would spread across the Channel, had undermined the English social contract. He was not the original leader of the mutiny, but he allowed himself to become its spokesman, and suffered for it.

He was born on 16 April 1767 at St Peter's churchyard, Exeter, Devon, the third child of Richard Parker, who was a successful Exeter baker and corn factor. His mother, Sarah, died when he was young. He was tutored by the Revd Mr Marshall, and learnt navigation from Mr Osborne, the quaymaster at Topsham, Devon. He entered the navy on 10 April 1782 with the help of his cousin Lieutenant Arthur, who got him signed as a volunteer in the two-deck *Mediator* (44) under the command of Captain Luttrell. He was rated able seaman and paid a bounty of £5 and two months' advance of £2 5s., but health problems following a voyage in the ship-sloop *Bulldog* (16) to the Gambia led to his being hospitalised at Haslar in Gosport in June 1784, and later at the hospital at Plymouth. He was discharged in August, and found work in the merchant service, sailing in Exeter ships to the Mediterranean and the East Indies. Following the French declaration of war in February 1793 he returned to naval service, but he was sent to Newgate prison on 15 May 1793 for some unknown crime, following which he joined the two-decked *Assurance* (44) under Captain Berkeley at Chatham, being rated midshipman in August. But again he failed, being court-martialled in December for refusing to carry his hammock aloft to be aired, work he considered inconsistent with his rate. He was, in consequence, disrated. In April 1794 he was back at Haslar with severe rheumatism, and shortly after signing into *Royal William* (100) in May was rehospitalised. He was discharged from his ship on 26 November, and his wife told the Admiralty at the time of his trial that his discharge was due to 'mental derangement', and that he was 'at times in a state of insanity'. *Portsmouth Gazette*, 26 June 1797

Soon after he was out of naval discipline he was arrested for debt. How he dealt with that is unclear, but he returned to Exeter, and there on 10 June 1795 he married Ann McHardy, who was a farmer's daughter from Braemar, Aberdeenshire. She had already baptised there a son, John Charles, the previous October; another son followed and was christened in Exeter in March 1796, and Parker's third child was born in May 1796. The Parkers were supported by Ann's brother, but Richard was arrested in Edinburgh for a debt of £23. He avoided prison only by rejoining the navy for a bounty of 20 guineas. When he entered the Leith tender he appeared to Lieutenant Watson as boastful, and eloquent, and to have a liking for drink.

He signed on board *Sandwich* (90) on 30 April at the Nore twelve days before the seamen there began to mutiny in support of their colleagues at Spithead, but the Nore was a mobilisation and manning depot, not an operational command, and the seamen lacked the coherence and discipline of the Channel fleet mutineers. The latter had made it clear they would go to sea if the French fleet sailed, or if a major convoy was expected, but at the Nore the mutineers hoisted a red flag on 23 May, and on 2 June commenced a blockade of Thames trade. There were even fears that they would take their ships to surrender to the Dutch, or would assist the expected Dutch invasion. Gunboats were organised under the orders of Commodore Erasmus Gower in the lower Thames to attack the mutineers, the buoys in the estuary were removed, and the forts at Sheerness, Tilbury and Gravesend were readied to fire hot shot. Admiral Keith was put in command at Sheerness near the Nore because he was thought to be popular with the seamen, and gradually ships' companies began to desert the mutiny. *Sandwich*'s crew surrendered on 13 June, and Parker was confined in Maidstone gaol.

Captain Mosse prosecuted him at court martial from 22 to 26 June with Vice-Admiral Sir Thomas Pasley presiding on the *Neptune* (98). It was established to the court's satisfaction that Parker was president of the committee from 14 May, that he had been involved in its decisions and punishments, and that he ordered ships to be fired on which sought to leave the conspiracy. But Parker maintained that he had only obeyed the delegates' commands, having signed on board a few days before the rising. He claimed to have prevented more violence, and denied that he was a Jacobin or traitor. Whatever was the truth, it is certain the government and the navy, which had been humiliated by the Spithead mutiny and very much frightened by that at the Nore, needed to make an example of him. He was hanged on 30 June from *Sandwich* (90), dressed in mourning clothes. Reportedly he jumped from the ship's rail to hang himself, with his wife watching from a small boat alongside. His body was hustled into the naval 'new burying ground' at Sheerness despite the request of Ann for her husband's body so that it could be buried like the gentleman he thought himself to be. She recovered it and took it to Rochester, where so large a crowd came to see and sketch him that the magistrates, fearing riots, ordered his burial in the vault of St Mary Matfelon, Whitechapel, on 4 July.

> Rated midshipman: August 1793
> Disrated by court martial: December 1793

PARKER

ADMIRAL OF THE FLEET SIR WILLIAM PARKER, BARONET, GCB, was one of Nelson's favourites. He wrote to the earl of St Vincent: 'Your nephew has very much pleased me, as indeed he always does.... I admire his spirit and resolution to attack... under all the disadvantages of situation: such conduct will some happy day meet its reward.'

He was born on 1 December 1781 at Almington Hall, Staffordshire, the third son of George Parker and nephew of Admiral Sir John Jervis, earl of St Vincent. He entered the navy on 5 March 1793 as a captain's servant on board *Orion* (74) commanded by Captain John Thomas Duckworth, and was rated midshipman at the time of the actions of 28 and 29 May and 1 June 1794. In March 1795 he transferred with Duckworth to *Leviathan* (74) and served in her in the West Indies. While in temporary command of the station, Duckworth appointed him in October 1796 acting lieutenant, and commander of the prize *La Magicienne* (26). During the next eighteen months he enjoyed considerable success cruising against enemy trade. In May 1798 he was appointed to the *Queen* (90), flagship of Sir Hyde Parker, and on 1 May 1799 he was appointed by him acting captain of the *Volage* (24), in which he continued his predation in the Gulf of Mexico and on the coast of Cuba. His lieutenant's commission was confirmed on 5 September, and his commander's was confirmed on 10 October, by which time he been moved into *Stork*, sloop. He returned in her to England the following year and served for nearly a year in the North Sea or attached to the fleet off Brest. He was promoted captain on 9 October 1801 and stayed

in employment during the peace of Amiens, commanding *Alarm* from March 1802 and moving into *Amazon* (38) in November.

At the renewal of the war in 1803 Parker was captain of the 18-pounder frigate *Amazon* (38) and was attached to the Mediterranean fleet under Nelson's command. He took part in the chase of Vice-Admiral Villeneuve and the combined Franco-Spanish fleet to the West Indies, but *Amazon* was subsequently detached on a cruise westward, and was not part of Nelson's fleet at Trafalgar. It was four and a half months after Nelson's death that Parker achieved the distinction which had been predicted for him. In December 1805 the *Amazon* was attached to the squadron under Sir John Borlase Warren, and on 14 March *Amazon* took a notable part in the capture of *Marengo* (74) and *Belle Poule*, frigate, taking the surrender of the latter ship.

Following this success, he was mostly employed on the coast of Spain and Portugal, returning to Plymouth in May 1810. While *Amazon* was refitting, Parker took three months' leave, and on 7 June he married Frances Anne, the youngest daughter of Sir Theophilus Biddulph, fifth baronet of Westcombe, Kent, in Birbury, Warwickshire. She was to give birth to two sons and six daughters. He returned to sea at the end of his leave, and served in the blockade of Brest until *Amazon* was so worn that she had to be paid off on 16 January 1812. Parker had commanded her for eleven years, and spent the next fifteen years ashore, purchasing Shenstone Lodge near Lichfield.

His honours and promotion were to be all that Nelson had predicted. He was nominated a CB on 4 June 1815 and knight grand cross of the royal order of St Ferdinand and of Merit (Sicily) in 1815. He was subsequently promoted KCB on 16 July 1834, GCB on 2 December 1842 and baronet on 18 December 1844; was awarded a good service pension on 26 April 1844, and was first and principal naval aide-de-camp to Queen Victoria from 10 December 1846 until his death.

These later honours represented his later services. He commanded *Warspite* (74) in 1827 and, having been promoted rear-admiral, was appointed second in command of the Channel fleet in April 1831, after which he served as a commissioner of the Admiralty from 1 August 1834 to 23 December 1834, and from 25 April 1835 to 25 June 1841. He was also member of parliament for Queenborough, Kent, in 1830, and member of parliament for Devizes, Wiltshire, from 1834 to 1836. He resigned only because he had been appointed commander-in-chief on the China station.

Having been promoted to vice-admiral on 23 November 1841, in February 1845 he was appointed commander-in-chief in the Mediterranean. In May 1846 he was also given command of the Channel fleet, and he briefly held a seat on the Admiralty Board from 13 July 1846 to 24 July 1846. In September 1849 he was, unusually, appointed to a second term in command of the Mediterranean fleet, returning home in March 1852, to be appointed chairman of the committee to enquire into the manning of the navy in July 1852. He was nominated an elder brother of the Trinity House in 1861, and appointed rear-admiral of the United Kingdom on 20 May 1862.

He died of an attack of bronchitis on 13 November 1866, aged eighty-four, at Shenstone House near Lichfield, Staffordshire, with the rank of admiral of the fleet.

Lt: 5 September 1799
Cmdr: 10 October 1799
Capt: 9 October 1801
R-Adm: 22 July 1830
V-Adm: 23 November 1841
Adm: 29 April 1851
Adm. of the Fleet: 27 April 1863

PASCO

VICE-ADMIRAL JOHN PASCO was famous as the senior lieutenant of Lord Nelson's flagship *Victory* (100) at the battle of Trafalgar on 21 October 1805, who missed his chance at promotion because he was serving as Nelson's signal lieutenant. He looked for his chief as the ranging shots were falling near the ship to request he be permitted to resume his duties as executive officer, but he found Nelson on his knees in prayer, and forbore to disturb him. When Nelson wanted to send his famous signal 'England Confides that Every Man will do his Duty', Pasco suggested that the telegraph signals would be much easier if he used the word 'Expects' instead of 'Confides'. He was wounded in the arm early in the battle, and was lying in *Victory*'s orlop deck when the dying admiral was brought in. He was able to tell him that the men were cheering the surrender of an enemy ship.

He was born on 20 December 1774, son of a caulker of Portsmouth dockyard, and entered the navy on 4 June 1784 as a captain's servant on board the *Druid* (32) under the command of Captain George A Byron. In 1786 he was rated gunner's servant, and therefore servant of the midshipmen's berth, in *Pegasus* (28) commanded by Prince William Henry. With him he served in the West Indies and North America. In 1787 he joined *Impregnable* (90) flying the flag of Admiral Samuel Graves, at Plymouth, and the following year he was rated an able seaman. In 1790 he was rated midshipman in *Syren* under Captain John Manley. In the following years he served in *Orion* (74) with Captain Duckworth, and on the French declaration of war on 1 February 1793 he was serving in *London* (90) under Captain Richard Keats.

Sir John Laforey gave him an acting commission as lieutenant in *Beaulieu* (40) commanded by his son Captain Francis Laforey, who had come to know Pasco when he had been a midshipman in *Pegasus*. Pasco served in the *Raisonnable* (64) under the command of Captain Charles Boyle from 1796 to 1799 in the Channel and at the Cape of Good Hope, and from December 1799 to October 1802 he served in the French prize *Immortalité* (36) commanded by Captain Henry Hotham on the coast of France.

In view of his lack of powerful connections he had progressed reasonably well through ranks, although his lieutenant's commission was still unconfirmed. But he was a man of character, and risked everything by complaining to the Admiralty when his father was dismissed from the dockyard, apparently for being one of those who took the occasion of the mobilisation prior to the Copenhagen campaign to demand higher wages. The earl of St Vincent, the first lord, was quite ruthless with the men, despite the distress they were in from rising wartime costs, perhaps largely because they were seeking under the pressure of the moment to obtain a long-term improvement of their condition. Pasco did get his appointment to *Victory* (100) in April 1803, but his prospects were seriously affected by his not serving as executive officer during Trafalgar, and more so by Nelson's death. Following Trafalgar he was paid a pension of £250 for his injury, but he had to wait until 24 December to be promoted commander, after which he was unemployed for three years. In May 1808 he was appointed to command the converted Indiaman *Mediator* (44) off Calais, and he moved in November to another former Indiaman, *Hindostan*, which was nominally a 54-gun ship but armed *en flute*.

On 1 September 1805, before sailing from Portsmouth for the rendezvous off Cadiz, Pasco had married Rebecca, daughter of J L Penfold of Plymouth dockyard. The couple were to have six sons, two of whom died in infancy, and three daughters. In the spring of 1809 following his appointment to command the *Hindostan*, he sailed to New South Wales and took Rebecca with him, returning around the world.

He left *Hindostan* on 24 November 1810, and his next command was the *Tartarus* (20), in which he continued after his promotion to post rank on 3 April 1811. In 1815 he was appointed to the *Rota* (38), and he retired from active service in September 1818 when he paid off the *Lee* (20). He remained ashore for the next twenty-eight years, and was next employed in 1846, as captain of *Victory* in Portsmouth harbour. He was promoted to rear-admiral on his retirement on 22 September 1847.

He married for a second time on 22 July 1843, uniting with Eliza, widow of Captain John Weaver, RM, and died with the rank of vice-admiral on 16 November 1854, aged seventy-nine, in East Stonehouse, Plymouth, Devon.

Lt: 15 July 1795
Cmdr: 24 December 1805
Capt: 3 April 1811
R-Adm: 22 September 1847
V-Adm: 11 September 1854

PASLEY

ADMIRAL SIR THOMAS PASLEY, BARONET, played a prominent part in the battles of the Glorious First of June. The injury he then suffered all but brought to an end a very long career.

He had been born on 2 March 1734 in Craig near Langholm, Dumfriesshire, the fifth son of James Pasley and his wife Magdalene, daughter of Robert Elliot of Middleholm Mill, Roxburgh. He entered the navy in October 1751 as a midshipman on board *Garland* (24) commanded by

Sir Thomas Pasley Bart.,
Vice Admiral of the Red Squadron,
engraving by Roberts after Lemuel F Abbot,
published by Burney and Gold, Shoe Lane,
1 December 1800.

Captain Saltern Willett, and in the following years served with Captains Cockburn, Webber and Robert Digby, the last of whom promoted him acting lieutenant in the small 9-pounder frigate *Biddeford* (20). In 1760 Pasley served with Captains Elliot and Hotham in the 12-pounder frigate *Eolus* (32). He was promoted master and commander on 9 August 1762, and post captain on 21 January 1771. In 1774 he married Mary, daughter of Chief Justice Thomas Heywood of the Nunnery, Isle of Man. The couple were to have two daughters.

He was actively employed during the American war. In 1780, in command of *Jupiter* (50), he was ordered to form part of the squadron under Commodore Johnson intended for service at the Cape of Good Hope and in the East Indies, and thus was in the action when Admiral de Suffren attacked the squadron in Porto Praya Road. He later served in the West Indies.

On the conclusion of the war he retired for a while from the sea. His wife died on 26 April 1788 in Avignon, France. In that same year he was appointed to command in the Medway, and hoisted his broad pendant as a commodore on board *Vengeance* (74). Later he moved to *Bellerophon* (74), in which he joined the Channel fleet during the Nootka Sound crisis in 1790, and again on the French declaration of war in February 1793.

He remained in *Bellerophon* on being promoted rear-admiral on 12 April 1794, when he was put in command of a reconnaissance squadron. This put him in the forefront of the engagement on 28 May 1794, when he was ordered to attack the French rear to prevent their escape. *Bellerophon* (74) engaged the *Révolutionnaire* alone for a considerable time before other ships came to his help. In the morning of the 29th *Bellerophon* was directly astern of Admiral Lord Howe's flagship, *Queen Charlotte* (100) when the French line was cut. Towards the end of the battle on 1 June, Pasley was severely wounded in his leg, which was amputated. In recognition of his contribution, not only did he receive a gold medal and chain from King George, but on 1 September he was created a baronet and awarded a pension of £1,000. The committee for the relief of wounded seamen presented him with a pair of goblets, valued at £500.

His injury put an end to his seagoing career, but he was promoted vice-admiral on 1 June 1795, and briefly employed in 1798 as commander in the Thames and Medway to oversee the trials of the Nore mutineers. In March 1799 he was appointed port admiral in Portsmouth.

He was advanced to admiral on 1 January 1801,

and died on 29 November 1808, aged seventy-four, at Cilland Cottage near Winchester. A memorial was erected in 1879 in St Swithin-Martyr, Worthy.

Lt: 10 October 1757
M-C: 9 August 1762
Capt: 21 January 1771
R-Adm: 12 April 1794
V-Adm: 1 June 1795
Adm: 1 January 1801

PELLEW

ADMIRAL SIR EDWARD PELLEW, VISCOUNT EXMOUTH, GCB, is known as a daring frigate commander in the American and French Revolutionary wars, and especially for his action in early 1797 in a full gale on the French coast when commanding a razee sixty-four, *Indefatigable*, in company with *Amazon* (28). Following the end of the war against the Napoleonic empire, he was to be the commander of the international force which obliged Algiers to agree to stop its centuries-old practice of enslavement. He was a hard man, and an effective commander.

He was born on 19 April 1757 in Dover, the second son of Samuel Humphrey Pellew of Flushing, near Falmouth, who was captain of a post office packet. His mother was Constantia, daughter of Edward Langford of Hawkes Farm, Alverton, Penzance. When her husband died in 1765 she moved to Penzance and sent Edward to the Revd James Parkin's school and Truro grammar school, but he ran away to join the navy in 1770 with the support of Lord Falmouth and the Boscawan family. He was taken into *Juno* (32) on 26 December by Captain John Stott as a captain's servant, and took part in the repossession of Port Egmont in the Falkland Islands. He transferred with Stott on 7 August 1772 to the 12-pounder frigate *Alarm* (32), in which he served in the Mediterranean, where he was rated master's mate and midshipman. But he and another midshipman so far disagreed with their captain as to be put ashore at Marseilles.

The Boscawan connection sufficed to get him rated a master's mate on *Garland* (24) under Captain Richard Pearson, from which ship he was sent to join the army on the Canadian lakes. He established his reputation by resolute action in the battle of Lake

Champlain on 11 October 1776 when command of *Carleton*, schooner, devolved on him. He not only saved his ship, but participated in sinking two American ships. In recognition of this service, he was commissioned to act in the capacity of lieutenant with command of *Carleton*. The following year, in command of a brigade of seamen, he took part in General Burgoyne's disastrous Saratoga campaign, following which he had to endure a period as an unexchanged prisoner on his parole.

After examination in 1778 at the Navy Office, St Mary-le-Strand, Westminster, his commission was confirmed on 9 January 1778. On 25 October he was able to go to sea as second lieutenant in the 12-pounder French frigate prize *Licorne* (32) under the command of Captain the Honourable Thomas Cadogan, with whom he served at Newfoundland. In April 1780 Captain Philemon Pownoll asked for him as first lieutenant of *Apollo* (32). When on 15 June 1780 Pownoll was killed in action against a French frigate off Ostend, Pellew again proved effective in action, driving the enemy into the neutral port. In consequence he was promoted master and commander on 1 July with appointment on the 12th to the ship-sloop *Hazard* (8), in which he was employed on the north-east coast of England until 24 January 1781; after this he was unemployed until 4 March 1782, when he was appointed to the command of *Pelican,* in which he served under the orders of Admiral McMillan on the coast of France. A fortunate encounter with three French privateers inside the Île de Batz, ending in their running ashore, led to his being made post captain on 31 May and appointed to command *Suffolk* (74). She was at the time in Plymouth dock, and he was *pro tempore* given an acting command of *Artois* (38) on the coast of Ireland, replacing Captain John MacBride.

He was unemployed during the first years of the peace, and took the opportunity to marry on 28 May 1783, uniting with Susan, second daughter of James Frowde of Knoyle, Wiltshire. The couple had four sons, of whom two became senior naval officers, and two daughters, who both married senior naval officers. During the peace he tried his hand at agriculture, but returned to sea on 27 April 1786

when he was appointed to the 12-pounder frigate *Winchelsea* (32) for Newfoundland service under Commodore John Elliott. He came ashore again on 5 July 1789, but was given command of *Salisbury* (50) on 1 June 1790 during the Nootka Sound crisis, coming ashore again on 2 December 1791.

Shortly before the outbreak of war in 1793, on 11 January, he was put in command of *Nymphe* (36) under Admiralty orders for Channel service. Despite the fact that she was largely manned with Cornish miners, he succeeded in capturing a French frigate, *Cléopâtre*, of equal force, after a hot action. This was the first such victory in the war, and in recognition he received a knighthood on 28 June 1793. On Christmas Day he transferred to *Arethusa* (32) under Rear-Admiral MacBride, in which he again beat a French frigate, *La Pomone* (44), into submission. He was moved into *Indefatigable* (44) on 2 February 1795, again under direct Admiralty control, and put in command of a detached section of the western squadron. On 26 January 1796 he boarded the wrecked transport *Dutton*, which had been part of Rear-Admiral Christian's fleet and deserted by her officers when stranded below the citadel at Plymouth, making use of a rope stretched from the ship to the shore. By his presence and authority, and with the help of unremembered boatmen, the lives of all on board were saved. In further recognition of his courage and ability he was created a baronet on 5 March 1796 and given the freedom of Plymouth.

On 16 November *Indefatigable* was the inshore vessel off Brest Road when Pellew was the first to see the ships of a French invasion force sail in freezing weather. It being night, he confused the situation as best he could by firing rockets and guns. The French reached Bantry Bay in reasonably good order, but failed to make good a landing, and lacking more than a few weeks' supplies, and expecting the Channel fleet under Lord Bridport to put in an appearance, they set course for Brest. On the return voyage the fleet became further disorganised as a result of heavy weather and the inexperience of the crews. On 13 January 1797 in a full gale, Pellew, with *Amazon* in company, encountered a straggler, *Droits de l'Homme* (74).

The high sea prevented the French two-decker opening her lower gunports, which gave Pellew a chance to engage on reasonably equal terms. The two frigates dogged her quarters until all three were in Audierne Bay south of Brest. In the murk, navigation became inexact. When land was sighted close under their lees all three ships broke off their fight to claw themselves clear. The *Naval Chronicle* writes that

> at this critical moment, the *Indefatigable* was close under the enemy's starboard bow, and the *Amazon* was as near to her on the larboard. Not an instant was to be lost. Every life depended upon the prompt execution of orders; and, to their credit, nothing could surpass the activity of the brave crew of the *Indefatigable*, who, with astonishing alacrity, hauled the tacks on board, and made sail to the southward. Before day-light, they again saw breakers upon the lee bow, and wore to the northward. Not knowing exactly on what part of the coast they were embayed, the approach of morning was most anxiously looked for; and, soon after it opened, the land was seen very close a-head: the ship was again wore, in twenty fathoms water, and stood to the southward. A few minutes afterwards, the *Indefatigable* discovered, and passed within a mile of, the enemy who had so bravely defended herself. She was lying on her broadside, a tremendous surf beating over her. She was afterwards found be *les Droits des Hommes*, of 74 guns, commanded by Captain, *ci-devant* Baron, le Cross; with 1,600 men, seamen and soldiers, on board; 170 of whom perished, exclusive of those killed in the action.

> The miserable fate of these brave men was, perhaps, the more sincerely lamented by the crew of the *Indefatigable*, from the apprehension of their experiencing a similar misfortune, their ship having, at that time, four feet water in the hold, the sea rolling heavily, and the wind being dead upon the shore.

> Sir Edward Pellew now ascertained his situation to be that of Audierne Bay; and perceived that the fate of himself, ship, and crew, depended on the chance of weathering the Penmark rocks. This, by the uncommon exertions of the men, notwithstanding their fatigued and almost exhausted state, in making all the sail that they could set, was happily accomplished at eleven o'clock; the *Indefatigable* passing about a mile to windward of the Penmarks. [NC 18.455]

Amazon had been less fortunate, and was wrecked, but with little loss of life.

Subsequent to his victory, Pellew was on 10 March 1799 put in command of *Impétueux* (74) in the Channel fleet, and on 1 January 1801 he was made colonel of the marines. Although it was a promotion, Pellew had avoided a move which would lose to him the chance of further prize money and put him too closely under the authority of Lord Bridport, for whom he had no respect. He also had to deal with mutiny in his ship at the end of May, which ended with three men hanged. Pellew was a driver, who drove himself equally hard. He left *Impétueux* on 15 April 1802 and moved into *Tonnant* (80) on 11 March 1803, in command of a squadron off Ferrol.

During the peace of Amiens he was elected in 1803 the member of parliament for Barnstaple, Devon, which seat he held in Addington's interest until July 1804. He spoke in March in support of the failing administration, and as a reward he was promoted rear-admiral on 23 April 1804 and appointed commander-in-chief in the East Indies. Leaving *Tonnant*, he hoisted his flag on *Culloden* (74) on the 30th. By the time he was to sail, Pitt was back in power, but Pellew secured his posting by resigning his seat in the Commons to a Pittite. The new first lord, Lord Melville, nonetheless took his revenge by sending Rear-Admiral Thomas Troubridge to India with orders to command the eastern half of the Indian Ocean. The conflict was not resolved in Pellew's favour until after Pitt's death in early 1806 led to a change of administration.

Being promoted vice-admiral on 28 April 1808, Pellew returned to England and came ashore on 14 July 1809. The following year he assumed command in the Scheldt, with his flag in *Christian VII* (80), moving on 27 April 1811 into *Caledonia* (120) as commander-in-chief Mediterranean. He hauled down his flag following his promotion to admiral on 4 June 1814, and in reward for services he was showered with honours. He was created Baron Exmouth of Canonteign, Devon, on 1 June 1814, and was appointed KCB on 2 January 1815 and GCB on 16 March 1816.

The battle which is associated with his name as Admiral Lord Exmouth occurred in 1816 as a result of the dey of Algiers violating the treaty abolishing slavery. Exmouth had returned to command in the Mediterranean, with his flag in *Boyne* (98), on 24 March 1815. For the Algiers operation he shifted his flag into *Queen Charlotte* (100) on 30 June 1816, and took command of an Anglo-Dutch force made up of five ships of the line, one vessel of fifty guns, nine frigates and various smaller warships, including four bomb ketches. Exmouth bombarded the defences of Algiers and its fleet for nine hours on 26 August, setting on fire the arsenal and every ship. The dey was obliged to release 1,200 slaves and renew the treaty. For this action Exmouth was advanced in the peerage to Viscount Exmouth on 10 December 1816, and received several foreign decorations. He struck his flag on 8 October. His last command was Portsmouth, from 13 September 1817 to 1 February 1821.

He was an elder brother of the Trinity House from 1823 until his death, and was made vice-admiral of the United Kingdom on 15 February 1832. He died on 23 January 1833, aged seventy-five, at his seat in Canonteign near Teignmouth, Devon, and was buried in Christow, Devon. His wife died on 29 October 1837, aged eighty-one.

Lt: 9 January 1778 (1)
M-C: 1 July 1780
Capt: 31 May 1782
R-Adm: 23 April 1804
V-Adm: 28 April 1808
Adm: 4 June 1814

PELLEW

ADMIRAL SIR ISRAEL PELLEW, KCB, was overshadowed by his elder brother, but like him was a highly capable captain, and also had the distinction of being blown up, nearly drowned by a squall and shipwrecked.

He was born on 25 August 1758 in Dover, the third son of Samuel Humphrey Pellew of Flushing near Falmouth, captain of a post office packet in Dover, and of his wife Constantia, daughter of Edward Langford of Hawkes Farm, Alverton, Penzance. He entered the navy as captain's servant in January 1771 and served three years in *Falcon*, brig-sloop (10), at Barbados under Commander C Baines. He left her in June 1774, and was a year ashore before he was rated midshipman in June 1775 on joining *Albion* (74), a guardship at Plymouth under the command of Captain Caster Allen. From her he moved in February 1776, following the outbreak of the American war, into *Flora* (14) under the command of Captain John Brisbane, with whom he sailed to New York, returning to England in *Leviathan* in December 1778 after *Flora* had to be sunk at Rhode Island to prevent her falling into the hands of the French. He then served in *Royal George* (100) and was commissioned a lieutenant on 1 April 1779. After service in the West Indies in *Drake*, sloop, which he joined on 1 April 1779, he was appointed in October 1782 to command *Resolution*, cutter (14), and distinguished himself by the capture in the North Sea of a Dutch privateer of sixteen guns. But he was not promoted master and commander until 22 November 1790, and he was never employed in that rank. He left *Resolution* in May 1788, and was appointed the following April first lieutenant of *Salisbury* (50) flying the flag of Vice-Admiral Milbanke as commander-in-chief Newfoundland, where he remained until December 1791.

In 1792 he married Mary, daughter of George Gilmore. The couple had a single son, Edward Pellew, who became a captain in the Life Guards and was killed by Lieutenant Theophilus Walsh, of the same regiment, on 6 October 1819 in a duel at Paris.

On the French declaration of war in 1793 he joined his elder brother Edward's ship *Nymphe* as a volunteer For his part in the capture of the French frigate *Cléopâtra*, he was promoted post captain on 25 June 1793. In August he was appointed to command *Squirrel* (24) in the North Sea and Channel, transferring in May 1795 to the 12-pounder frigate *Amphion* (36). That was very nearly the end of him. On 22 September 1796, while alongside a hulk in Plymouth, having completed repairs and ready for sea under the orders of his brother, *Amphion* was accidentally blown up. As she was a Plymouth ship, there were over 100 family and friends on board saying their farewells; a witness said:

> ...at about half past four P.M. I felt, whilst at Stonehouse, a violent shock like an earthquake; which extended as far off as the Royal Hospital, and the town of Plymouth. The sky towards Dock appeared red, like the effect of a fire: for near a quarter of an hour no one could discover what was the occasion; though the streets were crowded with people running different ways in the greatest consternation. When the alarm, and confusion, had a little subsided; it first began to be known, that the *Amphion* was blown up!... Captain Israel Pellew, and Captain William Swaffield, of his Majesty's ship *Overyssel*, who was at dinner with him, and the First Lieutenant, were drinking their wine: when the first explosion threw them off their seats, and struck them against the carlings of the upper deck, so as to stun them. Captain Pellew, however, had presence of mind sufficient to fly to the cabin windows; and seeing the two hawsers, one slack in the bit, and the other taut, threw himself with an amazing leap, which he said afterwards nothing but his sense of danger could have enabled him to take, upon the latter; and saved himself by that means from the general destruction; though his face had been badly cut against the

carlings, when he was thrown from his seat. [NC 3.197–202]

Few, apart from Pellew and the first lieutenant, survived the blast, which may have been caused by the gunner stealing gunpowder by concealing it in bags of biscuit, or was simply the result of the poor construction of the magazine, about which Pellew had already complained.

In April 1797 he was appointed to *Greyhound* (32) as part of the western squadron based on Falmouth, but was put ashore during the great mutiny, and was in consequence asked to resign his command in June. He moved in August to *Cleopatra* (32) and was employed in the Channel until November 1798, and then on the Halifax and Jamaica stations. The near-drowning occurred in 1800 when he was in command of *Cleopatra* and *en passage* north of Cape Hatteras:

> ...in a night rendered dark by a deep and jet black thunder-cloud which had obscured the moon, after very vivid lightning and a loud explosion, the wind shifted in a heavy squall, so as to bring the ship up several points, with her head to a very high and much-agitated sea, giving her at the same time fresher way through the water. The first plunge put the whole of the forecastle-deck under, and the officers on deck hardly expected to see her rise again. Captain Pellew, who was in his cot, got a severe blow by being dashed violently against the beams. The ship, however, rose, throwing a vast body of water aft, which burst open the cabin bulk-head, breaking loose very thing upon the deck but the guns. In this send-aft, the tafferel and after-part of the quarter-deck were far under water; luckily, only part of the after-hatchway was open, and no great body went below. [Marshall 1.454]

Early in 1801 *Cleopatra* grounded on one of the Bahamas and was floated off only by jettisoning her guns and part of her ballast. He left her in February 1802 following the conclusion of the peace of Amiens.

A year after the renewal of war, Pellew was appointed in May 1804 to command *Conqueror* (74) and in her took part in Nelson's pursuit of the combined Franco-Spanish fleet to the West Indies, and then in the battle of Trafalgar of 21 October 1805, in which she took possession of the French flagship, *Bucentaure*. In the confusion of battle, however, Vice-Admiral Villeneuve's sword ended up in Lord Collingwood's collection. Subsequently, *Conqueror* was employed under Sir Charles Cotton in the blockade of the Tagus. Following the internment of the Russian fleet, Pellew returned to England as superintendent of the ships afloat at Plymouth. He left his ship in August 1809.

He was promoted rear-admiral on 31 July 1810, and in 1811 was appointed captain of the Mediterranean fleet under his brother's command, in which exacting appointment he continued for the remainder of the war, coming ashore on 16 August 1814. He was made a KCB on 2 January 1815, and eventually promoted admiral on 22 July 1830. He died on 19 July 1832 after a long and painful illness, aged seventy-three, in Ham Street, Plymouth, and was buried in the parish church of Charles the Martyr, Plymouth.

Lt: 1 April 1779
M-C: 22 November 1790
Capt: 25 June 1793
R-Adm: 31 July 1810
V-Adm: 12 August 1819
Adm: 22 July 1830

PHILLIMORE

CAPTAIN SIR JOHN PHILLIMORE, CB, is somewhat unfairly best known for his eccentric query to the Navy Board. When he found that the allowance for paint was sufficient to paint only one side of his ship, he asked to know which side should be painted. When reprimanded for concluding a letter to the Board 'your affectionate friend', which was its own custom, he acknowledged his fault, and signed himself 'no longer your affectionate friend'. The allowance was afterwards doubled.

He was born on 18 January 1781, the third son of the Revd Joseph Phillimore, rector of Orton-on-the-Hill, Leicestershire, and his wife Mary, daughter of John Machin of Kensington, London. He entered the navy in June 1794 as a volunteer first class in *Nymphe* (36), and served his whole time as midshipman under Captain, later Sir George, Murray. He fought in the action off L'Orient on 23 June 1795 and, having followed Murray into *Colossus* (74), at the battle of Cape St Vincent on 14 February 1797. Afterwards he was shipwrecked in St Mary's harbour, Scilly, on 7 December 1798. With Murray he joined *Edgar* (74), but was serving in *London* (90) flying Admiral Hyde Parker's flag during the battle of Copenhagen on 2 April 1801. It was Phillimore as *London*'s acting signal lieutenant who sent Parker's unfortunate signal to Nelson to disengage. *Edgar*'s first lieutenant was killed in the action, and this led to a promotion of the junior officers on 4 April. Phillimore, who had been examined in 1800, was commissioned lieutenant. He subsequently continued to serve under Murray, in the two-decker French prize *Spartiate* (80) off Cadiz and in the Channel. He was promoted commander, for rank, on 10 May 1804, and the following year he was appointed to command *Cormorant* (20).

Towards the end of 1806 Phillimore was in command of *Belette,* brig (18), when that ship took part in Commodore Owen's attack on Boulogne in which it was attempted to use Congreve rockets to burn the enemy flotilla. He subsequently convoyed two transports laden with provisions and military stores to Colberg in Prussian Pomerania, in order to sustain the defence of that town by General Blücher until the peace of Tilsit. *Belette* then formed part of the force under Admiral Gambier which returned to Copenhagen in 1807. At the end of August, when anchored and becalmed, she was attacked by sixteen Danish gunboats, but managed to sink three of them before the boats of the British fleet arrived to tow her clear. In recognition of Phillimore's courage, Gambier employed *Belette* to carry his dispatches home to England, and as a result Phillimore was made post captain on 13 October 1807. But he was not immediately superseded, and in passage to Göteborg encountered the only two-decker in the Danish navy, which he escaped by sailing into shallow water.

After a period on half pay, Phillimore was appointed in 1809 to command the *Marlborough* (74) in the absence of Captain Graham Moore, and in her took part in the Scheldt expedition. On Moore's return to duty, Phillimore was appointed to command a troop ship, *Diadem*, a razee sixty-four. Until his effective protest, she was allowed stores, including hull paint, only on the basis of the thirty-two guns she carried. On 4 May 1813 he was put in command of *Eurotas* (38) armed with twenty-eight of Congreve's experimental medium 24-pounders, sixteen carronades and two long 9-pounders. This armament may have contributed to the defeat of *La Clorinde* (44) on 25 February 1814 after a protracted action in which Phillimore was severely wounded. *Eurotas* was dismasted in the action, but her first lieutenant, Smith, managed to clear away the wreckage and close with the Frenchman. The action ended when she struck to *Dryad* and *Achates,* which had sailed to the sound of the guns.

In recognition of his services, Phillimore was nominated a CB on 4 June 1815, appointed to command the *William and Mary,* yacht, on 13 April 1820, and was made a knight bachelor on 12 December 1821 by Earl Talbot, lord lieutenant of Ireland, whilst in attendance on the viceroy. When an account of *Eurotas*'s action with *La Clorinde* appeared in William James's *Naval History*, Phillimore felt it reflected badly on him, and thrashed the author with a stout stick, later paying him £100 damages.

He returned to a more active service in March 1823, in command of *Thetis* (46). He conveyed a commission of enquiry into the political state of Mexico, and returned with a cargo of $400,000 and 300 bales of cochineal from Havana. The following year he served in the Ashanti war, carrying a detachment of the Royal African corps to Cape Coast castle. In the long run, of greater importance were the steps he took to transform the post-war navy's treatment of the lower deck. He arranged for an advance of pay to be made each month, and obtained the men's agreement for the rum ration to be cut in half, with the value saved paid to their accounts.

He married on 17 February 1830 Catherine Harriet, the youngest daughter of Rear-Admiral Jeffery, Baron von Raigersfeld. The couple had two sons and a daughter, of whom the younger son was to become Admiral Henry Bourchier Phillimore. Captain Phillimore died on 21 March 1840, aged fifty-nine, and his wife died the same year.

Lt: 4 April 1801
Cmdr: 10 May 1804
Capt: 13 October 1807

PIGOT

CAPTAIN HUGH PIGOT is infamous for being the commander of *Hermione* who was murdered on 21 September 1797 when her crew mutinied. The evidence indicates that his leadership skills were of the lowest order, and his brutality was such that it suggests insanity. Unfortunately, the navy covered for him, rather than grasping the several opportunities it had to break him.

Pigot was born in Patshull, Staffordshire, the second son of Admiral Hugh Pigot and his second wife, Frances, daughter of Sir Richard Wrottesley, baronet. He entered the navy on 10 March 1782 as an admiral's servant on board the *Jupiter* (50) sailing to the West Indies, where his father was proceeding in *Formidable* (90). He was rated midshipman or master's mate on 1 October 1784, commissioned lieutenant on 21 September 1790, and promoted commander of the sloop *Swan* on the Jamaica station on 10 February 1794.

He was twice in collision with merchant ships. In May 1794 he managed to ram the merchant ship *Canada* in the Channel, despite which he was posted to *Success* (32) in September, only to collide with the American ship *Mercury* near San Domingo in July 1796. In both instances he blamed the merchant master, and in the second went so far as to have the American skipper seized and flogged. That led to diplomatic difficulties and to a court martial, which let him off with an apology. Admiral Sir Hyde Parker, commanding at Jamaica, thought he had been represented badly, and agreed to his transferring into the 12-pounder frigate *Hermione* (32) rather than returning to England.

Following his appointment 10 February 1797

he made a practice of giving preferential treatment to the sailors who had followed him from his previous ship. In May 1797 one of *Hermione*'s lieutenants, Harris, saved his ship from wreck, but the ship sailing in company went aground. Against all logic Pigot blamed Harris, and insisted on an enquiry. Harris was exonerated, and immediately left the ship for another. Pigot flogged midshipman Casey for contempt and relieved him from duty because one reef point had not been tied, and he had not apologised on his knees. He adopted the pernicious practice of flogging the last men down from work aloft. On 20 September three men were killed falling from the rigging as a result. Pigot had their bodies thrown into the sea, and flogged those who had stopped work at sight of the disaster. It is hardly surprising that he was murdered that night, and in view of the attitude of the navy, it is not surprising that the mutineers took their ship into La Guaira, near Caracas, and surrendered her to the Spanish governor. Nine others of her officers were also killed.

The Spaniards put *Hermione* into service, but they did not show much gratitude to the mutineers, who were given $25 each and the choice of joining the Spanish army, heavy labour or refitting their ship. Parker rightly calculated that they would be looking for ways to get to the United States or to the British islands. In order to apprehend them, he set up an intelligence system and offered rewards and pardons for informers. Thirty-three of the mutineers were captured and twenty-four were hanged and gibbeted. One man was transported, and eight were acquitted or pardoned. But Hyde Parker was so furious with Rear-Admiral Rodney Bligh, who had exonerated Lieutenant Harris and had granted the pardons to some of the mutineers, including one to a boy of twelve years of age, that against Admiralty regulations he ordered him to resign his command and return home. No doubt a factor in this story was the long history of violence, predation and hierarchy in the West Indies where slavery was a fact of life, and buccaneers had a disturbingly parallel 'libertarian' culture. Pigot had been effective in making captures, and Sir Hyde Parker

profited hugely from the admiral's eighth share of prize money.

Hermione was cut out of Puerto Cabello in October 1799 by Captain Edward Hamilton of the *Surprise* and returned to service, renamed *Retaliation* by Hyde Parker and *Retribution* by the Admiralty. Hugh Pigot's brother, General Henry Pigot, had a clash with Captain Alexander Ball, RN, in Malta, who commented that Pigot was the most unpopular man ever to command a garrison.

Lt: 21 September 1790
Cmdr: 10 February 1794
Capt: 1 September 1794

PITT

COMMANDER THOMAS PITT, BARON CAMELFORD, was another insane West Indian frigate commander who was only belatedly reined in by the navy.

He had been born on 19 February 1775 in Boconnoc, Cornwall, the only son of Thomas Pitt, first Baron Camelford, a member of parliament, and of his wife Anne, younger daughter and coheiress of Pinckney Wilkinson, a merchant from Hanover. His education was firstly at Neuchâtel in Switzerland in Mr Meuron's school, where he was sent in 1786, and then, for nine days only, at Charterhouse school in London in July 1789. His name having been on the books of a warship from September 1781, he entered the navy in September 1789.

His early service was of the most demanding kind, and he established a good reputation when the ship on which he was serving, the two-deck frigate-flute *Guardian* bound for New South Wales, struck a field of ice near the Cape of Good Hope. Most of the crew deserted in the boats, but her commander, assisted only by Pitt, brought the wreck into Table Bay in February 1790. Having returned to England with a very good report, Pitt joined 12 March 1791 the *Discovery* (8) being commissioned by Captain George Vancouver for Pacific exploration. This voyage was to reveal Pitt's character faults. During the passage up the west coast of America, Vancouver flogged him several times for misdemeanours, and at Hawaii he was dismissed and sent home in a supply vessel. His anger was stoked by his discovery *en route* that his father had died, which made him a peer and a very wealthy one at that. Nevertheless, he was still capable of doing service, and at Malacca he joined the two-decked frigate *Resistance* (44). He was soon made an acting lieutenant, showing his capacity and courage in the operations ending in the capture of Malacca from the Dutch. Returning to England on 21 September 1796 he twice challenged Vancouver to a duel, and finally beat him in the street. The lord chancellor bound him over to keep the peace.

In 1797 at Antigua he was appointed by the commander-in-chief at the Leeward Islands, Rear-Admiral Henry Harvey, acting commander of a sloop, *Favourite* (16), whose captain was ill. This was resented bitterly by Lieutenant Charles Peterson of *Favourite*, whose commission was senior, and he transferred to another ship, the captain of which soon afterwards left, as did the senior officer at English Harbour. This posed a question as to who was now senior officer, acting Captain Pitt, Baron Camelford, or Lieutenant Peterson, who was senior to Camelford on the lieutenants' list, and also acting for a senior captain. Both refused the other's orders, and open warfare between the armed marines of both ships was averted only by Camelford taking decisive action and shooting Peterson dead.

He was tried before a court martial at Martinique on 20 January 1798, and after five days' deliberation the court acquitted him on the grounds that if Camelford were indeed the senior officer, then Peterson was a mutineer. Probably no less important were the considerations that Peterson was already dead, and Camelford was a very wealthy peer. The public, however, did not agree, and so great was the opprobrium that Camelford left the Indies, reaching England in command of *Terror,* bomb, by July 1798.

He might well have continued in the navy but for an eccentricity of a high order, in setting out late in 1798 to visit France equipped with a letter to Barras, one of the French directors. He was intercepted, but despite it being a capital offence to travel to France, a special meeting of the privy council found him not guilty. Probably his social position continued to shield him. When he resigned his commission to *Terror*, however, he put an end to his naval career because the Admiralty refused to appoint him to another ship.

Thereafter his life continued along an ever more eccentric path which included two clandestine visits to France and the return to parliament for the rotten borough of Old Sarum, which he owned, of the Revd John Horne Tooke, who was a radical. It ended on 10 March 1804 when he died from a wound received in a duel with an old friend, Thomas Best, which had been provoked by a woman who falsely claimed that she and Camelford had been insulted by him. Camelford apparently knew the woman was lying, and knew his friend to be an excellent shot, but fought nonetheless.

Lt: 7 April 1797
Cmdr: 12 December 1797
Struck off the Navy List: 1799

POLE

ADMIRAL OF THE FLEET SIR CHARLES MORICE POLE, BARONET, GCB, was a friend of Horatio Nelson's, and served the navy both afloat and in parliament.

He was born on 18 January 1757 in Stoke Damerel, Devon, the second son of Reginald Pole and his wife Anne, second daughter of John Francis Buller of Morvall, Cornwall. He was educated at Plympton grammar school and the Royal (Naval) Academy, Portsmouth, where he was sent on 16 January 1770. He entered the navy in 1772 as a midshipman in *Thames* (32) under the patronage of Nelson's early friend, Captain Locker. He was then moved into *Salisbury* (50), in which he later served in the East Indies under Commodore Sir Edward Hughes. It was at this time that he first came to know Nelson. He was commissioned lieutenant on 26 June 1777 in *Seahorse* (24), Captain Panton, and when Sir Edward Vernon succeeded Hughes, Pole was moved into Vernon's flagship, the *Rippon* (54), in which he served during the siege of Pondicherry. He was promoted master and commander on 17 October 1778, put in command of a small prize taken during the siege, *Cormorant* (18), and sent to England with dispatches. This led to his being made post captain on 22 March 1779 in *Britannia* (100) flying Vice-Admiral George Darby's flag, and then put in command of *Hussar* (28), which unfortunately he ran aground on the Pot rock in Hell's Gates between New York harbour and Long Island Sound. He was then sent back to England and given command of a frigate still on the builder's ways, *Success* (32), which he commissioned. In 1782 he fought a brilliant action with a Spanish frigate, *Santa Catalina*. Commenting on the action, and Pole's report of it, Nelson wrote: 'in his seamanship he shewed himself as superior to the Don as in his gallantry, and no man in the world was ever so modest in his account of it. [NC 21.269]

Evidence of his good connections is the fact that during the peace Pole commanded a guardship, *Crown* (64), until 30 August 1786, then *Scipio* (64) during the so-called 'Dutch' mobilisation; in the crisis of 1790 he was on 10 May put in command of *Melampus* (36), and the following year he moved to *Illustrious* (74). In 1790 he was made groom of the bedchamber to the duke of Clarence, and on 8 June 1792 he married Henrietta, third daughter of John Goddard, merchant of Rotterdam and later of Woodford Hall, Essex. The couple were to have two daughters. He became a fellow of the Royal Society.

With the outbreak of war, he was put in command of *Colossus* (74), which formed part of Vice-Admiral Lord Hood's fleet sent to the Mediterranean, and then was attached to Rear-Admiral George Montagu's squadron in the Channel fleet. He remained in her when promoted rear-admiral on 1 June 1795 and sailed to the West Indies in Rear-Admiral Christian's armada, returning home with Christian in *Beaulieu* (18) in November. In March 1797 he was appointed Admiral Lord Bridport's captain of the fleet in the Channel, and this put him at the heart of the crisis caused by the mutiny at Spithead. His letters to Captain William Young, who was on the Admiralty Board, are an important source for understanding the course of events. Apart from that crisis, the

work of captain of the fleet was extremely demanding at a time when the fleet was learning the techniques needed to maintain a blockade of Brest in all weathers.

In June 1799 he commanded a squadron and flotilla action when the Spanish fleet under Admiral Gravina tried to get into Brest, but was diverted into Aix Roads, where they subsequently were blockad-

Sir Charles Morice Pole, Bart.,
Admiral of the Blue Squadron,
engraved by H R Cook (by permission of
Mr Asperne, proprietor of the *European Magazine*)
after James Northcote, RA, published by Joyce Gold,
103 Shoe Lane, 29 April 1809.

ed. On 2 July Pole attempted to dig them out with an attack on their prepared position moored between the Isle of Aix and the Boyart shoal and protected by a floating mortar battery, but the range of the Spanish artillery proved to be too great and Pole was obliged to order his ships to disengage.

On 1 May 1800 he was appointed governor and commander-in-chief at Newfoundland, being promoted vice-admiral on 1 January 1801 following his return to Spithead in November. On 2 June he was ordered to proceed to the Baltic to relieve Nelson following the battle of Copenhagen and the confrontation with Russia, after which he was created a baronet on 12 September 1801.

That was to be the end of his naval service. In the subsequent peace, he began a career in politics, being elected to the parliamentary seat for Newark-upon-Trent, Nottinghamshire, in 1802. He continued to hold the seat until 1806, when he was returned for that for Plymouth, which he retained until 1818. His brother, the Right Honourable Reginald Pole Carew, was under-secretary in the Addington ministry, and Admiral Pole was appointed to head the parliamentary commission looking into abuses of the civil management of the navy. He resigned on 10 February 1806 to take a place on the Admiralty Board, but left the board on 23 October. During the following years he spoke frequently in support of the navy and its officers, and it was his work as a politician which earned him the highest ranks and highest honours. He was promoted admiral on 9 November 1805. He was nominated a KCB on 2 January 1815, and was promoted GCB on 20 February 1818. King William IV made him master of the robes in July 1830, and he was promoted admiral of the fleet on 23 July. He died on 6 September 1830, aged seventy-three, in Denham Abbey, Hertfordshire, when the baronetcy became extinct.

Lt: 26 June 1777
M-C: 17 October 1778
Capt: 22 March 1779 (2)
R-Adm: 1 June 1795
V-Adm: 1 January 1801
Adm: 9 November 1805
Admiral of the Fleet: 23 July 1830

POPHAM

REAR-ADMIRAL SIR HOME RIGGS POPHAM, KCB, was a controversial figure, as well known for his invention of the 'naval telegraph' used at the battle of Trafalgar as for his unauthorised attack on Buenos Aires.

He had been born on 12 October 1762 in Gibraltar, son of Joseph Popham, linen-draper of Cork, Ireland, and consul-general in Tetuan, Morocco. His mother was Mary, née Riggs, of Waterford, and she died giving him birth. He was her fifteenth child, and her husband remarried, having another seven children. He did not follow the usual career path, first going to Brenton school and then to Cambridge University before entering the navy in March 1778 as an able seaman in *Hyaena* (24) under the command of Captain Edward Thompson. He spent three months as a prisoner of war when *Sheilah-Nagig* (14) was captured in May 1781, but was released on parole and was commissioned lieutenant on 16 June 1783.

Following the conclusion of the war he was employed in 1786 in the survey of south-west Africa undertaken by the sloop *Nautilus* (24). His achievements as a hydrographer were to be another major contribution to his profession, but they also set him apart from the majority of his colleagues.

In March 1787, having obtained permission from the Admiralty to engage in trade, he took command of an Imperial merchant ship at Ostend, which he reflagged in Tuscany, and sailed for India. He worked in the India and China trades, twice purchasing larger ships, and undertook some important surveys for which he was rewarded by the East India Company. Unfortunately part of the cargo carried on his last voyage to Ostend was owned by Frenchmen, and when his ship was taken prize in the English Channel in July 1793 after the outbreak of war, his finances were seriously affected. There was also a question about his infringement of the monopoly of the East India Company. The event became a *cause célèbre*, and it was not until 1805 that he received compensation of £25,000, less his legal expenses, for a loss to him of £70,000.

While at Calcutta he undertook a survey of the Hoochly, and when driven off course to Prince of Wales Island, Penang, he surveyed that island and found a new passage between the island and the coast, through which he took the East India Company's China fleet in 1792. He published *A Description of Prince of Wales Island* in 1791, and reprinted it with charts in 1799. He married in 1788, in Calcutta, Elizabeth Moffat, daughter of Captain Prince in the East India Company's military service. The couple had four sons and three daughters.

He had been removed from the navy list in 1791 for failing to renew his leave, but was reinstated in 1793 following the French declaration of war.

In the Flanders campaign, he was attached to the duke of York's army, with charge over inland navigation and eventually with responsibility for evacuating the army. On the duke's strong recommendation, he was promoted commander on 26 November 1794, but was left in his present occupation. On the conclusion of the Flanders operations, again on the duke of York's recommendation, he was promoted post captain on 4 April 1795. That his promotions should have come through the intervention of the army was held against him by his brother captains.

He had created a corps of sea fencibles for the defence of Nieuport, and on his return to England he engaged himself in the formation of a sea fencible force for the defence of British coasts. In 1798 he was put in command of that part of the force raised between Deal and Beachy Head and most immediately threatened by France. In May of that year he commanded the naval part of a raid he himself proposed on Ostend to destroy the Bruges canal sluices. Unfortunately, it proved impossible to re-embark the soldiers under Sir Eyre Coote, and they were taken prisoner. The following year he was sent to Kronstadt to persuade the tsar to supply Russian solders for service in the Netherlands. This was a remarkable responsibility, but he proved very effective at engaging the tsar's interest. The Netherlands campaign failed, but Popham's management of the inland navigation for Sir Ralph Abercromby's army, and the 10,000 Russian soldiers and his evacuation of them, were models of their kind. He was rewarded with a pension of £500 a year, and enrolment as a knight of Malta by Tsar Paul on 2 August 1799.

By that time he had begun his great work on telegraphic signals. He had been elected a fellow of the Royal Society on 18 April 1799, and in the spring of 1800 he first experimented with his dictionary code during Admiral Dickson's reconnaissance of Copenhagen, publishing his first version of *Telegraphic Signals, or, Marine Vocabulary* in 1803. This contained a numbered list of words and phrases commonly used to convey naval intelligence and orders, and the letters of the alphabet for spelling out other words. A simple two- or three-flag numerical hoist could be used to convey each word or phrase in sequence. At first these signals were used only unofficially by the navy, and Popham continued to improve his concept, but it was generally in use by the time Nelson employed it to communicate with his frigates before Trafalgar. It also enabled him to make his famous signal, 'England Confides that Every Man will do his Duty'. His signal lieutenant, Pasco, asked his permission to substitute 'Expects' for 'Confides' because the latter was not one of the words in the dictionary and would have needed to be spelt out. For the first time, commanders were able to issue orders they had not previously given their captains in writing, and scouts were able to send detailed reports. The code was to be officially adopted by the Admiralty in 1812, and Popham finished the definitive edition in 1816.

Sir Home Popham, K.M. and F.R.S., Commander of His Majesty's Squadron at the Capture of Buenos Ayres, &c, engraved by Cardon after a painting by Mather Brown in the possession of Lady Popham, published by Joyce Gold, 103 Shoe Lane, 1 November 1806.

Late in 1800 he was appointed to command *Romney* (50). He was first employed escorting a troop convoy with part of Sir Ralph Abercromby's army intended for driving the French from Egypt. Then he was sent by the secret committee of the East India Company to negotiate trade treaties with the sheriff of Mecca and other Arabian states. This was not his most successful effort, but he did obtain an agreement with the sultan of Aden. At Calcutta *Romney* was given a major repair, the expense of which was declared to be excessive by the Navy Board. The case against Popham was a fabrication perpetrated by Benjamin Tucker, secretary to the earl of St Vincent, the first lord of the Admiralty, who despised Popham. Popham published *A Concise Statement of Facts Relative to the Treatment Experienced by Sir Home Popham since his Return from the Red Sea*, and eventually the question was settled by the select committee of the House of Commons on the civil affairs of the navy, which, in July 1805, reported that the figures were in reality a tenth of what the Navy Board had assessed. Inevitably, Popham's many enemies preferred to remember the accusations. His important contribution to naval technology did not make Popham a popular character in a service which tended to be suspicious of intellectuals. And Popham's entrepreneurial efforts put him in conflict with the predatory profession of the navy.

In 1804, while his case was still being considered, he published the chart of the survey of the Red Sea that he had made during his trade mission, and in the summer he was appointed to command the anti-invasion light craft from *Antelope* (50) in the Downs, moving in December into *Diadem* (64). He adopted an aggressive policy of raiding the praams and barges moored close outside Boulogne, under the guns of many batteries along the shore and built on piles offshore, and in the autumn he brought to the problem new resources in the form of special pyrotechnic weapons. The *Naval Chronicle*'s account described the weapons as

> smacks... loaded with barrels of gun powder, covered with flint stones closely stowed together so as to make the greater explosion. The Smacks were sunk very low in the water, painted to resemble the sea, so that at night they could scarcely be distinguished from the water; they looked like a large chest, or a large plank floating; below them was hung a box of machinery, something like clock-work; it would go any

time from ten minutes to six hours, after a line was pulled, the person conducting it was to time the period of explosion, so that it might go off with most effect. [NC 12.329–35]

In the final approach to the enemy, they were to be towed by an oarsman in a catamaran. Home embarked with Lord Keith, who had overall command of the defences, and Lord Melville, the first lord, to witness the operation, but it was later admitted that it was not much of a success. His interest in pyrotechnics brought him into contact with the American inventor Robert Fulton, who was trying to sell submarine mines to the navy.

When he was exonerated of the financial charges, Popham was ordered to hoist a broad pendant and take command of the naval forces in an expedition to capture the Cape of Good Hope. But he was not content with simply carrying out his mission. In January 1806 he took the forces under his command with a detachment of the army garrison at the Cape to seize Buenos Aires and Montevideo. He claimed that the idea had been discussed at length with the prime minister, Pitt, but Pitt died the same month. Popham's actions again made him the centre of controversy. The operation had been undertaken because he believed that the South Americans detested Spanish rule, which they did. But the Spanish army rallied and the tiny British garrison was overwhelmed. Popham, who had already sent an open letter to London merchants inviting them to exploit the new opportunities for trade, could only seize the town of Maldonado as a bridgehead, and institute a blockade. He was relieved of his command by Rear-Admiral Stirling on 5 January 1807, and severely censured by a court martial when he returned to England.

This did not, however, put an end to his naval career. In 1806 he had been appointed groom of the bedchamber to the duke of Gloucester, which office he held until his death. Influence at court is always useful. He was also popular with the City of London merchants. In July he was appointed captain of the fleet under Admiral Gambier for the second Copenhagen expedition, despite the protest made by Captains Hood, Keats and Stopford.

Perhaps his appointment was a result of his familiarity with the navigational problems from earlier service there in 1800, but it is also likely that no one else would take the job in what was perhaps the only truly unpopular expedition during the war.

In 1809 he commanded the *Venerable* (74) in the Scheldt expedition under Sir Richard Strachan. In 1812, still in command of *Venerable*, he served on the coast of Spain in support of Spanish guerrillas. In this he was successful, and eventually captured Santander, but he received no particular notice for his achievement, probably because his name grated on the official mind.

That was the end of his wartime service, but he was promoted rear-admiral on 4 June 1814, and was nominated a KCB on 2 January 1815. During this period he was also active in politics, holding the parliamentary seat for Yarmouth, Isle of Wight, from 21 March 1804 until January 1806, for Shaftesbury, Dorset, in 1806 and 1807, and for Ipswich, Suffolk, from 1807 to 1812. His political support for Pitt had certainly helped his career, but not enhanced his popularity in the service. Following the war he served as commander-in-chief on the Jamaica station from 1817 to 1820, and was created a knight commander of the Guelphic order of Hanover in 1818. He returned to England only to die, on 11 September 1820, aged fifty-seven, in Cheltenham, Gloucestershire. His wife survived him by forty-six years, dying in 1866, aged ninety-four, in Bath, Somerset.

Lt: 16 June 1783
Struck from the Navy List in 1791, and reinstated in 1793
Cmdr: 26 November 1794
Capt: 4 April 1795
R-Adm: 4 June 1814

PROWSE

REAR-ADMIRAL WILLIAM PROWSE, CB, was one of the frigate captains summoned by Lord Nelson on board *Victory* as the fleets converged at the battle of Trafalgar on 21 October 1805, and given very broad instructions to help the captains of ships of the line find their way into action. What is especially remarkable about his career is that he was able to prosper despite very humble origins, because he caught the attention of a couple of senior officers who continued to ask for him when they had ships needing capable lieutenants and commanding officers.

Nothing is known of his birth or parentage, but it is believed that he was raised on board a merchant ship. He first entered the navy on 13 November 1771 as an able seaman in *Dublin* (74), which was serving as a guardship on the Hamoaze at Plymouth under the command of Captain Thomas (*or* Charles?) Herbert, and he remained in her an unusually long time, until 26 February 1776. It is possible that this was no more than a nominal muster, but it was unusual for such to be given an able seaman's rating. He was rated midshipman and master's mate in his next ship, *Albion* (74), by Captain George Bowyer on 31 August 1778 when he was serving at sea on the American station. He was present in her at the actions off Grenada on 6 July 1779, and near Martinique in April and May 1781. On 22 December he moved into *Atlas* (90) under Captain George Vandeput at Chatham, and on 14 April 1782 he joined the 9-pounder frigate *Cyclops* (28) commanded by Captain Brabazon Christian for service in North America, where he was commissioned lieutenant on 6 December 1782. He may have served in merchant ships between 1784 and the mobilisation in 1787, when he was employed for a few months in *Bellona* (74) under Bowyer. During the Nootka Sound crisis of 1790 he served in *Barfleur* (90) and *Stately* (64) under Captain Robert Calder, who also seems to have discovered his quality. From August 1791 to January 1793 he served in *Duke* (90) flying the flag of Lord Hood at Portsmouth.

On 20 March 1793 he was appointed to *Prince* (90) flying Rear-Admiral Bowyer's flag, and he followed him into *Barfleur* on 28 December. He was still serving in her at the time of the battle of the Glorious First of June in 1794. He was very severely wounded in that action when a large shot tore away so much of a leg as to oblige him to be invalided to hospital ashore, but he recovered and was ordered to serve as first lieutenant under Calder on board *Theseus* (74) in the West Indies and the Channel fleet. He continued to serve with Calder when the latter accompanied Sir John Jervis to the Mediterranean in *Victory* (100), travelling to join her in *Lively* (26) in November 1795. Jervis promoted him commander on 20 October 1796 in *Raven* (16). She was one of the repeaters at the battle of Cape St Vincent on 14 February 1797, after which Jervis put Prowse in command of one of the prizes, *Salvador del Mundo* (112). The Admiralty confirmed his commission as post captain on 6 March 1797. As so often happened, promotion put him out of employment for a while.

In August 1800 Calder asked for Prowse as flag captain of *Prince of Wales* (98) under orders for the West Indies. He was back in England on 22 June 1802, and on 4 August was appointed to command the 18-pounder frigate *Sirius* (36), in which he was employed in the Mediterranean and off Cadiz, remaining in her command for nearly six years. In 1805 she was employed in Calder's squadron watching Ferrol, and during the action of 22 July when Prowse had two men killed and three wounded. He came under Nelson's command when Calder was sent to Cadiz and then returned to Portsmouth to face his court martial. Following the battle of Trafalgar, Prowse continued to serve in the Mediterranean under Lord Collingwood. A reputation already well established was further strengthened by an action off the mouth of the Tiber on 17 April 1806 when he attacked a flotilla consisting of *La Bergère* (18), which he took, and three brigs and five heavy gun vessels, in all mounting seventy-six long guns and twenty-one carronades. He came ashore on 19 May 1808 and had nearly two years of shore leave.

è On 15 March 1810 he was appointed to command the *Theseus* (74), and he continued in her until 23 December 1813. He was nominated a CB on 4 June 1815 and a colonel of the Royal Marines on 12 August 1819. He died on 23 March 1826, aged seventy-two, in St Pancras, London, with the rank of rear-admiral, and was buried in St Pancras New Church. He was able to leave sums of £2,000 to his sisters.

Lt: 6 December 1782
Cmdr: 20 October 1796
Capt: 6 March 1797
R-Adm: 19 July 1821

PYM

ADMIRAL SIR SAMUEL PYM, KCB, has the unfortunate distinction of having suffered the worst defeat to the Royal Navy during the wars against the French Republic and Empire.

He was born in 1778, a son of Joseph Pym of Pinley, Warwickshire, and his wife, who is known to have been a daughter of Thomas Arnott, MD, of Cupar, Fife, and niece of Sir William Arnott, baronet. He was entered into the books of *Eurydice* (24) as a captain's servant in June 1788 under the command of Captain George Lumsdaine, and served in the Channel and Mediterranean. When he transferred in May or June 1792 to the *Zebra,* sloop (16), under Captain William Brown he was rated as an able seaman, and he almost immediately followed Brown into the brig-sloop *Kingsfisher* (18), in which he was rated a midshipman. He served on the Irish station until November, when he again followed Brown into the cutter *Fly* (8). Having spent all his early service in small vessels, in early 1794 he joined *Ganges* (74) commanded by Captain William Truscott, but he was on board her no more than a month before he returned under Brown's command, into *Venus* (36) serving in the Channel and North Sea. Together they moved to the 18-pounder frigate *Alcmene* (32) in February 1795.

When Pym was commissioned lieutenant on 7 March 1795 he was appointed to *Martin*, sloop, commanded by Captain William Grenville Lobb. He followed Lobb to the French prize 9-pounder frigate *Babet* (20), and later to the *Aimable* (32) in the West Indies. He was wounded in a boat action in January 1798 while in command of one of *Babet*'s boats, but nevertheless he succeeded in capturing *La Désirée* (6). While serving in the 18-pounder frigate *Ethalion* (36) he received over £5,000 in prize money from the capture on 16–17 October 1799 of two Spanish treasure ships near Cape Finisterre, *Thetis* and *Santa-Brígida*, freighted with specie worth nearly £700,000. Pym endured shipwreck on Christmas Day 1799 when *Ethalion* was wrecked on the Penmarks, off the south-west point of Brittany, but he survived and was taken for a last time back into a ship commanded by his friend William Brown, the *Robust* (74).

On 10 February 1801 he was promoted commander for rank, and on 1 January he was put in command of the sloop *Swan* commissioning at Portsmouth. On 29 April 1802 he was posted captain, following which, on 25 May, he married a daughter of Edward Lockyer of Plymouth. The couple had at least one child.

He then began to move more into the limelight, and for a few years served in capital ships. On 29 April 1804 he was appointed to command *Mars* (74) in the Bay of Biscay, and he moved in October to the *Atlas* (90), in which he took part in Sir John Thomas Duckworth's action off San Domingo on 6 February 1806, receiving a gold medal along with the other captains.

In October 1808 Pym was appointed to the 18-pounder frigate *Sirius* (36) and began his service in the Indian Ocean. On 21 September 1809 he served in the force under Commodore Josias Rowley which raided St Paul's in Isle Bourbon, then known as Isle Napoleon. The *Naval Chronicle*'s account of the first action reported that:

> The squadron went in and fired their broadsides, and then hauled out; the *Sirius* frigate, Captain Pym, stood in again, and anxious to avail himself of the only opportunity that presented itself, he asked leave, and was permitted, by signal from the Commodore, to anchor, and accordingly, in the most gallant style, carried his little ship in and placed her within pistol-shot of the beach, and half-musket shot of the *Caroline* French frigate, and the two East Indiamen and a French brig of war, and opened so heavy a fire on them from his English bull-dogs, that in 20 minutes (the troops at the same time charging through the town) the whole struck their colours. [NC 23.67-9]

Pym was given the principal credit for saving the two captured Indiamen, and participated in the later capture of the island in July 1810, in the mid-dle of the austral winter.

While Rowley was occupied with establishing British control of Isle Bourbon, Pym was senior officer of a frigate squadron consisting of the *Sirius*, *Iphigenia* (32), *Néréide* (36) and *Magicienne* (32), with the brig *Staunch*. These were employed in blockading the Isle de France (Mauritius), which was being used quite effectively as a cruiser base by a more powerful force of five French frigates. The fort on Isle de la Passe guarding the entrance to Port South East (Mahébourg) was taken by an assault force from two of the British frigates with the intention of preventing the French from bringing prizes in, but the French squadron commander later reported that French flags were kept flying on the fort and on the frigates, thereby effectively luring three French frigates, *Bellona*, *Minerva* and *Victor* into Port South West with their prize, the East India Company's ship *Ceylon*. Pym, who was reconnoitring Port Louis, hurried back to Port South East on 22 August and sailed into the anchorage to engage the enemy, not realising the extent of the navigational difficulties of the road. He wrote in his official report:

> At noon *Nereide* made signal ready for action; I then closed, and from the situation of the enemy, decided on an immediate attack; and when her master came on board as pilot, made signal to weigh, but when within about a quarter of an hour's run of the enemy, he unfortunately run me on the edge of the inner narrow passage. We did not get off (and that with wonderful exertion) until eight o'clock next morning. At noon on the 23rd the *Iphigenia* and *Magicienne* came in sight; the enemy having moved further in, and making several batteries, as also manning the East India ship, and taking many men on board the frigates, I called them to assist in the attack, having all the captains and pilot on board, and being assured we were past all danger and could run direct for the enemy's line, we got under weigh, and pushed for our stations, viz. *Sirius*

alongside the *Bellona*, *Nereide* between her and the *Victor*, *Iphigenia* alongside la *Minerva*, and *Magicienne* between her and the East India ship; and just as their shot began to pass over us, sad to say, *Sirius* grounded on a small bank, not known; Captain Lambert joined his post, and had hardly given the third broadside before his opponent cut her cable. *Magicienne*, close to *Iphigenia*, ran on a bank, which prevented her bringing more than six guns to bear; poor *Nereide* nearly gained her post, and did in the most gallant manner maintain that and the one intended for *Sirius*, until *Bellona* cut. All the enemy's ships being on shore, and finding *Sirius* could not get off, the whole of them opened their fire on *Nereide*; and even in this unequal contest, and being a-ground, she did not cease firing until ten o'clock, and sorry am I to say, that the captain, every officer and man on board, are killed or wounded. [NC 25.72]

Iphigenia, under Captain Henry Lambert's command, was caught in the act of trying to warp out of harbour under fire, and against the wind, with the men from *Sirius* and *Magicienne* on board, when three more French frigates arrived and forced her to strike. The British defeat was mitigated only by the loss of the French cruisers which had gone ashore.

Taken prisoner, Pym was freed when Isle de France was captured in the following December, and a court martial acquitted him of blame for the catastrophe. He was appointed in February 1812 to command the *Hannibal* (74), in which he was employed off Cherbourg, and in May he was moved to the French prize *Niemen* (38), in which he served for the next three years in Basque Roads and off Bordeaux, off Cherbourg, at Lisbon, on a voyage to St Helena and the Cape of Good Hope, at Bermuda, on the coast of America and in the West Indies.

He left the sea on 5 May 1815 at the end of the war, and on 4 June 1815 he was nominated a CB.

But that was not in fact to be the end of his naval career. He returned to sea in 1830 and 1831 in command of *Kent* (74) in the Mediterranean. He was nominated a KCB on 25 October 1839, served from 1841 to 1846 as admiral superintendent at Devonport, and in the autumn of 1845 commanded an experimental squadron in the Channel.

He died at the Royal Hotel at Southampton, with the rank of admiral, on 2 October 1855.

Lt: 7 March 1795
Cmdr: 10 February 1801
Capt: 29 April 1802
R-Adm: 10 January 1837
V-Adm: 13 February 1847
Adm: 17 December 1852

RADSTOCK – *see* Waldegrave

RAINIER

ADMIRAL PETER RAINIER is principally remembered for the period when he was commodore and commander-in-chief in the East Indies station. When he died, his estate was worth £250,000, of which he left 10 per cent to reduce the national debt in recognition that, because of his appointment to the East Indies station, he had acquired a fortune which far exceeded his 'merits and pretensions'.

He was born on 24 November 1741, the son of Peter Rainier of Sandwich, and Sarah, née Spratt. He attended a school in Tonbridge in 1754, and entered the navy in 1756 on board *Oxford* (50). As a young man he served in the East Indies, in *Yarmouth* (60), in which he arrived in March 1758, and in *Tiger* (60), in which he was present in the actions of 29 April and 3 August 1758 and 10 September 1759 against the Comte d'Aché, moving in June 1760 to *Norfolk* (74), flagship of Rear-Admiral Charles Steevens at the siege of Pondicherry and of Vice-Admiral Samuel Cornish at the siege of Manila in September to October 1762. The *Norfolk* was paid off in England in 1764, and Rainier may have spent the next decade employed by the East India Company. He was promoted lieutenant on 26 May 1768, but not appointed to a ship, the *Maidstone* (28) commanded by Captain Alan Gardner, until January 1774.

The American war brought faster promotion and a second period of service in the East Indies. On 3 May 1777 Vice-Admiral Clark Gayton promoted him to command *Ostrich*, sloop, and following the capture of a large American privateer on 8 July 1778, during which he was severely wounded, the Admiralty made him post captain on 29 October 1778, with appointment in January 1779 to *Burford* (64), which was under orders to form part of Sir Edward Hughes's squadron that sailed for the East Indies on 7 March 1779. There, Rainier took part in operations against Hyder Ali, including the capture of Negapatam in November 1781 and Trincomalee in January 1782, and the five actions against Admiral de Suffren.

At the end of the war he returned home, and in 1790–1 he commanded the *Monarch* (74) in the Channel, but with the French declaration of war in February 1793 he commissioned *Suffolk* (74), on which he hoisted his broad pendant and proceeded once again to Madras, arriving in November 1794 and finally returning to England in 1805 when he retired from the service. During that period he assisted at the capture of Trincomalee and eventually the surrender in August of all the Dutch posts in Ceylon. He took possession of Amboyna on 10 February 1796, and Captain Christopher Cole under his command took Banda Neira by surprise and by storm on 8 March. He provided security for British trade vessels, and at the same time became immensely wealthy from the prizes and booty taken by his captains. During his service in the East Indies he was promoted to rear-admiral and vice-admiral, and in the Trafalgar promotion of 9 November 1805 he was made admiral of the blue.

Rainier was returned to parliament in May 1807 as member for Sandwich. He died at his house in Great George Street, Westminster, on 7 April 1808 at the age of sixty-six and was buried in Sandwich.

Lt: 26 May 1768
M-C: 3 May 1777
Capt: 29 October 1778
R-Adm: 1 June 1795
V-Adm: 14 February 1799
Adm: 9 November 1805

REYNOLDS

REAR-ADMIRAL ROBERT CARTHEW REYNOLDS is best known for his part when commanding the 18-pounder frigate *Amazon* (38) in the engagement with *Droits de l'Homme* (74) on 13 January 1797, in company with a razee sixty-four, *Indefatigable*, under the command of Sir Edward Pellew.

He was born in Lamorran, Cornwall, the son of John Reynolds and his wife Elizabeth, and was baptised on 30 July 1745. He entered the navy in 1759 under the patronage of Captain George Edgcumbe commanding *Hero* (74), and may have been present in the battle of Quiberon Bay. Subsequently he served for a few months in *Brilliant* (28) commanded by Captain Loggie, for three years in *Pearl* (32) commanded by Captain Charles Saxton, and for nearly a year in *Venus* (36) under Captain Samuel Barrington. The *Venus* was paid off in June 1769, and on 1 May 1770 Reynolds passed his lieutenant's examination. However, he was not commissioned that year despite the mobilisation at the time of the Falkland Islands crisis, and had to wait until the conflict in the American colonies was threatening to become another world war. He was commissioned on 26 February 1777, and during the next five years served principally in the Channel fleet: in the *Royal George* (100), the flagship of Vice-Admiral Robert Harland; in the *Barfleur* (90); and in the *Britannia* (100), with Vice-Admiral Barrington. On 18 April 1783 Reynolds was promoted to command the armed storeship *Dauphin*, in which he served in the West Indies, and from 1786 to 1788 he commanded *Echo* (14) on the Newfoundland station.

Again he had to wait for promotion, not being advanced to post rank until 24 September 1790 at the time of the Nootka Sound crisis. He was appointed temporarily to the command of the *Barfleur* in November. In 1795 Reynolds commanded the frigate *Druid* (32), and he transferred in 1796 to the *Amazon*, attached to the flying squadron under Pellew. On 13 January 1797 in very heavy weather with reduced visibility they engaged *Droits de l'Homme* (74), until they realised they were embayed in Audierne Bay. All three combatants tried desperately to bring their ships about, but only *Indefatigable* succeeded in avoiding shipwreck. Estimates of the loss of life in *Droits de l'Homme* run up to 1,000 men, but *Amazon*'s people were more fortunate, or as the British press preferred, better disciplined. All but six officers and men got safely to shore, where they surrendered as prisoners of war. In the following September, Reynolds was exchanged, and was acquitted at the court martial for the loss of his ship.

Following his shipwreck and exchange Reynolds was appointed to *Pomone* (46), a frigate of the largest class, captured from the French in 1794 and rearmed with 24-pounders. He continued in her in the Channel or the Bay of Biscay until the end of 1800, when he was moved into the *Cumberland* (74), from which in 1801 he again moved, to the *Orion* (74) in the Channel fleet. In 1803 he commanded a corps of the Cornish sea fencibles; in 1804 he commanded the *Dreadnought* (98) in the Channel, and from 1804 to 1807 the *Princess Royal* (98).

His death in the wreck of the *St George* (98) occurred at the end of an appointment from 1810 to 1811 as second in command in the Baltic under Sir James Saumarez. On 1 November 1811 Reynolds sailed from Hanö in charge of a large convoy for England with his flag as rear-admiral hoisted on the *St George*. Bad weather forced them to put back three times, and it was not until 12 November that they could finally proceed. On 15 November, after the convoy anchored for the night in the Belt, a large merchant ship dragged its anchor and collided with *St George*, parting her cable so that she drove on shore, where she lost her rudder and her masts had to be cut away. With great difficulty she was got off and refitted in Wingo Sound, with jury masts and a jury rudder. In the opinion of the officers, she was capable of making the voyage, but it was 17 December, very late in the season, before she was ready to sail with *Defence* and *Cressy* (74s) in company. On Christmas Eve, in a north-west storm, the *St George* was driven towards the coast of Jutland, struck on a bank some 300 yards from the shore near Ringkøb, and broke up. All but twelve of her 850 people were drowned. The

Cressy escaped, but *Defence* commanded by Captain David Atkins was lost with all but five of her people. Reynolds's body was not recovered.

Tim Weatherside wrote to the *Naval Chronicle*:

> It certainly... does appear most extraordinary, that the *St George* should have been allowed to leave Wingo Sound, at such a season, under jury masts, and with only a temporary rudder: for as to having two ships to attend her, it is clear, that when a ship gets on a lee shore in a gale of wind, or even when at sea when boats cannot live, no other ship can be of service to her. [NC 27.119–21]

At some unknown date Reynolds had been married, and he had two daughters and two sons, of whom his second son, also named Robert Carthew, commanded the boats which cut out the brig *Curieux* from under the batteries in Port de France, Martinique, on 4 February 1804. He had been promoted to the command of the prize, but died of his wounds at the age of fifty-nine on 13 September.

Lt: 26 February 1777
M-C: 18 April 1783
Capt: 24 September 1790
R-Adm: 28 April 1808

RICKETTS – *see* Jervis

RIOU

CAPTAIN EDWARD RIOU died heroically at the battle of Copenhagen on 2 April 1801, aged thirty-eight, when his ship swung stern to the heavy fire from the Trekroner fort while obeying Admiral Sir Hyde Parker's order to withdraw.

He was born on 20 November 1762 at Mount Ephraim near Faversham, Kent, son of Captain Stephen Riou in the Grenadier Guards, of a Huguenot family, and of Dorothy, daughter of George Dawson of North Ferriby Grange, Yorkshire. He joined the navy at the age of twelve, served in *Barfleur* (90) at Portsmouth and *Romney* (50) at the Newfoundland station, and in 1776 was rated as a midshipman in *Discovery* (8) commanded by Captain Charles Clerke, with whom he sailed to the Pacific in company with the *Resolution* (12) on James Cook's third voyage. When Cook was killed at Hawaii, Riou transferred with Clerke to the *Resolution*. In October 1780, after his return to England, Riou was commissioned lieutenant. He subsequently served in the West Indies, at Portsmouth in *Ganges* (74), which was fitted as a guardship, and in Newfoundland. He was described by Jacob Nagle, a seaman in the *Ganges*, as a strict disciplinarian with a fanatical regard for cleanliness. He was also a religious man, but was an affectionate son and brother.

He was fortunate in 1789 to be appointed, with the patronage of the Townsend family, to command the two-decked frigate *Guardian,* which was pierced for forty-four guns but then armed *en flute*, and laden with stores for the British settlement at Botany Bay. He sailed from Spithead on 8 September, and on Christmas Eve, thirteen days out from the Cape of Good Hope and not far from Marion Island, *Guardian* ran onto the submerged part of an iceberg and was badly holed. Sails were fathered and stretched under the hull, but the pumps continually broke their chains, the men were exhausted, and as the ship was apparently in immediate danger of sinking, the boats were hoisted out. As many of the ship's people as was possible with the heavy sea running left the *Guardian* and got into the boats. Only fifteen of them survived. Riou refused to leave his command so long as any remained in the ship, and in the end she did not sink because of the buoyancy of her cargo, and was brought safely into Cape Town on 21 February 1790. There she had to be broken up. Riou arranged that the convict artisans he was transporting, those who had survived and had worked to save the ship, should be pardoned.

Although he was acquitted of blame for the loss of his ship, and became a popular hero, his promotions to master and commander on 21 September 1790 and subsequently post captain on 4 June 1791 were only for rank and half pay. He was not given command of a ship until 1794, when he was appointed to *Beaulieu* (40) serving in the West Indies. Ill health forced his retirement from

that station, and he was honoured with the command of *Princess Augusta,* yacht, despite his youth. His health unexpectedly improved, and in June 1799 he was appointed to command the 18-pounder frigate *Amazon* (38). He was still serving in her when she was attached to the Baltic force in the spring of 1801.

Prior to the battle of Copenhagen, Admiral Sir Hyde Parker, Rear-Admiral Nelson and other senior officers surveyed the coastal defences from *Amazon*. Riou was one of Parker's council of war at which it was decided Nelson should lead the attack from the south end of the moored Danish line, and he and Captain Thomas Foley helped Nelson draft the detailed battle plan on the night before the action. In fact, that plan had to be extemporised owing to ships grounding before they reached their station, and this put the *Amazon* into a highly exposed position. When the signal was received ordering withdrawal, Riou was too junior an officer to ignore it. Lieutenant-Colonel William Stewart, who commanded soldiers of the 48th Regiment during the battle, recorded the report that Riou

> was sitting on a gun, was encouraging his men, and had been wounded in the head by a splinter. He had expressed himself grieved at being thus obliged to retreat, and nobly observed, 'What will Nelson think of us?' His clerk was killed by his side; and by another shot, several of the marines, while hauling on the main-brace, shared the same fate. Riou then exclaimed, 'Come, then, my boys, let us die all together!' The words were scarcely uttered, when the fatal shot severed him in two. Clarke and M'Arthur 2.403

Lieutenant John Quilliam, who was to serve as first lieutenant on *Victory* (100) at Trafalgar, took over command after Riou's death and got *Amazon* away. A monument to Riou's memory was erected in St Paul's Cathedral, London.

Lt: 28 October 1780
M-C: 21 September 1790
Capt: 4 June 1791

ROTHERAM

CAPTAIN EDWARD ROTHERAM, CB, was flag captain to Vice-Admiral Collingwood in *Royal Sovereign* at the battle of Trafalgar on 21 October 1805.

The second son of Dr John Rotheram, MD, of Newcastle-upon-Tyne, and his wife, Catherine, née Roberts, a native of Hexham, Edward Rotheram was baptised in Hexham on 27 December 1753. His father and Dr Hutton at Head school in Newcastle instructed him in mathematics, and he acquired a practical knowledge of navigation in the Newcastle coal trade. He entered the navy on 14 April 1777 as an able seaman in *Centaur* (74), at first under the command of Captain Sir Richard Hughes. She was employed in the Channel, and Rotheram remained on board until 29 April 1780, successively under the command of Captains Phillips Cosby, Anthony (?) Parry and John Neale Pleydell Nott, while being rated as midshipman and then master's mate. He then transferred to *Barfleur* (90) flying the flag of Vice-Admiral Samuel Barrington, continuing in the Channel, until 13 October, when he was ordered to act as lieutenant in *Monarch* (74), commanded by Captain Francis Reynolds, with whom he served in the Leeward Islands and Jamaica; he was one of Sir Samuel Hood's squadron in the actions off Martinique and the Chesapeake on 29 April and 5 September 1781, at St Kitts in January 1782 and in Admiral Sir George Rodney's victory at the Saintes in April 1782. He was commissioned lieutenant on 19 April 1783.

Following the end of the war he was on half pay for four years. Nevertheless, in 1785 he married Dorothy Harls of Newcastle-upon-Tyne, and the couple had one daughter. In May 1787 he was appointed to *Bombay Castle* (74) under the command of Captain Robert Fanshawe serving in the Channel, and on 12 April 1788 he was appointed to *Culloden* (74) under the command of Captain Sir Thomas Rich, whom he followed to *Vengeance* (74) on 24 December 1790, and then back to *Culloden* as first lieutenant in December 1792. It was as such that he fought in the battle of the

Glorious First of June in 1794. This led to his promotion to commander on 6 July 1794 and appointment on 27 January 1795 to *Camel*, storeship in the Mediterranean, and subsequently to *Camilla* (20) in the Channel, *Hawke,* sloop, and the French prize *L'Unité* (34) in the North Sea and Leeward Islands, and finally *Lapwing* (28) in the Channel again. He was made post captain on 27 August 1800 and paid off in November 1802. After two years ashore he was appointed on 15 December 1804 Collingwood's flag captain in *Dreadnought* (98), and he followed him into *Royal Sovereign* (100) on 10 October 1805.

Collingwood had written contemptuously of Rotheram in a letter to his sister on 26 August 1805: 'such a captain, such a stick, I wonder very much how such people get forward.... Was he brought up in the Navy? For he has very much the stile of the Coal trade about him, except that they are good seamen.' [Collingwood no 92] Nelson felt it necessary to caution Collingwood that 'in the presence of the Enemy, all men should be as brothers'. But Collingwood's contempt for Rotheram's seamanship fell away when he fought with him, finding his courage in battle all that could be asked. Marshall reports the story that in the early part of the battle of Trafalgar 'A heavy shower of musketry had nearly swept the quarter-deck of the *Royal Sovereign*, when some of his officers requested ... [Rotheram] not to expose himself to the enemy's small arms men, by wearing his epaulettes and gold laced hat, "Let me alone," he replied, "I have always fought in a cocked hat and I always will."' [Marshall 2.298]

After the battle he was appointed to command *Bellerophon* (74) in the place of John Cooke, who had been killed, and remained in her until she was paid off on 7 June 1808. However, not all was well. He was court-martialled in 1807 for unacceptable behaviour to his lieutenants and the chaplain, and was reprimanded. Collingwood remarked to his sister that, although he thought Rotheram 'a stupid man' he had hoped for the best, recognising that his battlefield appointment had been 'the only chance he had of being in a ship'. [Collingwood no 205]

Bellerophon was indeed his last command. He

was made a CB on 4 June 1815, after three times of asking, and was appointed a captain of Greenwich hospital in 1828. He died of an apoplectic fit at the age of seventy-six on 2 November 1830 in Bildeston, Suffolk, and was buried in the churchyard of St Mary Magdalene.

Lt: 19 April 1783
Cmdr: 6 July 1794
Capt: 27 August 1800

ROWLEY

ADMIRAL SIR CHARLES ROWLEY, BARONET, GCB, coming from one of the more important naval families, served without attracting much attention until July 1813, when in command of the third rate *Eagle* (74) he played a spirited part in the capture of Fiume in the Gulf of Venice by a squadron taking their orders from Rear-Admiral Fremantle.

He was born on 16 December 1770, the fourth and youngest son of Vice-Admiral Sir Joshua Rowley, first baronet of Trending Hall, Suffolk. His mother was Sarah, daughter of Bartholomew Burton, deputy governor of the Bank of England. His name was entered on 1 January 1778 as a captain's servant on board the *Monarch* (74), but his real entry into the navy occurred in 1785. He was given passage in the 9-pounder frigate *Thisbe* (28) flying the broad pendant of Commodore Herbert (?) Sawyer out to the North American station, where in May he was rated an able seaman in *Assistance* (50) commanded by Captain Bentink. He also served in *Ariadne* (20) and *Resource* (28) prior to being rated master's mate on 8 December 1788. In November he joined *Pegasus* (28) under the command of Prince William Henry, duke of Clarence, whom he followed on 11 March 1788 into *Andromeda* (32), although he had to revert to the status of captain's servant. On 27 October he transferred to *Thisbe,* which was now commanded by Captain Samuel Hood, and was rated an able seaman. On 23 April 1789 he transferred again to *Salisbury* (50) flying the flag of Vice-Admiral Milbanke commanding at Newfoundland, who commissioned him lieutenant on 8 October 1789 and appointed him to command *Trepassey* (6), where he remained until February 1791. He

next joined *Bombay Castle* (74) under Captain Duckworth, with whom he served in the Channel from 20 June to 4 September, when he moved to *Niger* (32) under Captain Keats.

On 5 April 1793, two months after the French declaration of war, he followed Keats to *London* (90), and he served in her until 1 March 1794, joining *Resolution* (74) flying Rear-Admiral George Murray's flag on 28 April. He sailed with him to North America, where he was appointed acting captain of *Hussar* (28) on 16 December, and promoted commander on 20 April 1795 with appointment to the ship-sloop *Lynx* (16). He was posted captain of *La Raisen* (26) on 2 July, and commissioned on 1 August 1795. He was appointed on 8 November to *Cleopatra* (32), which he commanded until 23 May 1796, then transferred to *Hussar* (28), and on 5 October 1796 to *L'Unité* (38) in the Channel, where he remained until 21 August 1798.

He married on 17 December 1797 Elizabeth, the youngest daughter of Admiral Sir Richard King. The couple had five sons and two daughters.

On 22 November 1800 Rowley was appointed flag captain to Sir Charles Cotton in the *Prince George* (98), where he remained only until 27 January 1801. Having survived his scrutiny, he was appointed on 10 March to the 18-pounder frigate *Boadicea* (38), in which he took part in cutting out a Spanish warship from under the guns of Corunna. From 15 March 1804 to 8 November 1805 he served in the *Ruby* (64) as part of the force blockading the Texel under Rear-Admiral Thornbrough, and subsequently deployed to the coast of Spain, following which he was transferred into *Eagle*, which he was to command to 13 May 1814. In May 1806 he was placed under the orders of Sir Sidney Smith on the coasts of Naples and Sicily, in 1809 he served in the Scheldt expedition, in 1810 he was employed off Cadiz, and from 1811 he was in the Adriatic.

The attack was made on Fiume on 3 July 1813, and the plan went awry when the wind shifted. Nevertheless, the battery against which *Eagle* brought up, the second, was soon silenced, and when that fact was communicated by telegraph,

Admiral Fremantle ordered it to be stormed. Rowley led a force of marines himself from his gig against the second battery, while Captain William Hoste of the *Bacchante* (38) stormed the first battery. Rowley then led his men into the town, brushing aside the snipers in the windows of the houses, and finally flushed the garrison out of a large house in the central square with the aid of the squadron's boats armed with carronades.

Following the fall of Fiume, Rowley attacked the fortress of Farasina, which he demolished, and on 2 August 1813 he and Hoste attacked the harbour defences of Rovigno on the Istrian coast, which they silenced prior to taking the town and destroying its defences. The ships in the harbour had been scuttled by the enemy, but some were salved, and the rest were destroyed. He continued to play a prominent part under Admiral Fremantle in the capture of Trieste in October and the expulsion of the French from the gulf.

In recognition of his merits he was given permission to wear the insignia of a knight of the imperial military order of Maria Theresa, conferred on him by the emperor of Austria, he was promoted rear-admiral on 4 June 1814, and he served as commander-in-chief at the Nore from 1 November to 31 March 1818. From 24 August 1820 to 8 June 1823 he commanded at Jamaica. He was nominated KCB on 2 January 1815 and a GCH on 7 October 1835, created a baronet on 22 February 1836, and made GCB on 4 July 1840. He served as commissioner of the Admiralty from 23 December 1834 to 25 April 1835, and was appointed groom of the bedchamber to William IV. He died on 10 October 1845, aged seventy-four, in Brighton, with the rank of admiral.

> Lt: 8 October 1789
> Cmdr: 20 April 1795
> Capt: 1 August 1795
> R-Adm: 4 June 1814
> V-Adm: 27 May 1825
> Adm: 23 November 1841

ROWLEY

ADMIRAL SIR JOSIAS ROWLEY, BARONET, GCB, was the scourge of the French settlements in the south Indian Ocean, in 1809 and 1810 commanding the naval force which first raided then captured Bourbon, and playing a decisive role in the capture of Isle de France (Mauritius).

He was a grandson of Admiral of the Fleet Sir William Rowley, KB, vice-admiral of England and a lord of the Admiralty, who died on 1 January 1768, and an uncle was Vice-Admiral Sir Joshua Rowley. The second son of Clothworthy Rowley, barrister-at-law and member of parliament for Downpatrick, county Down, and of his wife Letitia, who was daughter and coheiress of Samuel Campbell of Mount Campbell, county Leitrim, he was born on an unknown date. On 1 November 1777 his name was entered as a captain's servant in the books of his uncle's ship, *Monarch* (74), when she was serving in the Channel fleet, and on 8 December 1778 he transferred to *Suffolk* (74) under the command of Captain Hugh Cloberry Christian, with whom he served in the West Indies. On 7 January 1780 he was rated midshipman in *Alexander* (74) commanded by Lord Longford in the Channel, moving on 18 July 1781 into *Agamemnon* (64) under the command of Captain Benjamin Caldwell as able seaman and midshipman. On 9 December he joined *Prothee* (64) under Captain Charles Buckner, with whom he returned to the West Indies, and on 16 March 1782 he rejoined his uncle in *Resource* at Jamaica, following him into *Diamond* (32) on 7 October. On 15 January 1783 he was rated master's mate in *Resistance* (44) under the command of Captain James King, who was succeeded on 26 November by Captain Edward O'Bryen. He was commissioned lieutenant on 25 December 1783, and continued to serve in *Resistance* until 23 April 1784. It was then apparently a time of settled peace, and he was not employed again until 17 April 1786, when he was appointed to the brig-sloop *Otter* (10) commanded by Captain J Parker Hardy. He served in her until 3 November 1788, and then was ashore again until the time of the Nootka Sound crisis in 1790, when on 17 May he was appointed to the 12-pounder frigate *Winchelsea* (32) under Captain the Honourable Alexander Cochrane and later Captain John Fish. He left her on 7 February 1791, and again was ashore until after the French declaration of war on 1 February 1793.

On 16 March he was appointed to *Magicienne* (32) under Captain George Master, with whom he served in the Channel, and he was transferred into *Alexander* (74) under Captain Henry West on 29 August.

He was promoted on 14 March 1794 to commander with appointment to *Lark* (16) in the North Sea, and his employment in the squadron which escorted Princess Caroline of Brunswick to England led to his promotion in little over a year to post captain on 6 April 1795. He then had to wait nearly two years for a command, until he was appointed on 5 August 1797 to *Braave* (40), in which he served at the Cape of Good Hope; he then transferred on 22 January 1799 into *Impérieuse* (38) for service in the East Indies. He returned to England in June 1802.

Following the peace of Amiens he was put in command of *Raisonnable* (64) on 15 April 1805 and in her fought in Sir Robert Calder's action off Ferrol on 22 July. The following year *Raisonnable* formed part of the expedition under Commodore Home Popham and Sir David Baird which recaptured Cape Town and then proceeded to the Rio de la Plata. Rowley commanded the detachment of sailors who were employed with Lieutenant-General Whitelocke's army to bring artillery through the swamps to Buenos Aires. That operation failing, British forces withdrew, and *Raisonnable* returned to the Cape of Good Hope station.

In August 1809 Rowley and Lieutenant-Colonel Keating decided that it was necessary to destroy the capacity of the Isle de Bourbon to support cruiser attacks on trade. In a well-organised operation, troops stationed on the Island of Rodriguez were collected, and landed on 21 September, to silence shore batteries prior to the squadron sailing into St Paul's harbour. There they recovered two British Indiamen and captured the French frigate *La Caroline*. The batteries and magazines were blown up. On 16 March 1810 Rowley transferred to *Boadicea* (38), and in July the squadron under his command returned to Bourbon with enough soldiers to finish the job. They were landed on the 7th and 8th, and the is-

land garrison capitulated on the 9th.

Rowley was still at Bourbon on 22 August when he learnt of Captain Samuel Pym's intended attack on the French frigates in Grand Port, Isle de France (Mauritius). He sailed immediately to assist, but before he arrived he learnt of the disaster which had happened after Pym seized the Isle de la Passe in the entrance to Port South West in order to prevent the return of French cruisers which had captured several Indiamen. They failed to stop all but one of them getting into harbour, and when Pym tried to cut them out, three frigates were lost by running on the reefs, and one and a brig were captured. This British disaster is the only naval victory listed on the Arc de Triomphe in Paris, but Vice-Admiral Albemarle Bertie, commanding the Cape station, wrote in his official dispatch:

> A momentary superiority thus obtained by the enemy has been promptly and decisively crushed by the united zeal, judgment, perseverance, skill, and intrepidity of Captain Rowley, in his Majesty's ship *Boadicea*; the value and importance of whose services, long conspicuous and distinguished as they have been, have fully justified the selection and detention of him as the senior officer conducting the blockade of this station; and who, in the present instance, almost alone and unsupported but by the never-failing energies and resources of his active and intelligent mind, under circumstances, as may be easily imagined, of extreme anxiety, mortification, and disappointment, in a few hours not only retook his Majesty's ships *Africaine* and *Ceylon*, but captured also the largest frigate possessed by the enemy in these seas, and has thus restored the British naval pre-eminence in this quarter, which his talents have long so successfully contributed to maintain. [NC 25.157]

The disaster at Port South West had been made much worse by the loss of *Africaine* (38), to two French frigates, as she was trying to join Rowley at Bourbon.

With the assistance of two sloops, *Boadicea* recaptured the *Africaine* the same afternoon and took her to St Paul's. The French frigates were in sight but forbore to interfere, and Rowley thought himself too weak to attack them. They returned to Port Louis, which enabled Rowley on the 18th to capture a third French frigate, *Venus*, and the company ship *Ceylon*, which she had taken prize. *Africaine* had originally been built for the French marine and captured by *Phoebe* in February 1801.

When Rowley was reinforced with several frigates in October he was able to establish a close blockade of Port Louis on Isle de France, prior to a full-scale invasion of the island being organised by the East Indies squadron with an embarked force commanded by Major-General the Honourable John Abercrombie. Bertie arrived from the Cape on 29 November. Against best service practice, because Isle de France was considered to be the responsibility of the commander-in-chief East Indies, he assumed command, and he entrusted Rowley with getting the army ashore over an exposed beach. Within four days the French capitulated. Rowley was then sent home with the victory dispatch.

He left *Boadicea* on 4 December 1810, and after a winter's leave was appointed on 9 April 1811 to command of *America* (74) under orders for the Mediterranean, where he displayed as much energy in his operations against shipping in the Gulf of Genoa. He was less successful in an attempted *coup de main* in December 1813 with the objective of seizing Leghorn, but succeeded early the following year in landing an army under Lord William Bentineck which captured Genoa. The spoils, however, had to be shared with a squadron of ships of the line under Sir Edward Pellew, the appearance of which had finally brought the French capitulation.

On 2 November 1813 Rowley was rewarded with a patent of baronetcy, and on 4 December was nominated a colonel of the Royal Marines. He was promoted to rear-admiral on 4 June 1814, and nominated KCB on 2 January 1815. He returned to the Mediterranean that summer with his flag in the *Impregnable* (100) under the command of his brother, Captain Samuel Campbell Rowley. He returned to England at the end of the war and came ashore on 10 November 1815. From 5 May 1818 to 9 December 1821 he was commander-in-chief on the coast of Ireland; and after his promotion on 27 May 1825 to vice-admiral he served as commander-in-chief in the Mediterranean from December 1833 to February 1837. It was customary at the time for the Maltese and Ionian Republic to appoint commanders-in-chief Mediterranean GCMG, an honour which was duly awarded on 22 February 1834, and he was to be further honoured as a GCB on 4 July 1840. He was elected member of parliament for county Kinsale in July 1821, and died with the rank of admiral on 10 January 1842, aged seventy-seven, in Mount Campbell, Drumsna, county Leitrim.

Lt: 25 December 1783
Cmdr: 14 March 1794
Capt: 6 April 1795
R-Adm: 4 June 1814
V-Adm: 27 May 1825
Adm: 10 January 1837

St Vincent

Admiral of the Fleet the Right Honourable Sir John Jervis, earl of St Vincent, GCB, is a controversial figure. As a young man he was known as a polished courtier, but as he aged he imposed an iron discipline on himself and especially on his subordinates. The perfection of routine paid off in the operational readiness of the fleets he commanded in the wars against the French Revolution and Empire. Of his management of the Mediterranean fleet in 1796 Horatio Nelson wrote: 'They at home do not know what this fleet is capable of performing; anything and everything... of all the fleets I ever saw, I never saw one, in point of officers and men equal to Sir John Jervis's, who is a commander able to lead them to glory.' [Nelson 2.229] Few but Nelson and Thomas Troubridge, however, found they had much enthusiasm for working under his command. St Vincent's officers were not treated as 'a band of brothers', and his methods ultimately debased the creativity of Royal Navy tactical control.

He was born on 9 January 1735 in Meaford near

Stone, Staffordshire, the second and youngest son of John Swynfen Jervis of Meaford, bencher of the Middle Temple, counsel to the Admiralty and auditor of Greenwich hospital. His mother was Elizabeth, daughter of George Parker, Esq. of Park Hall and sister of Sir Thomas Parker, lord chief baron of the Exchequer. He was educated at the free school in Burton-upon-Trent, and then at Weston's academy in Greenwich, where his father moved on being appointed solicitor to the Admiralty and treasurer of Greenwich hospital. His father planned that he should make a career in the law, but instead he entered the navy on 4 January 1749 under the patronage of Commodore the Honourable George Townshend as an able seaman in the *Gloucester*, commanded by Lord Colvill. Another important patron was to be Admiral Sir Charles Saunders, with whom he served in the Mediterranean and North America, Jervis making a good impression in the siege and capture of Quebec.

He had already been in the navy over thirty years when he took part in the battle of Ushant on 27 July 1778 in command of *Foudroyant* (80), second astern of Admiral Keppel's flag. Jervis's testimony was important in acquitting Keppel at the subsequent court martial. On 19 April 1782 while serving under Captain Samuel Barrington, who was a personal friend, he engaged and defeated *Pégase* (74), and as a reward was invested as a KB on 29 May. He took part in all three of the operations to relieve Gibraltar, under Admiral Lord Rodney in January 1780, in March 1781 under Vice-Admiral George Darby, and finally in that commanded by Admiral Lord Howe in October 1782. Following the conclusion of the war he entered politics, holding the parliamentary seats for Launceston, Cornwall, from January 1783 to 1784, for Great Yarmouth, Norfolk, from 1784 to 1790, and for Chipping Wycombe, Buckinghamshire, from 1790 to 1794. At the time a supporter of William Pitt, he spoke for fiscal and administrative reforms. He married on 5 June 1783 his cousin, Martha, daughter of Sir Thomas Parker, and was promoted rear-admiral on 24 September 1787.

In the general promotion which occurred on the outbreak of war he was promoted vice-admiral on 1 February 1793. He did not attend the parliamentary debate on the outbreak of war, because he viewed the policies of Pitt as a major contributing factor to the French declaration but did not want to take a public position. He did vote in favour of the opposition motion for parliamentary reform in May, but this did not prevent his being appointed to command of the fleet sent to secure the West Indian islands. Once he arrived on station he cooperated effectively with General Sir Charles Grey, who was a personal friend, in the capture of Martinique and Guadeloupe, and later in pillaging the islands. Both men were to be censured by the House of Commons for their excess, and neither was offered a peerage as reward for his services. Ill health obliged him to request permission to return home, but before the arrival of Lord Colvill to assume command he learnt of the arrival of a French force at Guadeloupe. This time the French prevailed against a fever-stricken British garrison. Jervis was to be involved in lawsuits with Colvill, and with Captains Nelson and Elphinstone over prize money.

In February 1795 he struck his flag at Spithead, but his property was still on board his flagship *Boyne* (98) when she blew up on 1 May. A month later he was promoted to admiral, but the controversy surrounding him raised doubts about whether he should be appointed to command-in-chief in the Mediterranean. His name had been put forward by Lord Hugh Seymour, and eventually the first lord, Lord Spencer, agreed. On 29 November 1795 Jervis replaced Vice-Admiral Hotham as commander-in-chief Mediterranean and began, with the help of his first captain Robert Calder, a thorough overhaul of fleet discipline and tactics.

He arrived in his command at a time of peculiar difficulty. The triumph of French arms in Italy, which forced the kingdom of Naples into neutrality, brought Spain into the war on the side of France. The odds against the Royal Navy in the Mediterranean were too great, and in September 1796 Jervis was ordered to retreat to the Atlantic, evacuating the British toehold in Corsica and Italy. Operating out of Lisbon, he took station off Cape

St Vincent to prevent any hostile movement out of the Mediterranean which might lead to such a combined fleet in the Channel as in 1779 had threatened invasion. Admiral Córdoba, who had put into Cartagena for repairs and then proceeded into the Atlantic, was watched as he approached, and on the morning of 14 February 1797 the Spanish fleet was sighted. As Calder counted them out, with the numbers eventually reaching twenty-seven to the British fifteen ships of the line, Jervis reportedly said sharply, 'Enough, sir, no more of that. The die is cast and if there are fifty sail of the line, I will go through them.'

In fact, the Spanish fleet numbered twenty-five ships, of which four were merchant urcas loaded with mercury under a strong local escort. The eight or nine ships of the convoy and its escort were separated from the main body. To Jervis, however, it appeared as though the Spanish fleet was divided. He steered to keep the two parts of the fleet separate so that he could retain control of tactical developments. In the confused tactical manoeuvring under fire, the British line became disconnected, and the main Spanish force seemed to be seeking to threaten the British rear and to close up the gap with the convoy escort. At a critical moment he signalled the rear squadron to steer for the closing gap, and Horatio Nelson, commanding *Captain*, had the moral and physical courage to wear out of the line without waiting for the rear-admiral. Jervis's and Calder's drilling of the fleet told against the poorly manned and drilled Spaniards, and at the end of the day the British had taken four prizes and demonstrated how capable they were of contesting any attempt at invasion. In recognition of his achievement, Jervis was created Baron Jervis of Meaford and earl of St Vincent on 23 June 1797.

Always tending towards despotism, St Vincent's reaction to the mutinies of 1797 was severe to the point of tyrannical. Far from feeling any sympathy with the very real grievances of the men, he used the full weight of naval discipline to eliminate any disaffection. It was only after his retirement that new and more liberal thinking about leadership began to be seen in the pages of the *Naval Chronicle*, when it came to be recognised that bat-

tles are not won by men who are kept by fear in obedience. When Vice-Admiral Charles Thompson complained in a public letter that St Vincent's action in hanging two men on the Sabbath was a profanation, St Vincent insisted that Thompson or himself should be ordered home. And later, when Vice-Admiral Sir John Orde objected to Nelson's being sent in command of a detached force to the Mediterranean although junior to himself, St

The Right Honourable Earl of St Vincent,
Knight of the Most Honourable Order of the Bath,
Admiral of the White Squadron,
engraving by William Ridley after
Lemuel F Abbot, published by
Burney and Gold, Shoe Lane,
1 August 1800.

Vincent became violently abusive and ordered him home. This was to lead to Orde's requesting a court martial on St Vincent, and then to calling him out. Eventually the strain of keeping the sea, while refitting ships at Gibraltar instead of permitting their captains to return to England, forced St Vincent to request supersession. Vice-Admiral Keith was sent with reinforcements, but St Vincent continued to command from Gibraltar, rejoining the fleet when the Brest fleet entered the Mediterranean. The divided command was not effective, and at last, on 15 June 1799 he struck his flag. He had been appointed colonel of the marines, apparently in 1785, and was promoted lieutenant-general of the marines on 26 August 1800.

When he had somewhat recovered his health in October, Orde made his challenge. St Vincent replied that he was not personally responsible for his public actions, but Orde made it clear that it was his personal conduct which he resented. However, they did not meet because word got out and the Admiralty conveyed to both of them that King George forbade their fighting.

Although still in far from perfect health, St Vincent then agreed to accept command of the Channel fleet, superseding Lord Bridport. His introduction of Mediterranean fleet discipline was anything but popular, and it appears that much of the real development in blockade methods had taken place during Bridport's period in command. Such orders as that forbidding officers on any account to sleep ashore had a serious effect on their family lives, but they may also have been important in maintaining a readiness for instant action. For 121 days from May to September 1800 the blockade of Brest was sustained without a break, and when the fleet returned to Torbay in November there were only sixteen men needing to be sent to hospital. Ushant became the fleet rendezvous, and the inshore squadron patrolled the rock-strewn waters between the Black Rocks and the Parquette shoal.

With the formation of the Addington administration in early 1801, St Vincent accepted the office of first lord of the Admiralty, which he held from 19 February 1801 until 15 May 1804. His first task was to prepare the fleet being sent to the Baltic, to do which he had to deal with a 'combination' of shipwrights who sought to use the pressure of events to obtain a permanent doubling of their pay. St Vincent offered a temporary allowance to compensate for wartime inflation, but when it was rejected he turned the delegates out into the street, and dismissed from the yards anyone involved in the labour action. Following the conclusion of peace, he turned with his usual energy and self-confidence to rooting out corruption in the dockyards and civil administration of the navy. The movement for reform was already under way

before his appointment, but he imparted to it his ruthless energy, and insisted on the formation of a royal commission on 29 December 1802. The reports of the commission over the next two and a half years laid bare the weakness of the administrative culture of the navy and were to lead to reform, which replaced the practice of collecting fees for services and selling unserviceable stores, by increasing the salaries paid for work. But the commission was not given the power to examine witnesses under oath, as St Vincent wanted, as this would have made possible legal proceedings against individuals who could thereby have been forced into resignation. His focus on discipline may have been at the expense of the much-needed repair of the fleet prior to the recommencement of war in 1803. William Pitt, now in opposition, made that charge, and when he returned to power in May 1804 there was no question but St Vincent had to resign from the Admiralty. The royal commission was replaced by one for the revision of the civil affairs of the navy.

The attacks continued on St Vincent following his resignation, but were rejected by a vote of the Commons, which went on to pass a resolution 'That it appears to this house that the conduct of the earl of St. Vincent, in his late naval administration, has added an additional lustre to his exalted character.' After Pitt's death in January 1806 St Vincent agreed to return to command the Channel fleet, with the rank of acting admiral of the fleet, but his health and the collapse of the Grenville administration in March 1807 led to his final retirement. He occasionally appeared in the House of Lords, and in 1808 spoke strongly against the attack on the neutral Danes.

He was a fellow of the Royal Society, and in 1806 became an elder brother of the Trinity House. He was promoted general of the Royal Marines on 11 May 1814, he was invested GCB on 2 January 1815, and his rank of admiral of the fleet was confirmed on 19 July 1821 at the coronation of King George IV. His wife died on 8 February 1816, and St Vincent followed on 13 March 1823, aged eighty-eight, at his seat of Rochetts, Essex. On his death, the earldom and barony became extinct, but the viscounty devolved to his only surviving nephew, Edward Jervis Ricketts. There is a memorial to him in St Paul's Cathedral, and another in St Michael, Stone, Staffordshire.

Lt: 19 February 1755
M-C: 15 May 1759
Capt: 13 October 1760
R-Adm: 24 September 1787
V-Adm: 1 February 1793
Adm: 1 June 1795
Adm. of the Fleet: 19 July 1821

SAUMAREZ

ADMIRAL SIR JAMES SAUMAREZ, BARON DE SAUMAREZ, GCB, was Nelson's second in command at the battle of the Nile, the victor of the July 1801 action east of Gibraltar, and Baltic fleet commander at a time when great diplomatic skills were required.

He was born on 11 March 1757 in St Peter Port, Guernsey, the third son of Dr Matthew Saumarez, MD, and his second wife, Carteret, daughter of James Le Marchant of Guernsey. He was placed on the muster books of the 9-pounder frigate *Solebay* (28) in 1765 as a volunteer, under the command of Captain Lucius O'Bryen, and served in the Irish Channel. In July 1770 he joined *Montreal* (32) as a supernumerary for passage to the Mediterranean, where he joined *Pembroke* (60) under Commodore Charles Proby, who was commander-in-chief Mediterranean. He later joined *Winchelsea* (32) under Captain Philip Durell on the same station. He was rated midshipman in *Levant* (28) under Captain Samuel Thompson, and appropriately proceeded for service in the Greek archipelago. In March 1775 he left his ship, and in October was examined at the Navy Office at St Mary-le-Strand in Westminster, and then immediately joined *Bristol* (50) as a passed midshipman under Commodore Sir Peter Parker. On the voyage to New York, *Bristol* carried Lord Cornwallis as a passenger; he offered Saumarez a commission in the army, which he declined. The very heavy punishment that *Bristol* received from American batteries during the capture of Charlestown, after which Saumarez was left the only man alive in his gun crew, finally bought him promotion. In recognition of his services he was commissioned on 25 January 1778 to command of *Spitfire*, an armed galley employed in cruising for American privateers. It was later burnt at Rhode Island to prevent it falling into the hands of the French.

Saumarez returned a passenger to England, where he was appointed in June 1779 to serve in *Victory* (100) flying Sir Charles Hardy's flag during the critical time when the Franco-Spanish invasion fleet was in the Channel in overwhelming force. By 1781 he had risen to being her first lieutenant. When Vice-Admiral Hyde Parker succeeded Hardy, and in June hoisted his flag in *Fortitude* (74), he took Saumarez with him as second lieutenant, where he served during the battle of the Dogger Bank on 5 August 1781. In recognition of his services he was promoted master and commander on 23 August and appointed on 7 February 1781 to *Tisiphone,* fireship. She was serving as a scout for Admiral Kempenfelt in December when Saumarez sighted a French fleet escorting a convoy of transports for the West Indies, of which more than twenty were captured. Saumarez was then sent to the West Indies to warn of the expected arrival of the remainder of the French convoy. Sir Samuel Hood made him post captain on 7 February 1782 in *Russell* (74) when he was only twenty-four years old, and he accounted very well for himself at the battle of the Saintes on 12 April 1782, cutting the French line even before Admiral Rodney. He was sent home with dispatches, but with the coming of peace there was no employment for him.

Saumarez apparently occupied himself working for the establishment of Sunday schools, and visited France to inspect the new breakwater at Cherbourg. He married on 27 October 1788, in Guernsey, uniting with Martha, only child and heiress of Thomas Le Marchant. The couple were to have four sons and four daughters.

In January 1793, shortly before the French declaration of war, he was ordered to hoist a broad pendant on board the *Crescent* (36), for which he provided half the crew from Guernsey islanders who volunteered to serve with him. He soon made a spectacular capture of a French frigate, *La*

Réunion, close to the mole at Cherbourg, and was rewarded with being made knight bachelor on 6 November 1793.

Saumarez was attached to the squadron under Rear-Admiral John MacBride in support of the expedition commanded by Lord Moira intended to assist the French royalists. On 8 June 1794 he was in command of a small squadron when he encountered a very superior French one in mid-Channel. Ordering the slower-sailing ships to make their escape, he amused the enemy by apparently sailing into their trap, only to make use of the superior local knowledge of his master, Jean le Breton, to enter St Peter Port, Guernsey, by an uncharted passage.

In March 1795 he was put in command of *Orion* (74), which formed part of the Channel fleet under Admiral Lord Bridport, although for three months from April to 8 June he took temporary command of *Marlborough* (74) for Lord Radstock. *Orion* was detached in 1797 as part of a squadron under Rear-Admiral Sir William Parker to join the Mediterranean fleet before Cadiz. Arriving prior to the battle of Cape St Vincent on 14 February, *Orion* was engaged singly with *Salvador del Mundo* (112) for over an hour and forced her to strike. But *Victory* took the credit, and when *Orion* had fought *Santisima Trinidad* (136) and brought her not only to strike, but to hoist British colours, Admiral Jervis ordered the fleet to wear before she could be secured.

Later, Jervis, the earl of St Vincent, ordered Saumarez to take command of the inshore squadron off Cadiz, and on 30 April 1798 he commanded the detachment from the Mediterranean fleet ordered to join Rear-Admiral Nelson, who had been sent to observe the armament at Toulon.

Sir James Saumarez, Bart., Rear Admiral of the Blue Squadron, engraving by William Ridley after Philip Jean, published by Burney and Gold, Shoe Lane, 1 September 1801.

He was thus second in command to Nelson during the pursuit of Vice-Admiral Bruey and at the battle of the Nile on 1 August 1798, although Nelson did not recognise the fact. Saumarez admitted to his journal that he was of too nervous a disposition to have handled the stress of the pursuit, but he did well enough in the battle. *Orion* was the third ship to anchor inshore of the enemy line, and was hotly engaged. Saumarez was injured by a large splinter but remained on deck, and when the firing died down in the van, and he learnt that Nelson was severely wounded, he sent a boat through the fleet to instruct those ships which were able to slip their cables to move towards those French ships which were still resisting in the rear of their line. After the action he was put in charge of taking the damaged captures to Gibraltar, and during the passage he took the opportunity to supply the Maltese with arms from the French ships.

Saumarez felt that Nelson had not given him enough credit in the victory dispatch, but he was nominated a colonel of the Royal Marines on 14 February 1799, and was appointed the same day to command *Caesar* (80) in the Channel fleet. When St Vincent succeeded Lord Bridport, he decided to create an advanced squadron off Brest which was to keep station by the Black Rocks throughout the winter, a station which became known in the fleet as 'Siberia'. To this difficult and dangerous post Saumarez was appointed. When he was promoted rear-admiral on 1 January 1801 he hoisted his flag in *Caesar*, and on 28 January returned to his station off the Black Rocks. During severe gales, he ran for shelter into Douarnenez Bay, where he could observe the interior of Brest harbour. Evidently he had mastered his nerves. He was rewarded by being created a baronet on 13 June 1801, and put in command of the blockade of Cadiz.

It was there that on 5 July he learnt that three French ships of the line and a frigate under the command of Admiral Linois had put into Algeciras. With six of the line, Saumarez attacked the three French ships sheltering under the guns of Algeciras, but paid the price of hubris. The wind failed, and *Hannibal* (74) grounded under fire and eventually had to surrender when the rest of the squadron, badly battered, were towed by their boats back to Gibraltar. The ships' companies set to work to repair battle damage, but the odds were considerably lengthened when a Spanish squadron of six ships under Admiral Don de Moreno broke out of Cadiz and collected the French. *Pompee* was so badly damaged that her crew was employed refitting the other ships. It was thought *Caesar* could not be put into condition for service, and Saumarez shifted his flag into *Audacious* (74), but by Herculean exertions the crew of *Caesar* were able to get out of harbour in time to recover their admiral. Saumarez was able to pursue with five ships, Captain Keats in *Superb* (74) having arrived from off Cadiz. This time Saumarez was lucky. Moreno adopted a defensive line abreast, with the three French in a second line ahead of the Spaniards. This was a weak formation which Saumarez was able to exploit by sending *Superb*, in the dark, to engage from the landward side. Two Spanish ships began to fire on each other, caught fire, and both blew up in the dark with the loss of nearly all hands. The *St Antoine* was captured, and the rest of the enemy squadron were forced back into Cadiz. For these actions Saumarez was invested a knight of the Bath on 5 September 1801, and made a freeman of the City of London. He declined the offer of command in the Mediterranean in May 1802 after the end of the war, preferring to return to Guernsey, and in 1803 he was awarded a pension of £1,200 a year.

With the renewal of the war in 1803 he hoisted his flag on 11 March in the *Vindictive* (28), which had been hulked to serve as a stationary flagship at the Nore, and then assumed command in the Channel Islands, with his flag at first in *Grampus* (50) and later in *Diomede* (50). Once the threat of invasion was passed, this became a quiet command. At St Vincent's prompting, a special promotion of flag officers was ordered by the Admiralty in order to raise Saumarez to the list of vice-admirals on 13 December 1806. In January 1807 he became second in command in the Channel fleet, hoisting his flag in *San Josef* (110) and later moving to *Prince of Wales* (98) and in August to *Hibernia* (110).

Following the treaty of Tilsit in July 1807, which transformed Russia into an ally of France, Saumarez was in May 1808 put in command of a squadron intended to operate in the Danish islands and to co-operate with Sweden, hoisting his flag in *Victory*, with Sir Samuel Hood and Sir Richard Keats as his rear-admirals. Several Spanish regiments which had been incorporated into the French army were extricated by Keats under Saumarez's command and repatriated to Spain. So tactfully did he deal with the Swedish problem that he was awarded by King Charles XIII (Bernadotte) the grand cross of the military order of the Sword. Russian ports were blockaded to force them to resume a clandestine trade with Britain, but no aggressive action was taken which would have extended the nominal hostility with Russia. He hauled down his flag on 10 November 1812.

He was promoted admiral on 4 June 1814, invested knight grand cross of the Bath on 2 January 1815, and appointed rear-admiral of the United Kingdom in July 1819, being promoted vice-admiral in December 1821. Between 24 March 1824 and 10 May 1827 he returned to active service as commander-in-chief Portsmouth, flying his flag in *Britannia* (100). He was created Baron De Saumarez of Saumarez, in the island of Guernsey, on 15 September 1831, and made the last general of the Royal Marines on 13 February 1832. He was an elder brother of the Trinity House in 1834 and vice-president of the Naval Charitable Society. Nevertheless, King William IV had a prejudice against him, and he was violently rebuked at a levee for not attending Sir Richard Keats's funeral. Perhaps Sailor Billy felt he was shown up in a poor light by Saumarez's religious convictions.

Saumarez died on 9 October 1836, aged seventy-nine, in Saumarez, Guernsey, and was buried in the churchyard of St Marie du Castel. His wife survived him until 17 April 1849, when she died aged eighty.

Lt: 25 January 1778
M-C: 23 August 1781 (2)
Capt: 7 February 1782
R-Adm: 1 January 1801
V-Adm: 13 December 1806
Adm: 4 June 1814

SCHOMBERG

CAPTAIN ISAAC SCHOMBERG had the misfortune in April 1786 to be appointed first lieutenant of *Pegasus,* which was the first command entrusted to Prince William Henry, the future William IV.

Schomberg had been born on 27 March 1753 in Great Yarmouth, the eldest surviving son of the ten children of Ralph Schomberg, physician and author, and of his wife Elizabeth, daughter of Joseph Crowcher, a London merchant. In October 1770 he entered the navy in *Royal Charlotte,* yacht, commanded by Captain Sir Peter Denis, transferring six weeks later to *Prudent* (64) commanded by his uncle Alexander Schomberg at Spithead. In June 1771 he returned to Denis, who had been promoted to rear-admiral; he served with him for most of the following three years, and then served in succession under Rear-Admiral Robert Duff and Vice-Admiral John Montagu. Following his commissioning on 21 August 1777 whilst on the Newfoundland station he commanded the schooner *Labrador* and the brig *Hinchinbrook,* returning home in November 1778 as second lieutenant of *Europe* (64). In April 1779 Schomberg transferred to the *Canada* (74) as second lieutenant, and in October he became first lieutenant on the recommendation of Captain Sir George Collier. He was present at Vice-Admiral George Darby's relief of Gibraltar in April 1781. Under the command of Captain William Cornwallis, but, still in *Canada,* he fought in the actions at St Kitts in January and near the Saintes on 12 April 1782.

An important development in his career occurred a week later when he transferred to Sir Samuel Hood's flagship, *Barfleur* (90). It was to be a mixed blessing. The posting was to be of short duration because of the end of hostilities, but Schomberg's introduction to Hood led to his being selected in April 1786 as first lieutenant of the *Pegasus* (28) under the command of the royal prince. The potential for career advancement was very great. One of Schomberg's fellow officers, Captain Henry Harvey, had been employed fitting *Pegasus* for service while the prince was still her lieutenant, and was well rewarded for his service. Schomberg and the prince, however, were not compatible personalities. The latter was only twenty when he was made post captain, had only been a lieutenant for one year, and liked hard drinking. Schomberg was thirty-three, had been a lieutenant for nine years, and was interested in books. Making matters far more difficult, the two had previously served together when the prince had been a midshipman and Schomberg already a lieutenant. The prince did not like receiving advice, especially from a more experienced man.

Eventually in January 1787 Schomberg was provoked into applying to the senior officer on the station, Captain Horatio Nelson, for a court martial on himself to clear his name. The prince then persuaded Nelson to send Schomberg and himself to Jamaica so that a court could be assembled, but the officer commanding on that station, Alan Gardner, persuaded Schomberg to withdraw his request. He was thus saved from a certain disgrace. Eventually he was sent back to England, arriving on 22 July, when he was put on half pay.

Schomberg, however, did not in fact have to pay a very heavy price, because Hood rescued him from the beach and appointed him second, and later first, lieutenant of *Barfleur* (90), his flagship as commander-in-chief Portsmouth. From there, in October 1788 Schomberg was appointed first lieutenant of the *Crown* (64), flagship of Commodore the Honourable William Cornwallis, commander-in-chief East Indies. When on 3 March 1790 *Crown's* captain was invalided home, Schomberg was made temporary flag captain with the rank of commander. On 10 July he was put in command of *Atalanta.*

Apart from his difficulty in suffering privileged fools gladly, Schomberg could himself play the fool, as he did on 13 September 1790 when he complained violently and in writing that the East India Company fort at Madras did not hoist its colours when he, an acting commander appointed to *Atalanta*, was entering the roads. That sort of thing should have been left to the senior naval officer present, Captain Strachan. When Commodore Sir William Cornwallis arrived, he felt that Schomberg had greatly exceeded himself, and ordered him to return to England for trial, although he also wrote the Admiralty suggesting the matter be dropped.

On 22 November 1790, before Cornwallis's report reached London, he had been promoted captain. However, he was not offered employment on the outbreak of war with France in February 1793. Nevertheless, on 13 August 1793, at Pangbourne, Berkshire, Schomberg married Amelia, daughter of the Revd Lawrence Brodrick of Stradbally, Queen's county. The couple had several children, of whom four sons survived infancy.

At the end of the year he commanded *Vanguard* (74) for a month, and in April 1794 he took command of the *Culloden* (74), which at the battle of 1 June 1794 was on hand to accept the surrender of *Vengeur*. Her captain and 127 men were saved by *Culloden*'s boats before *Vengeur* sank. However, the honour of her defeat really went to *Ramillies* (74) and *Brunswick,* which had beaten her soundly before *Culloden* came up. Between November 1794 and November 1795 Schomberg commanded *Magnanime* (44), employed in convoys out of Cork, and then he retired from active service at sea.

Apart from his writing, he occupied the following years commanding units of sea fencibles, in 1801 commanding between Southend and Harwich, and in 1802 he published, in five volumes, *Naval Chronology, or, An Historical Summary of Naval and Maritime Events from the Time of the Romans to the treaty of peace, 1802.* In the long run Schomberg's later career as a naval historian was of greater interest than his service at sea. After the renewal of war in 1803 until the regiment was disbanded in 1808 he commanded the Hastings district of the sea fencibles, and appar-

ently it was at his suggestion that they were disbanded, the threat of invasion being a thing of the past. In reward, he was appointed in December 1808 to the Navy Board.

He died at the age of fifty-nine at Cadogan Place, Chelsea, on 21 January 1813, and was buried in the family vault in St George-in-the-East, Stepney, London, on 28 January.

Lt: 21 August 1777
Cmdr: 3 March 1790
Capt: 22 November 1790

SEYMOUR (CONWAY)

VICE-ADMIRAL LORD HUGH SEYMOUR CONWAY is best known for his intemperate life, and for his share of the misfortunes of war. He was very well born, but his friends, apparently, were of his own making.

He was born on 29 April 1759, the fifth son of Francis Seymour Conway, first marquis of Hertford, and of his wife, Isabella, the youngest daughter of Charles Fitzroy, second duke of Grafton. Educated at Bracken's academy at Greenwich, the Navy Office credited him with first going to sea in 1770 as a captain's servant in the *William and Mary* (yacht). He was rated a midshipman when a year later he joined *Pearle* (32) on 21 April 1771 under the command of the Honourable Levison Gower, who was a relative. He remained in that rate while serving in *Portland* (50), *Princess Amelia* (80), *Royal Charlotte* (armed transport), *Alarm* (cutter), and *Trident* (64), finally being rated an able seaman in *Alarm* in which he served for over two years before passing his examination on 4 July 1776. [ADM 107.6.356] He was commissioned lieutenant on 10 August 1776 while serving in *Alarm* commanded by Captain John Stott. *Alarm* was employed in the Mediterranean, and there on 18 June 1778 he was promoted commander of *Minorca* xebec. The step to post captain followed on 8 February 1779, with appointment to command the 18-pounder frigate *Latona* (38) in the Channel fleet. He was still commanding her when he took part in Lord Howe's relief of Gibraltar in 1782.

He was unemployed during the years of peace,

and fell into low company, leading a life of dissipation as an intimate of the prince of Wales. This chaos came to an end when on 3 April 1786 he married Anne Horatia, daughter of James Waldegrave, second Earl Waldegrave. The couple had six sons and two daughters. Seymour Conway entered into a political career, holding in succession the parliamentary seats for Newport, Isle of Wight, from 1784 to March 1786, for Tregony, Cornwall, from 16 June 1788 to 1790, for Wendover, Buckinghamshire, from 1790 to 1796, and for Portsmouth from 1796 to 11 September 1801. He also held the court appointment of master of the robes and keeper of the privy purse to the prince of Wales from May 1787 to March 1795, after which, for four months, he occupied the appointment of lord of the bedchamber to the prince of Wales.

At the time of the Nootka Sound crisis in 1790 Seymour Conway was appointed to command *Canada* (74), and on a trial passage he was struck violently on the head by a sounding lead. Before the concussion had been properly healed, his condition was greatly worsened by the firing of some saluting guns, and he had to go ashore and remain in almost complete isolation for the following year. In February 1793, on the French declaration of war, he was sufficiently recovered to be able to take command of *Leviathan* (74), which formed part of the Mediterranean fleet under Lord Hood. He was sent home with dispatches after the occupation of Toulon, and then brought *Leviathan* home to join the Channel fleet prior to the battles of the Glorious First of June in 1794, following which he was promoted colonel of the marines on 4 July 1794. He dropped the surname of Conway ten days later, and was promoted rear-admiral on 1 June 1795, hoisting his flag on one of the prizes, *Sans Pareil* (80), in the Channel fleet under Lord Bridport's effective command. She was one of the ships in collision when in December 1796 Bridport attempted to sail from Spithead to intercept the Brest fleet, which had sailed to support the invasion of Ireland. Seymour was a commissioner of the Admiralty from March 1795 to September 1798, but spent most of his time at sea.

He was promoted vice-admiral on 14 February 1799, and arrived in the West Indies as commander-in-chief of the Jamaica station in August, when he took possession of the Dutch settlement of Surinam. But his service at Jamaica was not to be long, for he died of the yellow fever on 11 September 1801, aged forty-two. His body was sent back to England, where his wife had predeceased him on 12 January. One of his officers wrote:

If it be a satisfaction to surviving friends, to know that the latest hours of one they loved, was attended by the most tenderly solicitous friends, that is now a consolation most justly to be felt; as the group which surrounded the dying Hero, and performed the last offices to his person, was formed of friends who loved, and dependents who revered him, and who will ever lament his loss, and respect his memory. NC 6.463

Lt: 10 August 1776
M-C: 18 June 1778
Capt: 8 February 1779
R-Adm: 1 June 1795
V-Adm: 14 February 1799

SEYMOUR

REAR-ADMIRAL SIR MICHAEL SEYMOUR, BARONET, KCB, is best known for a notable night action he fought when in command of *Amethyst* (36) against the French frigate *La Thétis* (44) on 10 November 1808 close to the island of Groais [Groix].

He was born on 8 November 1768 at Glebe House, Palace, county Limerick, the second son of the Revd John Seymour, rector of Palace and of Abington and chancellor of Emly. His mother was Griselda, second and youngest daughter and co-heiress of William Hobart of High Mount, county Cork. He was educated at the University of Dublin and entered the navy on 15 November 1780 as a captain's servant in *Merlin*, sloop, under the command of the Honourable Captain James Luttrell, with whom he moved to *Portland* (50), *Mediator* (44) and *Ganges* (74). When Luttrell retired, Seymour served in the West Indies with Vice-Admiral James Gambier in *Europa* (50), with Captain Robert Causzar in *Antelope* (50) and with Captain John Pakenham in *Janus* (44), returning to England in poor health in September and October 1785. His rating had progressed to able seaman and midshipman, back to able seaman, then to master's mate and finally back to able seaman. He then served as a midshipman under Captain Samuel Marshall in *Pegasus* (28), which was fitted as guardship at Portsmouth, and as master's mate in June 1787 in *Magnificent* (74) commanded by Captain George Cranfield Berkeley, an old friend of Luttrell.

He passed his examination in 1787 but was not commissioned lieutenant in *Magnificent* until 28 October 1790, at the time of the Nootka Sound mobilisation. When *Magnificent* was paid off in October 1791 he spent a year and a half at his family home before he was appointed to *Marlborough* (74) under Berkeley's command on 27 March 1793 following the French declaration of war. He served as junior lieutenant at the battle of the Glorious First of June in 1794, when he was so severely wounded in his arm that it had to be amputated. In compensation he was awarded a truly pitiful pension of only 5s., but in February 1795 he was able to rejoin Berkeley, who was then in command of *Formidable* serving in the Channel. He joined the French prize *Commerce de Marseilles* (120) commanded by Captain the Honourable George Grey at Spithead on 12 June 1795, and transferred to *Prince* (90) under Captain Charles Powell Hamilton on 2 August. He was appointed acting commander of *Fly* (8) in June 1796 and was moved on 9 August into *Spitfire,* sloop, which he was to command for four years. Lord Spencer confirmed his promotion to commander on 20 August 1795, and at the end of his commission on *Spitfire* on 11 August 1800, Spencer again promoted him, to post captain. He was not appointed to a ship before the peace of Amiens.

During his period in command of *Spitfire* he married, on 20 January 1798, Jane, third daughter of Captain James Hawker, RN, and sister of Admiral Edward Hawker. Jane gave birth to six sons and seven daughters, of whom the third son was Admiral Sir Michael Seymour. Two of her grandsons were Vice-Admiral Sir Edward Hobard Seymour and Admiral Sir Michael Culme-Seymour.

With the renewal of the war, Seymour was employed as acting captain in a succession of six ships, until at last in 1806 Lord Barham appointed him to command *Amethyst* (36) armed with 32-pounders. His action with *La Thétis* over two years

Captain Michael Seymour, R.N.,
engraved by H R Cook after James Northcote, RS,
published by Joyce Gold,
103 Shoe Lane, Fleet Street,
28 February 1809.

later made his reputation. *La Thétis* was a very serious opponent, having on board 360 seamen and 106 soldiers who had served together for years under Captain Pinsun, a respected officer.

About seven the flash and report of cannon were distinctly seen and heard from a battery on the French coast, in a direction contiguous to the alarm and signal post. The conjecture of the moment supposed it in consequence of the near approach of the *Amethyst*; but it was in reality directed against their own frigate, of the sailing of which they were ignorant. About half-past seven a sail was descried just ahead: it was supposed a small armed vessel, or something still more contemptible, and the deception of night favoured the supposition. A musket was ordered to be fired: no notice was taken: she grew larger. The *Amethyst* still continued under an easy press of sail. A gun was now fired, and the crackling noise of this shot was heard as it passed through the cabin windows. This by the enemy was instantly returned, and the veil of darkness which had hitherto obscured her was now removed, by the lights flying in every part of her; every inch of canvass was set; her boat cut from her stern, and a ship of war appeared anxious for escape, though capable of resistance. The *Amethyst* immediately spread more canvass, but allowed her to gain a little, lest her apprehensions might induce her to run on that shore which was then so near them. About nine, however, those apprehensions were at an end, and the *Amethyst* closed fast. Her adversary, now finding all hopes of escape at an end, made her best dispositions to receive the *Amethyst*, and before ten o'clock the action commenced, which continued, with very little intermission, until about twenty minutes after twelve. The French ship fell on board the *Amethyst* a little after ten. She extricated herself from that situation; but, at a quarter past eleven, she intentionally laid the *Amethyst* on board; and from that time, until the moment of her surrender, which was about an hour, the contending ships were locked together, the fluke of the *Amethyst*'s best bower anchor having entered the foremost main-deck port of *la Thétis*. After great slaughter, *la Thétis* was boarded and taken possession of, and some prisoners were received from her, before the ships were disengaged. [NC 21.94]

Two hundred and thirty-six French had been killed or wounded before they surrendered.

In acknowledgment of his capture, Seymour was awarded a gold medal, the Patriotic Fund awarded him £100 and a piece of plate, and the city of Limerick made him a freeman.

He returned to sea in *Amethyst* on 8 February 1809, and fought and won another hard action in company with *Emerald* early on 6 April, off the Île d'Ouessant. At the end of the engagement the French frigate *Niémen* (38), which was armed with long 18-pounders and 32-pounder carronades, had lost 120 men killed and wounded. In recognition, Seymour was created a baronet on 31 May 1809 and in October he was appointed to command the *Niémen*, to which the officers and crew of the *Amethyst* turned over.

On 10 May 1812 he was appointed to *Hannibal* (74), which he commanded in the Channel for two years, capturing the French frigate *Sultane* on 26 March 1814. When *Hannibal* was paid off on 6 September, Seymouth moved ashore near Kingsbridge in Devon. On 3 January 1815 he was nominated a KCB, in December of that year his pension was increased to £300 a year, and he was nominated knight bachelor on 20 April 1816. He then accepted a series of inactive appointments: from September 1818 commanding *Northumberland* (74), which had been fitted as a guardship at Sheerness; in August 1819 moving to one of the royal yachts, *Prince Regent*; in 1825 moving to the *Royal George*, which was the king's own yacht; and in January 1829 being appointed commissioner at Portsmouth. All of these appointments he held while living for the most part on shore at Blendworth House, which he had bought, close to Portsmouth. Apparently his duties left a great deal of time for reading and gardening.

He returned to a more active life when the Navy Board was abolished, eliminating the position of resident commissioner. He was promoted to rear-admiral on 27 June 1832, and in February 1833 hoisted his flag as commander-in-chief South America in the prize taken thirty-five years previously at the battle of the Nile, *Spartiate* reduced to a 76-gun ship. It is believed he accepted this appointment largely to promote the career of his son

Michael. His command was based on Rio de Janiero, where he died at the age of sixty-five on 9 July 1834. He was buried in the English cemetery at Rio de Janeiro, and a monument to his memory was erected there.

Lt: 28 October 1790
Cmdr: 20 August 1795
Capt: 11 August 1800
R-Adm: 7 June 1832

SHORTLAND

CAPTAIN JOHN SHORTLAND took an active part in the founding of New South Wales, and died fighting against impossible odds in a frigate action.

He was born on 5 September 1769, the first son of Commander John Shortland, RN, and first went to sea in 1781 with his father, who was travelling to Quebec as agent for transports. He joined the navy on 2 August 1783 as an able seaman on board the *Vulture*, and then served in *Latona*, Captain Boston, in the West Indies, and was rated midshipman or master's mate on 18 February 1785. When he returned to England in 1787 the first fleet to Australia was fitting out, with his father as agent for transports, and young Shortland was taken on board the 18-pounder frigate *Sirius* (36) commanded by Captain John Hunter, with Commodore Phillip flying his broad pendant. They sailed on 13 May and reached Botany Bay in January 1788. *Sirius* then carried some of the settlers to Norfolk Island, because there were not enough provisions at Port Jackson, but after landing the people, the ship was driven onto a reef in a storm and totally destroyed. Shortland was there for the next eleven months, and did not get back to England, by way of Batavia, until April 1792.

He was commissioned lieutenant on 10 October 1793, and appointed to *Arrogant* (74), Captain James Hawkins Whitshed, but when at the beginning of 1795 Captain Hunter was appointed to the government of New South Wales, he asked for Shortland as his first lieutenant in *Reliance*. This he later regarded as a poor career decision as it took him away from the sea of glory for five years, although it took him to the Cape, Tahiti and New Zealand.

On his return to England he was promoted commander on 1 January 1801, and appointed as agent of the Transport Board on *Pandour*, a 44-gun 'flute' frigate employed carrying troops to Egypt. He was then appointed to command another troop ship, *Dolphin*, and later *Trompeuse*, sloop (14), under orders for Guinea, where he was made post captain in *Squirrel* (24) because of the death of her captain. The promotion was confirmed on 6 August 1805.

The late Captain Shortland, R.N.,
engraved by H R Cook after George Field,
published by Joyce Gold,
103 Shoe Lane, Fleet Street,
31 July 1810.

Whilst in command of the *Junon* (38), he was badly wounded on 13 December 1809 when she was captured by *La Renommée* and *La Clorinde* off Guadeloupe, West Indies. He had been drawn into action with four French frigates by their use of Spanish colours and knowledge of the private fleet signal. Both his legs and his left arm were wounded and he had a wound in his side. He was taken thirteen miles in a canoe to the hospital at Guadeloupe, where his right leg had to be amputated. He died of exhaustion on 1 January 1810, aged forty, at the hospital of Guadeloupe, and was buried at Basseterre with military honours.

The *Naval Chronicle* published an account the following year of Shortland's dog, which he had brought up from a puppy, and named Pandour, after his ship. He evidently accompanied his master in the canoe to the Guadeloupe hospital and remained with him until his death, but after he was repatriated to England, he was stolen. He turned up with a sailor at Halifax, where he was recognised. Admiral Borlase Warren was called in to adjudicate and, after watching the dog carry out the tricks Shortland had taught him, arranged for his return to England and his old family.

Lt: 10 October 1793
Cmdr: 1 January 1801
Capt: 6 August 1805

SMITH

ADMIRAL SIR WILLIAM SIDNEY SMITH, GCB, was described in the *Naval Chronicle*: 'The genius of this gentleman appears, from his earliest entrance into the service, to have been particularly adapted to the most arduous and desperate enterprises.' ᴺᶜ ⁴·⁴³⁵ Smith was certainly an officer of very great courage and resource, but those who had to work with him found him a loose cannon, and foolish. 'Of all the men whom I ever knew who have any reputation,' wrote the duke of Wellington, 'the man who least deserves it is Sir Sidney Smith.' Croker 1.348–9

He was born on 21 June 1764 in Park Lane, London, son of Captain John Smyth of Midgham, Hertfordshire, gentleman usher to Queen Charlotte and aide-de-camp to Lord George Sackville Germain. His mother was Mary, daughter of Pinkney Wilkinson, merchant, and sister-in-law of Lord Camelford. According to the *Naval Chronicle*, he entered the navy in June 1777, but the Admiralty later calculated that it must have been in 1775. ᴬᴰᴹ ⁹/² ᶠ ⁴¹ After serving in several ships on the American station he was commissioned lieutenant on 25 September 1780 and appointed on 22 May 1781 to *Alcide* (74), under orders for the West Indies. In her he fought at the battles of the Chesapeake, St Kitts and Dominica. He was promoted master on 6 May 1782, being appointed to

command *Fury* (18) at Jamaica, and then made post captain on 7 May 1783 in *Alcmene* (32) at the age of eighteen. Soon after, with the end of the war, he was ordered home and *Alcmene* broken up, upon which Smith was unemployed for five years. He travelled to France, and learnt the language to perfection. He also toured the coastline extensively. In 1787 he similarly toured the coast of Morocco.

In 1788 he paid a visit to Sweden, and with war looming between Sweden and Russia he requested permission to accept a command in the Swedish fleet. He received no answer to his request, but served nonetheless as a volunteer, for which he was awarded the insignia as knight grand cross of the Swedish order of the Sword on 16 May 1792. It was more usual for Britons to serve in the Russian fleet, so Smith's decision was unpopular in the navy, and he came to be known as 'the Swedish Knight'.

Still unemployed in England, he paid a visit to his brother John Spencer Smith, who was to become in 1795 secretary in charge of affairs at the British embassy in Constantinople. He may have intended to volunteer for service in the Turkish navy, but learning of the recall of British seamen on the French declaration of war on 1 February 1793, he made his way to Toulon just at the time when it was being evacuated by Lord Hood, and volunteered his services for the destruction of the French arsenal and the ships in the harbour. He destroyed ten ships of the line and the works ashore, but the operation was not a complete success. Eighteen ships were left in a condition in which they could be salved by the returning French navy. Possibly that was because Smith was not in the Mediterranean fleet, and the responsibility he was given was resented. Certainly, Hood should have made more effective arrangements.

Finally, on 3 April 1794, Smith was given command of a ship, *Diamond* (38). One of his assignments was to transport Lord Spencer to Flushing, and he took the opportunity to request command of a flotilla of small craft. This he was accorded after Spencer was sworn in as first lord of the Admiralty in December. Smith was able to put to good use his knowledge of the French coast and language to conduct partisan operations. On 18 April 1796, while cutting out a French privateer at Le Havre, he was captured and taken a prisoner to Paris. Exchange was refused, and he was kept two years in the Temple prison, on the excuse that his burning of the ships at Toulon while not carrying a commission to one of the ships in the Mediterranean fleet was an act of piracy, and that he had been involved in espionage inside France. What followed was a daring escape, using forged documents and royalist friends dressed as policemen to effect his release from the Temple.

On 8 May 1798 he was taken by Lord Spencer to be presented to King George, and then on 2 July he was put in command of *Tigre* (80). He was under orders to join St Vincent at Cadiz, but he also was given a commission from the Foreign Office appointing him and his brother joint plenipotentiaries to the Porte. There was confusion about whether he had an independent command or, as was eventually decided, he came under Nelson's authority. His apparent usurpation was very much resented by Nelson, but he later came to appreciate Smith's better qualities.

At Constantinople, Smith was made a member of the sultan's dewan, and given command of Turkish naval and military forces being assembled at Rhodes in response to the French invasion of Egypt. On 3 March 1799 he also took command of the two ships blockading Alexandria, and learnt that same evening that the French army of Egypt had captured Jaffra, where they were to be guilty of murdering their captives. Smith concentrated his forces at Acre, and landed 800 seamen and marines to stiffen the defence of the city. General Napoleon Buonaparte launched twelve assaults, the last of which nearly penetrated the defences.

Sir William Sidney Smith, K.S. of Sweden, drawn and engraved by William Ridley, published by Burney and Gold, Shoe Lane, 1 January 1801.

When the French were in the breach, and Turkish reinforcements were delayed by calms, Smith landed at the head of a party of seamen and drove back the assault.

He was showered with honours and awards, including a pension of £1,000, and as had happened to Nelson after the Nile, they all went to his head. As a nominal Turkish commander he took part in the two attempts by the Turkish forces at Rhodes to effect a landing in Egypt. When these failed, he negotiated a truce with the French, and on 24 January 1800 initialled the treaty of El Arish, by which he agreed to transport the French army of Egypt home to France. This Admiral Keith refused to countersign without instructions from London, and many more lives were to be lost in the reconquest of Egypt in 1801, in which Smith played a part. In recognition of his important role in the eventual defeat of the French, however, he was entrusted with Keith's dispatches.

On his return, he resigned his command on 6 September, and was elected member of parliament for Rochester, which seat he held until 1806. He attacked in the house the efforts of Addington's first lord, the earl of St Vincent, to reform the naval administration, and to reduce expenditure by the rapid reduction of the fleet following the peace of Amiens.

With the recommencement of war, he was given employment under Lord Keith in the Channel defences, perhaps in order to get him away from Westminster, taking command of a new fourth rate, *Antelope* (50), on 12 March 1803. He was made colonel of the Royal Marines on 23 April 1804, and ordered to assume the duties of a commodore commanding light craft operating on the Flemish coast. But he was more interested in experimentation with unconventional warfare, building catamarans modelled on those of the Polynesians, which were used to tow Robert Fulton's pyrotechnics to attack the invasion forces at and around Boulogne. He bankrupted himself in the process, and was for a while in 1805 in the King's Bench prison for debt.

Lord Barham, who had replaced Viscount Melville as first lord, concluded that Smith was better kept in a subordinate position. He was promoted rear-admiral on 9 November 1805, and in January 1806 hoisted his flag in one of the prizes taken out of Toulon in 1793, *Pompée* (80), to serve under Lord Collingwood. He was sent on detached service to the coast of Naples, where his vanity made co-operation with General Sir John Moore extraordinarily difficult. However, his energy and ability transformed the campaign, leading to the victory at Maida.

In August he was ordered to put himself under the command of Vice-Admiral Sir John Duckworth, and it was in a subordinate role that he took part in the contested, and futile, passage of the Dardanelles to Constantinople in February and March 1807. There were many voices that questioned why he, with his great experience of relations with the Porte, had not been made to command the expedition, when he might have been able to reassure the Turks that Britain was their friend.

In the summer he returned to England, and then in November he was sent to the Tagus with his flag in *Hibernia* (110). There he had to deal with the invasion of Portugal by General Junot, and took the chief part in persuading the Portuguese court to accept British protection, and to go into exile in Brazil. In February 1808 he was himself sent out to Rio de Janeiro to take command of the South American station, but a quarrel with the British minister, Lord Strangford, led to his recall in 1809. He was invested by His Most Faithful Majesty as a knight of the military order of the Tower and Sword.

He married on 11 October 1809 Caroline, widow of Sir George Rumbold, baronet, consul-general in Hamburg.

He was promoted vice-admiral on 31 July 1810, and was sent out as second in command in the Mediterranean, but his health gave way, and he retired from active service. In 1815 he was in Paris when Napoleon returned from exile in Elba. Riding to Brussels, he accompanied General Wellington to the field of Waterloo. He was not permitted 'any of the fun' but was the first Englishman out of uniform to congratulate the victor.

He was invested a KCB on 2 January 1815, and a knight of the Spanish royal and military order of San Fernando, was promoted admiral on 19 August 1821 and lieutenant-general of the Royal Marines on 28 June 1830, and was advanced in chivalry to GCB on 20 July 1838. He was a fellow of the Royal Society. His wife had died in May 1826, in Paris. He died on 26 May 1840, aged seventy-five, at 6 rue d'Anjou, and was buried in Père-Lachaise Cemetery.

Lt: 25 September 1780
M-C: 6 May 1782
Capt: 7 May 1783
R-Adm: 9 November 1805
V-Adm: 31 July 1810
Adm: 19 August 1821

STANHOPE

ADMIRAL THE HONOURABLE SIR HENRY EDWYN STANHOPE, BARONET, was a most unusual officer, being as committed a scholar as he was a warrior.

He was born on 21 May 1754, the only son of the Honourable Edwyn Francis Stanhope, cousin of the fifth earl of Chesterfield, and his wife Catherine, daughter and coheiress of John Bridges, marquis of Carnarvon, and widow of William Berkeley Lyon. He studied with the Revd Dr Wharton at Winchester College, and was admitted to Oxford University, but was soon persuaded that he was more fitted for the navy. He joined *Rose* (20), Captain Caldwell, in May 1768 and sailed to the American station. He served for a while in *Romney* (50) under Commodore Hood, and then returned to the *Rose*, and when she paid off he prepared to return to Oxford. He also studied for a while at Mr Charles Bettesworth's naval academy at Portsea. He took his degree, and in

March 1775 he sailed for Boston in the brig-sloop *Otter* (14), Captain Squires, and took a part in the battle of Bunker Hill. His service during the American war was active until he was captured in Newport and imprisoned. He twice escaped, and eventually made his way to Halifax, reaching Plymouth in March 1777. He was commissioned lieutenant in *Nonsuch* (64) on 10 March, and sailing for New York, he continued in active service against the Americans. He was one of those who had to set fire to his ship at Newport to prevent its being captured when the French fleet under the

The Honourable Henry Edwyn Stanhope,
Vice Admiral of the Blue Squadron,
engraved by William Ridley from a miniature
painting, published by
Joyce Gold, 103 Shoe Lane,
28 February 1806.

———

Comte d'Estaing arrived. After taking part in the desperate defence of the fort, he was able to escape by rowing a whale boat through the middle of the French fleet, eventually arriving at New York.

In April 1779 he was appointed first lieutenant of *Portland* and sent to Newfoundland. He was promoted master and commander on 6 August 1779, but fell out with his admiral, and requested

a court martial, at which he was vindicated. He returned to England in 1780. Admiral Rodney made him post captain in *Terrible* (74) on 16 June 1781. He commanded *Russell* (74) at the action off St Kitts, and then was sent home with dispatches in such a poor state of health that it was questionable whether he would live. But he recovered and carried the text of the definitive peace treaty to New York. He married on 14 August 1783 Margaret, daughter of Francis Malbone of Newport, Rhode Island. She gave birth to one son, Captain Sir Edwyn Francis Scudamore Stanhope, and four daughters.

During the peace he retired to his scholarship, but in September 1794 he returned to active service, being appointed to *Ruby* (64). His service in this war was to be much less active, owing to failing health. He was entrusted in October 1795 with bearing home the dispatch telling of the capture of the Cape of Good Hope, but was received coolly because of reports of an injury committed to a junior lieutenant, of which in fact he had been cleared by a court martial. He was restored to favour in court, and appointed in March 1796 to command *Neptune* (98), on board which the court martials of Richard Parker and the other Nore mutineers were to be assembled. The proceedings took two months, after which he sailed to the Nore and handed over command to Captain Erasmus Gower. In early 1799 he was forced to retire from sea service, although he commanded the sea fencibles in Cornwall and Devon for a while.

He was promoted rear-admiral on 1 January 1801, vice-admiral on 9 November 1805 and admiral on 12 August 1812, was created a baronet on 13 November 1807, and devoted his time to the study of Hebrew and translating the Old Testament. He died on 20 December 1814, aged sixty, in Clifton, Gloucestershire.

Lt: 10 March 1777
M-C: 6 August 1779
Capt: 16 June 1781
R-Adm: 1 January 1801
V-Adm: 9 November 1805
Adm: 12 August 1812

STEWART

CAPTAIN JOHN STEWART had a remarkable career as navigator and warrior. His service in the coastal defence of England against invasion virtually invented a new category of naval staff officer, and his single-handed operations in the Aegean may be considered the beginning of British support for Greek independence.

He was born on 21 December 1774, the second son of William Stewart of Castle Stewart, Galloway, Dumfriesshire, and of his wife, the sixth daughter of Lord Fortrose. In 1788 he was sent to the naval academy at New Cross, Deptford, and on 9 May the following year he joined the navy as a midshipman in *Rose,* frigate, commanded by Captain Jacob (?) Waller.

After making two voyages to Newfoundland, he joined the *Discovery* (8), Captain George Vancouver, on 16 January 1791 on a voyage of exploration to the north-west coast of North America. He accompanied Vancouver on his boat voyages amongst the archipelagos. Talking later to his friends of one confrontation with the aboriginal inhabitants, he said:

> My station was in the stern sheets, where providentially lay a pair of large horse pistols. I took one of them, and a midshipman, who stood by me, took the other. We had scarcely done this, when two tall, strong, horrid looking savages, rushed into the water, within a few feet of us, dressed in their war dress of buffalo hide; each armed with a long spear, and their faces painted with all sorts of colours. The savage who was opposed to me, threw himself back a little, elevated his spear, and seemed in the very act of hurling it through my body; when suddenly his eye caught mine, and he observed that the muzzle of my pistol was directed to his breast. He instantly was horror struck, and remained fixed in his terrific attitude. Aware of the efficacy of fire arms, he dreaded instant death, if he made his intended throw at me... [NC 28.2]

One of his friends on this voyage was the notorious Thomas Pitt, Lord Camelford, who was discharged by Vancouver at Hawaii.

When *Discovery* reached St Helens on 3 November 1795 Vancouver recommended Stewart to Vice-Admiral Elphinstone, later Lord Keith. He was immediately examined, and on the 6th was commissioned second lieutenant of *Arab* (16), but she was wrecked on the coast of France, and Stewart, rescued from drowning but having lost all his money, could not pay for provisions on parole and had to go to prison with his men. After being exchanged, he served with Lord Keith on board *Queen Charlotte* (100) in 1797, but was ashore in Leghorn when she caught fire on 17 March 1800.

> Lieutenant Stewart's ardour in the cause of humanity was only equalled by his judgment in affording us relief, when he had reached the *Queen Charlotte*; which lay at the distance of twelve miles from the shore. He judiciously dropped his Tartan under the bows, where almost all the remaining crew had taken refuge. Little more than an hour had elapsed, after this assistance had been given, before the ship blew up. All that had been left unburnt, immediately sunk down by the stern; but when the ponderous contents of the hold had been washed away by the waves, she, for an instant, recovered her buoyant property; and was suddenly seen to emerge almost her whole length from the deep; and then immediately turning over, she floated on the surface, with her burnished copper glistening in the sun. Amidst the various wonders of the deep, which are beheld by those who go down to the sea in ships; this certainly formed a most sublime and awful event. [NC 28.7]

Stewart was left in Leghorn to intercept supplies being freighted for the French army until 29 April 1800, when he was put in command of *Mondovi,* sloop (14), in which he continued to enforce an embargo of grain shipments from the ports of

Tuscany. On 25 December he was promoted to commander, but was left in *Mondovi*. He sailed with Lord Keith to Marmorice Bay, where training was conducted for the landing of General Abercromby and the British army at Aboukir for the reconquest of Egypt. Stewart's particular job was to liaise with Turkish authorities at Rhodes, who were supposedly supplying small craft. He played a central role in the actual landing of the army, and went ashore on 13 March 1801, slept in the British camp, and witnessed the French counter-attack on the 14th, during which Abercromby was killed.

The late Captain John Stewart, R.N.,
engraved by R? Page from a drawing in the
possession of William Adam, Esq. published by
Joyce Gold, 103 Shoe Lane, Fleet Street,
31 May 1812.

On 10 April 1801 he was promoted to command the *Africaine* (38), being confirmed in post rank on 6 August 1801. He continued to be employed in support of the army in Egypt, taking command of a troop ship, the *Haarlem*, to transport General Fox from Minorca. Only with the signing of the peace of Amiens did he return to England. In 1802 he was awarded the Turkish gold medal for distin-

guished services on the coast of Egypt.

On the resumption of war in May 1803 Lord Keith was appointed to command in the North Sea and in the Channel as far as Southsea Bill. This complicated responsibility could be undertaken only from a convenient station on shore, and Stewart was appointed to command the 12-pounder frigate *Ceres* being used as a hospital ship, specifically so that he would be available to Keith as a staff officer. For this purpose he was given a general leave of absence from his ship, and resided in the Isle of Thanet. From there he travelled, establishing signal stations, conducting reconnaissance of the enemy coast and ordering raids, which were not always of great value. Of that on Boulogne at the beginning of October 1804 he wrote:

> Lord Melville made his appearance in the night, in a frigate, and saw the whole. To be sure, nothing could be grander as a sight – the whole enemy's coast a line of fire, with every now and then a great explosion. On our part not a single shot fired. All was still. I know Lord Melville was much disappointed, as he and others expected great things from it. [NC 28.18]

When Stewart's health could no longer take the strain, he spent some time with relations, and then in early 1806 was commissioned to command the 18-pounder frigate *Seahorse* (38) serving off Cadiz. In 1807 he was sent to the Greek archipelago to look after British interests following the peace between France and Russia and Duckworth's futile raid on Constantinople. The Turks were vulnerable to both their former enemies, but also determined to enforce their suzerainty over the Greeks. Stewart's work suppressing privateers amongst the Greek islands had political implications. He wrote in 1808:

> In working to the N. amongst the islands, I found the consternation of the Greeks general: from each place I received accounts of the Turkish ships being out, and most of the accounts exaggerated. As I

knew that whatever the Turkish force was, it would be certainly much superior to my ship, I devised in my head most of the cases likely to arise; and determined, if the disparity of force was not excessive, to attack them, and if they were under sail, to do so in the night. I felt my situation critical. I was alone; and could not get assistance for some time. If I were driven out of the Archipelago, the whole of the islands would be instantly over run by the Turks, and our character and influence suffer in consequence. NC 28.34

In early July he caught up with the Turkish squadron of two frigates and a gunboat, with which he toyed until dark, then closed, sank the smaller frigate and captured the larger. He sent the Turkish seamen to Constantinople, and wrote the Captain Pacha 'telling him that he must have fore-seen what would happen, after all that had passed, and Lord Collingwood's answer, if he sent out ships. I recommended his not sending any more, as it would only irritate the two nations against each other, who I was sure both wanted peace.' NC 28.35 He carried the British commissioner the Right Honourable Sir Robert Adair to the Dardanelles, and peace was signed.

His last services were in the western Mediterranean, and in June 1811 *Seahorse* was paid off at Woolwich, as worn as was her commander. He died on 26 October 1811, aged thirty-six, at the house of George Hathorn in Brunswick Square, Shoreditch, London.

Lt: 6 November 1795
Cmdr: 25 December 1800
Capt: 6 August 1801

STIRLING

VICE-ADMIRAL CHARLES STIRLING was a hard-fighting and honest sailor, who took a prominent part in the battle of Algeciras, in Sir Robert Calder's action, and in the combined operations against Montevideo, but came unstuck when he offend-ed the commercial interests of Jamaica.

He was born on 28 April 1760, the second son of Captain Sir Walter Stirling, RN, of Faskine, Lanarkshire, and of his wife Dorothy, daughter of Charles Willing of Philadelphia. His name was placed on the books of his father's ship *Rainbow* (44) in September 1763, as captain's servant, when he was only three. His father transferred his name to each ship to which he himself moved (*Seaford*) and it is possible that he served in *Portland*, which he would have joined in August 1771. Probably, however, he did not himself go to sea until he was rated midshipman in *Southampton* (32) in 1773 by Captain George Vandeput, with whom he would have served in the Channel. In September he sailed with Sir Edward Hughes in *Salisbury* (50) to the East Indies, and he continued there until April 1778, when he transferred into *Formidable* (90) in the Channel fleet. He was commissioned lieutenant on 12 June 1778, moving in quick suc-cession to *Defence* (74), the former French *Pallas*, renamed *Convert* (32), and *Robust* (74), where he remained from March 1779 to May 1780 under the command of Captain T Cosby on the North American station. He served at the capture of Charlestown, and Vice-Admiral Arbuthnot pro-moted him on 15 May master and commander of *Avenger* (14). In the next two years he com-manded *Vulture* (14), *Savage* (14) and *Termagant* (22), all in North America. Rear-Admiral Thomas Graves would have promoted him post captain after a spirited action against an American frigate, which ended in the loss of his ship, but saved sev-eral merchant ships trying to cross the bar into Charlestown. So difficult had become the situation of the navy in New York by then, however, that he had to wait until 15 January 1783, before the first lord, Admiral Keppel, promoted him on the rec-ommendation of Lord Howe, and appointed him to command *Dictator* (64) on the river Thames.

By then it was peacetime, and he retained his command only until April, and spent the follow-ing seven years ashore. He married in 1789 Charlotte, second daughter of Andrew Grote of Blackheath, Kent, who was a London banker. The couple had four sons and one daughter.

At the time of the Nootka Sound crisis, in March 1790, he was appointed to command the 9-

pounder frigate *Lapwing* (24) in the Channel fleet under the command of Lord Howe, but was employed for only three months. Some time after the French declaration of war in February 1793 he was appointed to command *Venus* (36) cruising in the North Sea under Vice-Admiral John Dalrymple, transferring on 25 December 1795 to the two-year-old 18-pounder frigate *Jason* (38), which was employed under the orders of Sir John Warren and Sir Edward Pellew in the western squadron based on Falmouth, and at Quiberon in support of the French royalists. After a very active service he was wrecked on 13 October 1798 in Douarnenez Bay. On his return from captivity he was appointed in March 1799 to command *Pompée* (80) in the Channel fleet under the command of the earl of St Vincent, then sent to the Mediterranean, the West Indies and finally on a winter tour off the Black Rocks, watching Brest.

During Sir James Saumarez's unfortunate attack on 6 July 1801 on Admiral Linois's three ships of the line at Algeciras Bay, Stirling skirted close to the shore, and to the batteries along it, to hold his wind until he reached Linois's flag, the *Formidable*, where he moored fore and aft within pistol shot of his enemy. But scarcely had the broadsides started, when *Pompée* swung her head towards the enemy, and was only able to take punishment without returning any. Stirling refused to cut his cable without an order from the admiral, although it was obvious that his ship could not long survive. He caught his young son in his arms to put him in a boat, but the signal to disengage then was seen, the cable was cut and soon the tide had carried *Pompée* clear. As she was so badly damaged, she was towed into Gibraltar, and her men were employed refitting the rest of the squadron for a renewal of the action, which took place with such satisfactory results on the 12th.

Following the peace of Amiens, in 1804, Stirling accepted the Navy Board appointment of resident commissioner at Port Royal, Jamaica. It is uncertain whether he ever proceeded to his employment. He was promoted rear-admiral on 23 April 1804, and in June 1805 hoisted his flag on board *Glory* (90) in the Channel fleet, taking command of five ships of the line watching Rochefort.

In July Admiral Cornwallis ordered him to place himself under the command of Sir Robert Calder cruising to intercept the combined fleet under Vice-Admiral Villeneuve, which was expected in European waters from Martinique with Lord Nelson in pursuit. He was thus second in command during the action of 22 July. Because the blockade had been raised on Rochefort, Calder decided not to re-engage in the subsequent days, believing that the Rochefort squadron would be summoned by telegraph.

In 1806 Stirling was transferred to *Sampson* (64) and ordered to supersede Sir Home Popham, who had violated his instructions and on his own initiative sailed from the Cape of Good Hope to seize Spanish possessions at Buenos Aires. Stirling was very reluctant to take on the job, as the people there had not asked to be 'liberated', and indeed fought back to good effect. Major-General Beresford and the little army committed to the operation were forced to surrender following heavy street fighting in Buenos Aires. Reluctantly Stirling provided the necessary support for the siege and capture of Montevideo as a secure post for the army, but resisted the soldiers' enthusiasm for an advance up the Rio de la Plata. He was superseded in command when Rear-Admiral George Murray arrived on 14 June, and was left guarding Montevideo when the combined arms moved up the river to meet a signal defeat, after which General Whitelocke was glad to purchase his withdrawal by a promise to leave the South Americans in peace. He then proceeded to the Cape of Good Hope in *Diadem* (64), returning home on 7 April 1808.

After several years ashore, Stirling was appointed commander-in-chief at Jamaica in October 1811. Unfortunately his authority was undermined when in 1812 Sir John Borlase Warren was appointed to command on the coast of North America, with Jamaica reduced to a subordinate command. This led to dissension, which ended with charges of abusing his position by hiring out naval ships to escort merchantmen. A subsequent court martial found the charges 'in part proved', and he was condemned to be put permanently on the half-pay list and not included in any future promotions. There were many objections to the proceedings of the court, and perhaps the real crime on Stirling's part had only been that he was so honest that he became a target for more pliable men. [Ralfe 3.73]

Charlotte died in March 1825, and he died on 7 November 1833, aged seventy-three, at Woburn Farm near Chertsey, Surrey.

> Lt: 12 June 1778
> M-C: 15 May 1780
> Capt: 15 January 1783
> R-Adm: 23 April 1804
> V-Adm: 31 July 1810

STOPFORD

ADMIRAL THE HONOURABLE SIR ROBERT STOPFORD, GCB, is best known for his part, when in command of *Phaeton* (38), in Lord Cornwallis's famous fighting retreat on 16–17 June 1795. Subsequently he fought in the battle of San Domingo, and in the action at Brest Roads in October 1808.

He was born on 5 February 1768, the third son of James Stopford, second earl of Courtown. His mother was Mary, daughter and coheiress of Richard Powys of Hintlesham Hall, Suffolk. In 1779 he was sent to Eton College, and he entered the navy on 31 May 1780 in the *Prince George* (98) flying the flag of Rear-Admiral Robert Digby. Amongst the lieutenants serving in her at the time were Richard Keats and Sir Thomas Foley. Prince William Henry, later the duke of Clarence, was acting as midshipman. Stopford seems to have profited from and valued these connections throughout his life.

His ship was in Vice-Admiral George Darby's fleet sent to relieve Gibraltar in 1780, in Rear-Admiral Thomas Graves's at the Chesapeake on 5 September 1781, and with Sir Samuel Hood at the battle of the Saintes on 12 April 1782. On 13 December he was rated midshipman in *L'Aigle* under Captain William Tooks, and 17 January 1783 he transferred into *Atalanta* under the command of Thomas Foley, in which he was ordered to act as lieutenant, and was employed in settling American loyalists near Annapolis Royal in Nova

Scotia, clearing trees and building houses and barns for the refugees. As his commission had not been confirmed by the Admiralty when *Atalanta* was ordered back to England, Stopford made an exchange on 29 February 1784 with another lieutenant. He remained in Nova Scotia in his acting rank, sailing to Cape Breton Island and into the St Lawrence, where his new ship, the 12-pounder frigate *Hermione* (32), was heavily beset with ice. When she returned to England in 1785 Stopford was commissioned lieutenant, on 15 July. The following spring he was appointed on 8 March fourth lieutenant of *Salisbury* (50), Captain Erasmus Gower, flying the broad pendant of Commodore John Elliot, who was appointed commander-in-chief and governor of Newfoundland.

On 1 May 1789 he joined *Aquilon* (32) as second lieutenant, and on his arrival at Gibraltar he was, on 2 June, promoted master and commander of *Ferret,* sloop (14). On 4 December that year he was ordered to take command of the 12-pounder frigate *Ambuscade* (32), but his commission was not approved by the Admiralty and he returned to his former command on 18 May. His opportunity came with the Nootka Sound incident the following summer, when he was ordered to observe the state of Spanish mobilisation at Cadiz and then report to London. There he was promoted on 12 August 1790 and appointed to command *Fame* (74). He left her on 27 October, and served briefly in command of *Lowestoffe* (32) that November, and then was unemployed until after the French declaration of war on 1 February 1793.

He was appointed to *Aquilon* (32) on 29 April, and was actively employed, in particular in the transport of HRH Prince Augustus, duke of Sussex, from Leghorn to England and back. He fought as part of the Channel fleet in the actions of 28 and 29 May and 1 June 1794, in the last engagement taking *Marlborough* (74) in tow when she was totally dismasted and surrounded by French ships. This service established his reputation with Lord Howe, who moved him on 15 July to command of *Phaeton* (38). His part in Cornwallis's retreat added to it. On discovering the approach of the greatly superior force of the Brest fleet, Stopford reported his intelligence. The following morning, when it was clear that it would be difficult to avoid defeat and capture, Cornwallis sent Stopford a note directing him, as soon as the firing started, to crack on sail and when well ahead of the squadron let fly the top-gallant-sheets and fire guns, the well-known signal for a fleet in sight. Having carried out his orders, in the afternoon he stood back to the admiral's ship, *Royal Sovereign* (100), and gave her three cheers. The combined effect of Cornwallis's resolute formation and *Phaeton*'s tactical deception was that the French broke off contact. It was no less to his credit that the crew of *Phaeton*, which he commanded from July 1794 to July 1799, refused to take any part in the Spithead mutiny.

On 13 July 1799 he was transferred to *Excellent* (74) for service in the Channel and West Indies, during the latter period acting as commodore with a captain under him. Later he was transferred to the 12-pounder frigate *Castor* (32) and ordered to fly a broad pendant.

Following the peace of Amiens, and the renewal of the war, Stopford was appointed on 1 January 1804 to the *Spencer* (74) and in August was ordered to join the Mediterranean fleet under Lord Nelson, with whom he sailed the following year in pursuit of the Toulon fleet to the West Indies and back to Europe. He was serving with Lord Collingwood off Cadiz when Nelson arrived to assume command, but *Spencer* was so affected by scurvy after nearly a year at sea that she was one of the ships ordered to Gibraltar just prior to the battle of Trafalgar, and did not rejoin until 28 October 1805. Nonetheless Stopford was nominated colonel of the Royal Marines on 9 November.

He made up for missing that battle, however, by playing parts in some of the most important operations in the next decade. In 1806 he was a part of the squadron under Sir John Duckworth which was dispatched to the West Indies, and there fought the battle of San Domingo. He ran for parliament in the afterglow, and was elected the member for Ipswich, Suffolk, which seat he held for a year. But this did not interrupt his naval service. He was or-

dered to take command of a troop convoy carrying 5,000 soldiers to the Rio de la Plata, but Rear-Admiral Murray did not meet him at his rendezvous at Porto Praya, and eventually he took his exhausted soldiers to the Cape of Good Hope. In July 1807 *Spencer* was ordered to form part of Admiral Gambier's fleet before Copenhagen, and Stopford was one of those who objected to Sir Home Popham being appointed captain of the fleet, ostensibly because of his lack of seniority.

Stopford was promoted rear-admiral on 28 April 1808, and played a major part in the attack on Basque Roads. This operation commenced with his being placed in command of the blockade of Basque Roads with his flag flying in *Caesar* (80) and with two other of the line and five frigates, of which three were detached to L'Orient. On 23 February 1809 he attacked four French frigates under the batteries of Sable d'Olonne and left them all on their beam ends in a falling tide. Ten enemy sail of the line which had sortied returned to Basque Roads in April, and he advised Lord Gambier, who joined him and assumed command. It was decided to employ fireships against the moored ships, and it was very much of a surprise when the Admiralty sent Lord Cochrane to carry out the operation.

Stopford married Mary, seventh daughter of Captain Robert Fanshawe, RN, resident commissioner of Plymouth dockyard, on 29 June 1809 at Stoke church, Plymouth. The couple had three sons and four daughters.

At the conclusion of Lord Gambier's trial, at which Stopford was called upon to give evidence, he was appointed in September 1810 commander-in-chief at the Cape of Good Hope with orders to capture the Isle de France (Mauritius). By the time he arrived, however, that operation had been successfully undertaken. Early in 1811 he was informed of the death of Rear-Admiral Drury, commander-in-chief East Indies, and that an amphibious assault on Java was in preparation. In the circumstances, he resolved to depart from his command in order to take charge in the East Indies from Captain Broughton, which resolution was later approved by the Admiralty. He met the assault force at Batavia and assumed naval command, co-operating effectively with Lord Minto and Sir Samuel Auchmuty. Broughton requested that Stopford be court-martialled 'for behaving in a cruel, oppressive, and fraudulent manner, unbecoming the character of an officer, in depriving me of the command of the squadron', but the Admiralty refused the request.

On his return to England in April 1813 he hauled down his flag and was not again employed until 1 May 1827, when he was appointed commander-in-chief at Portsmouth, which post he held until April 1830. He was made a KCB on 2 January 1815, and a GCB on 6 June 1831. In 1837 he was appointed commander-in-chief Mediterranean, hoisting his flag in *Princess Charlotte* (104), but unfortunately his last command did nothing for his reputation. He no longer had the flexibility of mind to deal with the complex situation which developed when the Egyptian rebel Mehmet Ali took possession of a Turkish naval squadron. The British government supported the sultan, but was concerned that France would support Mehmet Ali, and wanted quick action. Stopford favoured Mehmet Ali, and the foreign secretary, Lord Palmerston, found it easier to work through Stopford's second in command, Commodore Charles Napier. Stopford eventually carried out a bombardment of Acre, after which Napier negotiated a convention with Mehmet Ali.

On 10 May 1837 he had been appointed knight grand cross of the order of St Michael and St George of Malta and the Ionian Republic, as was then the custom for newly appointed commanders-in-chief Mediterranean. He had been appointed rear-admiral of the United Kingdom in April 1834, and he was promoted to vice-admiral of the United Kingdom in May 1847. But Palmerston refused him a peerage. He was governor of Greenwich hospital from 1 May 1841 until his death with the rank of admiral on 25 June 1847, aged seventy-nine, in Richmond, Surrey.

> Lt: 15 July 1785
> M-C: 2 June 1789
> Capt: 12 August 1790
> R-Adm: 28 April 1808
> V-Adm: 12 August 1812
> Adm: 27 May 1825

STRACHAN

ADMIRAL SIR RICHARD JOHN STRACHAN, BARONET, GCB, is best known for the capture of four French ships of the line in November 1805 as they fled from the battle at Trafalgar. But he should be known for his command of the naval forces in the 1809 Scheldt expedition.

He was born on 27 October 1760 in Plymouth, the first son of Lieutenant Patrick Strachan, RN, and his wife Caroline, daughter of Captain John Pitman, RN. The Navy Office credited him with entering the service as an able seaman in *Ranger*, sloop, and in *Edgar* (74), before serving as a midshipman in *Orford* (64). But it is believed he actually entered the navy in 1772 in *Intrepid* (64), Captain James Cranston, in which he was taken to the East Indies to join his uncle, Sir John Strachan, commanding *Orford* (68). He served with Commodore Hotham and Lord Howe during the American war, was rated an able seaman and midshipman in *Albion* (74), and served out the rest of his time as midshipman in *Preston* (50) and *Eagle* (64), before passing his examination on 7 January 1779. [ADM 107.7.92] He was commissioned lieutenant in the West Indies on 5 April 1779. He returned to England and was appointed to the *Hero* (74), in which he served in Commodore George Johnstone's expedition to the Cape of Good Hope, in the action at Praya and in all the actions between Sir Edward Hughes and Admiral Suffren. Hughes promoted him commander in January 1783 and post captain on 26 April in the French prize *Naiad* (30).

Strachan returned to England at the end of the war, and in 1787 was appointed to command *Vestal*, in 1788 sailing to take the Honourable Charles Alan Cathcart *en embassy* to China, but Cathcart died in the Strait of Banca and Strachan returned to England. The following year he was again sent to the East Indies. Joining the squadron under Commodore the Honourable William Cornwallis, he was transferred to *Phoenix* (36). In 1791 he was ordered by Cornwallis to intercept a French convoy which was believed to be carrying contraband to Mangalore for Tippoo Sahib, with whom Britain was at war. This was not accomplished without an action in which there were fairly heavy casualties on both sides. No contraband was found, and Strachan refused to accept the surrender of the French frigate *Résolue*, which had struck. Cornwallis ordered him to tow her to the French commandant at Mahé.

On the outbreak of war in February 1793 Strachan returned to Europe and, on *Phoenix* being paid off, was appointed to *Concorde* (36) in Rear-Admiral John MacBride's squadron of the Channel fleet. In April 1794, while serving under Sir John Borlase Warren, he was in action again with *Résolue* but was able to capture only her consort, *L'Engageante* (34). Subsequently he commanded the 18-pounder frigate *Melampus* (36), moving into another, *Diamond* (38), in 1796 when her captain, Sir Sidney Smith, was captured, and finally into *Donegal* (74) in 1802, in which ship he remained during the peace of Amiens. Following the renewal of the war he sailed to the Mediterranean, served briefly under Lord Nelson, and then was posted off Cadiz. Spain was not at war with Britain at the time, but when a Spanish frigate sailed on 23 April 1804 he chased her for twenty-four hours, engaged her, and brought her a prize into Gibraltar, where she was eventually condemned. He subsequently was given command of *Caesar* (80) and placed in charge of a squadron watching Rochefort. He was nominated colonel of the Royal Marines on 23 April 1804.

Sir Richard Strachan's action, as it was called, occurred during 2 and 3 November 1805. Strachan reported to Admiral William Cornwallis,

> Sir, Being off Ferrol, working to the westward, with the wind westerly, on the evening of the 2nd we observed a frigate in the N.W. making signals; made all sail to join her before night, and followed by the ships named in the margin, [*Caesar* (80), *Hero* (74), *Courageux* (74) and *Namur* (90); *Bellona* (74), *Aeolus* (32), *Santa Margarita* (40), far to leeward in the southeast] we came up with her at eleven at night; and at the moment she joined us, we saw six large ships near us. Captain

> [Thomas] Baker informed me he had been chased by the Rochefort squadron, then close to leeward of us. We were delighted. I desired him to tell the captains of the ships of the line astern to follow me, as I meant to engage them directly; and immediately bore away in the *Caesar* for the purpose, making all the signals I could, to indicate our movements to our ships; the moon enabled us to see the enemy bear away in a line abreast, closely formed; but we lost sight of them when it set, and I was obliged to reduce our sails, the *Hero*, *Courageux*, and *Aeolus*, being the only ships we could see. We continued steering to the E.N.E. all night, and in the morning observed the *Santa Margarita* near us; at nine we discovered the enemy of four sail of the line in the N.E. under all sail. We had also every thing set, and came up with them fast; in the evening we observed three sail astern; and the *Phoenix* spoke me at night. I found that active officer, Captain Baker, had delivered my orders, and I sent him on to assist the *Santa Margarita* in leading us up to the enemy. At day-light we were near them, and the *Santa Margarita* had begun in a very gallant manner to fire upon their rear, and was soon joined by the *Phoenix*.

> A little before noon, the French finding an action unavoidable, began to take in their small sails, and form in a line, bearing on the starboard tack; we did the same; and I communicated my intentions, by hailing to the captains, that I should attack the centre and rear, and at noon we began the battle: in a short time the van ship of the enemy tacked, which almost directly made the action close and general; the *Namur* joined soon after we tacked, which we did as soon as we could get the ships round, and I directed her by signal to engage the van; at half past three the action ceased, the enemy having fought to admiration, and not surrendering till their ships were unmanageable. *NC* 14.426–7

The prizes proved to be from the van division of the combined Franco-Spanish fleet at Trafalgar.

Two days prior to his dispatch reaching the Admiralty, on 9 November 1805, Strachan was promoted rear-admiral, and he was rewarded with an appointment as KB on 29 January 1806. He was also included in the thanks of both houses of parliament for the victory at Trafalgar, and awarded an annuity of £1,000.

Later that year he was dispatched with a squadron to intercept a French one believed to be heading for the West Indies, but did not fall in with them. The following year he was employed in watching Rochefort, but being short of supplies was obliged to raise the blockade. On 17 January the French sailed, and he chased them into the Mediterranean, where they went into Toulon. He joined the fleet under Lord Collingwood before returning home, where he was appointed to command *Venerable* (74).

The Scheldt operation in 1809 was the largest amphibious expedition hitherto launched from Britain, designed to destroy the shipyards of Antwerp that Napoleon needed if he were to recover from the defeat at Trafalgar. Strachan had command of thirty-five ship of the line, of which twenty-five had their lower guns removed to accommodate soldiers, two ships of fifty guns, twenty-one frigates, thirty-three sloops, five bomb-vessels, twenty-three gun-brigs, five carrying mortars, seventeen hired cutters, fourteen revenue vessels, five tenders and eighty-two gunboats, and he had to transport 30,000 soldiers across the Straits of Dover and up the Scheldt against well-positioned French batteries. This proved a very demanding command. Heavy surf made the intended landing beaches unusable, and Strachan had to improvise, taking the main fleet through the channels of the estuary so that the soldiers could be landed from the Veer Gatt onto Bree Sand. Flushing and Walcheren Island were successfully captured, but then the army became bogged down and began to fall ill. Walcheren fever claimed thousands of lives, and the army had to be withdrawn, eventually even evacuating the toe-hold in Flushing. The operation proved a disastrous failure. The army commander,

the earl of Chatham, who had been first lord of the Admiralty at the time of the outbreak of war in 1793, was unable to deal with the complexity of operations in the Scheldt estuary, and Strachan did not have the experience in amphibious operations which might have enabled him to overcome the army's problems.

Chatham exploited his position in cabinet to meet with King George, and tried to lay the blame for the failure of the Scheldt operation on Strachan. This unconstitutional proceeding was seen by the service and by parliament for what it was, but Strachan was not again employed. He was appointed a GCB on 2 January 1815, and with that honour, cheapened by being bestowed on almost all senior officers on the same date, he had to be content.

He married in April 1812 Louisa Dillon, but there were to be no children. He died on 3 February 1828, aged sixty-seven, in London, survived by Louisa, who died in 1868 in Naples.

Lt: 5 April 1779
M-C: January 1783
Capt: 26 April 1783
R-Adm: 9 November 1805
V-Adm: 31 July 1810
Adm: 19 July 1821

SUTTON

REAR-ADMIRAL SAMUEL SUTTON is best known for his part in the battle of Copenhagen on 2 April 1801, when he commanded *Alcmene* (32), one of the frigates ordered by Lord Nelson to pass along the disengaged side of the British line of battle and engaged the head of the Danish line and the Trekroner fort. He was also Nelson's flag captain in *Amazon* (38) following the battle, and in *Victory* (100) after the collapse of the peace of Amiens, until he exchanged with Thomas Masterman Hardy off Toulon on 30 July 1803.

Little is known about his origins apart from the year of his birth, 1760, and the simplest details of his service record. He entered the navy on 9 April 1777 as an able seaman, and later was midshipman in *Monarch* (74) under the command of Captain Joshua Rowley, with whom he served in the Channel fleet until December 1778 when Rowley as a rear-admiral hoisted his flag in *Suffolk*

(74) with Hugh Cloberry Christian his flag captain. Sutton followed him and served in the West Indies, shifting when he did in December 1779 into *Conqueror* (74) under the command of Thomas Watson, and to *Terrible* (74) in June 1780, and then in July into *Princess Royal* (98), both under Captain John Thomas Duckworth. He was ordered to act as lieutenant in *Princess Royal*, and continued to do so when he was transferred in July 1781 to the sloop *Jamaica* (16) under Captain Manley Dixon. In December he moved again, into the French prize *Le Du Guay Trouin* [*Guay Troin*] (18) under Captain Benjamin Hulke. In May 1782 he moved into *London* (90) commanded by Captain James Kempthorn, and with Rowley's flag once more. In December he moved with Rowley into *Ajax* (74) commanded by Captain N Chasington. And in March 1783 he moved yet again, into *Preston* (50) commanded by George Martin. His commission was finally confirmed on 21 April 1783, when he was twenty-two years old, without his ever having been formally examined. He then returned home in *Childers* (10) and in March 1785 was appointed to *Merlin*, sloop, under Captain Edward Pakenham, with whom he served at Newfoundland until December.

He spent the next four and a half years ashore, but was appointed to *Iphigenia* (32) under Captain Patrick Sinclair on 22 June 1790 at the time of the Nootka Sound crisis, but came ashore again on 7 February 1791.

Just prior to the French declaration of war on 1 February 1793, on 3 January, he was appointed to *Culloden* (74) flying the flag of Rear-Admiral Sir Thomas Rich in the Channel fleet. In November 1794 he was appointed first lieutenant of *Mars* (74) under Sir Charles Cotton, and continued in the Channel fleet. He took part in Vice-Admiral Cornwallis's famous retreat from a superior force on 16 June 1795. On 1 September he was promoted commander of the ship-sloop *Martin* (16), in which he served on the coast of Africa, and in the North Sea, where he transported the Duc d'Angoulême from Leith to Cuxhaven. Promotion comes fast in wartime, and in reward for his service to aristocracy he was made post captain on 27

June 1797. He was then ashore for over a year, but on 3 September 1798 he was appointed Sir Richard Onslow's flag captain in *Monarch* (74) in the North Sea, and on 13 March 1799 he was transferred to *Prince* (90) as Sir Charles Cotton's flag captain. He was appointed to the *Alcmene* (32) on 23 February 1801.

Following the battle of Copenhagen he was transferred into the 18-pounder frigate *Amazon* (38) to take the place of Captain Riou, who had been killed, and served as flag captain to Nelson in the Baltic and later when he commanded the anti-invasion forces in the Downs. Nelson hauled down his flag in July 1802 with the conclusion of the peace of Amiens, but Sutton remained in command until November, and read his commission on board *Victory* (100) on 9 April 1803 prior to delivering her to Nelson in the Mediterranean off Toulon. When he left the *Victory* there in July or August, he exchanged with Thomas Masterman Hardy into *Amphion* (32), in which Nelson had travelled south, and in her was actively employed in the Mediterranean station. On 5 October 1804 she was one of the frigates sent to intercept the Spanish treasure ships. *Amphion* was opposed to *Mercedes*, second astern of the Spanish admiral's ship, which blew up ten minutes after the commencement of the action, killing all but forty of those on board, including many women and children.

Apparently the prize money from this action was enough to cause him to drop out of the service in October 1805. He was married and had children but the date of his marriage is unknown. He was promoted rear-admiral on 19 July 1821, and died in June 1832, aged seventy-two, in Ditchingham, Norfolk.

Lt: 21 April 1783
Cmdr: 1 September 1795
Capt: 27 June 1797
R-Adm: 19 July 1821

THOMPSON

VICE-ADMIRAL SIR THOMAS BOULDEN THOMPSON, BARONET, GCB, fought with Nelson at Tenerife, the Nile and Copenhagen. Although several of his contemporaries had humble origins, and succeeded in rising to high rank and great honours, Thompson's story must be the most remarkable.

He was born on 28 February 1766 in Barham near Canterbury, Kent, probably the son of M Boulden and his wife Sarah, who was daughter of Richard Thompson. One source has it that his parents were too impoverished to provide their son with a proper education, but that Sarah's brother, Captain Edward Thompson, RN, provided the necessary means, and later undertook himself to teach Thomas navigation. There is also a report that in

Sir Thomas Boulden Thompson, Knight,
engraved by William Ridley after Englehart,
published by Joyce Gold, 103 Shoe Lane,
1 August 1805.

fact Edward Thompson was the boy's father and Sarah's maiden name was Boulden. Thomas did certainly change his name to Thompson. In June 1778 Captain Thompson was appointed to command *Hyaena* (24) and took his nephew, or son, into the ship's company as able seaman or midshipman. He was commissioned lieutenant on 14 January 1782, and stayed with his uncle, or father, when in July 1783 the latter was appointed commodore on the African station, young Thomas acting as second lieutenant in the *Grampus* (50). In

January 1786 Commodore Edward Thompson died. Captain Trip suceeded to command of the squadron, and his first lieutenant waived his own claims to command *Nautalis*.

Thomas Thompson was promoted to post captain on 22 November 1790, but was not appointed to a ship until after the outbreak of war, and in 1796 was placed in command of *Leander* (50), which was stationed in the North Sea. Escort of a convoy in 1797 took her to Gibraltar, where Admiral the earl of St Vincent ordered her to form part of the squadron under Rear-Admiral Nelson which was to cut out a valuable galleon from the harbour of Santa Cruz de Tenerife. Thompson was one of those wounded trying to advance from the mole into the town.

In 1798 *Leander* was one of the ships attached to the squadron that Nelson was ordered to take into the Mediterranean to deal with the threat posed by an armament at Toulon and the Italian coast under General Buonaparte's command. Although only a 50-gun ship, *Leander* was part of the line at the battle of the Nile on 1 August. When a shot cut the cable of *Le Peuple Souverain* so that she drifted away and left a gap between *L'Orient* and *Franklin*, Thompson was able to place the small *Leander* where he could direct a raking fire into both.

On the 5th Thompson sailed from Aboukir with Captain Berry as a passenger, bearing dispatches to Admiral St Vincent, but *Leander* ran into *Le Généreux* (74), one of the French ships to survive the battle of the Nile, and after fighting for six and a half hours was forced to surrender. Both he and Berry were wounded, and the treatment afforded the prisoners was not consistent with the standards civilised Europe had come to expect. After his exchange, Thompson was tried for the loss of his ship, and the court declared that it was 'of opinion, that the gallant and almost unprecedented defence of Captain Thompson, of the *Leander*, against so superior a force as that of the *Généreux*, is deserving of every praise this Country and this Court can give'. [NC 14.12]

He was invested a knight bachelor on 13 February 1799, awarded a pension of £200 per annum, and twelve days later married Anne, daughter of Robert Raikes of Gloucester, the founder of the Sunday schools. She gave birth to three sons and three daughters, of whom his second son was Vice-Admiral Sir Thomas Raikes Trigge Thompson.

In 1801, in command of *Bellona* (74), he was ordered to form part of the fleet under Admiral Sir Hyde Parker sent to deal with the formation of the Armed Neutrality, and was in the action at Copenhagen on 2 April under Vice-Admiral Nelson's immediate command. *Bellona* unfortunately ran aground, but was still able to take an effective part in the action, during which Thompson had one of his legs shot off.

His pension was now increased to £500, and he was put in command of *Mary*, yacht, stationed at Deptford. The *Naval Chronicle* concluded its biographical memoir of Thompson with a comment on the striking resemblance of his portrait: 'he possesses a manly, expressive, and interesting countenance; he is above the middle size, of a vigorous make, and graceful figure. The latter, however, is now losing somewhat of its proportion; as, from the loss of his leg, he is incapable of taking much exercise; except on horseback, and a tendency to corpulence becomes daily more and more visible.'

He was made a baronet on 11 December 1806, promoted vice-admiral on 4 June 1814, and nominated KCB on 2 January 1815 and GCB on 14 September 1822. Entering politics, he held the parliamentary seat for Rochester from 1807 to 12 June 1816, taking a right-wing stand on issues of criminal law reform and Catholic emancipation. He was comptroller of the navy from 20 June 1806 to 24 February 1816, and treasurer of Greenwich hospital and director of the Chatham Chest from 1816 to his death on 3 March 1828, aged sixty-two, in Manor Place, Hartsbourne, Hertfordshire. Anne survived him to 9 September 1846.

Lt: 14 January 1782
M-C: 27 March 1786
Capt: 22 November 1790
R-Adm: 25 October 1809
V-Adm: 4 June 1814

THORNBROUGH

ADMIRAL SIR EDWARD THORNBROUGH, GCB, had established a strong professional character by the time of the battle of the Glorious First of June in 1794, in which he was senior frigate captain. On 11 October 1798 he played a major role in the defeat of a French invasion attempt.

He had been born on 27 July 1754 at Plymouth dockyard, the only son of Commander Edward Thornbrough, RN, and entered the navy on 20 June 1761 as lieutenant's servant to his father in *Arrogant* (74) under the command of Captain John Amhurst. He spent two years in the Channel and the Mediterranean, and then at the age of nine was placed on the books of a guardship at Plymouth, *Firm* (60), on which he was rated an able seaman. The supposition is that he was sent to school. When he returned to active service, on 22 March 1768, he was to rejoin his father in *Temeraire* (74), which was fitted as a guardship at Plymouth and commanded by Captain Edward Lecras. He was rated a midshipman. He joined *Albion* (74) at Spithead, under the command of Captain the Honourable Samuel Barrington, in the middle of December 1770 during the mobilisation for the Falkland Islands crisis, but left her on 3 April on the settlement of the dispute, and joined *Captain* (64), in which his father was first lieutenant and Rear-Admiral John Montagu flew his flag. *Captain* was under orders for North America, where she proceeded in June 1771, returning in August 1774, having spent most of that time at Boston. While there, Edward Thornbrough was commissioned lieutenant on 16 April 1773, and in his précis of his service, he remembered that he was appointed to *Cruizer*.

On 13 October 1774 he was appointed first lieutenant of *Falcon*, brig-sloop (14), and returned to Boston, where his ship was employed in support of the army at Bunker Hill on 17 June 1775. On 8 August he was injured and taken prisoner in an attempt against an American schooner. After he was exchanged he was invalided home, but he was able to join *Richmond*, frigate, on 13 March 1776 and served for three years, mostly in North

America. On 5 September 1779 he was appointed to *Garland* (24) under the command of John Stanhope, and he served for seven months escorting a convoy to Newfoundland and back. On 26 April 1780 he was appointed first lieutenant of *Flora* (36), the first 18-pounder frigate in the Royal Navy. He proved himself the following August in action with *La Nymphe* (36), when the French succeeded in boarding *Flora* but were driven back by her people led by Thornbrough, who pursued them into their own ship, which was then taken prize.

In recognition of his service, he was promoted on 14 September master and commander of *Britannia,* armed ship (24). He returned to the American theatre and on 21 September 1781 was there promoted by Rear-Admiral Thomas Graves to post captain in *Blonde* (32). Unfortunately, he lost his ship on rocks near Seal Island at the mouth of the Bay of Fundy, and was rescued from the uninhabited island only by the humanity of two American cruisers. He was acquitted at his court martial, and appointed on 14 January 1783 to command *Egmont* (74). She was employed between Spithead and Plymouth, with the intention that she should go to the East Indies, but with the coming of peace Thornbrough left her on 17 April 1783.

After a few months ashore, he was appointed on 3 October to command the French prize *Hebe* (38), which had been taken the previous year in the Channel by Captain Henry Trollope in *Rainbow*. Thornbrough remained in her command in Channel service through the peace until 21 October 1789. In June 1785 Prince William Henry, on his being commissioned lieutenant, was appointed to *Hebe* for a nine-month cruise around Great Britain.

During the Nootka Sound incident in 1790 Thornbrough was appointed on 19 July to the *Scipio* (64), moving to the 18-pounder frigate *Latona* (38) on 21 December 1792. Serving in the Channel fleet, Thornbrough made a strong reputation for himself following the French declaration of war by boldly engaging a squadron of French ships and frigates, although he was unable to effect any capture. In the initial cruise leading to the series of actions collectively known as the battle

of the Glorious First of June, *Latona* was one of the advanced scouts kept under Lord Howe's direct command. In the engagement of 28 May she was in the thick of the action, Thornbrough taking his chance to fire a raking broadside into *Révolutionaire* (44). On the evening of the 31st he was called on board the *Queen Charlotte* (100), where he was instructed by Lord Howe to take a position between the hostile fleets within night vision of the French. In the action on 1 June *Latona* again engaged damaged ships of the line, and in the evening took possession of *La Juste* (80).

On 10 July following the return of the fleet in triumph to Spithead he was appointed to command *Robust* (74) in the Channel fleet. At the time of the Quiberon operation in 1795 he claimed to have given passage to two French dukes, five field marshals, four admirals and a total of fifty officers. In late 1798 he again distinguished himself when *Robust* formed part of a squadron commanded by Sir John Warren which was detached in pursuit of a French squadron carrying soldiers intended for an invasion of Ireland. It was discovered off Tory Island on 11 October, and in the general chase which followed, *Robust* was the first to bring the enemy to action, at about 7am on the 12th. Her opponent proved to be the *Hoche* (84). With the support of *Magnanime*, frigate, commanded by Captain the Honourable Michael de Courcy, Thornbrough forced her to strike after an engagement of three hours. *Hoche* having had 1,224 people on board, including soldiers, of which 200 were killed, her carnage was terrible. *Robust* suffered twelve killed and seventy wounded, and her rigging had been so badly cut up by fire from French frigates that they were able to disengage and get away.

Following the actions of 28 May to 1 June 1794, the service on the French coast in *Robust* and the capture of the *Hoche*, Thornbrough was on 14 February 1799 nominated colonel of the marines. He was also appointed on 21 February to command *Formidable* (98), and was ordered to fly a commodore's broad pendant in the Mediterranean, where he played a part in Lord Keith's pursuit of Vice-Admiral Bruix back to Brest. He was then promoted rear-admiral on 1 January 1801.

On the renewal of the war in 1803 he held a succession of flag commands in the North Sea, the Channel and the Mediterranean. On 22 March 1805 he was appointed first captain of the Channel fleet under Admiral Lord Gardner, serving in *Hibernia* (110). He was promoted vice-admiral on 9 November 1805, and hoisted his flag in *Prince of Wales* (98) to command in the Channel fleet and off Rochefort. In June 1806 he shifted his flag to *Ville de Paris* (110), striking it on 14 October for a few months ashore and raising it again on 2 February 1807 in *Royal Sovereign* (100) for service in the Mediterranean; he returned home on 21 December 1809 and struck his flag. Between 4 August 1810 and 16 November 1813 he was commander-in-chief on the Irish station, flying his flag on the fir-built 18-pounder frigate *Trent* (36). And he ended his career following the war as commander-in-chief Portsmouth from April 1815 to May 1818. He was nominated KCB on 2 January 1815, GCB on 11 January 1825 and vice-admiral of the United Kingdom on 30 January 1833.

He was married three times, first to Anne, second daughter of Commissioner Lecras, who had been his commanding officer when he served as a boy in *Temeraire*. The couple had two sons and four daughters, but Anne died in 1801, in Exeter. One of her sons was named William Henry, at the request of the prince, and already had a commission as lieutenant when he died at the age of fourteen. Thornbrough's second marriage, on 4 December 1802, was to a daughter of Sir Edward Jeynes of Gloucester and sister-in-law of Admiral Sir William Hotham, GCB, and of Captain Thomas Young, RN. Her name is not recorded, and she died without children in November 1813, in Bishop's Tawton near Teignmouth, Devon. His third wife was Frances, third daughter of Commissioner Lecras and sister of his first wife. He died with the rank of admiral on 3 April 1834, aged seventy-nine, at his residence in Bishops Teignton, Devon.

Lt: 16 April 1773
M-C: 14 September 1780
Capt: 21 September 1781
R-Adm: 1 January 1801
V-Adm: 9 November 1805
Adm: 4 December 1813

TOBIN

REAR-ADMIRAL GEORGE TOBIN, CB, is remembered in Marshall's *Naval Biography*, which tells us that in 1793 Tobin received letters while away from England 'informing him that Captain Horatio Nelson,... had kept the third Lieutenancy of the *Agamemnon* (64), open for some time, in hopes of his joining her; but little calculating on the subsequent greatness of that officer, Mr. Tobin was rather pleased than otherwise at being out of the way of accepting the offer, and particularly so when, a few months afterwards, he found himself second lieutenant of the *Thetis* (38), a fine frigate, commanded by the Honourable Alexander Cochrane.' MARSHALL 2(Supp).630

George Tobin was born on 13 December 1768 in *Salisbury* (50), the second son of James Tobin, merchant and landowner in Nevis, West Indies, and of his wife Elizabeth, eldest daughter of George Webbe of Nevis, who was related to Lady Nelson. James Tobin was an acrimonious defender of slavery, but his first son, James Webbe Tobin, became an important abolitionist. After attending the King Edward VI school in Southampton, George entered the navy with the patronage of Admiral Herbert Sawyer. On 1 June 1780 he was rated midshipman when he joined *Namur* (90), under Sawyer's command and with Captain Robert Fanshawe in subordinate command. *Namur* proceeded to the West Indies with Admiral Rodney, and there Tobin took part in the actions of 9 and 12 April 1782. When *Namur* was put out of commission on 7 June 1783 at the end of the war, Tobin joined *Bombay Castle* (74) fitted as a guardship at Plymouth, again under Captains Sawyer and Fanshawe. He followed Sawyer into *Thisbe* (28) on 6 February 1785, as a supernumerary, his patron having now been ordered to fly a commodore's broad pendant, and in August while in the Halifax station followed him into *Assistance* (50), where he was rated a midshipman. They moved again in September 1786 into *Leander* (50), but he was out of employment from June 1787.

Between the autumn of 1788 and the summer of 1790 he made several voyages in East Indiamen to Madras and Canton, and then he joined *Tremendous* (74) at the time of the Nootka Sound crisis with a commission as lieutenant dated 14 November 1790.

The threat of war passing, in the spring of 1791 he accepted a commission as third lieutenant of *Providence* (16), Captain William Bligh, under orders to proceed to Tahiti and take on a cargo of breadfruit for transplantation in the West Indies. This was the sequel to the *Bounty* voyage which had ended in mutiny. During this voyage, Tobin painted beautiful coastal views into his journal, and he was to continue an accomplished amateur painter the rest of his life. Having escaped a career with his kinsman Horatio Nelson, he next served in *Thetis* (38) in Nova Scotia waters, and was eventually appointed her first lieutenant. Following a short probation in *Resolution* (74), flying the flag of Vice-Admiral George Murray, he was promoted commander on 12 July 1798 and appointed to a new cedar-built sloop, *Dasher*. By now he had repented of his dismissal of Nelson, and he attempted to get orders to the West Indies so as to be near his now famous kinsman, but failed and spent the last years of the war on the French coast trying to stop the passage of coastal convoys.

Tobin was made post captain on 29 April 1802 and with the renewal of the war was appointed on 21 September 1804 to *Northumberland* (74) as flag captain to Rear-Admiral Alexander Cochrane. He married on 13 June 1804 Dorothy, daughter of Lieutenant Gordon Skelly, RN, and widow of Major William Duff. This marriage brought a daughter into his family, and Dorothy also gave birth to two of his children, a son and a daughter.

On 20 September 1805 he was placed in command of *Princess Charlotte* (38), and on 5 October off Tobago he captured *Cyane*, a French corvette. Knowing he could not overhaul the French ship, Tobin disguised his ship and succeeded in attracting the Frenchman within range. In the summer of 1806 Tobin escorted a homeward convoy, and then was attached to the Irish station, with passages to Barbados, Jamaica and St Helena to bring home the trade. In January 1812 the name of his ship was changed to *Andromache*, and he was ordered to serve

in the squadron under Sir George Collier during the siege of San Sebastian. On 27 March 1814 *Andromache* led the squadron under Rear-Admiral Penrose when it forced the passage of the Gironde, and in June 1814 she was part of the fleet assembled at Spithead for the review by the allied sovereigns.

She was paid off at Deptford on 23 July, and Tobin went on half pay, living at Teignmouth, where he knew the marine painter Thomas Luny. When Emperor Napoleon Buonaparte surrendered to *Bellerophon* (74) and was waiting on board in Plymouth Sound, Tobin visited and painted a picture of the scene. He was nominated a CB on 8 December 1815, and promoted rear-admiral on 10 January 1837. He died on 10 April 1838, aged sixty-nine.

> Lt: 14 November 1790
> Cmdr: 12 July 1798
> Capt: 29 April 1802
> R-Adm: 10 January 1837

TOMLINSON

VICE-ADMIRAL NICHOLAS TOMLINSON is best known for his part in the battle of Copenhagen, although perhaps his troubles with the Admiralty and Navy Boards are more interesting.

He was born in 1764, the third son of Captain Robert Tomlinson, RN, and his wife, Sarah, only daughter of Nicholas Robinson, MD, of Christ's Hospital, London, president of the College of Physicians. He entered the navy on 15 March 1772 as a captain's servant or volunteer first class on the books of *Resolution* (74) commanded by Captain William Hotham, in which ship his father was serving as first lieutenant. He transferred into *Thetis* (38) on 5 January 1776, and when a Captain John Gill succeeded to command on 9 March 1778 they proceeded to the American theatre. He came ashore on 14 December, and on 3 March 1779 was rated able seaman when he joined the 18-pounder frigate *Charon* (44) under the command of the Honourable John Luttrell. Two weeks later, on 17 March, he was rated midshipman when Captain Thomas Symonds succeeded to command. In *Thetis* he served in North America until 10 October 1781, when he came ashore to join the army under

General Cornwallis, and was taken prisoner at Yorktown on 18 October. He was then appointed to a cartel ship commanded by Symonds, which carried part of the defeated army home to England. There he was exchanged and commissioned lieutenant on 23 March 1782, and fought as first lieutenant of *Bristol* (50) under Captain James Burney in the East Indies in the last engagement between Sir Edward Hughes and Admiral Suffren in September 1784. He was badly injured in an explosion on board the East India Company ship *Duke of Athol* at Madras, and obliged to return to England to recover, arriving in March 1785. On 23 June 1786 he was well enough to be appointed first lieutenant of *Savage* (14), and he remained with her until March 1790. In June, during the Nootka Sound crisis, he joined the impress service at Greenock under the command of Captain Jaheel (Sr.) Brenton, until the dispute with Spain was settled in October.

Peace appearing to be settled, he accepted employment in the Russian navy as captain of a man of war, but as soon as war was declared by France in February 1793 he returned to England and offered his services. He was appointed on 11 July lieutenant of the two-deck frigate *Regulus* (44), under Captain Edward Bowater, and then at the particular request of Sir Sidney Smith, who was engaged in intelligence and covert operations on the coast of France, given in July 1794 command of the gun vessel *Pelter*. He was employed in close support of operations ashore, notably in connection with the royalist expedition to Quiberon Bay. 'At length, in consequence of incessant fatigue, thirty out of fifty of the crew of the *Pelter* were confined to their hammocks. The vessel herself also was greatly shook and damaged, by repeated actions and the firing of her heavy guns, so that an immediate return to England became indispensable.' [NC 25.93] She was towed across the Channel, but could not work to windward and had to enter Dartmouth. There she was repaired, at greater expense than would have been the case at Devonport yard. Fourteen years later this was to cause him great difficulties.

He married in 1794 Elizabeth, second and youngest daughter and coheiress of Ralph Ward of Foxburrows near Colchester, Essex. She was to give birth to four sons and four daughters.

After a very short period as first lieutenant of *Glory* (90), and another brief period as lieutenant commanding the gun vessel *Vesuve*, he was promoted commander on 29 November 1795 and appointed to *Suffisante*, sloop (14). 'To whatever extent boarding and cutting out the enemy's vessels from under forts, &c. may have since been carried,' noted the author of *An Appeal to the Public, in Behalf of Nicholas Tomlinson,* 'Captain

Captain Nicholas Tomlinson, R.N, engraved by R? Page, published by Joyce Gold, 103 Shoe Lane, Fleet Street, 28 February 1811.

Tomlinson believes, he had the honour to set the example in the late war (at least in Europe), by cutting out a lugger, in a single boat, in open day light, while lying within pistol-shot of a battery, with the adjoining sand hills covered with soldiers.' He was voted a piece of plate worth £50 by the Committee for Encouraging the Capture of French Privateers.

His troubles really began as a result of being promoted post captain, 'for rank', on 12 December 1796. This put him out of employment, and he was still unemployed in 1798, which brought him to the decision to fit out a privateer, the *Lord Hawke*. As the Admiralty did not approve of his commanding her, he hired a captain, and sailed in her as a passenger as far as Oporto. The *Appeal* continued:

> On this occasion, Captain Tomlinson, for the first time, incurred the displeasure of the Lords of the Admiralty, by the use of the private signals for the Channel fleet; and although his sole view was merely to prevent any of the English cruisers from running off their stations, by chasing the *Hawke*, which he knew to be a fast sailer, unnecessarily and without any advantage whatsoever; yet he himself has been ever ready to allow, that these reasons amount rather to an apology than a justification of his conduct.

In December 1798 he was struck off the navy list for this breach of protocol, and his appeal fell on deaf ears.

Whether in hope of ingratiating himself at the Admiralty, or simply from frustrated feelings of patriotism, in April 1801 he volunteered to serve under Admiral Sir Hyde Parker as a pilot during the Baltic campaign. He was one of those who laid the buoys which made possible Rear-Admiral Nelson's attack on the Danish line at Copenhagen, and he provided Parker with the local knowledge of Revel and Kronstadt which would have been invaluable had not Tsar Paul's assassination ended the new alliance between Russia and France. This activity served Tomlinson's purpose, and the king restored him to the navy list with the rank of post captain, dated from 22 September 1801.

He was then employed in the sea fencibles under Captain Philip Beaver at Malden, and remained there from July 1803 to 17 September 1806, when he was promoted to command of the South End district. He resigned in June 1809 when the Admiralty accepted his plan of operations for fireship attacks on the enemy shipping at Antwerp, but he would have been better advised staying at home. The Navy Board did not supply the required combustibles, and the fireship was wrecked. Tomlinson

employed himself in the destruction of the basin, arsenal and sea defences of Flushing, but the complaint he had made to the Navy Board backfired. The enquiry being conducted by parliament into the civil affairs of the navy may have been the real cause of their action, but it chose to issue a warrant for Tomlinson's arrest on the grounds that one of the vouchers for the 1795 repair at Dartmouth was a forgery. The *Appeal* was written as part of his defence against a truly Dickensian legal process which cost him at least £600.

He returned to commanding in the sea fencibles at Southend until they were broken up on 28 February 1810, when he went on the retired list. He died on 6 March 1847, aged eighty-two, in Newick Park, Sussex, with the rank of vice-admiral.

Lt: 23 March 1782
Cmdr: 29 November 1795
Capt: 22 September 1801
Superannuated R-Adm: 22 July 1830
Restored on the Active List
V-Adm: 23 November 1841

TOWRY

CAPTAIN GEORGE HENRY TOWRY's name became well known in the navy following a remarkable action which took place on 24 June 1795 off Minorca. When in command of *Dido* (28) and *Lowestoffe* (32) he encountered two considerably more powerful French frigates, *Minerve* (40) and *Artémise* (36). *Minerve* was so much heavier than *Dido* that her captain attempted to run her down, but Towry swerved in time, and hooked her bowsprit with his mizzen, both of which went by the board. While they were clearing away to renew their action, *Lowestoffe* came to *Dido*'s support, and dismasted *Minerve*. At that point *Artémise* fled, leaving her consort with no option but surrender. Nelson, for one, felt 'quite delighted at the event'. Nelson 2.48 Towry was put in command of the prize.

He was born on 4 March 1767, the son of George Philipps Towry, who was a commissioner of victualling. His mother's name is not known. He was sent to school at Eton, and joined the navy in June 1782 in *Alexander* as a captain's servant under Lord Longford. He was present at the relief of Gibraltar under Lord Howe, and served under the command of Captains Anthony (?) Molloy, William Cornwallis, Edward Thornbrough and Prince William Henry in *Carnatic*, *Royal Charlotte* (100), *Europa* (50) and *Pegasus* (28). These were all valuable patrons. Towry was commissioned lieutenant on 23 October 1790, and at the request of Lord Hood he was appointed to *Victory* (100) shortly after the outbreak of war in February 1793. After serving with him in the Mediterranean, Hood promoted him commander on 14 September 1793 and posted him to *Dido* on 18 June 1794.

After his triumphant action, he was not long left in command of his prize, *La Minerve*. In April 1796 Sir John Jervis moved him to *Diadem* (64), in which he served under Commodore Nelson, who flew his broad pendant on board during the evacuation from Corsica in October. Towry fought in the battle of Cape St Vincent on 14 February 1797, and returned late in the year to England, where he was appointed in December 1798 to command *Uranie* (38), later being transferred to *Cambrian* (32). During the peace he was ashore, and like so many sailors took the opportunity to get married, uniting with Elizabeth, elder daughter of Captain George Chamberlayne. The couple had a son, who survived childhood. Following the renewal of the war, in July 1803, he was appointed to a powerful new 18-pounder frigate, *Tribune* (36), in which he served in the Channel until January 1804, when he had to take sick-leave. He was appointed to command the yacht *Royal Charlotte*, and was later made a commissioner for the transport service. At some time he also served as deputy chairman of the Victualling Board. But he retired in 1806, possibly because of the death of his wife, and he died when aged forty-two, on 9 April 1809. He was buried at St Marylebone.

Lt: 23 October 1790
M-C: 14 September 1793
Capt: 18 June 1794

TROLLOPE

ADMIRAL SIR HENRY TROLLOPE, GCB, is known for a remarkable action in a single ship against a French squadron, which proved the value of carronades for main armament.

He was born on 20 April 1756 in Bucklebury, Berkshire, the second son of the Revd John Trollope and his first wife. He entered the navy in April 1771 as a midshipman in *Captain* (64), serving in North America with Rear-Admiral John Montagu and later in *Asia* (74) under Captain George Vandeput. After only six and a half years in the service, he was commissioned lieutenant on 25 April 1777 in the *Bristol* (50), in which he returned to North America and was employed in the brigade of boats on the Hudson attempting to make contact with General Burgoyne. In April 1778 at his own request he was put in command of *Kite*, cutter, in the Channel, and he remained in her when promoted master and commander on 16 April 1779. He was made post on 4 June 1781 and appointed to *Myrmidon* (20), moving in February 1782 into *Rainbow* (44).

The prologue to Trollope's demonstration of the power of the carronade occurred on 4 September 1782, when he was off the Île de Batz. *Rainbow* was armed with forty-four carronades – 68-pounders on the gundeck, 42-pounders on the upper deck and 32-pounders on the quarterdeck – and was on the lookout for a convoy carrying naval stores under the escort of *La Hébé* (38). The French captain was game enough, but struck to *Rainbow* as soon as he discovered what weight of shot was being fired. Pleased with this success, Trollope was determined to try his luck with a ship of the line, and waited off Ferrol, hoping without success that one or more of the ships there would come out. He was so long waiting that it was assumed *Rainbow* was lost. *Hebe* was subsequently purchased for the navy, and became the model for a long series of frigates, two of which, *Unicorn* and *Trincomalee*, are still in existence.

Trollope married in 1782 Fanny Best, a native of London, who had been educated in Brussels. The couple had no children, but during most of the peace lived the good life in rural Wales, where they acquired a castle near the sea. During the crises of 1789 and 1790 he was employed, taking command of *La Prudente* (36) in the Channel on June 1789 and transferring in December to *Hussar* (28) for Mediterranean service, coming ashore in

January 1791. He did not return to sea until over two years after the French declaration of war on 1 February 1793.

In May 1795 Trollope was appointed to command the *Glatton,* which had been built with iron hanging knees for the India trade, and converted for naval use by arming her with fifty-four 68-pounder and 42-pounder carronades, using arrangements devised by Trollope and approved by Lord Spencer against the advice of the Navy

Sir Henry Trollope, Knt., Vice-Admiral of the Blue Squadron, engraved by H R Cook after Robert Bowyer, published by Joyce Gold, 103 Shoe Lane, 30 November 1807.

Board. On 16 July 1796, encountering in the North Sea a Dutch squadron of six frigates, a brig and a cutter, Trollope closed with them and ordered their commodore to strike his colours,

which he returned with a broadside, and I believe was well repaid by one from the *Glatton* within twenty yards; after which the action became general with the enemy's squadron, the two headmost of which had tacked, and one of the largest had placed herself alongside, and another on our

weather bow, and the sternmost had placed themselves on our lee quarter and stern. In this manner we were engaged on both sides for a few minutes, with our yard-arms nearly touching those of the enemy on each side; but I am happy to acquaint you, that in less than twenty minutes the weight of our fire had beat them off on all sides, but when we attempted to follow them, we, much to our regret, found it impossible.
NC 18.358

To Mr Wells, the constructor who had converted *Glatton* for naval purposes, he wrote that she was 'in every respect the best ship I ever was in'. For this action he was made a knight bachelor.

Following his success, for which he was richly rewarded by the London and Russia company merchants, and given the freedom of the boroughs of Yarmouth and Huntingdon, he made a cruise to the Shetlands and then started on leave while *Glatton* was given repairs. When it was learnt, however, that Cuxhaven was threatened by a French naval force he was recalled and put in command of *Leopard* (50) and four frigates. Within forty-eight hours he was in the Elbe, where he remained despite the dangers of ice until January 1797. When in May *Glatton*'s people heard of the mutiny at the Nore they mustered on deck and told Trollope that they must comply and sail to the Nore, although they said they had no complaint with any of their officers. Trollope was allowed to discuss the matter with Admiral Duncan, who agreed nothing could prevent *Glatton* sailing, but told Trollope that he must prevent her being taken to the Nore. While she was becalmed off Harwich there was nearly bloodshed, but in the end Trollope persuaded *Glatton*'s crew to submit. Trollope took her to the Downs. There he found the *Overyssel* (64) and the *Beaulieu* (50) in open mutiny, but *Glatton*'s crew did not flinch when he threatened to fire into the mutineers, and both ships agreed to return to rejoin Duncan's flag at the Texel.

Lord Spencer was so impressed by Trollope's conduct that he made him the questionable offer of appointment to command the *Russell* (74), which had been in the forefront of the mutiny at Spithead. Duncan made it clear that Trollope could refuse if he wanted, but the appointment was accepted and Trollope soon had the loyalty of his new crew.

The sequel was played out in the battle of Camperdown, five months later. In command of a small squadron, Trollope made the initial contact with the Dutch fleet under Admiral de Winter and delivered them to Admiral Duncan at Camperdown shoal on 11 October 1797. *Russell* was in Vice-Admiral Richard Onslow's division, opposite the *Delft* (56) in the line. Carrying out Duncan's tactical order to cut the Dutch line in line abreast, Trollope silenced the *Delft* and then went to the assistance of Onslow in *Monarch* (74), then engaged *Jupiter* (74), Admiral Reyntjes's flagship. After she surrendered, he passed on to take the *Wassenar* (64). *Russell*'s losses were light, as was often the case when a ship was well drilled and had a heavier armament, but her rigging was badly damaged. Trollope brought eleven prizes into Yarmouth. His brother, Lieutenant-Colonel Thomas Trollope, RM, commanded the marines on *Venerable* (74) in the battle. A half-brother had been killed near Camperdown a month before.

Following the battle, he and Duncan's other captains, were presented with gold medals, and when King George came downriver in the *Queen Charlotte,* yacht, to visit the fleet at the Nore, Trollope was at the wheel. The review had to be cancelled because of strong adverse winds, but before George went ashore at Greenwich, he created Trollope a knight banneret. Or he thought he did, but the privy council later decided it was an order which could be invested only on the field of battle or on the quarterdeck of a ship that took part in the action.

Trollope remained in command of *Russell*, but was transferred to the Channel fleet, where he was employed off Brest under the command of Lord Bridport. In June 1799 he was appointed to the prize taken at the battle of the Glorious First of June, *Juste* (80), but he quarrelled with the earl of St Vincent, Bridport's successor, over a verbal supplement to written orders. Trollope accused St Vincent of un-officer-like conduct. St Vincent, of course, took violent offence, and Trollope declined to serve under him. On the union of Ireland with Great Britain on 1 January 1801 there was a general promotion in which Trollope was promoted rear-admiral. St Vincent's appointment as first lord of the Admiralty, however, put Trollope's prospects to an end.

The *Naval Chronicle* asked:

> Why, in times of such active service as the present, so brave, and so able an officer should remain unemployed – unless it be from a want of personal interest – is a question, the solution of which we are unable to divine. Perhaps it would be well for the service, and for the nation at large, if, when fresh expeditions are fitting out, the Admiralty Board, disclaiming all feelings of partiality towards individuals, would refresh their memory by glancing over the Navy List. NC 18.344

Declining health, however, might have kept Trollope from accepting employment. His wife died in Bath in 1816, and, although he was nominated a KCB on 20 May 1820 and GCB on 19 May 1831, he became increasingly morose and paranoid until he blew his brains out on 2 November 1839, aged eighty-three, in Freshford near Bath.

Lt: 25 April 1777
M-C: 16 April 1779
Capt: 4 June 1781
R-Adm: 1 January 1801
V-Adm: 9 November 1805
Adm: 12 August 1812

TROUBRIDGE

REAR-ADMIRAL SIR THOMAS TROUBRIDGE, BARONET, was a fighting captain whose career in his early years was closely associated with that of Horatio Nelson. During the campaign leading to the battle of the Nile, Nelson wrote to the earl of St Vincent, 'Troubridge possesses my full confidence, and has been my honoured acquaintance of twenty-five years standing.' NC 23.24 St Vincent was equally enthusiastic, and Troubridge was to be his principal staff officer. But Troubridge lacked the mental strength to stand the strain of higher command when he had to deal with powerful men outside the navy and the alienation which occurred with Nelson following his seduction at Naples. The very humble circumstances of his birth may have been a factor. It was doubtless a result of his anger and impatience that he and the crews of two ships of war drowned in the Indian Ocean.

Sir Thomas Troubridge, Bart.,
Rear-Admiral of the White Squadron,
engraved by H R Cook after Samuel
Drummond, published by
Joyce Gold, 103 Shoe Lane, Fleet Street,
31 January 1810.

He was born in or about the year 1758, the only son of Richard Troubridge, an Irish baker of Temple Bar and of Cavendish Street, St Marylebone, London. His mother was Elizabeth, née Squinch, of Marylebone, afterwards Mrs Smith and Mrs Freame. He is believed to have first gone to sea as a cabin boy in a West Indiaman. Admiral Sir Charles Saunders took an interest in him, and he entered the navy on 8 October 1773 as an able seaman on board *Seahorse* (24) under the command of Captain Farmer. Nelson joined a few days later, and they served together in the East Indies

during a period when men were quickly tested. On 24 March 1774 he was rated midshipman, and on 25 July 1776 he was rated master's mate. He subsequently served in several different ships but returned to *Seahorse* on 1 January 1781 when Sir Edward Hughes commissioned him lieutenant. He fought in the battles of Sadras on 17 February 1782 and Trincomalee on 12 April 1782, following which Hughes moved him as junior lieutenant into *Superb* (74), a ship in which he had previously served. In that capacity Troubridge fought in Hughes's third and fourth actions against the French. On 10 October 1782 he was advanced to first lieutenant of the *Superb,* and on the 11th he was promoted commander of *Lizard* (10). Hughes made him flag captain of *Sultan* (74) on 1 January 1783, less than ten years after he joined *Seahorse.*

On his return to England he married on 20 December 1787 Frances, daughter of Captain John Northall and widow of Governor Richardson. His wife lived only until 13 June 1798, before which she gave birth to a son, the future Rear-Admiral Sir Edward Thomas Troubridge, and a daughter.

At the time of the Nootka Sound crisis in 1790 he was put in command of *Thames* (32) and served for two years in the East Indies under Commodore the Honourable William Cornwallis. The French declaration of war in February 1793 found Troubridge commanding *Castor* (32), and on 10 May he had the ill fortune to be captured by a division of the Brest fleet while escorting a convoy to Newfoundland. He was on board *Sans Pareil* (80) as a prisoner when she was captured during the battle of the Glorious First of June. After she surrendered, he took charge of effecting necessary repairs, and brought her into Spithead.

He was then put in command of *Culloden* (74), and after working for a while in Gibraltar convoys, served in the Mediterranean fleet under Admiral Jervis. He and Nelson were employed in watching the Toulon approaches, and Troubridge made a very positive impression on his chief. That impression was further strengthened at the battle of Cape St Vincent on 14 February 1797, when *Culloden* led the British line.

Troubridge anticipated Jervis's order to tack in succession to divide the Spanish fleet, bringing *Culloden* about as the signal flags conveying the order were cracking out.

In the July attempt to seize a galleon at Santa Cruz de Tenerife, Nelson, now a rear-admiral, put Troubridge in command of the initial landing attempt, which was frustrated by currents and had to be cancelled. In the landing the following night, Nelson's wounding left Troubridge in command of the survivors who managed to get into the town. He was obliged to ask for a capitulation from the governor. The British were permitted to retire without their arms on condition that they did not make another attempt on the islands, but contemporary hype translated this into an act of bravado in which Troubridge remained in control of events.

At the battle of the Nile on 1 August 1798 *Culloden* ran aground cutting a corner into the anchorage where the French fleet lay, and missed the action, although Troubridge sent men to support the other ships. Adding to his distress was the news received soon after the battle that his wife had died. At the strongly stated requests made by Nelson and Jervis, who was now earl of St Vincent, he was given a Nile gold medal. The convention that the first lieutenants be promoted following a major engagement was also extended to *Culloden*.

Following Troubridge's return to Palermo, and the repair of *Culloden*, he was employed in the reconquest of Naples. The *Naval Chronicle* noted:

> The arduous nature of the service in which Captain Troubridge was now employed, can be conceived only by those who were present, and who participated with him in its toils and fatigues. All the principal traitors and Jacobins that were taken in the island were secured and distributed amongst the ships of his squadron, to await the punishment due to their crimes. Captain Troubridge solicited the presence of a Neapolitan judge, to try the offenders; but it seemed to be the wish of the imbecile ministry, to cast the odium of every execution upon the English. NC 23.24

He was then employed in the reduction of Fort St Elmo and in taking possession of Roman territory after the withdrawal of the French army, after which he was put in charge of the blockade of Malta. His feeling about the callousness of the Sicilian monarchy, in failing to supply the basic needs of the people in the liberated territories and in Malta, added to Troubridge's growing anger, which he also expressed in writing to his brother officers. His investment by His Sicilian Majesty in the order of St Ferdinand and of Merit was no redress. He was also invested an English baronet on 30 November 1799, and in May 1800 *Culloden* was ordered back to England. Troubridge left deeply unhappy about Nelson's obsession with the Sicilian court and Lady Hamilton, but was gratified when Nelson persuaded the Neapolitan government to pay him an annuity of £500.

Three weeks after he returned home, apparently in desperate need of a rest, he was serving with St Vincent in the Channel fleet, where he supported the work of his chief to introduce the more stringent standards of discipline from the Mediterranean. He was made colonel of the marines on 1 January 1801, and when St Vincent was appointed first lord of the Admiralty by Addington on 19 February 1801, he took Troubridge with him to support him on the Board. As an Admiralty commissioner he had a share in the decisions to employ Nelson in the defences against invasion, and then under Sir Hyde Parker at Copenhagen. Nelson suspected that he was being deliberately kept at a distance from Lady Hamilton. He became increasingly vicious in his letters, and brought his friendship to an end. Troubridge was no less unbalanced in his secondment of St Vincent's witch hunt for embezzlers in the navy's civil affairs. His entrance into politics, as member of parliament for Great Yarmouth from 1802 to 1806, was brought about by St Vincent to forward the business of reform. Troubridge, however, did not have the temperament for politics, and wisely took little part.

Troubridge was promoted rear-admiral on 23 April 1804, but on Pitt's return to power he was out of a job at the Admiralty, leaving the Board on 15 May. A hint to Nelson that he would like to be at sea was ignored. In April 1805, however, he was appointed by the new administration commander-in-chief of the East Indies station eastward of Point de Galle on the south-west coast of Ceylon (Sri Lanka). This may have been occasioned by Addington's decision to join Pitt, on condition that employment was found for the members of St Vincent's board. But it is very likely that another reason for creating this new, and divided, command was to express Pitt's dislike of Sir Edward Pellew, who had previously been appointed by St Vincent to command the entire East Indies station.

Troubridge hoisted his flag in *Blenheim*, a worn-out three-decker cut down to a 74-gun ship. Off Madagascar he encountered a French squadron under Admiral Linois, who avoided action. For his part, Troubridge was unable to force one, owing to *Blenheim*'s poor sailing and because of the need to provide for the safety of a convoy in his charge.

Pellew objected bitterly to dividing his command, refused to do so, and appealed to the Admiralty, which changed its mind and appointed Troubridge to the Cape station. Impatient to leave India, Troubridge insisted on sailing in *Blenheim* for the Cape, possibly with the intention of returning to England and retirement. *Blenheim* had been aground at Sumatra and neither she nor the Dutch prize *Maria Reijersbergen*, which had been re-named *Java* (32), survived a cyclone which struck on 1 February 1807 *en route* to the Cape.

Lt: 1 January 1781
Capt: 1 January 1783
R-Adm: 23 April 1804

TUCKER

REAR-ADMIRAL THOMAS TUDOR TUCKER is known for the supporting part he played in the capture of USS *Essex* off Valparaiso on 28 March 1814.

He was born on 29 June 1775, the third of Frances and Henry Tucker's eight sons. She was the eldest daughter of George Bruere, governor of the Bermudas, and Henry was secretary of the Bermuda council. Thomas first went to sea with the East India Company, but after two voyages he entered the navy in 1793 as master's mate of the

Argo (44) under the command of Captain William Clark, with whom he also served in *Sampson* (64) and *Victorious* (74). In 1796 he served in *Monarch* (74) flying the flag of Vice-Admiral Sir George Keith Elphinstone at the Cape of Good Hope and in the East Indies. Continuing on the East India station, on 21 March 1796 he was appointed acting lieutenant of *Suffolk* (74), in which Rear-Admiral Peter Rainier was flying his flag. Subsequently he served in *Swift*, cutter, under Captain John Sprat Rainier, but was able to return to service with Captain Clarke again in *Victorious* between 1797 and 1799. When he left him, it was to join *Sceptre* (64) under the command of Captain Valentine Edwards. He was nearly drowned when she was wrecked in Table Bay on 5 November 1799.

He was informed that his commission had not been confirmed when he returned to London in May 1800, but he was then examined and given a commission dated the 20th. He was appointed in June to *Prince George* (98), in which he served in the Channel under the command of Captain James Walker, moving with him in August or September into *Prince* (90).

The peace put him out of work. On the renewal of the war he was appointed in June 1803 to *Northumberland* (74) flying the flag of Rear-Admiral Sir Alexander Cochrane, and served in her off Ferrol and in the West Indies, where he fought in the battle of San Domingo on 6 February 1806. After the action he was again given an acting rank, to command *Dolphin* (44), which was a post ship although reduced to serving as a store-ship, and then transferred to several other ships in West Indies service, with the Admiralty finally confirming him in the rank of commander on 15 February 1808. He was appointed to command *Epervier* (16), and almost immediately transferred to *Cherub* (18), in which he captured several enemy ships and assisted in the capture of Guadeloupe in February 1810. He remained in her until she was paid off in August 1815.

On 23 January 1811 he married Anne Byam Wyke, the eldest daughter of Daniel Hill of Antigua. The Tuckers were to have two sons and three daughters. He established such a strong reputation with Sir Francis Laforey, the commander-in-chief, that he persuaded the Admiralty to promote Tucker to post rank on 1 August 1811 while leaving him in command of *Cherub*.

In September 1812 he escorted a convoy to England, and there was ordered to refit *Cherub* for foreign service. It was remarkable that he permitted his crew to take leave, and that they all chose to return to the ship. He sailed for the Pacific coast of South America in December and rendezvoused with *Pheobe* at Juan Fernandez, Tucker coming under the command of Captain James Hillyar. *Cherub*'s main role in the capture of USS *Essex* was to watch the entrance to Valparaiso harbour. Of the battle itself, the *Naval Chronicle* remarked on *Essex*'s 'obstinate defence, attended by the destruction of more than half her crew. In this event,' it continued, 'owing to our superiority of force, we have nothing to boast, any farther than the smallness of our own loss, and the diminution of the enemy's naval resources.' NC 32.82 Tucker was one of the few casualties, being severely wounded but not prevented from bringing his ship home in August 1815, after which she was paid off.

He briefly commanded the American prize *Hannibal*, renamed *Andromeda* (24), when she was paying off at Woolwich in December 1815 and January 1816, and then moved to *Comus* (22) at Deptford and Northfleet, but after May 1816 he had no further employment. He was nominated CB on 4 July 1840, and died with the rank of rear-admiral on 20 July 1852 at Portman Square, London.

Lt : 20 May 1800
Cmdr: 15 February 1808
Capt: 1 August 1811
Retired R-Adm: 1 October 1846

TURNOR

CAPTAIN JOHN TURNOR came from humble origins, was propelled along a royal road to promotion and gained considerable wealth, but died young.

He was probably born in 1764, in Crugmaur, Llangoedmor, Cardiganshire, the third son of John Turnor and his wife, Margaret, née Gyon, of

The late Captain John Turnor, R.N.,
engraved by H R Cook after a family picture,
published by Joyce Gold,
103 Shoe Lane, Fleet Street,
31 December 1810.

Fynnawn Coranau, Pembrokeshire. He entered the navy on 8 December 1777 as an able seaman on board the *Fame* (74) commanded by Captain Colby. He was rated midshipman or master's mate on 31 December 1777, and established his reputation at the action off St George's Bay, Grenada, on 6 July 1779. While serving in *Preston* (50), Captain Alexander Graeme, he fought in the battle of the Dogger Bank on 5 August 1781. During the peace, having been introduced to Prince William Henry, later duke of Clarence, he transferred to the *Pegasus* (28) commanded by the prince, and sailed in her to North America. On 22 November 1790 (taking date from the 18th) he was appointed first lieutenant of *Camilla* (20).

With the French declaration of war in February 1793 he was appointed fourth lieutenant of *Robust* (74) commanded by Captain the Honourable George Keith Elphinstone, later Lord Keith, and with him saw service at Toulon. He was entrusted with the task of embarking the troops, being the last man to leave Toulon. He was fourth lieutenant of *Glory* (90) at the battle of the Glorious First of June in 1794, and third lieutenant of *Monarch* (74), Rear-Admiral Keith's flagship, in the expedition to the Cape of Good Hope. Respecting the duke's known preferences, Keith took the opportunity to promote Turnor commander in October 1795, and master of the *Star*. Later he was moved into *Echo* (14) and in her participated in the capture of Colombo, when his share of the prize money was more than £12,000. He was also at the capture of the Dutch fleet in Saldanha bay on 17 August 1796, which further increased his wealth and led to his being made post captain on 26 December 1796 in *Tromp* (54), a captured Dutch ship. He next served with Vice-Admiral Rainier in the East Indies, but while in command of *Trident* (64) on 1 January 1801 he died.

> Lt: 18 November 1790
> Cmdr: October 1795
> Capt: 26 December 1796

USSHER

REAR-ADMIRAL SIR THOMAS USSHER, CB, set such a high standard in coastal raiding that his example inspired Winston Churchill in the development of the commando forces of the Second World War.

He was born in 1779 in Dublin, the eldest son of the Revd Henry Ussher, senior fellow of Trinity College and astronomer royal of Ireland. His mother was Mary, née Burne. He entered the navy on 27 January 1791 as a midshipman in *Squirrel* (24) under the command of Captain William O'Brien Drury; on 19 September 1793 he joined *Invincible* (74), commanded by Captain Thomas Pakenham, and while serving in her he took part in the actions of 29 May and 1 June 1794. Pakenham assisted in the capture of *Le Juste,* and when he was given her to command, Ussher followed. On 14 October he joined *Prince George* (98) flying the flag of Rear-Admiral Sir Hugh Cloberry Christian, with whom he served in the West Indies, following him into *Glory* (90) on 21 November 1795 and *Thunderer* (74) on 11 March 1796.

When he had been in the navy only five years he was made acting lieutenant of the *Minotaur* (74) under Captain Louis on 7 May, and served in her,

and in a fir-built brig-sloop, *Pelican* (16), from 20 June, both afloat and ashore in the West Indies. His commission was eventually dated 17 July 1797. In April 1798 he was wounded and captured while trying to cut a privateer out of Cumberland Harbour (Guantanamo Bay, Cuba). While serving in *Pelican*, Ussher was engaged in more than twenty boat actions before he was appointed on 17 May 1799 third lieutenant of the fir-built 18-pounder frigate *Trent* (36), commanded by Captain Robert Waller Otway; he then continued to specialise in boat work. By the time he returned to England in 1801 he had accumulated so many wounds, in addition to being threatened with lockjaw, that he obtained a survey by the college of surgeons, who recommended him as having suffered the equivalent of the loss of a limb. Nevertheless, he was not pensioned until 1814.

Against the advice of the surgeons, he applied for another command, and was appointed on 11 June 1801 to *Nox,* cutter, attending on the king at Weymouth. But even contact with royalty did not lead to his being made post at the general promotion in April 1802. He moved on 26 September 1802 into a cutter, *Joseph* (12), and again on 16 April 1804 into *Colpoys,* brig. In October 1804 he undertook in a four-oared gig a reconnaissance into Brest harbour preparatory to a fireship attack, rowing the entire length of the twenty-one ships lying to moorings. The attack was cancelled at the last minute. Later he raided a signal station with only six men and captured the code book. *Colpoys* was then attached to the Mediterranean fleet, and Ussher continued his raiding work in that theatre, but in the summer of 1806 the exertion became more than he could endure. An old wound broke open, and he was obliged to give up command of his ship.

Admirals the earl of St Vincent, William Cornwallis and Thomas Graves each gave him strongly worded letters of recommendation, and the promise of command of an 18-gun sloop, *Redwing,* seems to have worked wonders on his health. He was appointed on 18 October 1806 and returned to the Mediterranean, where he was employed between Cadiz and Gibraltar escorting trade, for which he painted *Redwing* like a Portuguese merchantman. On one occasion he attempted to recapture a merchantman under tow by Spanish gunboats, towing *Redwing* until the coastal batteries forced him to disengage. Two hours later, riding on horseback in the neutral ground on the glacis of the battery, he encountered the Spanish commanding general, O'Reilly, who complimented him on his gallant conduct. In an action on 7 May 1808 he ordered that each of *Redwing*'s guns should be shotted with one round shot, one grape, one canister and a bag of 500 musket balls, and to ensure that this lethal cocktail was fired to most effect he lowered *Redwing*'s boarding net to encourage the enemy to close. The outcome was that he sank two schooners, drove two gun vessels and four merchantmen into heavy surf, and captured seven merchantmen and an armed mistico. This success finally sealed his promotion, and he was made post on 24 May 1808, but left in command of *Redwing*. With the end of the Spanish war he returned home for a much needed rest.

In March 1809 he was put in command of *Leyden* (64), which was to serve as mother ship for a flotilla of thirteen gunboats in the Kattegat, but the abdication of the king of Sweden prevented that operation, and *Leyden* was employed in the Scheldt operation, ferrying home sick soldiers. *Leyden* soon had to be taken out of service, and Ussher was on half pay until April 1811, when he was appointed to command *America* (74). This was a temporary command, and Ussher had to deal with a mutiny, which he did by ordering the captain of marines to bayonet any sailor who refused his duty.

He then took command on 20 May of a post sloop, *Hyacinth* (20), and returned to the Mediterranean. He found it impossible to disguise his ship to fool the privateers which were raiding the Gibraltar trade, and so obtained a flotilla of smaller craft, which he used to raid them at their moorings at Malaga. They were protected by a battery of fifteen long 24-pounder guns on the molehead. Ussher personally led an advance force which cleared the battery, turned the guns against the

Spanish fortress overlooking the harbour, and then signalled by rocket for the main attack to advance. The outcome was not entirely satisfactory, because the wind failed, making it difficult to bring away the prizes, and because of the large butcher's bill, but service opinion regarded it as a 'brilliant affair'. Another of Ussher's raids, following his transferral to command of *Euryalus* (32) on 17 November 1812, was right into the mouth of Marseilles harbour. To his surprise the French batteries suddenly ceased firing. He later learnt from the French governor that 'as he had dared to carry off a vessel lying under the muzzles of their guns, he was considered deserving of a better reward than being blown out of the water, and was therefore allowed to depart quietly with his well-earned trophy'. _{Marshall 3 (Supp) 352}

Ussher was left in command on the French coast in the winter of 1813–14, transferring on 14 February 1813 into the 18-pounder frigate *Undaunted* (38) and on 19 July 1814 into *Duncan* (74). Reportedly he was before Marseilles on 21 April 1814 when by the illumination of the town he concluded that the citizens were celebrating the abdication of Napoleon Buonaparte. He was at first rebuffed by a battery commander who opened fire, but later the mayor came off to apologise, and *Undaunted* was permitted to enter the harbour. Soon afterwards, Ussher was put in charge of conveying Buonaparte to his exile on the island of Elba.

Ussher was made a knight bachelor, and on 4 June 1815 was nominated a CB, with promotion to KCB on 12 April 1831. He married Elizabeth, daughter of Thomas Foster of Frove House, Buckinghamshire, and niece of Frederick William Foster, bishop of the Moravian church at Jamaica, West Indies. The couple had three sons and two daughters. Ussher was promoted rear-admiral on 9 November 1846, and died on 6 January 1848, aged sixty-eight.

Lt: 17 July 1797
Cmdr: 18 October 1806
Capt: 24 May 1808
R-Adm: 9 November 1846

VINCENT

CAPTAIN RICHARD BUDD VINCENT, CB, was described by the officers of *Arrow* as 'a most pleasant, mild, gentleman-like Commander, yet at the same time a strict officer; one of the best and ablest in the British navy. It is needless to mention his courage; that has already spoken for itself.' [NC 17.269]

He was born in 1770 in Newbury, Berkshire, son of Osman Vincent, who was a silk-merchant and banker. His brother John Paynter Vincent studied medicine and eventually became president of the Royal College of Surgeons, but Richard Budd entered the navy on 15 July 1781 as an admiral's servant, or volunteer, on board the *Britannia* (100) flying the flag of Vice-Admiral Barrington in the Channel fleet, and served in the relief of Gibraltar by Lord Howe and in the engagement with the Franco-Spanish fleet off Cape Spartel in October 1782. In 1783, following the end of the American war, he joined *Salisbury* (50) flying the flag of Vice-Admiral Campbell, commander-in-chief Newfoundland, and was successively rated able seaman and midshipman. In 1787 he joined the sloop *Trimmer* (14) under Captain Charles Tyler and served on the coast of Wales, and later that year he was transferred to *Pegasus* (28) commanded by Captain Marshal at Plymouth. He was serving in *Carnatic* (74) flying the broad pendant of Commodore Samuel Goodall at the time of the Nootka Sound crisis in 1790, and was transferred to the *Prince* (90) flying the flag of Rear-Admiral Jervis, who commissioned him lieutenant on 3 November 1790 and appointed him to *Wasp* sloop, Captain Thomas Lee, on 10 April 1791. On 22 December 1792 he was appointed third lieutenant of *Terrible* (74) commanded by Captain Skeffington Lutwidge, and he saw service in the squadron sent to the Mediterranean under Vice-Admiral Cosby in May 1793. He was at the occupation and evacuation of Toulon and the sieges in Corsica.

His prospects suffered when on 11 October 1794 he was taken into Admiral Lord Hood's flagship *Victory* (100) only to have Hood unexpectedly ordered to strike his flag at Spithead the following April, but on 5 May he was employed as second lieutenant of *Triumph* (74) commanded by Sir Erasmus Gower, and he was present at the famous fighting retreat of Admiral Cornwallis on 17 June 1795. During the mutiny in 1797 Vincent was for a time left in sole charge of *Triumph* and did his best to moderate the indiscipline of the ship's people. He rose to first lieutenant, but again his prospects were thwarted by the bad luck of leaving *Triumph* only a few days prior to the battle of Camperdown of 11 October 1797.

Captain Richard Budd Vincent,
engraved by H R Cook, published by
Joyce Gold, 103 Shoe Lane,
30 April 1807.

His new ship was the Dutch prize *Zealand* (64) serving as Admiral Lutwidge's flagship at the Nore, and Vincent had hope that he would be promoted, as was customary, when King George visited the fleet to view the Dutch prizes from Camperdown, but the visit was cancelled owing to the strong easterly wind, which prevented the royal yacht getting below Greenwich. Lutwidge transferred to another Dutch prize, *Overyssel* (64), on 23 May, with Vincent accompanying him, to take part in the invasion of the Netherlands. But Vincent's prospects were again to be disappointed when the Dutch fleet at the Texel surrendered without a fight.

He continued with Lutwidge when he transferred into the 18-pounder frigate *Amazon* (38) on 4 January 1802, and again into *St Albans* (64) on the 11th. Only on 29 April, with the general promotion which took place at the peace of Amiens, was Vincent promoted commander. He was then lucky with an appointment, on 17 May, to command *Arrow*, sloop, armed with twenty-eight 32-pounder carronades. She was built to an experimental design proposed by Sir Samuel Bentham, and proved unsuccessful for customs prevention work as her unusual appearance made her too recognisable. She also found it difficult to attract seamen, who distrusted novelties. Eventually she was paid off and recommissioned, and ordered on foreign service with a full complement drafted to her from the receiving ships, whereon Vincent sailed in July 1803 to the Mediterranean, Adriatic and Aegean. Lord Nelson wrote on 8 June 1804:

> I approve of the line of conduct you mean to pursue in the execution of your orders; and also of your correspondence with his Excellency, Mr. Stratton, our Minister at Constantinople, relative to the conduct of the Governor of the Castle on the European side, on entering the Dardanelles; and make no doubt that the Ottoman Government will sufficiently account for the conduct of the Castle's firing upon the *Arrow* and convoy, and make the necessary reparation to our Minister for the insult. [NC 17.269]

Eventually *Arrow* was found to be in need of major repairs, and on 2 January 1805 Vincent sailed from Malta for England, escorting a convoy. Vincent told the subsequent court martial:

> Early in the morning of the 3rd of February, per log, the *Dutchess of Rutland* transport, which had been missing some days, joined. The weather was then quite moderate, with light breezes from the N.E.

> At 8 A.M. I made the signal for the convoy to steer W. by N.; Cape Caxine in sight, bearing south; the *Acheron* [8 guns] and 32 sail in company.... At ten minutes past [4 P.M.], made the *Dutchess of Rutland*'s signal 'to lead the convoy, steering the same course, &c' and 'the convoy to follow her motions, thought the men of war acted otherwise.' At a quarter past, made the signal 'for the convoy to make all sail possible.' About one, I tacked to the northward, and shortened sail for the *Archeron* to close me. At a quarter past she made the signal 'the strange ships were enemies;' ditto, made the signal to the convoy 'that an enemy was in sight, to make all possible sail, and proceed to the appointed rendezvous;' which was enforced by several guns at different times, and repeated by the *Archeron* in the same manner; also by Lieutenant Coggan, Agent of transports, in the *Triad* brig bomb tender, which remained with the convoy.... [The next day] as the night had been very dark, I was anxious for daylight to ascertain the general position of the convoy, that I might act in the best manner for its defence; seeing the action was inevitable, without being able to get to my assistance the armed vessels as intended. The [enemy] frigates stood from us to the westward, and at dawn of day the wind being light and variable, their heads to the southward, I observed the headmost with French colours up, and she soon after hoisted a broad pendant at the main. At 6 I made the *Dutchess of Rutland*'s signal for 'action;' and the *Acheron*'s 'to close.' The former being the most effective ship of the convoy, probably would have been of service, had she immediately obeyed the signal and bore up, by the very appearance only of coming to my assistance; but she did not even answer it. I then made sail on the starboard tack, to get between the enemy and protect the rear of the convoy.

Vincent summed up:

> Though His Majesty's ships fell a sacrifice to superior force, I have no hesitation in believing the damage and delay caused to the enemy by this event, afforded the greater part of my charge time to effect their escape. And when I reflect that three vessels only were captured by them out of thirty-two sail, I cannot but express my admiration and thanks to the officers, crews, and passengers of His Majesty's ships *Arrow* and *Archeron*, for their zeal and courage in so unequal a contest…

Arrow's hull flared above the gunports, and with short guns, the blast set her on fire several times. When finally Vincent struck she was sinking so fast that there was barely time for the French to get her people out. *Archeron* performed a noble service in leading the enemy away from the convoy, before she struck, when the French found her so damaged that they set her on fire. *Dutchess of Rutland* was one of the ships captured, and her captain did not take care to destroy the convoy signal book, which was used a few days later to decoy a ship. Vincent and his men were then plundered by their captors, but were humanely treated by the Spaniards at Cartagena, and the officers were eventually exchanged, reaching England on 4 June 1805. Vincent was acquitted by the court martial, and on the following day, 8 April 1805, made post captain. The Patriotic Fund presented him with a sword valued at £100 and a piece of plate. Provision was also made for the ordinary sailors 'who have lost their own property in so resolutely defending that of others' with a fund of £477 10s.

Vincent married on 30 July 1805, in Droitwich, Worcestershire, Philippa, the youngest daughter of Captain Richard Norbury, RN. On 11 May 1806 he was appointed to command the 9-pounder frigate *Brilliant* (28) at Cork, but he resigned owing to ill health in October and was not re-employed until 1808, when on 12 April he was appointed first to *Cambrian* (32) in the Mediterranean, and then transferred on 1 July to *Hind* (28). But he did not stay long afloat. On 10 September he accepted Rear-Admiral Sir Alexander Ball's invitation to take charge of the port of Valletta as captain of *Trident* (64); he remained in this job under Ball's successors until 1815, when, after a brief period at sea in the 12-pounder frigate *Aquilon* (32), he returned to England and retired. He was invested KCB on 4 June 1815, and died on 18 August 1831, aged sixty-one.

Lt: 3 November 1790
Cmdr: 29 April 1802
Capt: 8 April 1805

WALDEGRAVE

ADMIRAL SIR WILLIAM WALDEGRAVE, BARON RADSTOCK, GCB, the second son of John, third earl of Waldegrave, and of his wife Elizabeth, sister of Granville Leveson Gower, first marquis of Stafford, could claim such social standing that he was formally appointed ambassador, albeit to the bey of Tunis. But his status does not in other respects appear to have cut him much slack with the navy.

He was born on 9 July 1753, and spent seven years at Eton before entering the navy on 17 May 1766 on board *Jersey* (60) commanded by Commodore Richard Spry, with whom he remained for three years in the Mediterranean. After serving in a succession of ships, he was in March 1774 appointed to the *Medway* (60), flagship of Vice-Admiral Robert Man commanding in the Mediterranean; Man promoted him master on 23 June 1775, and commander of *Zephyr* (10). He was made post captain on 30 May 1776 in *Rippon* (54), which proceeded to the East Indies station as flagship to Sir Edward Vernon, but Waldegrave found his health affected by the climate and returned to England in September. Perhaps he should have listened to his mother, who had given firm instructions that he should not be sent to the East Indies, but the navy put him in command of *Pomona* (28) as soon as he arrived home, under orders to the West Indies. There he had some success against American privateers, capturing the *Cumberland* in January 1779. He was subsequently transferred into the 12-pounder frigate *Prudente* (36) serving in the Channel fleet, and in July 1780, with the assistance of another 12-pounder frigate, *Licorne* (32), he captured a large French frigate, *Capricieuse*, after a four-hour battle, following which he had to burn his shattered prize. In April 1781 he made a good impression on Vice-Admiral George Darby during the relief of Gibraltar; in December he was at the capture by a squadron under Rear-Admiral Richard Kempenfelt of twenty sail of a French convoy in the Bay of Biscay; and in March 1782 he was put in command of *Phaeton*

The Right Honourable Lord Radstock,
Admiral of the Blue Squadron,
engraved by William Ridley after
James Northcote, RA, published by
Joyce Gold, 103 Shoe Lane, Fleet Street,
31 October 1803.

(38), in which he took part in Lord Howe's relief of Gibraltar in 1782.

During the peace he travelled, and in Smyrna he married on 28 December 1785 Cornelia, second daughter of David Van Lennep, Dutch consul-general and president of the Dutch Levant Company in Smyrna. Cornelia gave birth to three sons and six daughters.

At the outbreak of war Waldegrave was appointed to the *Courageux* (74) and served in the Mediterranean fleet under Lord Hood, who sent him home with dispatches following the occupation of Toulon. He travelled across Spain from Barcelona to Corunna, and thence by sea to Falmouth, returning to the Mediterranean by way of Germany with orders for Hood. He was promoted to rear-admiral on 4 July 1794, and returned home. In May 1795 he was briefly in command of a squadron in the Channel, but he was promoted to vice-admiral on 1 June 1795, and ordered to hoist his flag in *Barfleur* (90). Yet again he returned to the Mediterranean fleet, now under the command of Admiral Sir John Jervis, who ordered him to proceeded to Tunis with a squadron of five sail of the line to ensure the continuation of supplies for the fleet, to deny French cruisers the use of Tunisian harbours and to recover the British frigate *Nemesis* (28). This was both a naval and a diplomatic mission, and to strengthen his hand Sir Gilbert Elliot, earl of Minto and viceroy of Corsica, commissioned him ambassador to the court of Tunis. Eventually he achieved his latter objective by ordering Captain John Sutton on the night of 9 March 1796 to cut *Nemesis* and the French warships out of the bay, one of them being taken.

Waldegrave was not one of Jervis's favourites, but he was still serving with the Mediterranean fleet when on St Valentine's day 1797 the battle was fought off Cape St Vincent. In recognition of their parts in the action Vice-Admiral Charles Thompson and Rear-Admiral William Parker were created baronets, but Waldegrave refused the baronetcy he was offered as beneath his present status in the peerage as an earl's son. In November 1800, however, on his return after three years commanding in Newfoundland, he was created Baron Radstock on the Irish establishment. With his promotion to admiral on 29 April 1802 his opportunities for employment were limited.

He was made the first ever GCB on 2 January 1815. He was president of the Naval Charitable Society, and died on 20 August 1825, aged seventy-two. Cornelia died in 1839.

Lt: 1 August 1772
M-C: 1775
Capt: 30 May 1776
R-Adm: 4 July 1794
V-Adm: 1 June 1795
Adm: 29 April 1802

WALKER

REAR-ADMIRAL JAMES WALKER, CB, fought in the battles of Camperdown and Copenhagen, and was an intimate of Portuguese royalty.

He was born in 1764, a son of James Walker of Inverdovat, Fife. His mother was Mary Leslie, third daughter of Alexander Melville, fifth earl of Leven and Melville. He entered the navy on 18 December 1776 in *Southampton* (32) under the command of Captain William Garnier, and was rated midshipman in January 1777 before sailing to Jamaica. He returned for service in the North Sea and in the Channel fleet under Sir Charles Hardy during the crisis in 1779 when the combined Franco-Spanish fleet entered the Channel. In August, Garnier was succeeded by Captain Affleck, and *Southampton* returned to Jamaica, where in June 1781 Walker joined *Princess Royal* (98) flying the flag of Rear-Admiral Rowley; while serving on board he was ordered to act as lieutenant. He served in *Torbay* (74) in Sir Samuel Hood's engagements at St Kitts on 26 January 1782 and in the battle of the Saintes on 12 April. He was commissioned on 8 May 1783, and at the conclusion of peace travelled in Europe before returning to active service with an appointment on 11 September 1789 to *Champion* (24) under Captain Sampson Edwards, with whom he served at Leith. On 24 January he transferred to the 12-pounder frigate *Winchelsea* (32) under the command of Richard Fisher for Channel service, leaving her in February 1792 for nearly a year at home. On 2 December he was appointed to *Boyne* (98), and served in the escort of an East India Company convoy to the tropic of Capricorn. He remained with her until 24 June 1793, after the French declaration of war in February, when he joined *Niger* (32) under the command of Captain the Honourable Arthur Kaye Legge.

At the time of the battle of the Glorious First of June in 1794 he was signal lieutenant in *Niger*, which was employed as a repeating frigate, and in recognition of his services he was commissioned commander on 6 July 1794. Despite its being the early days of a war, he had to wait over a year for appointment, on 15 July 1795, to *Trusty*, sloop.

He almost immediately blotted his copybook in a serious way by violating his orders to return to Spithead, proceeding instead to Cadiz. As a result he was dismissed from the service on 26 September 1795 by the verdict of a court martial. His excuse was that he had heard of a convoy awaiting escort, and the reason for his conviction was probably the complaint made by the Spanish government that he had smuggled out of Cadiz a large quantity of money which was the property of English merchants. His justification was the imminent alliance between Spain and France, and following the Spanish declaration of war he was restored by order in council in March 1797 to the navy list. He recovered his standing at the Admiralty three months later during the Nore mutiny when he proposed using heavily armed gunboats against the mutineers, and was commissioned on 10 June to do so. But he had not proceeded further than Gravesend below London when word was received that the mutineers had submitted.

Following the collapse of the mutiny he was on 16 July put in command of the former *Sibyl* (28), renamed *Garland* in 1795, to escort a convoy to Elsinore. He transferred on 20 August to *Monmouth* (64) in the North Sea fleet under the command of Admiral Duncan, and this put him at the centre of the action with the Dutch at Camperdown shoal on 11 October 1797. It fell to his responsibility to engage the *Delft* and *Alkmaar*, both of which he compelled to surrender. 'My lads, you see your enemy,' he is reported to have declared to *Monmouth*'s people. 'I shall lay you close aboard and give you an opportunity of washing the stain off your characters in the blood of your foes. Now, go to your quarters and do your duty.' [Ralfe 4.160] In recognition of his service he was confirmed in his post rank on 17 October.

He took command of *Veteran* (64) on 8 February 1798, and transferred in rapid succession to *Draaknel*, *Prince George* (98), *Prince* (90) and *Isis* (50) on 7 October 1800. He served in the North Sea, the Skagerrak and the Baltic, and in the grand fleet in the Channel. He was still in *Isis* at the time of the battle of Copenhagen on 2 April 1801, and bore a heavy part of the action against two Danish block-ships and a 14-gun battery. Because of the temporary grounding of *Elephant* (74) flying Nelson's flag, *Isis* had to take on *Elephant's* intended opponent as well as her own, and when eventually Nelson was able to proceed along the line, he left *Isis* at her work and took another position. Nine officers and 103 men in *Isis* were killed or wounded in this action.

On 1 July, Walker obtained command of the 18-pounder frigate *Tartar* (32), with orders to convoy merchantmen to Jamaica. There on 27 January 1802, despite the drastic demobilisation ordered by St Vincent following the peace of Amiens, he received an Admiralty commission to command *Vanguard* (74). On the renewal of war he was employed in the blockade of San Domingo, when he captured *Creole* (44) and *Duquesne* (74), co-operated with the black generals Dessalines and Christophe, and obtained the surrender of the starving garrison at St Marc, which was glad to escape the vengeance of the blacks. On 2 March 1804 he was put in command of his prize, *Duquesne*, which he brought home from Jamaica to Chatham.

Walker was appointed on 1 March 1805 to *Thalia* (36), in which he escorted convoys to the East Indies and Newfoundland, before being employed in command of a small squadron based on Guernsey. In October 1807 he was transferred to *Bedford* (74), which was employed under Sir Sidney Smith in the escort of the Portuguese royal family to Brazil. Following a gale, *Bedford* was the only ship in close company with the Portuguese ships carrying the royal family. Walker remained in Rio de Janeiro for the next two years, became a confidant of the court, and was to be nominated by the prince regent on 30 April 1816 a knight commander of the Tower and Sword.

Bedford was employed in the blockade of Flushing, and in September 1814 Walker took command of a squadron carrying the advance guard of the force under the orders of Major-General Keane intended to occupy New Orleans. As Sir Alexander Cochrane and Rear-Admirals Pulteney Malcolm and Codrington all went ashore during the disastrous campaign, Walker was left with the heavy responsibility of managing a fleet, the large ships of which had to be kept a hundred miles offshore because of the shoal water.

In the summer of 1814 he was selected to accompany the duke of Clarence to Boulogne to collect the tsar of Russia and the king of Prussia. He continued in active service following the peace, commanding *Albion* (74) and *Queen* (90), until 10 September 1818, when he paid off *Northumberland* (74). He was nominated a CB on 4 June 1815, and promoted rear-admiral on 19 July 1821.

Little is known about Walker's private life but that he married a daughter of the Right Honourable General Sir John Irvine, KB, who was commander-in-chief in Ireland. The couple had no children, and after his wife died he remarried, but again without recording a date. His second wife was Priscilla Sarah, fourth daughter of Arnoldus Jones, afterwards Skelton, who was an army officer from Branthwaithe Hall, Cumberland, and member of parliament for Eye, Suffolk. Walker died on 13 July 1831, aged sixty-seven, in Blachington near Seaford, Sussex.

Lt: 8 May 1783
Cmdr: 6 July 1794
Capt: 17 October 1797
R-Adm: 19 July 1821

WARREN

ADMIRAL THE RIGHT HONOURABLE SIR JOHN BORLASE WARREN, BARONET, GCB, was almost a dilettante admiral, but despite a deficiency in seamanship, he proved to be an effective commander. In September 1798 he was to play an important part in keeping Ireland British.

Named John after his father, of whom little is known, he had been given birth by Bridget Borlase Warren, daughter and coheiress of Gervase Rosell of Radcliffe-upon-Trent, Nottinghamshire, on 2 September 1753 in Stapleford, Nottinghamshire. He was intended for the Church. He studied with the Revd John Prinsep in Bicester, enrolled in Winchester in 1768, and was admitted on 23 September 1769 as a fellow-commoner in Emmanuel College, Cambridge. He apparently stayed there until 1771, when the death of his elder brother led to his changing his plan of life. He was borne on the books of *Marlborough* (74), guard-ship in the Medway, on 24 April 1771, but con-tinued his studies, and at one point was entered as a deserter in the muster. He was rated on 9 April 1772 a midshipman in *Alderney*, sloop, and em-ployed in the customs prevention service, but con-tinued a part-time student and took his degree in 1773. He was discharged from *Alderney* by Admiralty order on 17 March 1774, and was elect-ed the parliamentary member for Great Marlow, Berkshire, in his own interest, which seat he held until 1784. On 1 June 1775, on the death of his father, the baronetcy was restored in him. In 1776 he took his master's degree and purchased Lundy Island in the Bristol Channel, and a yacht.

His extravagances were to make prize money important to him and on the outbreak of war in America he decided to take the navy a little more seriously. Between 1777 and the end of the war he was in active service. He was commissioned fourth lieutenant of *Nonsuch* (64) on 19 July 1778, dis-charged and returned home in October, appoint-ed in March 1779 to *Victory* (100), and commis-sioned master and commander on 5 August 1779 of *Helena*, sloop. In February 1781 he was moved to the *Merlin*, sloop, and he was made post cap-tain on 25 April 1781 with appointment to *Ariadne* (20). In March 1782 he was moved into the *Winchelsea* (32). With the coming of peace he went on half pay. Although on active service he offered himself for re-election at Great Marlow in 1780, which led to his experiencing financial difficulties, and his expenses were increased when he mar-ried on 12 December 1780 Caroline, daughter of Lieutenant-General Sir James John Clavering, KB.

During this period his continued interest in naval service was expressed by his accepting the office of vice-president of the Society for Improvement of Naval Architecture, and by his publication in 1791 of *A View of the Naval Force of Great Britain*. He urged the value of creating a naval reserve comparable to the French *inscription mar-itime* which would free the navy from dependence on the press gang in wartime. His political career was supposed to support his naval one, but failed to do so. However, his connections were strong.

He was appointed groom of the bedchamber to the duke of Clarence in 1787.

In 1793, following the outbreak of war, he was appointed to command the 18-pounder frigate *Flora* (32) flying the flag of Rear-Admiral John MacBride. Early in 1794 he was ordered to hoist a broad pendant as commodore, and take com-mand of a small squadron on the coast of France which was intended to track down a French squadron doing great damage to the trade. He brought it to action on 23 April and captured three of the four frigates, in recognition of which he was invested a knight bachelor on 30 May 1794. In

Sir John Borlase Warren, Bart., K.B.,
engraving by William Ridley after
John Opie, published by
Burney and Gold, Shoe Lane,
1 June 1800.

early 1795 he was ordered to support a royalist landing in Quiberon Bay, and then returned to his commerce raiding, capturing no fewer than 220 enemy sail in the Channel in 1796. The Patriotic Fund rewarded him with the presentation of a sword and 100 guineas.

In 1797 he was appointed to command *Canada* (74) serving in the Channel fleet. When command-ing a small squadron of three ships of the line and five frigates, he received intelligence of a French attempt to land soldiers on the north-west coast of Ireland. On 12 October he brought them to action, capturing the *Hoche* (84) and three of the eight frigates accompanying her, a further three being captured later. Warren reported:

> The enemy bore down and formed their line in close order upon the starboard tack; and from the length of the chace, and our ships being spread, it was impossible to close with them before seven A.M. when I made the *Robust*'s signal to lead, which was obeyed with much alacrity, and the rest of the Ships to form in succession in the rear of the van.
>
> The action commenced at twenty minutes past seven o'clock A.M. the Rosses bearing S.S.W. five leagues, and at eleven, the *Hoche*, after a gallant defence, struck; and the frigates made sail from us: the signal to pursue the enemy was made immediately, and in five hours afterwards three of the frigates hauled down their colours also; but they, as well as the *Hoche*, were obstinately defended, all of them being heavy frigates, and, as well as the Ship of the line, entirely new, full of troops and stores, with everything necessary for the establishment of their views and plans in Ireland. [NC 3.353]

Although the French had been heavily outgunned, this action made Warren very popular. He had been elected to the parliamentary seat for Nottingham on 11 November 1797, and he retained it until 1806. He was promoted rear-admiral on 14 February 1799 and in July put in command of *Téméraire* (98) in the Channel fleet, mostly serving off Brest. The following year he commanded a detached squadron in the Bay of Biscay, and later off Cadiz. In 1801 he was in the Mediterranean in support of the army in Egypt, one of his sons being killed in the landing, and later he was in charge of the western Mediterranean.

Following the peace of Amiens he was made a privy councillor, and sent as an ambassador to Russia to complement the accession of Tsar Alexander. He remained at his post on the renewal of war, although he would have preferred command of a cruiser, which might have restored his wealth. It fell to him to advise the tsar that Britain had no intention of letting him acquire Malta.

Returning to England in 1804, he was offered a seat on the Admiralty Board, but preferred service at sea. He was promoted vice-admiral on 9 November 1805, and in January 1806 hoisted his flag on the *Foudroyant* (80) in command of a small squadron of six other ships of the line ordered to cruise south and west of the Channel with orders to seek squadrons commanded by Admirals Leissègues and Willaumez that had escaped from Brest. More by good luck than by effective strategic judgement, he fell in with and captured *Marengo* (74) and *La Belle Poule*, frigate, homeward bound from the East Indies under the command of Admiral Linois. Apparently, the earl of St Vincent had little regard for Warren's capacity on detached service. Warren was ordered to sea again, but failed to intercept his prey, which did considerable damage to British trade.

Nevertheless Thomas Grenville, the first lord of the Admiralty, helped Warren to return to parliament on 23 March 1807 as member for Buckingham, although he held the seat for only a little over a month until the general election in May. And in October 1807 Warren succeeded Vice-Admiral George C Berkeley as commander-in-chief of the North American squadron based at Halifax. He was probably selected less for his abilities as a warrior than for his capacity as a diplomat, following Berkeley's injudicious orders to compel American warships to surrender British deserters. This had led to the engagement between HMS *Leopard* and USS *Chesapeake* off the Virginia Capes on 22 June 1807. Apart from the routine patrols by his cruisers, Warren also was involved in the construction of a permanent naval station at Bermuda.

At the end of his three-year term he was relieved, and promoted on 31 July 1810 to the rank of full admiral, but he was sent back to North America on the outbreak of war with the United States in 1812, with command extending from Jamaica and the Leeward Islands to Canada. He was criticised for the slowness with which he instituted a blockade of the American coast, but at the time there was some prospect that the New England states could be persuaded to secede from the union as they had no enthusiasm for Mr Madison's war. It was his strategy to use pressure on the southern United States to relieve that on Canada, where an American army had taken the offensive, but the execution of the strategy was to await Warren's replacement by a more aggressive admiral, Vice-Admiral Sir Alexander Cochrane. Warren's order in 1813 to hand over his command was justified by his rank being too high for the level of responsibility. He returned home in the spring of 1814.

He was invested a GCB on 2 January 1815, and a knight grand cross of the Guelphic order. He died on 27 February 1822, aged sixty-eight, at Stapleford Hall, Nottinghamshire, his wife surviving him to 28 December 1839.

Lt: 19 July 1778
M-C: 5 August 1779
Capt: 25 April 1781
R-Adm: 14 February 1799
V-Adm: 9 November 1805
Adm: 31 July 1810

WESTCOTT

CAPTAIN GEORGE BLAGDEN WESTCOTT was killed in action in command of *Majestic* (74) during the battle of the Nile on 1 August 1798. She was one of the last of the *ad hoc* line of battle to round Aboukir Point and get into action, by which time it was dark and difficult for Westcott to judge the best course to place her where she could deliver more fire than she received. She came up against the French *Heureux* (74) in a position where she had to endure heavy fire from her batteries and from the musketeers, one of whom killed Westcott by shooting him in the throat.

His date of birth is unknown, but he was baptised at Honiton on Otter, Devon, on 24 April 1753. His father was Benjamin Westcott, who may have been a baker. His mother's name was Susanna. He first joined the navy in 1768 on board *Solebay*

(28) under the command of Captain Lucius O'Bryen, where he was rated as master's mate, and later as able seaman and midshipman. He served as midshipman for three years in the *Albion* (74) under the command of Samuel Barrington and John Leveson-Gower, and he was commissioned lieutenant of *Valiant* (74) on 6 August 1777. He continued in her when Samuel Granston Goodall assumed command, and fought at the battle off Ushant on 27 July 1778. He was in the Channel fleet under Sir Charles Hardy in the crisis of 1779 when the Franco-Spanish fleet entered the Channel, and under Vice-Admiral George Darby at the relief of Gibraltar in April 1781. That November he was transferred into *Victory* (100), flying the flag of Rear-Admiral Kempenfelt during the attack on a French convoy on 12 December, and she was the flagship of Lord Howe in the 1782 relief of Gibraltar. He continued in employment during the greater part of the subsequent peace, serving in *Medway* (60) and as first lieutenant in *Salisbury* (50), Commodore John Elliot's flagship as commander-in-chief Newfoundland. After his promotion to commander on 1 December 1787 he was appointed to *Fortune*, sloop, and was promoted to post rank on 1 October 1790 during the Nootka Sound crisis. He was flag captain to Admiral Goodall in *London* (90) during the Russian mobilisation of 1791, and then went on half pay until September 1793, seven months after the declaration of war by the French Republic.

He fought in the battle of the Glorious First of June as flag captain to Rear-Admiral Benjamin Caldwell in *Impregnable* (90). He came to command *Majestic* (74) when Caldwell was transferred into her and sent to the West Indies. Sir John Laforey replaced Caldwell, but Westcott remained as flag captain of *Majestic*, and brought Laforey home to England in June 1796. Then *Majestic* became a private ship. In her he served in December in the Channel fleet off Brest under Admiral Colpoys; he was at Spithead during the mutiny in April and May 1797, and later in the year he joined St Vincent off Cadiz. *Majestic* was one of the ships he ordered to join Nelson in the Mediterranean to deal with the crisis caused by the naval and military armament at Toulon and in the western ports of Italy, which ended with the battle of the Nile and Westcott's death.

He was not one of Nelson's confidants prior to the battle, but Nelson made a point of asking his widow and daughter to breakfast with him in January 1801, and he gave her his own Nile medal. He also visited his mother, who was not well off. Somewhat condescendingly he wrote that 'had they been chimney-sweepers it was my duty to show them respect.' Gamlin 1.64

> Lt: 6 August 1777
> Cmdr: 1 December 1787
> Capt: 1 October 1790

WHITBY

CAPTAIN HENRY WHITBY played a sad part in the growing hostility between Britain and the United States, and was one of the heroes of the battle of Lissa in 1811, but died young.

He was born on 21 July 1781, the seventh and youngest son of the Revd Thomas Whitby of Creswell Hall, Staffordshire. His mother was wife Mabella, youngest daughter of John Turton of Angrave. He entered the navy in January 1795 as a midshipman on board *Excellent* (74), flagship of the Honourable Rear-Admiral Cornwallis, on which his brother, John Whitby, was flag captain. Reportedly he was confined to his hammock with measles on board *Royal Sovereign* (100), to which Cornwallis had transferred his flag, at the time of the celebrated retreat of 17 June, and only a direct order kept him from standing to his gun. Later he served on board *Alcmene* (32) under Sir Richard Strachan, then in a succession of ships, until he was commissioned lieutenant on 4 June 1799 and appointed to the *Prince George* (98) under the command of Sir Charles Cotton. He was a witness of the battle of the Nile from a frigate, and in April 1801 he was appointed to *Leviathan* (74) flying the flag of Rear-Admiral Duckworth commanding at Jamaica. Duckworth promoted him commander, and made him acting post captain of the *Proselyte* (32), but unfortunately Whitby ran her on a reef, she sank, and word of this misfortune reached the Admiralty before it had confirmed him in his rank.

He had the mortification of being sent back to *Leviathan*, but eventually Duckworth again promoted him commander on 28 April 1802, in *Pelican* (16), and made him post captain on 6 February 1804.

In the summer of 1805, when in command of *Centaur* (74) and under orders to join Nelson's

Captain Henry Whitby, R.N.,
engraved by R? Page, published by Joyce Gold,
Shoe Lane, Fleet Street, 31 October 1812.

squadron, he was struck by a hurricane which dismasted his ship, and capsized her. Eventually the wind diminished, and the ship righted itself, and was towed into Halifax. There he met Captain Inglefield, the resident commissioner, and soon was engaged to marry his daughter Catherine Dorothea.

In 1806 Whitby, then commanding *Leander* (50), was employed in trade control off the American coast, and was accused, probably falsely and for political reasons, of firing into an American coaster and killing a sailor. According to the *Naval Chronicle*, the American government

> demanded Captain Whitby from our government, to try him by their own laws, or to hang him at any rate without justice.

Nothing less than his life could satisfy their fury: and, can it be believed, that one of the cabinet of this country, the friend of liberty, and the rights of the British people, then high in office, and the peculiar protector of the heroes of the navy [*i.e.* the first lord of the admiralty, Lord Mulgrave], proposed, or gave it as his opinion, that the demand of the Americans should be acceded to? Can it be possible? NC 28.271

Instead Whitby was tried by a British court martial, which decisively acquitted him. Nevertheless, the United States government ordered the exclusion of British warships from American ports, and banned the sale to them of supplies. To placate the Americans, Whitby remained unemployed. Later, however, he obtained convincing proof that the man he was supposed to have killed could not have been a victim of a shot from *Leander*, and further that this fact was well known to the American government.

He was able to convince the Admiralty, and was appointed to command *Cerberus* (32) under orders to join the Baltic fleet commanded by Sir James Saumarez. His health, always precarious, was affected by the strain of service in the Baltic, and he was expected to die at sea. He did not, but on returning home he found his wife dying of tuberculosis, which carried her off on 17 January 1810.

There were no children to comfort Whitby, but he was able to persuade the Admiralty to send *Cerberus* to the warmer seas of the Mediterranean. On 13 March 1811 she formed part of a squadron of four frigates under Commodore Hoste which engaged a French squadron of six frigates and some small craft off Lissa. It was a famous victory, and a hard-fought one. *Cerberus*, fifty men short of her complement of 254 at the beginning of the action, lost a further eighty dead and wounded. Of Whitby's performance, a brother officer wrote: 'He was an ornament to his profession, an honour to all who knew him; and, had it pleased the Almighty to have restored him once again, it would not have been long before he would have stood one of the very first, and most conspicuous characters that

grace our annals.' On his return to England he was feted by the mayor and corporation of Stafford, and he was presented with a gold medal by the Admiralty, which also appointed him to a new 18-pounder frigate, the *Briton* (38). But his health deserted him, and he lived only to see her commissioned, dying on 5 May 1812, aged thirty.

Lt: 4 June 1799
Cmdr: 28 April 1802
Capt: 6 February 1804

WHITSHED

ADMIRAL OF THE FLEET SIR JAMES HAWKINS WHITSHED, BARONET, GCB, is perhaps most interesting for the manner in which he lived between the conclusion of the American war and the French declaration of war in February 1793. There is no record that he had even been to school prior to his entering the navy in 1774 in *Kent* (74) under the command of Captain Charles Fielding, but when the war was over he decided to attend lectures on astronomy at Oxford University. In 1789 he travelled with a friend, Vice-Admiral William Bentinck, through the Netherlands to Hamburg and Lübeck, Revel, where they went to sea with the Russian squadron, St Petersburg and Copenhagen. In Copenhagen they resided for some time before returning to England via The Hague. Hawkins then visited Paris to witness the events of the French Revolution, following which he and Bentinck built a small yacht in which they sailed by way of the Texel and Friesland to Hamburg. This experience was no doubt important in securing for Hawkins a command in 1791 in the fleet planned for Baltic service, but it did not in the end sail. On 11 December 1791 he married Sophia Henrietta, Bentinck's sister, and assumed the additional surname of Whitshed. The couple had two sons and four daughters.

He had been born in 1762 in county Louth, the third son of the Right Revd Dr James Hawkins, bishop of Raphoe, and his wife Catherine, née Keene. The vicissitudes of naval life may explain his interest in academic study. On his first cruise an accident happened when a burning wad from a cannon firing a salute blew back on board and, exploding badly stored gunpowder on the poop, killed and wounded forty-two men. He then sailed to the Newfoundland station, where, while serving in *Canada*, schooner, the anchor dragged in a storm and she quickly broke to pieces on the rocks. He was given an acting commission as lieutenant in *Rainbow* (44), commanded by Sir George Collier at Halifax, but when Admiral Byron arrived at Halifax with sickly crews, *Rainbow* was stripped of men, and Whitshed reverted to the lower deck.

James Hawkins Whitshed, Esq.,
Vice Admiral of the Red Squadron,
engraved by H R Cook after James Northcote, RA,
published by Joyce Gold,
103 Shoe Lane, Fleet Street,
30 November 1809.

However, his commission had been confirmed by the Admiralty on 4 September 1778, and eventually he was appointed to the 18-pounder frigate *Amazon* (36). At the end of 1779 he was transferred into Sir George Rodney's flagship, *Sandwich* (90), and at Gibraltar on 10 February 1780 he was promoted by him master and commander of a purchased vessel, which he took to the West Indies with Rodney, and was there made post captain on 18 April 1780 in *Deal Castle* (20). That ship remained in the Indies during the hurricane season,

and was cast away on Porto Rico. After surviving yellow fever and his court martial, he continued in active service for the rest of that war.

On the outbreak of war in 1793, Whitshed was appointed to command *Arrogant* (74), and then was moved into *Namur* (90) fitting for foreign service. In 1796 he served in the Channel fleet, and in January 1797 he sailed with Rear-Admiral Parker to join Sir John Jervis in time to take part in the action on St Valentine's day, 14 February 1797, off Cape St Vincent. On his return to England he was transferred to *Formidable* (98), in which in remained in command until he was promoted rear-admiral on 14 February 1799. He hoisted his flag in *Queen Charlotte* (100), served under the earl of St Vincent, returned to the Channel fleet in *Barfleur* (90), then shifted his flag into *Téméraire* (98), in which he remained until July 1801, when he succeeded Sir William Parker in command of the Halifax station.

He resigned during the peace of Amiens, but following the resumption of hostilities he was sent to Ireland to organise its naval defences. In the spring of 1807 he succeeded Lord Gardner in command of the Irish station, and he remained in that command for three years. He was promoted to a full admiral on 31 July 1810, and retired from active service. On 2 January 1815 he was nominated KCB, and he continued to receive honours, on 17 November 1830 being nominated GCB and on 16 May 1834 being made a baronet. He died on 28 October 1849, aged eighty-seven, in St Marylebone, London, his wife surviving him to 20 January 1852.

Lt:	4 September 1778
M-C:	10 February 1780
Capt:	18 April 1780
R-Adm:	14 February 1799
V-Adm:	23 April 1804
Adm:	31 July 1810

WILLIAMS

ADMIRAL SIR THOMAS WILLIAMS, GCB, had a long and distinguished career. He never took part in a major naval battle, but was credited with several sharp actions while in command of frigates. He may be best known for the period when he was in command of *Endymion*, a 40-gun frigate that was armed with 24-pounders, while attached to the North Sea fleet under Lord Duncan in October 1797.

He was born in 1762, son of Captain William Williams, RN, who placed his name as captain's servant on the books of all the ships he commanded from 1770 to 1776, the last being the 9-pounder frigate *Active* (28) in Sir Peter Parker's squadron. On this ship Thomas is actually supposed to have served, and no doubt in recognition of his six years of fictional service, he was now rated a midshipman. He immediately saw action of the most desperate kind, *Active* being the lead ship in the attack on the fort at Sullivan's Island near Charlestown. He continued to be strenuously employed throughout the American war. In 1777 he joined *Prince of Wales* (74) under the command of the Honourable Captain Samuel Barrington, which was a Plymouth guardship but was fitted for service in the West Indies following the French intervention in the rebellion. He was commissioned lieutenant on 8 December 1779 and appointed to *America* (64) under the command of Captain Samuel Thompson, and served on the North American station. From May 1781 to May 1783 he served in *Assurance* (44) under Captain William Twiney, and then, having been promoted master and commander on 15 April 1783, he was appointed in May to *Rhinoceros* (10), in which he continued in the American station until March 1784.

He was then out of employment for five years during the peace until June 1789, when he was appointed to *Otter* (10) and served in the North Sea. He was promoted post captain on 22 November 1790, but then had to wait for employment until 1792, when he was appointed to *Lizard* on the coast of Portugal and in the North Sea. In December 1792 he married Jane, daughter of Edward and Jane Cooper, and a cousin of the novelist Jane Austen.

On the outbreak of war on 1 February 1793 he served in the transport to the Netherlands of three battalions of the guards. In 1794 he was appointed to command *Daedalus* (32), and in the winter of 1795 he brought home from the Ems the sick from British forces in Germany, dealing with

river ice and the enemy, who controlled one bank of the river. In recognition of his service he was transferred in July into *Unicorn* (38) stationed on the coast of Ireland. On 8 June 1795, with *Santa Margaretta* under his command, he encountered two French frigates and a corvette, which the two ships engaged, capturing both frigates, including the *Tribune* (44) commanded by an American, Commodore Moulston. In January 1796 when the Brest fleet sailed to Bantry Bay with an invasion force, Williams carried the intelligence to Vice-Admiral Robert Kingsmill at Cork, and then captured a large flute carrying 450 French hussars and a cargo of military stores, which prize he managed to get out of the centre of the French fleet. He was nominated a knight bachelor on 13 July 1796.

Williams, having been put in command of *Endymion* in April 1797, was attached to the North Seas fleet on 12 October 1797, the day following the battle of Camperdown. When close off the coast of the Netherlands, he encountered a Dutch 74-gun ship, *Brutus*, anchored close against the sand in a strong lee tide. It was possible for Williams to make only one pass, tacking across her bows to deliver two broadsides and with difficulty clearing her bowsprit. The next day when joined by the 18-pounder frigate *Beaulieu* (40) he prepared to make another attack, but *Brutus* cut her cable and crossed the bar into Goree, evidently having lightened ship by jettisoning her guns. The following day, Williams encountered *Jupiter* (74), which had been captured from the Dutch at the battle of Camperdown but was now in distress, dismasted and anchored on a lee shore in a hard gale. Williams stood by overnight, and then towed her into the Nore.

Williams then returned to the Irish station, at the request of Vice-Admiral Kingsmill. In August 1798 his wife died in the Isle of Wight, when a runaway dray horse threw her from her gig. He remarried in November 1800 in Salisbury, uniting with the eldest daughter of Charles Whapshare.

In February 1801 Williams was appointed to the *Vanguard* (74) and ordered to serve with the Baltic force being formed under Sir Hyde Parker and Horatio Nelson, remaining there under Sir Charles

Pole after the battle of Copenhagen, and then join-ing the force blockading Cadiz. After the renew-al of the war in 1803 he was appointed in May 1804 to *Neptune* (98) but was soon obliged to go ashore for health reasons. He was given com-mand of the Gosport division of the sea fencibles, until he was well enough to be reappointed to the same ship in August 1807. He then served in the Channel fleet, and in the squadron under Sir John Duckworth sent to the West Indies in pursuit of a French squadron. In September 1808 he was sent back to the West Indies to strengthen Sir Alexander Cochrane's squadron.

He had been nominated colonel of marines on 28 April 1808, and was promoted rear-admiral on 25 October 1809. He hoisted his flag in *Venerable* (74) in May 1810, serving off the Scheldt under Sir Richard Strachan, and in September transferred his flag to *Hannibal* (74) as second in command of the Channel fleet. In October he was ordered to pro-ceed with a squadron to the Tagus to co-operate with Lord Wellington in the defence of the lines of Torres Vedras in front of Lisbon, and in the subsequent movement against the enemy. In October 1811 he was appointed commander-in-chief at the Nore, striking his flag on 30 November 1814.

He was nominated KCB on 2 January 1815 and GCB on 13 September 1831, and served as groom of the bedchamber to the duke of Sussex. His wife died on 17 December 1824 in Brighton, Sussex, and he died with the rank of admiral on 10 October 1841, aged seventy-nine, at Burwood House, Surrey.

Lt: 8 December 1779
M-C: 15 April 1783
Capt: 22 November 1790
R-Adm: 25 October 1809
V-Adm: 4 June 1814
Adm: 22 July 1830

WILLOUGHBY

REAR-ADMIRAL SIR NESBIT JOSIAH WILLOUGHBY, known as 'the immortal' to his men, was a fire-eater who lived at the edge. The hero of numerous desperate boat actions, he was also a quarrelsome subordinate and a shipboard tyrant.

He was born on 29 August 1777, the fifth son of Robert Willoughby of Cossall and Aspley Hall, Nottinghamshire, and of Kingsbury in Warwickshire, and his second wife Barbara, daugh-ter of James Bruce of Kinloch. He entered the navy in May 1790 as a volunteer in *Latona* (38) under the command of Captain Sir Albemarle Bertie, and served in a succession of ships at home prior to joining *Orpheus* (32) commanded by Captain Henry Newcome in February 1793, in which ship he served on the coast of west Africa and then in the East Indies.

His first boat action was in August 1795 during the capture of Malacca. He was at the capture of Amboyna and Banda, and after joining *Suffolk* (74), flagship of Rear-Admiral Peter Rainier, in November 1797, he was ordered on 13 January 1798 to act as lieutenant in *Victorious* (74). Her captain soon had him put under arrest for insub-ordination, and when the case came to trial a year later he was sentenced to be dismissed from his ship. For some reason, however, Admiral Rainier thought he should be given another chance, and the following day, 14 June 1799, he was appoint-ed to command *Amboyna*, brig. His health having suffered from his year's confinement in the trop-ics, he was invalided home, but during his passage in *Sceptre* (64) he volunteered to lead the ship's boats through a reef at Rodriguez to capture a French privateer. He was ashore when on 5 November *Sceptre* was wrecked in Table Bay with the loss of her captain and many of her crew.

On reaching England, and recovering his health, he was appointed in August 1800 to *Russell* (74), which was one of the ships commanded by Vice-Admiral Nelson at the battle of Copenhagen on 2 April 1801. Again Willoughby commanded the boats, taking possession of the Danish ship *Prøvesteenen* under heavy fire. *Russell*'s captain or-dered him to be cheered when he returned, but soon he was in trouble again, and had to face more charges of insubordination. He also brought charges against his captain, William Cuming, of tyranny and oppression, which were disposed of by the court before he was found guilty of insolence and con-tempt, and dismissed from the service.

Again he found an admiral willing to give him another chance. On the renewal of the war in 1803 Sir John Duckworth agreed to take him as a volunteer in his flagship to the West Indies, and on his recommendation Willoughby was restored to the navy list, with a commission as lieutenant dated 26 October 1803. Within a month he had demonstrated his value by negotiating the surrender of *Clorinde*, a French frigate which had run aground attempting to escape from Cap François, where the Haitian people, under the leadership of General Dessalines, were in the process of establishing their independence. As *Clorinde* was exposed to the batteries of the town when she went aground, Willoughby was only able to get her off by negotiation with Dessalines. In February 1804 he again established his value during the abortive attempt to capture Curaçao. He commanded a battery which was subjected to such strenuous attack, and exposed to such disease, that nearly the entire force died. A year later he returned to England with Duckworth, as first lieutenant of *Acasta* (40) under Captain Dunn. The intention to promote him on arrival in England was frustrated by the Admiralty's disapproval of Duckworth's removal of Captain Sir James Athol Wood from command. Duckworth, however, continued to employ him, and he served on board his flagship *Royal George* (100) in the Dardanelles and Marmora operations in 1807. Again, danger brought out the best in Willoughby, who on 14 February, when the *Ajax* was destroyed by fire, saved many lives at great risk to himself and to his boat's crew. After the contested passage of the straits, he was in the forefront of another boat action, in the Sea of Marmora, and was hit by two pistol shots, one of which lodged near his brain where it could not be extracted.

In July 1807 he was appointed to the ship-sloop *Otter* (16) under orders for Montevideo and the Cape of Good Hope. There on 10 January 1808 he was promoted to command *Otter*, the commission being confirmed by the Admiralty on 9 April, and employed under Captain Robert Corbet of the *Néréide* cruising off Mauritius, from there continuing to Bombay. Corbet's influence on Willoughby's leadership skills was anything but positive, and he

was again tried by court martial, this time on a charge of 'cruelty and unofficer-like conduct' following a complaint made by *Otter*'s people, 'one and all'. The evidence presented at the trial between 9 and 14 February was clearly against him. He bragged about enjoying punishments. But Corbet was one of the court, having been acquitted of a similar charge the previous day. Willoughby was also acquitted, with a recommendation 'to adopt more moderate language on future occasions'.[ADM 1/135] On 14 August he commanded *Otter*'s boats in cutting out a ship anchored under the batteries at Black River on Isle de France (Mauritius), and on 21 September he commanded the seamen who were landed at Saint-Paul on Isle Napoleon (Bourbon) to destroy the French cruising squadron and the port batteries.

He was then promoted by Rear-Admiral Albemarle Bertie to command *Néréide* (36), although his post commission was not confirmed until 5 September 1810 following a series of desperate actions. He charged the French batteries at Jacotel in full dress uniform on 30 April; he was nearly killed on 15 June when a musket burst, shattering his jaw and laying bare his windpipe; and he was still swathed in bandages when he landed the troops which captured Isle Napoleon on 7 July. On 10 August, following the capture of Isle de la Passe at the entrance to Grand Port, Isle de France, by a squadron commanded by Captain Sir Samuel Pym, Willoughby was left in possession when Pym sailed around to Port Louis. On the 20th a French squadron arrived, and Willoughby lured them with French flags into the harbour in order to prevent them surprising Pym. Once in with a following wind, they did not try to extract themselves under fire, and moored close to the shore where they were protected by reefs. Willoughby sent a warning to Pym who returned in *Sirius* (36) on the 22nd. What followed was the only naval victory for the French recorded on the Arc de Triomphe. Willoughby signalled to Pym 'Ready for action' and added, incorrectly, 'Enemy of inferior force'. His court martial was later to characterise this latter as 'injudicious'. Fortunately, *Sirius* ran aground, and the attack could not be made until the following day, when the remaining two frigates under Pym's command arrived. At 4pm on the 23rd, Willoughby, knowing the harbour, led in *Néréide*, but the others did not follow closely enough. Two ran aground and were lost, and his was the only ship to reach its firing position. He was heavily outgunned, and after an action of three and a quarter hours he was obliged to strike his colours, by which time it was so dark that the French continued firing all night. The butcher's bill was ninety-two killed and 137 wounded, including Willoughby, who was injured by a splinter from her fir gunwales which tore out an eye.

He was freed when Isle de France was captured in December, and exonerated by a court martial. On 4 October 1811 he was awarded a pension of £300, which was increased on 1 July 1815 to £550. He was not considered fit for employment, but this was by no means the end of his adventures. He made his way to the Baltic, where he offered his services to Sir Thomas Byam Martin, and when rejected he continued to St Petersburg, where his offer to serve with the Russian army was accepted. In September 1812 he was made prisoner by French hussars, and despite making a friend amongst his captors, he suffered terribly in the retreat of the French army. The tsar made a personal appeal on his behalf, but Napoleon refused to exchange him, and confined him as a secret prisoner in the Château de Bouillon. He remained there for nine months until he was moved to Péronne ahead of the advancing allied army, and managed to escape.

Apart from his increased pension, he was rewarded on 4 January 1815 for his services and suffering with nomination as CB. He was also able to return to active service, commanding from 1818 to 1822 the 18-pounder frigate *Tribune* (36) on the coast of Ireland and in the West Indies. Later he was knighted, twice, on 30 June 1827 at the request of the duke of Clarence, then lord high admiral, and on 21 August 1832 again by the king when he was nominated a KCH. A good-service pension was awarded on 14 January 1839, and on 30 November 1841 he was appointed a naval aide-de-camp to the queen. He died on 19 May 1849, unmarried and with the rank of rear-admiral, at his house in Montagu Street, Portman Square, London.

Lt: 13 January 1798
Dismissed the service: 23 June 1801
Restored in 1803, by Order in Council
Seniority: 26 October 1803
Cmdr: 9 April 1808
Capt: 5 September 1810
R-Adm: 28 April 1847

WOOD

REAR-ADMIRAL SIR JAMES ATHOL WOOD, CB, is best known for his disastrous encounter with the naval hierarchy when Admiral Duckworth decided to relieve him of command of *Acasta* (40) in the West Indies, so that he could convey himself, and a great deal of illegal cargo, back to England with one of his own captains, Richard Dalling Dunn. That disappointment was by no means the first in Wood's life, nor was it to be the last.

He had been born in 1756, the third son of Alexander Wood of Burncroft, Perthshire, and his wife Jean, daughter of Robert Ramsay of Banff. His name may have been entered in the muster of a ship of war in 1772, but he started his sea career on board an East India Company ship, and entered the navy only in August or September 1774 as an able seaman in *Hunter*, sloop, serving on the Irish station and in the defence of Quebec. He was rated a master's mate when in June or July 1776 he joined *Barfleur* (90) in home waters flying the flag of Vice-Admiral Sir James Douglas and under the command of Captain Mark Milbanke. Wood followed him in April 1777 to *Princess Royal* (98), in which in succession Sir Thomas Pye and Admiral John Byron flew their flags. On 15 February 1778 Wood was made acting lieutenant in *Asia* (74) under the command of Captain Vandeput, and he served in her in the Bay of Biscay until the end of April or early May. He was then ashore for some five months until his commission was confirmed on 18 October, when he was appointed to *Renown* (50) under Captain George Dawson, and served in her in the American theatre until February 1780, reportedly rising to being her first lieutenant. He subsequently served ashore at the siege of

Charlestown in 1780; then returned to England in *Squirrel* (24); joined *Juno* (32) in September or October 1781 under Captain James Montagu, with whom he served on the coast of Portugal; and in November joined *Anson* (64) for service in the West Indies under a succession of captains. He was second lieutenant in *Anson* at the battle of the Saintes on 12 April 1782, succeeding as first lieutenant when Captain William Blair was killed.

Following the conclusion of the peace of Paris in 1763, Wood spent several years in France, where it was cheaper to live, and developed a friendship

Captain Sir James Athol Wood, R.N., engraved by H R Cook after a family picture, published by Joyce Gold, 103 Shoe Lane, Fleet Street, 30 September 1810.

with the Comte de la Tour du Pin, one of France's foremost sailors. In 1787 he visited a brother in India, and purchased a ship to enter into the country trade, but soon was obliged by poor health to return in her to England. At Cape Coast Castle a British privateer seized his ship, put him and all the ship's officers on shore, and took it to Barbados, where it was condemned. Wood followed when he could, and obtained an annulment in the Court of Admiralty, but recovered little of his property.

However, as Britain and France were again at war, he offered his services to Sir John Jervis, and in December 1793 or January 1794 was appointed a lieutenant in *Boyne* (98), Jervis's flagship.

He was almost immediately transferred by Jervis to *Six Brothers*, transport, in command of a fleet of cartel ships carrying prisoners from Martinique home to France. Unfortunately he arrived at St Malo during Robespierre's reign of terror, and Wood and all his officers were thrown into prison without his friends being able to discover his fate. He was released from the Abbaye prison in April or May 1795, and managed to obtain the release of other British in the same situation. On his return to England he was promoted commander, on 8 July 1795, and appointed to *Favourite*, sloop, in which he returned to the West Indies. There he made a good account of himself in action against privateers, provided effective support for the garrison of Grenada during the revolt, and took a notable part in the reconnaissance prior to the capture of Trinidad. He was rewarded in February 1797 by being put in command of *San Damaso* (74) taken as a prize, in which he returned home at the end of November with a convoy. His promotion to post captain was confirmed on 27 March 1797. As the prize was not taken into British service, he was transferred in February 1798 into *Vindictive* (28), and then into *Garland* (28), in which he served at the Cape under Admiral Hugh Christian.

When reconnoitring a large French merchantman at Port Dauphiné at Madagascar he had the misfortune to run on a sharp rock and sink almost immediately, but the French had run their ship ashore on the approach of the frigate, and fled in their boats. There followed a race as to who should obtain possession of the wrecked merchantman, which *Garland*'s people won. This gave them the supplies they needed to survive and to build a vessel for their escape, but after five months they were relieved when a ship arrived from the Cape.

On his return to England his old patron Admiral Jervis, now earl of St Vincent and first lord, put Wood in command of *Acasta* (40) on 12 April 1802. Following the renewal of the war, he served in her under Cornwallis off Brest, before he was sent in November 1804 to the West Indies in charge of a convoy, and entrusted with the orders for the recall of Admiral Duckworth which brought so much misfortune to him. When Duckworth ordered Wood's supersession, the latter protested that his appointment had been made by the Admiralty. Nonetheless, he had to follow as a passenger. By the time he reached England, the Admiralty had reinstated him in his command, and tightened the regulations to prevent similar abuse of authority in the future. Unfortunately, before he was informed of these developments, Wood had libelled Duckworth for a court martial. Courts tend to favour superior officers, and not only was Duckworth acquitted, but Wood was severely censured, his complaint being judged as 'gross, scandalous, malicious, shameful, and highly subversive of discipline'. Clearly he was out of his depth. A petition he subsequently made to the Admiralty was without effect, and a motion made by his brother Sir Mark Wood in the House of Commons that the proceedings of the court be laid on the table of the house was turned down despite Duckworth's own admission that he had freighted the *Acasta* with mahogany logs not intended for ships' stores.

Public opinion was on Wood's side, and viewed him as having fallen into the gears of the navy machine. Probably the Admiralty Board thought so as well, although they felt discipline required them to support Duckworth. At any rate, Wood was appointed to command *Uranie* (38) in August or September 1805, and then in April 1806 transferred to *Latona* (38) for service off Brest and in the West Indies. But his experience appears to have unhinged his mind. He swore out a deposition against Duckworth in which he described him as a coward and a dirty rascal. He became a shipboard tyrant, and St Vincent described him as 'a very dangerous man'. [Markham 55]

Nevertheless, he was to prosper greatly as second in command under Charles Brisbane in the capture of Curaçao in December 1806, being awarded a gold medal and a knighthood, which was conferred on 1 November 1809. He was also elected member of parliament for Gatton, Surrey, in 1806, although he retained his seat only until 1807. He continued to serve in the West Indies and Nova Scotia until 1809.

It must be presumed that his change in fortune also effected a change in his relations with his officers, because he continued to be employed. In December he was given command of *Captain* (74), transferring on 1 August 1809 to *Neptune* (98), in both ships being employed escorting convoys to the West Indies. On 20 March 1810 he was put in command of *Pompée* (80) in the Channel, and employed escorting Mediterranean convoys. On 10 March 1812 he found himself in charge of a small squadron off Ushant when a superior French squadron was sighted, with what appeared to be two further ships of the line joining. Wood felt it best to put about before dark, and during the night made such efforts to escape that he pumped eighty tons of fresh water overboard. Only in the morning did he discover that the other ships were British. He was court-martialled and found to have been too hasty in his judgement, but the verdict amounted only to a mild admonition. He was left in command of *Pompée* and later sent to join Admiral Lord Exmouth in the Mediterranean, resigning his commission only on 27 November 1815, at the end of the war.

He enjoyed the revenues of vendue master, or auctioneer, at Curaçao from 1812 to 1815, was advanced in chivalry to CB on 4 June 1815, and was promoted rear-admiral on 19 July 1821. He died in July 1829, aged seventy-three, in Hampstead, London.

Lt: 18 October 1778
Cmdr: 8 July 1795
Capt: 27 March 1797
R-Adm: 19 July 1821

WRIGHT

COMMANDER JOHN WESLEY WRIGHT was more an intelligence agent than a naval officer. He worked closely with Sir Sidney Smith, and died in suspicious circumstances in the Temple prison in Paris.

He was born on 14 June 1769 in Cork, Ireland,

a son of Captain James Wright. Early in his life his family moved to Minorca, where he studied music and French, and he entered the navy in February 1781 as a volunteer in *Brilliant* (28) commanded by Sir Roger Curtis, serving at Gibraltar during the siege. He returned to school at Wandsworth from 1783 to 1785, when he entered a business house in the City of London. He was sent probably in 1788 on a mission to Russia, where he stayed for five years. In 1794 he met Sidney Smith, and persuaded him to accept him on board *Diamond* (38) as his 'clerk' with the naval rank of midshipman. This work involved liaison with French royalists, including clandestine intelligence-gathering missions ashore. With Smith he was captured in 1796 and imprisoned in the Temple prison, and together they effected their escape two years later.

When Smith was appointed to command *Tigre* (80) he joined as acting lieutenant, his commission being confirmed on 29 March 1800. He participated in the defence of Acre, contributing materially to the mobilisation of Arab resistance to the French. He served with Smith on the Egyptian coast, and was promoted commander on 7 May 1802 with command of *Cynthia*, sloop, which he took to England. He was awarded the Turkish gold medal for distinguished services on the coast of Egypt.

During the peace of Amiens he travelled under an assumed name without a passport to Paris, gathering intelligence, which was smuggled out, before returning to England the day before Britain declared war on France on 18 May 1803.

With the renewal of war, Wright was appointed to command the *Vicenjo,* brig, and served on the coast of France. On 23 August 1803 he landed General Georges Cadoudal, and on 16 January 1804 Charles Pichegru, who was met by Cadoudal. Both Revolutionary generals, they had become royalist conspirators, and were planning a coup to assassinate Napoleon Buonaparte and instal a royal government. Headquarters for these operations was Walmer Castle, where William Pitt, temporarily out of government, was lord warden. One of his aides was General Edward Smith, Sidney Smith's uncle. The French police foiled the

plot, and the pretender, the Duc d'Enghien, who was living in neutral territory close to the French border, was kidnapped. The haul was completed on 8 May 1804 when Wright had the ill fortune to be becalmed in the mouth of the Vilaine, where he was surrounded by seventeen gunboats and taken prisoner.

The Late John Wesley Wright, Esq.,
Captain in the Royal Navy,
engraved by T Blood from an original portrait
painted at Malta by Gaetano Calleja, published
by Joyce Gold, Naval Chronicle Offices,
103 Shoe Lane, London,
31 July 1815.

He was repeatedly questioned about whether he had landed royalist agents, but steadfastly refused to answer. He was brought up as a witness at Cadoudal's trial, but refused to testify. On 27 October 1805 it was announced that he had committed suicide but there is no reason to suppose that was the case. His name was kept in the navy list until the autumn of 1807.

Lt: 29 March 1800
Cmdr: 7 May 1802

YEO

CAPTAIN SIR JAMES LUCAS YEO, KCB, was marked for his abilities commanding landing forces and for flotilla warfare. To him must go a good part of the credit for saving Canada from American conquest.

He was born on 7 October 1782 in Southampton, son of James Yeo, formerly agent victualler in Minorca. He was educated at Mr Walter's academy at Bishop's Waltham, near Winchester, before joining the navy in February 1793 as a boy volunteer in *Windsor Castle* (90) flying the flag of Vice-Admiral Phillips Cosby. He served at Toulon and in Corsica, returning to England with Cosby in *Alcide* (74) at the end of 1794. In the spring of 1795 he joined *Orion* (74) under the command of Captain John Duckworth in the Channel, and transferred with him to *Leviathan* (74) under orders for Jamaica. When Duckworth was appointed commodore in September 1796 he gave Yeo a lieutenant's commission in *Albacore* (16), which was confirmed on 20 February 1797. Invalided home in 1798, Yeo was appointed on 18 May to *Veteran* (64), Captain Moss, and served in the North Sea. As first lieutenant in *El Corso,* brig, in 1800 he was engaged for several weeks bombarding the defences of Genoa from the boats of the fleet, and later with *El Corso*'s boat, in burning the shipping in the harbour of Cesenatico in the Adriatic. At the peace of Amiens, he returned to England as first lieutenant of *Généreux* (80) captured from the French.

Following the return to war, he was appointed first lieutenant of *Blenheim* (74), and later, of the 18-pounder frigate *Loire* (46) commanded by Captain Frederick Lewis Maitland. On 4 June 1805 *Loire* entered Muros Bay and anchored opposite a battery, intending to destroy it and capture a large French privateer. Yeo, Maitland wrote, was sent with a landing party:

> having landed under the small battery on the point, it was instantly abandoned; but hardly had he time to spike the guns, when, at the distance of a quarter of a mile, he

perceived a regular fort, ditched, and with a gate, which the enemy (fortunately never suspecting our landing) had neglected to secure, open a fire upon the ship; without waiting for orders he pushed forward, and was opposed at the inner gate by the governor, with such troops as were in the town, and the crews of the French privateers. *NC 24.270*

He killed the governor with one blow, and captured the fort, enabling *Loire* to capture the privateer, which was taken into service as a ship-sloop, *Confiance* (22). Yeo was appointed on 21 June to her command.

He served two years at Lisbon, taking an active part in the negotiations leading to the Portuguese court accepting British escort to Brazil, before being sent home with Rear-Admiral Sir Sidney Smith's dispatches. In recognition of his services he was made post captain on 19 December 1807, and as further compliment to him, he was permitted to remain in command of *Confiance,* which was made a post ship and ordered back to the Tagus; from there he accompanied Rear-Admiral Smith's fleet to Rio de Janeiro. He persuaded the governor of Para that the French post at Cayenne could be captured, and with an Anglo-Portuguese force of 400 men he attacked the heavily fortified garrison of 1,200 and over 200 cannon. It took Yeo five weeks to defeat his enemy, and on its surrender he had to guard over 1,000 prisoners. When finally he was relieved, he returned to England to recover his health, and then returned to Rio, where he was invested in the Portuguese order of St Benedict of Aviz on 17 March 1810. King George later granted him permission to wear the decoration, and also invested Yeo a knight bachelor on 20 June.

On 3 January 1811 Yeo was appointed to command *Southampton* (32) on the Jamaica station, and on 3 February 1812 he engaged a formidable privateer, the *Amethyste*, which had been stolen from the Haitian Emperor Christophe and manned with Carribbean toughs. Eventually the *Southampton*'s prevailed, and *Amethyste* was returned to Haiti. *Southampton* was wrecked on a reef with USS *Vixen,* which she had just captured, and Yeo came home a passenger.

On 19 March 1813 he was appointed commodore and commander-in-chief of the flotilla on the Canadian Great Lakes, and he arrived at the naval station at Kingston in May. There he was faced with great difficulties. A pre-emptive raid on the American naval station at Sacketts Harbour was rendered nugatory by the weakness of General Prevost, who ordered the troops to be recalled before all the American ships were destroyed. Yeo

Sir James Lucas Yeo, Knt., Captain R.N.,
engraved by H R Cook after Buck,
published by Joyce Gold,
103 Shoe Lane, Fleet Street,
1 November 1810.

fought a drawn battle against the superior American flotilla at Niagara on 10 August but was then driven back to a defensive position at Kingston. Over the winter, both sides worked to expand their shipping, and Yeo was the first afloat in the spring, destroying American ordnance stores at Oswego and blockading Sacketts Harbour to prevent the fitting-out of the new American ships. But eventually he had to lift the blockade, and then he was again blockaded at Kingston. The deci-

sive move in the war on the lakes was the construction of *St Lawrence*, a first rate ship of the line, at Kingston. It was never launched, but remained on the ways as deterrence.

When operating against the Americans along the line of Lake Champlain, Prevost pressured the captain of a vessel just fitting out to take aggressive action against an American position which ought to have been taken by the army. The results were disastrous, and Yeo libelled Prevost for a court martial. The man who had taken the fort at Moros and captured Cayenne was not in favour of useless heroics. Writing to the admiralty secretary, Craker, he stated:

> there was not the least necessity for our squadron giving the enemy such decided advantages, by going into their bay to engage them; even had they been successful, it would not in the least have assisted the troops in storming the batteries; whereas, had our troops taken their batteries first, it would have obliged the enemy's squadron to quit the bay, and given ours a fair chance. NC 33.254-7

Prevost died before the court could assemble.

In 1815 Yeo was nominated KCB, and appointed commander-in-chief on the west coast of Africa with a broad pendant on board *Inconstant* (36). In October 1817 he moved into *Semiramis* (36) and sailed to Jamaica. His long service in hot climates had repeatedly affected his health, and he died on 21 August 1818, aged thirty-five, on passage home from Jamaica.

Lt: 20 February 1797
Cmdr: 21 June 1805
Capt: 19 December 1807

NOTE ON SOURCES

For those naval officers who were still in the navy in 1818, the ADM 9 series of documents in the National Archives, London, is a vital source. Each officer was requested to draw up a summary of his service record, to the best of his memory. In many cases, that memory was defective, but an Admiralty clerk went through the reports and made corrections. In the hierarchic traditions of the service, flag officers' records were put into volume 1, with subordinate officers being entered in subsequent volumes. However, that system soon broke down, and ADM 9/2–7 contain the records of officers of all ranks.

ADM 9/1: H Bayntun, f 88; R H Bickerton, f 15; H Blackwood, f 108; I Coffin, f 27; M Dixon, f 51; P C H Durham, f 68; T Foley, f 49; E J Foote, f 91; J Gambier, f 7; J Gore, f 101; B Hallowell, f 71; E Harvey, f 36; W J Hope, f 79; W Hotham, f 97; R G Keats, f 46; R King, f 89; C H Knowles, f 11; A Legge, f 65; G Martin, f 39; T B Martin, f 75; G Montagu, f 3; G Moore, f 85; J N Morris, f 74; H Neale, f 63; W Otway, f 121; E Pellew/Exmouth, f 26; I Pellew, f 69; C Rowley, f 115; J Saumarez, f 23; C Stirling, f 76; R Stopford, f 47; E Thornbrough, f 21; H Trollope, f 17. ADM 9/2–7: F W Austen, f 135; F W Aylmer, f 319; T Baker, f 51; R Barrie, f 280; F Beaufort, f 505; E Berry, f 39; C Boyle, f 54; E Brace, f 131; E P Brenton, f 453; J Brenton, f 132; J Brisbane, f 166; P B V Broke, f 163; W Broughton, f 37;

C Bullen, f 230; J Bullen, f 22; R Byron, f 236; P Campbell, f 158; T B Capel, f 97; J S Carden, f 333; P Carteret, f 352; G Cockburn, f 82; C Cole, f 191; G R Collier, f 192; W P Cumby, f 324; W C C Dalyell, f 1273; H Digby, f 30; H Downman, f 96; H Duncan, f 328; C Ekins, f 31; M Fitton, f 2464; A Fraser, f 70; J A Gordon, f 318; E L Graham, f 304; E Grey, f 688; E Hamilton, f 50; T M Hardy, f 85; J Harvey, f 102; J Hayes, f 252; P Heywood, f 286; J Hillyar, f 293; H Hope, f 438; W Hoste, f 183; H Hotham, f 103; S P Humphreys, f 303; T H Hurd, f 202; F P Irby, f 190; M Kerr, f 41; W King, f 417; J Lind, f 296; F L Maitland, f 165; J W Maurice, f 458; D Milne, f 119; W Mounsey, f 474; J Nisbet, f 94; Northesk, f 25; E W C R Owen, f 72; E Palmer, f 404; J Pasco, f 573; H Paulet, f 80; J Phillimore, f 414; W Prowse, f 40; S Pym, f 276; E Rotheram, f 142; J Rowley, f 104; M Seymour, f 140; S Smith, f 41; S Sutton, f 53; G Tobin, f 238; N Tomlinson, f 175; T T Tucker, f 597; T Ussher, f 459; R B Vincent, f 374; J Walker, f 63; T Williams, f 55; N J Willoughby, f 514; J A Wood, f 43; J L Yeo, f 426.

Two important modern resources have also assisted in the preparation of this collection. The first place must be given to Patrick Marioné, *The Complete Navy List of the Napoleonic Wars, 1793–1815*, Brussels, 2003. The other is the *Oxford Dictionary of National Biography*, Oxford, 2004.

KEY TO BIBLIOGRAPHIC REFERENCES

ADM: Admiralty records, housed in the National Archives, London.

Allardyce: Alexander Allardyce, *Memoir of the Honourable George Keith Elphinstone, K.B., Viscount Keith*, Edinburgh and London, 1882.

Bridport: Bridport Papers, British Library, London, Additional MS 35201.

Charnock: John Charnock, *Biographia Navalis: or, Impartial Memoirs of the Lives and Characters of Officers of the Navy of Great Britain from the Year 1660 to the Present Time…*, London, 1794–8.

Clarke and M'Arthur: James Stanier Clarke and John M'Arthur, *Life of Admiral Lord Nelson K.B. from his Lordship's Manuscripts* (first published 1794–8), London, 1840.

Coleridge: *The Collected Works of Samuel Taylor Coleridge*, ed Barbara E Rooke, 2 vols, London, 1969.

Collingwood: *The Private Correspondence of Admiral Lord Collingwood*, ed Edward Hughes, Navy Records Society, vol 98, London, 1957.

Collingwood (2): *A Selection from the Public and Private Correspondence of Vice-Admiral Lord Collingwood, Interspersed with Memoirs of His Life*, ed G L Newnham-Collingwood, 5th edn, 2 vols, London, 1837.

Croker: John Wilson Croker, *The Croker Papers, 1808–1857*, 3 vols, London, 1885.

DNB: *Dictionary of National Biography*, micro edition, London, 1975.

Elliot: *Life and Letters of Sir Gilbert Elliot, First Earl of Minto, from 1751 to 1806*, ed E E E Elliot-Murray-Kynynmound, countess of Minto, 3 vols, London, 1874.

Farington: Joseph Farington, *The Farington Diary, – Selections*, 8 vols, ed James Greig, London, 1933.

Farington (2): *The Diary of Joseph Farington*, ed Kenneth Garlick, Angus Macintyre and Kathryn Cave, 16 vols, New Haven, 1979.

Gamlin: Hilda Gamlin, *Nelson's Friendships*, 2 vols, London, 1899.

Hoste: G H Hoste, *Service Afloat; or, The Naval Career of Sir William Hoste*, London, 1887.

Jackson: T Sturges Jackson, ed, *Logs of the Great Sea Fights, 1794–1805*, 2 vols, Navy Records Society, vols 16 and 18, London 1900.

James: William James, *Naval History of Great Britain from the Declaration of War by France, in February 1793, to the Accession of George IV in January 1820*, London, 1826 (first published 1822–3).

Le Fevre and Harding: Peter Le Fevre and Richard Harding, *Precursors of Nelson*, London, 2000.

Markham: *Selections from the Correspondence of Admiral John Markham*, ed C Markham, Navy Records Society, vol 28, London, 1904.

Marshall: John Marshall, *Royal Naval biography, or, Memoirs of the Services of All…*, 4 vols, with supplements, London, 1835.

Mon: Nelson Museum, Monmouth.

Nagle: John C Dann, *The Nagle Journal: A Diary of the Life of Jacob Nagle, sailor, from the Year 1775 to 1841*, New York, 1988.

NC: *The Naval Chronicle*, periodical, 40 vols, London, 1798–1818.

Nelson: *The Dispatches and Letters of Vice-Admiral Lord Viscount Nelson*, ed Nicholas H Nicolas, 7 vols, London, 1844–6.

NMM: National Maritime Museum, Greenwich, manuscript collections.

PRO: Public Record Office, National Archives, Kew, London.

Ralfe: James Ralfe, *The Naval Biography of Great Britain*, 4 vols, Boston, 1972 (first published London, 1828).

Schomberg: Alexander Wilmot Schomberg, *How His Majesty's Ship Glatton (56 guns) Defeated a French Squadron on the 15th July, 1796*, 7 pp, 1938.

Tucker: J S Tucker, *Memoirs of Admiral the Rt. Hon. the Earl of St. Vincent*, 2 vols, London, 1844.

Wellington: *Some Letters of the Duke of Wellington to His Brother, William Wellesley-Pole*, ed C Webster, Camden Miscellany, XVIII, Camden Society, 3rd series, vol 79, London, 1948.

Wellington (2): *The Dispatches of… the Duke of Wellington… from 1799 to 1818*, ed J Gurwood, 13 vols in 12, London, 1834–9.

INDEX OF PERSONS

Main entries are indexed in bold